For Ida   *For Ilene*

Alternative Scriptwriting Beyond the Hollywood Formula

Fifth Edition

Ken Dancyger and Jeff Rush

Focal Press
Taylor & Francis Group
NEW YORK AND LONDON

First published 2013
by Focal Press
70 Blanchard Rd Suite 402
Burlington, MA 01803

Simultaneously published in the UK
by Focal Press
2 Park Square, Milton Park, Abingdon, Oxon OX14 4RN

Focal Press is an imprint of the Taylor & Francis Group, an informa business

Notices
Knowledge and best practice in this field are constantly changing. As new research
and experience broaden our understanding, changes in research methods, professional
practices, or medical treatment may become necessary.

Practitioners and researchers must always rely on their own experience and knowledge
in evaluating and using any information, methods, compounds, or experiments described
herein. In using such information or methods they should be mindful of their own
safety and the safety of others, including parties for whom they have a professional
responsibility.

Product or corporate names may be trademarks or registered trademarks, and are used only
for identification and explanation without intent to infringe.

Library of Congress Cataloging in Publication Data
Dancyger, Ken.
  Alternative scriptwriting : beyond the Hollywood formula / Ken Dancyger, Jeff Rush.
  —Fifth edition.
      pages cm
  ISBN 978-0-240-52246-3 (paper back)
  1. Motion picture authorship. 2. Motion picture plays—Technique.
  I. Rush, Jeff. II. Title.
   PN1996.D36 2013
   808.2'3—dc23
                                        2012041004

  ISBN: 978-0-240-52246-3 (pbk)
  ISBN: 978-0-240-52247-0 (ebk)

Typeset in TrumpMediaeval
Project Managed and Typeset by diacriTech
Printed and bound by CPI Group (UK) Ltd, Croydon, CR0 4YY

Contents

Preface

When we first wrote *Alternative Scriptwriting* in 1990, the formulaic approach to structure of the Hollywood screenplay was dominant. By exploring alternatives to that model, we hoped to contribute to the deeper question of what makes a compelling, creative screen story.

Today, the world of screen stories still struggle with this challenge. But much has changed. Who would have thought that the center of formula—television—would become in the first decade of the twenty-first century the dynamic creative center of screen storytelling? And who would have foreseen the explosion of screenwriting books, gurus, and screenwriting programs all over the world?

It is with these phenomena in mind that we include in this fifth edition chapters on television series screenwriting and deeper deliberations on the role of genre in the writing of and teaching of writing screenplays.

We hope these new chapters will add to the deepening of teaching and learning of screenwriting and to their outcomes—the scripts to come.

Acknowledgments for the Fifth Edition

In support of the fifth edition of this book, we'd like to thank Carlin Reagan at Focal Press. Jeff would also like to thank his colleagues in Film and Media Arts at Temple—particularly Nora Alter, Allan Barber, Chris Cagle, Rod Coover, Eran Preis, Mark Rosenthal, Michael Ryan, Elisabeth Subrin, and Paul Swann—for continued discussion about film and narrative. We'd especially like to express our appreciation to students in different parts of the world who, in their curiosity and in their work, keep making us feel that our own work on story is an ongoing creative investigation into what makes story work. Thank you all.

1

Beyond the Rules

There are many different schools of thought with regard to becoming a better screenwriter. Some value convention, while others stress experimentation. Some focus on character, while others rely on plot. Because there are so many different opinions, we feel it's best to state our biases at the outset.

First, we think of the screenwriter as a storyteller who happens to write for film. Many screenwriters write for more than one medium. Steve Tesich (*Breaking Away*) and Harold Pinter (*The Handmaid's Tale*) write for both theater and film. David Hare (*Strapless*), William Goldman (*Butch Cassidy and the Sundance Kid*), and John Sayles (*Baby It's You*) write both fiction and screenplays, as have many others throughout the short history of screenwriting. Our point is that you, as the scriptwriter, are part of a broad storytelling tradition. To cut yourself off from other forms of writing or to view script-writing as an exclusive art form is to cut yourself off from a large cultural community of different types of writing that have more in common than you might realize.

Second, a screenplay should be more than structurally sound. The screenwriter is often referred to as a technician—the equivalent to the draftsman in architecture. Although there are screenwriters who are content to be technicians, many are not. Nor do we feel you should be a technician. One of our goals in this book is to suggest ways to move beyond structure.

Third, you have to know everything about structure in order to move beyond it. It isn't possible to reinvent the process without knowing it in detail. Consequently, we illustrate the conventions of screenwriting so that you will be able to break from them.

Now that you know our biases, we can state our simple approach. We outline conventions and then proceed to suggest practical ways to undermine or alter those conventions. We use specific examples to illustrate the points we're trying to make. Our ultimate goal is to help you develop better screenplays. To do this, we talk about form, content, character, and language, while pressing you to develop alternative narrative strategies that prompt you to write the best screenplay you can write. As Melanie Griffith says to the conventional Jeff Daniels in Max Frye's *Something Wild*, "I know you, you're a closet rebel." Just as she sees beyond his superficial characteristics, we want you to look beyond the surface of scriptwriting, beyond form. You'll be surprised at what you find.

Conventions

There are some fundamental story devices that remain constant regardless of your scriptwriting approach. All screen stories use plots in which the premise is expressed in terms of conflict. The focus on conflict is so central to storytelling that its use can be traced from the original Ten Commandments to the two film versions of the story. Discovery and reversal are two more conventional storytelling devices because surprise is important to all stories; without it, the story is flat and tends to become a mundane series of events, rather than a story that invites the viewer to get involved and stay involved. A turning point is another device that is typically used in storytelling. The number of turning points varies from screen story to screen story; but their usefulness is critical. All of these elements—conflict, discovery, reversal, and turning point—are the technical devices you use to involve the reader in your story. Beyond these devices, however, the choices are limited only by your willingness to explore your imagination.

Structure

In the past 10 years, structure as applied to film has come to mean Act One, Act Two, Act Three. Each act has its own characteristics: Act One introduces character and premise; Act Two focuses on confrontation and struggle; Act Three resolves the crisis introduced in the premise. Operating in each act are various plot devices intended to intensify conflict, develop characters, and propel the plot forward. We discuss structure in more detail in Chapter 2.

Noteworthy, however, is how the scriptwriting structure differs from other structured forms of storytelling. Most plays have only two acts, and most books have more than three chapters. Although many operas do have three acts, the unfolding of the narrative to suggest the greater importance of subtext over text indicates how far removed opera is from film (but here, too, the screenwriter can learn something from another medium).

Premise

The premise, sometimes referred to as the concept, central concept, or central idea, is what the screenplay is about. Usually, the premise is presented in terms of the central character's dilemma at a particular point in her life (the point at which the screen story begins). For example, the premise in *All About Eve* is: What happens to a great actress (Bette Davis) when age threatens her physical beauty and her career? In *Inside Moves*, a story about a young man, played by John Savage, the premise is: What happens when this young man decides to kill himself and then fails?

Premise is usually presented in terms of conflict. *In All About Eve*, the conflict offers two options: to accept ageing regardless of the emotional and professional consequences that option suggests, or to struggle for intimate relationships and roles beyond natural reason. This struggle and its outcome form the basis of the script. When Bette Davis makes her decision, the screen story is over.

In *Inside Moves*, Rory, John Savage's character, attempts suicide, but survives. Consequently, he has two options: to try again, or to find a way to make a life he can live with, even enjoy. Life or death is the basis of this screen story. Once Rory makes his decision and commits to one option, the screen story is over. The premise, then, is central to the screen story and is best posited in terms of the central conflict for the main character.

A variation worth mentioning is the existence of two particular types of premises. We mention them because they have become part of the industry parlance. The two variations are high concept and low (or soft) concept. High concept refers to a plot-oriented premise and implies excitement. Low concept refers to a premise that is softer on the plot and consequently relies more on the strength of the characters. A simple way to discern the two is to view a high-concept premise as a plot-intensive story and a low-concept premise as a character-intensive story. During the 1980s, the desirability of high-concept premises had considerable economic value, and they were more likely to be produced.

The Role of Conflict

Conflict is the central feature of the screen story. Man against man, man against environment, and man against himself portray the classic versions of conflict found in the screen story. Variations of sex, age, religion, and culture provide variety to the conflict. Polarities (i.e., extreme opposites) make conflict operational in screen stories. In the Western genre, the most obvious polarity was the hero's white horse and white clothing, and the villain's black horse and black clothing. Policeman/criminal, lawyer/accused, rich/poor, hero/villain—all are polarities that exemplify the character conflicts featured in different screen stories.

All screen characters are developed using polarities—opposites in physical appearance and in behavioral characteristics. In *On the Waterfront*, the main character is the only character who is physically fit. His brother, a criminal, looks older, dresses differently, and speaks differently. The main character is dark; the young woman he falls in love with is a blonde. It should come as no surprise that she speaks better and behaves more intensely than the main character does. When she is committed to a decision, the main character hedges. The polarities go on and on. When we look at all the other characters' physical variations (slim and heavy), age variations (young and old), and aggression variations (violent and meek), we see that they permeate the screen story. Polarities are the most obvious, useful devices for instilling conflict in your story.

Character

The main character of the screen story is the primary means for the audience to experience the story. The audience will be involved in the story to the extent that it identifies with the character and his dilemma. On the surface, the character may be recognizable via a dominant physical or behavioral characteristic. However, during a moment of private revelation or a moment when the character allows himself to appear foolish or vulnerable, our empathy for that character is realized and our identification with the character is secured.

Generally, the main character is energetic and exposed to sufficient conflict to propel her through the story. The main character differs from secondary characters in a variety of ways. The primary difference is that the main character undergoes a metamorphosis during the course of the story. On the other hand, the secondary characters do not change and, in fact, necessarily serve as a source of contrast to the main character. Through interaction with the main character, secondary characters help to move the story along.

All the characters (main and secondary) have distinct goals in the screen story. Generally, these goals parallel the premise. Secondary characters take each side of the issue and the main character is faced with the conflict. In *On the Waterfront*, Marlon Brando's character is faced with these questions: Can he, a washed-up boxer, be a more moral person than his brother, the criminal? Should he be a criminal or a saint? Actors Lee J. Cobb and Rod Steiger, who play gangsters in the film, are important secondary characters, along with Eva Marie Saint and Karl Malden, who play the roles of saints. The secondary characters prod Brando to join their respective side. The screen story draws to its conclusion once Brando has made his choice.

Dialogue

Since 1927, films have had sound, comprising dialogue, sound effects, and music. When dialogue is used in film, it fulfills three roles. First, dialogue characterizes. Speech patterns tells us whether the character is educated, from where the character originates, the profession of the character, the approximate age of the character, and the emotional state of the character. Second, dialogue helps define the plot. What the character says depends on the role of the character in the story. Louis, in *Four Friends*, is a dying man who loves life, as opposed to the central character's tentative approach to life. Louis's function is to highlight, through dialogue, his joy of living, his enthusiasm for science and for sex, and all of those elements absent from the main character's life. The third function of dialogue is to relieve tension, through humor, when it occurs in a script (an inevitable state given the writer's attention to conflict). Humor serves to put us at ease with the characters; we like people more readily after we've shared a laugh with them.

In a more general sense, dialogue has an additional overarching purpose—to make the characters more believable. The writer's first objective is to make the audience believe the story, or, more specifically, believe the characters in the story. If the dialogue is working, the audience will be more inclined to believe in the characters. When dialogue does not work, the characters tend to be less believable. Consequently, dialogue plays an important role in the creation of character credibility.

Atmosphere

When a reader reads a screenplay, she is confronted with a good deal of description and then dialogue. So how can the writer create atmosphere? Doesn't atmosphere come from visualization when the screenplay is filmed? Not entirely. Atmosphere, in a screenplay, is the accumulation of details that creates the illusion of a single, coherent world on the page.

The writer creates a spatial, or three-dimensional, sense of believability when the dialogue is credible and when the depictions of time and place are so convincing that the reader can say "I know that person, I've been in that place or situation." Detail is the key. When there is enough detail, the atmosphere of the screenplay moves from generic to particular, from mechanical to meaningful.

Action Line

Action line is frequently referred to as the story line or the plot. The term *action line*, however, is most appropriate for film, because the visual nature of the medium suggests visual action as the preferred form of characterization. Also, action line is occasionally referred to as the foreground story, or the major story line, as opposed to the background story, or the secondary story line.

The term *foreground story* implies the more important aspects of the story, which isn't always true. Indeed, in many stories the more subtle background (or minor story line) involves the deeper elements of the story, the characters' relationships as opposed to the larger events that drive the story. For an audience, these relationship elements are frequently the most meaningful, emotional link to the screen story. Consequently, the background story can be just as, if not more, important for the audience.

Often, the action line, although more sensational, is more superficial in its meaning. For simplicity, the action line can be viewed as the exterior action of the story, and is definitely conflict oriented. The background story can be viewed as the interior (main character) action of the screen story. Background story is identification oriented.

Rising Action

Rising action carries the action line from the beginning to the end and implies that the level of conflict that confronts the major character increases as we move through the screen story. The level of conflict is greatest in Act Three. There is a dip in the rising action at the beginning of Act Two and Act Three.

Subtext

Subtext is the background story or the interior struggle of the main character to choose the most appropriate solution to his interior conflict. Subtext is often expressed in terms of general human emotional states: love–hate and life–death. Not every screen story deals with such primal feelings, but many memorable films have these dimensions to their stories. At the deepest level, subtext can reach the audience in a more complex and gripping manner than action can. The screen stories you most likely remember have a strong subtext.

Discovery

As we mentioned earlier, the element of surprise is important in a screenplay. Whether it refers to plot or character, unexpected revelation—no matter how trivial—maintains our interest. Discoveries made later in the screen story must be greater in scale than those found earlier in the screen story.

Reversal

Plot twists manifest as reversals of fortune for the main character. This form of setback creates tension and concern for the fate of the character. Reversals are used more sparingly than are other plot devices. Too many reversals in a screen story tend to depreciate the impact of the reversals. Use reversals with care to allow for maximum impact.

Turning Point

Sometimes referred to as plot points, turning points yield surprise, anticipation, and tension, and help maintain our interest in the screen story. Turning points are classified as minor or major, while reversals tend to be major turning points. Minor turning points take place frequently throughout the screen story. Early major turning points open up the story and provide a broader spectrum of options for the main character. Late major turning points help to focus the story by pointing the main character toward the resolution of his crisis.

Going Against Structure

Structure is such an important characteristic of the screenplay that we devote Chapters 2 through 9 to discussing structure, counter-structure, genre, and working against genre. As previously mentioned, the structured approach uses three acts to tell the screen story, and, if you choose, the use of a particular genre to deliver the three acts.

The central question you face if you don't wish to use the conventional three-act structure is: What is available to you? Can you, for example, tell a story in one act? Probably not. Can you tell a story in two acts? Yes, as evidenced in *Full Metal Jacket*. In four acts? Yes, as evidenced in *Mo' Better Blues*.

Although the setup–confrontation–resolution approach to structure remains the predominant form, the absence of resolution in *Full Metal Jacket* and the addition of a second optional resolution in the fourth act of *Mo' Better Blues* add a dimension to the films that is not present in the classic case. The potential benefit of the fresh addition of a second resolution is to alter the meaning of the film.

A limitation of scriptwriting is that a screen story must be set up and must have some level of conflict or confrontation. Consequently, a story that is all setup, or all confrontation with no setup (the one-act option), is too limiting and too similar to a fragment of a larger story, rather than being a feature-length screen story.

One qualification to this argument about going against structure is to pose this question: When Julie Dash wrote *Daughters of the Dust* was the circularity of the story going against conventional structure or was she opting to tell the story in a manner most sensible to her? Similarly, is she opting for a group of characters over a single goal-oriented main character, and does that choice imply working against convention, or again, is it a case of a woman telling a story in a manner most sensible to her? The manner in which men and women tell stories is not an issue easily resolved, but for those interested in the issue we refer you to a fascinating book that does imply gender difference. The title is *Women's Ways of Knowing* (Basic Books, 1986), and the authors, Mary Field Belenky, Blythe McVicker Clinchy, Nancy Rule Goldberger, and Jill Mattock Tarule, make a persuasive argument that women are less interested in linear storytelling and far more empathetic with the circular approach used by Julie Dash.

In regard to genre, the scriptwriter's options increase. Genres, or particular types of films such as gangster or horror, have particular characteristics that audiences identify with those films. For example, audiences identify the monster antagonist with the horror film, and the urban setting with the gangster film. You can use a particular genre as the vehicle for your structural choice, or you can challenge a particular genre motif. For example, in a Western, the protagonist is generally positive, moral, and faces his challenges alone. However, as evidenced in *The Wild Bunch*, the scriptwriter challenges the genre motif of the wholesome protagonist by making the main character an outlaw and a murderer and surrounding him with people who are worse.

The violation of genre needn't relate to character. It can relate to any motif of a genre. A scriptwriter can vary the presentation of the antagonist, the nature of the confrontation, and the resolution. For example, the female sniper in the war film *Full Metal Jacket* breaks from the conventional onscreen depiction of the villain. More often, the villain is the Teutonic German, such as in *Saving Private Ryan*, who brutally murders the sole Jewish member of the American patrol. De facto, in *Full Metal Jacket*, the enemy becomes a fellow American in the first half of the film.

Another challenge to genre is the use of mixed genres to alter meaning. *Blade Runner* and *Something Wild* are examples. This particular scriptwriting technique became popular in the 1980s. Given the number of genres, many options are available to the scriptwriter. Not all genres mix with success, but attempts to mix even the most unlikely genres have yielded interesting results. For example, by mixing the musical and film noir genres, *Diva* is fresher than it would have been had it been presented as a straight musical or film noir screen story.

An ultimate challenge to conventional storytelling has been put forth by Woody Allen in his film *Crimes and Misdemeanors*. Not only does Allen alter structure (he presents two three-act stories in one film), he also mixes genres and challenges particular motifs in each of the genres. The result is a startling screen story during which the shifts in our expectations and moods are so rapid that we are left dazed and dazzled by his audacity. Allen's *Crimes and Misdemeanors* suggests audiences will tolerate a good deal of experimentation and are sufficiently film-experienced to know what to expect from conventional structure and genres. Allen challenges these expectations on as many levels as he feels are manageable.

Character Alternatives

If the classic main character is active, likable, and central to the story, alternative approaches challenge each of these qualities. These character alternatives are explored in detail in Chapters 12 through 14.

What happens to your screen story when the main character is more passive, more voyeur than the participant? What happens when your main character is not admirable or even likable? What happens when your main character is overshadowed by one or more secondary characters? Do these initiatives undermine the effectiveness of your screen story? The answers to these questions yield a new range of possibilities. They can weaken your story, or alter the experience of your story in new and interesting ways. In all likelihood, you will have to adjust your treatment of all the characters and of the amount of narrative necessary to tell your story. This is especially true for the role of the antagonist.

Taking up the issue of the unconventional main character, we can find examples throughout the history of film. Diello (James Mason), the main character in Michael Wilson's *Five Fingers*, is a spy trying to sell secrets to the Nazis, including the time and place of the Normandy invasion of France. Hardly a person to admire, Diello is, nevertheless, a fascinating and involving character. Travis Bickle (Robert De Niro) in Paul Schrader's *Taxi Driver* is an alienated, highly disturbed war veteran. He is sufficiently antisocial and prone to violence to have little appeal as a main character. Rupert Popkin (Robert De Niro) in Paul Zimmerman's *King of Comedy* is even less appealing. Delusional and desperate, Popkin wants to be a television celebrity.

In each of these cases, the scriptwriter was faced with presenting characters and action in a way that allowed the viewer to identify with the main character. In *Taxi Driver*, the uncaring, callous nature of the majority of characters makes Travis Bickle seem more sensitive, and he becomes a victim rather than a perpetrator. Consequently, we identify with Travis Bickle in spite of his neurotic behavior. This is the sort of adjustment the writer has to make if it is desired to move away from the classic presentation of the main character.

You can also use an ironic character as an alternative character. An ironic character promotes distance between us and the character, and allows us not only to sympathize with the character's plight, but also to wonder why events and people seem to conspire against him. Often, the ironic character is portrayed as an innocent victim of a person or system. This type of character is very useful when you feel that the ideas are more important than the people in your screen story.

Dialogue Alternatives

Dialogue in a screen story enhances the particular credibility of the character. Whether it's used to advance the plot or develop the character, audiences expect film dialogue to be believable. This is in keeping with the illusion of realism in the film medium. Events on film look real; therefore, behavior and appearance of performers must support that illusion. What if the screenwriter wants to use dialogue to undermine credibility or to supersede the sense of realism? If so, the quality and function of the dialogue in the screenplay broadens considerably and invites the influence of other storytelling forms—the play, the performance, the burlesque—all of which are dependent on dialogue in more elaborate ways.

Dialogue can be more highly charged and more emotional than conventional movie dialogue. Paddy Chayefsky uses this approach in his screenplay *Network*. The old-time producer (William Holden) and the new-style programming executive (Faye Dunaway) argue eloquently about their conflicting philosophies. The dialogue illustrates this conflict. Dialogue can also be stripped of feeling and abstracted so that the viewer relates to the dialogue as a metaphor for his state of mind, rather than with a sense of plausibility. David Hare uses this approach to dialogue in his screenplays *Plenty* and *Strapless*.

A third option for dialogue is to use language ironically in order to destroy the most literal meaning of the language. This type of dialogue is often associated with the Marx Brothers; Groucho was constantly trying to undermine meaning. For example, Groucho plays Rufus T. Firefly in Bert Kalmar and Harry Ruby's *Duck Soup*. Firefly is the new leader of Freedonia, a fictional middle European state. Fanfare announces the arrival of the leader. In the palace, he is greeted by Mrs. Teasdale. The regal guests eagerly await his arrival. Rather than following the pomp expected in such circumstances, the dialogue trivializes the ceremonial dimension of the scene, reducing it to the level of a social card game in a community hall. The exchange of dialogue follows:

```
            MRS. TEASDALE
We've been expecting you.
      (she gives him her hand; pompously)
As Chairwoman of the reception
committee, I extend the good
wishes of every man, woman and
child of Freedonia.

            FIREFLY
Never mind that stuff. Take a
card.
      (he fans out a pack of cards)

            MRS. TEASDALE
A card? What'll I do with a
card?
      (she takes it)

            FIREFLY
You can keep it. I've got
fifty-one left. Now what were
you saying?
```

Another dialogue alternative is used in screen stories that have very little action and subsequently may be subject to a loss of screen energy. Often this situation is compensated for using energized dialogue, which is sufficiently charged so that the dynamism of the story is brought out. This alternative necessitates a great deal more dialogue because dialogue becomes considerably more important than in the conventional screen story. Spike Lee's *She's*

Gotta Have It is a recent example of this type of dialogue. Budget limitations can also promote the use of excessive, energized dialogue in order to avoid costly action sequences. Quentin Tarantino's use of dialogue scenes to replace action sequences is a good example of this impulse.

Atmosphere Alternatives

Atmosphere is created by visual detail and lends a visual credibility to your screen story. If your goal is to challenge credibility or to add another level of meaning to your story, manipulation of environmental details becomes your most direct tool to alter atmosphere.

In *Local Hero*, Bill Forsyth uses detail to subvert and alter the original direction of the narrative. *Local Hero* is the story of a Texas oilman's efforts to buy land in Scotland. The purpose of the purchase is to exploit offshore oil. To underscore the corporate dimension of the story line, we would expect offices, oil rigs, and the material benefits of the exploiters and the exploited. Forsyth has little interest in this type of detail. Instead, we are presented with a sensual otherworldly presentation of the land and its hypnotic effect on the would-be exploiters. The result is that the oilmen, by the end of the narrative, don't get what they came for but they don't seem to mind. The owner of the company, a mystic portrayed by Burt Lancaster, and his salesman, portrayed by Peter Riegert, have been changed by their exposure to this mystical landscape. They are sensually enriched, but materially worse off.

Francis Ford Coppola and Michael Herr use the atmosphere of *Apocalypse Now* to move that story from a realistic treatment of the Vietnam War to a metaphor of war and Vietnam as hell. In his screenplay *The Untouchables*, David Mamet moves his gangster film about Al Capone and Elliot Ness to a story about the struggle of good and evil. The metaphor moves us away from the events of the story toward the subtext of good and evil.

Finally, the scriptwriter has the option of altering atmosphere by using details that undermine the sense of place developed from preceding details. A good example of this alteration is found in David Lynch's *Blue Velvet*. A tranquil, pastoral town is presented—beautiful flowers, contented inhabitants, and, of course, rosy-cheeked children. Then, suddenly, Lynch shows us the ants and insects living beneath the surface. Shortly after this shot, the viewer's initial impression of the town is shattered when the main character finds a severed ear. The tranquility is broken, and we can't trust our expectations for the balance of the screen story.

Foreground and Background Story Alternatives

The scriptwriter has broad options in the area of foreground and background stories. Film stories have long been divided between personal interest stories and adventure (action) stories. Often, the personal interest story is more literary and the action story is linear. Today, the action story is called the high-concept premise and the personal interest story is called the low-concept premise. The high-concept film, particularly since *Star Wars*, has become the dominant type of screen story. Foreground stories are the prevalent form and the resulting schism has screenwriters scurrying to maintain their positions in the marketplace. In spite of the market, screen stories benefit from having both strong foreground and background stories, as described in Chapter 17.

It should be noted that the current international dominance of the American film is attributable to the success of the foreground, plot-oriented story. Films such as *The Terminator* series, the *Lethal Weapon* series, as well as the earlier *Indiana Jones* and *Star Wars* series employ stars, special effects, and production values, but at heart are all linear stories with memorable set pieces of action. When European films such as *La Femme Nikita* or Australian films such as *The Road Warrior* employ a similar narrative strategy, they too, are great international successes. This does not mean, however, that writers should now all devote themselves to the action genre. Indeed, the success of films such as *Sleepless in Seattle* and *Forrest Gump* demonstrates that audiences also want low-concept or character-driven stories.

For the scriptwriter, alternatives begin to develop when working with the balance of foreground and background. The key ingredient in creating foreground and background balance is the main character. If the scriptwriter positions the main character in a deeply personal dilemma, the outcome of the story is less predictable. Background stories, which dwell on the interior life of the main character, tend to be less predictable because the interior life is not linear.

Although foreground stories are the current dominant form, much attention has been paid to background stories, as evidenced in *Moonstruck*. Screen stories that are more background story oriented tend to have particular characteristics beyond their character orientation. Often, dialogue moves away from realism toward a more literary quality and is distinctive and eccentric. Playwrights are accustomed to using dialogue—literary, charged dialogue—because there is less action on stage. Emotional levels intensify through language and dialogue. The dialogue in *Moonstruck* shouldn't come as a surprise, since the scriptwriter, John Patrick Shanley, is a playwright. So, too, are Sam Shepard, Ted Tally, Steve Tesich, Hanif Kureishi, David Hare, and David Mamet, all interesting playwrights who also happen to write screenplays with strong background stories.

When the writer uses the background story, the main character becomes more personal to us, and the narrative more open ended. The result invites a deeper involvement from the viewer.

Rising Action Alternatives

When writers use a stronger background story, they open up possibilities in varying the convention of rising action. Generally, the action of the screen story gradually rises to a climax, except for a brief pause at the beginnings of Acts Two and Three. These pauses allow the writer to set up the parameters for the acts that follow. When using a background story, the scriptwriter can devote more time to the characters, although this does not necessarily advance the plot or move the story toward the climax. A good example of this alternative approach to rising action is found in Louis Malle's *My Dinner with Andre*. Less extreme, but no less interesting, is Jean-Claude Carriére and Louis Malle's *May Fools*. In these films, the shift from rising action affords the audience a greater opportunity to know the characters.

As we mention in Chapter 4, moving away from the three-act model results in a more open-ended sense of character and structure. A similar result occurs when the scriptwriter moves away from rising action. To make this step effective, however, the screenwriter must make the focus on the characters worthwhile. The characters must be interesting, and the dialogue has to be as involving as new plot developments would be. This means charged, witty, and surprising dialogue. If these elements are not present, the viewer will experience a flatness that does not serve the interests of the screen story.

This idea of modulating rising action applies only to Act Two of the screenplay. The screen story still needs the rise in action during the setup in Act One and the continued rise in action to the resolution in Act Three—unless, of course, you choose not to use an Act Three.

Developing Narrative Strategies

There are various ways to tell a screen story, more than the conventions of screenwriting suggest. This message is the central theme of this book. In order to tell your story, you need to develop a narrative strategy that is best suited to your idea. First, you need to answer the following questions: Who is your main character? What is the premise of your story? What is the most exciting action line for this story? Does the action line best highlight your main character's dilemma? Is your main character's dilemma situational, or is it deeply rooted in her personality?

The choices you make when answering these questions are inherently dramatic choices. You, as a screenwriter, must make the best dramatic choice. Bear in mind that the choice that is most interesting is not necessarily the most obvious.

A central issue for all scriptwriters is the creation of a story that invites the viewer to identify with the main character or with that character's situation. If your narrative strategy employs characters who don't invite accessibility, you can't guarantee that the viewer will stay with you for the length of your story.

What are the narrative strategies available to the writer? There are many, and you have options with every element in the screenplay, including character, language, atmosphere, action line, background story, and structure. In regard to the main character, for example, you can opt for an active main character, a more passive one, or a less likable one. Your choice depends on the type of character that best elicits the dramatic results for which you are looking. In regard to dialogue, you do not have to be limited by character function, and in terms of structure, you can vary or mix genres, challenge the convention of the three-act structure, or vary the foreground–background mix. In all cases, exploring alternative ways to develop your narrative strategy yields a fresher approach to your story and more open-ended characters.

The scriptwriter must be flexible to ensure that what he takes away from one area of the screenplay is compensated for elsewhere. If we don't like your main character and the challenge is to create a situation in which we identify with that character (in spite of our reservations about the character), there are certain steps you must take to reach this goal. You may have to shift your approach to the other characters; your dialogue may have to be more emotionally charged and more intense, and you may need a more elaborate plot. Alfred Hitchcock, in his work with writers Ben Hecht and Raymond Chandler, exemplifies the ability to capture viewer empathy in spite of the use of less-than-admirable main characters. In *Psycho*, *The Birds*, and *North by Northwest*, it's the situation—rather than the character—that brings us into the story. In *Notorious* and *Strangers on a Train*, the unsympathetic main characters are offset by extreme antagonists, people we like to hate.

A scriptwriter also has to be concerned with the issue of stimulation for the viewer. Audiences go to movies to enjoy themselves. Whether stimulation comes from a complex plot or witty dialogue, there is an element of charm and stimulation that is necessary in relating the screen story to the audience. What happens to this element when you begin to challenge screenwriting conventions? It begins to fade. Therefore, you have to include stimulation in some other form. Spike Lee challenges conventional structure in *She's Gotta Have It*, but his additional charm comes from the dialogue. Whatever narrative strategy you use, audience identification and stimulation are critical factors in determining the success of your screenplay. If you select an alternative strategy, these factors will still have to be present.

Conclusion

In this chapter, we discussed conventions and counter-conventions to scriptwriting. Conventions are critical building blocks to tell your story. Counter-conventions can make that story fresh and more exciting. In order to use new strategies, however, you have to know the conventions of scriptwriting. Throughout this book, we highlight the creative opportunities that lie between these conventions and counter-conventions.

Reference

1. George Seaton, Kalmer Bert, and Will B. Johnstone *The Marx Brothers: Monkey Business, Duck Soup, and A Day at the Races* (London: Faber and Faber, 1953).

2

■ ■ ■ ■ ■ ■ ■ ■

Structure

In this chapter, we will begin an extended examination of structure—looking at how it is used both in mainstream and alternative films. We will consider the relationship of structure to character development and change, internal and external conflict, story meaning, and the relative positioning of character and audience.

Consider the story line of a mainstream film. In *The Verdict* (Sydney Lumet, 1982), Galvin, an alcoholic lawyer who has lost faith in the law, is given a lucrative open-and-shut case to settle out of court. But, finding himself moved by the injustice the case represents, and seeing an opportunity to redeem himself, he decides to bring it to trial. We know this is crazy, and, sure enough, he runs the case into the ground. At this point, there's nothing left and the script may as well end with Galvin's return to his dissolute life. But now, Galvin digs down and seizes the story. He finds "something in himself," and when everyone else wants to quit, he persists. At the "darkest moment," Galvin comes up with the clue that leads him to the critical witness. He wins the case and achieves personal redemption.

Now contrast this story line with that of an alternative film, *She's Gotta Have It* (Spike Lee, 1986). Nola Darling, speaking directly to the camera, tells the audience that she is consenting to this film in order to clear her name. We are then taken back into her past where, in a series of interviews and documentary-like scenes, we learn that Nola refuses to choose between her lovers. She insists that she wants them all. The lovers, however, aren't so understanding, and Jamie, the one she cares most about, finally dumps her. This event throws Nola into a period of despair. Her desire for freedom has backfired, and the cost is loneliness and bitterness. To escape this, she decides to drop her other lovers and return to Jamie. However, at the last moment, we are brought back to the present and learn that her attempt at monogamy was a mistake. "I'm not a one-man woman," she says.[1]

During the next four chapters, we're going to analyze the contrast between the approaches to narrative structure illustrated by these two stories. Before we do, however, we want to stop for a moment and consider how different these approaches feel. In the first story, there is a clear progression, a developing connection between the acts. The end of the story is a consequence of all that has taken place before. In the second story, the end seems to contradict the loneliness and bitterness that precedes it (although, actually, it makes perfect sense and may seem more believable than the change in *The Verdict*). In the first story, Galvin changes; he overcomes his past humiliation and regains his self-respect. In the second story, Nola seems to be the same person at the end of the film as she is at the beginning, only more so. In the first story, the structure is linear; in the second story, the structure is coiled. Furthermore, that Nola, and other characters, speak directly to the audience, through the camera, allows the audience to engage with the narrative in different ways. They become a participating member of the narrative, while at the same time engage critically with the film as it unfolds.* The events in *The Verdict* are transparent; they are expressions of, and serve to articulate, character change. The events in *She's Gotta Have It* are less clear; they seem arbitrary and open to conflicting interpretations. In *The Verdict*, recognition of failure leads to new strength and redemption. In *She's Gotta Have It*, the notion of failure is revealed to be a success.

Both of these stories are structured, but the structure works in opposing ways. In *The Verdict*, the structure contains the meaning of the story. Because Galvin reaches into himself when events look hopeless, he finds an inner strength that allows him to overcome injustice and find personal redemption. Everything in the script works to develop this movement. In *She's Gotta Have It*, the structure doesn't contain the meaning of the story. While Nola reaches into herself after she loses Jamie, her self-examination does not have the outcome we expect—her taking one lover and accepting domestic life. Instead, the expected connection is blatantly violated and we are invited to look elsewhere for the meaning of the film—to the documentary style, the flatness of the image, the picaresque quality of the scenes. While *She's Gotta Have It* is clearly structured, the film does not reveal its meaning through structure in the same way as *The Verdict* does. These differences are critical and profoundly affect the way we respond to the two films.

Understanding how structure works and the options it offers greatly expands our potential as scriptwriters. To start our exploration of the alternative screenplay, we are going to look at variations in structure by distinguishing between scripts that foreground structure (as seen in *The Verdict*) and those that challenge, undermine, or underplay this structure (as seen in *She's Gotta Have It*). In this chapter, we look closely at the most common articulation of the structural model—a version of the traditional three-act form that we call restorative three-act form. In the next chapter, we examine the fictional world that the restorative three-act structure

---

*The playwright and dramatic theorist Bertolt Brecht identified this dual perspective, sometimes called a distancing technique, as a component of "epic theater." It has been subsequently used by a number of filmmakers, most noticeably by the French writer and director Jean-Luc Godard.

tends to create. In Chapter 4, we examine alternative ways of structuring screen stories.

The Restorative Three-Act Structure

The basic screenwriting texts introduce some variation of three-act form, which is claimed to be the basis for every mainstream American screenplay. Three-act form is derived from Aristotle's broad notion that all dramas have a beginning, a middle, and an end, and that these parts are in some proportion to one another. Unfortunately, this formulation is so general that it tells us very little. (After all, was Aristotle completely serious when he said, "A middle is that which is itself after some other thing and after which there is something else"?[2])

A more specific variant of the three-act form has become the dominant model for mainstream films. This variant is derived from the well-made play, developed by the French playwright Eugene Scribe in the 1820s. Characterized by a clear and logical denouement, this conservative model of storytelling was the most popular dramatic form of the newly dominant French and English middle class that emerged in the "safe" Europe after the Napoleonic wars. By requiring a return to complete order, the well-made play allows us to act out our fantasies of breaking the rules, without in any way threatening the structural framework of society. "It is not supposed to have any 'remainder' or unsolved quotient to puzzle the audience."[3] Hence, our name *restorative three-act structure*.

Before we examine the restorative three-act structure, let's first review the basic foundation of three-act structure as it is presented in textbooks:

- A 120-page feature script is divided into three acts. The first act is roughly thirty pages long, the second act is sixty pages, and the third act is thirty pages.
- Each act rises to a point of crisis, or greatest intensity, which is called the *act curtain scene*[†] or the *plot point*. The resolution of this plot point throws the story into the following act.
- The plot point "hooks into the action and spins the story around in another direction."[4]
- The first act is concerned with setup, the second act with confrontation, and the third act with resolution.
- There is a period of relaxation at the start of each act before the act begins to build. Each act builds to a greater intensity than existed in the previous act.

[†] The term "act curtain," of course, comes from the theater where the curtain falls at the end of the most intense moments of conflict, which mark the act breaks. It is designed to keep the audience wondering what will happen after intermission. In television, the build of intensity is used to keep the audience watching through the commercial breaks.

Let's apply this outline to *The Verdict*:

- *The Verdict* is a 123-page script. The first act is twenty-eight pages long, the second is sixty pages, the third is thirty-five pages.
- Each act rises to a plot point.

The first-act plot point occurs when Galvin chooses to turn down the out-of-court settlement and bring the case to trial. While holding the settlement check in his hand, he says, "If I take that money I'm lost. If I take it I'm just going to be a rich ambulance chaser."

The second-act plot point occurs when, after Gavin has mishandled the defendant on the stand, he walks out of the courtroom in despair and the case seems doomed.

Once Galvin decides to take the case (end of first act), everything changes. Instead of wandering dreamily, Galvin strides determinedly, aggressively putting together his attack. However, the change is still superficial, and he's in over his head. His witness drops out; he tries to settle his case again, but this time he cannot; someone seems to be protecting a possible critical witness. His new expert witness is limited, and Galvin's court manner is rusty. Meanwhile, the defense anticipates his every move, waiting for him to fail; finally, he does.

However, after the case seems lost (end of second act), Galvin refuses to give up. Now in another turn, he discovers a new sense of purpose. Through sheer perseverance, he finds the critical witness. Galvin also learns of the duplicity of his lover and refuses to go back to her. He regains his self-respect and wins his case.

- The first act is concerned with setup, the second act with confrontation, and the third act with resolution.

In the first act, we meet all but two of the principal characters: the surprise witness (who is being held for the third act) and the new expert witness (who is not needed until Galvin's first-act witness drops out). The first-act dropout witness is the only character set up in Act One who does not appear later in the film. As Galvin ponders whether to bring the case to trial, we learn the essential expository information about it. The first act ends with the confrontation drawn, but not yet developed.

The second act follows the playing out of that confrontation until it appears to defeat Galvin. With the exposition out of the way, complication may be piled on top of complication. There is no way out. If we ended the film at the end of the second act, the resolution would feature the total defeat of Galvin.

In the third act, Galvin, having come to terms with himself, is able to move the case toward resolution. Once he engages in his quest for the critical witness and comes to terms with his false lover, we sense that he holds his fate in his hands. All he has to do is follow his instincts and we are sure he will prevail.

- There is a period of relaxation at the start of each act before the act begins to build. Each act builds to a greater intensity than was seen in the previous act.

After Galvin decides to take the case (end of first act), there is a period of relaxation and he is quite confident that he will win. Only when his expert witness drops out does he start to have doubts, and only then does the tension begin to build. After Galvin appears to lose the case (end of second act), there is another period of relaxation, during which he lets himself be taken over by his doubts. Only when he decides to press on and seek out the missing critical witness does the story begin to move toward its climax.

The second act (Galvin's apparent failure) has much greater dramatic impact than does his decision to take the case at the end of the first act. And of course, the climatic third-act victory in the courtroom dwarves all that comes before it.

The Verdict is a textbook example of restorative three-act structure. The clear-cut pattern of transgression and recognition (the Act One and Act Two plot points) is followed by sufficient opportunity for the character's redemption and restoration. Galvin figures things out just in time to fit his life back together. Also, *The Verdict* is straightforward and lacks irony or any other narrative device that undercuts the significance of this structure. These two elements—sufficient time for restoration and lack of irony—characterize the restorative three-act structure. As we see in later chapters, alternative screenplays, along with many other narrative forms, challenge both of these elements.

We have stated that different structures have distinct and characteristic forms that condition how we respond to them. To understand how structure determines our response in restorative three-act structure, we need to look at the way acts are used to structure not only the action, but also character development and the progression of our viewing experience.

Character Change

Restorative three-act stories are character driven. They are not about action alone, nor are they about characters incidentally caught up in events. Rather, they are about the intersection of a particular action and a particular character so that the working out of the action is a simultaneous working out of the character. One of the most difficult challenges in writing a three-act, character-driven story is to devise plot points that not only feed into the action, but also articulate character development.

This is true even in most generic action films. *Jurassic Park*, for example, at first glance appears to be structured entirely around the dinosaur attack. However, such a structure alone would so minimize our investment in character that even the T. Rex would not faze us. To gain our investment, a simple but essential character line is laid down that both involves us in the characters and uses the wonder/fear of the dinosaurs to develop this. In the first act, Grant rejects children and the whole notion of parenting, while at the same time he inadvertently demonstrates, through his affection for the newly born dinosaur, his fundamental caring nature. The second act brings him to the realization that the children are important to him. The third act plays out this caring, giving him any number of opportunities to put himself on the line for the children and suggests that this dry man of the past has discovered a hitherto unknown life force in himself. We can see this character development if we compare the strained smile of his partner/lover Ellie at the end of the first act, when she watches his contempt on being introduced to the children, and her loving smile at the end, when both children lean gratefully against Grant in the helicopter. The three acts thus structure the character change by articulating a series of progressive stages of character development.

The Central Character

By definition, restorative three-act stories are structured around one central character. Although there may be many characters of interest, there is only one character who carries us through the act breaks. *Bull Durham* is a good example of how act structure focuses on a single character. Although the film opens with Annie's long voiceover and then moves to the ballpark where we meet Nuke, Crash Davis is the central character because the act breaks turn on him. Act One ends when Crash walks out (after Annie brings the two men home to audition as her lovers), leaving Annie with Nuke, and himself estranged from the woman he clearly desires.

During the entire second act, Crash fights his pride and eventually loses. The second act ends at the low point—the moment when, after guiding Nuke to the major leagues, Crash is released from the team.

The stimulus that starts the third act also comes from Crash; he decides to go to Annie, and the movement through the act comes from his need to prove himself. The story ends only after he hits his record home run, reconciles himself to becoming a manager, and returns to Annie. Thus, although Annie provides a running voiceover throughout the script, and Nuke is the only character who breaks out of the minors, Crash is the character whose movement defines the dramatic spine of the story. All other action is ultimately subordinated to his change.

Relating Internal and External Conflict

In restorative three-act stories, the action is designed specifically to foreground a particular form of character psychology. This psychology is presented in a particularly stark, either/or form of conflict. We can see this when we watch how act breaks chart the character's development.

Bud, the central character in *Wall Street*, is torn between respect for his father and his father's values, and overwhelming greed and a desire to escape from his father's life. In the first act, greed seems to win, and Bud worms his way into the graces of takeover king Gordon Gekko by selling inside information that Bud obtained from his father. His success gives him a taste of the good life. However, Gekko is not interested in a one-shot deal; he wants Bud to make a career out of gathering and using insider information. Bud agonizes over this career choice and then agrees to support Gekko.

Thus, the first act of *Wall Street* is a victory for one side of Bud's character. But this is meaningful only if we see that Bud has another side, the one represented by his father, because only then will we know how much his pact with Gekko is costing him.

The second act follows Bud's rise in the financial world. He pulls off deals, buys a fancy East Side apartment, and gets the girl who, anyone except Bud can see, is just along for the money. There are a few glitches in his new life, but nothing he can't overcome. He doesn't even hear his father's warning that he's become Gekko's whore until his new world comes crashing down. When Gekko decides to take over the airline that Bud's father worked for all his life, his boss's actions are too much for Bud. Bud destroys his fancy apartment and lets his girlfriend walk out the door—end of Act Two.

Now the other side of Bud's character asserts itself. By helping to save the airline, Bud's character is redeemed in the third act, even though we leave him on the courthouse steps awaiting sentencing.

A critical technique in restorative structure is building the plot so that self-realization can come before external payback. Although the Stock Watch investigation brings the whole swindle down in the third act of *Wall Street*, Bud's fall in the second act comes not from external intervention, but rather from his realization that he's lost himself. This makes redemption possible. In *Rookie of the Year*, the twelve-year-old Henry becomes an all-star rookie relief pitcher by virtue of the mysterious strength he gains in his pitching arm after it heals from a break. We know that something will happen to Henry to cause him to lose his magical strength. However, if the film's resolution turned on this alone, if the loss of his strength ended the second act, the story would have a degree of arbitrariness we don't usually accept in a mainstream film. The story's motivational force would be medical rather than dramatic. Instead, the second act ends when, after losing his friends and his childhood, Henry decides to retire from professional baseball so that he can experience his life. His arm has to be brought back to normal for the story to end, but that happens in the third act after the key second act character decision has been made.

Either/or character tension is central to restorative three-act structure. In *Wall Street*, the cold-hearted tycoon Gekko, without this binary character tension (or possibly with more complex tension), would never destroy himself in this way. If *Wall Street* were Gekko's story, the structure would be two acts—he succeeds and he gets caught. Restorative three-act structure allows for character realization, which leads to character redemption and restoration. A character may not escape the law in a restorative three-act story, but he will have opportunity to redeem himself before he is arrested, to show that the real punishment came from within himself.

Not all restorative three-act stories are as blatant as *Wall Street*, but all pose this kind of decision. In *Bull Durham*, Crash must give up his pride to be with Annie. In *The Verdict*, Galvin must give up his naive notion of justice and get his hands dirty to win his case. In *Rookie of the Year*, Henry must give up his major league career in order to have his life.

First-Act Characteristics

The Point of No Return Unlike picaresque, slice-of-life, or other, flatter forms of storytelling discussed in the next few chapters, restorative three-act stories seize a particular period of time and make it the single defining moment in the character's life. The first-act curtain functions as a one-way gate. Once the character moves through the gate, he has entered a unique situation and can never return to the way things were before this moment. The gate is different for each picture and is given significance by the difficulty the character has in passing the turning point and by the role it plays later in the story. For example, once Benjamin makes love to Mrs. Robinson in *The Graduate*, he becomes the vulnerable character in the second act. He could have made love to Mrs. Johnson, who does not have any daughters, and it would not have mattered. The importance of this turning point is underscored by the fact that it takes him most of the first act to get up the nerve to make love to Mrs. Robinson and, later, by the fact that his action appears to have doomed his affair with Mrs. Robinson's daughter, Elaine.

False Solution The first-act plot point is a solution to the central character's dilemma because it seems to answer the dramatic problem raised in the first part of the film. Will Crash Davis become Annie's lover? Will Galvin take the case? Will Bud work for Gekko? However, the solutions are false; if they weren't, the story would be over. The false solution splits the character's intimate perspective of, "It's my life. I've got things under control" from the audience's long-term perspective of, "The movie's not over yet. Don't do that. You're going to get in trouble." The first-act curtain scene, while appearing to solve the crisis, opens up a whole new set of problems.

The false solution can be an obvious wrong turn, such as Benjamin sleeping with Mrs. Robinson, Bud working for Gekko, and Crash walking out on Annie; or it can be a turn in the right direction with insufficient understanding or preparation, such as Galvin deciding to bring his case to trial without coming to terms with his rustiness, his drinking, and his innocent belief that the injustice in his case is so obvious it will speak for itself.

Second-Act Characteristics

Act of Consequence The second act is the act of consequence—when the character finally catches up to the viewer. Act Two reaches its climax when the character finally has to face the implications of the false solution at the end of the first act. This recognition provides the opportunity for insight, which leads to resolution and restoration in the third act. The second-act curtain scene is given particular impact by a kind of double resolution. The character finally realizes her mistake, while we, the viewers, are finally satisfied that the character has come back to us. Frequently, this is the moment of highest identification. We are in sync with the character.

Moving Ahead of the Character One of the surprising elements of the restorative three-act structure is that for much of the story, we are ahead of the character. This is particularly true during the second act, when the character seems oblivious to her fate. It is as if the character is running away from her history, her background, and her circumstances with a rubber band tied to her waist. The character doesn't see the rubber band, but we do. We wait for the band to be stretched to its limit and snap her back.

In some screen stories, the central character's obliviousness in the second act is overt, and the internal conflict seems to vanish. For most of the second act in *Wall Street*, Bud does not question his actions. In fact, a scene in which he wonders who he is calls attention to itself precisely because it comes out of nowhere. In other stories, the character is not so much oblivious to his fate as he is working to deny it. Crash Davis's bitterness seems to evolve from a growing awareness that his playing days are numbered and he will never again make the big leagues. However far ahead of the character we are, the tension works the same way. We wait for things to go bad, and we wait for the moment when the character is forced to face what he has done to himself.

Character Assertion The end of the first act tends to thrust a decision upon the central character. In many cases, the structure leads us to believe that if the character had made a different decision, the story would be over. All of our sample stories would end if the characters had decided differently—Bud would turn down Gekko, Galvin would settle out of court, Crash would win over Annie the first night, and Benjamin would refuse Mrs. Robinson's advances.

The feeling at the end of the second act is quite different. The story appears to recede and leave the character lost. Although we are with the character, our momentum is exhausted because we have just seen the character defeated by the events we knew would defeat him. The cost of the character's earliest mistakes is not so much punishment as it is indifference.

Therefore, the character needs to reassert his importance to the story. The character's willingness to do this propels us into the third act. Now the character leads us, amazes us with resourcefulness, connects insight to success, and proves that once he has faced himself, he will triumph. Bud's success in pulling off the deal that challenges Gekko comes only as a result of the righteousness of his motivation—to help his father's airline.

Third-Act Characteristics

Recognition and Restoration The restorative three-act story has an upbeat ending. Having recognized his failure, the character is able to rise and overcome internal tension and story conflict. Usually, the resolution of internal conflict comes first. Self-realization is sufficient to allow Crash to finally overcome his pride and make love with Annie, Galvin to recognize that innocence alone won't win a case, Bud to reunite with his father in the hospital room, and Ben to face that he had to take control of his life even if it means breaking up Elaine's wedding.

The remainder of the third act is the playing out of the external conflict, which is now approached with a single-minded purpose. For Crash, this event is simple—he must hit his record home run. But for Bud and Galvin, the rest of the third act is melodramatic. Will Bud succeed in freeing Blue Star Airlines from Gekko and in saving his father's job? Will Galvin overcome a corrupt judge and his deceitful lover and win his case? Will Ben convince Elaine that his affair with her mother was meaningless?

Once internally resolved and armed with a goal, the character is given the chance to triumph over the odds. The external events of Act Two have led to recognition, not irredeemable disaster. Recognition comes in time to stave off tragedy; this is the key to the feel of restorative three-act stories. There is always a second chance; personal redemption and restoration are more significant than events, and actions are less important than motives.

The restorative three-act structure is a gentle form of storytelling. Characters are expected to make mistakes—that's part of life. The real test comes when the mistakes are laid bare, when the character realizes what we, as viewers, have already figured out—how false the character has been to himself. Out of this understanding comes the character's chance to prove himself and earn redemption.

Working It Out: Restorative Three-Act Structure

Before we go on, we will look at a few hints for working with the restorative three-act structure.

Three-Act Skeleton

One of the major advantages in working in any three-act structure is that it breaks down a two-hour story into more manageable units. You will find this story breakdown most useful if you think about it as an ongoing process, rather than as something you do only once. Writing is anything but a step-by-step process; the breakdown of acts is continually refined and rethought. The following suggestions are some useful ways to conceptualize the three-act structure:

- Write a paragraph for each act.
- Write the whole story in a paragraph using one sentence for each act.
- Convey the whole thematic movement implied by the acts in one sentence. For instance, for *Wall Street* we could write, "The realization that one's greed has caused the loss of one's identity and the destruction of loved ones' lives leads to a rethinking of values and the knowledge that self-awareness and love are more important than money."

Notice how the thematic sentence reveals the critical force of the restorative three-act structure. The active verb, *leads*, comes between the second and third act, between realization and restoration.

Build

Acts must build progressively. Unless you are purposely trying to thwart the viewer's expectations, you are committed to topping your first act. If your story goes flat in the second and third acts, it may be due to a lack of progressive development, or it may be because you are giving too much away in the first act. If you find you cannot top your first act, then pull it back and see if you cannot hold your build until later in the story.

Focus

Act structure demands focus. It is frequently said that each dramatic scene must do at least two things: it should develop character, provide texture, or cause us to laugh or cry, and it should move the plot. Specifically, the scene must refocus the act's tension and move us toward resolving that tension. Benjamin's inviting Mrs. Robinson to the hotel refocuses the question of whether Benjamin will sleep with Mrs. Robinson, while it also moves toward resolving the tension.

Align Action With Character

The most difficult thing about the restorative three-act structure is aligning the act breaks, demanded by the action, with the stages of development, needed for clear characterization. Once this has been done, the progress of events will be inevitable. There are many ways to separate Bud from Gekko other than by the potential destruction of Bud's father's airline. The most obvious is to move the Stock Watch investigation into the second act. However, only the potential destruction of the airline would trigger that one line of vulnerability in Bud, causing him to break down.

As you work to align character with action, you may find it helpful to use one of the three-act structure conceptual aids previously listed to chart act development. Make two parallel breakdowns—one for the development of the action and one for the development of the character. At first, you may find that there is little correspondence between the breakdowns, but as you work with the story, you should find that they eventually align. When they are aligned, you will find that a three-sentence summary of the action of the story also summarizes character development and change.

Relationship of the First Act to the Third Act

When a story goes bad in the third act, usually the problem can be traced to the first act. Restorative three-act stories are not about surprises; rather, they are about the playing out of events that have already been set up.

Frequently, an inexperienced scriptwriter will reach the end of the second act (the point of recognition) and get stuck, unable to make a believable character change. The potential for character change must be planted in the first act. We have to see Bud's love for his father early in the story in order to know how that love is being compromised in the second act. The energy that comes from recognizing the compromise causes the character to change.

Directionality

In the restorative three-act structure, the acts tend to move in opposite directions. In most cases, the climax of the first act frantically pushes the story upward and outward, and the climax of the second act is downward and inward. The story ends with a consolidation—an upward and outward push that is no longer frantic.

If you find that your acts are all going in the same direction, you have effectively written a one-act story. We discuss what you can do with a one-act story later in this book. However, if you have unwittingly written a one-act story, you have most likely removed the interim victories and disappointments of the restorative three-act structure, and your story will be unrelenting. Go back and see if you can modulate the act breaks. Give us something at the end of the first act before you take it away.

More Examples

We will end by looking at examples of three-act structure in films which represent three different genres.

In *Knocked Up* (2007) a Judd Apatow romantic comedy, Ben, a slacker who lives on disability in a communal house, has a one night stand with Alison, an up-and-coming television host. She becomes pregnant and, when, against everyone's advice, she chooses to keep the baby, Ben has to decide whether he wishes to become involved. After a conversation in which his father says, "You're the best thing that ever happened to me,"[5] Ben agrees to support Alison at the end of act one. But Ben does not understand what he has gotten into. Their relationship builds, and then collapses when Alison finds out that Ben did mushrooms on a road trip to Las Vegas suggesting that he will turn out like her problematic brother-in-law. Finally recognizing that his life has reached a dead end, Ben's second long talk with his father leads him to take charge of his life. The third act begins when he gets a job and moves into his own apartment. When Alison calls but does not leave a message, Ben is ready. He rushes her to the hospital, and, out of the shared birthing experience, they develop a more grounded relationship. Instead of doing mushrooms, Ben drives home with baby and Alison, trailing a line of cars behind him. "These guys can honk all they want. I ain't going faster than twelve."[6]

At the end of the first act of *Avatar* (2009), a James Cameron science fiction film, Jake in his identity as an avatar agrees to be trained by Neytiri in the ways of the Na'vi, the people living on the planet that Jake has come to plunder as a representative of the RDA Company. Despite his love affair with Neytiri, by the end of the second act, Jake must admit to the assembled Na'vi that he is a company spy. They turn on him as a result. Yet when Grace, the scientist with whom he works, is dying, he decides to seek the Na'vi's help. By becoming a Toruk Makto, one of six individuals who have ever successfully ridden the ferocious Great Leonopteryx monster, he gains the respect of the Na'vi and begs them to intercede for Grace. It is too late for Grace, but he subsequently wins the trust of the Na'vi by turning on and fighting back his own people. In the end, he severs his connection with the human Jake and permanently becomes his avatar.

Matt's extended family's inheritance of a large parcel of Hawaiian land is about to expire and, prior to the beginning of the film, the family has agreed to sell it for development. Also, before the film begins, Matt's wife has fallen into a coma as a result of a boating accident. The first act of *The Descendants* (2011), an Alexander Payne drama, ends when Matt learns that his wife had been having an affair with Brian. The script describes Matt's reaction as follows, "Matt stands up, walks in a little circle—he literally does not know which way to turn. Then he knows."[7] The transition from circular, undirected reaction to knowledge marks the act change.

Matt spends the entire second act tracking down Brian, learning in the process that he is connected to the developer to whom Matt's family is hoping to sell the land. The two story lines converge. If the deal goes through, Brian, his wife's lover, stands to make a great deal of money from Matt's property. It is at this point that Matt first speculates on scuttling the deal to his Cousin Hugh, the family member who is its biggest supporter. Cousin Hugh pushes back and says that he will be at the family meeting to discuss the deal. The script describes Matt's reaction, "TRACK TO . . . MATT'S FACE as he process this horrifying news delivered so casually."[8] And then it all goes to hell for Matt as he thinks, "Why can't a nuclear bomb blow the whole island up right now?"[9]

Finally Matt acts. He confronts Brian, but chooses not to tell Brian's wife about the affair, instead giving her an unexpectedly erotic kiss to which she responds. At the gathering to ratify the sale of the land, he tells his family that, over their objections, he will not sell it. He talks about protecting the land, and we understand that this is part of his reasoning, but we also suspect that it is also his way of punishing Brian. After scattering his wife's ashes in the ocean, the movie ends with Matt and his daughters on the couch, eating ice cream and watching television. Matt has made peace with the affair and the death of his wife.

Although these are three very different films, their use of three-act templates is similar. The characters' own initiatives in each drive them into the second act. In *Knocked Up*, Ben does not have to support Alison's pregnancy, but his conversation with his father suggests there is something to be gained by doing so. In *Avatar*, when asked to give an answer about why he is there, Jake says "To learn,"[10] which is the answer the Na'vi wish to hear. As a result, Neytiri is ordered to tutor him. Although it is his daughter who informs Matt of his wife's infidelity in *The Descendants*, the action that carries the film into the second act is Matt's choice to pursue it. And the first acts in all three movies serve as one-way gates. Once Ben gives Alison his promise to support her, he cannot go back on that at the risk of losing her. Once Jake convinces the Na'vi to teach him their ways, he cannot admit his role with the company at the risk of losing his connection with them. Once Matt learns about the affair, he cannot regard his dying wife in the same way. Further, the pursuit that marks all three character's movements into the second act is a false solution because it represents character action with incomplete understanding. No matter how much he supports her, Ben cannot win Alison until he moves out of his group house and gets a job. Jake will have to both admit that he is a spy and ultimately turn against the company before he can be accepted by the Na'vi and win Neytiri. Matt will need to understand the relationship between his wife's affair and selling his land, between violations among couples and between inhabitants and the land. Because of the film's genre, this is a more metaphorical and ephemeral connection then we see in the other examples.

In all three cases, we as viewers move ahead of the characters in understanding what they will have to face so that we are not surprised when each character falls in the second act. Ben is dumped by Alison for doing mushrooms in Las Vegas. Jake is captured by the Na'vi after he admits that he represents the Sky People. Matt wishes that the island be nuked after coming to understand he must turn on his family. Finally, each character will come to some understanding at the end of the second act that propels him forward into the third act. Ben's father tells him, "You can go around blaming everyone else, but in the end, until you take responsibility for yourself, none of this is going to work out." Ben pleads, "Just tell me what to do,"[11] and then realizes it is up to him to figure it out. He takes a job as a web designer and moves into his own apartment. Befitting the genre, Jake's understanding is more action-based. To return as an avatar to the Na'vi, Jake tells us in voice-over, "Sometimes your whole life boils down to one insane move,"[12] but the insane move causes him to understand that he must remain with the Na'vi. Conversely Matt's realization is more character-based. He connects his wife's betrayal of him to his potential betrayal of the land.

At the films' conclusions, all three character have acted as a result of what they have learned and all reach resolution as a result of it; Ben grows up and wins Alison, Jake commits to being a Na'vi and servers his connection to his human self, Matt prevents the land sale and comes to terms with the loss of his wife, both physically and romantically, while forging a new relationship with his daughters.

Thus, in these examples, which span a range of genres, we see that the three-act character template still applies. Characters make mistakes, come to understand them, and grow as a result. While the depth of understanding and the actions necessary for characters to achieve their goals may vary in each genre, the pattern of their development remains the same.

Conclusion

The restorative three-act form that organizes most mainstream American screenplays is one of many means to structure a screen story. Most restorative stories share certain characteristics, such as a central, sympathetic character who drives a story line that clearly relates external conflict to internal tension. Each act provides the impetus for the next act; the story moves forward, with each act building the tension toward the ultimate restoration in the third act.

Because restorative three-act structure gives characters maximum opportunity for redemption and restoration, this form of storytelling is very positive.

Typically, the first act sets up the conflict and allows the character the opportunity to find a solution to her problems. During most of the second act, the audience is ahead of the central character, waiting for the character to fall as a result of her poor first-act solution. This is the act of consequence, because at the very end, when the character finally recognizes the false solution and catches up with the audience's awareness, she usually reaches her lowest level in the story. This recognition leads into the third act, where the character has the opportunity to redeem herself.

In the next chapter, we need to look deeper at the kind of fictional world the restorative three-act structure tends to create. Then we'll move on to the alternatives.

Notes

1. Spike Lee, *She's Gotta Have It* (New York: Simon and Schuster, 1987), 361.
2. Aristotle, *Poetics* (Chicago: Henry Regnery, 1967), 15.
3. Tom F. Driver, *Romantic Quest and Modern Query, A History of the Modern Theatre*, 1st ed. (New York: Delacorte Press, 1970), 48.
4. Syd Field, *Screenplay: The Foundations of Screenwriting* (New York: Dell, 1982), 9.
5. Judd Apatow, *Knocked Up*. Web. Accessed June 15, 2012,. http://awards .universalpictures.com/pdf/knockedup.pdf, 46.
6. Ibid., 139.
7. Alexander Payne and Faxon, Nat and Jim Rash. 2012. *The Descendants*. Web. Accessed June 15, 2012,. http://genecartwright.com/Oscar/The%20 Descendants.pdf, 36.
8. Ibid., 86.
9. Ibid., 87.
10. James Cameron. *Avatar*. Web. Accessed June 15, 2012,. http://www.cinefile .biz/script/avatar.pdf, 47.
11. Apatow, op. cit., 113.
12. Cameron, op. cit., 117.

3

Critique of Restorative Three-Act Form

In restorative three-act stories, there is an implied contract between the viewer and the filmmaker, a tacit agreement that although the characters will err, we are never to lose sight of the costs. Although part of us may wish that the heroine gets away with something, we need the satisfaction of payback to fulfill our sense of dramatic completion.

But this need for payback is not inevitable; there are many stories that satisfy us precisely, because the character is not governed by such a fixed moral system and its consequent need for retribution. Rather, we seek payback in most mainstream films because of the way that the restorative three-act structure organizes our expectations. Because we are invited to identify with the transgressing character, which is clearly defined at the end of the first act, we are positioned both to understand the character's motivation and to see her mistakes.

This helps explain that familiar feeling of sitting in a theater and begging the character on the screen not to do something. She always does, and the thing she does always comes back to haunt her. Thus, in the broadest sense, the premise of most restorative three-act stories is that crime doesn't pay, that good will triumph over evil, and that there is no confusion over which is which.

But suppose this simple morality is foreign to us? Suppose the world we know is more likely to be marked by small missteps, unexpected tenderness, and, most of all, a lack of overriding predetermined purpose or clarity? Suppose we realize that the corruption of money and power is much subtler than that portrayed in *Wall Street*? Suppose we know that situations are rarely as unambiguously unjust as the one faced by Galvin in *The Verdict* and that good deeds are frequently tainted with blurred motivations? Forget corporate raiders and do-good lawyers. Suppose we find ourselves asking questions such as: Why do our lives seem to slip by in a succession of little details that appear so unimportant? How do we reconcile material success with personal malaise? Are we free of values long considered traditional, or do they haunt us in unexpected ways? How do we respond to the call of the larger world?

The creative screenwriter may not find it possible to answer these questions in a restorative three-act script. Although many restorative three-act films have less naked and less emphasized act breaks than do *Wall Street* and *The Verdict*, that structure still, like all forms of storytelling, suggests a point of view. No matter how we disguise it, a story with a clear violation followed by recognition and redemption seems like a moral tale, a reaffirmation of a preexisting, commonly understood ethics.

Are we saying that to write a thought-provoking script, you have to abandon the restorative three-act structure? Absolutely not. The purpose of this book is not to prescribe but to explore. No one can tell you in which style to write. If you allow someone to do so, you are ceding your power as a writer. We can, however, look at the things that are communicated by different styles and different approaches, and invite you to consider whether these correspond to the way you see the world.

You can go even further and ask: Is the form of the story really that important? Is there such a thing as neutral form, one into which we can pour any story? The answer is No. This is the focus of this chapter. Nothing is neutral; form is inextricably linked to content. There is no single way to tell a story, no right way, because the choice of form is a creative decision. The scriptwriter's choice of form communicates a basic feel and a point of view that fundamentally determines how we understand the story.

Before we look at alternative structures, we need to examine in more detail the point of view suggested by the restorative three-act form. When we decide on how we will tell our stories, we need to know what comes along for the ride, whether we want it or not. We will see how the restorative three-act structure implies broad perspectives on issues of free will, the relationship of character to society, our ability to change ourselves, and the transparency of motivation.

Story Over Texture

In the beginning of the previous chapter, we stated that restorative three-act stories disclose their essential meanings through the playing out of their structure. Although all stories reveal their meanings over time, restorative three-act stories are particularly horizontal in design. If we halt their forward plot movement, we have little left to organize the story.

To create the forward movement, each major scene must push the story toward the plot point, which, with its own circular logic, gains its significance, because it is the moment toward which the story is carefully built. This progression leads to a clear hierarchy of values for the viewer—we understand what is important (which brings us closer to the plot point) and what is merely background (texture and detail). In a restorative three-act script, forward movement comes at the expense of texture, resonance, and ambiguity.

One of the fundamental problems in grasping real-life experiences is that these experiences have no inherent focus. A million things compete for our attention. How do we know what is important? Once we find what's important, how do we maintain the clarity to follow it? If we are to write scripts that reflect this ambiguity, we have to go beyond the clear-cut order of the restorative three-act structure to suggest the sheer overabundance of detail and stimuli in contemporary life.

But the scriptwriter should be cautioned. When we talk about writing from the complexity of experience, we are not talking about transcribing reality. If you attempt to merely copy the disorder of direct experience, if you write with a million things competing for your attention—shaving, washing the dishes, tying shoes, coping with the death of a lover, feeding the cat—then all you'll create is disorder. Reproducing disorder is not a matter of writing in a disorderly fashion. The trick to writing about reality is to find a way to bring to the foreground the conflict between focus and confusion. Although the meaning points in a different direction, this approach requires as much control as does the restorative three-act structure.

Consistency of Tone

To be intelligible, all stories must have some form of tonal consistency. As in a game, the rules can be arbitrary, but once they are established, they must be maintained. Otherwise, events and actions will have no meaning.

In a restorative three-act story, however, tonal experimentation is particularly limited by the need to serve the progression of the act breaks. The film *Heathers* provides an example of this limitation. An apparent black comedy, the first act of *Heathers* ends with Veronica and her devilish boyfriend, J.D., killing her tormentor Heather (one of the high school's three most popular girls, all with the same name) and then covering up the crime with a fake suicide. This is an outrageous stuff, and it cries out to be pushed further. But by the end of the second act, after two more sets of killings, Veronica's had enough. She breaks off her relationship with J.D. and, in the third act, seeks revenge. The movie ends with her finally killing J.D., who has been the driving force behind her rage. Simple morality takes over; Veronica is redeemed. She has killed the evil force and now accepts the least popular person in the school, her old friend Martha Dumptruck. The chaos suggested in the first act, the outrageous acting out of impetuous teenage rivalry, is tamped down and made tame in the same way that the more freewheeling tone found early in the movie has been contained to service the plot.

Decision-Making Space

Acts tend to start out loosely structured and then gradually focus, constricting the character and forcing some decision. As we reach the act climax, we get the feeling that all action would stop and that the movie would end if the character did not make the decision that moves the story into the next act.

It is impossible to mistake the fact that a decision is being made or the importance of that decision. The overall structure of the script builds to and is dependent on the decision-making moment. Often, the moment is slowed down, exaggerated, or frozen. This clear-cut articulation can be thought of as a decision-making space, a moment that is emptied of any distractions aside from the decision.

In *Wall Street*, Gekko and Bud are riding in a limousine when Gekko proposes that Bud work for him. As the car stops, Bud has a moment to make up his mind before the limousine pulls away, leaving Bud alone on the street corner and with the promise of Gekko's wealth literally disappearing in front of him. There is no mistaking what Gekko is asking nor that Bud will have any later chance to accept it. Thus, Bud is fully aware of the one-way gate he is passing through.

Rarely do we experience decisions in these clear-cut moments when we can isolate and weigh the consequences and then decide our fate. By decisions, we are referring to the millions of things that define us (the kind of people we like, what we enjoy doing), which are so fundamental to our character that we rarely think of them as decisions at all. If we thought of decisions this way, then Bud would not stand outside his experience enough to weigh the pros and cons of this choice. Rather, all his small actions, his step-by-step revelation of himself that led to his getting involved with Gekko, would serve to make the decision for him. If he did later become aware of what he had gotten into, he would not be able to point to one single moment where that had happened. Of course, if we imagine Bud's character drawn this way, then reversing his fate would be that much more difficult, if not impossible.

Understanding Motivation

Restorative three-act stories are character driven: The action turns on character decision, and the motivations that underlie the decision are made accessible to the audience. In fact, the essence of the restorative three-act structure is that action is an expression of motives, of character conflict.

Clearly, if we are to write a story about human actions, we must have some way to read motivation. However, the manner in which motivation is portrayed is variable. In restorative three-act stories, it is very rare for the central character to make a decision that hasn't been carefully prepared for the viewer. The first-act breaks of all the films we've discussed—*Wall Street*, *The Verdict*, *Bull Durham*, and *The Graduate*—have been calculated, so that we understand the conflicting forces underlying the decision being made. The fact that we weigh the options as we wait for the character to decide gives us a feeling of participating in the decision-making process.

By contrast, in *She's Gotta Have It*, Nola's final decision to abandon Jamie appears, at least initially, to come out of the blue. Her decision makes sense only when we look back on the rest of the film and put things together. Our understanding is not instantaneous. We are supplied with clues not only from the movement of the story but also from the texture, the details, and, most importantly, from the ellipses, the things not there. Our understanding is more reflective, and its full impact may not hit until the film is over.

Binary Character Psychology

In order to be distinct, acts tend to inflict extreme choices. Bud is either with Gekko or he is not; Crash is either with Annie or he isn't; there is no middle ground. As the strength of the restorative three-act structure is its use of progressive acts to chart a progression of character, we see the either/or quality transposed onto character. To side with Gekko, Bud has to turn on his family and their values. To reject Annie, Crash, overtaken by his pride, rejects his romanticism.

In some restorative three-act stories, the third act represents a return to innocence, as in Bud's return to his family at the end of *Wall Street*. However, this shedding of all that happens to him during the course of the film may seem unsatisfactory. To return to his family, Bud rejects the greed and ambition that drove his actions for most of the film. The residue of this ambition is never accounted for. How did he come to terms with it? Where did it all go?

In other restorative three-act stories, the third act represents a compromise between the extremes of the first two acts, and we feel that the character's experiences are more satisfactorily accounted for. In *The Verdict*, Galvin attempts to defend a case based solely on justice. In the second act, his cocoon-like innocence is shattered. It is only when he is willing to misrepresent himself—to lie and to open other people's mail—he gets to the one witness who will help him win the case. At the end of the film, the two sides of Galvin's character have been integrated. Galvin can now seek justice and play the game at the same time.

The force of the restorative three-act structure comes from a certain willful blindness on the part of the character. In the second act, the character is not aware of what we know about him. This willful blindness allows the second act to build while we wait for the character to fall. This obliviousness generates dramatic force at the expense of self-awareness. The character develops precisely, because he does not notice what is perfectly plain to us. When he does, the character tends not to adjust by making small accommodations but to snap back into place.

At first glance, the restorative three-act structure appears to bring us closer to the characters. Its paradox is that upon closer examination, the comfortable awareness of the first-act transgression places us safely outside of the story. As discussed in the next chapter, other forms of stories—those that don't have such a clear-cut first-act climax—tend to leave the viewer much less certain about the circumstances and the morality of the situation in which the character finds herself. As we are not pre-positioned, we have to work constantly to reassess the meaning and the relative morality of the character's actions. In fact, these kinds of screen stories tend to do away with the larger ethical questions and suggest less the affirmation of general morality than the struggle to deal with an ambiguity that is as problematic to the viewer as it is to the character.

History as Backdrop

The underlying assumption in a restorative three-act script is that the character is restrained by her conflict, her flaw, and her psychology. Even though the conflict is externalized (i.e., there is a real dramatic problem), the problem expresses an internal conflict. Once the character stops fighting herself (usually in the beginning of the third act), she tips the plot in her favor and eventually triumphs.

So what is the problem with this? Nothing, except that this form of scriptwriting doesn't account for the particular historical, social, political, economic, and familial circumstances that also condition fate. History, as an event or impersonal force, serves merely as a vehicle for psychological development. The film scholar David Bordwell cites an example of the appropriation of history as a plot device: "As an old Russian émigré says at the end of *Balalaika*: 'And to think that it took the Revolution to bring us together.'"[1]

We see this even in films without an apparent political perspective. Consider *Jurassic Park* for a moment. Ellie's role as a professional woman who treats an ailing stegosaurus and who braves the raptors to switch on the power would seem to suggest a much more progressive view of women than is traditionally presented in mainstream film. This is quickly dispelled, however, when we look at Ellie's dramatic role in the film. She has no doubts, no hesitation, and no conflict or growth, so that her actions indicate nothing about her internal life. Instead, her dramatic function is to smile knowingly at Grant when he is around children, thus serving merely to mark his progress through the acts. Although she is portrayed with the mannerisms of a feminist, her dramatic role is that of a static signpost against which we measure the male character's growth. It is worth noting that even though *Jurassic Park* is not advertised or thought of as a political film, it conveys, as do all films, a political meaning nonetheless.

Although the use of history as a backdrop to psychological development is not always as obvious, barriers of race, gender, class, and history are still presented as secondary to the transcendence of individual will. If we find ourselves suspicious of this worldview, if we feel our history has shown us the limitations and corruptions that underlie our illusion of free will, then we must be leery of the restorative three-act structure. If we are not, we may find ourselves reinforcing, through the structure of our screenplays, the very conservative notions we wish to challenge in our stories.

Motives Outweigh Events

Action in restorative three-act stories services, and gains importance as an expression of, character conflict. The physical world and the force of history are subordinate to their roles as reflections of the character's personal redemption. The effect of subordination is to coddle the character and to make the consequences of action less important than motives. Redemption is not only spiritual but also a literal reconstruction of the circumstances of the character's predicament. The character is never allowed to get in so deep that he can't get out.

To understand this coddled form of storytelling, compare the restorative three-act structure to classical tragedy. In *King Lear*, Lear falsely condemns his one true daughter, Cordelia, in the first act. The rest of the play depicts the consequences of that condemnation. His recognition of his wrong, wrought by four acts of hardship and disintegration, leads him to kneel when he finally meets Cordelia again. Yet, such recognition is too late. Although he is finally able to see, he cannot transform the world into a reflection of his own psychology. Forces larger than his motives and desires have been set into motion. He may recognize them, but it is too late to stop the tragedy of his death and the destruction of his kingdom.

In contemporary literature, stories often work the other way. Instead of being faced with the destruction of a whole kingdom, characters confront the stone-cold indifference of the material world. In the short stories of contemporary American writers such as Raymond Carver, Bobbie Anne Mason, and Annie Beattie, the most remarkable elements are the limits of human expression and the lack of a clear-cut ethical imperative in a world that is resistant to universal meaning.

The restorative three-act structure doesn't work that way. It is a moralistic form of storytelling with the basic premise that good motives triumph and that the world is understandable, consistent, manageable, and responsive to goodness and truth. As a result, external events are rarely arbitrary; instead, they are earned. In a three-act structure script, the character's fate is not only in her own hands, but as long as she is willing to admit her mistakes, the consequences of her actions can be eradicated.

The Effaced Narrator

One of the dominant aspects of mainstream film is the extent to which it seeks to erase the evidence of a storyteller and to imply that what takes place on the screen would take place regardless of whether a camera were recording it. The screenwriter should be aware of this distinction between showing and telling, dramatizing and narrating. Aristotle makes a distinction between the poet "imitating everyone as acting" and the poet narrating "by being himself and not changing."[2] The poet imitating everyone stands effaced and is an ideal, invisible agent that reproduces, without comment, events that have happened. The poet being himself and not changing is present as a storyteller who stands between us and the events and consciously interprets them. In the first instance, the story is understood to be transparent; the subject is the event. In the second instance, the story is understood to be an indeterminate interaction between the events and the narration. The events may be so minimized that the story is largely about the voice.

Clearly, there is no such thing as a story without a storyteller. No matter how much the storyteller seeks to disappear, there is always an interpreting sensibility or point of view that structures the action for us. Yet, the restorative three-act structure is based on a conventional structure that is designed to divert our attention from narration and to suggest that the story tells itself.

In a novel, we expect to find a narrator, a voice that speaks directly to us. Unlike the more omniscient narration used by nineteenth-century writers such as George Eliot, most twentieth-century literary fiction implicates this voice in the story. Thus, we have degrees of unreliable, first-person narrators or third-person narrators inflected with the voice and emotional charge of characters within the story. We talk about this in Chapter 22. In fact, this overt narrative shaping is one of the reasons why novels can frequently turn on events that have less obvious import than do those in films.

In most plays and films, there is no overt narrator who speaks directly to the camera and interprets events. However, this does not mean that there is no narrator. Rather, the narrator is implied, in large part, through a dramatic structure. This is why we say that restorative three-act films reveal themselves through their structure—the structure itself functions as the narrator. Structure modulates our interest and gives significance and meaning to events without calling attention to itself, as though the story just happened and the characters really control their own fates.

It is critical that we understand the narrative role of the restorative three-act structure. If we want to work with other forms of stories, we have to find other means to serve this function. As we see in the next chapter, one of the things that happens when we break out of restorative three-act form is that the effaced narrator becomes increasingly visible and overt.

Conclusion

The pattern of transgression, recognition, and redemption makes the restorative three-act structure a very comforting form. It allows us to identify with characters who have gone beyond acceptable behavior, while at the same time remaining aware that they will be forced to confront their behavior. The three-act structure privileges the individual over any social, historical, economic, and familial limitations. Although this may be underplayed, we cannot avoid the implications of the form altogether. If the feel of transgression, recognition, and redemption is what we want, then there is no better way to express this than by using the restorative three-act structure. But to create a different feel, to find a way to respond to the arbitrariness and indifference of the contemporary world, we have to look elsewhere.

References

1. B. David, J. Staiger, and K. Thompson, *The Classical Hollywood Cinema. Film Style & Mode of Production to 1960* (New York, NY: Columbia University Press, 1985), 13.
2. Aristotle, *Poetics* (Chicago, IL: Henry Regnery, 1967), 5.

4

Counter-Structure

As we have seen, stories cast in restorative three-act form tend to be conservative, suggesting an orderly, clear-cut world in which characters control their own fates and action is redeemable by motive. These stories don't speak to the more ephemeral sense of experience that we mentioned in the previous chapter. To express a more disjointed world, changing content is not enough; structure, too, must function in more ambiguous ways. Sometimes, it is placed in the foreground and made very obvious. By calling attention to itself, structure suggests the artificiality of form over the chaos of day-to-day experience. At other times, structure becomes flattened and apparently minimized, creating the illusion of documentary randomness.

We can comfortably define the restorative three-act structure, because it provides a framework that tends to promote the story, or, as Syd Field says, if you know the three-act paradigm, "you can simply 'pour' your story into it."[1] However, counter-structures, which evolve organically from less preplanned needs, are as open-ended and various as are the stories from which they grow.

The following examples are not meant to indicate preexisting categories or a definitive list but rather to demonstrate some of the options open to the scriptwriter.

Structure in the Foreground

We will start by looking at a central paradox that governs all art. By definition, art demands some shaping to give it a meaning. The problem is how then to represent a world whose organization seems elusive at best. One way to do this is by making structure obvious. By calling attention to itself as the fundamental organizing principle, this use of structure exaggerates its artificiality. Because it is shown to be artificial, it organizes the story without reducing the feeling of chaos underneath.

Ironic Three-Act Structure

In *Chinatown*, Syd Field clearly demonstrates how acts function. The first act ends when the real Mrs. Mulwray shows up at Gittes's office. As Field points out, this spins the plot around: "If she is the real Mrs. Mulwray, who hired Jack Nicholson? And who hired the phony Mrs. Mulwray, and why?"[2] Gittes must find out who set him up. The second act ends with the discovery of the eyeglasses in Mrs. Mulwray's saltwater pool, apparently implicating her in the death of her husband. Having shielded her from the police inquiry and then becoming her lover, Gittes now realizes his mistake.

The act structure clearly delineates the development of Gittes's character, from the cool outsider to the emotionally involved lover. By the time he makes love to Mrs. Mulwray, we know that he's tied up with the same personal demons that drove him out of Chinatown in the first place. We can speculate on those demons—an unwillingness to take orders and the inability to separate personal commitment from professional judgment—whatever they are, his super-cool indifference in the first scene, during which he gloats as his client studies pictures of his wife's adultery, has changed into a personal entanglement that goes beyond simple justice in the second act.

We believe that Gittes will overcome this personal entanglement because of the self-conscious detective story genre that *Chinatown* plays on. We know that the detective will spurn love in favor of justice, will destroy highly placed criminals because he lives on the margin of society, and will be most dangerous when apparently defeated.

However, while evoking the classic detective genre, *Chinatown* also distorts it, setting up another line of expectation. Unlike the classic detective whose failure to fit into the domestic world is presented as heroic, Gittes is portrayed as somewhat incomplete. We sense a sorrow under his glibness and a loss we will later learn is connected with Chinatown. Unlike the classic detective whose life, not his emotions, turns on the working out of the plot, Gittes's whole personality is threatened by his growing involvement with Mrs. Mulwray. We don't expect him to be sitting calmly at his desk the day after Mrs. Mulwray is shot, waiting for whoever comes over the transom, the way we do with Sam Spade at the end of *The Maltese Falcon*. At the end of *Chinatown*, we believe Gittes is emotionally destroyed.

Chinatown evokes not only the detective genre but also the restorative three-act genre in which a character's vulnerability is exposed, addressed, and then overcome. This double expectation of triumph—justice will be done by the detective and he will overcome his vulnerability—is turned topsy-turvy when the criminal, Noah Cross, defeats the detective by getting away with his crimes, and Mrs. Mulwray, the only person to have touched Gittes since his last fling in Chinatown, is shot. The story gains its power precisely because of the extent to which it invites us to believe that our expectation of a happy ending will triumph over a darker reality. When our expectations are not met, the darker reality seems all that much more oppressive, because it has penetrated the apparently safe frame of the story.

Ironic three-act structure, then, involves setting up the expectation raised by coherently developed act breaks and foiling it at the end. The extent of the unexpected turn of events is tricky, because, even though it breaks the logic of the acts, it must conform to a deeper story logic to satisfy us.

For instance, although Buck Henry's screenplay *The Graduate* follows the restorative form (with Ben busing off triumphantly with Elaine), Mike Nichols's film adds a twist to this ending. Nichols focuses on the lovers in the back of the bus for what seems to be an uncomfortably long time, allowing them to reveal themselves. At first, they look at each other apparently with joy, then they stare forward without a word, until we become uncomfortable. Have they triumphed, or are they condemned to the same unfulfilling life that Mr. and Mrs. Robinson started in the back of their Ford?

The ending works because the ironic reading keeps us close enough to restorative expectations to satisfy ourselves, while at the same time teasing us with something more. Thus, although we had expected both Benjamin and Gittes to triumph, we can reconstruct the logic of their failure by rethinking what has gone on before. The fact that Ben seems to have nothing to say to Elaine is consistent with the circumstances of their courtship. Thus, ironic three-act stories don't break the structural logic so much as they turn it in other directions.

Exaggerated Ironic Three-Act Structure

By contrast, at the conclusion of *Blue Velvet*, Sandy and Jeffrey regard mechanical robins as though they were real and buy into a notion of small-town happiness without ever addressing the implied voyeuristic perversity that earlier involved Jeffrey with Dorothy. Nothing quite adds up, yet because we are aware of this from the beginning (by the exaggerated small-town images), the playing out of the film still somehow satisfies us. Unlike *Chinatown*, which lets us believe the story might all work out, *Blue Velvet* never ceases to remind us of its ironic distance.

From the opening credit sequence, we are teased with the multiple meaning of images. The heightened icons of innocence—the white picket fence, the yellow tulips, and the slow-motion fire truck—set against Jeffrey's father's stroke both suggest and parody small-town harmony. The presence of evil is constantly overstated, so that everything, from the heavily underscored pan shot of the Lincoln street sign (after Jeffrey had been warned to stay away from that neighborhood) to Frank's gratuitous use of the word *fuck*, serves to make us suspicious of, rather than comforted by, the simple good/evil dichotomy.

Despite the multiple meaning of the images, *Blue Velvet* relies on the three-act structure to drive the story. The tension between the restorative organization and the exaggerated representation of small-town life gives the film its particular irony.

The first act comes to a close when, determined to pursue the mystery of Dorothy and the disembodied ear, Jeffrey breaks into Dorothy's apartment and steals her key. The long second act follows Jeffrey's growing involvement with both Dorothy and Sandy, to the point that he is warned off the case by Sandy's father. Jeffrey's impotence is underscored at the act break when, powerless, he watches a man he knows to be criminally implicated visits Sandy's father. The final act kicks toward resolution when Dorothy shows up at Jeffrey's house naked and beaten. This event leads to the final showdown, after which order is restored to Timberton, but it is an order as artificial as the mechanical birds.

Does *Blue Velvet* rely on the three-act structure? Yes. But set against the exaggerated representation of good and evil—the stagy meetings in the malt shop and the dreams of the robins coming home—the three-act structure seems equally artificial. The undeveloped decision to go after Dorothy, the coincidence of the toilet flushing that covers the honking of the car's horn, the banality of the evil, all exemplify and parody the structure and its happy ending. Like *Chinatown*, *Blue Velvet* uses the three-act structure, but whereas *Chinatown* teases us with the possibility of a restorative ending, *Blue Velvet*, by making both its structure and the world it represents into a cliché, mocks even the aims of restoration: Restore what? A small-town myth that existed only in the movies?

One of the classics in film history also uses this technique. Jean Renoir produced *Rules of the Game* in the spring of 1939, and it opened in Paris just weeks before the outbreak of World War II. *Rules of the Game* borrows liberally from French farce. The butler is named Corneille, the hijinks upstairs are matched with the amorous misadventures downstairs, and both the conflict and its resolution are infused with a Mozartian delight.

However, it doesn't all quite fit. Both by evoking a genre from the past and by miming its innocent tenderness while exposing its incongruity, Renoir is able to suggest that the closure the film achieves comes from the artifice of art, of genre, rather than from any order in the lives being portrayed. We are invited to appreciate the magnificent symmetry of the form while also recognizing the impotence, rot, and isolation of the particular social world that form represents. Less than 9 months after the film's release, the German army tore through France in 10 days, and that impotence was revealed to the rest of the world. The film is simultaneously exquisitely beautiful and starkly terrifying.

Filmmaker as Antagonist

We don't watch *After Hours* for very long before we are aware that something is off center here, too. But, unlike in *Blue Velvet*, where the characters do not know that the birds are mechanical, in *After Hours*, Paul gradually becomes aware that he is being affected by something that exists outside of the story. At a climactic moment, as the camera pulls up and away, Paul gets on his knees and yells into the lens, "Why are you doing this to me?" This action breaks down the fundamental assumption of realism—that no one in the story is aware of being observed. Once this happens, the whole notion of a structure that organizes the story for a viewer, but is not apparent to the characters, is undercut. Instead of the structure being concealed behind the actions of the character, it becomes the exact opposite—both obvious and antagonistic to the character. The character becomes aware that something is controlling his life, and, in this way, he must face how limited his freedom is. He is forced to fight something so deeply embedded in his existence that he can't step outside and confront it. As we see in Chapter 22, this tension between the character and the narrator can be a way to express the tension between our illusion of complete freedom and the subtle ways that, unbeknown to us, the outside pressures of society, class, gender, and history condition our choices.

Documentary Randomness

In contrast to the previous examples, other scripts flatten and minimize structure, creating the illusion of documentary randomness.

Indifferent Three-Act Structure

Badlands has two distinct turning points that resemble act breaks—the moment when 14-year-old Holly runs off with her boyfriend, Kit, who has just killed Holly's father, and the moment when, after several murders, Holly finally decides to leave Kit. Certainly, these two decisions would function very well in a redemptive mode, suggesting a story about an adolescent's mistake and the realization of its costs. The difference in *Badlands* is that Holly, who provides the blank, emotionless voiceover narration, does not seem to learn anything.

Let's look in detail at the treatment of Holly's decision to run off with Kit. On page 19 of the script, Kit shoots Holly's father in the back. Holly kneels by her father, then goes into the kitchen, followed by Kit. Then Kit, followed by Holly, comes back into the living room, feels Holly's father's heart, and says, "He don't need a doctor."

Cut to Kit dragging Holly's father into the basement (script page 20). An indefinite period of time has passed. Kit picks up a toaster and brings it up to the kitchen, where Holly slaps him. She walks into the living room. He follows and then decides to leave for a while. She sinks down on the couch.

Cut to the exterior of the house at night (script page 21). More time has passed. Cut back to the interior. Holly comes up the stairs and looks through the bedroom window at two boys playing outside.

Cut to the train station (script page 21). Same time period. Kit puts a coin in the slot of a gramophone booth and makes a record on which he confesses that Holly and he plan to kill themselves. Kit leaves the booth.

Cut to gasoline being poured over the piano (script page 22). Leaving the record playing, Holly and Kit set the house on fire and run to the car.

Cut to Holly collecting her books from her locker at dawn (script page 23). In a voiceover, she tells us she could have sneaked away, but her destiny now lay with Kit, for better or for worse.

What has been carefully cut out of this sequence is the moment when Holly decides that her destiny lies with Kit. In place of this moment, we have static, almost tableau-like scenes that seem inappropriate to what is happening. Because we do not see them as transitions or attempts to come to terms with the killing, we can only try to make sense of them by attributing our own emotions to them and assume that Holly is mourning her father. However, our assumptions of Holly's mourning are confused when, inexplicably, she runs away with Kit. When her voiceover expresses no feeling at all for her father, we realize that we have no way to penetrate the images. Why is everything photographed so beautifully? Why does the main character have such limited reactions? We don't know. But what better way to convey the coldness we associate with a mass killing spree than that eerie, inexplicable distance?

To understand the power of this oblique structure, we can look at a film like *Bonnie and Clyde*. Despite the number of bullet holes, the violence in *Bonnie and Clyde* feels like abstract movie violence, while the killing in *Badlands* casts an unrelenting oppressiveness over the viewer that lingers long after the end of the film.

Badlands uses a technique worth noting. As we watch, we struggle to relate the time of the voiceover to the time of the events in the movie. Because the voiceover seems so immature and so undisturbed by the violence it is describing, and because it seems to cast Holly's actions as adventures in a romance novel, we tend to place it very close to the time of the images. However, as this movie draws to a close, we learn that Holly is speaking from a perspective distanced by a number of years from the events on the screen. This makes the perspective of the movie even more chilling. Although this much time has passed and she has thought about what she has done, Holly is still unable to recount the horror or even the unromanticized dreariness of what she has gone through.

Ironic Two-Act Structure

She's Gotta Have It makes no attempt to answer restorative expectations. In fact, the film ends with a deliberate flouting of our expectations. We expect Nola Darling, having lost the man she seemed to love, to abandon her free-spirited lifestyle, but she does not. Yet, we find Nola's declaration of indifference perfectly satisfying, unlike our response to *Chinatown*, in which we would be totally lost if Gittes declared that he was no longer interested in Mrs. Mulwray. In *Chinatown*, we move through a clear first-act transition when Gittes, threatened by Mrs. Mulwray, decides to take her on. This transition engages us and draws us into the second act; our participation commits us to its playing out. *She's Gotta Have It* has no such first-act turning point. In fact, its flashback structure discourages a linear, three-act reading. Nola moves ahead of us throughout the whole film. Although we first assume that she has a monogamous relationship with Jamie, we are not explicitly told this. When we later learn about her other lovers, we are learning about something that has already been decided, rather than participating in a newly made decision. Thus, unlike Gittes in *Chinatown*, we are not implicated in the shaping of Nola's life; we are presented with her lifestyle as given.

She's Gotta Have It does have something akin to an act break. After Jamie leaves her, Nola decides to drop her other two lovers and go back to him. However, because we have not been involved in Nola's initial decision to have three lovers, and because we are not positioned to see the taking of the three lovers as a first-act mistake, we do not feel this break serves as a consequence of some earlier misdirection. Unlike a traditional second-act break, we have no sense of her coming back into sync with us. Rather, we stand outside and watch, wondering what she is going to do without being able to prejudge her actions. When she does not stay with Jamie, we are left trying to put the pieces of the story together to figure out why.

One-Act Structure

Although *She's Gotta Have It* is structured in two acts, Martin Scorsese's *Mean Streets* has no act breaks at all. *Mean Streets* follows one line: Charlie's attempt to find salvation in the streets by backing Johnny-Boy. Within the first 10 minutes of the film, we learn that Charlie has guaranteed Michael's loan to Johnny. When Johnny throws away what little money he has, Charlie pulls him aside to get it sorted out. This scene has all the makings of a first-act curtain. We know, even though Charlie does his best not to notice, that Johnny is a disastrous credit risk. Yet, as Charlie's decision has already been made, all this scene does is affirm and deepen action that began in the backstory—Charlie will stick with Johnny until the end.

At the beginning of the film, Charlie is warned against guaranteeing Johnny's loans. This is essentially a second-act scene, a scene that heightens the cost of the decision traditionally made at the end of Act I, and one that the rest of the film continues to develop. Throughout the rest of the movie, Charlie is repeatedly warned off Johnny-Boy, while at the same time Johnny becomes the source of Charlie's salvation—a cross he has chosen to bear. This pressure slowly builds until Johnny, fleeing with Charlie, is killed, leaving Charlie to live without salvation.

Without plot turns, without small victories or misdirections, a one-act script is extremely difficult to sustain for 2 hours. But, when it succeeds, it carries a relentless accumulation of power that is hard to achieve in a more segmented story. Such a story starts with a conflict that is already well engaged and runs through a long, slow, second-act arch. Frequently, the conflict is so intense and fundamental; it is beyond a defining, third-act character resolution. For example, Charlie's struggle between salvation and family is no closer to a resolution at the end of *Mean Streets*.

Although divided into thirds, *Stranger Than Paradise* provides a similar example. Each of its three parts moves in the same direction and gives us the same single-minded directionality that we see in *Mean Streets*. Whatever itch Eddie is seeking to scratch, his trips to Cleveland, Florida, and, finally, Budapest propose the same kind of solution. Eddie will feel displaced wherever he is, which we knew right from the beginning of the film. Thus, rather than reveal or expose character, flattened structure tends to confirm and deepen what we already know. It also tends to cast doubt on any possibility of change. What will Eddie discover in Budapest? We don't know, but would be surprised if he finds it to be any different than Cleveland. In Lizzie Borden's *Working Girls*, the central character, after spending a dull, grueling day and night as a prostitute, decides to quit. Because we are never invited to ask why she's become a prostitute in the first place, because this has been predetermined before the film starts, we regard her decision with skepticism.

Mixed Modes

We have artificially separated forms into those that place structure in the foreground and those that flatten it. In practice, most alternative screenplays use both tendencies. Jean-Luc Godard's *Masculine/Feminine* is a perfect illustration of playing out the tension between two opposite ways of approaching structure.

Masculine/Feminine, which follows Paul's involvement with the rising pop singer Madeline, is subtitled "15 Precise Acts." The action is punctuated with numerical intertitles, which progress erratically toward the number 15. For instance, we don't see number titles for a time, and when we do we see 4, 41A, then nothing, then 7 and 8 in the middle of other titles. These numbers, however erratic, provide an obvious and self-conscious structure. We know the film will be over by the time we reach 15.

By contrast, the scenes are flat, under-lit, and highly documentary in style. They are structured like imperfect interviews, with the suggestion that the most important information is always that which cannot be said. Words are a poor approximation of what is meant; the world appears heavy, opaque, uninterpretable, and impervious to emotion. Characters are observed at a distance. There are few transitions, and all point-of-view shots are ambiguous.

The film plays on this paradox between the artificial and the documentary. By providing an explicit, overt, narrating structure (the progressive numbers), the script acknowledges its artificiality, freeing it from hiding the coincidences that determine all narrative structure. We cannot miss this sense of external control, the implication that the characters are not controlling their own lives. They seem lost in a world that provides them only with advertising slogans. Paul speaks to Madeline through a record machine, unable to find his own words to express his feelings for her. At the same time, this narrative presence is rendered suspect by the documentary style.

No matter how many interview questions are asked and how hard the camera seeks to penetrate, the flat, opaque surface of the world reveals little, neither to the characters nor to the narrator.

One of the functions of narration is to signal the end of a film. In a mainstream film, the story ends without calling attention to whatever actually structures a sense of ending. The questions raised by that structure seem to resolve themselves. In *Masculine/Feminine*, by contrast, the end is intentionally arbitrary—the title, 15, flashes on the screen. Madeline and one of her roommates sit in a police station, answering routine questions. Everything is emotionless. We learn that Paul came into some money, bought an apartment, and, when showing it to Madeline, stepped back too far and fell to his death. The film ends. Self-consciously structured to the point of overt manipulation, *Masculine/Feminine* becomes a reflection of larger elements—advertising, culture, class, and history—that affect our lives, while at the same time, seeking, like Paul, to find meaning in a world that has lost emotion or connection.

Some Brief Additional Examples

We conclude with a few brief examples of alternative structures. We will return to many of these films later.

Julie Dash's film, *Daughters of the Dust*, takes place on the day in 1902 in which the Peazant family is due to leave the South Carolina island of Ebo Landing to head north. The opening title leaves no doubt that they will in fact go, and so the forward narrative tension is diverted into a circular mediation on the departure's meaning. The timelessness of this moment is rendered with particular perspective, because one voiceover narrator is the great-grandmother, Nana Peazant, looking back, whereas the other is an unborn child looking forward.

Swoon is based on the famous 1924 case involving Nathan Leopold and Richard Loeb's gratuitous murder of a young boy. However, rather than presenting this event as though we are there, our perspective is given context throughout by a number of anachronisms that emphasize the mediated notion of this history. We never forget we are watching these events from the viewpoint of today, and this mediation turns our attention from the event itself to the treatment of homosexual love in the 1920s and today and to the need to declare oneself through violent, defining actions.

Both *Nashville* and *Slacker* make a city and its culture (the films occur in Nashville, Tennessee, and Austin, Texas, respectively) their central focus. They do this by introducing a large cast of characters whose relationship to one another seems so tangential that we feel all that is unifying the story is the place itself. *Nashville*, however, repeatedly returns to the same groups of characters and finally brings the pieces together in an ending that either seems coincidental or so intentionally manipulated as to call attention to its organization. *Slacker* remains serial throughout, moving from incident to incident without returning to any of them. This flattens our expectation of an extended dramatic build, and instead, as we watch each incident, we struggle to make connections between it and the other incidents. The film seems to be structured around a random train of alternative lives whose very lack of direction defines a cross-section of the city.

To Sleep with Anger is structured around an ambiguity of genre. Harry, a trickster/storyteller, visits a middle-class family of old friends in Los Angeles and overstays his welcome. At one level, the conflict is between the old and the new, about a past catching up to characters, about personalities and how they change. However, underneath, the story is inflected with a hint of magic realism and, for most of it, we are never quite sure whether we are watching a family melodrama or a mythic confrontation, until the last 10 minutes, when the story declares itself in favor of the mythic. The celebration over Harry's dead body that marks the end of the film pulls us out of the limited perspective of the family story and makes us understand that we cannot only respond to these characters through their individual histories but that we must also confront the larger cultural forces that inform their world.

Conclusion

We have demonstrated two contrasting alternatives to the restorative three-act structure. Sometimes, structure is emphasized and made very obvious. In this case, it calls attention to itself, suggesting the artificiality of form over the chaos of day-to-day experience. Ironic three-act structure twists the standard form, turning it in unexpected directions, whereas exaggerated three-act structure parodies the norm and undercuts the value of restoration. At other times, structure may be flattened and minimized, creating the illusion of documentary randomness. For example, indifferent three-act structure creates a sense of inevitability by not providing the standard insight into character motivations or the meaning of their actions. One- and two-act structures narrow the screenplay's focus to just one conflict or goal and tend to confirm what we already know about the character or situation.

Many alternative screenplays mix structural emphasis and structural minimization, playing on the tension between the two impulses. Alternative structures should grow organically out of the needs of the individual work. The possibilities are infinite. In Chapter 6, we detail the specifics of creating the stories themselves.

References

1. S. Field, *The Foundations of Screenwriting* (New York, NY: Delacorte Press, 1982), 11.
2. Ibid., 9.

5

More Thoughts on Three Acts: Fifteen Years Later

Many of the questions that we have been asked since *Alternative Scriptwriting* was first published in 1990 center on three-act structure: Is three-act structure always as problematic as you say? Aren't most films written in three acts? If not three acts, what else? Can there be more or less reliance on structure, depending on the film? Has the emphasis on three acts changed over time?

Since the first edition of this book, the gap between mainstream and alternative films has closed considerably. Today, major studios have branches for acquiring and distributing "smaller" films. Many more "smaller" films are recognized in major film festivals. At least on the surface, many stylistic devices first introduced in alternative films have been appropriated by the mainstream, just as independent films have adapted those of the mainstream. Many independent films today do use three-act structure.

Given this, we thought it was time to look back on what we wrote about three acts and nuance it a little finer. In so doing, we would like to move the discussion from the question of whether many alternative films use three acts to how they use them.

A Little Context about the Three-Act Discussion

Three-act structure has been a major concern of the wave of screenwriting books, beginning in 1979 with Syd Field's *Screenplay: The Foundations of Screenwriting*[1] and continuing today. On the first page of *Screenplay*, after defining a screenplay as a story told with pictures, Field says "All screenplays contain this basic linear structure" (Field 7–13). Then he draws a diagram of three-act structure, identifies it as a paradigm, and calls it the foundation of all good screenplays.

This becomes the defining "paradigm" of almost all the screenplay texts that followed. Shortly after *Screenplay* was published, William Goldman, in *Adventures in the Screen Trade*[2] (1983), proclaims "SCREENPLAYS ARE STRUCTURE" [caps are Goldman's] (Goldman 195). Linda Seger starts *Making A Good Script Great* (1987) with four chapters on act structure. In *How to Write a Movie in 21 Days* (1988), Viki King proposes writers begin by thinking of a 9-minute movie, a conceptual device that allows her to stipulate that movies must have nine structural signposts, which articulate three acts. For instance, the first three signposts mark the build to number four, "The Act I Turning Point" located on screenplay page 30. This is followed by signpost number five, "The Act II Metaphor," and so on. In *Writing Screenplays That Sell*[3] (1988), Michael Hauge features a structural checklist that includes much of what we have discussed and then subsequently critique in Chapter 2 of *Alternative Scriptwriting*—showing "the audience where the conflict is going to lead them" or assuring that "every scene, event and character in the screenplay must contribute to the hero's outer motivation" (Hauge 87). Lew Hunter, in *Screenwriting 434* (1993), proposes a 2-minute movie, which he divides into three acts. More than 200 of his 343 pages concentrate on structure. Robert McKee, whose popularity is both celebrated and mocked in the film *Adaptation*, dedicates the first five chapters of his book *Story: Substance, Structure, Style, and the Principles of Screenwriting* (1997) to structure. And in Chapters 2–4 of this book, we, too, talk about a structural model, even if we end up critiquing it.

What strikes us, looking back on these key texts, is not that they discuss structure, which we agree is an important component in all screenplays, but rather how much attention they put on structure in proportion to everything else. We can speculate on some reasons for this. One is that structure may be easier to teach or to write about, compared to other elements of good writing. To say that there needs to be a plot point on pages 25–27 requires less sustained analysis than is required to discuss the depth of character conflict or theme that makes the plot point meaningful. It is certainly easier for those who evaluate screenplays to turn to the pages identified by the paradigm and assure themselves that the act breaks are happening where they should. A second reason may be that the first wave of the push for structure (Field and Goldman) occurred in the late 1970s/early 1980s, when the intellectual movement called structuralism, even though it had peaked in France (where it was invented), still had great influence in the United States. Many strands of structuralism (beyond the similarity in name) concentrate on the syntagmatic line, or the dimension that unfolds in time—said to mark the deep structure, or universal mental construct—which underlies all stories. This concentration on a hidden, latent truth, at the expense of a surface that evokes many, possibly contradictory readings, may have influenced the focus on three-act structure.

Reframing the Three-Act Discussion

Whatever the reason, we would like to examine three-act structure again, not in terms of how it functions (we have covered that thoroughly in Chapters 2–4), but in terms of how it is used in four contemporary films. To do this, we will propose a spectrum that has at one end an aggressive three-act approach that tends to subordinate multiple meanings to one dominant, overarching structure and at the other end a relaxed three-act structure that on close examination reveals three acts but that encourages a more open range of meanings.

It will be useful to start by making a distinction between plot and structure. Plot is usually defined as two or more non-simultaneous events that are connected by cause and effect. In its purest sense, plot has nothing to do with communicating this cause and effect to the audience. Structure, at least in the way it is used in most screenplay discussions, assumes plot but goes further. It is the articulation of plot in such a way that it is shaped or organized for the viewer. Some aspects of structure serve to orient the viewer in time, relative to the progress of the story. Others serve to draw particular attention to important story points. To demonstrate how much of structure has to do with communication with the viewer, eight of the first ten items in Michael Hauge's structural checklist refer explicitly to communicating the audience's relationship to the story:

1. ⋮
2. ...show the audience where the story is going to lead them.
3. ⋮
4. Accelerate the pace of the story.
5. Create peaks and valleys to the action.
6. Create anticipation in the reader.
7. Give the audience superior position.
8. Surprise the audience and reverse the anticipation.
9. Create curiosity in the reader.
10. Foreshadow the major events of the screenplay (Hauge 87–93).

Structure, then, is a form of narrative voice, a direct address to the viewer (see Chapters 22 and 24). Most examples of narrative voice in mainstream film are minimized or hidden beyond character action, in order to create the illusion that character, rather than some outside force, is driving the story. However, structure is one exception to this rule. Structure must call attention to itself if it is to have an effect on the audience. This is most apparent at act breaks, when it is frequently articulated by music, change in rhythm, and/or lyrical scenes of character reflection. If the audience does not feel this articulation, then there is no sense of structure shaping the story—this lack would cause the story to be perceived as flat and undifferentiated.

In Chapter 22, we argue that the alternative film tends to make more obvious use of narrative voice than does the mainstream. That is, alternative films tend to more consistently and explicitly recognize communication with the audience, not just at act breaks, but at other times as well. Because of this, even when alternative films use three-act structure, it may function as just one of many organizing principles. Thus three-act structure, although present, may be more relaxed, because it does not tend to dominate the way it does in mainstream films. This will not necessarily flatten the story, because the other narrative articulations give it shape.

Two provisos are necessary here. The distinction between aggressive and relaxed three-act structure is sometimes easier to make when viewing the final film than when reading the script. Many of the elements that add to the relaxed feel (quality of the image, shooting patterns, importance of production design, to name a few) depend on directorial interpretation (the broader expression of narrative voice) that builds on the script and more clearly distinguishes its approach. However, although this is true, it is still important to consider the approach to three-act structure that you are suggesting to the director when you write. An intensely action-based script with strong act breaks will not have much room for personal reflective moments, no matter what the director wants to add, just as a flattened, personal screenplay most likely will resist the director's desire to stage a serious car chase.

Secondly, the distinction between aggressive and relaxed three-act structure is a continuum, rather than an either/or. Different readers/viewers respond differently to structural clues. We are proposing this spectrum in celebration of the increasing overlap between various approaches to film storytelling, rather than as an unbridgeable distinction between them.

Let's now make this concrete by looking at some examples.

The Constant Gardener

The Constant Gardener (2005), adapted from a John Le Carré novel of the same name, is a good place to start. Directed by the Brazilian Fernando Meirelles, *The Constant Gardener* in many ways demonstrates the changes in mainstream narrative filmmaking over the past 15 years. It contains images of raw African poverty that we would not have expected to see in the mainstream films we cited in previous chapters, such as *The Verdict* or *Wall Street*. Handheld or steadicam images are more restless than are those contained in earlier films and allow a looseness of frame that suggests a much broader sense of context. There is a pronounced filtering of images to heighten their dramatic functioning (and encouraged by computer-based editing), along with greater activity in the frame, which creates a richer sense of environment. The script combines a love story with an adventure film, so that the film is positioned to deal with the texture between the personal and the political. Yet, despite all of this, the film features an aggressive three-act structure.

The Constant Gardener tells the story of a British diplomat serving in Kenya, Justin, who is more interested in gardening than in power. When he learns that his wife, Tessa, was killed after going into the bush with Arnold, an African doctor, he seems to accept the common wisdom that they had been having an affair and that her death is the result of a lovers' quarrel. The first act fills in the backstory to make such an interpretation believable.

Yet, Justin doesn't quite buy it. In the second act, after learning that Arnold is gay and regards Tessa as a colleague, not a lover, Justin backtracks to London, where he determines the couple had been pursuing a pharmaceutical conspiracy that has been killing innocent African victims. While there, Justin is shut down by the foreign service and must surrender his passport. The act ends with him gathering the courage to violate his diplomatic training, leaving London on a false passport, and beginning to track down the corruption that killed his wife.

As this is a drama/thriller, the third act is extended and follows the now convinced Justin as he tracks down the pharmaceutical conspiracy. Although costing him his life, his actions lead to the exposure of British complicity in the conspiracy and terminates the drug testing that has been responsible for so many African deaths.

We find that the openness of its filmmaking style is contradicted by its aggressive reliance on three-act structure. The first act's function is to misdirect us into believing the affair between Tessa and Arnold, while discounting the conspiracy they might be unearthing. All the action, including the images that so reveal the texture of Africa, is bent on serving this purpose. For instance, Tessa's pregnancy leads to a hospital scene in which she nurses an African baby. We are encouraged to believe that this is her child with Arnold, before we learn that her own baby died in childbirth. She is actually nursing the baby of a dying African woman in the next bed, a woman whose murder is related to the plot that Tessa and Arnold are seeking to stop. The writer's choice to blatantly manipulate the audience expectations comes at the expense of exploring the depth of character or situation. Rather than a fully developed character, Tessa is treated as an agent or expression of the misdirection required by the structure.

Because the first act is so focused on creating the illusion that Tessa is cheating on Justin, our sense as experienced film watchers tells us that it cannot be true. This constructed first-act untruth, a frequent strategy of aggressive three-act structure, has the effect of undercutting the rawness of the images of Africa. If the first act is so palpably manipulated to create a suspicion we suspect will later be proven false, we learn to distrust much of what we learn there—including the texture of the African reality the film seeks to expose.

The simple flip-flop of Justin's skepticism to true belief, which occurs in the second act, has the black and white quality so typical of aggressive three-act films. It suggests a worldview that can only encompass extremes. Although this injects us into the conspiracy action movie that makes up the third act of *The Constant Gardener*, it leaves us feeling that the shattering representation of this part of the world cannot stand up to the personal sense of character either/or that so characterizes aggressive three-act structure.

Hustle and Flow

Craig Brewer's *Hustle and Flow* (2005) opens in flattened, documentary style with DJay, a middle-aged pimp, reflecting on the differences between men and dogs. Set in Memphis, the film initially feels open-ended, featuring a series of small encounters. DJay sells some dope at a bar, picks up one of his prostitutes from a club, hangs out, is given a toy piano in exchange for dope, and shops for a popsicle. Underlying this is a vague discontent that is particularly interesting, because it is not focused on a specific action or solution. This vagueness gives the film a deeper reality than does all the stuff about whores, street life, and hustling. We know that dissatisfaction—how its seeps into us and cannot be easily named or addressed—even if we do not know the street life through which it is represented.

After about 25 minutes, however, the film slips into the more aggressive three-act mode. The toy piano, along with the chance meeting of a childhood friend who works as a sound engineer, leads DJay to decide to cut a rap demo. He plans to pass the demo on to Skinny Brown, a rap singer due to perform in Memphis.

The second act builds on the first, focusing on the cutting of the demo. Although there are a number of obstacles, most are external (e.g., getting a better microphone), having little to do with character. The greatest character development comes when a secondary character's wife comes to understand what her husband is doing. Beyond that, the focus is on the community that develops around the recording.

In the third act, DJay fails to get Skinny Brown to listen to the demo. DJay's subsequent violent outburst lands him in prison. However, one of DJay's prostitute's, Nola, hustles the demo to radio stations, where it is picked up and becomes a hit. When the prison guards hand DJay their demo, he generously promises to listen, saying, "Everyone needs a dream."

The act structure is anomalous because, although it focuses the action, it does not do much to develop character. Between the first act and the third, the unease that underlies the first few scenes is suspended in favor of the making of the demo. Thus, DJay's violent outburst in the third act is rather abstract, representing a rage and a frustration that has not been progressively dramatized. Depending on one's reading, this schematic outbreak of violence represents the frustration underlying a generic social situation (DJay's been struggling financially and socially, which means he is, ipso facto, angry) or a reluctance to fully explore his character. The one blowup between DJay and his producer, Key, in the second act is too generically a creative falling out, soon patched up, to bring us further inside of DJay.

We can see what this structure does to the texture of individual scenes. The film opens with DJay's ruminations as he sits in his car, seeking to find a john for his prostitute Nola. His monologue about being a man, not a dog, has a longing, a striving for some sense in his life, that allows us to feel the depth of this man's need. In a subsequent car scene, still in the first act, Nola cuts her own deal with a john, wondering what DJay is even there for. Yet, by the time we move into the second act, DJay is focused, his vague longings addressed, and now he gives an inspirational speech to Nola, claiming "We in charge." Although this is a successful pep talk, it does not suggest the complexity of feelings he expresses earlier in the film. Later we learn how much in service of the structure this speech really is. His repeating "We in charge" to Nola before he goes to jail gives her the courage to go out and push the demo, eventually getting it on the air. It also suggests the kind of feel-good ending that aggressive three-act structure frequently encourages.

Buffalo 66

Vincent Gallo's *Buffalo 66* (1998) follows a newly released con, Billy, who "kidnaps" a young woman, Layla, in order to pretend to his parents that she's his wife. At the same time, Billy is determined to kill the former Buffalo Bills' place kicker, whose missing an easy Super Bowl field goal led to Billy's losing a bet that he must pay off by serving someone else's jail time.

The film is deadpan and flat, with limited, relaxed articulation. However, close analysis enables the viewer to make a case for three acts. In the first act, Billy sustains a pretense that his life is coherent and full by presenting Layla as his wife, while not confronting the emptiness that lies underneath his charade. In the second act, the pretense collapses, when, after pretending he no longer needs Layla, Billy cannot bring himself to leave her. In the third act, Billy is able to admit to intimacy with Layla, finally substituting this for his desire to shoot the Bills' place kicker. Billy develops through modulated steps that chart his growth, yet none of these turns is particularly marked. The film rarely plays its theme, rather allowing it to inform, but not be reduced by, the deadpan flatness.

What is marked are three heightened moments that lend the film an unexpected staginess. Billy's father lip synchs to a Sinatra song, Layla tap dances in the bowling alley, and Billy's fantasy shooting of the Bills' place kicker is rendered in dramatic stop time. Unlike the rest of the film, which is flat and unresponsive to the wishes of character, the lighting and stop motion in these scenes are highly theatrical and dramatically inflected. We read these stylizations as more than just representing the subjectivity of the characters; they are such startling, overt interventions they must also represent a direct communication to the audience, the narrative voice. Long after we may have forgotten the act structure, these moments stay with us, marking the vividness and texture of the fantasies that in relaxed, three-act structure may be more important than the overall movement of the story.

Elephant

Gus Van Sant's *Elephant* (2003) provides another example of a relaxed, three-act structure by dividing the story into three parts but giving them only temporal, rather than dramatic, meaning. *Elephant* dramatizes a high school shooting. Act I introduces the students on the day of the shooting. It is a normal day as far as they know; nothing is amiss. Yet, Van Sant manages to suggest something threatening about the ordinariness; the scenes have an exaggerated concentration, but the focus is not on character, but rather on the idea and fragility of youth itself, its energy, its wonder, its sense of a social hierarchy. Act II flashes back (mainly) and introduces the preparation of the two shooters, Eric and Alex. Although we see them making plans, there is no discussion about what they are about to do nor do we ever see them making the decision to attack the school. Act III follows the two boys on the day of the shooting, their attack once they reach the school, and the game played by the last boy before his final shooting.

The act structure tells us about time, but beyond that reveals little. The shooters do not even appear in the first part of the film. The motivation for the break from Act I to Act II is narrative rather than dramatic; a student sees the shooters arriving and waves to them. The student has no sense of whom they are; it is the narrative voice that at that point takes us back in time. Aggressive act structure is usually organized around one character whose actions (or reactions) trigger the act breaks. *Elephant* is deliberately unclear about whose story this is—Eric's, the boy who initiates the shooting, some of the other students in the school, or the school itself. This unwillingness to provide a definitive answer is heightened by an act structure that is not character-based but rather abstractly thematic.

Traditionally, aggressive three-act structure charts the development of motivation. Given how difficult it is to understand the motivation of the characters dramatized in this film, we might expect a careful step-by-step explanation of what drove these boys to this act. As the role of the first act is to dramatize the forces that motivate action, that is, where we typically expect to get this explanation. But in this film, the boys do not even appear in the first act. When we do meet them in the beginning of the second act, their motives are purposely opaque. Eric is hazed in the classroom when someone throws a spitball at him, yet before he can process his resentment, he is already casing the cafeteria, planning for the shooting. If this indicates that he has already decided to shoot up the school, we are left out of the decision making. If that comes later, we are not clued in. In fact, the film plays with false explanations, video game violence, distant parents, a documentary about Hitler, and a kiss between the two boys, while explicitly denying the release of an answer.

As we have said, structure is an expression of narrative voice; both in mainstream and independent films, it is an articulation for the audience of where they are in the story and the relative importance of events. In *Elephant*, the events and the shooter's motivations are inexplicable. The narrative voice, as expressed in the act structure (and in every element in the design of the film), does not function to explain the act, but rather as an articulation of time, almost a ticking clock, that heightens the inevitability of what is about to happen.

Another aspect of narrative voice is intertextuality, a recognition of the social/cultural context in which a film will be seen. *Elephant* depends on the audience's awareness of the wave of school shootings that took place in the United States during the late 1990s, particularly the one at Columbine High School. Without this, the writer would be forced to dramatize much more of the circumstances, the buildup, and the motivation for the shooting, convincing us that it could happen. This push to a more aggressive three-act structure might have made a film that stands better outside of history, but one whose very neatness would have diminished its bewilderment over how such a thing could happen. *Elephant* is more of a sketch structured around the audience's presumed common knowledge. As such, it is freed from having to offer a definitive explanation or even to convince us that it could happen. It can instead use a relaxed three acts, an increasing warning of what we know is going to come, to suggest its (and our) inability to understand, a representation without explanation.

Summary

In this chapter, we have looked back at our previous discussion of three acts (Chapters 2–4) and nuanced it to reflect the increasing overlap between mainstream and independent films. We have acknowledged that as a result of this overlap, many independent films are using three-act structure, although the emphasis on story structure is frequently less pronounced than in mainstream films. In order to articulate the difference, we are proposing a spectrum that runs from aggressive to relaxed three-act structure.

One distinction we have looked at is that between plot and structure, where structure is the use of the narrative voice to articulate the cause and effect inherent in plot. In a subsequent chapter, we talk more about the narrative voice and how it tends to be hidden in mainstream film behind the action of characters. The major exception to this is in aggressive three-act structure, where the act breaks are heightened to communicate their importance to the viewer. As narrative voice is frequently foregrounded in alternative film, communicating directly with the viewer is accomplished by other means that allow three-act structure to be relaxed. The more relaxed story structure yields moments such as Layla's tap dance in *Buffalo 66* or the multiple explanations for the random violence in *Elephant*, in part by suggesting that the pleasure of these films is not only how it all comes out but also the sampling of textures and moments along the way.

References

1. S. Field, *Screenplay: The Foundations of Screenwriting*, new expanded edition (New York, NY: Delacorte Press, 1982).
2. W. Goldman, *Adventures in the Screen Trade: A Personal View of Hollywood and Screenwriting* (New York, NY: Warner Books, 1983).
3. M. Hauge, *Writing Screenplays That Sell* (New York, NY: McGraw-Hill Book Co., 1988).

6

Narrative and Anti-Narrative: The Case of the Two Stevens

In this chapter, we look at the work of two important film storytellers, Steven Spielberg and Steven Soderbergh. They represent two extreme impulses. Spielberg's impulse is classic linear storytelling, clearly plot-driven, and very effective (so effective, in fact, that it underpins the most commercially successful career in film history). Soderbergh's impulse is ambiguous, experimental, and quirky. We call it anti-narrative. The impulse of Steven Soderbergh is, above all, a strategy to opt for creative rather than overtly commercial narrative solutions. That is not to say that Steven Spielberg has not experimented or sought creative solutions in his own work. Nor is it to say that Steven Soderbergh has not sought out linear, commercially viable narratives in his career. However, for the most part, Steven Spielberg has embraced one type of narrative and Steven Soderbergh has embraced the opposite. For this reason, an exploration of their work will highlight these two extreme options available to the *filmic storyteller*, a term that illuminates the role of filmmakers who either write or have a powerful influence on the scripts before production.

To give the chapter a deeper context, it's useful to highlight the two contrasting impulses of Spielberg and Soderbergh from a career perspective. To put it most simply, Spielberg's career has been marked by the popular impulse. Aesthetic concerns and socio-political concerns have taken a distant second place. In terms of narrative strategies, this has produced structural clarity and goal-oriented main characters that are easy to identify with. Spielberg is also more attracted to genres—the action-adventure film and the science fiction film in particular.

When he has taken on a melodrama, it has always been fused with a plot-oriented overlay, as in the war films *Empire of the Sun* and *Schindler's List*. And even in his more recent work, where he embraces important socio-political material, such as in *Amistad*, he still gravitates to plot, focusing on the trial instead of the characters.

An important question to consider is whether the entertainment impulse in a storyteller is an asset or, in the most elitist, critical sense, a deficiency. When we look at the early careers of Charlie Chaplin, Woody Allen, or Federico Fellini, we can see the primacy of this impulse. We see it also throughout the career of Alfred Hitchcock. The entertainment or commercial impulse has not compromised the reputations of any of these filmic storytellers.

Perhaps a more productive way to look at this impulse is to consider it a definite strategy in a field in which there is a full range of strategies. In this sense, Steven Spielberg is a storyteller, always mindful of holding his audience. He is a storyteller who views his creative life as an amusement park, with his films as the various rides. Clearly, he prefers the rides that emphasize charm over darkness, thrills over meditations, and action over reflection.

With Steven Soderbergh, another cluster of strategies prevails. Over the course of his career, Soderbergh seems to favor the creative impulse over the commercial impulse. And instead of dwelling on genres of wish fulfillment, Soderbergh has focused principally on character-driven genres, the melodrama and the film noir; he has dwelled upon genres of the nightmare or the incursion of darkness into realist melodramas, such as *King of the Hill*. He has also upgraded the character layer in plot-driven genres, such as in his gangster film *The Limey*.

Although Soderbergh has made commercial, straight-line narratives, such as *Erin Brockovich*, his distinct preference is to subvert narrative conventions, the consequence of which is a series of unusual narrative experiences. One might almost call them experiments. In *sex, lies, and videotape*, he is experimenting with structure, and in *Out of Sight* and *Kafka*, he is experimenting with tone; the result is what we would classify as anti-narrative.

Steven Spielberg: The Approach to Character

When we look at Spielberg's characters, we find that they are most often extreme. Polarities create conflict, and Spielberg wants as much conflict as possible to drive the narrative. Consequently, the young/old, black/white, Jewish/Gentile grid (schematic or narrative polarity) is applicable to the main character/antagonist relationship in Spielberg's work. To articulate this relationship, we turn first to the presentation of the main character.

The Main Character

Spielberg's main characters share two qualities, regardless of their age. The first is a childlike innocence. The result may be playfulness, such as one finds in Jim, the young boy in J.G. Ballard, Tom Stoppard, and Menno Meyjes's *Empire of the Sun*. Although Jim is caught in Shanghai during the Japanese invasion, and although he will be imprisoned, separated from his parents, and placed in considerable danger, he remains open to seeing the world through a curious, individualistic, and playful perspective. The same can be said for Indiana Jones in George Lucas, Phillip Kauffman, and Lawrence Kasdan's *Raiders of the Lost Ark*, and for Dr. Alan Grant in Michael Crichton and David Koepp's *Jurassic Park*. Although Indiana Jones and Dr. Alan Grant are adults, they each retain a childlike enthusiasm and belief in their work. They are the opposite of jaded characters.

Second, Spielberg's main characters typically display a great amount of reluctance. This is not to say that they are passive or ambivalent, but rather that they are characters not easily or impulsively affiliated with a goal. However, once they do commit to a side, they do so to the fullest. Captain John Miller in Robert Rodat's *Saving Private Ryan*, Oskar Schindler in Steve Zaillian's *Schindler's List*, and the lawyer Roger Baldwin in David Franzoni's *Amistad* are examples of this personality trait.

As expected, all of these characters are goal-oriented and will compassionately see that goal through to its successful conclusion. Sheriff Brody will do all he can to eliminate the threat of a shark against the people of Amityville in Peter Benchley and Carl Gottlieb's *Jaws*. Roger Baldwin will do all he can to defend Cinque in the slave revolt in *Amistad*. Elliott will do all he can to save the alien in Melissa Mathison's *E.T.* And once committed, Oskar Schindler, in *Schindler's List*, will do all he can to save as many Jews as possible from extermination in Nazi death camps. In each case, the main character's initial reluctance gives way to heroic effort and achievement of the goal.

The Antagonist

For the actions of the main character to be experienced as heroic, you need a very powerful antagonist. The more powerful the antagonist, the greater the likelihood that the main character will be perceived as heroic, even if the character is a child or a reluctant adult. The antagonist consequently plays a key role in the Spielberg narrative. The essence of evil Nazism is embodied in Amon Goeth, the commandant of the Nazi labor camp in Poland. Goeth personifies the power, the arbitrariness, the cruelty of the Nazis toward the Jews. As the antagonist, he poses the greatest threat to Oskar Schindler's goal of saving as many Jews as possible from Nazi extermination.

Nazism is replaced by slavery in *Amistad*. The persecution of Cinque, the leader of the slave revolt, represents the injustice of slavery. Roger Baldwin's defense of Cinque represents an attack on this injustice. Unfortunately, in this Spielberg film, we have no character equivalent to Goeth; consequently, Baldwin's efforts don't reach the heroic level of other Spielberg main characters. Here, the absence of a good antagonist affects the experience of the main character and the narrative as a whole. There will be more on this issue in the discussion of plot.

For the most part, however, Spielberg does work with powerful antagonists, such as the shark in *Jaws* and various dinosaurs (particularly raptors) in *Jurassic Park*. The magnitude of this threat from the antagonist makes the actions of Sheriff Brody and Dr. Grant appropriately heroic. In more human form, the antagonist in *Raiders of the Lost Ark* is the rogue archaeologist—he has affiliated himself with the Nazis who are pursuing the Lost Ark to harness its spiritual and physical power for their own material and evil purposes. Because of his level of understanding of the historical religious importance of the Ark as an archaeological artifact (aesthetics over materialism), this archaeologist is a truly dangerous man, whereas the Nazi masters are simply crude wielders of power. Together, however, they push Indiana Jones to heroic proportions in his effort to secure and protect the ark for more enlightened purposes. As a result, the main character becomes the hero.

Another example is Captain John Miller in *Saving Private Ryan*. Captain Miller must take his company into enemy territory to retrieve Private Ryan, the last living son (three have died) in his family. The time is the D-Day invasion of Europe. The French countryside is clearly teeming with the German enemy. Although the Germans are the antagonists, Spielberg wants to emotionalize the antagonist. During the search for Ryan, the patrol comes upon a German. Many of the patrol members want to kill the German, but Captain Miller decides to free him. Later, in the climactic battle scene, this same German soldier will cruelly kill the one Jewish member of Miller's patrol. Such cruelty gives additional weight to the power and determination of the antagonist, and it gives a palpable and heroic quality to Captain Miller in his effort to save Private Ryan. This heroic quality is heightened even more when Captain Miller gives up his own life to achieve the goal of saving Private Ryan. Here again, the characterization of the antagonist gives scale to the achievement of the main character. He is a hero.

The Issue of Identification

Writers use a number of strategies to enhance the audience identification with the main character. Spielberg's use of the antagonist is one example. There are other strategies that Spielberg favors and others that he sidesteps. He is not drawn to a charismatic main character. In fact, quite the contrary, he takes pains to establish that his main character is ordinary. Sheriff Brody in *Jaws* is a simple family man concerned about his kids and about doing his job responsibly. Elliott in *E.T.* is an ordinary young boy—playful, earnest, naive. Jim in *Empire of the Sun* is curious and creative. But both he and Elliott are very sensitive. They are neither bullies nor nerds, but rather are somewhere in-between. Indiana Jones is boyish and enthusiastic, a bit irresponsible with regard to relationships, but well intentioned. Even Dr. Grant is a stiff academic. None of these characters is charismatic. So what is it about them that invites us to identify with them?

We've mentioned the "Everyman" qualities of Spielberg's main characters. Spielberg also likes to position the main character in a dilemma—call it situational or moral, the decision the character will make clarifies his values. In *Jaws*, Sheriff Brody must decide whether his job is to protect the economic well being of Amityville or to protect lives. Dr. Grant faces a parallel dilemma in *Jurassic Park*, as do Oskar Schindler in *Schindler's List* and Roger Baldwin in *Amistad*. By choosing human values over material values, these main characters affirm their own humanness.

The moral stakes rise when life itself is on the line. For Captain Miller in *Saving Private Ryan*, each life saved is a virtue; each life lost is profoundly felt. Miller's struggle is to value life, to view life as a temporary gift to be treasured. Elliott in *E.T.* chooses to save an alien life, which makes his plight all the more innocent and decent. E.T. becomes "another kind of being," equally deserving of being saved. This struggle over the primacy of human values in Spielberg's main characters makes them easy to identify with. Even an ambiguous character such as Oskar Schindler visibly transforms himself from opportunist to humanist. This movement helps us to identify with him.

A final strategy that makes identification with the main character possible is the deployment of plot. In a sense, Spielberg uses plot the way Hitchcock and Polanski use plot—to attempt to victimize the main character. By operating as if the threat of a man-eating shark or a man-eating raptor or a man-eating war will destroy the main character, we in the audience quickly identify with the potential victim who avoids being victimized and who, in fact, becomes a hero by overcoming the forces against him. There is never a cynical last twist that defeats the character. He always succeeds in the end, and by doing so, he emerges a hero, a very easy character with whom to identify.

The Approach to Structure

One of Spielberg's approaches to structure relies on the narrative being both centered and linear. If the goal-directed main character keeps moving relentlessly toward resolution in the face of a powerful antagonist, at complete odds with the plot, that movement becomes heroic. But to be considered a hero, there must be resolution, an answer to the question: Has the main character achieved his goal? In Spielberg's films, this answer is always answered in the affirmative; there is always a sense of closure by film's end. This struggle leading to closure characterizes classic Hollywood narrative at its most effective.

To understand the specifics of this structure, we need to look at the operation of the plot, or foreground story, as well as the background story, or character layer. We need to look also at the balance of these two layers. Finally, we need to look at the trajectory, the dramatic arc from critical moment to resolution (the organization of the three-act narrative). We turn first to the deployment of plot in Spielberg films.

The Role of Plot

Plot-driven narrative is a major reason for Hollywood's international success. Steven Spielberg isn't obsessed with plot, but, as we stated earlier, he has gravitated toward plot-driven narratives. One of his earliest films, *Duel*, is essentially all plot. A motorist angers a truck driver on the road, and then the truck driver begins pursuing him with murderous intent. *Raiders of the Lost Ark* and *Indiana Jones and the Temple of Doom* are entirely plot driven. Although there is a modest father–son character layer in *Indiana Jones and the Lost Crusade*, that narrative is also dominated by plot. As well, *Jurassic Park* and *The Lost World: Jurassic Park* are both essentially dominated by plot.

When Spielberg has veered away from plot—in *Empire of the Sun* and *The Color Purple*—the films have been less successful commercially; consequently, he has been very mindful of plot in his latest films. The plot is set up to oppose the goal of the main character. If that opposition is successfully structured, the plot should maximize conflict, thus serving as the primary challenge the main character will be forced to overcome. Consequently, our involvement and participation in the main character's plight will also be maximized.

Let's turn to three examples of this plot structure in Spielberg's work. The plot of *Schindler's List* is the relentless attack on the Jews by the Nazis. The creation of the ghetto, the liquidation of the ghetto, the transport to the labor camp, the random killing of Jews in the labor camp, and the transport of Jews to Auschwitz are all plot sequences in the film. Each event illustrates the atrocities being committed against the Jews.

The goal of the main character then becomes saving the Jews from extermination. To do so, Schindler creates a fictitious factory where Jews work in his business enterprises. In fact, the real goal is to save as many Jewish lives as possible—this goal directly opposes the plot. In the course of the plot, many more Jews are killed than are saved. Schindler's efforts only scratch the surface, but his efforts are heroic relative to the scale of the Nazi killing machine.

In *Amistad*, the plot centers on a slave revolt aboard the ship Amistad— the slaves' overtaking of the ship, the capturing of the ship in American waters, and the subsequent trial of the captured slaves (the focus is on the leader, Cinque). The goal of the main character as the defense lawyer for Cinque is to seek acquittal for his client. The fact that slavery is legal makes the slaves' revolt illegal. Consequently, the goal of the lawyer is to condemn and overturn the immoral, yet legal, practice of slavery. In fighting against such great odds, which in essence is the plot, the actions of the lawyer are morally justified, and so heroic.

In *Saving Private Ryan*, the goal of the main character, Captain Miller, is to save the lives of his men or, at the very least, to prevent them from dying. The plot, the progress of the war from the D-Day invasion of France to securing Private Ryan, who is the last surviving son in his family, works to challenge the goal of the main character.

In each of these examples, plot is working in the classic narrative style, which is to work directly against the goals of the main character. This is the dynamic we find working so well in the work of the most effective classic film storytellers—Alfred Hitchcock, Fred Zinnemann, and Robert Zemeckis, to name a few. All of these storytellers are attuned to the use of plot to amplify the dynamic of the dramatic arc. But no one has understood the usefulness of plot better than Steven Spielberg.

The Role of the Character Layer

In Spielberg's work, the character layer plays a secondary role to plot. Both the genres chosen and the approach to character suggest a discomfort or, at best, a reluctant acknowledgment of the usefulness of the character layer. To understand how Spielberg has used the character layer, an explanation is needed of how this layer and the film's premise are linked, because this linkage is central to the experience of the film narrative.

The character layer, or background story, is key to our emotional relationship with the narrative. Plot is exciting, filled with action, surprise, twists and turns, but it is the character layer that invites us into an emotional relationship with the narrative. Not until the father–son layer of *Indiana Jones and the Last Crusade* was there an emotional connection with the character of Indiana Jones. We enjoyed the action of the first two films of the series, and we related to the boyish enthusiasm of Indiana Jones, but we weren't emotionally rooted in the series until Spielberg and writer Jeb Stuart implemented this character layer in the narrative. In a sense, this is the key to understanding the means Spielberg uses to emotionalize his films. To state the structural choices in a different way, Spielberg uses plot for conflict and excitement, and he uses character in a subsidiary fashion to emotionalize his narratives.

Another approach to the issue of the character layer is to link Spielberg to Stanley Kubrick in his narrative approach. Where possible, Kubrick replaces character layer with plot. He does this in the search for excitement, as in the journey of the main character in *Eyes Wide Shut* (rather than exploring the husband–wife relationship) and in following men through training and battle in *Full Metal Jacket* (rather than more deeply following the course of peer relationships). In contrast, Spielberg doesn't eschew the character layer in *Saving Private Ryan*; he simply embeds it deeply into the course of the plot.

We get the character layer, but we never forget its subsidiary role to plot. The opposite unfolds in Raoul Walsh's *The Naked and The Dead* and in Ed Dmytryk's *The Young Lions*.

The character layer in *Amistad* unfolds in the progression of plot, principally the trial, whether the relationships are white/black, free/slave, or lawyer/defendant. The same is true in *Empire of the Sun*. The progress of the war and its implications—capture, incarceration, the struggle to survive—for the main character, Jim, are constantly put in the foreground, with an emphasis on how Jim experiences these events. The character layer—with its issues of child/adult, Chinese/English (servant/master), Japanese/Caucasian (master/slave), English/American, male/female—is subsidiary to the drive of the plot. An exception to this approach to the character layer is found in *Schindler's List*. In this case, Spielberg, with writer Steve Zaillian, in effect mixes two genres: the war film, in which the plot layer (the war against the Jews) dominates, and the melodrama, in which the character layer dominates. In that character layer, Oskar Schindler is a powerless person challenging the power structure of the Nazi war machine. The primary relationships that are explored here are the Nazi relationship with Amon Goeth and the Jewish relationship with Itzhak Stern, the Jewish accountant at Schindler's plant, a plant created to save Jews. In exploring these two relationships, Spielberg articulates the two choices for Oskar Schindler. One is to experience total power over the people who work for him and whom he is saving. This option, emotionally articulated, represents the apogee of human corruption. The other option is to view an employee as an equal, to share feelings and mutual respect for and with another. By his actions, Schindler chooses the second option. That choice and its implications are the through line for the melodrama layer. *Schindler's List* represents the exception in Spielberg's career. More often, plot prevails.

The Centrality of Linearity

When we speak of linearity at its most orthodox, we think of a narrative that begins with a goal-directed character introduced at a critical moment—indeed, a point of crisis. In short order, the character meets the roadblocks produced by the plot and the antagonist. He moves forcefully through the first-act turning point that opens up the narrative. In Act Two, the act of confrontation, the action intensifies, with the additional press of the character layer. The act ends with a second turning point, an event that forces the main character to make his or her choice. Finally, the character moves through Act Three toward resolution. The level of effort rises to new heights. The plot is resolved. The character layer resolves. The main character either achieves or does not achieve his goal in the resolution. The resolution is definitive in the narrative. Closure is achieved. This is the pattern of the linear narrative. Few film storytellers embrace that closure and the linear pattern to reach closure more vigorously than does Steven Spielberg. In many ways, he represents the quintessential linear storyteller.

We've already discussed the plot orientation of the Spielberg narrative, but to highlight the linearity, two points denote the tightness of that structure: the critical moment at which we join the story and the resolution of the narrative. The slave revolt on the ship is in progress as *Amistad* begins, while *Jurassic Park* begins with the characters making arrangements to visit the park. In spite of its prologue, the critical moment for *Saving Private Ryan* is the D-Day beach landing. *Jaws* begins with the shark attack on the first victim. There are, of course, exceptions—both *Schindler's List* and *Empire of the Sun* begin with an introduction to the main character. In *Empire of the Sun*, that introduction is quite lengthy, giving us a look into Jim's mind, his psychology. For the most part, however, Spielberg quickly launches us into the story.

Resolution is equally resolute. Indiana Jones retrieves the ark in *Raiders of the Lost Ark*. At the conclusion of *Saving Private Ryan*, Private Ryan has been successfully saved. At the end of *Schindler's List*, the war against the Jews has ended and the Jews who were saved by Schindler acknowledge their debt to him. At the end of *Amistad*, Cinque is acquitted, and, implicitly, the practice of slavery has been discredited in the United States. At the end of *E.T.*, E.T. returns home. At the end of *Empire of the Sun*, Jim is freed from internment and is reunited with his parents. In the linear Spielberg narrative, the resolution is definitive.

The Approach to Voice

The tone of the narratives in Spielberg's films is best described as genre-appropriate. His action-adventure and science fiction films are optimistic, sunny, and hopeful, and his war films are realistic. If there is a Spielberg voice—and we believe there is—it is an optimistic voice, hopeful even in tragic circumstances. The voice is the quintessential American voice—celebratory of individuality and of decency. Another layer of that voice is Spielberg's liberal view of social issues, as is seen in his two films about Blacks in America. Where possible, Spielberg also advocates children's rights in a world dominated by adults.

The Approach to Genre

The choice of genre essentially sets the parameters for the storyteller. Screenwriters do have the choice of altering genre, as the Coen brothers, the Dahl brothers, and the Wachowski brothers often do. In each case, the film is definitely a film noir or an action-adventure film, but by altering a motif or by mixing genres, the experience of the narrative changes (which we will discuss in Chapter 9). Steven Spielberg is much more orthodox in his work with genres. First, Spielberg has a distinct preference for genres that involve wish fulfillment. The majority of his films have been action-adventure or science fiction. In both of these genres, the actions of the main character are challenged by the plot—life in the character's world will be adversely affected if the character doesn't succeed. And both of these genres are dominated by plot. *Jaws, Jurassic Park, Raiders of the Lost Ark*, and *Close Encounters of the Third Kind* all exemplify Spielberg's approach to action-adventure and to science fiction.

Another explanation of the appeal of these genres to Spielberg is the dramatic arc at their core; science fiction centers on the struggle of technology against humanity. The action-adventure film focuses on a local or global catastrophe, the effects of which are overcome by the efforts of the main character. In both genres, success creates a hero.

This view of the main character's transformation is central in Spielberg's realist films—the war films such as *Saving Private Ryan*, and *Schindler's List*. The same can be said for his biographical film, *Amistad*. Although the fate of the main character in the war film can veer toward a wasted life, as in Robert Aldrich's *Attack* and *Too Late the Hero*, or toward the surreal good fortune of appearances, as in Agnieska Holland's *Europa Europa*, Spielberg needs to see the actions and fate of his main character in heroic terms. The same can be said of the dramatic arc in *Amistad*.

The genres chosen, the approach to character, and the shape of the dramatic arc all point to a maximization of classical narrative strategies. For Spielberg, classical narrative is used to celebrate the potential in character. Even if life is sacrificed, it's a choice the character makes. Plot exists to energize that struggle, to make a hero of the main character or to acknowledge that views of children can be wise, sometimes wiser than the views of adults. It's a romantic vision. It represents the classic narrative impulse at its clearest.

Steven Soderbergh: The Approach to Character

If Steven Spielberg's characters are ordinary people who reluctantly take heroic action and succeed, Soderbergh's characters are more often ordinary people who take action and fail. With two exceptions, which we'll shortly address, Soderbergh's characters find themselves in circumstances or relationships that overwhelm them. Some survive, but most find themselves condemned to the netherworld where one finds all film noir characters— betrayed or buried. Soderbergh characters occupy a world somewhere between realism and the dark side, the nightmare world, quite the opposite from Spielberg's characters.

The Main Character

Soderbergh has presented two characters who, through their will, succeed in the face of considerable adversity. Erin Brockovich in Susannah Grant's *Erin Brockovich* and Aaron Kurlander in Soderbergh's *King of the Hill* are classic melodrama main characters—powerless and looking for power in their particular time and place. And each survives and emerges heroic despite the impossibility of the task.

In *King of the Hill*, Aaron is faced with the problems of economic survival; he is a 12-year-old with a marginally employed father and a sick mother. The family's living arrangement in a hotel is vulnerable, his brother has to be sent to a relative in order to save a dollar a week, and the repo men are about to repossess the family car if they can find it. Aaron is looking at personal disaster. The only help Aaron has is his intelligence and his attitude; his optimism helps him survive.

In the case of Erin Brockovich, the problem is also economic; she's a single mother and needs a job to support her children. At a deeper level, she needs to restore her self-esteem. To do so, she assertively pursues a job in a lawyer's office and, shortly after getting the job, she pursues the cause of victims of toxic waste dumping in a nearby small town. Her target becomes the power company responsible for the toxic waste. Erin's challenge is immeasurable. In both films, it is the attitude of the main characters that enables their survival and, indeed, their triumph.

More typical of the Soderbergh character is Jack Foley, from Scott Frank's *Out of Sight*, a very successful bank robber who keeps being caught because of his consideration and decency. The usual gangster character is a driven character, an ambitious character, neurotic, filled with desire for success. Foley is not typical of the gangster main character. He is more reminiscent of George, the main character in Neil Jordan's *Mona Lisa*; he is too emotional to be a successful criminal. Wilson, in Lem Dobbs's *The Limey*, is also a main character overwhelmed with emotion. Wilson's goal is to get revenge for the death of his daughter. For various reasons, Wilson was never much of a father to his daughter. His actions are not intended to further his career; rather, they are intended to restore his identity as a father. Likewise, Michael Gallagher in Sam Lowry and Daniel Fuch's *The Underneath* is a man pulled back home to restore the relationship with the girlfriend he had abandoned. To reconnect with her, he will use others, turn to crime, and betray his family. He is the classic film noir character. Desire blurs his judgment and his actions end up destroying him.

This cross-section of Soderbergh characters shows that he favors vulnerable characters. But none is more vulnerable than Ann Millaney in Soderbergh's *sex, lies, and videotape*. She is a depressed and passive character; she awakens only once she has a relationship with Graham, her husband's old friend, and discovers that her husband has been unfaithful to her with her own sister. Although Ann does awaken, the aura of vulnerability and sadness that she exudes dominates the narrative.

With few exceptions, Soderbergh's main characters are rarely heroes. More on display is their humanity and vulnerability. The narrative becomes the microscope through which to observe their behavior. How we feel about that behavior is an issue to which we'll return in the discussion about identification. But first we turn to the role of the antagonist in Soderbergh's films.

The Antagonist

The role of the antagonist is complex in Soderbergh's work. In fact, sometimes, Soderbergh does not use an antagonist at all. When he does, the antagonist doesn't prompt the main character to heroic action. At best, the complexity and humanness of the antagonist make that character as vulnerable as the main character. We could even go so far as to say the emotional nature of the antagonist adds to the humanity, the emotionality, of the main character.

In *sex, lies, and videotape*, Ann's husband, John, is the antagonist. He is a liar as well as a lawyer, and is insecure in his relationship with Ann's sister. He is the antagonist, but he is a flawed one; he is victimized by his own actions. Flawed but dangerous are the words that best describe Mad Dog, the antagonist in *Out of Sight*. Just as we see Jack Foley with his decency as well as his determination, we see Mad Dog with his insecurity as a killer. Both main character and antagonist play against our expectations. Terry Valentine, in *The Limey*, is a rich, opportunistic but nervous music promoter. Soderbergh goes a long way to show us how vulnerable, how all-too-human, Terry is. The result is that each of these antagonists is diminished dramatically so that the main character's actions are experienced as human, as opposed to heroic. In this sense, we could say the manner in which Soderbergh uses the antagonist contributes to the anti-narrative feel of his narratives. It certainly slows the sense of linearity in the narrative.

A second form of antagonist, which also contributes to the anti-narrative feel in Soderbergh's work, is the use of an institution or an event as antagonist. An example of this is the Depression in *King of the Hill*. Its length and depth promote antagonistic behavior on the part of the hotel manager, but not enough to imply he is the antagonist. Here, the event, the Depression, creates an aura where personal behavior, in this case that of the hotel manager, reflects the desperation it has promoted. The Depression becomes the real antagonist.

Similarly, in Lem Dobbs's *Kafka*, it is the Castle—the center of government power and bureaucracy—that prompts Kafka's paranoia. A police officer and the head of medical records become stand-ins for that power and its abuse, although they do not become the antagonists. The Castle, in its imposing position and its role in the death of two of Kafka's colleagues and friends, fulfills the role of antagonist.

The Issue of Identification

Soderbergh does not go out of his way to invite us to identify with his main characters. Kafka is intense and paranoid; Ann Millaney is depressed; Michael Chambers is self-absorbed and self-destructive; Jack Foley is self-assured and ironic; Wilson is intense and angry; Aaron

Kurlander makes up stories about himself. These are not characters we automatically connect with. We identify with Erin Brockovich—an exception in Soderbergh's films—because she is the underdog. More often, we watch the characters at a distance rather than being invited into an intense relationship with them. Even in Steve Gaghan's *Traffic*, we watch the three main characters, Javier, Helena, and Robert, from a distance. All of these characters find themselves in a relationship dilemma that forces them to choose between their professional and personal interests. It's not so much that we are invited to identify with these characters; rather, we are invited to watch them work out their essentially moral dilemmas. As a general principle, we tend to like Soderbergh's characters, but we don't readily identify with them.

The Approach to Structure

When examining the structure of Soderbergh's films, one notices immediately that it is not necessarily linear. Indeed, Soderbergh is most experimental with the structure of his work, using anti-narrative to avoid closure, employing an unexpected mix of plot and character layers, or softening the goal-directedness of the main character.

We begin with Soderbergh's most classic or linear film, *Erin Brockovich*. Here, the goal of the main character is to regain her self-esteem. This will provide a baseline for how far Soderbergh can move away from classic structure. The plot layer of the narrative is Erin's career advancement, in spite of Erin having no formal preparation to be a paralegal. The majority of the plot focuses on building the lawsuit against the power company. It's a medical suit based on the health damage to the residents adjacent to the power plant. The character layer explores two relationships—a personal, or love, relationship with a neighbor and a professional, or respect, relationship with the lawyer who is Erin's employer. The structure of *Erin Brockovich* is such that the plot is the challenge to Erin's goal of regaining her self-esteem. At no point does the character layer do more than humanize Erin. It does not undercut the linearity of the narrative. When we meet Erin, she is at a low point in her self-esteem; by the end she is rich and her self-esteem is secured. There is closure in as certain a manner as in a Spielberg film. *Erin Brockovich* is classic linear narrative. To understand Soderbergh's penchant to challenge linearity, we now turn to his use of plot in other films.

The Role of Plot

Plot provides a classic narrative with linearity, as well as with twists and turns that make it both exciting and satisfying. To understand how Soderbergh uses plot, it's best to look at his anti-narrative work. In this work, he undermines plot when we expect him to capitalize on it. He does this either through his approach to character or through the introduction of a greater character layer, sometimes employing the main character and/or the plot against expectations. For example, the videotaping (the plot) in *sex, lies, and videotape* enables rather than challenges the main character. Turning to plot-driven stories, we can see how Soderbergh challenges expectations.

Out of Sight is clearly a gangster film. In the gangster film, the career of the gangster is the plot. The main event for Jack Foley's career in *Out of Sight* is the Detroit theft of uncut diamonds from a rich former fellow inmate, Richard Ripley, the Wall Street ripper. The heist will give Foley the financial freedom he has long sought. The problem is that another fellow former inmate, Mad Dog, and his gang, also have their eyes on the diamonds. Also problematic is that Jack is being pursued by the FBI and by his love interest, Federal Marshall Karen Cisco. In *Out of Sight*, Soderbergh subverts the plot by exploring two relationships—Jack's loyalty to Buddy, his accomplice, a loyalty bordering on brotherhood, and his relationship with his most relentless pursuer, Karen Cisco. This adversarial relationship becomes a love relationship that keeps undermining the plot. She is his captive in Act One—they are intimately secured in the trunk of a getaway car. Are they captor and captive or are they having their first date, albeit unorthodox? In Act Two, they become lovers, and in Act Three, she captures him, shooting him in the leg to keep him alive. At the end of the film, she seems to have masterminded his escape from captivity. Essentially, the character layer takes over from the plot layer, working against genre expectations. *Out of Sight* becomes a character-driven gangster film.

The Limey is another example of a plot-oriented narrative that is subverted by the character layer. *The Limey* is essentially a revenge tale, and the plot progression is clear. The grievance or betrayal occurs in Act One, and Acts Two and Three are used to secure revenge. The more distant the target—the heads of the mob in *Point Blank*, the Emperor of Rome in *Gladiator*—the more challenging the plot to reach the source of grievance. In these narratives, the plot moves with the speed of a rushing train. In *The Limey*, we have the requisite distance between the main characters Wilson and Terry Valentine, so that the plot can be as forceful as needed. But instead of getting on the train and pushing the throttle, Soderbergh keeps taking us off into the character layer. Here Wilson reconnects with being a father. We see scenes from the past of his daughter Jenny growing up and recent scenes where her surrogate parent is her acting teacher. The teacher sharply chastises Wilson about his relationship with Jenny, and tells him Jenny's perceptions of it. In effect, she fills in the missing parts. The plot layer would relegate Wilson to his role as avenger, but the character layer allows Wilson to be a father. The character layer thus subverts the power of plot in *The Limey*.

The Role of the Character Layer

Film noir is dominated by a character layer in which the main character is victimized by the very relationship explored in the film. Michael, in *The Underneath*, pursues his ex-girlfriend Rachel throughout the story, and it is because of Rachel that he comes up with the plot to rob an armored truck as it makes a pickup at a bank (he is the driver of the armored truck). Although Rachel is implicitly the femme fatale who leads to his destruction, Soderbergh subverts the expectation that she alone destroys him. Instead, Michael is his own antagonist, in the sense that he knows he can't resist going back to her, just as he knows his gambling and his poor judgment contribute to his fate. It's as if Michael is no good and knows he is no good. That awareness makes him his own antagonist rather than the classic film noir character, a victim of his love interest. In fact, numerous relationships are explored here—Michael's Cain/Abel relationship with his brother, his favored son relationship with his mother, his parasitic relationship with his new stepfather, and his parasitic relationship with the female bank employee. A second structural incursion into the nature of the character layer is to use the plot—robbery and its aftermath—as a sign of the moral corruption of the main character. Because of the plot, the implication is that Michael deserves his fate, again an unusual characteristic in film noir.

King of the Hill offers another example of the subversion of expectations. The narrative is essentially a melodrama, a character-driven genre about a powerless character trying to gain power. Generally, this is undertaken through relationships. Not so in *King of the Hill*. Here, plot replaces the character layer. The plot is Aaron Kurlander's efforts to master the behavior needed to deal with the personal effects of the Depression. This means pretending to be someone he is not and trying to earn the money his father has such great difficulty earning. Aaron will fail in these endeavors, but, paradoxically, the very fact that he attempted them keeps his spirit from being crushed. As a result, he does survive the Depression. The plot enables Aaron to cope, and the fact that he coped prepares him for the successful future that surely awaits this character. In *King of the Hill*, the use of plot alters the experience of the melodrama and energizes the narrative.

Working Against Linearity

Steve Gaghan's *Traffic* is an excellent example of how Soderbergh subverts linearity. Traffic is three stories with three main characters. Although each story follows the arc of its characters, what links the three stories together is the traffic in drugs.

The first story focuses on Mexican police officer Javier Rodriguez. The choices for Javier are to be an honest cop or a corrupt one. The majority of this story takes place in Mexico. The second story focuses on Robert Wakefield, an Ohio State Supreme Court justice who is appointed by the President to be the new anti-drug czar. The choices for Robert are to be an effective professional or to be an effective father. The complication in this story is that his daughter Caroline, a high-achieving privileged teenager, becomes addicted to cocaine and heroin. The majority of this story takes place in Ohio. The third story focuses on Helena Ayala, a pregnant California housewife, whose husband Carlos is arrested on drug trafficking charges. If he is convicted, Helena's lifestyle will change dramatically. The choices for Helena are to be a docile housewife or to do what she has to do to protect her family. The majority of this story takes place in southern California.

Although there is plot in each of these three stories, Soderbergh focuses on the character arc rather than on following the plot to its resolution. By following character, the drive of the plot is undermined. If the three stories were about plot, there would be more emphasis on the flow of the drugs. In *Traffic*, the emphasis is on the choices made by the characters. The middle story illustrates the point. Although Robert is the drug czar, in the end he resigns, primarily because he feels the battle he has to win is a battle to restore his relationship with his daughter and to save her from being destroyed by drugs. Robert himself chooses character over plot (the drug czar versus the drug story). Also, because the character arc is more critical than the plot arc, we get the feeling that the drug culture will carry on as it did. Helena has succeeded in getting Carlos freed. She has affiliated with Carlos's boss in Mexico and has killed Edouardo, the main witness against Carlos. She has saved her family, but the drug war will continue and Carlos may yet land in jail. There is in this sense no real closure. What we have experienced is an episode in the drug wars.

In addition, these three stories have a code of survivalism that overshadows the morality of the drug issue. In the Mexican story, Javier's relationship with his partner Manolo, who becomes corrupted, and the consequent sense of responsibility Javier has toward Manolo's widow far outweigh his career moves in importance. Just as Helena does what she has to do to survive, and just as Robert does what he has to do to help his family survive, Javier acts to save a corner of dignity in his life. The progress of the drug trade proceeds. There are no heroes in *Traffic*—that would require more use of plot; here, there are only human beings whom we watch affirm their humanness. The result is that *Traffic* is far from a linear experience.

The Approach to Tone/Voice

As stated earlier, genre films unfold within expected tonal parameters. Do Soderbergh's films unfold within tonal expectations? Melodramas such as *Erin Brockovich* or *sex, lies, and videotape* unfold in a realistic tone. And for the most part, these two films exhibit the expected realistic tone.

Traffic actually uses three genres. The Mexican story unfolds as a police story with a large character layer. The Ohio story devolves into a melodrama, although it has a thriller's devotion to using plot to discover the threat. The third story unfolds as a crime story revolving around Helena's becoming "the criminal." Again, there is plot, but there is a stronger character layer. All of these genres are realistic and thus proceed realistically. Meanwhile, film noir is expected to unfold with an overheated expressionism, and *The Underneath* has that heated, literary character we affiliate with the genre.

Although Soderbergh works within genre expectations, he breaks them just as often. It is to these examples that we now turn. Although Soderbergh has a preference to move to the intense nightmare dimension in his work, we don't expect this quality in a melodrama. Nevertheless, Soderbergh uses this tone in *King of the Hill*. If Act One is a romanticized view of real life, Acts Two and Three gradually move into the subjective nightmare sense of the Depression. In *King of the Hill*, Soderbergh is experimenting with a tone he had more elaborately explored in Lem Dobbs's *Kafka*. Ostensibly, *Kafka* is a story about a writer who is also employed in insurance. The character looks first into the disappearance of a friend and his death, and then into the disappearance of a second friend, both of whom had worked with him. He feels that somehow the key to the disappearances lies in the Castle, the center of power, the seat of the bureaucracy. The time is 1919, the place is Prague. Kafka infiltrates the castle, clashes with the head of medical records, and is pursued by the two men who recently became his assistants at the insurance company. Whether his experiences are real or just a paranoid dream isn't made clear. What is critical is the tone of paranoia, dream, possibility. The atmosphere and feeling are more important than the plot. In a sense, it's an experimental narrative about an important writer's state of mind. It is important that Kafka's inner state is effectively created. If we feel his anxiety, his dread, as our own, Soderbergh has achieved his narrative intention. Plot here is an excuse rather than an informing narrative strategy.

Another example of a tonal shift away from expectation is Scott Frank's *Out of Sight*. Gangster films tend to proceed realistically. *Out of Sight* is not a situation comedy in the vein of *Midnight Run*; rather, it is a genre film in the vein of the Coen brothers' *Fargo*, and it veers between comedy and realism as Robert Benton and David Newman's *Bonnie and Clyde* did. Whether the ironic tone originated with the novel by Elmore Leonard or not, *Out of Sight* surprises us. The structured choice of focusing on the character layer over the plot, along with the self-reflective and wry Jack Foley, together create a space for a tone that keeps shifting away from genre expectation.

The Approach to Genre

Steven Soderbergh has a clear preference for genre films—melodrama, above all—but he is equally attracted to the police story, gangster film, and film noir. As we have mentioned, Soderbergh is interested in stretching genre, or, at the very least, in reversing the expected course. Consequently, *The Limey* begins to look more like a melodrama than a crime film, and *Traffic*, a police/melodrama/crime film, has powerful overtones of melodrama. Likewise, *Out of Sight* could be framed as a romantic comedy-cum-gangster film, with the romantic comedy more prominent. Only *Erin Brockovich* comes off as a straightforward melodrama.

All of this suggests that Soderbergh is as interested in elevating his voice via the experience of narrative as he is in telling the story. In this sense, the rise of Soderbergh as a storyteller is very much in line with the ascent of voice in film storytelling.[1] His approach to genre consequently plays an important role in his anti-narrative experimentation.

Conclusion

In this chapter, we looked at two different storytellers. Each approaches character, structure, story form, and tone from a different perspective. Steven Spielberg has an optimistic, romantic perspective and a desire to engage his audience in a direct, powerful connection with his narrative. He prefers the classic linear narrative, from critical moment to resolution to closure.

At the other extreme, we find Steven Soderbergh using what we have termed anti-narrative. In his very different approach to character, structure, form, and tone, Soderbergh is restless and experimental. At times, this can result in a more distant or open experience. Our temptation may be to suggest that Soderbergh is consciously seeking to be creative or is more interested in the medium than in its audience. Whatever the reason, he has opted for a more open-minded approach to narrative, and the mix of strategies he deploys is more idiosyncratic than is the work of Steven Spielberg. But when they work, such narratives are surprising and fresh.

The two Stevens represent two narrative impulses at opposite ends of the spectrum. Spielberg invites us to enter into a relationship with his main characters, while Soderbergh keeps his main characters a bit distant from us. This is where the divergence of their paths begins. To understand this more fully we now turn to a discussion of genre, and in later chapters, a full discussion of character and voice. Each of these chapters will yield a deeper understanding of why the two Stevens represent the opposite creative polarities for the screenwriter.

Reference

1. Ken Dancyger, pp. 153–163, "The Ascent of Voice", chapter in GLOBAL SCRIPTWRITING, Focal Press, 2001.

7

Multiple Threaded, Long-Form Television Serial Scripts

Over the past 15 years, some of the most interesting screen-based drama has been on long-form television serials that use a multiple threaded story structure. In his book *Everything Bad Is Good for You*, Steven Johnson discusses how multiple threaded, long-form television (TV) serials expand viewers' cognitive perceptions by opening spaces in the narrative.

> Narratives that require that their viewers fill in crucial elements take that complexity to a more demanding level. To follow the narrative, you aren't just asked to remember. You're asked to analyze. This is the difference between intelligent shows, and shows that force you to be intelligent.[1]

While I agree with Johnson's argument regarding viewers' reception, these scripts are not as open-ended as he suggests. If so, they would not likely be produced. The question faced by the writer, then, is how to introduce the complexity made possible by multiple story lines and still give the script coherence. Addressing these questions is worth a complete book in itself. However, in this chapter, we will look broadly at several seasons of serials and argue that these multiple threaded scripts are highly dependent on theme and premise, character line, and tone to organize their stories.

Theme and Premise: Soprano's Season 5, Episode 61 "Unidentified Black Males" 2004

Theme is an extension of what we call narrative voice in this chapter—the component or agency of storytelling that organizes the story and communicates it to the audience. This focus on narrative voice is particularly important in serials because, while their story at the dramatic or character level may seem chaotic, at the organizational and communications level, they tend to be more coherent. Narrative voice shapes the meaning of events so that they come together for the audience—in order to do so, the writer must determine a theme, an area of interest which he/she wishes to emphasize in the story, and a premise, an active point-of-view toward that area of interest. Theme is usually expressed as a noun, whereas premise is expressed as a verb. The translation of theme into premise converts the idea into action and helps drive the story.

We have not talked about theme a great deal in this book because it can take the writer away from the concrete texture of experience that we see as so important in alternative styles. An overt concentration on theme can cause the writer to attempt to focus everything around the way story serves to illustrate meaning and undercut the randomness we think is so central to alternative film. But if the writer is working on a story designed to run 7, 12, or 13 episodes over a number of seasons, it is almost impossible to submerge randomness. In this case, concentration on theme provides useful working technique to help pull the details of the story into coherence.

One possible theme for the six seasons of *The Sopranos* centers on the idea of impotence. Turning this into a premise, we might express it as follows: an underlying sense of powerlessness or impotence leads to an overcompensating need to be overly in control, causing the violence that drives Tony's life, as well as his inability to open up and accept the benefits of his therapy.

Before we go further, we need to make one observation. We are not claiming to identify the one defining theme in any of the scripts we will be discussing in this chapter. Part of theme's evocative power is its slipperiness, and the fact that it speaks in a number of ways to different viewers. We are instead developing our notion of the theme to illustrate our point. As you study stories, we invite you to consider alternative themes and then demonstrate for yourself how they are woven into the scripts.

The "Unidentified Black Males" episode of *The Sopranos* provides a good example of our theme. After an introductory scene, the episode begins with Finn, the boyfriend of Meadow, Tony Soprano's daughter, attempting to pay for a family dinner. Tony aggressively rebuffs him, saying, "You eat. I pay." Immediately we see Tony's obsessive need to control, as well as Finn's need to challenge it. Four scenes later, Meadow bangs futility on an old window air conditioner, trying to get it to cool, as Finn stands by, unable to do anything. Circling around their inability to make up their minds, Finn and Meadow then argue about their future together, now that he's graduated college. Neither of them is able to make a decision. Thoroughly exhausted by the end of the scene, they cannot even decide what movie they want to see to avoid the heat.

Setting up the irony of the episode which will be echoed in its ending sequence, Meadow goes shopping with her mother Carmelo and declares that she will never be dependent on a man, saying, "There are options in life." Carmelo, currently seeking a divorce from Tony, responds, "You have options. I have a lawyer."

Later, after Meadow has found him a job on one of Tony's construction sites, Finn gets sick after watching a fight between two members of the gang. Bringing this emotion back to the apartment, Finn asks Meadow what it was like growing up with the mob. She claims never to have seen any violence and then defends the mob, speaking about the powerlessness and vulnerability its originating members had faced in the Messogiorno, "All higher authority was corrupt." Back at the construction site, Finn will not answer a sports question, fearing a wrong answer will get him beat up.

Into this cloying atmosphere of indecision, Finn happens upon his boss Vito receiving oral sex from another man. Later that day, calling him his "arch nemesis," Vito bullies Finn into accepting an invitation to a Yankees game. Instead of going, Finn runs home to pack, to get out of town. Finally, exhausted after a long fight with Meadow who accuses him of refusing to commit, Finn proposes that they should just get married. The motivation behind Finn's propose is unclear—he may simply think that being married into Tony's family will assure his protection from Vito. But in any case, Meadow is thrilled. The double irony of Carmela's line, "You have options. I have a lawyer" comes together at the end of the episode. First, Carmela learns that no lawyer is willing to take her divorce because of Tony's possible retaliation. Then, returning home, she finds Tony taunting her by floating in their pool and must pretend to be delighted by Meadow's telephoned news of her engagement.

The theme of a persuasive impotence leading to an excessive need for control is echoed in other scenes in the episode. Tony cannot talk about his marriage and instead walks out of the restaurant when Carmela asks him for a divorce. In mangled, suffocated English, gang leader Little Carmine decides to go after Johnny Sack. Discovering that his cousin, Tony B, the man he has been protecting throughout the season, has killed another mobster, Joey Peeps, and precipitated a mob war, Tony collapses with a panic attack. Instead of confronting him as he plans, Tony gives Tony B a promotion that he then brags about to his psychiatrist.

In the pilot, Tony says to his therapist, "It's good to be in something from the ground floor. I came too late for that and I know. But lately, I'm getting the feeling that I came in at the end. The best is over." This sense of entering after the good times have passed him by structures the whole serial, which turns on Tony's progressive rise, but which is constantly shadowed by this fate, the circumstances that he is born into to. "Because of RICO," he explains to his psychiatrist. "Is he your brother?" she asks. This thematic line gives coherence to the whole serial. Its ending, where the audience is left uncertain as to what happens to Tony, transfers this desire for control (in the form of clarity and resolution) from the character to the audience. We as viewers suffer the same impotence as do the characters.

The Pilot as Introduction of Theme and Premise

The theme needs to be set up in the pilot and the premise. We will see how this is done in two serials, HBO's *Boardwalk Empire* and AMC's *Breaking Bad*. Both shows use a structure that twists the plot, starting at a point of action and then flashing back. This heightens the way that this action, the first thing we see, becomes the defining event that focuses the theme.

The theme of *Boardwalk Empire* through its first two seasons deals with the blindness that comes with power and the way it distorts relationships. Stated as a premise, it might read like this: great power undercuts the holder's ability to trust others' reactions, uncertain whether they are genuine or self-serving. This causes powerful people to depend, sometimes blindly, on people who promise rebirth, innocence, and love.

Boardwalk Empire's pilot opens with two masked men hijacking a truck of Canadian Club whiskey, smuggled ashore and bound for New York. It then flashes back three days to the coming of prohibition, where Nucky Thompson, the powerful and corrupt treasurer of Atlantic City, celebrates its possibilities, "We got a product that a fella's got to have. Even better's, we got a product he ain't *allowed* to have." Nucky's protégé, Jimmy Darmody, is introduced as an eager young player, just back from the war, bitter that he is not been given the opportunity to advance quickly through Nucky's organization. In order to make a name for himself and stick it to his boss, Jimmy and Al Capone, another comer, hijack the truck of whiskey, headed for the gangster Arnold Rothstein in New York, and in the process kill five of Rothstein's men. Disgusted at Jimmy's misplaced enthusiasm, Nucky is at first unable to find him, when Jimmy appears, offering a cut of the take.

This scene demonstrates how the script dramatizes the theme. Before passing Nucky the money, Jimmy challenges him, "You can't be half a gangster, Nucky. Not anymore. That much I know." Nucky in response to the money says, "I didn't ask for this." Jimmy answers, "You didn't have to." Nucky could have Jimmy picked up and delivered to Rothstein, thereby ending the incipient feud and the conflict that drives the season. This would have been the rationale action of someone who was not conflicted, not "half a gangster." Instead Nucky says affectionately, "What am I going to do with you?" and then walks off, taking the money. In the filmed scene, he puts the envelope in his jacket.

With the exception of how he acts with his wife-to-be Margaret that we will discuss below, Nucky's success turns on his ability to make shrewd and unemotional decisions about what is best for him. For instance, he does not hesitate to turn on his brother whenever it is expedient. Yet in as much as he is capable of affection, Nucky feels it for Jimmy, his protégé, much in the way that Nucky was the protégé of the Commodore, the man responsible for the financial success of Atlantic City. This is the theme of possible rebirth and love—held by those most close to him, those he has the greatest difficulty in seeing through, and those it turns out he will have the most reason to fear.

This theme is repeated throughout. When Nucky in Chicago learns that his brother has been shot, he calls Margaret and asks her to hide the ledger of his illicit financial dealings in his office desk. In response to her question about why she should be the one to do it, he says, "I don't know what's happening right now and until I return, I would prefer to rely only on you. Can I do that?" Margaret of course looks at the ledger, giving her important knowledge of Nucky's dealings that will drive subsequent episodes. In season two, Nucky signs over the deed to his road lands to Margaret in order to protect them in the case of his conviction. Instructed to sign them back to him at the end of the season, she instead signs them over to the church. Nucky never once considers that this is possible. Although season three has not been released, we can imagine that Nucky's rage once he discovers this betrayal will not only focus on his loss of income, but his, now too apparent, misplaced trust in Margaret.

Breaking Bad's pilot similarly opens *in medias res** with a pair of pants floating down into the desert. After flinging them out of an Recreation Vehicle's window, Walter White, driving like a mad man, eventually runs the vehicle off the road and, under the pressure of an approaching siren, records an apologetic video to his wife and son. "I want you to know that . . . no matter what it may look like . . . I had all three of you in my heart." He picks up a gun and aims it at the oncoming sound.

The show flashes back 3 weeks to the very work-a-day life of Walter, a high school chemistry teacher who, although he says to his class, "chemistry is the study of matter. But I prefer to see it as the study of change," suffers from his own stasis on the day of his 50th birthday. Walter is presented as an everyman. In that role, he is financially strapped, tepidly happy, and certainly not living the life he had dreamed. He is contrasted to Hank, his Drug Enforcement Administration brother-in-law who has no children and recounts his adventures on local TV news. Needing money to pay for the treatment of his recently discovered lung cancer, Walter decides to cook meth with his former high school student Jessie. When asked by Jessie why he is doing it, Walter attempts to blame it on his need for money, then considers and finally says, "I am . . . awake."

The theme circles around the idea of what it is to be "awake" in contemporary America. It suggests that everyday, middle-class life in America is a form of sleepwalking, a catatonic state grounded in a fear of not being able to pay the bills and not being able to act because the little you have built might collapse. The premise might be similar to that of many rock songs and teen movies—that it is better to live a wakeful, short life than a longer, somnambulant and safe one. Actually, just an aside, this is not a premise, but a moral. To make it a premise, we need to make it active, something like this, "taking control of your life, even at the expense of your safety, leads to the a sense of purpose that transcends the danger."

---

*Literally "in the middle of things." It refers to stories that start in process, then either flashes back or fills in the beginning.

We can see it dramatized throughout the pilot, but we can make an example out of a key scene that precedes Walter's first attempt to cook meth. His son, Walter Junior, who has cerebral palsy and must use crutches, is mocked by some jocks because his parent must help him buy pants. Walter, whom we sense would have bit his tongue in his old life, vanishes out the back door of the clothing store and then reappears in the front, beating on one of the jocks. After they leave, defeated, the stage direction says, "Standing here, Walt feels a kind of *power*—one brought on by an absence of fear." Earning this absence of fear drives his character as the serial progresses. It comes from challenging and then overcoming increasingly more powerful threats as he gets deeper into the drug trade.

Character Lines

This book makes the argument that restorative three-act structure is not merely a means of structuring a story, but a strategy for developing characters. In restorative structure, the character makes a false decision that violates her own values or turns in the right direction with insufficient preparation to sustain it, and then must face its consequences. Confronted with these, the character must acknowledge and adjust to overcome them. This usually requires her to integrate heretofore conflicting pieces of her personality. The resultant change leads to personal redemption—the character changes in time for her mistakes to be corrected—while the cracks in society that have motivated her initial conflict are smoothed over. By the end of the film, the character is clearly defined. In learning the lesson the film teaches, by seeing and then addressing her flaws, she is no longer doomed to fall victim to them again. We considered a number of consequences of this structure including that: story dominates texture, tone is consistent, motivation is clearly accessible, the character change is essential, and that social conflict is less important than character conflict.

We contrasted this structure with the more open-ended structures in alternative films. Although we considered a range of films with a number of different strategies, we identified some recurring characteristics of this structure including: structure does not lead to final character definition and that, even after the film ends, characters frequently still contain irresolvable contradictions. In most of these films, social conflict is foregrounded rather than dismissed by resolution of character conflict.

Long form serials use character development strategies that draw from both models. While not offering the clear-cut character resolution we see in restorative thee-act structure, they are also not as open-ended or socially focused as are some alternative films. This stylistic hybridity is a consequence of many things, one of which is the frequency of their episodes and their extension over a number of seasons. Serials must balance their need for sufficient closure to satisfy the season's viewer against keeping the conflict open for subsequent seasons. They also must have sufficient variety to warrant continual viewing.

Having sufficient variety is complicated by the fact that, in order to be coherent, characters tend to be focused around a limited set of conflicts. Thus, while subsequent seasons have different story elements, their plots tend to reprise the same set of fundamental conflicts. So for instance, Tony Soprano's underlying impotence becomes more pronounced in each season of *The Sopranos* as does the intensity of his response to it; yet, each cycle moves no closer to his character's resolution—as long as he is alive, there are no final answers to the contradictions in his character or his situation. In a sense by reiterating the conflict and having it lead to similar outcomes (for instance, Tony's killing Ralphie and then Tony B in subsequent seasons), Tony becomes increasingly more like the essence of Tony, defined not by his resolution, but by the structural permanence of his conflict.[†]

The reinforcement, rather than the resolution, of character contradiction suggests that the character lines in serials not only develop through a sequential line, but also through an increasing composite picture that the viewer forms by superimposing character lines of previous seasons against that of the current one. Character's line and motivation become more complex or ambiguous by virtue of this juxtaposition. The circling around, or folding back upon, the same set of issues suggests that we view the development of a serial character line as a spiral, a recurring cycling action that gradually penetrates deeper into the character.

Taking this into consideration, let's look at Walter White's development in *Breaking Bad*. After the pilot, the next two episodes center on whether he can bring himself to kill Krazy 8, the drug distributor who survived the first episode and is chained in Jessie's basement. Walter, looking for a way out, asks Krazy 8 for a reason to spare his life. "Sell me," Walter begs. Krazy 8 makes the most of Walter's hesitation, engaging him in a heart-to-heart that ends with Krazy 8 getting Walter to admit that he has not told his family about the cancer. Even when Walter realizes that Krazy 8 is only playing him and that he must strangle the drug dealer, this unexpected intimacy does not let up. The killing is close-up, hand-to-hand, and unescapably personal. When Jessie returns home, he finds Walter has cleaned the basement out. The slate has been wiped clean. We assume that Walter has had enough. Upon his return home, he finally tells Skyler that he has cancer.

Yet, Walter's return to his family does not last. After announcing he is thinking of not undergoing treatment because of the cost, his son's contemptuous reaction is, "Go on Dad. Just give up and die." When a former colleague from graduate school offers to pay for the treatment, Walter tells his family that he deserves the right to make a choice and that he will not do it. Then,

---

[†]Of course, this is assuming the Tony has any conflict beyond that of his survival. It is also possible to read him (at least one character suggests this) as a sociopath entirely lacking in conflict.

after some thought, he changes his mind and agrees to treatment. But rather than taking his former colleague's money, he decides to pay for it himself—by returning to cook meth. We can possibly read this as simply an act of pride—that he does not want someone else to support him—but the structure of the serial does not leave it like that. In episode 10 in the second season, he learns that, with his cancer in remission, his immediate financial worries are over. Instead of celebrating, Walter does not know what to do with himself. He has a manic binge, in which he frantically repairs the substructure of his house. While stocking up at the building supply store, however, he cannot resist giving advice to someone he presumes to be a competitive meth cooker. Pondering this as he makes his home improvement purchases, Walter finally makes up his mind. He leaves his cans of paint in the checkout line, approaches the cooker in the parking lot and warns him to, "Stay out of my territory." In the next episode, he has back to work with Jessie. Two seasons later when his brother-in-law begins to target Walter's old assistant, Gale, a misdirection that could deflect attention from him, Walter almost blows his cover by insisting that Gale is not capable of such a high quality of work.

In order to understand how this pattern of cycling compares to that of the three-act model of character development, we need to consider is how we understand Walter's meth cooking. In a restorative three-act model, we would be clearly positioned. Not only would the cooking and the violence that goes along with it be a false solution that marks the end of the first act, but we would understand that Walter is violating his own value system and that at some point he will have to come to terms with it. Even if he could get away with (in dramatic terms) the initial meth cook in the pilot, the killing of Krazy 8 is the kind of violation that we expect needs to be accounted for. Further the meth and the killing, both of which takes three episodes, would be an action that Walter works up to in the course of the first act, not one that he does in the pilot. Yet, the fact that happens so early in the life of the serial intentionally blurs its moral consequences. It is a given. If you watch the show, you accept it. As such, we understand that we are expected to be unclear how to read it.

Secondly, we do not know how to take the end. At the time of this writing the series is not completed, but we suspect that when it is, Walter will pay with his life. What we do not know is how and what it will mean. But we can speculate, at least broadly. If his cancer remains in remission and he dies from the violence associated with the meth, the series will suggest that it may have been a mistake to become Heisenberg, that a slow and steady life remaining asleep may be the best way to live after all. If he dies of cancer while still reigning as Heisenberg, it might suggest that being "awake" was worth it, that it gave the last part of his life a meaning. Finally, if he dies from something unrelated, it will challenge our confidence that there is any meaning in the story world at all—that the narrative voice is a different order of organization than the chaos of life. This would be the most radical of possible endings because it would not only take us in a different direction in the story world, but cause us to retroactively question our faith in the organization of the story telling itself.

The fact that we do not know is, of course, important. Because of the length of long-form serials, the ambiguity of their stories linger in a different way than do single episode features (this is obviously different in features that are part of a series). As we have mentioned previously, endings causes us to retrospectively revisit stories and reinterpret, where necessary, their meaning in light of the finality of their conclusion. The lack of an ending means a lack of a final frame of reference. This allows the viewer of a long-form serial to engage the character outside of the final frame of the narrative and draw consequences uncontained by the completed character line. Paradoxically, such release from knowledge of the overall story structure may encourage an openness, a sense of imagination, in the viewer which reinforces Johnson's quote about shows that "force you to be intelligent" by filling in crucial elements. Sometimes stories seem more alive before they end. Serials may evoke this kind of excitement by virtue of their very seriality.

Because it is spread over a number of characters, *Boardwalk Empire* does not have the same intensity of single character line as does *Breaking Bad*. The range of characters we follow means that cumulative meaning of the series is focused on their interweaving. For our purposes we will concentrate on the line of Jimmy Darmondy, which is tightly woven around that of Nucky and is completed in the first two seasons. Imagined as restorative three-act structure, Jimmy's first act false solution might have been to turn against Nucky. He would ride the success of this, even after the viewer begins to anticipate that Jimmy lacks Nucky's decisiveness and ruthlessness. Jimmy would get in further over his head until he falls, only then beginning to understand his own limitations. In the third act, he would realize that he can play in this game only as a sidekick and seek to rejoin Nucky, who would accept him back.

The beginning of *Boardwalk Empire* is developed in just this way. Although Jimmy steals Rothstein's liquor and kills his men, he does so not in rebellion, but in service to Nucky, believing he is completing his mentor's unspoken wish. Jimmy's rebellion only begins to build when he is sent to Chicago and then again in his negotiations with Nucky who wants Jimmy to return to Atlantic City. Jimmy really begins to peel away from his mentor when Nucky cuts a deal with Rothstein. Jimmy's false solution, his turn into the second act, comes at the end of the first season when Jimmy intently listens to the Commodore's rant against Nucky. He begins plotting against his former mentor at the beginning of the second.

In the course of the second season, Jimmy's star rises and then falls in much the way we would expect of a restorative second act. Yet, he never truly breaks free from his mentor. Talked into sanctioning an attempt on Nucky's life, he approaches Nucky just prior to the shooting, hands out, palms up, with an equivocal statement, "It doesn't make a difference whether you are right or wrong. You just have to make a decision." It is unclear whether this is a warning or an apology, but it emphasizes Jimmy's uncertainty, his lack of commitment to his own second act. Trumped by Nucky's importation of real Irish whiskey, Jimmy can only passively agree when his partners decide to sell off their cheap stuff. By the end of the season, Jimmy is ready to return to Nucky's good graces. In the last episode, he asks for a chance to set things right. As the *Boardwalk Empire* showrunner, Terence Winter, puts it,

> One of the things I wanted to do by design in the finale is make the audience pissed off [at the start of the episode]. I wanted people to say [when it seemed like Nucky and Jimmy would reconcile], "Oh great, after all that, it's all going to be forgotten and Jimmy is going to be back in Nucky's good graces." I wanted them to think right up to the very end that Nucky is going to forgive him and take him back.[2]

Thinking he has succeeded, apparently earning his way back by killing off the witnesses lined up to testify against Nucky, Jimmy shows up at a final rendezvous only to have Nucky shoot him. What Jimmy has learned does not matter. He is not allowed to get away with his transgressions and redeem himself.

In fact, the learning may all be with Nucky. The tracking of Jimmy's line illustrates how the movement of one character is interwoven with that of another. Terence Winter puts it this way,

> In the pilot, Jimmy told Nucky: "You can't be half a gangster anymore." We wanted with the first two seasons to follow that trajectory, where he goes full season from being the guy who doesn't want to get his hands dirty to actually pulling the trigger himself. And what's the strongest version of that? To pull the trigger on the very guy who told him, "You can't be half a gangster anymore."[3]

Tone: The Larger World

Finally, as consistent with other discussions in this book, we will look at what these serials suggest about the world beyond the story. As in other chapters, we will not focus on the explicit content of the serial (i.e., is the story explicitly political), as much as how it uses its tone and manner of presentation to imply broader meaning.

Full of period touches, particularly in costumes, appliances, music and sets, *Boardwalk Empire*'s representation of the 1920s is respectful, almost worshipful. Like many series explicitly set in an historical period, the serial carefully works external events (Harding's election, Jack Dempsey's fights) into its story. Through its sympathetic treatment of characters who violate prohibition at the same time it dwells on the hypocrisy of the Agent Van Alden, the agent who is supposed to enforce it, the serial shares with the audience the implied agreement that prohibition was a mistake. But they do it in a gentle way. The scripts do not convey a superior position to the characters in the story, but share a world-weariness with them, a sense that this kind of behavior is expected. The joke, if anything, is on the government and the belief that natural human appetites, such as alcohol, can be legislated.

While also careful to work in historical events, *Mad Men*, by contrast, is targeted to a knowing audience laughing, at least at times, at the mistakes of the past. The most obvious of these easy targets is in the serial's portrayal of ethnic and gender stereotypes, as well as advertisings close relationship with the tobacco industry. The pilot, entitled "Smoke Gets in Your Eyes," turns on Don Draper's attempt to come up with an advertising slogan for his firm's biggest client, Old Gold cigarettes, after the Federal Trade Commission has forbidden advertisements that make cigarette health claims. His solution is to come up with a slogan—"It's toasted"—a solution that the company find acceptable because, even though it is true of all cigarettes, diverts concern from the health issues. When Joan introduces Peggy to her new job as secretary, she says of the electric typewriter, "Now try not to be overwhelmed by all this technology. It looks complicated, but the men who designed it made it simple enough for a woman to use."

The net effect of this is to put the viewer at a safe distance from the action. Whatever the overt point-of-view of the serial—women's inability to advance in corporate America for instance—the formal structure remains reassuring and unchallenging. From our vantage point today, it is easy to mock the trade commission's timidity or the sexual hypocrisy of the fifties without recognizing our own blindness to our prejudices of today. As many of the mainstream examples we refer to in this book, *Mad Men* proposes change in its content but assures us that we are insulated from change by its narrative perspective.

Homeland, as did *24* before it, draws from the cultural zeitgeist and the subsequent wars following September 11. But if we contrast it to *24*, we can see how the environment has changed, not only in terms of conflict, but also in narrative structure. *24* presents the terrorist threat as shadowy and unabashedly evil, giving us initial villains in each season who are duped or naïve, and them moving on to terrorists, and politicians who are stereotypically evil. Except in rare moments, the center of our identification is with Jack Bauer rather than with the terrorists. Even when Jack goes overboard in his interrogations, we are consistently reminded that such excess is necessary for the safety of the country. The scripts do this by presenting the terrorists as images, seen largely through surveillance devices.

Homeland, by contrast, richly characterizes Brody, the planted terrorist who does not complete his mission in the first season. By lingering on his difficulties in returning to his wife who has fallen in love with his best friend, the serial positions the audience to identify with Brody. While first duplicating *24* by showing us Brody's life only through surveillance, we soon see him directly. In fact, the serial credits his inner life sufficiently to include a series of his flashbacks that explain why he has come to be a terrorist. This identification with a character who would had been treated as the abject other in *24* deepens the viewers' confusion about how to take Brody's actions and raises questions about the politics of identification. In doing so, it suggests a richer and more ambivalent approach to terrorism that had previously been presented. Time has changed how we see terrorism and this has resulted in formal changes in our storytelling.

In the pilot of *Girls*, an HBO series about three young women in their early twenties living in New York, one of the character talks about her love of the earlier HBO series, *Sex and the City*. But where *Sex and the City* features women in their thirties and forties who had found professional, but not romantic, success, the characters in *Girls* seek not only romantic success, but their professional identities. The *Sex and the City* pilot opens with Carrie narrating the breakup of a well-heeled English journalist for her "Sex and the City" column; *Girls* opens with the struggling Hannah, the main character, both being financially cut off by her parents and losing her non-paying internship. Carrie's column is advertised on the side of a bus; Hannah who also wants to be a writer is unknown and unpublished. Carrie's relationship breakup is the end of a quick, but very romantic courtship. Hannah confesses her financial cutoff to her sometimes boyfriend who never leaves his apartment and treats her as his sex toy.

This intertextuality[‡] works in ways that are not dissimilar to the spiraling we see in the character line. While the scripts in *Sex and the City* purport to a toughness, they still glamorize romance, disconnecting it from the drudgery of building a career or the logistics of sex. The urgency for romance in *Girls* is juxtaposed with a restlessness, a looking for purpose, a grittier sense of how little control the characters have over their own lives. Sex is more explicit, but also more mechanical and unsatisfying. If we read *Girls* in the context of the earlier *Sex and the City*, the contrast between the two adds a dimension to the later serial's world. The impact of the financial crises has shifted the possibilities that had been opened to the characters. They live in contrast to the dreams they saw represented when they were younger.

We may read the plane crash that ends the second season of *Breaking Bad* as an ironic extension of Walter's actions from the individual to a larger social context. In response to the crash, indirectly caused by Walter, his high school holds a memorial where he is asked to speak. Thus, Walter is not only a cause of the suffering, but also a member of a community of sufferers who are expected to share this common tragedy. He is both cause and mourner.

The irony of Walter's position works well, but it also illustrates one key difference between television serials and some of the alternative films we have considered in this book. While the plane crash succeeds in juxtaposing the individual's actions to the reaction of the larger community, it does not dramatize the disconnected sense of unexplained contingency we sometimes see in contemporary life. By fully foreshadowing the crash—we see moments of its aftermath before many of the preceding episodes—the serial makes its actual occurrence a satisfying resolution of these hints. However, the very foreshadowing diminishes its randomness or contingency. In this sense, it feels

---

‡The relationship between texts.

very different than does the reoccurring twenty dollar bill that blows out the window of the cab in Scorsese's *After Hours* or the earthquake that turns the story in Altman's *Short Cuts*. This need to overexplain or setup may be part of the compromise build into the structure of long-form television serials. For events to pay off in the course of the season, they must be foreshadowed in most, if not all, the previous episodes. Or, if they are important events from the serial's deeper past, they must be recapitulated in the reminder sections that begin many episodes. This tends to undercut the randomness of subsequent events. The very need to keep viewers up-to-date also diminishes the element of chance or accident that gives many alternative films their power.

Summary

Multiple threaded, long-form television serials have opened up storytelling possibilities for writers who have previously seen their aesthetic interests limited to alternative features. Because of their multiple plot elements, serials foreground theme as a central core that unifies individual episodes and entire seasons. Thus, they give the writer more opportunity to concentrate on ideas than do mainstream features. Because viewers may live with a serial over a number of years before it is resolved, they get used to complexities and contradictions in the characters. Therefore, the writer's treatment of character can be richer than that it is in both traditional television and in more mainstream feature films. Further, instead of experiencing serials as the linear development of character lines, viewers may also see them in terms of the juxtapositions across seasons. As a result, the restorative three-act model of character build and resolution becomes more complex, and the viewer is able to accept that characters may never resolve fundamental contradictions. Finally, by evoking historical moments, earlier treatments of social issues or stories that foreground theme, serials may raise complex relationships between the story and the broader world. Foregrounding these contrasting representations can connect scripts to larger realities in ways that go beyond what we had previously believed television could do.

References

1. Steven Johnson, *Everything Bad Is Good For You* (New York: Riverhead Books, 2006), 63–64.
2. James Hibbert, 2011. "*Boardwalk Empire* showrunner explains finale, talks season 3," *Entertainment Weekly*, December 11, 2011. Web. Accessed June 1, 2012, <http://insidetv.ew.com/2011/12/11/boardwalk-empire-finale/>.
3. Ibid.

8

Why Genre?

Scriptwriting as a pedagogy has been dominated for the past three decades by an obsession with three-act structure. A parallel perception that actually seeks a deeper structure, the journey of the hero, sources from the writings of Joseph Campbell. Before the dominance of these two approaches, Aristotle and his theatrical descendants focused upon the rising action of conflict organized into a narrative. The primary struggle of the protagonist and antagonist was the baseline of every story.

In the midst of all these activities applied to the understanding of screenwriting, genre was either a reference to style such as the visual stylization of a film noir or a particular narrative story form such as the gangster film that lent itself to visual stylization. The only other reference to genre was within literary theory. Northrop Frye in his seminal work, *The Anatomy of Criticism*, refers to large general categories of genre—comedy, tragedy, and romance. Within these general categories, he describes particular motifs and tropes, specific to the larger categories.

In this chapter, we suggest that genre is the missing link in the pedagogy of screenwriting. We also suggest that every film narrative fits into one genre or another and that there are two general categories of genre. The first, the classical genre, fits in the three-act structure, whereas the second, *voice-oriented* genres, does not. The latter grouping is discussed in Chapter 13.

With regard to the classical genre, we'd like to suggest that the contemporary pedagogy of screenwriting is incomplete without consideration of genre. Genre is the meta-structure of the screenplay. It organizes premise, character, and structure. As the specific genre has its own character arc and dramatic arc, it is impossible to move the screenplay forward effectively until a determination of the genre of the narrative is made. It is the genre decision that tells the writer whether the character arc is positive or negative and whether enough plot is being used in the narrative's dramatic arc. Until a genre is chosen, the writer can only stumble forward in the writing process. Choosing a genre, in short, is a critical decision that will enable the writer to progress his or her screenplay. Understanding genre enables the writer to choose the genre appropriate to his or her narrative.

The Progression of Screenwriting

A screenplay usually begins with a character, a situation, or an incident. A particular place or time period may equally incite the beginning of a screenplay.

Depending on the writer's experience, a series of tropes may provide a general structure to the idea. Examples of such tropes might be the following:

1. My first serious relationship.
2. An adventure that turns bad.
3. The workplace has its own rules.
4. Avoid commitment at all costs.
5. Good intentions are never enough.
6. Ambition helps one and hurts many.
7. Leaving home.
8. My father the disappointment.
9. Technology is a threat.
10. I win the lottery.

From the above list, the writer decides whether he or she wants to explore a life lesson, apply a coming of age or loss of innocence matrix, focus on character, or focus on plot. The exploration of an ethical challenge or the nature of morality in a particular character, time, or place also avails to the writer the capacity to grow his initial idea.

The next narrative step is to populate the story with dramatically suitable characters and of course to decide upon a beginning, middle, and an end for the story.

Further informing the writer about the narrative is the answer to a series of self-reflective questions.

Why does this story grab my imagination?
What does it mean?
What would I like to say in this story?

The answers to these questions will move the story away from stereotype and hopefully toward creative uniqueness.

The next sequence in the screenplay's evolution requires consideration of the nature of an audience's relationship with the main character of the screenplay.

Is the main character likeable, sympathetic, and empathic?
How can the writer enhance these qualities in the main character?
Is there a structural intervention (the plot) that will strengthen the identification of the audience with the main character?
How can other characters including the antagonist be deployed to strengthen the audience's relationship with the main character?

In relation to the story progression, another set of questions come into play.

Does the main character change in the course of the narrative?
Is there enough change to justify the anticipated length of the screenplay?
How is that change affected?
How substantial is a device, surprise, deployed in the screenplay?
Does that surprise enhance the rising action within the structure of the screen story?

The next consideration can be described as the positioning of the main character in the narrative. Ideally the main character should be positioned in the middle of the narrative. A double check on positioning is to pose the questions who is helping the main character and who is opposing the main character? Here too balance is important. If no one opposes the main character, does this flatten the dramatic properties of the screen story to this point? To turn this issue on its head, is there a premise operating for the main character in the screen story? The premise sometimes referred to as the spine or the central conflict of the screen story needs to be present throughout the screenplay.

One working definition of the premise is to consider two opposing choices for the main character. Love or money for Rose in James Cameron's *Titanic* (1997); ongoing dishonor or regained honor for Frank Galvin in Sidney Lumet's *The Verdict* (1983); selfishness or humanness for C.C. Baxter in Billy Wilder's *The Apartment* (1959). A useful organization of the character population around the main character is to see one group representing option 1 of the premise and the balance representing option 2.

No dialogue has been written. A tone for the screenplay has not yet been determined.

It is at this fork in the narrative road that particular pedagogical strategies will focus on sharpening structure or defining the voice of the writer and planting it deep in the narrative or simply focusing on telling the story in as effective and engaging a way as possible. Any of these approaches will move the screenplay ahead possibly even to a reasonable conclusion. Our suggestion however is that the narrative journey will be faster and stronger if the matrix of genre is applied at this point.

The Benefits of Genre

There is no single genre that is meant for a particular story. Rather it is more useful to see genre as a series of potential pathways each taking the viewer on a different journey. There's no one right journey. Each genre shapes the narrative differently. Knowing about genre will however help the writer make the choice best suited to tell the story the writer is trying to tell.

At its core, every genre positions a character in the story differently. Genre choice also influences the resolution of the story, the deployment of plot versus character in the story, and reflects a tone that enables the audience to believe in the narrative's outcome. This must all sound terribly self-serving about genre's importance in narrative. Genre is important; genre is the critical decision in the writing of the screenplay. It's time to explain why.

The Character Arc

At the beginning of the screenplay, we join a main character at a critical moment in his/her life. For dramatic purposes, let's call that critical moment a crisis. In the course of the screenplay, we are going to follow that main character and watch him/her adapt or change to meet the crisis. By the resolution of the screenplay, the main character will have changed either for the better or for the worse, depending on the genre. That change is enabled by a relationship or relationships. If the relationship is extremely central, we might call the character pushing for the change a transformational character. If that character is negative or powerful in their opposition to the main character and his goal, that character is the antagonist. Plot can also put pressure on the main character and force adaptation or worse. The character arc then is a reflection of how the character under duress (usually the main character) changes from the beginning to the end of the screenplay. Genre choice influences the critical moment, the beginning, the end, the nature of the character population, positive and negative, the degree of character change, and the credibility of that degree of change. Let's turn to each of these points in the character arc and its shape, in turn.

The Critical Moment

An arrogant scientist decides to experiment upon himself resulting in a behavioral shift with self-destructive consequences in *Dr. Jekyll and Mr. Hyde* (1933), a horror film. A self-defeating actor can never get an acting job, because he knows more than the director, in *Tootsie* (1985), a situation comedy. An unworldly naïf is asked to save the world from evil in *The Lord of the Rings* (2001), an action-adventure. A relentless and famous detective has an almost fatal heart attack while pursuing a killer in *Blood Work* (2002) a police story. An uneducated but ambitious young man arrives in the East to take up his rich uncle's offer of a job, if he comes East, in *A Place in the Sun* (1951), a melodrama.

In a sense, the action of the main character in the critical moment of the screenplay points us, the audience to a particular resolution appropriate to the genre. The arrogant risk-taking of Henry Jekyll at the beginning of *Dr. Jekyll and Mr. Hyde* makes his later destruction very much in keeping with genre expectations.

In *Tootsie*, Michael's arrogance as an actor who knows more than the directors auditioning him makes his decision to audition as a woman who becomes a very successful actor as a woman, very much in line with the clash of values, the source of comedy in the situation comedy.

Frodo's naivety and goodness make him a less than likely superhero who can best the super-villains amassed against him and his allies in the action-adventure film *The Lord of the Rings*. It also makes Frodo appealing in a genre permeated by wish fulfillment rather than realism.

Here we come to an important point about genre. *Blood Work and A Place in the Sun*, a Police Story and a Melodrama, are genres whose credibility is based upon how realistic they are. Consequently their crisis points, where we enter these stories, has to be equally realistic. Frodo on the other hand is not a realistic main character at all. As action-adventure is all about wish fulfillment, the journey of Frodo from naïf (even his physical size is anti-heroic) to superhero is at best a metaphor for the notion that goodness will always trump evil in the world, at best a wish if we look at the history of the past century.

Turning to the dark turn of events in *Dr. Jekyll and Mr. Hyde*, we see the cautionary tale in full flight. Fly too high and you will die. Accept the natural order or die. In the horror film, the nightmare dominates the form. Humans beware.

Resolution

Just as the critical moment in its relationship to the main character's goal and nature will differ from one genre to another, so too will the resolution.

An insurance salesman flirts inappropriately with a client's wife in *Double Indemnity* (1943). Whether he does so out of boredom or out of desperation, this critical moment starts him on the journey that will lead to his own destruction. Destruction of the main character is the resolution of the character's arc in film noir.

The arc in situation comedy is far more hopeful. In *The Apartment*, the main character also works for a large insurance company. As we meet him, he is lending his apartment for a night to an insurance executive. He does so in the hope that the executive will enable his promotion within the company. His behavior is as ignoble as the main character in *Double Indemnity*. Nevertheless his fate is quite different. He chooses to become a better person, a more humane person at resolution. This positive ending is in keeping with the situation comedy just as the dark ending is the resolution audiences expect from film noir.

The resolution is more extreme in the action-adventure. Indiana Jones, a risk-taking archeologist, survives death at the critical moment of *Raiders of the Lost Ark* (1981). By its resolution, he has evaded hordes of Nazis, outfoxed an equally-clever archeologist, and essentially rescued mankind by preventing the Nazis and said rival archeologist from possessing the ancient all-powerful Ark of the Covenant. In short, Indiana Jones has become a superhero.

Of course this is an absurd outcome but very much in keeping with action-adventure film, a story form brimming with wish-fulfillment (as opposed to realism). The key point here is that it's the genre choice that will determine whether a resolution is realistic, the outcome of wish, or the outcome of a nightmare.

The Nature of the Character Population

In general terms, the character population will be extreme in genres of wish-fulfillment such as the action-adventure film and in genres of the nightmare such as the horror film and the film noir. In the more realistic genres such as the melodrama and the situation comedy, the character population will be realistic, as recognizable as a neighbor, a friend, or family.

More specifically, the character population is determined by their service to the premise. Another variable that will determine the character population is the tone of the film. The lighter the characters are, the more enabling they are for the main character. The more intense dark or powerful they are, the greater the threat to the main character and his/her goal.

To illustrate genre differences in character population, we turn to four films, two thrillers, a melodrama, and a situation comedy. Because all are realistic genres, the character populations have to be credible and realistic.

Steven Frear's *Dirty Pretty Things* (2001), written by Steven Knight, is the story of Okwe (Chiwetel Ejiofor), an illegal immigrant in London from Nigeria, trying to make his way. He works with West Indians, Yugoslavs, and Turks; his best friend is Chinese, and his primary employer is Spanish. The character population with the exception of two British immigrant officials is immigrants, strangers in this strange white land, London. The plot surrounds the exploitation of immigrants. They sell their vital organs for British passports. Formerly a doctor in Nigeria, Okwe because of his illegal status is doubly exploited as a doctor and as an illegal.

Aside from making the point that all these immigrant groups, legal awaiting legality or illegal, all live on the margins. All are also either victims or perpetrators in this world of immigrants. Senay (Audrey Tatou) is a Turkish national, not allowed to work but working as a cleaner in a hotel, to make her way. Juliette (Sophie Okonedo) is a black prostitute. Guo Yi (Benedict Wong) is a legal immigrant working in a morgue as an attendant, to make his way. All share status and support with Okwe.

Jan (Sergi Lopez), manager of the hotel where Okwe, Juliette, and Senay work, is the antagonist who runs the sale of illegal organs business. He is Spanish, powerful, and the clear antagonist for Okwe and the other illegals. But he is not alone. A sweatshop employer elicits sexual favors from Senay to keep a job. British immigration officials hunt down Senay relentlessly, as if she were an animal rather than a woman from Turkey seeking to improve her life.

The point here is that the character population aligns with the premise (does an illegal have to act illegally to become legal?) around the issue of personal behavior vis-à-vis others, ethical or exploitative. And in keeping with a central motif of the thriller—can an ordinary person (Okwe) in unusual circumstances (illegal status) overcome a powerful antagonist whose goal is to use him up?

Guillaume-Canet's *Tell No One* (2006), a thriller, is based on American Harlan Coben's novel. The screenplay is by Canet and Philippe Lefebre. The critical moment is the murder of Alexandre Beck's (Francois Cluzet) wife Margot (Marie-Josee Croze). Eight years later, he has not recovered from the loss but finds himself the prime suspect in her murder. Unless he learns why/how/if she died, he will suffer the fate of the accused and convicted. The narrative concerns itself with the consequences of his becoming the prime suspect and the unfolding of the search for the real killer if his wife is indeed dead. She is not and he is not.

The character population is principally three groups—the family and friends of Margot and Alexandre. This is widely interpreted to include a gangster, Bruno, whose son is a patient of Alexandre. The second group is the investigators—police and lawyers who are working to prove or disprove Alexander's guilt. The third group is the actual perpetrators of the attempt to kill Margot and now to kill Alexandre. They represent the true harmers in the narrative.

Tell No One has an unusually large character population. Canet weaves it tight by including "guilty" people among the friends or helpers. Margot herself, her father (a police captain), Alexandre's sister, Margot's best friend have participated in deceiving the main character Alexandre. But each has deceived out of love for the main character or to protect him.

The antagonist, Senator Neuville (Jean Rochefort) has enlisted criminals to act on his behalf and to punish Margot for the death of his son, years earlier. The son, a sexual predator and violent character, was killed because of his violence toward Margot years earlier. Alexandre learns of his history only in Act III.

The character population in *Tell No One* is trying to either protect or harm Margot. Alexandre just happens to be the husband. In her absence (death or disappearance), he becomes the target. To survive, he needs to understand and escape the rush to judgment by the police and the rush to murder on the part of the senator's cohorts. Protecting or harming becomes the rationale for the character population in *Tell No One*.

What is notable about the character population in both the thrillers is the presence of a powerful antagonist who essentially drives the plot. A second feature of the character population is that even those characters who are helpers to the main character play a key role in endangering the main character. Margot in *Tell No One* and Senay in *Dirty Pretty Things* as they face the ultimate threat to their lives force the main character to save them, thereby posing the greatest level of threat to the main character.

This immediately differentiates them from the situation we find in the Melodrama. *After the Wedding* (2006), Susanne Bier's film, has no true antagonist and only a modest plot.

Jacob (Mads Mikkelson) is a childcare worker in an orphanage in India. He is called back to Denmark to secure desperately needed funding for the orphanage. The benefactor Jurgen (Rolf Lassgard) invites Jacob to the wedding of his daughter. There Jacob meets his former girlfriend once more, now Jurgen's wife, and at the wedding, the bride announces that Jurgen is not her real father.

In short order, Jacob discovers he is the girl's real father. What will he do? His situation is complicated when he learns Jurgen is dying of cancer. The premise for Jacob is to stay in Denmark or to return to India. The first option represents responsibility and the second idealism.

The character population in *After the Wedding* flesh out the stay or go options. In Denmark, Jacob's daughter, his former girlfriend, and Jurgen are important, as is his daughter's husband. In India, the primary character is Pramod, a young boy who Jacob has raised from infancy.

Although the daughter's husband Christian misbehaves, there is no real antagonist here. Jacob's struggle is an internal struggle. In this sense, he is his own antagonist. Because there is very little plot, the character population is much smaller than in the thriller.

Lucas Moodysson's *Together* (2000) is a situation comedy set in a commune in 1975 Stockholm. Goran, the de facto leader of the commune, has a sex-obsessed girlfriend whose quest for orgasm trumps her relationship with Goran. He believes in open relationships in principle. He is after all an openminded male. The narrative opens when his conventional sister, Elisabeth, and her two children leave her physically abusive alcoholic husband Rolf. Can Elisabeth change for the better by living in the commune? Can the commune survive its internal stresses and contradictions? This is the narrative as well as the source of the comedy in *Together*.

The character population of *Together* divides among the membership of the collective and those outside it. Inside the collective, the characters are deeply unhappy. Goran's girlfriend Lena is always betraying him. Lasse's ex-wife Anna lives in the collective now as a lesbian. He has not recovered from the breakup. Klas, a gay man, longs for Lasse. Eric, a banker's son, angrily embraces doctrinaire Marxism. None of these characters are happy hippies.

Among the conventional characters, Elisabeth and Rolf and their two children struggle with the consequences of alcoholism in their family. Both sets of characters are struggling with the everyday problems of life essentially relational breakdown and human experiments in different belief systems to help them cope with those problems.

Moodysson uses a larger than average character population to drive home his belief that unhappiness is more often than not the human condition. There is no plot here, and there are no real antagonists. In this sense, the title of the film is ironic. In the film, we at last see the enemy and discover that the enemy is us. Here the large character population fleshes out Moodysson's premise in a mixture of funny and sad. In this particular genre, the character population flesh out the premise and realistically struggle with each other and themselves.

The degree of character change in the screen story also varies with genre. More specifically, if we look at Okwe's change in *Dirty Pretty Things* and Alexandre's change in *Tell No One*, both thrillers, we notice that by the resolution both have survived and are happy. But on a deeper level, both are the same people they were when we met them at the critical moment. This is typical of character change in the thriller.

In the case of Elisabeth and Goran in *Together*, a situation comedy, and of Jacob in *After the Wedding*, the character change that takes place is altogether deeper. The values of the character and their belief systems have faced a challenge, and in each case, those beliefs are either confirmed or modified. Notable is that in each case, the character has changed. Whether something has been lost or gained, the depth of challenge and change for Elisabeth, Goran, and Jacob is significant and deep. It's also emotionally wrenching. This too is more typical of character change in the melodrama and in the situation comedy. And we speak here only of character change among three realist genres. Character change is far greater in genres of wish fulfillment and of the nightmare. Because those genres are more extreme in narrative as well as character, they require a degree of belief suspension that simply doesn't operate in realistic genres. The point here is that genre choice dictates all the characteristics of the character arc mentioned here, and they differ from genre to genre. Deciding on the genre of a screenplay consequently is one of the more important decisions the writer will make.

The Dramatic Arc

The romantic comedy is dominated by progress of a particular relationship. Boy meets girl, or boy meets boy, or girl meets girl. After these two very opposite natures meet, we follow the course of the relationship. The resolution accentuates that relationship's success. The dramatic arc of the romantic comedy is the course of the relationship.

Every genre has a distinct dramatic arc that differentiates one genre from another. The dramatic arc in the sports film is the career of the main character. The dramatic arc of the gangster film is also a record of the career of the gangster, but it has a rise and fall shape ending in the destruction of the gangster, whereas the sports film focuses primarily on the rise.

The dramatic arc of the police story follows a crime-investigation-apprehension shape. The dramatic arc of film noir follows the progress of a relationship, but it's far from the romantic comedy. It's a bad relationship that will lead to the destruction of the main character. A subplot is the crime that proves the main character's love; it's the nail in the main character's coffin. The dramatic arc of the thriller is a chase that tends to work out well for the main character. The dramatic arc of the horror film is a chase as well, but its outcome is not a good one for the main character.

The dramatic arc of the melodrama and the situation comedy are shaped by a particular sort of power struggle. In both, the main character is a powerless person seeking power from the power structure. The main character may be a young person in an adult world, a woman in a man's world, a minority character in a majority world, a gay person in a heterosexual world. The positioning of the main character and the goal of empowerment characterize the dramatic arc of the melodrama and the situation comedy. In the situation comedy, the main character tends to succeed in their goal; the result is more mixed in the melodrama.

The dramatic arc expands in its ambition in genres of wish fulfillment. It's nothing less than good and evil in the action-adventure with good embodied in the main character and his or her cohorts and evil embodied in the antagonist and his or her cohorts. The struggle takes on a moral character in the Western and a more particular struggle between humanity and technology in the science fiction film. In all cases, there is an epic quality to the nature of the struggle in the dramatic arc. Clearly all these stories of wish fulfillment are intended to make their audiences feel better just as genres of the nightmare in their particular dramatic arcs are intended to unsettle their audiences. Here, the key is that the dramatic arc of each genre will differ from that of other genres.

What else needs to be said is that writers will often layer in a melodrama dramatic arc to emotionalize the screen story and to reach out more deeply to its audience. To be more specific, the main character in *Lawrence of Arabia*, T.E. Lawrence, is a bastard son of a lord in the class-driven upper ranks of the British army. He feels himself to be an outsider. The power he acquires is as the leader—mastermind of the Arab revolt during World War I. That war in the deserts of the Middle East is the plot of *Lawrence of Arabia*.

Similarly Clarice is positioned as a powerless character in *Silence of the Lambs*. She acquires power in this police story by killing Buffalo Bill. Lisbeth Salander is a powerless marginal person in the thriller, *Girl with the Dragon Tattoo*. She acquires power by revenging herself against men who have abused her and by helping Mikael Blomkvist in the plot to find other abusers/killers of women in the Vanger family. In each of these films whether a war epic, a police story, or a thriller, the dramatic arc has been elevated by the addition of a melodrama frame for the main character. Think of it as the deployment of two dramatic arcs in a single screen story. In each case, the melodrama layer has deepened the impact of these films on their audiences.

This same principle is what is operating in the great television successes of the past decade. From *The Sopranos* to *Breaking Bad* to *Downton Abbey* to *Deadwood*, the use of deeper melodrama dramatic arcs for a number of the characters have complemented the gangster film arc in *The Sopranos*, the heist film arc in *Breaking Bad*, and the morality tale arc in *Deadwood*, making these films deeper experiences in the gangster film, the heist film and the Western, respectively.

But each of them begins in a genre. Writers can take the narratives deeper or remain within the classic genre frame. The richness of each however begins with an appreciation and application of a specific genre. That's the why of it.

9

Working with Genre I

One of the most observable characteristics of American film is the continuing strength of genres or story forms. Genre is more than formula. More often, it is a type of story that has a visceral appeal to its audience. The scriptwriter who ignores the strength of that appeal does so at considerable cost. The Western, the gangster film, and the musical are forms synonymous with Hollywood. Film noir and the horror film, although originating in Europe, have proved to be enduring in North America. The popularity of genres means that most scriptwriters, during the course of their careers, will have to work with genre. Consequently, the screenwriter should understand genres and how to work with them. They are, in effect, a shorthand to structured types of stories. By knowing this shortcut, the scriptwriter is free to explore aspects of the genre that have more personal relevance.

Genre and the Audience

Film sociologists have long probed the relationship between movies and the audience, but the most insightful views of genres and their relationship to the audience have come from a less scientific perspective. Writers such as Susan Sontag, Paul Schrader, and Robert Warshow have examined particular genres and found complex relationships between the fears and aspirations of audiences and the genres that speak to these feelings. Warshow,[1] for example, examines the hero in the gangster and Western genres and suggests that the gangster is the same as most other citizens. He is a new arrival, an immigrant who wants to succeed in this society. He differs from most of us in the means by which he chooses to succeed—criminality. Warshow suggests that all of us want to succeed, but in the modern milieu of the city, many fail. The gangster's failure leads to the ultimate failure, his death, and therein lies the tragedy.

The more optimistic view of the hero is present in the Western genre. The hero in the Western genre functions on a plane of morality unavailable to the gangster in modern life. In the idealized world of the Western, simpler resolutions to conflict and to ethical aspirations afford an audience the kind of wish fulfillment that is associated with a simpler, pastoral time. Warshow is careful to underline that neither genre is about history. Facts are not as important as are dreams in genres, thus serving as dreamscapes for their audiences.

Dreams and nightmares are the emotional baselines for storytelling in the genre approach. The world of the nightmare is central to the horror film and to film noir. A world where dreams come true is central to the Western, the adventure film, and the musical; and, of course, more recognizable people, situations, and behavior are the bases of the more realistic genres—the documentary, the melodrama, and the situation comedy.

The writer, however, should be aware that just as audiences change over time, so, too, do genres, in order to tell classic stories in a new guise. One could not make a classic Western without taking in the events that have affected audiences' views about Western heroes, villains, Indians, the land, and civilizing forces. With the nuclear age, space has become our new frontier, thus making the Western set the old frontier. In the past 25 years, we have seen at least four Westerns set in space—*Outland*, *Star Wars*, *Aliens*, and *Planet of the Apes* (remake). All these films have many characteristics of the classic Western, thus showing how genres change and adapt to circumstances of the time.

Genres

It is not our intention to tell the history of genres in this chapter, but some sense of both the classic genre and its contemporary equivalent is valuable to the development of genre shorthand. We deal with the following genres in detail:

- The Western
- The gangster film
- The film noir
- The screwball comedy
- The melodrama
- The situation comedy
- The horror film
- The science fiction film
- The war film
- The adventure film
- The epic film
- The sports film
- The biographical film
- The satire film

In terms of understanding genres and using dramatic components in writing genres, it's best to consider particular common features of genres. These features are:

1. The nature of the protagonist
2. The nature of the antagonist
3. The shape of the dramatic action

4. The catalytic event
5. The resolution
6. The narrative style
7. The narrative shape
8. The tone

Each genre has its own distinct characteristics, and those characteristics will differ from one genre to another. For example, the protagonist or main character in the horror film tends to be a victim, whereas the main character in the Western is a hero. By highlighting some of the differences among genres, our goal is to show how the writer can best use these features in writing genre stories and then in working against the genre expectation to make a story seem fresh.

The Nature of the Protagonist

The main character and the character's goal are the primary focus of the story in any genre. Although the main character in the Western is heroic and tends to be romanticized and the main character in the horror film is a victim, the main characters in war films tend to be far more realistic. In the musical, main characters tend to be presented energetically, whereas in film noir, they are typically constricted and desperate. The qualities of the main character within a particular genre tend to be consistent, which makes the shorthand dimensions of that character readily available to the writer.

The Nature of the Antagonist

The importance of the antagonist is constant across genres, but the nature of the antagonist depends on the level of realism associated with particular genres. Where the presentation of the main character exclusive of realism is heroic—the adventure film or the Western—the antagonist becomes more evil, more powerful, and sometimes more than human. Where the genre is nightmarish, as in the horror film and film noir, the antagonist is equally extreme.

Only in the realistic genres, such as the war film, the melodrama, and the gangster film, does the antagonist take on more human rather than superhuman qualities. In these genres, the goal of the main character is more understandable and more realistic; consequently, the antagonist, although still important, takes on a more human dimension.

The Shape of the Dramatic Action

Gangster stories tend to be shaped around the rise and fall of a gangster. Police stories are shaped around the perpetration of a crime, its investigation, and its successful resolution, which is the apprehension of the perpetrator. All genre films have a very particular dramatic shape. And all begin with the expected opening: A soldier is inducted into the army to fight in a foreign war; a cowboy dreams of acquiring land and a cattle herd; a poor boy from the Midwest wants to improve his life in the industrial Northeast.

In the course of the dramatic action, we will find out whether the soldier survives, what personal sacrifice is necessary for the cowboy to improve himself, and what transgressions are necessary for the young Midwesterner to get ahead. In each case, the fate of the character will differ in accordance with genre expectations. And in each case, the characters' attempts to fulfill their goals will dictate the shape of the dramatic action.

Catalytic Event

Stolen cattle, a friend's death, the end of the Civil War, an Indian raid—all are the catalytic events in different Westerns. Each propels the main character to find and resolve the consequences of the flow of action resulting from the catalytic event. Every genre has its own kind of catalytic event. A crime is the catalytic event of the police story. In a horror film, a young family moves into a reputedly haunted New England home. The critical catalytic event should occur quickly or the dramatic vitality of the genre is dissipated. The audience expects a quick start.

The Resolution

Dramatic action leads us, of course, to the resolution. But not every genre leads us to the same kind of resolution. Although the fate of our Midwesterner in the melodrama tends toward the tragic, this is not the case in the classic Western or in the war film. In the Western, although the main character pays a price for his ambition, he does tend to succeed and become a hero in the effort. That effort requires a ritualized demonstration of heroism—the climactic gunfight. In the war film, although there is a climactic battle, the character's fate is determined not by his individual actions but by the superior forces of the protagonist's side; the resolution may come though superior air power or through a simple, arbitrary act that allows the character to survive the battle. Whatever the reason, resolution does not come from the individual action of the main character; consequently, the sense of the main character as a hero is less apparent than in the Western, where individual action is central to the resolution.

Narrative Style

Every genre has a particular narrative style that the audience expects and enjoys. Westerns, for example, tend to be punctuated by gun fights, deployment of weaponry, expertise in horsemanship, and survival skills in what is essentially a rural, primitive wilderness. Violence and violent resolution to conflict characterize the genre. This is not the case in melodrama, where relationships, their evolution, and their outcome are central; although there may be a tragic outcome in melodrama, the violence is emotional rather than physical.

Narrative Shape

Different genres exhibit different shapes. Although Westerns such as *High Noon* take place in a single day, this is not at all typical of the Western. In fact, many Westerns have an expansive time frame—years in the case of *Red River* and *The Searchers*. This is unusual, however, in film noir, where the character is running out of time; this is his last chance. Consequently, film noir stories tend to have a far more intense narrative shape. The time frame collapses, as does the accelerated presentation of a desperate relationship for the main character. Time is critical in the adventure film and in the thriller; it is far less important in the situation comedy and the war film. Consequently, the narrative shape in each of these genres differs considerably.

The primary consideration here is the level of intensity the genre requires to be in tune with the goals of the main character. In film noir, the main character is desperate, trying to survive his tragic fate. In the adventure film, the level of threat to the main character has to be constant, so that the audience stays interested in the plot. In the Western and the situation comedy, the relationship with the main character is relatively more relaxed; thus, the narrative shape is also more relaxed.

Tone

Although tone will be discussed in detail in a later chapter, it is important to consider it here as an element of genre. Tone can range from the fantastic in the adventure film and the musical to the realistic in the war film and the melodrama. Tone also ranges from the ironic in the screwball comedy and the satire to the engrossing in the thriller and the horror film.

As with all the elements mentioned in this section, the clarity of these elements offers the writer clear opportunities to alter or challenge these conventions in order to make the story seem different or fresh. However, for the purposes of this chapter, we assume constancy within genres. We turn now to the genres themselves.

The Western

The Western genre has an elaborate, rich history. The central themes of the Western play themselves out in the classic Western, which was the predominant form until 1950. The central motifs of the classic Western are as follows:

- The hero, a man alone, functions with a worldview that is both moral and decent.
- The hero has a distinct skill with guns and horses.
- The antagonist has mercantile goals—the accumulation of money, land, and cattle—and will recognize no person or ethic that stands in his way.
- The land plays a pastoral, but critical, role. It not only represents freedom, but also primitivism.
- Civilization is represented by those forces that represent an organizing influence on life—the town, the army, married life, and children.
- The struggle between the forces of primitivism (such as the land and the Indians) and those of civilization (such as the army and the town) forms a particular dilemma for the Western hero. In which world will he reside? His heart sides with the forces of primitivism, but his head sides with the forces of civilization. This is the classic conflict for the Western hero.
- The drama plays itself out in a ritualized form—gunfights and cattle drives—and individual conflicts are acted out rather than negotiated.

Having characterized the classic Western, we should also recognize how the Western has changed since 1950. Revisions to the classic Western have been attempted, as their primary goal, to make the Western less innocent. The hero is systematically demystified: in *The Gunfighter*, Gregory Peck, the hero, is a victim of his reputation; in *Winchester '73*, James Stewart portrays a neurotic hero; and in *The Wild Bunch*, William Holden's hero is a killer without a hint of the tenderness of the classic hero. Other Westerns have focused on the issue of civilizing forces. Armies have been presented as more primitive than the primitives (i.e., the Indians)—as in *Apache, The Outlaw Josey Wales*—and towns have been hell rather than heaven—as in *High Plains Drifter*. The nature of the central character's struggle has become much more jaded and much less idealistic. Indeed, both *The Culpepper Cattle Company* and *Heaven's Gate* are about the loss of idealism.

More recently, there has been a resurgence in the Western, and here, too, we see subtle and not-so-subtle shifts in the genre. The idealism of the classic Western is again challenged in *Wyatt Earp*. The myth of Wyatt Earp is as much a target of the writers as are the historical events or the dramatic opportunities provided by the gunfight at the OK Corral. *Tombstone*, released the same year (1994), conforms more closely to the typical Western, but again the struggle is less primitivism against civilization than it is about opposing material goals. This theme of the materialism of the main character is particularly notable in *Unforgiven*. In this film, the hero is less a hero and more a man of the 1980s than of the 1880s.

So, the Western has changed, but the dreamscape—a frontier where the struggle between primitivism and civilization unfolds—has not. Western film stories have just moved to another frontier.

The Gangster Film

The classic gangster film, like the Western, concerns itself with a very particular story—the rise and fall of a man who has no patience to progress through the ranks. The gangster is a man in a hurry; his time is running out. The motifs of the classic gangster film are as follows:

- The hero is an immigrant who is low in status but desires higher status.
- The city is the home of the gangster; it establishes his struggle to move up the social order.
- Power comes from the willingness to take power. This means courage, cunning, and a willingness to murder those who object to sharing power. This is the law of the jungle.
- The hero is loyal to his immigrant roots.
- The antagonist is the society that cannot tolerate the law of the jungle. The representatives of the society are the police and the FBI. They are the front line of combat against the law of the jungle.
- The symbols of success are material—such as guns and cars—and women.
- Getting ahead is everything, and the ends justify the means.

The classic gangster film is an ongoing dimension of American film; *The Godfather* and *The Untouchables* are popular examples. However, the genre has been too important a representation of modern life to contain itself solely to the character of the gangster. The gangster has been joined by other central characters—the cop (*Dirty Harry*), the detective (*The Big Sleep*), and, on the international level, the spy (*The Spy Who Came In From the Cold*). All these characters seek to find a way of succeeding in their particular jungles. As with the gangster, the struggle for position in the existing social order involves pushing out the other spy or killer who challenges the existing order. In all cases, the struggle is to the death. Their worlds will be subverted under any other outcome.

Recently, gangster films have added an existential dimension to the struggle. It is as if hope has dimmed and a kind of nihilistic death wish pervades the gangster and his fate. Whether focused on the individual (*The King of New York*) or a gang (*Reservoir Dogs*), betrayal has become the focus for the fate of the gangster. This dramatic shift crosses ethnic barriers, and we see the gangster's fate more tragically magnified in the Puerto Rican ghetto (*Carlito's Way*), in the Black ghetto (*Clockers*), and in the Irish ghetto (*State of Grace*). Whether it is the encroaching effectiveness of the law or the feeling that there is overpopulation in the urban jungle and Malthus's law of population control has come into effect, these stories portray a less hopeful, more desperate gangster hero—a hero who is less heroic and more violent. His struggle is the last act of a condemned man.

As to the settings, Harry Callahan lives in San Francisco, Phillip Marlowe works in Los Angeles, Elliot Ness lives in Chicago, and Don Corleone lives and works in New York City. These are the distinct battlegrounds of the gangster drama. The identifiable locale gives a particular credibility to the gangster film, but make no mistake, the subject matter of the gangster film is not a documentary on urban life; rather, like the Western, it is a dreamscape and nightmare of urban life. Gangster films are psychodramas, the equivalent of modernized tales of gladiators and Christians. For all these characters in this genre, there is nothing less at stake than their lives.

Because these stories are primal and male, there is little scope in this genre for male–female relationships. The genre does have memorable women— Bonnie in *Bonnie and Clyde*, Cagney's mother in *White Heat*, and Gloria Grahame in *The Big Heat*—but in each case, the role of the woman is catalytic to the action of the gangster. In no case is the woman a stand-alone character functioning in an interesting way in her own world. Whether they be sibling, mother, virgin, or whore, women play supporting roles in gangster films.

A final word: If fictional prose foreshadows genre activity in film, in the near future we will soon see detectives who are Indians working on reservations (Tony Hillerman) and Eskimos working in the Arctic (Scott Young). We will see rural cops (Ted Wood) and more international manifestations of the gangster genre (David Thompson). All these authors have portrayed detectives in different or unusual settings that have struck a chord with the public. Hollywood producers have taken note, particularly in telling stories of international gangsters (e.g., *Red Heat, The Russia House*).

The classic gangster film's search for success is taking on an international dimension, and the world is beginning to look like an oversized jungle in which the stakes of human drama grow increasingly dangerous. The gangster genre has never had more material with which to work.

The Film Noir

Beginning in the pessimistic 1920s in Germany, film noir as a genre appealed to the darker fears of an increasingly urbanized population. Film noir could be subtitled "the genre of betrayal"—personal betrayal, national betrayal, and international betrayal. The characteristics of film noir are as follows:

- The desperate central character lives on the edge; he merely exists. We can't call him the hero, as is the case in the gangster and Western genres, because the personal behavior of the central character in the film noir is anything but heroic.

- The central character thinks that his chance at a better, richer, more vital life can only be found in another character—usually a woman. This may be his last chance, and he certainly acts as if it is.
- The relationship between the central character and his savior is a highly charged, sexual relationship.
- The central character will be betrayed in this relationship.
- A by-product of the relationship is violence.
- The key root of the problem with the relationship is the city, the stand-in symbol for modern life. The city saps the generosity out of the relationship. All that is left is deception and betrayal.
- There are no children in film noir. Married couples have no children. Children represent hope, and there is no hope in any relationship or in the future.
- Sexuality and violence coexist and seem to be cause and effect.
- The sense of aloneness in the central character is palpable. It represents an existential state.

Film noir is a genre that symbolizes our nightmares. The classic of the genre is represented by Billy Wilder's *Double Indemnity*, a film of murder for the promise of love and the discovery that there is no love, only more murder. More recent representations of film noir are *Body Heat*, *Chinatown*, *Raging Bull*, *Basic Instinct*, and *Romeo is Bleeding*. For such a pessimistic genre of film, film noir seems to elicit many creative premises. As a genre that depicts the worst in human beings, it brings out the best in writers and directors—an interesting irony.

The Screwball Comedy

The screwball comedy is funny film noir that has a happy ending. The characteristics of this genre are quite similar to those of film noir:

- The central character is an isolated male.
- He looks desperately for a female to overcome his isolation or anxiety.
- The premise of the film is about the struggle in their relationship.
- During the course of the struggle, which is highly sexually charged, the maleness of the central character is challenged. The female is the dominant character in the relationship. This role reversal is central to the screwball comedy.
- Whereas the outcome of film noir is tragic, the outcome of the screwball comedy is happy.
- The urban setting of the genre is as much a jungle in screwball comedy as it is in film noir.
- There are no children but only troubled married couples in the screwball comedy.
- The aggression in this genre is the source of the humor, in contrast to the violence it evokes in film noir.

The screwball comedy is a genre that requires more risk and more aggression than is seen in the situation comedy. Consequently, few screwball comedies are made. *Shampoo* and *Something Wild* are modern examples of this genre, but few writers are developing scripts akin to the 1930s-era *Bringing Up Baby* and *Monkey Business*. Screwball comedies make most male writers very nervous, because the genre threatens masculinity and dominance or desired dominance in relationships. The genre is, however, very lively and energetic.

Both *Tootsie* and *Mrs. Doubtfire* borrow the dynamic from screwball comedies, but neither follows through in the classic screwball comedy sense. Both work with the masculine–feminine side of their main characters, and *Tootsie* particularly characterizes the male side as the antagonist of the story. This New Age approach moves both films into the safer realm of the situation comedy and away from the dangerous shoals of the screwball comedy.

The Melodrama

The melodrama is frequently associated with soap operas. This generalization is unfair, because, as a genre, melodrama is closest to the people, issues, and events of our times. This is not to say that the melodrama is a dramatized documentary of our own lives. Perhaps it is safer to suggest that the melodrama is the dramatized lives of our neighbors. The characteristics of the genre are as follows:

- The central character is more often female than is typical in many other genres. However, the central character can be male.
- The presence of a distinct social order is a barrier to the central character and indicates the power structure in the city, region, town, or country.
- The central character transgresses the power structure. This is usually attempted through a relationship with someone from within the power structure.
- Beauty and intelligence are not equivalent to the traditional symbols of power—money and social or political connections.
- The central character's behavior while transgressing the power structure is as much a threat to her own family as it is to the powerful family of which she would become a part if the new relationship is a success. The central character is unsupported in her goal.
- The conviction of the central character is fueled by the belief that life must be and can be improved. The status quo (such as the original family or unsuccessful marriage) is an insult to her sense of self.
- The vitality of the melodrama is, in part, supported by its modernity. Period melodramas are less successful, because they are too distant from the audience. More successful melodramas reflect the people, lives, and issues of the contemporary audience.
- Idealism, cynicism, sexuality, and aggression reflect the attitudes of the characters and, more important, support the central characteristic

of the melodrama—a story of power and powerlessness set against an inflexible social and political structure.

Perhaps the most important power struggle of the 1980s was the battle of the sexes. The sexual revolution and the rise of feminism, together with rapid economic change, fueled a redefinition of the male–female relationship. Attitudes toward career, childrearing, and marriage were all in flux. Yet, the male–female relationship, as it has been for centuries, is a central dimension of our existence. It is no surprise that *thirtysomething* was one of the most successful television shows of the decade. Some of the most memorable films of the period—*Kramer vs. Kramer, Independence Day, My Beautiful Laundrette, Breaking Away*—are melodramas. Societal change has unleashed a torrent of films about power relationships at all ages and stages. *Fast Times at Ridgemont High, Crossing Delancey*, and *Beaches* have much in common. They are all melodramas, and each film has a woman as its central character; the only difference is the women's age.

Melodrama can also be examined as a reflection of the political power structure in a society. Within this framework, the male–female dynamic is just one axis of a larger political construct. Another axis is the politics of the family. Here the struggles of fathers and sons are reflected in films such as *East of Eden* and *A River Runs Through It*. The rebellious son was made an archetype of the era in *Rebel Without a Cause*. The daughter who dared to be different was the focus of *Peyton Place*.

The framework of politics itself is the theme of Rossen's famous *All the King's Men* and the not-so-famous but equally interesting John Sayles's take on urban politics, *City of Hope*. Add race and we have Euzhan Palcy and Colin Welland's *A Dry White Season*. In this complex melodrama, it is the liberal white man, portrayed by Donald Sutherland, who challenges the laws of his native South Africa to defend the dignity of his black gardener. His challenge and his punishment, death is the classic consequence for the main character in melodrama.

This fate, death, in *Lorenzo's Oil*, is challenged by Susan Sarandon and Nick Nolte, parents who are told their son has an incurable disease and will die. These parents do not accept the conventional wisdom of the medical power structure. They spend time, money, and energy to find a cure for their son's illness. And they do. This melodrama about the politics of health and medicine is a victory for the parents, but the experience of the screen story highlights the power of the melodrama to realistically take us to the darkness and tragedy that is part of life.

The Situation Comedy

The situation comedy is very similar to the melodrama, although the outcome differs. Often, the outcome in a melodrama is tragic or at least has a dimension of tragedy. The mother leaving the family at the end of *Ordinary People* is a good example of a tragic melodrama. In situation comedy, the tragic potential dissipates, and a more satisfying outcome results. A good example of the situation comedy is depicted at the end of the film in *Ruthless People* when Bette Midler's character kicks her husband, played by Danny DeVito, into the ocean. Of course, humor is the result of all the character conflict in the situation comedy. The characteristics of this genre are as follows:

- The central character is more often male than female. Examples of male central characters in situation comedies are Dudley Moore in *10* and *Arthur*, John Ritter in *Skin Deep*, Michael Caine in *Blame It On Rio*, Bill Murray in *Groundhog Day*, and Ben Stiller in *There's Something About Mary*.
- The setting is contemporary.
- The central character transgresses not the power structure but the values of the power structure.
- Money and social connections are not enough; the central character needs to recapture values he feels are lost (such as idealism and vitality).
- As in the melodrama, the central character's transgressions isolate him from everyone—friend and foe.
- The situation comedy readily embraces current issues, uses them to the disadvantage of the central character, and promotes a search for new values. *An Unmarried Woman* and *Moscow on the Hudson* are examples of quality situation comedies.

Just as *The Apartment* was the situation comedy that heralded the end of the 1950s, so, too, do the filmic meditations of Woody Allen on urban life in *Crimes and Misdemeanors*, which reflects the end of the affluent 1980s. *Forrest Gump* was the quintessential situation comedy of the 1990s. Acknowledging the limits and the cruelty of the surrounding society, this mentally limited character has the emotional capacity to transcend that society. As he did in *Big*, Tom Hanks captures a sensibility at odds with everyone around him, and by doing so teaches them a valuable life lesson. But just as the comedies reflect their time, they also reflect enduring qualities. The characters that surround the main character in *The Apartment* are as self-absorbed and self-serving as are the characters that populate situation comedies such as *Groundhog Day*, *Dave*, and *Bullets Over Broadway*, made 30 years later.

To be more specific, the dissonance between character and society is also the theme of two recent important situation comedies, *Dave* and *Groundhog Day*. *Dave* focuses on the presidency, whereas *Groundhog Day* focuses on the media. In each, the transcendence of the individual characters over their deficiencies affirms a hopefulness in a bleak time. These films differ from the populist comedies of Frank Capra, which fused the transcendence of the individual to the potential for good in American society. These 1990s comedies are less optimistic about society as a whole; their focus is on the individual as his own salvation. The society itself is portrayed as the source of the problem, whereas for Capra it was the true source of strength for the individual.

Another important theme in the situation comedies of the 1990s is the dysfunctional family. *Mrs. Doubtfire* focuses on a dysfunctional husband. *Home Alone* focuses on one of the children accidentally left at home by the hurried parents. *It Could Happen to You* depicts an unhappily married couple who wins the lottery. The dysfunctional family and dissonant characters are important sources for the situation comedies of the 1990s.

The Horror Film

The horror film, originating from the nineteenth-century literature of Stevenson, Poe, and Shelley, is principally a reaction (as was the literature) to the veneer of civilization that comes with the material successes of modern life. Monsters, unbridled aggression, and sexuality—the inhabitants of our nightmare world—have a continuing popularity, particularly with young people. The world of our unconscious is the central source of material for the horror film. The characteristics of the genre are as follows:

- The central character is a victim, rather than a hero.
- The antagonist is often manifested from a technological aberration (such as Frankenstein's monster) or a social aberration (such as Freddy Krueger).
- Unbridled aggression and sexuality play an important role. Cruelty knows no relative form; this is a genre of absolutes.
- Technology, science, and scientific activity often unleash the antagonist. Fears about the future are as important as are our fears about the past.
- Religion is viewed as an intermediary that can influence the outcome of events. The central conflict is often portrayed as a struggle between God and Satan (such as in The Exorcist, Rosemary's Baby, and The Seventh Sign).
- Children have special powers in this genre. Children exhibit vision, insight, and tolerance; adults exhibit the opposite traits.
- Relationships can't save the central character. Very often, the victimizer is a member of the family.
- The location (such as the house, village, and archaeological find) has a special significance that influences the outcome of events for the central character.
- The supernatural has a significant role in the horror film genre; most events can't be explained rationally. As the genre dwells on the irrational, some form of understanding devolves from a supernatural explanation.
- In the 1990s, the horror film returned to a key dimension of the horror novel: the humanity of the monster. James V. Hart's screenplay of Bram Stoker's Dracula focuses on the historical evolution of Count

Dracula and poignantly suggests that immortal love has created Dracula and that compassion rather than cruelty will do him in. Similarly, Amanda Silver focuses on the creation of a nanny as the monster in The Hand That Rocks the Cradle. These films depict more empathy for and understanding of the monster than do the horror films of the 1970s and 1980s.

The Science Fiction Film

The science fiction film is to society what the horror film is to the person—a tale of catastrophe, a story of our worst nightmares. In the science fiction story, an ecological catastrophe (*The Naked Jungle*), a technological accident (*2001: A Space Odyssey*), or the unwelcome meeting of two worlds (*The Day the Earth Stood Still*) all serve to remind the audience that the inhabitants of Earth don't have enough respect for the environment, for science, or for each other; if this tendency persists, Earth will be destroyed or will destroy itself. In this context, the science fiction film is analogous to the biblical epic—both are morality plays celebrating past moral victories, while warning us to renew our moral fervor or there will be no future. The characteristics of the science fiction genre are as follows:

- The central character is an innocent bystander who is victimized by a technological accident or an unnatural phenomenon of another world.
- The central character may or may not overcome the challenge of the antagonist. The Invasion of the Body Snatchers is a good example of a science fiction film in which the main character begins and ends the story as a victim.
- The existence of relationships promises respite and perhaps an element of hope in light of the daunting scale of the struggle.
- The antagonist may be a scientist or the product of science or nature. The scale of the antagonist is so great (the ants in the Naked Jungle), that the central character is reminded not only of her mortality but also of how very human she is.
- The outcome in the science fiction film story is often more hopeful than are the outcomes in either the film noir or the horror film.
- There is a certain nobility that devolves to the central character based on her attempt to overcome her struggle with the supernatural (Aliens).
- The environment can be urban or rural, earthbound or otherworldly. In any case, the environment is a benign, but necessary, host for the antagonist. The presence of Earth and how the environment (Earth or space) is presented reminds us of our place in the natural order.
- The story line of the science fiction film is often plot intensive and presents a specific threat to the natural order. The plot outlines the central character's response to the threat.

The War Film

The war film genre is a national melodrama; these films are about transgression and power. How does the individual survive intact, physically and mentally? How are we, the audience, to feel about a particular war or about war in general? Many of the greatest films in the brief history of film have concerned themselves with war—*All Quiet on the Western Front, The Big Parade, La Grande Illusion, Kanal, They Were Expendable, Paths of Glory, Dr. Strangelove Or: How I Learned to Stop Worrying and Love the Bomb*—and those behind the lines who tried to cope with the war and its aftermath—*Open City, The Best Years of Our Lives, Forbidden Games, Who'll Stop the Rain?* Films such as *Europa Europa* and *Schindler's List* focus on the noncombatants as victims of war.

War, because it threatens all of us, is an important genre. The characteristics of the genre are as follows:

- The central character has one primary goal: survival. This may mean personal survival, national survival, or the survival of the personal or political values he believes in.
- The character's values are tested.
- The polarities of human behavior—altruism and barbarism—coexist and are as much in combat as are the combatants.
- Violence plays a central role in this genre.
- Relationships, male–male and male–female, take on particular importance.
- Each film carries a particular political perspective of war. Many films are critical of war; others suggest that war brings out the best and the worst in the characters.
- There is a primal quality and intensity to personal behavior.
- The antagonist is often never seen. Paths of Glory and Full Metal Jacket are good examples.

The point of view of the war genre ranges from romantic (*Sergeant York*) to cynical (*Too Late the Hero*). Whatever the perspective, the individual character is the focal point of the war genre. War isn't simply a test of character in these films; more often, it is a plea to reflect upon the issues of war. As Jean Renoir said about his great 1937 antiwar film *La Grande Illusion*, "two years later they fought again, but this time a bigger, more violent war."[2] It appears the genre will continue to appeal to audiences.

The Adventure Film

What the situation comedy is to melodrama, the adventure film is to the war film. James Bond and Indiana Jones are positive cartoon heroes who not only survive war but also seem to thrive on it. In their fantastic, aggressive adventures, there is a reassurance that men may start wars, but boys such as these can stave off the consequences. The characteristics of this genre are as follows:

- The central character, most often a male, rather than trying to survive, plays a messianic character whose role is to save either the nation or the world.
- The main character is thoroughly capable in terms of mastery of the tools and weapons of salvation, whether they be cerebral or physical.
- The main character exhibits a playfulness that can be childlike or childish.
- The challenges to the main character are considerable and numerous. This is a more plot-intensive genre as compared to most other genres.
- The antagonist is very often imbued with almost superhuman intelligence, strength, or other powers. Whether it be the joker or a shark, the more formidable the antagonist, the greater the success of the central character.
- Humor and self-depreciation are often characteristics of the genre.
- Relationships are superficial. There is no time for intimate relationships in this genre.
- Sexuality and violence, although present, are neither sensual nor visceral. Again, there is no time to dwell.
- Ritual and mythology are more important than are realism and complexity. Consequently, the genre readily embraces less realistic actions and modes; farce and technology coexist in this genre.
- Stereotypes abound in the adventure genre. Examples range from the mad scientist in Dr. No to the mindless thugs in Indiana Jones and the Temple of Doom. The racism implicit in the latter film and films such as First Blood are by-products of the stereotyping rampant in the adventure genre.

The adventure film has been a staple for the past decade or so. Indeed, many of the most successful films ever made were adventure films produced in the 1980s. The Indiana Jones series, the Superman series, the Rambo series, and the Batman series are the best examples. So successful has been the genre that characters from other genres (*Dirty Harry* and *Lethal Weapon*) have veered, at least in the sequels, toward adventure film and away from the genre of the original.

Adventure films have also been borrowing the dysfunctional family motif from the situation comedy, evidenced in *The Last Action Hero*, which borrows the alienated teenager from the melodrama. Although the mix does not work well in *The Last Action Hero*, the situation-comedy element in *True Lies* does offset the soft plot of this particular adventure.

The Epic Film

The epic film is very often presented as a serious adventure film. The struggle of the main character is heroic but realistic. The main character may be a historical figure whose exploits have been memorialized in print (T.E. Lawrence's *The Seven Pillars of Wisdom*) or in literature (Joseph Conrad's *Lord Jim*). The epic film may be biographical or historical, but its main appeal is the moral or ethical dilemma (the personal issue) tested against a larger panorama—war (*Patton*) or colonialism (*Gandhi*). Inevitably, the interweaving of personal and historical stories makes the epic film one to experience.

Writers who excel in this form are Robert Bolt (*Lawrence of Arabia, A Man for All Seasons*, and *The Bounty*) and Carl Foreman (*Bridge on the River Kwai* and *The Guns of Navarone*). Numerous contemporary writers are interested in this form. Robert Towne wrote *Greystoke: The Legend of Tarzan and Lord of the Apes*; Paul Schrader wrote *The Last Temptation of Christ*; and Bob Rafaelson wrote *Mountains of the Moon*. The characteristics of the genre are as follows:

- There is a charismatic central character.
- The antagonist is so powerful that the efforts of the central character elevate the central character to a heroic position.
- There is a historical crisis, such as World War I and the Arab Revolt in Lawrence of Arabia, and Henry VIII's desire to remarry, against Catholic canon, leading him to establish his own church, in A Man for All Seasons.
- The moral struggle by the protagonist is so overwhelming that success seems impossible. Colonial India and the struggle for nonviolent freedom by Mahatma Gandhi in Gandhi is an example.
- There is a depiction of the real world, rather than fantasy. Therefore, when violence is displayed, it is all the more shocking. Violence plays an important role in this genre, because it signals the central character's willingness to sacrifice his life for a just cause.
- There is often poetic subtext. In the midst of all the violence of the story, the central character is sufficiently moral that his stand seems romantic, old-fashioned, and poetic. Consequently, the central character in an epic film is often immensely appealing.
- There is a complex central character. Paul Muni as Émile Zola in The Life of Émile Zola and Paul Scofield as Thomas More in A Man For All Seasons are good examples of complex characters. This trait also contributes to the appeal of this character.
- There is a sense of mission in the central character that is rarely exhibited by central characters in other genres. While Harrison Ford is an ambivalent Indiana Jones, Jeremy Irons is anything but ambivalent in The Mission.
- The complex story line blends two stories—the personal story of the central character and the historical incident.
- The central character is tested. As a result of the test, he is challenged to pursue a course of action.
- The central character meets a tragic fate. In this sense, the epic film story is closer to the melodrama than to the adventure film.

The Sports Film

The sports film is a particular sort of adventure film. It can be real (*Champion*), cynical (*Raging Bull*), or fantastic (*Field of Dreams*). Unlike the adventure film, the focal point can be personal (*Bang the Drum Slowly*) rather than apocalyptic. This doesn't mean that the sports genre is less exciting. *Rocky* is as exciting an experience as the best of the adventure films and is more emotionally satisfying than some. The characteristics of the sports film are as follows:

- The central character is a gifted athlete.
- He tests himself within the parameters of a particular sport.
- Only sports that have a broad appeal to society make a good background for this genre. Boxing, football, and baseball have been the sports of choice. The best films have been boxing films in which the character has much at stake, physically and spiritually. No one has made a good film about a tennis player! Only Downhill Racer has succeeded aside from the three main sports (boxing, football, and baseball), although Heart Like a Wheel, Chariots of Fire, and The Hustler were successful.
- The apparent antagonist—the other team, the manager, or the owner—is not as important as is the interior struggle of the central character. He is his own worst enemy, as evidenced in The Hustler.
- Relationships, whether they be male–female or male–male, are crucial to the emotional well-being of the central character.
- A mentor (a father, a coach, or another professional) plays a key role.
- Family is an important component in this genre. Melodramas and gangster films are the only other genres in which family figures so prominently.
- The ritual—in this case, the big game or the big fight—plays a central role in the sports genre.

The Biographical Film

Biography, as in prose, is an important genre. What are our leaders, authority figures, great artists really like? We are fascinated with their greatness and talent. We want to know all about them. Underlying our fascination is our wish for immortality. In their own way, the subjects of biographical films (by their actions, achievements, or character) have achieved immortality. The characteristics of the biographical film are as follows:

- The central character has a particular talent and a nonconformist personality.
- The central character's talent develops in conflict with the conventions of society.
- The drive for actualization is singular.

- The antagonist is not physical; rather, it can be time (The Life of Louis Pasteur), ignorance (The Life of Émile Zola), or conventional thinking (Patton).
- The seminal event is acted out in a public manner.
- The psychological makeup of the central character allows her to overcome the tragedy of life and succeed. Although Van Gogh dies at the end of Lust For Life, his success is evident in his life's work.
- There is a sense of mission that is religious in its overtone. Patton is as zealous, in his way, as Gandhi.
- Personal relationships often fail, but this only adds to the spiritual side of the central character.
- The critical moment, whether it is a discovery or a religious or political conversion, is the most important point in the story, far more important than the public acknowledgement of the character's achievement.
- The tragic aspect of the character's life is also important in this genre. Whether it be Patton's dishonor, Gandhi's assassination, or Zola's death, the reminder of mortality acts as ballast to the mythical subtext of these stories.

The Satire

Satire is a special form of genre. It is not often found, but its strength is such that you should know about the genre. The characteristics of the genre are as follows:

- The central conflict relates to a crucial social or political issue of the day. The environment, health care, the power of television, and nuclear war are all examples of recent satires.
- The film has a distinct point of view about the issue.
- Humor mixes freely with aggression.
- The central character is a vehicle to promote an issue.
- Fantasy and unreality are acceptable in this free-form genre.
- The level of aggression mounts rapidly, escalating to absurd levels before the film ends.
- Relationships can only be transient, given the urgency of the posed social or political threat.
- Random irrationality reminds us of the horror film. The genre succeeds when we see ourselves as victims of the danger and threat of society.
- This is a vigorous, energetic genre and is not at all tied to realism, like the melodrama or the film noir. High energy is rampant in these films.

Satire experienced a resurgence in the 1990s. Two themes stand out: the film industry and urban life in the city of dreams, Los Angeles. Both *The Player* and *Mistress* focus on the loss of humanity in the film industry.

The main character in *The Player*, a studio executive, brutally kills a writer and not only gets away with murder but then advances in the corporate hierarchy of Hollywood. The characters in *Grand Canyon* and *Short Cuts* are ordinary people living in Los Angeles who also seem to have lost their way and, in *Short Cuts*, also their humanity. The result is the need to escape—to the Grand Canyon in *Grand Canyon*—or to have no means of escape, in *Short Cuts*. The nastiness of each of the characters in *Short Cuts* suggests that malice and murder are not the province of the studio executive or of the ghetto—they're everywhere. Whether Robert Altman is criticizing all modern urban life or strictly Los Angeles is unclear, but what seems certain is that his interpretation of Raymond Carver assures that Los Angeles, for so long the city of angels and dreams, is now the city of the nightmare, the modern equivalent of a Hieronymous Bosch painting.

Conclusion

Working with genre is probably the most topical and typical activity of today's screenwriters. Whatever story you choose to write, you're probably working with genre. Consequently, it is critical that you be familiar with the motifs of each genre. To involve the audience more rapidly in your story, use the expected signposts of the genre, which are a shorthand that audiences absorb from their earliest viewing.

References

1. R. Warshow, "The Gangster as Tragic Hero" and "Movie Chronicle: The Westerner," in *The Immediate Experience* (New York, NY: Doubleday, 1962), 83–106.
2. S. Kauffman, "The Elusive Corporal and Grand Illusion," in *A World on Film* (New York, NY: Delta, 1996).

10

Working with Genre II: The Melodrama and the Thriller

The melodrama and the thriller represent two extremes of genre. Although both are genres whose tone is realistic, they are opposites in terms of their structure. Simply put, the melodrama is a character-driven genre, while the thriller is a plot-driven genre. In this chapter, we will explore these two story forms not only to highlight these differences, but also to illustrate the way they incorporate narrative characteristics from each other that enhance the power of both.

The Classic Melodrama

In profiling the classic melodrama, it is useful to look at its dominant qualities. They are as follows:

- The presentation of the main character.
- The deployment of plot (how it is used in the melodrama). To put it another way, there is a genre bias for character layer over plot in the structure of the melodrama.
- The dramatic arc.
- The amplitude of the dramatic arc (which determines whether the melodrama will be a soap opera or a tragedy).
- The relationship of the dramatic arc to an issue of the day.
- Voice (which will determine whether we empathize with the main character or feel contempt toward the main character).

Although we will fully discuss these qualities of the melodrama, it is worth noting that the dramatic level of the melodrama will correlate to the sources of conflict deployed. For example, the goal of the main character is directly opposed by the antagonist. The antagonist is the principal harmer. The vigor with which the main character pursues his or her goal in spite of the antagonist will also raise the energy level in the narrative. Now we turn to the first quality, the main character in the melodrama.

The Main Character's Goal

The first notable quality of the melodrama, the main character, is that he or she is a powerless person in pursuit of power. The power resides in a prevailing power structure that wants to maintain the status quo, thereby excluding the main character. The profile of the powerless person might be a child in an adult world, a woman in a man's world, a senior citizen in a society obsessed with youth, a minority character in a majority world. This latter characterization might mean an immigrant, an African-American in a white majority, an Asian character in a white majority, or, conversely, a Caucasian character in an Asian majority. The matrix might also profile a homosexual character in a heterosexual society. Whatever the main character's age, status, class, or color, the key is that the character be a powerless person in a society where the power resides in a majority that differs, in age, status, class, and/or color, from the main character.

The second notable feature of the main character is that her goal is to acquire power. Beth in Lee Tamahori's *Once Were Warriors* wants a normal family life within the Maori culture of New Zealand; she must oppose a fractured, dysfunctional, destructive family in order to achieve her goal. In Steven Soderbergh's *King of the Hill*, 10-year-old Aaron wants to believe he can overcome the hardships the Depression has placed on his family. In Mike Nichol's *Wolf*, the middle-aged main character, Will Randall, is fired from his editorial position to make way for a younger, aggressive man. In Agnieska Holland's *Washington Square*, the young woman, Catherine, is rejected by her father and manipulated by a handsome suitor, Morris Townsend. Although her goal is to find love, men's motives, status, and privilege clash with her goal. In a man's world, the limits on a woman are profound. This paradigm is explored in the adaptations of Jane Austen's novels, as well as in contemporary narratives such as Joseph Mankiewicz's *All About Eve*, Deepa Mehta's *Fire*, and Kimberly Pearce's *Boys Don't Cry*.

Again, the main character's goal in the melodrama is to acquire power. Positioned as a powerless person, the main character can only assume power by challenging the prevailing social and political structures.

The Dominance of the Character Layer

Because melodrama so often concerns family issues of identity and life crises, the psychological or interior life of the main character prevails over issues of career, competition, and society. In this sense, the melodrama is far more concerned with the internal life of the main character than with that character's external life. This doesn't mean that melodramas are not set in schools, sports arenas, or corporate towers. What it does mean is that stories set in schools, like John Duigan's *Flirting* or Tony Bill's *My Bodyguard*, are stories of outsiders coping with that status in a school setting that cruelly excludes them. They are not so much stories of social adjustment as they are about the more psychological or interior issues of coming of age. Another alternative presents itself in Terrence Rattigan's *The Winslow Boy*. Here the story is about the loss of innocence. Rigid school roles are applied to a young boy. He is accused of a theft. Such conduct demands expulsion, an action that will blacklist the boy from society for life. Here the application of those rules tests the strength of the boy's family and implies that the school, one of the pillars of societal power, will crush the individual or the family that challenges that power. From the point of view of the family, the matter becomes one of honor. If the boy is acting honorably, he is innocent. The father then acts to uphold that honor even if the legal fees bankrupt him. How far is the father willing to go to support the family honor? This is the journey shared by both father and son in *The Winslow Boy*.

The measure of commitment, the psychological risk—these issues work themselves out in the character layer of the melodrama. In the character layer, the main character will explore two significant relationships that imply opposite options for the main character. The full exploration of those relationships will determine the status of the main character at the end of the narrative. In Michael Mann's *The Insider*, that means for both main characters, Jeff Wigand and Lowell Bergman, that exploration will mean professional integrity or personal self-interest (careerism and its material rewards). In Naomi Foner's *Running on Empty*, it means Danny, the main character, will have to choose between two options, remaining a key supporter of his family or leaving the family to fulfill his own ambitions (to study music). This set of options is complicated by a plot in which the FBI pursues Danny's parents for a political crime committed 15 years earlier. The character layer explores the two options by developing the relationship between Danny and his father, who represents the stay option, and Danny's relationship with a young woman whose father is the local high school music teacher. The young woman represents the freedom or self-interest option. The story evolves along a coming-of-age arc, with Danny choosing at the end to leave his family to study music at Juilliard.

A third example of the importance of character layer in the melodrama is Mike Van Diem's *Character*. Here the relationships that are explored are, on the one hand, Jacob's relationship with his parents—both of whom are cold, withholding, and in a sense emotionally abusive—and, on the other hand, Jacob's other relationships related to work—interestingly, one male, the other female. Both Dr. de Gaankelaar and Miss Te George offer what Jacob's parents cannot or will not offer—acceptance and emotional support.

What is important about the exploration of the character in each of these cases is that, based on the outcome, the character will or will not survive. The main character's very existence seems to depend upon the outcome. The reason is clear: issues of identity, personal growth, and emotional independence can make or break a character. They are real issues that are visceral for all of us. We recognize them and we easily relate to them. Because of this, character layers are critical to the melodrama's effectiveness.

The Dramatic Arc and Its Amplitude

The dramatic arc of the melodrama is the journey the main character will make in the course of the narrative. That journey can be interior or exterior. If it is the latter, the journey is enhanced if it relates to the moral education of the main character. If no moral lesson is learned, we are in essence left with a journey of behavior without reflection. We experience this kind of journey as a soap opera. If the journey is a self-reflective journey or, at the very least, insight is gained at its end, we have an emotionalized experience that moves beyond soap opera. If the dramatic arc is internal and visceral, with the very existence of the main character at stake, we experience the melodrama as a tragedy. The greater the amplitude of the dramatic arc, the more intense the experience of the melodrama.

Issues of career (*Boiler Room*, by Ben Younger) and significant relationships (*The Best Intentions*, by Bille August) can be presented along a very steep arc. Although these issues may be intense, they may not carry the impact of more interior narratives—stories of identity such as Kimberly Pearce's *Boy's Don't Cry*, or stories of personal morality such as Horton Foote's *To Kill a Mockingbird*, or stories of loss such as Lasse Hallstrom's *My Life as a Dog*, or stories of limited parental acceptance such as Robert Anderson's *I Never Sang for My Father*, or stories about aging such as Joseph Mankiewicz's *All About Eve*, or stories about life crises such as John Sayles's *Passion Fish*. These latter stories essentially address life crises and test the resolve of their characters. How the characters manage these crises is the dramatic arc of the narratives. In each case, the quality of the character's life is at stake.

Four examples of relationship stories illustrate the point. Pamela Gray's *A Walk on the Moon* tells the story of Pearl, a thirtysomething married woman in 1969. Pearl has two children and a hard-working husband, and she feels she has given up her dreams. That summer, sequestered from her husband by cottage life, Pearl falls into an affair with an itinerant, handsome young man. Will she give it all up, or will she face her life as it is—responsibilities, dour husband, etc.? These are the choices for Pearl. In the end, she opts to return to her husband. In *A Walk on the Moon*, the dramatic arc is gradual rather than steep.

In Diane Kurys's *Entre Nous*, the main character, a young Jewish woman, marries the man who rescues her from the Nazis. The time is 1943 and the place is southern France. After the war, the main character has two children. Increasingly unhappy—or rather unfulfilled—in her marriage, the main character turns to a fun-loving female friend. These two relationships, the husband and the friend, are the two choices for the main character. Choosing her friend, the main character leaves the marriage, with bittersweet consequences for her and her daughters. In *Entre Nous*, the dramatic arc is more elevated than that in *A Walk on the Moon*. Because of this, the main character's final choice makes for a more powerful emotional experience.

In Mogens Rukov and Thomas Vinterberg's *The Celebration*, a parent–child relationship, rather than a marriage, is explored. Christian, Helene, and Michael are the surviving adult children of Helge, a 60-year-old patriarch. Materially successful, Helge celebrates his sixtieth birthday with all of the members of his extended family. The day of the celebration and its immediate aftermath set the time frame for the narrative. The dramatic arc here, although presented in this brief time frame, is very steep. The question for Christian is whether he will accept the status quo (successful father, emotionally unsuccessful children) or whether he will challenge the myth of his father, the power of his father, and share the truth about his father—that his father raped him and his now-dead twin sister when they were children. If Christian succeeds, he and his siblings may be able to move on and be more emotionally complete adults (and consequently successful). Indeed, the challenge is effective, and, in the end, both of his siblings and even his socially graceful and superficial mother turn against Helge. In *The Celebration*, the dramatic arc is steep because, for a child, even if adult, challenging the father represents the ultimate power struggle; much can be gained but everything must be put at risk.

The fourth example is Emir Kusterica's *The Time of the Gypsies*. The main character, Perhan, is reared by his grandmother. He helps care for his crippled sister, and his unemployed uncle lives with the family as well. The relationships that are critical in the narrative are Perhan's relationship with women (his grandmother, his sister, and his fiancée) and his relationship with men (his uncle, his criminal patron). The issue is what kind of man Perhan will be—will he be deceitful, manipulative, and destructive like his uncle and his patron, or will he be responsible and nurturing like his grandmother? Unfortunately, Perhan opts to emulate the other gypsy men; consequently, in the end, he destroys himself. Although the dramatic arc follows the course of his relationships from young man to husband, from son to father, the dramatic arc actually becomes a life cycle, or, rather, a life circle. Perhan will come full circle as do the other gypsy men in the film; each destroys himself before his time.

Key to understanding the importance of the dramatic arc of the main character is the notion of journey for the main character. Will the journey be external, such as career advancement, or will it be internal, such as a coming of age or an adjustment to a life crisis? And will there be a measure of self-reflection in this journey? And finally, to what extent is the journey about personal values—morality—and to what extent is the journey an existential journey, concerning itself with the quality of the character's existence? The nature of the arc will determine the depth to which we experience the melodrama.

Issues of the Day

Issues of the day are typically a reflection of clashing social and political values. These clashes are magnified by the media, thereby capturing the public consciousness. Understandably, the media's subsequent obsession with these issues is particularly amenable to the melodrama. Issues such as the relations between men and women, the position of children in society, the newfound power of the youth culture, the mythical appeal of material culture, and the struggle for spiritual values each serve as fertile ground for the melodrama. Issues of the day change. Fifty years ago, women's rights were viewed as a radical issue, the melting pot overshadowed minorities, there was no youth culture, and old age was an esteemed status. The melodrama adapted accordingly.

Seventy years ago, a woman who wanted too much would experience a tragic fate. She would end her life loveless, abandoned even by her children. This is Stella's fate in Henry Wagstaff Gribble and Gertrude Purcell's *Stella Dallas*. For her hubris, for her spiritual independence, Stella loses everything that she values. She's a woman who wanted too much. Such is not the fate of ambitious women in Marlene Gorris's *Antonia's Line* or in Callie Khouri's *Thelma & Louise*, or, for that matter, in Emma Thompson's modern treatment of Jane Austen's *Sense and Sensibility*. In these films from the 1990s and in those of today, the fate of the ambitious woman is vastly different from what it was in the 1930s. This is reflected in the films of each period.

These changes in societal perspective are nicely illustrated in melodramas about postwar adjustment. Melodramas about the aftermath of World War II differ profoundly from melodramas set in the post-Vietnam war period. Robert Sherwood's *Best Years of Our Lives* and Nancy Dowd, Robert C. Jones, and Waldo Salt's *Coming Home* make the point. In both narratives, there are characters who manage to make the adjustment and there are characters who don't. But it is the public's attitude toward the war that infuses all characters. And in both cases, it is that attitude partnered with the issue of postwar adjustment that makes these films gripping but so very different from one another.

Turning to issues that capture our attention today, if we look at stories about relationships, the issue is whether an individual's rights are more important than the collective rights of the family. To put it another way, is a family a destructive trap, or is it a refuge? This is the subject matter of Alan Ball's *American Beauty*, Tod Solondz's *Happiness*, and Ethan and Joel Coen's *Fargo*. Although each of these narratives adds a layer of satire, each also has a layer of melodrama.

Another issue today is the contemporary obsession with the material world. This is the subject of Ben Younger's *Boiler Room* and of Neil LaBute's *In the Company of Men*. Corporate life and material wealth and their influences on relationships within families and within male–female relationships, as well as within male–male relationships, form the dramatic arcs of these narratives.

And, of course, the melodrama is an apt form to explore the contemporary obsession with celebrity. Paul Thomas Anderson's *Boogie Nights* focuses on a young man's career as a porn star. Michael Mann and Eric Roth's *The Insider* works with the subject of a "60 Minutes" episode. Jacques Audrard's *A Self-Made Hero* deals with a real-life character who recreated a more heroic army life for himself. And he succeeded!

The melodrama meshes easily with issues of the day. From a character point of view as well as from an identification point of view, the issues of the day intensify our interest in, and our relationship with, the main character. The consequence is a more intense experience of the melodrama.

Voice and the Melodrama

Voice in the melodrama tends, for the most part, to be realistic. Consequently, Joe Mankiewicz's *All About Eve*, a melodrama set in the theater world, conforms to the behavior and atmosphere we expect from that world. So, too, does the presentation of the Los Angeles porno scene in Anderson's *Boogie Nights*. There have, however, been challenges to this expectation of realism. The dark claustrophobia of Alan Ball's *American Beauty* creates irony in most of the narrative, an irony that distances us from the main character until the last act. Irony and distancing is in play in Tod Solondz's *Happiness*. The result is a stylized, almost MTV presentation of each member of a family, which prompts us to criticize the family rather than advocate the individual members.

A somewhat different experience is available in Paul Auster's *Smoke*, a melodrama about a group of people who come together in a Brooklyn smoke shop. Each character comes to realize that friendship is important; it can save lives and it can save relationships; it can resurrect abandoned families and it can yield a sense of belonging in the midst of excessive transience. Friendship crosses gender, racial, age, class, and status boundaries. This modest but critical dramatic arc is facilitated by a highly stylized voice that accelerates realism and heightens the reaction of each of the characters in the narrative. In every sense, *Smoke* is the opposite of *Happiness*; however, each is far from realism.

Finally, Erick Zonca's melodrama *The Dreamlife of Angels* is the story of two marginalized young women. As in the work of his Belgian contemporaries, Luc and Jean-Pierre Dardenne (*Rosetta*) and Frederic Fonteyne (*An Affair of Love*), Zonca uses a hyperrealism to involve us with these two marginalized young women, Isa and Marie. They are on a path to nowhere. We follow Isa in a relationship with a young girl in a coma. The relationship is impossible, and yet the young girl comes out of her coma. Isa, spiritually sound, also survives, and we suspect she will thrive. Marie, on the other hand, is an angry young woman who always makes poor choices. Self-destruction in relationships leads to personal self-destruction. In the end, she has broken with her only true friend, Isa, and invested herself in a relationship with a rich young man whose only desire is to amuse himself with Marie. He uses her sexually and predictably discards her. Abandoned, Marie commits suicide.

What is critical about the voice in Zonca's melodrama is that he deeply respects, indeed loves, these two characters. As a result, we move into a close relationship with them. We move so close to Isa and Marie that the experience of the narrative is both spiritual and emotional, to the point of almost being unbearable. The same can be said of *Rosetta* and of *An Affair of Love*. This new intimacy is the voice of Zonca and the Dardennes and of Fonteyne; it differs significantly from the genre expectation of melodrama.

To pull together all of these characteristics of the classic melodrama we now turn to the analysis of a single melodrama, Deepa Mehta's *Earth*.

■ ■ ■ A Case Study of Classic Melodrama: Deepa Mehta's *Earth*

Earth takes place in Lahore, India, in 1947. The British will soon leave India, and the film covers the Muslim–Hindi conflict that preceded partition into Pakistan and India. The main character is Lenny, an 8-year-old Parsi girl. Although hindered by polio, forced to use leg braces, she is a spirited, curious young girl. The principal secondary characters are Shanta, her beautiful Hindu nanny, her parents, privileged and trying to stay neutral, and Shanta's two suitors, both Muslim. The plot focuses on the political situation in Lahore, beginning with the British intention to leave, and ending with the Muslim slaughter of Hindus and Sikhs. The character layer is driven by the love triangle between the Muslim Ice Candy Man, the Muslim Hasan, and the Hindu Shanta. In Act Three, Ice Candy Man will be responsible for the death of his fellow Muslim Hasan after Shanta has committed to him. Ice Candy Man will also initiate the destruction of Shanta with the aid of Lenny.

Earth is a loss-of-innocence story focusing on Lenny. She begins hopeful, curious about the world. She particularly relies on a vicarious sexual relationship with Shanta. She is showered with attention by the men who admire Shanta. Because Shanta always looks after Lenny, Lenny enjoys the attention she is accorded by the two handsome suitors. Lenny is also privy to the conversations of all the young handsome friends, Sikh, Muslim, and Hindu. She hears of the politics but all she sees is attractive adults arguing with affection and happiness because they are together. Lenny also witnesses the marriage of a young, less privileged friend. For women in this culture, marriage is the obligation and the apogee of their lives. This reality, too, fans Lenny's curiosity. To this point, life is good; Lenny is budding sexually and continues to experience new things. But then the dark side of events and personal behavior begins. Ice Candy Man's relatives are massacred on a train.

Both Ice Candy Man and Lenny witness Hasan's sexual success with Shanta, who commits to marry Hasan, who will convert and become Hindu. But events accelerate. Hasan is killed, and a mob led by Ice Candy Man invades Lenny's home, whose parents have now hidden Shanta. But Ice Candy Man uses his charm and invites Lenny to tell him where Shanta is. Lenny does. Shanta is taken away by the mob, in all likelihood to be brutalized and killed. The narrative moves forward

40 years. Lenny is now an adult. She tells us that she never recovered from the loss—the personal loss and the loss of innocence—that day. The death of Shanta ended Lenny's childhood.

Lenny, as a child in an adult world, is the powerless main character. She has as her goal to make her way in the world and to understand that her curiosity will be rewarded with knowledge and security. She does gain knowledge, but her sense of security about the world is totally altered by her experience. What she learns about tolerance, specifically religious tolerance, is challenged by her relationships with Shanta and the Ice Candy Man. Ice Candy Man turns to hatred and violence when his personal desires are thwarted, and Lenny becomes an accomplice in the destruction of Shanta when her desire, albeit immature, for special attention from the Ice Candy Man leads her to tell him where Shanta is hiding. This act and the consequent destruction of Shanta alter Lenny's sense of security in the world. Anxiety and guilt supplant curiosity and openness. Lenny, as she tells us, is changed forever.

In terms of an issue of the day, religion and racial and tribal differences are an ongoing problem worldwide. At its heart, *Earth* is as much about tolerance of difference as it is about the Muslim–Hindu–Sikh schism that led to the partition of colonial India in 1947. Appropriately telling the story from a child's hopeful and optimistic point of view, Deepa Mehta mixes realism with romantic warmth. It's as if childhood is about seeing the world in this romantic hue. Because she doesn't show us the change but rather implies it, the romantic story dominates Lenny's narrative.

The Classic Thriller

If the dominant quality of the melodrama is essentially deter-mined by the inner life of the main character, the dominant quality of the thriller is the opposite—the existence of the main character out in the world. The focus on externalities doesn't make the thriller superficial or devoid of psychology—it simply means that the thriller will be primarily plot driven. Time will be important, often becoming the equivalent of the antagonist in the screen story. Time is not on the side of the main character.

In order to fully flesh out our portrait of the classic thriller, we turn once again to the role of the main character and his goal, the role of the antagonist, the structural dominance of plot over the character layer, the dramatic arc, the role of the antagonist in the shape of that arc, the issues of the day, and the voice of the writer or writer/director.

The Main Character's Goal

The main characters in the thriller tend to be ordinary peo-ple with recognizable traits. This is necessary because the structure of the thriller puts them in extraordinary circumstances and forces them to fashion an escape. The character may be a charming advertising executive, such as Roger Thorndike in Ernest Lehman's *North by Northwest*, or an awkward computer whiz such as Angela Bennett in Irwin Winkler's *The Net*. In both cases, the character is initially no match for the antagonist. The antagonist is a professional spy or killer and the main character is an amateur. This makes the main character's victimization all the more likely, confounding the odds for survival and success.

Although the majority of main characters resemble Richard Kimble in *The Fugitive*—a man accused of murdering his wife, and who, although innocent and not a detective, must find the killer in order to survive—some thrillers involve characters who are experts in a particular field. Sergeant John Gallagher in Andrew Davis's *The Package* helps an assassin infiltrate a U.S. government agency and then must stop the military plot to assassinate the head of the Soviet Union; the main character and the antagonists are professional soldiers. Similarly, in Alfred Hitchcock's *Vertigo*, Johnny is a professional detective, just as the antagonists are criminals, albeit not professional criminals. In this sense, the main character in *Vertigo* should have an advantage. Another Hitchcock irony in this film is that Johnny is emotionally disadvantaged: he is an acrophobic, a man afraid of heights. In both *The Package* and *Vertigo*, the professionalism of the main character doesn't detract from the effectiveness of the narrative. The main character, professional or amateur, is put in the position of victim by the plot. Whether he or she will survive is the substance of the thriller.

The goal of the main character in the thriller is to survive. To do so, the main character must first understand what he or she is up against and then must stop the antagonist from fulfilling his or her goal. By doing so, the main character will save himself and simultaneously be transformed from a potential victim into a hero.

The Role of the Antagonist

There are various aspects about the antagonist that are critical if the thriller is to work. First and most important, the antagonist operates with a clear goal that is in fact the key to the plot. The murder of Richard Kimble's wife in *The Fugitive* was a horrible accident. The killer had meant to kill Kimble, but Kimble wasn't at home. To know this and to know the why of it is the key to Kimble's dilemma. This discovery is made by the main character at the end of the second act. Until then, he is pursued by the antagonist.

Second, the antagonist is powerful. He represents a force, political or economic, that empowers the antagonist and dwarfs the main character. Richard Hannay in Hitchcock's *Thirty-nine Steps* has only his wits and his survival instinct to thwart the antagonist, who has "a foreign power" supporting him. In *The Package*, the antagonistic force is the CIA and its Russian equivalent.

In William Goldman's *Misery*, it's not so much powerful institutions as it is a powerful will—Annie, a fan obsessed with novelist Paul Sheldon. Beginning as his rescuer and nurse, she devolves into his "would-be editor," and then eventually his kidnapper. Since he is injured in the accident, Paul Sheldon is seemingly helpless in the face of her demands and her threats.

The antagonist essentially seeks the destruction of the main character, and the main character understands that fact. But, coupled with this goal, there is often an admiration, even love, between the protagonist and the antagonist: consider Madeleine in *Vertigo* or Annie Wilkes in *Misery*. And although it's not love in *The Package*, the antagonist–protagonist relationship has similarities to those in *Vertigo* and *Misery*. The Henke imposter, Boyette (Tommy Lee Jones), is more like Gallagher (Gene Hackman), as compared to the antagonist–protagonist in Davis's *The Fugitive*. Although Jones's character is aligned with the real antagonist, the CIA colonel, the mutual admiration between Henke (Boyette) and Gallagher is unexpected and analogous to that between Madeleine and Johnny in *Vertigo*. This admiring obsession may lead to love or obsession or both, but it complicates the relationship of the antagonist to the main character in a powerful fashion.

The Dominance of Plot

Think of the plot of the thriller as a chase. The main character's goal is to prevail, but along the way he or she must figure out the why of it and then the how of it, all while being pursued. Numerous genres are dominated by plot and have as their dramatic arc a chase. The horror film is certainly one. A Western such as David Peoples's *Unforgiven* also uses a chase as its arc, as does Waldo Salt's *The Wild Bunch*. What differentiates the thriller from these other genres, however, is its realism. The events of the plot have to be not only plausible, they also have to echo real-life events. A second feature of the dominance of the plot is that there is very little character in the thriller. Although Irwin Winkler deploys a character layer in Act One of *The Net*, it simply slows down the film rather than deepening it. More often, plot simply steamrollers the efforts at character layering. Jonathan Mostow's *Breakdown* and Andrew Marlowe's *Air Force One* illustrate the primacy of plot. The focus shifts to the twists and turns of plot and what is at stake if the main character fails to survive. The audience understands all too well the meaning of the main character's failure, as in the president failing to achieve his goal in *Air Force One*.

One of the few films to manage a successful incorporation of character layering in this genre is Alex Lasker and Bill Rubenstein's *Beyond Rangoon*. Here, the east–west meditation on loss (the main character's son and husband are murdered in Boston) is as well articulated in the character layer of the narrative as are the challenges to the main character as she attempts to flee the threat to her life (the plot) in Myanmar. But *Beyond Rangoon* is the exception.

One last point: Plot can dominate because so often the character doesn't have an internal conflict as in the case of the main character in *Beyond Rangoon*. The main character can then devote his or her energies and intelligence to survival, the ultimate goal of the main character in most thrillers.

The Dramatic Arc

The dramatic arc of the thriller ranges from political to personal to existential. Andrew Marlowe's *Air Force One* and Lorenzo Semple Jr. and David Rayfiel's *Three Days of the Condor* are about political values. Which political system will prevail? Will power move to more authoritarian hands? This is also the core issue in *The Package*, *The Net*, and *Enemy of the State*. In each of these stories—whether the main character is the president of the United States, a CIA operative, or an ordinary lawyer, the values of the free world are riding on his or her success.

More personal issues, such as survival and quality of life, are at stake in *The Fugitive*, *Breakdown*, and *Misery*. But the arc can deepen when the quality of that survival is spun out with a spiritual dimension, such as in *Beyond Rangoon* or in the Carl Schultz thriller *The Seventh Sign*. No modern thriller has more effectively added an existential layer to the dramatic arc than has M. Night Shyamalan's *The Sixth Sense*. Clearly, there is an ample set of options in the thriller genre to give the dramatic arc amplitude, ranging from the political to the deeply psychological. Most important to the operation of the dramatic arc is the urgency of the main character. Not to act with urgency would invite the character's destruction, the very outcome the main character seeks to avoid.

Issues of the Day

Because issues of the day play such an important role in realistic genres, their role is also important in the thriller. During the Cold War, the subject of espionage was at the core, as illustrated by *Three Days of the Condor* and Robert Garland's *No Way Out*. In the 1990s, the issue of terrorism became a prominent concern within the United States, as portrayed in Andrew Marlowe's *Air Force One* and in Erin Krueger's *Arlington Road*. Although the 30-year-old adaptation of the Thomas Harris novel *Black Sunday* was about foreign terrorism within the United States, the later examples of films from the 1990s can be attributed to the heightened sense of the threat of national terrorism of that time—as evidenced by the World Trade Center bombing and the Oklahoma City bombing. Terrorism is no longer theoretical or distant, as it was in the 1970s; it's very much an issue of both social and political concern today.

More personal but no less a concern today is the safety of one's children. Few films have exploited this fear more effectively than Amanda Silver's

The Hand that Rocks the Cradle. Shyamalan's *The Sixth Sense* dwells on a similar issue. The key here is that there are public or political issues of the day, and there are personal issues that grip the public. When these issues become paramount, they, too, become ideal subject matter for the thriller. Any issue that threatens the well being of the central character is potential material for the thriller.

Tone

As expected, the tone of the thriller is realistic in order to harness believability in the character and in the situation the character finds himself in. A good baseline thriller to illustrate realism is Bill Wittliff's *A Perfect Storm*. The natural challenge to the characters and the storm that takes their lives is that it must appear to be the most powerful storm ever recorded. Believability is the key to the effectiveness of this narrative.

Having suggested *A Perfect Storm* as the baseline for the genre, we move back to the work of the primary creator of the genre, Alfred Hitchcock. The first thing we notice is that he broadens the definition of realism in the genre. The original *The Man Who Knew Too Much* focuses on the inner state of the main character, who suffers guilt from a childhood trauma; this internal conflict is as realistically presented as is the external reality of murder.

To illustrate how liberal Hitchcock felt with tone, we need only look at how varied the tone could be when he worked with different screenwriters. When Hitchcock worked with a very serious writer, such as Brian Moore on *Torn Curtain*, the work tended to be almost weighted down by that seriousness; it became less believable. On the other hand, when he worked with Ben Hecht on *Spellbound* and *Notorious*, the romantic dimension of the story (the character layer) seemed to dominate the realism of the plot; consequently, the plot seemed farfetched. When Hitchcock worked with Ernest Lehman on *North by Northwest*, comic characters, together with the irony of the main character, made the plot playful and fun—anything but realistic. The sense of self-deprecation together with a sense of indignation about fate is also found in the main characters in *Thirty-nine Steps* and the *Lady Vanishes*. In a sense, we could say that Hitchcock, the master of the thriller, felt quite free to shift tone from light (*The Trouble with Harry*) to realism (*The Wrong Man*) to horror (*Psycho*).

Few filmmakers proceed as confidently as does Hitchcock. Consequently, a vast majority conform to the realist genre expectation. Even in cases where the supernatural plays a role, as in W.W. Wicket and George Kaplan's *The Seventh Sign* and in William Peter Blatty's *The Exorcist*, the narrative is carefully balanced to enhance believability in the behavior of the main character, in the antagonist (the devil), and in the struggle to survive. Physical and emotional credibility are at the tone's core in both of these films. A more conventional thriller, Jonathan Mostow's *Breakdown*, reconfirms the commitment of this genre to the expected tone, realism. Only Europeans such as George Sluizer (*The Vanishing*) and Claude Chabrol (*La Femme Infidèle*) implement the irony and the tonal variety found in the work of the genre's master, Hitchcock.

■ ■ ■   A Case Study of the Classic Thriller: Amanda Silver's The Hand that Rocks the Cradle

The Hand that Rocks the Cradle takes place in Seattle. The main character, Claire Bartel, has a 5-year-old daughter, a wonderful husband, and is pregnant. She is part of the perfect family. The catalytic event occurs when she visits a new obstetrician. He gives her a medical examination that she feels crosses the boundary of professional behavior into sexual assault. She files a complaint. Other patients step forward to file complaints, and the doctor kills himself.

The action shifts to the doctor's wife. She is pregnant. The death of her husband and the imminence of legal action against his estate leave her bereft of emotional and financial support. She miscarries and the resulting procedure results in a hysterectomy to save her life; she will never be able to have children. The story moves to 6 months later. Claire Bartel has had her baby, and she has been advertising for a nanny. Peyton Flanders, the doctor's wife, presents herself as the prospective nanny, and Claire hires her. Petyon proceeds to ingratiate herself to all the members of the Bartel family. Unbeknownst to Claire, Peyton begins breast-feeding the new baby. Peyton is attempting to take ownership of the family; in a sense, her first goal is to take over the children. After doing so, her next goal will be to get rid of the real parents. In Peyton's mind, Claire destroyed her life, and this will be Peyton's revenge.

In the thriller, the dramatic arc is a pursuit. The catalytic event begins the chain of events that can lead to the destruction of the main character. In *The Hand that Rocks the Cradle*, the turning point in Act One is Peyton's entry into the Bartel household. Although Claire, the main character, doesn't know it, the chase has begun, and it is only at the end of Act Two that Claire realizes the dangerous dynamic at play. At that point, she takes action to save herself and, in this case, to restore the rightful familial line. This will mean overcoming Peyton, the antagonist, and, as is the case in the classic thriller, the main character rises to the occasion and heroically survives. The antagonist dies in the struggle and the family is restored.

The thriller unfolds within the personal domain, the home. Other films, such vfor the classic thriller. Whether political or personal, both follow the arc of an "ordinary person" caught in extraordinary circumstances. Whether president or housewife, the dramatic arc is a pursuit, and in the end, the main character moves from danger to insight to victory over the antagonist. This is the arc that typifies the classic thriller. And the tone is, of course, realistic.

Variations

Although the melodrama and the thriller are distinct genres, the similarity in tone and the notion of trading structural characteristics has enhanced individual stories. Essentially, there is a swap—the melodrama borrows the plot layer from the thriller, and the thriller borrows the character layer from the melodrama. The result is an interesting hybrid. Three case studies will exemplify this variation.

■ ■ ■   A Case Study of Thriller–Melodrama Hybrid: *Sudden Fear*

Lenore Coffee and Robert Smith's *Sudden Fear* is a thriller about a spinster (Myra Hudson) who is a successful playwright, but not lucky in love. She falls in love with a younger man, Lester Blaine, whom she fired from an acting job in her current play. Returning from New York to her home in San Francisco, she takes to this younger man, who will marry her, but with a goal that differs from her own. His revenge for the firing will be to kill his new wife, Myra, and steal her money. If this were a film noir, he would succeed. But as a thriller, Myra, in order to save herself, has to reverse the situation by exposing and undermining Lester's goal. And she does.

Sudden Fear varies from the usual thriller because the plot layer is less pronounced; it's offset by a big character layer where Myra's relationship with Lester is fully explored. The alternative relationship for Myra is one with her devoted lawyer, a man of her own age and status. This character layer results in a far more complex set of characters than is usually found in a thriller. The extreme stereotypes, or at least weaker characterizations of the conventional thriller, are offset by the level of characterization more typical of the melodrama. Although the dramatic arc follows the course of the relationship, it isn't as interior as it would be in a melodrama. Because Lester's intent is murder, the plot is, in fact, an external cat-and-mouse arc more typical of the thriller. In this sense, we could call *Sudden Fear* a thriller with a significant melodramatic character layer.

■ ■ ■   The Case of Lorenzo's Oil

Nick Enright and George Miller's *Lorenzo's Oil* is a melodrama that has taken on the structure of a thriller. The main characters are Augusto and Michaela Odone. They are the powerless characters who challenge the medical power structure. Their 5-year-old son Lorenzo is diagnosed with a fatal illness. The plot focuses on their decision to fight the disease, which is said to have no cure. In a melodrama, the main characters would struggle with an internal issue, such as ambition, identity, or class. But there is no internal conflict, only a refusal to accept their son's cruel fate.

The plot, in essence, takes them on a search, first within the medical establishment and then beyond it. They are looking for a way to overcome a terminal disease. In a sense, the plot has the time element of a thriller (time is against them), and it has the chase dimension (trying to find a cure). In the end, Lorenzo's parents find a cure and do halt the progress of the disease. Here, a large plot layer replaces the large character layer of the melodrama. Since the narrative is based on a real-life event rather than a fiction, the plot layer gives the film more believability, a sense of psychological and physical realism that is heightened by this reliance on the thriller characteristics. In this case, the melodrama looks more like a thriller.

■ ■ ■   **The Case of The Insider**

Eric Roth and Michael Mann's *The Insider* is a melodrama with two main characters, Jeffrey Wigand and Lowell Bergman. Wigand is a scientist who was fired from his research position at a large tobacco company. Bergman is a CBS producer for "60 Minutes," and he wants to tell the story of the tobacco industry's cover-up regarding the health hazards of smoking. Wigand will be the subject. Each man is cast as a powerless person trying to fight the power structure of corporate America (tobacco and the television industry). It's a David vs. Goliath story, with Wigand and Bergman sharing the role of David.

What differentiates *The Insider* from most melodramas is that it presents itself as a thriller. The plot is the investigation, production, and distribution (airing) of the "60 Minutes" segment on Jeffrey Wigand. At every step, corporate muscle is used to bribe, gag, and finally intimidate, first Wigand and eventually Bergman. The initial antagonist, Big Tobacco, gives way to CBS, a second antagonist. Here, corporate strength is used to represent ruthlessness and immorality, crushing anyone who stands in the way—in this case Wigand and Bergman. In the end, Wigand and Bergman succeed (the "60 Minutes" segment is aired), but at a cost: Wigand has lost his family and his economic well being, and Bergman has quit his job.

The Insider uses plot as the thriller does—the pursuit of the broadcast. As in William Goldman's *All the President's Men*, the plot implies that far more than a television program is at stake—in this case the integrity of broadcast journalism, the immorality of corporate advertising, and the issue of personal ethics in the 1990s. Unlike *Lorenzo's Oil*, which eschews the usual character layer of the melodrama, *The Insider* retains its character layer. In this case, we have complex characters and interpersonal relationships, as well as a riveting plot. *The Insider* uses plot and character layer equally, as opposed to the primacy of character over plot in the traditional melodramas.

Recent Trends in Melodrama

There is little question that writers are striving to make the melodrama look more modern. Whether this means adapting a surprising tone, as in Alan Ball's *American Beauty* or in Tod Solondz's *Happiness*, or using multiple main characters, as in *Happiness*, Eric Zonca's *The Dream-life of Angels*, or Paul T. Anderson's *Magnolia*, the search for novelty is nowhere more pronounced than in the mixed-genre melodrama. Melodrama has been effectively mixed with most of the key genres. A strong example of this tendency is illustrated in *Silence of the Lambs*. Although the plot layer of *Silence of the Lambs* follows the classical arc of the detective genre (FBI agent Clarice Starling's hunt for the serial killer, Buffalo Bill), the character layer of the film is melodramatic. In essence, the question is: Can a powerless main character, a woman, make her way in a man's world, the FBI? If Clarice can't, she will fall victim to the power of men. The key helpful relationships that are explored are those with her boss, Jack Crawford, and, ironically, with a notorious serial killer, Dr. Hannibal Lector. Other powerful men, Dr. Frederick Chilton and Buffalo Bill, try to victimize her. *Silence of the Lambs* has an unusually significant layer of melodrama, quite possibly because the film revolves around a woman in a traditionally male world. This issue of the day makes the plot-driven police story more compelling and more meaningful to the audience.

Steve Zaillian's *Schindler's List* is another realist genre film (in this case, war) that benefits from a significant melodramatic layer—an industrialist making his way in the Nazi power structure. Schindler's goal, to save Jews, directly opposes the progression of the plot layer, which is aimed toward killing the Jews. Arif Aliev, Sergei Bodrov, and Boris Geller's *Prisoner of the Mountains*, also a war story, uses a Tolstoy novel as its base to explore the Chechnyan conflict in the 1990s. The plot is the progress of the Russian Chechnyan war.

Will Vania, a young army recruit, survive? The melodramatic layer explores Vania's relationships with his captors and with his fellow Russians (his fellow captive Sacha and his mother). Is the relationship with family more important than national identity, honor, history—the factors that have led to the war? This is the emotional core of the narrative for the viewer. Again, it is the layer of melodrama that strengthens the emotional core of the narrative.

James Gray's *The Yards* is a gangster film whose career-oriented plot gives way to a melodrama about family relationships. Much more modest than the character layer in Coppola's *The Godfather*, the character layer in *The Yards* focuses on a paroled ex-convict, Leo (Mark Wahlberg). Leo returns home to a sick mother and a successful aunt who is married to the head of a subway repair company. Although the uncle's business dealings have been corrupt (bribery is the entrepreneurial grease, political connections its tracks), he is successful—he has a big house and a big car. Exploring these relationships and his own values, Leo is the classic melodrama character, a victim of the power structure of family and of business. And, as in the earlier examples, it is the character layer of melodrama that emotionalizes the narrative.

In the examples discussed so far, there is a compatibility in the mix; both plot and character layers proceed on a realistic basis, and they work well for one another. But writers have also mixed melodrama with genres of wish fulfillment, creating a plot tone that is romantic and poetic. Here, the mix is more challenging. In the *Ballad of Little Jo*, Maggie Greenwald mixes a Western plot with a melodrama character layer. The main character, Josephine, goes West, into a man's world. To survive, she pretends to be a man. Greenwald succeeds in linking the story to an issue of the day—the role of women in society, the inequity of the sexes. By doing so, she brings this Western to a modern audience. The link to an issue of the day makes the melodrama more powerful for its audience. It simultaneously disappoints those who expected more of a Western.

Lars Von Trier's *Dancer in the Dark* is a musical and a melodrama. The melodrama layer is the story of a foreigner in the United States. She is a woman, a laborer with a congenital disease that will make her blind, trying to raise a son who has the same genes but doesn't know his prognosis; this is an ideal melodrama character—she is powerless. Her fascination with singing adds the musical layer. The result is a powerful dose of realism in a genre where wish fulfillment has always prevailed. In contrast to the tragic arc of the melodrama, the arc in the musical has traditionally concluded with the main character finding success on both a personal and professional level. Von Trier reverses the course in this musical.

Recent Trends in the Thriller

As already noted, the thriller tends to be a plot-driven, realistic narrative where the ordinary main character is caught in extraordinary circumstances. Whether the narrative functions on a personal or a political level, the arc of the story essentially looks like a chase, which dominates Act Two. Act Two ends with the newfound understanding by the main character. Once the characters know why they are being pursued, they can formulate a defense for Act Three. In Act Three, they are transformed from would-be victims to heroes. This is the classical thriller.

Recent thrillers have taken their cue from filmmakers such as Hitchcock and Chabrol. They have become less orthodox about the balance between plot layer and character layer, and some have loosened up with regard to tone. Most of the interesting work within the thriller genre has come out of Europe. Regis Wargnier and Sergei Bodorov's *East/West* is a thriller with a very significant character layer. After World War II, Marie, a Frenchwoman, and her son and her Russian-born husband return to his native Russia. They are idealistic about helping restore the new Russia (a country that suffered 50 million fatalities in World War II). The catalytic event comes once they are in Russia. Marie is abused and accused of being a spy, and then has her passport destroyed. Instead of being in a new, altruistic adventure, she finds herself in a prison. While her husband, a doctor, is valued, she is under constant suspicion; she is a foreigner. Language, expectations, and history separate her from her Russian neighbors. The family is given a room in a formerly grand apartment. All are watched, under suspicion. Her goal from this point on is to escape from Russia, to return to her native France, and thus freedom. The balance of the narrative is devoted to the escape. The price of escape is, at its most basic, the marriage, and it takes years to plan. Marie will be helped by a famous French actress known for her left-wing causes, by her first landlord's grandson, by a competitive swimmer, and, unknown to her, by her husband. Other than these people, all the power of Stalinist Russia stands in her way.

The character layer explores two relationships—Marie and her husband, and Marie and the swimmer. The first, her marriage, crumbles under the pressure of staying. As her determination grows, her husband's concern for her is replaced by a survivalist mentality. The marriage fails. The swimmer moves into Marie's room upon the imprisonment of his grandmother. The young man represents passion, rebellion, hope, and a will to support and join Marie in escape. Because he can travel abroad for swimming competitions, he becomes an important conduit for the escape plan. He also becomes Marie's lover. *East/West* employs a significant character layer to amplify Marie's passion for freedom. It is everything for her, and in the end, this character layer enhances the thriller plot, her escape from Russia.

Kristian Levring's *The King Is Alive* goes even further in elevating the character layer and in downplaying the plot layer. Levring also alters the nature of the antagonist. A group of British, American, and French tourists is in transit on a bus in sub-Saharan Africa. Unbeknownst to them, the bus's compass is broken and they end up lost. They arrive at an abandoned mining site. One of the members must walk for 5 days to the nearest town to try to effect a rescue. The others must organize to capture rainwater to survive. They have only canned carrots to eat; they will have to find ways to keep their spirits positive. At the end, the surviving members will be rescued, but not before the experienced member is found dead in the desert, another has died from food poisoning, and yet another has hanged himself.

By making the antagonist inanimate, the thriller shifts in meaning. Instead of an external meaning, this thriller takes on an interior and existential meaning. Specifically, *The King Is Alive* joins a cadre of narratives in which nature itself plays antagonist. Nature and nitroglycerin combine as antagonist in Clouzat's *Wages of Fear* and in the remake, Friedkin's *Sorcerer*. The desert is also a formidable antagonist in Robert Aldrich's *Flight of the Phoenix*. As in all of the above-mentioned films, it is human nature that is as formidable an antagonist as nature in *The King Is Alive*. Levring proceeds to explore the relationships within marriage, between men and women, and between Caucasians and the black bus driver, and few come out of the exploration unscathed. The very existence of the characters—its quality—becomes the subject of *The King is Alive*.

Under the guise of filling time, one of the men, a writer and former actor, decides to stage *King Lear*. The characters from the play and the actual characters of the movie fuse as Levring exposes human nature at its worst. There is no theatrical nobility here, only power seeking exploitation of the other. The will to power is as important as is the will to survive. Plot gives way to character in Levring's intriguing thriller. Plot provides the frame for a narrative theme more often found in the melodrama. Dominik Moll and writer Gilles Marchand's *With a Friend Like Harry* echoes the tone of Hitchcock's *The Trouble with Harry*. Of course, the issue in Hitchcock's story is that at the outset Harry is dead. What to do with the body becomes a narrative thread. In *With a Friend Like Harry*, Harry is very much alive and, although the main character begins to wish him dead by the end of Act Two, it takes all of Act Three to achieve the goal. Harry is the antagonist to the main character, a high-school idol of Harry's but whose current life is beset by the economic limits of being a teacher with three kids, a wife, a mortgage, and an old car. On top of that, he has irritating parents who are generous but controlling. He and Harry bump into each other in a gas station restroom while traveling south for vacation. Harry drives a big Mercedes, has a beautiful fawning fiancée, and is flattering, even obsessed, with his memories of the main character. Independently wealthy, Harry begins to weave himself into the main character's life. As the antagonist, Harry is very much driving the story. He buys the main character a big, new SUV, and he flatters him until he begins writing again.

For the first half of the narrative, it's all character layer, with Harry's motives still ambiguous. In the second half of the narrative, the plot kicks in. Harry must eliminate all of the barriers to the main character's creative potential. In short order, he kills the parents, the brother, and even his own fiancée. It is only when Harry suggests killing the main character's wife and three children that the main character acts. He kills Harry. And he has found his muse. His wife feels that the latest story he has written is brilliant.

The tone of *With a Friend Like Harry* is ironic, verging on farce, but never fully becoming farce. It is a tone Hitchcock used in *The Trouble with Harry*, and Marchand and Moll have captured it very well. *With a Friend Like Harry* has a significant character layer, but it is the unusual tone that engages us in the narrative.

What has happened in the Hollywood thriller is more modest. Although the plot-driven thrillers such as *Clear and Present Danger* and *Air Force One* have dominated, there have been variations. An interesting character-driven thriller with a political plot and an effort to personalize the issue of the day for its audience is Rod Lurie's *The Contender*. Focused on the issue of choosing a vice president and the effort to undermine the president's choice—who is a woman—*The Contender* is a powerful character-driven thriller. Lurie has focused on power and how it is wielded by elected officials. The president, his chief of staff, a senator who wants to gain power by undermining the president and his choice, an ambitious congressman who sees the hearings for the new vice president as an opportunity to move ahead in the political pecking order, a governor who believes he is the best vice presidential nominee, and the female senator who is the nominee—all are participants in the game. Person or politician, power broker or effective social and moral leader, these are the choices each character faces and must make. *The Contender* effectively raises the character issue while not giving up on plot. It represents a balanced approach to the thriller, borrowing heavily from the melodrama.

Erin Krueger's *Arlington Road* is a classic thriller that borrows heavily from film noir and an issue of the day to capture the audience's attention. The context for *Arlington Road* is the Oklahoma City bombing. The narrative implies that if we were more attuned to the warnings, such a tragedy wouldn't occur. The main character, Professor Farraday, is a specialist in terrorism. However, the impact of terrorism isn't strictly academic. His wife, an FBI agent, died during a raid on suspected terrorists. He raises his son on his own. He is a traumatized main character obsessed with preventing a repeat of this kind of tragedy in his life. But that's exactly what happens in *Arlington Road*.

The narrative begins when Michael Farraday saves a young boy, dazed, walking in the middle of the road, bleeding profusely. He takes the boy to the hospital. Later he discovers that the wound was caused by an explosion and that the boy is a neighbor who moved in recently. The boy's parents, Oliver and Cheryl Lang, are very grateful, and the focus of Act One will be the budding relationship between these neighbors. Since his wife's death, Farraday has been isolated, and he welcomes a friend in the neighborhood. His own son quickly becomes friends with the injured boy. But small bits of information—a letter from an eastern alma mater, architectural plans that look suspect—raise a suspicion in the main character's mind: Oliver Lang isn't who he claims to be.

Act Two is taken up with Farraday trying to prove that Lang isn't who he claims to be. In fact, Farraday suspects that Lang is actually a terrorist with a plan. Farraday's girlfriend is totally skeptical, but it is her death that ends Act Two. Act Three, the act of resolution, is taken up with the main character trying to prevent Lang from bombing a federal facility. To slow down Farraday, the antagonist kidnaps Farraday's son. Now he has a very personal stake in what is to occur. He follows the antagonist and believes he has stopped him, but in fact, he has been used. The explosives have been planted in his own car. He has driven the car into the FBI garage, and as he realizes where the explosives are in fact located, the bomb goes off, killing many, including the main character. The narrative ends with the accusation that the main character was the mad bomber, that he carried out the bombing against the FBI as revenge for the death of his wife. The antagonist and his family move on, presumably to the next attack on the federal government.

In *Arlington Road*, the antagonist is victorious and the main character has been the ultimate victim, a fate we associate with film noir rather than with the thriller. By adapting the resolution of film noir, Krueger is issuing a caution—be careful. Your neighbors may not be who you think they are. Or to put it another way, the mad bombers are among us—they are us. This dark vision may be appropriate given the turn of terrorism in the 1990s, but it is an adaptation that alters the traditional genre expectation—that the main character in the thriller will survive and by doing so will be a hero.

Different Reading, Different Genre

Patricia Highsmith, the novelist responsible for such misanthropic thrillers as *Strangers on a Train*, is also the author of T*he Talented Mr. Ripley*. The novel has been filmed twice, in 1962 by Rene Clement and in 2000 by Anthony Minghella. The first version was called *Purple Noon*; the second appeared as *The Talented Mr. Ripley*. The two versions are intriguing because they provide very different versions of the same source material. To be more specific and to put it in the context of this chapter, the first version is presented as a thriller with a character layer; the second is presented as a melodrama with a plot layer. What is instructive about the two versions is that they illustrate how important the story frame or genre can be to the experience of the story. Indeed, this narrative decision determines how we experience the story.

Tom Ripley is a young man from the wrong side of the tracks. His talent is his ambition and his amorality. His initial assignment was to convince Dick Greenleaf (Phillip in the first version), a spoiled, rich young man traveling in Europe, to return home. He fails, falling under the spell of the money and the aesthetic opportunity wealth offers. There are no rules for the rich. Ripley likes that. He kills Greenleaf and assumes his identity. He develops a friendship with his girlfriend. He taps his bank account. Will he be found out? Will he get away with it?

Rene Clement and Paul Gegauff's *Purple Noon* (*Plein Soleil*) follows the thriller structure. In Act One, Ripley is supposed to encourage Phillip to return home. He admires Phillip, but he is very much a parasite. He tries on his clothes but is caught. He watches Phillip make love to his girlfriend Marge and imagines what it would be like for him. Phillip has a sadistic personality. He torments Tom, eventually putting him in a small boat attached to the larger sailboat. Tom suffers burns and dehydration. This torment will be useful in gaining our empathy for Tom. They put the girlfriend on shore. Tom has been instrumental in promoting an argument between the two. Phillip intends to beach the main character. He pushes him. The abusiveness is palpable and Tom kills his idol. He returns to shore and begins to create the illusion that he is Phillip. To the girlfriend he remains an empathic friend.

The killing marks the end of Act One. From this point on, the narrative turns to plot. Will Tom be caught? A friend who can give Tom away shows up. Tom has to kill him. The police inquire about the disappearance of Phillip. Acts Two and Three follow Tom's efforts to get away with murder.

The narrative ends with Tom being caught. The body has washed up on shore. The mystery is solved. Acts Two and Three in *Purple Noon* are tense with the requisite twists and turns of the plot-driven thriller. In the end, the amoral main character of this thriller is caught.

Minghella's *The Talented Mr. Ripley* makes one element of the earlier narrative more overt—that Ripley's attraction to Dick Greenleaf is not entirely based on class distinction or on privilege. In this version, Ripley is gay and clearly has a homoerotic attraction to Dick. Act One concerns itself with the melodrama frame of the powerless Ripley wanting power. He is not abused by Dick Greenleaf but rather admires the young man so much that he wants to be at one with him. The killing is more an assertive action of desire rather than retribution, as it was in *Purple Noon*. Consequently, the desire to become Dick Greenleaf is far more a character issue than a plot issue. It is more psychological than material. As a result, it is the relationships that Minghella explores—the girlfriend Marge in this version is very suspicious of Ripley (rather than trusting). And in this version, the second killing, Teddy, is an act of self-defense, a protection from a predator, rather than an act to preserve material well being. Indeed, at each step, murder is an act of self-defense. By framing *The Talented Mr. Ripley* as a melodrama, Minghella has told the story as a reaction to being a gay, poor man, marginalized because of his sexual preferences and his economic circumstances. As one would expect, plot becomes secondary in this version, whereas plot dominates in the thriller reading of *Purple Noon*.

11

Working Against Genre

Because genre provides a writer with a shorthand that audiences readily understand, less time is needed to establish its characteristics. Just as character stereotypes are useful to the writer, so, too, are genres. However, stereotypes don't sustain our interest, nor do they fascinate us enough to carry us, through curiosity or tension, through the balance of the story. In order to sustain an audience's attention, the writer must give us the unexpected and must challenge our expectations.

As mentioned earlier, genres are often influenced by current events. These historical, political, and social changes suggest new perspectives. For example, technological advances were a powerful feature of the decades following World War II. Dalton Trumbo, in his 1962 modern Western *Lonely Are the Brave*, decided that in his conflict with primitivism and civilization, civilization would be represented by technology. Indeed, in the film, technology is the antagonist to Kirk Douglas's modern cowboy protagonist. Helicopters, jeeps, trucks, and advanced weaponry are the inanimate antagonists that challenge Douglas's character. Even a Social Security number poses a challenge to what he stands for—the values of a former age, freedom, or, as he puts it, "A girl Paul and I grew up with...a wild-eyed mountain girl...her name is Do-what-you-want-to-do-and-the-hell-with-everybody-else."[1]

How did the 1960s influence other genres? Perhaps the most striking gangster film of that decade was *Bonnie and Clyde*, whose main characters are very different protagonists compared to Tony Montana in *Scarface* or Rico in *Little Caesar* or Diggs in *The Asphalt Jungle*. The first difference is in their ages; the young age of the protagonist was a central feature of the films and plays of the 1960s. The society of the 1960s was gripped by the young and the attendant foment in social values. The sublimated energy and idealism of the young are the central feature of *Hair*, and the subverted energy and consequent cynicism are the central focus of *The Manchurian Candidate*.

The second difference in the protagonists of the 1960s is in their characterization. Bonnie and Clyde are depicted as innocents victimized by a society that offers no options to young people. This life-as-a-trap view, however, was also present earlier, in William Wyler's 1937 version of the Sidney Kingsley play *Dead End*.

So far, the changes we have discussed are aligned with society's changing perceptions and issues. To explore the idea of working against genre, we now turn to more dramatic alternatives.

Changing a Motif

Genres characteristically have consistent motifs that recur in all film stories. Motifs usually relate to the main character, the antagonist, the environment, the nature of the conflict, and the tools for resolving the conflict. Underlying attitudes about the past, present, and future are also important qualities.

What happens when a writer challenges an important motif within a genre? By examining four particular genres, we will see how a writer can make a genre seem fresh, rather than simply giving it a contemporary sensibility.

The Western

Few significant writer-directors are as exclusively identified with the Western as is Sam Peckinpah. While Peckinpah's film work parallels the period of the Western's decline, his films *Ride the High Country* and *The Wild Bunch* are among the most important in the genre. When we look at Peckinpah's work, we see a recurring effort to challenge the traditional presentation of the Western hero. In the classic Western, externalized action affords the hero the opportunity to be true to himself. Generally, he is not a character given to introspection, nor is he a character of psychological complexity. Only Borden Chase and Phillip Yordan's heroes, portrayed by James Stewart in a series of films made by Anthony Mann in the 1950s, and the tormented Billy, the Kid in Gore Vidal and Leslie Stevens's screenplay *The Left-Handed Gun*, suggest a psychological complexity that motivates the hero to externalized action. Peckinpah takes the psychological framework of the Western hero and tries to make him more complex, more realistic, and more difficult. The simple hero of the classic Western is replaced by one who is presented to us not only as that classic Western hero, but also as his alter ego.

In *Ride the High Country*, two old men, former famed gunfighters, are the composite heroes. Interestingly, the two men are played by Randolph Scott and Joel McCrea, each of whom portrayed classic Western heroes for the preceding 25 years. In addition to drawing upon our movie memories of these two actors, Peckinpah presents them as two men with diverging views about their present: One of them remains faithful to his past; the other wishes to improve his present by becoming a thief. The clash of values between them, represented by their past (the myth of the West) and their present (discarded but honorable), is really the clash between alter egos, the good and the evil present in all three-dimensional heroes. The casting adds a layer of movie mythology to the Western mythology.

Peckinpah carries on his exploration of composite heroes in *Major Dundee*. Dundee and Tyreen (Charlton Heston and Richard Harris, respectively) portray the stubbornness (Dundee) and nobility (Tyreen) crucial to the hero's survival in the hostile environment of the West. The historical backdrop for this film is the Civil War, but the action of the film takes place in primitive Mexico, far from standing armies and urban centers.

Mexico is also the backdrop for the action of *The Wild Bunch*, set during the Mexican Revolution of 1913. Peckinpah again presents us with a composite hero in Bishop Pike (William Holden), the leader of the Wild Bunch, together with his alter ego, Dutch (Ernest Borgnine), who portrays the cruelty and the camaraderie that forms the moral code of the Wild Bunch. Even in its unusual depiction, this code remains recognizable as the code of the Western hero. By splitting the character, however, Peckinpah again presents a more complex and realistic hero. The composite hero is more difficult to relate to, but he is the 1968 manifestation of those heroes who stand for the struggle of primitivism versus civilization—a theme central to the Western.

This process of character splitting is not exclusive to Peckinpah and the writers with whom he worked. William Goldman does the same in *Butch Cassidy and the Sundance Kid* as does Michael Cimino in *Heaven's Gate*. The gain in psychological complexity has made the Western hero in each of these films profoundly different and fresher than the classic one.

What if the central character in the Western is no longer a hero? What if he is as much a killer as Bishop Pike is, without the redeeming circumstance of being surrounded by characters who are even worse? This is the central feature of the protagonist in David Webb Peoples's *Unforgiven*. Bill Mooney (Clint Eastwood) was a gunfighter who gave it up to appease his wife, and after her death, he finds himself with children to care for but no money to support them. When a reward is posted by a group of prostitutes to bring to justice the two men who mutilated one of them, Mooney takes the job because he needs the money. Throughout the search, he maintains his sobriety and his dead wife's values. But it does not last. Whether it is the cruelty of the town sheriff, the loss of his friend, or just the reassertion of the old demons, Mooney reverts to what he was, a killer without remorse or glory.

This Western hero is not psychologically troubled like Lyn McAdam (Jimmy Stewart) in *Winchester '73*, nor is he relentlessly pursued as Bishop Pike (William Holden) is in *The Wild Bunch*. Mooney is the antithesis of the Western hero. Peoples altered the nature and goal of the main character and made a pursuit Western seem to be a meditation on the values of the classic Western.

Maggie Greenwald has a similar goal when she makes the central character a woman who must dress and act like a man in order to make her way in the West. *The Ballad of Little Jo* alters the gender issue, and the result is very effective. *Bad Girls*, by Ken Friedman and Yolanda Finch, is another film that alters the gender of the conventional male protagonist and is a catalogue of what not to do if you want your screenplay to succeed. A momentary comparison between *The Ballad of Little Jo* and *Bad Girls* illustrates this point very well: although both films focus on a female Western protagonist, it is here that the linkage to other Western motifs ends. In *The Ballad of Little Jo*, the main character takes on the characteristics of the male Western hero—she dresses like a man and acquires the skills men need to survive. She becomes capable with horses, guns, and so on. In *Bad Girls*, the group of young female prostitutes does not acquire much in the way of skills. At least four times, one of them is captured and needs to be rescued by a man. In *The Ballad of Little Jo*, the main character achieves a level of mastery that allows her to become part of the primitive rural values of the West (the opposite of the censorial civilized East she runs away from at the beginning of the film). There is no mastery or progression of the main character in *Bad Girls*. The plot simply does not afford such opportunities for growth.

Another motif that has been challenged by writers of the Western is the presentation of the town. In the classic Western, the town was viewed as a civilizing force, a place that represented the future. The church, the general store, and the marshal's office all represent the spirit of commerce and the law and order of the West. In the past three decades, writers have tried to challenge the presentation of the town. Dalton Trumbo, in *Lonely Are the Brave*, presents the town as one large holding center, a jail for the spirit. Ernest Tidyman, in *High Plains Drifter*, presents the town as a place much worse: it is the center of barbarism and, as is Sodom in the Bible, a place to be destroyed.

Less malignantly, but no less terminal, Miles Hood Swarthow and Scott Hale, in *The Shootist*, present the twentieth-century Western town as a good place to die. In this film, John Bernard Books, grandly portrayed by an ailing John Wayne, is a gunfighter dying of cancer. He visits a town doctor (James Stewart) whom he had known in better times. Upon hearing the news that he will die, Books chooses to die in the town, but on his own terms—in a gunfight with three worthy town villains.

Tombstone presents the town as a center of opportunity, a place where a man can make a living. The central character, Wyatt Earp, has moved to Tombstone to improve his material well-being after having been the sheriff in Dodge City, Kansas. Here, the town does not have the negative connotations it has in the classic Western. When trouble comes from the Clantons and the McCowerys, it is as if two sets of entrepreneurs were competing with each other, and after a time, they revert to guns rather than to opposing advertising campaigns.

In all these films, the town is not viewed as it is in High Noon or in 3:10 to Yuma. In each case, the town is a central but different feature in the film. In each case, an old story is renewed.

The Gangster Film

The gangster film continues to be presented in its classic form. Mario Puzo's *The Godfather*, Oliver Stone's *Scarface*, and David Mamet's *The Untouchables* attest to its continuing importance. However, as with the Western, variations and challenges to the motifs of the genre result in fresh and exciting films. To accomplish this, as in the Western, the presentation of the hero is challenged.

In the classic gangster film, the gangster hero is killed for transgressing the usual means to succeed in society. But against a backdrop of an increasingly drugged, corrupt society, more and more gangster heroes are not killed. They survive and are, in their way, heroic, given the levels of corruption surrounding them. The first of these heroes can be seen in Walker, played by Lee Marvin in *Point Blank*. Walker's vengeful attempt to retrieve money stolen from him by his partner takes him on a journey through the organization to which his partner now belongs. As Walker eliminates level after level of the organization, his revenge has less meaning, as does the money he seeks to retrieve. Walker is a thief, but he is portrayed as an existential hero. He has the same energy and intuitive drive of the classic gangster hero, but he has modern self-doubt that makes him particularly empathetic, given that he is as much a killer as is Tony Montana in *Scarface*.

The same characteristics—energy and intuition—are combined with decency in the James Caan character in *Thief*. He, too, is an existential hero, and he, too, lives to walk away from those who are dishonest with the thief.

Perhaps the most interesting gangster hero is Lou, the petty criminal portrayed by Burt Lancaster in *Atlantic City*. Lou is an aging bodyguard to a once-famous criminal's moll (Kate Reid). With the good old days behind him, Lou finds a new lease on his reputation via Sally (Susan Sarandon). She is young and in trouble because of her criminal brother-in-law and former husband (Robert Joy). But in rescuing Sally, Lou is forced to kill again in the process. Yet, he walks away happier than before. In a world of criminality and corruption, Lou is an empathetic hero, and he lives on.

Police and detectives as heroes have also been presented in a different light. The messianic *Serpico* is not dissimilar from Dan Banion in *The Big Heat*. Both have a moral fervor we associate with the energy needed to turn back the forces of criminality that challenge the social order, but there are variations. In *Bullitt* and *Madigan*, the main characters, played by Steve Mc-Queen and Richard Widmark, respectively, have upper-class tastes. In *Tightrope*, the main character, portrayed by Clint Eastwood, suffers from a guilt complex arising from his troubled domestic life. He is a single parent as well as a busy detective with a major murder case on his hands. Is he protagonist or antagonist? This blurring of the distinction takes on new levels in a film such as Barry Keefe's *The Long Good Friday*. The gangster is the protagonist, and an active political movement, the IRA, is the antagonist.

Not only are the gangster and the cop presented differently, but so is the traditional environment of the gangster film—the big city. The city is presented as the seat of power, particularly material power. In two noteworthy films, buildings became cities unto themselves. In *Die Hard*, a postmodern tower is the center of power where a policeman (Bruce Willis) must stop a high-stakes robbery. In this milieu, the gangsters are robbers posing as international terrorists. In *Someone to Watch Over Me*, the center of power is the building in which a wealthy murder witness lives. The detective assigned to guard the witness falls in love with her. This cross-class entanglement suggests another path to material success—climbing the social ladder—that moves beyond the gangster's approach of theft and murder.

A cross-cultural perspective on the center of power is explored in *Witness*. In this film, the main character, John Book, escapes from his corrupt colleagues who threaten to kill him and the murder witness he is protecting. Book and his witness escape to rural Pennsylvania, the home of the Amish, where the murder witness will be among his own people and thus harder to find. This shifting of the environment for the gangster film is the second challenge to a genre motif.

A third challenge is the alteration of the expected narrative shape of the gangster film. Characteristic of this genre is the strong plot: foreground over background action. Also characteristic is the drive of the main character to succeed in rising to the top in the gangster world, to solve the crime for the police.

In *Carlito's Way*, David Koepp explores a gangster trying for a different kind of personal success—he wants to leave the life of crime and live a normal life. Unfortunately, Carlito (Al Pacino) is loyal to his family and friends, which ultimately draws him back into the life of crime; consequently, he must suffer the classic fate of the gangster hero, death. This shift in the character's goal alters the balance of the foreground and background stories in the film. The result is a less exciting but more deeply felt sense of the character, his fate, and the impression that in certain ethnic communities, the fate of the members is predetermined and tragic.

Another example of the shift between plot and the interior concerns of the character is David Mamet's *Homicide*. Here the central character is a Jewish policeman named Gold. The plot has Gold and his colleagues trying to apprehend a young black drug dealer. The background story concerns Gold as a Jew, how he feels about it, and how he is pushed to try to be loyal to other Jews. An old Jewish woman has been murdered, and Gold's growing interest in the case involves him with a Jewish terrorist organization. Should he help them? Should he break the law, go against his own code of behavior to validate himself as a Jew? The meditation that proceeds in the background story eventually supercedes the hunt for the drug dealer. Although the plot does resolve itself, the background story leaves Gold as confused as he was early in the film. Nevertheless, the shape of this police story, with its shift away from plot toward the interior life of the main character, provides a striking example of working against genre expectations.

Film Noir

Film noir, the genre of deception and betrayal, provides writers with a narrow band of options to reorder. The protagonist, unlike the Western or gangster protagonist, is a victim and doesn't lend himself to redefinition (at least not yet). The antagonist, on the other hand, provides writers with considerable scope. Generally, the antagonist is the spider woman (*Black Widow*) that destroys its mate or alcohol (*The Lost Weekend*) or drugs (*The Man with the Golden Arm*) that destroy the main character. However, writers have been increasingly adventurous in their antagonists; politics and history have helped.

A number of the key film noir works of the past decades have made antagonists representatives of the government. Beginning with the Angela Lansbury character in George Axelrod's screenplay of *The Manchurian Candidate* (updated in 2004 by Jonathan Demme), the government and those in power, or closest to power, have manipulated the main character for political ends. In *The Manchurian Candidate*, Lansbury has her own son trained as a killer for the purpose of political assassination. This satire-tragedy puts political goals above personal affiliation. Here a mother sacrifices her own son to the cause.

No such personal sacrifice is at stake in William Goldman's *All the President's Men*, but the belief that the government functions "by the people and for the people" is challenged. This sobering tale, based on the Bernstein–Woodward book on the Watergate scandal, has terrifying overtones. This view of the antagonist is also present in Alvin Sargent's *The Parallax View*, in Robert Stone's *Who'll Stop the Rain?*, and in Robert Garland's *No Way Out*.

Another variation in film noir is the addition of pimps, promoters, and sociopaths as frightening antagonists. In Paul Schrader's *Hardcore*, the principal antagonists are the purveyors of pornography; in Elmore Leonard's *52 Pick-Up*, the antagonist is a sadistic purveyor of pornography; and in *Klute*, the antagonist is the pathological client of hooker Bree Daniels. As sexuality and aggression are motifs of film noir, the blending of two motifs, aggressive sexuality and the antagonist, brings a less personal, but no less menacing, position to the role of the antagonist. It is as if the workplace in film noir has become as dangerous as the home is.

Film noir has also invaded the terrain of other genres. The pastoral small town is the setting for *Blue Velvet*, but in this story of voyeurism and violence, a small town is no haven for its characters. Instead, it is the scene for nightmarish aggression and a level of sadistic sexuality rare in film noir. The small town no longer projects the good-neighborliness of *It's a Wonderful Life*. Nor does the Pentagon prove to be a safe haven in *No Way Out*. It is as fraught with danger as the city is in a classic film noir.

Film noir tends to play itself out through the actions of a desperate main character at a critical moment in his or her life. A good example is *Sunset Boulevard*. We meet Joe Gillis when he is a down-and-out writer in Hollywood, at the point where his car is about to be repossessed. Without a car in Los Angeles, his career will be over; he might as well give up his dream of being a Hollywood scriptwriter. It is at this point that the main character enters a relationship with a woman who he hopes will rescue him from what appears to be his fate. In *Sunset Boulevard*, the woman is Norma Desmond, whose driveway Joe has entered to evade the repo men pursuing him. In film noir, the fate Joe meets at the hands of Norma Desmond is far worse than anything the repo men could have done. This is the narrative shape of classic film noir. The relationship and the consequent betrayal embrace the degradation the main character must accept if he is to strengthen this false, final relationship. He erroneously believes that the sexual-aggressive nature of the relationship will strengthen him.

What happens when the writer tries to alter this classic narrative shape? Paul Schrader, who is responsible for a number of excellent film noir stories, including *Hardcore, American Gigolo, Taxi Driver*, and *Raging Bull*, also wrote *Light Sleeper*, a film that alters the narrative shape of film noir by including a relatively happy ending. *Light Sleeper* tells the story of John LeTour (Willem Dafoe), a former drug addict and current drug dealer. He works for Ann (Susan Sarandon). In the course of the story, he meets Mary Ann (Dana Delaney), his former wife, who left him because of his drug abuse. He genuinely wants to rekindle their relationship and tells her he is drug free, but she does not believe him. He persists and visits her dying mother. His kindness touches Mary Ann, and she agrees to go with him. They make love, but she tells him it won't happen again. He carries on his passion for her. When he drops off drugs to a classy client (Victor Garber), LeTour sees Mary Ann in the apartment in a drug-induced state. We are surprised that she is on drugs. He waits outside for her, but she jumps from the balcony of the apartment to her death. Angry, hounded by police to become an informer, he tells the police where he last saw her alive. The furious client arranges to have LeTour killed, but LeTour turns the tables and kills the man and his bodyguards. Although LeTour goes to jail, Ann has decided to wait for him. They decide that their relationship, first presented as mother–son, is genuine and can last. There in jail, hands together, the new lovers patiently vow to stay together after LeTour is released.

This optimistic ending of *Light Sleeper* is but one alteration to the classic narrative shape of film noir. There are many others. As the main character is a desperate man, we expect him to relapse into drug use and eventually die, but he doesn't. He does enter a desperate final relationship with his former wife, but his fate and hers are the opposite of what the genre leads us to expect. Nor is he killed in the attempt to kill the client who provided his wife with the drugs that killed her. The fact that in the end, the main character is alive, happy, and in love again leaves us with some hope, a state utterly foreign to film noir. The narrative shape of *Light Sleeper* resembles the dreamy sequel to a film noir story. It's as if LeTour has hit bottom just before the beginning of the film and the film is about his resurrection. In this sense, *Light Sleeper* begins where classic film noir ends. Whether this more hopeful vision of the urban nightmare is Schrader's redefinition of film noir for the 1990s or whether he simply wanted to create a Christ parable with a changed ending, *Light Sleeper* changes our experience of the film noir genre.

The War Film

Rather than choosing the combatant as the protagonist, as usual, two noteworthy films chose a young noncombatant whose life is very much influenced by war as the protagonist. In both *Empire of the Sun* and *Hope and Glory*, the protagonist is a 12-year-old boy. In one case, the boy has to cope with the Japanese occupation of Shanghai during World War II and with subsequent imprisonment in a concentration camp; in the other case, the boy has to cope with the London Blitz and its consequences. The boys identify with the romance of war and discover its reality as well. The challenge to the motif is that the protagonists are not totally absorbed with survival, as their youth allows for a much broader engagement with the war and its meaning. They are as involved with growing up as they are with the war.

Forbidden Games and *The Tin Drum* also use young protagonists. Each film is placed in the native country of the protagonist, and *Forbidden Games* takes place during World War II. Because these protagonists are not combatants, they have very different perspectives on war and on the issue of survival.

Another war film that treats the protagonist differently is *Full Metal Jacket*. In the story, Matthew Modine is an observer. The passive nature of this character is discussed in a later chapter. For now, it is useful to point out that this protagonist functions as much as a witness as an active participant. He watches and photographs the brutality of war in Vietnam as it occurs around him. The more classic protagonist is Charlie Sheen's character in *Platoon*. He wants to survive and does, albeit with less idealism. The two characters couldn't be more different.

▪ ▪ ▪   Mixing Genres

For the writer, challenging a motif within a genre offers an opportunity to present a story in a fresher way, whereas mixing two distinct genres in one story offers a different, more radical opportunity. Some genres often have such different meanings to an audience that mixing two can have a dissonant, troubling impact. With other genres, the mix may be more complementary and can make the film seem more energetic, fresh, and renewed. In both cases, the impact can be surprising. Mixing genres has resulted in some of the most startling and important films of the past decades, such as *Raging Bull, Blade Runner, Diva, Something Wild, Raising Arizona*, and *Blue Velvet*.

▪ ▪ ▪   A Case Study of Opposites I: The Stalking Moon

No two genres could be more different than are the Western and the horror film. Yet, in Alvin Sargent's *The Stalking Moon*, we have both genres. As a Western, the film is the story of an army scout (Gregory Peck) who is about to retire. On his last assignment, to capture a group of Indians who have escaped from the reservation, he finds a white woman and her Indian son. The woman (Eva Marie Saint) is to return to her white family in the East. To expedite her leaving, she goes with the scout, who eventually takes her to his home in the mountains. There they await the arrival of her vengeful Indian husband, the chief of the band, who will do anything to return his son to his side. So far, this is a Western with a surrogate family in the making—scout, white woman, and Indian boy. However, the horror genre intercedes when the Indian chief, who we never see until the last 5 minutes of the film, inflicts horrible death on all who stand in his way. The sudden violence and the scope of the killing suggest an inhuman power. The chief, Salvahee, takes on a primitive and supernatural destructive power as he wreaks insurmountable terror on those with whom he comes in contact, including the surrogate family.

The mixing of the two genres, Western and horror, one that focuses on the world of dreams and the other on the world of nightmares, is effective because those two worlds are flip sides of each other. They coexist in the subconscious, and it's not hard to imagine one quickly turning into the other. The fact that they are opposites helps the two genres coexist. The result is a dramatically effective story that is certainly unexpected.

▪ ▪ ▪   A Case Study of Opposites II: *Wolf*

The horror film embraces the nonrealistic manifestations of the nightmare; the melodrama tends to be about realistic people in realistic situations. The blend of nonrealistic horror story and realistic melodrama is the mix of opposites we find in Jim Harrison and Wesley Strick's *Wolf*.

Wolf tells the story of Will Randall (Jack Nicholson), an editor with a large publishing house. Mature and middle aged, he is about to be replaced by his young, aggressive protégé (James Spader). Driving in Vermont late at night, he accidentally hits a wolf, then tries to move the body off the road. The wolf, which is not dead, bites him and runs off. As expected, Will becomes a werewolf. In the classic werewolf tale, the wolf victimizes and destroys those he loves and eventually is destroyed. In *Wolf*, Will is not destroyed but is instead renewed, made young, by becoming a werewolf. The tired, middle-aged man becomes sexually vigorous and vocationally effective. His newfound aggressiveness applied in the corporate world makes him succeed over his rival. The horror dimension follows the story line of the main character—how he deals with becoming a werewolf when the moon is full, his fears that he murders people (including his estranged wife). He ends up biting both his rival and his lover (Michelle Pfeiffer).

In the horror genre, the main character needs to be destroyed, because the surfeit of aggression and sexuality makes him a danger to himself and society. Implicit is the idea that the character is evil and thus must be destroyed. In *Wolf*, the writers carefully separate good from evil. A good man who becomes a wolf may be sexually active and aggressive in business, but, essentially, he will be a good wolfman. An evil man (Spader) who becomes a wolf will become a killer and deserves to be destroyed. Simply becoming a wolf is no longer a reason for the main character's destruction, a deviation from the fate of the typical protagonist in the horror genre. In *Wolf*, the main character transcends victimization, a point we will return to later.

In the melodrama, the main character challenges the power structure, but in the end becomes its tragic victim despite a heroic effort. The melodramatic layer in *Wolf* centers on Will's age. Although highly thought of by his writers, his publisher (Christopher Plummer) wants someone with a more aggressive marketing-oriented approach. It is the classic case of the broom that follows the corporate takeover; the main character is swept aside. The concern with his age reflects the fascination with youth in the media; studio executives in Hollywood and reporters on newspapers are younger than ever. Even the character's wife is having an affair with his young successor. Will challenges the publisher and the age issue by devising a strategy to keep the writers with him in a new company and by taking up with the young, troubled daughter of the publisher.

The Nicholson character offers some compatibility between the two story forms—the horror film, where the main character is a victim, and the melodrama, where he struggles valiantly but in the end fails, a victim of the power structure. The same is true of the antagonist. In both genres, Spader's character—the young, evil, and ambitious male—is the antagonist. *Wolf* uses elements of the horror film— sexuality and aggression—to overcome the weakness and powerlessness typical of the melodrama protagonist. The main character uses these qualities to overcome the by-products of aging, fatigue, and depression in order to renew himself and be successful. Because he is essentially good, he can use the sexuality and aggression for positive purposes. Although this alters the narrative shape of both genres, it seems to work. The result is a touching, adult sense of the fate of the monster. By altering the narrative shape, these opposite genres work well together.

■ ■ ■   A Case Study of Similar Genres: *Blade Runner*

The science fiction genre is similar to the horror film genre. Often, it focuses on apprehensions about the future and technology, with the negative tradeoff of humanist values. The protagonist may be like Captain Kirk, struggling with the issue of aging (*Star Trek: The Wrath of Khan*), whereas the antagonist is a mad man, Khan, who may bring about Armageddon.

The protagonist in the science fiction film always has hope, whereas the protagonist in film noir displays a desperation that precludes hope. In film noir, the protagonist views life experiences more as a last chance, and the antagonist is much more personable than Khan is. Indeed, the protagonist–antagonist relationship in film noir is often characterized as a dance of death, with the dancers as two lovers rather than foes. Science fiction and film noir, although both proximate the world of the nightmare, are not a natural mix. Indeed, at the levels of protagonist, antagonist, and setting, they conflict with one another. In *Blade Runner*, we can explore where the mixing of the two genres works and where the contradictions are so great that they undermine the drama's credibility.

This science fiction story is the story of an ex-cop, Deckard (Harrison Ford), who is now a blade runner. A blade runner tracks down and destroys replicants, which are technical duplications of human beings used as slave labor on the Off-world space colonies. The manufacturer of these combinations of commerce and technology, the Tyrrel Corporation, works with the motto, "More human than human." Six replicants have escaped and returned to the polluted, polyglot metropolis of Los Angeles, and the blade runner must track them down and destroy them. Machines that become more human than human are a genuine danger.

The film noir story is that of Deckard, the desperate ex-cop who falls in love with the replicant Rachel (Sean Young). Does he destroy her or does he become more human than human, too? The film noir is framed by the futuristic metropolis of Los Angeles—a jungle of technology, overpopulation, and constant rain.

The *Blade Runner* script is both inventive and disappointing. The struggle between humanity and technology—the basis of the science fiction story— introduces elements of pathos and hope into the film noir story, which in turn provides a believable context for the science fiction element. We can imagine the Los Angeles of 2019 as something like the city we discover in *Blade Runner*. However, in dealing with the protagonist and the antagonist, the two genres contradict each other and eventually defeat a fascinating narrative effort.

In film noir, the protagonist is a victim. In the science fiction film, he is an idealist who struggles with the abyss toward which technology pushes him (and us). It is hard to imagine a cynical victim and a romantic idealist in the same person, yet this is precisely what *Blade Runner* proposes in Deckard. In terms of the antagonist, the science fiction story suggests that Tyrrel, who invented the replicants, is the antagonist. In a sense, he is the antagonist in the film noir story as well. He did ask the police to destroy the runaway replicant, Rachel, with whom Deckard falls in love. More important, however, he is the man who incorporated a finite life span in Rachel and thus put a very short term on the duration of Deckard's and her love. Rachel is destined to die sooner than one would expect in a love relationship with a human; Deckard is destined to be alone.

As an antagonist, Tyrrel is an eminent, but not gripping, presence in both stories. Although he is rarely present, there is considerable ambivalence about Tyrrel, commerce, and technology. However, there is nothing visceral in this antagonist; he is little more than a symbol. The demands of the two genres have pushed him, as the antagonist, far into the background. In the end, the mixing of the two genres undermines the effectiveness of either. The film script remains a fascinating failure.

A similar mix was attempted in Edward Neumeier and Michael Miner's *Robocop*, with more success. The protagonist, Murphy (Peter Weller), is believable as a victim. He is a policeman who is killed in the line of duty and is recreated as a robot-policeman, a Robocop. His personal struggle is that he was once human and is now the product of technology. By the end of the film, he finds some humanity, despite his technological makeup. The part of the antagonist is split between Murphy's murderer and the corporate head of security, in whose department Robocop's construction was requisitioned (a surrogate inventor). Particularly with regard to the protagonist, this mixed-genre film works.

∎ ∎ ∎   A Case Study of the Police Story as Nightmare: *The Fugitive*

Writers Jeb Stuart and David Twohy mix the police story and film noir in *The Fugitive*, which was based on the famous television series, which in turn was heavily inspired by Victor Hugo's novel, *Les Miserables*. The police story uses its central character Richard Kimble (Harrison Ford) to solve a crime. He is a man accused of killing his own wife, and it is up to him to both prove his innocence and seek revenge for his wife's death while being hunted by the authorities. After Act I, he spends as much time searching for the true murderer as he does evading Lieutenant Girard (Tommy Lee Jones), the man who is relentlessly pursuing him. In film noir, the main character is a victim, so the pursuit maintains Kimble as a victim on one level, giving it the principal duality that prevents *The Fugitive* from being seen strictly as a police story. The victim quality increases our sympathy for Kimble.

The screen story opens with the murder of Richard Kimble's wife. Kimble, a well-known surgeon in Chicago, returns home to find a one-armed man in his home; he struggles with him, but the man escapes. Kimble is accused of the murder, found guilty, and sent to prison to await execution. En route to prison, another prisoner shoots the bus driver and, in the resulting accident, Kimble escapes. The balance of the police story deals with Lieutenant Girard's hunt for Kimble, who eventually returns to Chicago to try to find the one-armed man.

By looking for an amputee with a prosthetic similar to the one Kimble detached from the killer the night his wife was killed, Kimble does find the one-armed man and he leads Girard to him. The investigation, however, brings Kimble face to face with the true antagonist, his friend Charles, also a heart surgeon. Charles, in the employ of a drug company, had hired the one-armed man to assassinate Kimble, not his wife. The plot ends with the real killer, Charles, apprehended, and Kimble, now in the protective custody of Girard, soon to be a free man.

These two genres of police story and film noir tend to have complementary shapes, with the police story being plot driven and the film noir story being driven by the background story about the relationship that will bring destruction to the victimized main character. In *The Fugitive*, the differing shapes do not undermine one another, whereas in the police story, both Girard and Kimble are working to solve the crime, despite Girard's pursuit of Kimble. In the film noir dimension of the story, Kimble is the classic victim protagonist, and the destructive antagonist, usually a woman, is a policeman. The drive, the relentlessness of Girard's pursuit of Kimble, parallels Javert's endless drive to capture and destroy Jean Valjean in Hugo's *Les Miserables*. Girard, in this sense, carries literary weight as the false antagonist in *The Fugitive*. Although Kimble and Girard are rarely together in the conventional sense, the strongest relationship in the film is between these two men, and until the final scene in the hotel, it is clear that Girard means to bring Kimble to justice and to death. Because of the common characters, the two story forms do not undermine one another. If anything, the emotionally powerful film noir dimension helps the viewer overcome the disappointing foreground resolution of the plot. The Girard–Kimble relationship is simply far more interesting than is Kimble's relationship with the one-armed man or Charles. The result is a film that seems to have the best of both genres—an exciting plot in the police story and a powerful emotional relationship in the film noir tradition. The sum is greater than the parts.

■ ■ ■ A Case Study of Screwball Comedy: *Something Wild*

The screwball comedy is the flip side of film noir. In both genres, the (usually male) protagonist is viewed as a victim, and the antagonist is often the woman he chooses (or is chosen by) and with whom he gets involved. The prime difference between the genres is that the outcome of the screwball comedy is happy, whereas the outcome of film noir tends to be tragic. The action line in both genres is the story of their relationship.

Max Frye's screwball comedy *Something Wild* is the story of Charlie Diggs (Jeff Daniels), a corporate executive with a rebellious side. He is picked up by Lulu (Melanie Griffith), who virtually kidnaps him for a weekend, one that becomes wild beyond all expectation when they meet Lulu's ex-husband. The relationship between Charlie and Lulu is prone to much role reversal and sexual aggression. She is unpredictable, seductive, and dangerous, but she appeals to the rebel in him, and he falls in love.

The film noir story in *Something Wild* has much to do with deception. Lulu deceives Charlie, and Charlie deceives Lulu. When they meet her ex-husband, played by Ray Liotta, the deception becomes lethal. Lulu's ex-husband wants to kill Charlie and almost succeeds. The principle of deception is pervasive. It goes on in the city as well as in rural settings; it takes place within relationships as well as within families. Lulu and her mother have an elaborate code of interaction, all based on a series of lies and delusions. This is the perfect milieu for the tragic outcome of film noir.

The upshot of mixing screwball comedy and film noir, however, steers us away from the logical tragic conclusion toward a happier outcome. The film provides considerable tension between the two genres. The goals differ and, consequently, the treatment of protagonist and antagonist differs. The screwball comedy aspect of the film softens our sense of the protagonist as a victim. Indeed, he has to overcome his victimization if he is to transcend the classic film noir protagonist. There is some loss of credibility in this leap. A similar fate is cast for the antagonist. Lulu moves from being a predator to being a pussycat, and the transition gives her little to do in the second half of the story. To keep the story going, her ex-husband becomes the antagonist. The result is not only a dramatically mixed experience, but also a rich one in terms of the alternating of comic and tragic goals. The energy that results from the clash of the two genres heightens our fascination with the story and with what might happen next. However, the shifting natures of protagonist and antagonist result in a less emotionally involving experience than if the film focused on one of the genres. This particular experiment in mixing genres is designed to appeal to us as voyeurs, rather than as participants.

■ ■ ■   ## A Case Study of Genders and Genres I: *The Ballad of Little Jo*

Many Westerns have introduced a dimension of melodrama into their stories. *The Gunfighter*, *The Left-Handed Gun*, and *High Noon* all include an overlay of melodrama, but few Westerns have used it as a major element. *The Ballad of Little Jo*, however, relies on melodrama as much as on the typical Western form.

Maggie Greenwald has written a story of a young eastern woman who must leave home. The woman, Josephine, has had a child out of wedlock and now, shunned by her family, is traveling West to make a life for herself. What she quickly discovers is that, as a woman, she will be viewed as chattel suitable only for sexual pleasure. To avoid this fate, she takes on the appearance of a man—in her clothing, hair, and affectation. At first unsure and shy, she begins to live and work in a mining town. Fearful that she will be discovered, she takes work as a winter sheepherder. Here, she believes she can avoid having her true identity discovered. She enjoys the solitude, and her growing competence is clear. She begins to acquire the survival skills that men have mastered. Eventually she earns enough to start her own farm. One day in town, she takes on a Chinese rail worker as her cook, to prevent him from being hanged. He quickly discovers her true identity, and they become lovers. Suddenly she has companionship. As time passes, her happiness is threatened by the local cattle company, which through intimidation and murder has been buying adjacent land. In the end, she decides to defend her land and stays. Both she and her lover die on the land, and it is only when she dies that the town discovers she is actually a woman.

As a Western, *The Ballad of Little Jo* has many of the classic elements. The main character is heroic. The story is shaped around the struggle between primitiveness and civilization, although, uncharacteristically, the central character here opts for primitivism, with its tolerance of individuality— Little Jo's relationship with a "Chinaman" and her deception. The *Ballad of Little Jo* presents a violent milieu, but there is little ritualized killing on-screen. Most of the killing takes place off-screen, and there is no gunfight at the end of the film. The story's resolution certainly differs from that in the conventional Western. There is no fierce antagonist to make Little Jo's actions stand out more heroically. The land, however, does play the classic Western role. Beautiful but dangerous, it offers opportunity to the character, but in the end the harshness of land ends Jo's life.

As a melodrama, *The Ballad of Little Jo* is the story of a woman challenging the male power structure. By pretending to be a male, Jo demonstrates her desire to participate in society in the same way men are able to. At one point, her Chinese lover warns her that if the men of the town find out she is a woman, their humiliation will be such that they will kill her. The film deviates from melodrama, however, by adopting the Western convention of the victorious main character.

Although the melodrama tends toward realism and the Western less so, Maggie Greenwald has not presented an elegiac West. The Western dimension of this screenplay is realistic rather than heroic and ritualized, which reduces the conflict between the two genres. If there is a genuine difference between this Western and most others, it is in the absence of an antagonist. Here, the melodrama form helps. By providing the entire male population as a power structure opposed to women, every male encountered before the Chinese man becomes at one point or another a threat to Little Jo. In this sense, men in general become Little Jo's antagonists, and her struggle to avoid discovery, even in both instances when her true identity is revealed, becomes heroic given the level of threat. Although the two genres do not share many elements, their combination in the movie strengthens and makes the nineteenth-century story into a modern struggle. *The Ballad of Little Jo* is an excellent example of mixing genres to good effect.

■ ■ ■   A Case Study of Mixing Genders and Genres II: *The Crying Game*

The Crying Game, which is on one level a political thriller about IRA terrorists, is also a melodrama about gender and sexual preference. The film opens with the IRA kidnapping of a black British soldier, Jody; from a bar where he is socializing with a woman, Jude; Jude is an IRA member who is part of the kidnapping plot. If the British do not release IRA prisoners, the soldier hostage will be killed. Fergus (Stephen Rea), who is assigned to guard the soldier, becomes his friend; Fergus is eventually supposed to kill Jody but doesn't, although Jody dies accidentally. The kidnapping plot ends disastrously for the IRA, because of Fergus. Before his death, Jody asks Fergus to take care of Dil, his lover back in London. Fergus agrees.

The next phase of the film, in London, focuses on Fergus's efforts to get to know Dil, and his gradual falling in love with Dil. All is well until he discovers that Dil is male. This apparently ends the budding love affair, but it is soon rekindled, as Fergus simply cannot get Dil out of his mind. Fergus's IRA cohorts, including Jude, resurface in London and demand his participation in the assassination of a government official. He has no choice, but Dil innocently prevents him from fulfilling the obligation, believing only that Fergus wants to leave to take up with Jude. With the mission betrayed, Jude returns to kill Fergus, but Dil kills her instead. Fergus sends Dil away and stands in as the murderer. In jail, Fergus is visited by Dil, who is impressed with his commitment to her. The film ends with the fantasy of their possible future love together.

In the political side of the story, Fergus is the main character. He is in the IRA for life. If he does not kill, the IRA will kill him, and the British might kill him anyway. The main character is presented as a potential victim attempting to avoid a particular fate. When a plot provides enough surprises, the sense of excitement and emotion around the fate of the main character can be considerable. (*The Day of the Jackal* is a good example of a plot-centered thriller.) However, *Crying Game* director Neil Jordan is not very interested in plot, and there is a minimal investment in surprise here. It looks to the melodrama to engage and move us.

The melodrama in *The Crying Game* focuses on a heterosexual white male who, against his previous disposition, begins to fall in love with a black male transvestite. His tragedy is, in the end, an altruistic sacrifice, but he is alive and eventually he will be able to return to Dil. As he did in *The Miracle*, in which incest was the taboo, Jordan flirts with the possibility that love can overcome boundaries of race and gender.

The success of *The Crying Game* stems from Jordan's interest in the melodrama, which helps compensate for the plot flaws in the thriller. Indeed, the melodrama is so provocative that it all but makes the audience forget that *The Crying Game* began as a political thriller. The script is also aided by the fact that both genres rely on realism. Compatibility in the role of the main character in both the thriller and the melodrama, essentially realistic, also strengthens the film. The absence of a strong antagonist in the melodrama leaves the role to poor Jude from the thriller. Her death, on one level, kills off the female rival to Dil, but on another level makes no emotional sense in the way the fate of a true antagonist should.

■ ■ ■ A Case Study of Adventure Film as Satire: *Raising Arizona*

The Coen brothers' *Raising Arizona* is both an adventure film and a satire. As both genres move away from naturalism, or realism, this particular mix of genres is both stimulating and fresh. The adventure film genre is narrative intensive and pits a romantic protagonist against a mythic antagonist. The levels of conflict between protagonist and antagonist are increasingly intensified and fantastic as we move through the story. In the end, the goal of the adventure genre is to claim goodness over evil and to have a good time doing it. The genre is based on adolescent wish fulfillment.

In the case of satire, the goals are much more serious. The satire genre tackles serious issues of social concern with a sense of aggressive comedy. The genre is critical, pointed, funny, and fast. Energy is essential. The antagonists are the issues of the day—television, nuclear war, medical incompetence, and government bureaucracy. The protagonist, in a sense, becomes the audience, because it is we who suffer the antagonistic effects depicted in the film.

Raising Arizona is about a couple's (Nicolas Cage and Holly Hunter) desire to have a child. They can't; hence, so they decide to kidnap one from a rich businessman whose wife has given birth to quintuplets. The kidnapping, and the subsequent efforts to prevent others from taking the child, is the heart of the story. In the end, the desperate couple decides to return the baby to its family. The adventure story relates to the kidnapping and the efforts of two convicts and a bounty hunter who try to steal the child from the kidnappers. The satire on contemporary American values revolves around children. This most precious resource, the story suggests, is nothing more than a valuable commodity; like bonds or gold; the baby is no more than a possession. The story satirizes this view of children by making the childless thieves desperate for a child to fill their empty lives. The Coen treatment is energetic and filled with action. Car chases, robberies, and explosions occur with startling frequency around the baby, pointing us toward the question of the value of children in today's society.

The mixing of the adventure and satire genres works in *Raising Arizona* because of the freedom inherent in both genres. Anything goes. There are few restrictions on protagonist–antagonist interaction, except that in both genres, it tends to be intense, active, and frequent. Pace, energy, and comic aggression are key to mixing these two genres. The Coens fulfill that requirement, and the result is a fresh, funny, and touching film about family values in the 1980s.

We have suggested that writers can work against genre expectations by challenging the motifs of particular genres or by mixing two genres to tell their story. In either case, the result is an unexpected and often more energized view of what could otherwise have been a formulaic story.

■ ■ ■   **A Case Study of Failed Mixed Genres: *Basic Instinct***

Mixing the police story and film noir can work effectively, as in *The Fugitive*, but the mixture fails in *Basic Instinct*. The reasons for this failure provide important lessons for aspiring screenwriters.

Joe Eszterhas's *Basic Instinct* tells the story of Nick Curran (Michael Douglas), a San Francisco detective with a troubled past. He has been drug- and alcohol-dependent, and he has killed bystanders in the line of duty. The plot unfolds when a woman kills a rock star with an ice pick during intercourse. The woman suspected of the murder, Catherine Trammell (Sharon Stone), is a novelist whose last book included a scene about killing a rock star with an ice pick. She also seems to know a lot about Nick; we soon find out that he is the research for her next book.

The police story proceeds along the lines of a criminal investigation. For half the story, Catherine is the primary suspect. But at one point in the investigation, suspicion shifts to someone trying to frame her. That person increasingly seems to be Beth, the police psychologist (Jeanne Tripplehorn), who knew Catherine when both were psychology students at Berkeley. Catherine's bisexuality alludes to an affair between them, an affair that led to the death of Catherine's faculty advisor. The instrument of death was an ice pick. As the film draws to a close, Beth is apprehended and then shot after having killed Gus, Nick's partner. The original crime seems solved, as does the older crime, as Beth's actions imply she is the killer.

The film noir dimension of *Basic Instinct* unfolds through Nick's fascination with Catherine. She knows a great deal about him, and he is provoked by her taunting him about his past—his wife's suicide, his drug and alcohol abuse, and his penchant for masochistic sex. The fact that Catherine seems more interested in him as research is compounded by her narcissistic excitement and her desire for women, specifically her lesbian lover Roxy (and earlier, Beth). His is a true "noir" love in that he is driven by passion and excluded from a permanent relationship by implication. Catherine is absolved of the opening murder, and the story ends with her and Nick in bed. She prepares him for sadomasochistic sex, and the film ends as she reaches for an ice pick.

Beyond the lack of credibility in the plot (it is hard to believe that Beth is the killer), it is difficult to believe that an investigation by the Internal Affairs Department could be conducted with such a dearth of intelligence. The police story fails, because the red herring of Catherine as the false antagonist is at odds with her role in the film noir story, her role as the true antagonist. Which brings us to Nick Curran. We have a contradiction in our expectations of Nick in the police story and in the film noir. In the police story, he is the hero who solves the crime. Yet in the film noir, we expect him to be the victim of the antagonist. We are faced, then, with a character who has to be both hero and victim, two roles that are at best difficult to reconcile. Coupled with the complication of an antagonist who is the antagonist in the film noir but a false antagonist in the police story, we have a situation of dramatic incongruity. Joe Eszterhas is a clever screenwriter, but he is not a magician. The result is the use of irreconcilable deployments of the protagonist and the antagonist in each of the two genres. The resulting loss of credibility is understandable, and the result is a failed screenplay.

■ ■ ■   ## A Case Study of Changing Motifs and Mixing Genres: *Crimes and Misdemeanors*

Woody Allen's *Crimes and Misdemeanors* is a remarkable example of audacious storytelling. Allen tells two independent stories linked by a single character, a rabbi, and an idea that morality is both relative and relatively elusive in our modern urban world. It is a complex enough challenge to combine two stories in one film; it becomes even more complex when the two stories are presented in different narrative forms—a straight melodrama and a situation comedy. Allen then goes one step further and decides that within each story—the melodrama and the situation comedy—he will challenge the most important motif—the fate of the protagonist.

The melodrama is the story of ophthalmologist Judah Rosenthal (Martin Landau), a man whose mistress threatens to ruin him unless he leaves his wife. Judah relies on two people with whom he shares this pending disaster. One person is a patient, a rabbi, who, in spite of going blind, is optimistic and encouraging to Judah. The other is his brother, a small-time hoodlum, who suggests that the only way to deal with the situation is for Judah to get his mistress out of his life permanently. How Judah deals with this personal crisis is the story line of the melodrama.

Judah's sense of immorality and his anxiety are central to the decision he makes and the range of feelings he experiences once the decision is made.

The situation comedy follows the efforts of Cliff (Woody Allen) to sustain his integrity in the face of a career during which he has experienced limited success and a marriage that has been a total disaster. Cliff makes documentary films and is currently working on a film about Professor Levi (a character based on Primo Levi, the writer and Auschwitz survivor), a concentration camp survivor who postulates on the meaning of love and morality in modern life. Enter his brother-in-law (Alan Alda), a successful television producer. To appease his sister, Alan Alda's character offers Cliff a job making a documentary about himself. Cliff fools himself into thinking that he's taking the job for the money. He hates everything his brother-in-law stands for. In Cliff's mind, you can't have both wealth and integrity. Naturally the story line displays his ambivalence.

The documentary on his brother-in-law brings about a crisis, both professional and personal. While making the film about his brother-in-law, Cliff meets an associate producer, Hallie (Mia Farrow), with whom he falls hopelessly in love. He also botches the film. In the end, Cliff loses both the film and the relationship with Hallie. Not even Professor Levi can help Cliff overcome the cesspool of materialism that swirls about him. The professor inexplicably kills himself, thus ending the film project that would have at least provided Cliff with some integrity.

Cliff's moral position is vulnerable on every level, and he is left perplexed and saddened by the various outcomes—all of which are bad. In rereading this description, it doesn't sound very funny, but the story line of all situation comedies might be tragic from a different point of view. As Alan Alda's character says, his definition of comedy is tragedy plus time. So, too, is the situation comedy about Cliff tragic. The melodrama in *Crimes and Misdemeanors* is about recognizable people in a power struggle. Judah's melodrama story, on the contrary, reflects the most important power struggle of the 1980s, the battle of the sexes. In *Crimes and Misdemeanors*, the melodrama and situation comedy genres work to complement each other. There are points where the differences add a level of tension, a dissonant chord, that surprises us and helps move the story beyond our genre expectations.

In terms of character, the central character in each story is recognizable—the ambitious Judah Rosenthal and the idealistic Cliff. Each character is ambivalent and has an interior conflict about his value system. Each wants to be perceived as a success, but each carries a family history. Judah has a religious background. His father's words continually resonate, "The eyes of God are on us always." To find his way, Judah becomes an ophthalmologist, but (according to his father) he is always losing his way. Cliff has a history of failed relationships. Both he and his sister share this penchant and its implications, and they both fail in life.

The two stories are also similar in the types of conflict that prompt their respective crises. In both cases, the source of the conflict is a woman—Judah's mistress or, in Cliff's case, a wished-for mistress. Both characters desperately deal with these two women. In each case, the character convinces others to aid him in his struggle.

Judah uses his brother; Cliff uses Professor Levi. In each case, the struggle unleashes an intense, almost desperate attempt to cope with the resulting events.

The two stories differ primarily in their resolutions. Woody Allen twists each tale away from the genre convention. Melodrama usually ends in the tragedy of the thwarted ambition of the central character—the execution of Montgomery Clift's character in *A Place in the Sun*, the absence of the mother from her daughter's wedding at the end of *Stella Dallas*. This is not the case with Judah Rosenthal. Although a party to murder, he is not arrested, nor will he be absent from his daughter's wedding. Judah is scot-free and has freed himself from his anxiety and guilt as well.

In the situation comedy, the main character usually finds success in the end: Jack Lemmon loses his job but gets the girl at the end of *The Apartment*, and James Garner gets the girl (or boy, depending on your interpretation) at the end of *Victor, Victoria*. No such luck for Cliff. His resolution is closer to that found in melodrama. Cliff loses everything—his wife, the girl of his dreams, the film he didn't want to make (about his brother-in-law), and the film he wanted to make (about Professor Levi). Cliff, the man who is interested in ideals, ends up power-less, and Judah, the man who is interested in power, ends up with even greater power. The mix works in this case because of the proximity of the two genres. Situation comedy is the flip side of melodrama. Film noir and the screwball comedy are also mirror images of each other. Consequently, a film like *Something Wild* has a greater likelihood of working than does a film that uses wildly different genres—the horror-comedy *An American Werewolf in London*, for example. It is easier to succeed with genres that share basic qualities.

In *Crimes and Misdemeanors*, Allen poses numerous narrative challenges for himself and his audience. By telling two different stories, by using two differ-ent genres, and by twisting genre characteristics within each story, he creates a modern parable. What is the nature and role of love and morality in our lives? Allen's meditation is structured, formal, rather than alluded to as an afterthought or aside. He doesn't use the classic qualities of an empathetic main character or a monstrous antagonist. He confidently proceeds to tell two stories, using two genres, and allows us to ponder the questions in our lives.

Conclusion

It is critical for the writer to understand genres in order to write mixed-genre screenplays. Clearly, writing against genre has become the crossword puzzle of the screenwriter—difficult but addictive. Know your genres and you will be able to work against them; you'll be able to move beyond formula into other interesting and energetic options. Mixing genres offers the writer much in the way of narrative opportunities—surprise and novelty at the very least. But there is also the option of layering the story in new and interesting ways. Just as challenging a genre motif alters our experience of the screen story, the mixing of genres can undermine our expectations and provide new dimensions to old stories to entice the fickle film audience.

The examples mentioned in this chapter only scratch the surface of mixed-genre screenplays. Hence, many of the big films released in the early 1990s were mixed-genre films—*Dick Tracy, Die Hard II, Total Recall, The Fugitive, Schindler's List*—that mixed-genre stories may now be viewed as the standard, and genre stories may be the exception.

Reference

1. D. Trumbo. Screenplay for the film, *Lonely Are the Brave* (Universal Pictures, 1962).

12

The Flexibility of Genre

Genre characterizations, both academic and not, conjure up a singular look and feel to the genre film. A Western has a moral main character and the antagonist has an immoral character. They settle their conflict violently against a backdrop of beautiful vast open spaces.

The gangster film has an urban setting that makes the gangster's struggle modern. But the means of conflict resolution remain violent.

These characteristics are accurate but limiting. Genre has always been flexible, pliant to creative reinterpretation as well as the audience's insatiable craving for novelty. Although we will use specific genres to illustrate genre flexibility, it might be useful to contextualize the range of flexibility, by looking at two particular storytellers who in their work not only capture the advantages of genre film, but also seek their own imprint on those films.

Quentin Tarantino, Genre Riffs

Quentin Tarantino has made a career by adapting a particular genre and playing with the form. Two striking examples make my point. *Pulp Fiction* (1994) is a gangster film, albeit an unusual one.

The gangster film tends to proceed in a straight line from the beginning of the gangster's career to its bloody end. The gangster's rise from obscurity to his precipitous fall is the plot of the gangster film. The characterization is equally particular. The gangster is a recent immigrant with strong roots in family. He wants the good life for his family and his career as a gangster is the means of access to the good life.

In *Pulp Fiction*, Tarantino abandons a linear structure and frames three episodes, short films rearranged to present out of a time chronology. He organizes the three episodes around a robbery that bookends the entire film. At the end, we realize the robbery takes place before the three short episodes occur. Neither the frame nor the three episodes bring logic and linearity to the overall screen story.

The first story introduces us to two hit men en route to their work, the killing of an outlier client and his team. The tone of the episode is garrulous, funny, and when the violence is unleashed, it's shocking given the humorous exchange between the two hit men. Tonal variance from the classic gangster film masks the violence *Pulp Fiction* shares with *Scarface* and other classic gangster films.

Comedy and violence characterize the second and third episodes of *Pulp Fiction*. The third episode drifts away from the classic in its philosophical musings about remaining in the profession. Here the dialogue aims for something much deeper than its use in the first episode. Tarantino in both cases has used and overused dialogue to replace the action we expect in the gangster film.

In *Inglorious Basterds* (2009), Tarantino is using the war film as the basis for his riff. In the war film, a main character, usually a soldier, tries to survive. The plot may be a battle or an incident. Opinion about war and its influence on human behavior, articulates the voice of the writer and/or director on the issue of war. The tone tends to the realistic.

In *Inglorious Basterds*, the tone ranges from the realistic (Chapter 1) to the absurd (the killings of the Nazi hierarchy in the theater). What is at stake in war? Is it life itself? Is it adventure? Perhaps is it all about personal survival as opposed to belief? Perhaps. Tarantino is making a war film and at the same time deconstructing its motifs and satirizing them. As a result, there are no real heroes, villains are more interesting than heroes, and revenge trumps all other human values. This leaves us thinking about the war film just as *Pulp Fiction* left us thinking about the gangster film. It's as if Tarantino wants us to believe that there is both more and less to genre than critics would have us believe. In any case, his films do illustrate the pliant characteristics of genre.

Billy Wilder and the Dramedy

Bill Wilder is best known for having made *Some Like It Hot* (1958), one of the greatest farcical Situation Comedies and *Sunset Boulevard* (1950), one of the most realistic film noirs. He also made hybrid genre films, too dark to be described as a melodrama. Recently, these hybrid films have come to be called dramedies. Dramedies in their nature are useful examples of how elasticity in the narrative events and tone push a genre in the direction of a different, opposite genre.

Billy Wilder's most celebrated dramedy is *The Apartment* (1960). C.C. Baxter, an insurance company employee, wants to advance up the corporate ladder and so he lends his apartment out for trysts to his superiors. He is ambitious but lonely.

He does move up the corporate ladder and is heartened to pursue the elevator girl at work. He asks her for a date. She never shows up because she is having an affair in his apartment with his boss. On Christmas day, she attempts suicide in his apartment. All will work out for C.C. Baxter in the end but the journey is about how much is lost when ambition displaces humanity as a way of life. Serious theme! Serious film and yet everything works out, except for his boss.

In *Avanti*, (1972), a corporate executive flies to Italy to bring back his father's body for proper burial in the United States. There on an island in the Mediterranean, he discovers that his father has been coming to a resort for 20 years, to carry on an affair with another woman. He meets the woman's daughter who has come to Iscia to recover her mother's body. It seems the lovers chose to die together. The narrative highlights how the uptight "moral" main character, initially horrified by his father's behavior, falls for the daughter who is anything but uptight. In the end, the main character and his new lover decide to bury the dead couple on Iscia and to carry on annually in their parents' tradition. The film ends with their vows to meet next year in Iscia.

In *Avanti* as in *The Apartment* serious, even tragic events, suicide, infidelity mix with true love and values that transcend social convention. The dramedy typically navigates the space between the comedic and the dramatic.

We turn now to specific classic genres to illustrate ongoing flexibility and the narrative purposes served by that flexibility.

The Heist Film

The heist film is a more specific subset of the gangster film. If the gangster film follows the rise and fall of the career of the gangster, the heist film focuses on that job, late in the gangster's career, that precipitates the fall. The heist itself can be seen as the final attempt to secure the benefits of crime, money or fame, whether the main character-gangster has been a success or never been. The degree of desperation in the narrative relates to the former status of the main character. The narrative itself will focus on the gathering of a gang or team to carry out the heist, the heist itself and the consequences of the heist. Generally, the difficulty of the heist will illustrate the skills of the main character and his team, or the lack thereof. Just as in the case of the gangster film, relational dimensions—family, father–son, love— will elaborate the emotional stakes attached to the meaning of the heist.

The classic heist film is best represented by John Huston's *The Asphalt Jungle* (1950). Robert Siodmak's *Criss Cross* (1948) and Robert Wise's *Odds Against Tomorrow* (1958) are equally powerful although *Criss Cross* veers toward film noir, using the femme fatale as the source of the main character's fall, whereas racism within the gang is the source of the main character's fall in *Odds Against Tomorrow*.

In *Asphalt Jungle*, the release from prison of Doc Riedenschneider (Sam Jaffe) kicks off the plot, the plan to rob a jewelry store. This heist promises great reward. This will be his last job, but he needs a gang and he needs finance. He finds both but his financier is a desperate "respectable" man (Louis Calhern) and plans to rob Doc once he has successfully robbed the jewelry store. The main character is Dix Handley, a hooligan who is honorable and is looking to use his share to buy back the family farm in Kentucky. His problem is he's a compulsive gambler and consequently is always in debt.

The robbery succeeds with one member shot and dying (the explosives expert). Dix is shot by the "respectable" man's hooligan. Doc is captured by the police, having admired a teenager dance to the jukebox he has been supplying with coins. He simply was too admiring of the young girl and so delayed leaving. Dix dies having reached his family's former farm in Kentucky. Although the heist has succeeded, all its participants have failed. This is the classic narrative structure for the heist film.

The heist film has lent itself to shifts in tone. At one extreme it has been the basis for numerous comedic treatments from *The Lavender Hill Mob* (1951) to the darker *The Ladykillers* (1955) to *A Fish called Wanda* (1988). It's not that the thieves get away with the material benefits of the heist. They don't. But in each of these cases, it's the characters who undo themselves rather than the abilities of law enforcement.

More believable in tone but more upbeat in outcome are films such as *Robbery* (1967), *The Italian Job* (1969), and *The Bank Job* (2008). Here, the heist gangs are at a distinct advantage. They succeed, but not all the members of the gang survive.

Mixing the comic and realist impulse in the heist film, we have the enormously popular *Oceans 11* series made by Steven Soderbergh. Gang members do survive and manage to overcome a powerful antagonist, the head of the casino to be robbed. The skills of all parties are foregrounded. The heist is as elaborate as the Jules Dassin heist films *Riffifi* (1955) and *Topkapi* (1963). Tonally, *Topkapi* is similar to *Oceans 11*. It's a fun take on a genre that in its classic form tends to the dark side.

Although the central features of the heist film putting together the gang, the difficult challenge of the robbery itself, and the outcome of the robbery for the participants are all a presence in all the above mentioned, there are differences. Those differences are essentially tonal; they focus on the nature of the relationships within the gang (loyalty vs. rivalry), motivations for the robbery, and variations in the outcome—negative being the expected, positive being the exception.

In tonal terms, writers such as Ben Maddow and John Huston in *Asphalt Jungle* and Walter Hill and Jim Thompson in *The Getaway* (1972) have given their films an existential layer embedded in the desperation of their main characters. Charles Crichton had no such ambitions in *A Fish called Wanda* or in *The Lavender Hill Mob*. That very range within the heist film best illustrates its flexibility as a genre.

The Thriller

In the current chapter in this book entitled "Working with Genre II: The melodrama and the thriller," I write about the thriller without focusing on its flexibility. It's useful for this chapter to briefly illustrate how very flexible this popular genre is.

Within the thriller category, there are three subcategories—the personal thriller, the political thriller, and the psychological thriller. *The Hand that Rocks the Cradle* (1992) and *Breakdown* (1997) are personal thrillers. *Air Force One* (1997) and *Arlington Road* (1999) are political thrillers while *Repulsion* (1965) and *The Vanishing* (1988), Dutch version are psychological thrillers.

Both the personal thriller and the political thriller lend themselves to tonal variance while the psychological thriller much less so. Consequently, a lighter approach to the political thriller is exemplified by *Air Force One*. Serious events occur, people are killed, but the president prevails over his kidnappers, is heroic, and saves the world from the next calamity. If this sounds like an Action-Adventure approach, it's because it is.

Arlington Road on the other hand proceeds as a cautionary tale about home-grown terrorists. The main character dies, the terrorists are victorious, unusual in the political thriller.

In the personal thriller films such as *The Firm* (1993) and *The Pelican Brief* (1993) exemplify the earnest but ultimately successful main character's effort to thwart powerful antagonists. These films represent the classic approach to the personal thriller. *North by Northwest* (1950) on the other hand represents an altogether lighter approach. At no point do we feel the main character played by Cary Grant is under threat. And his being put out by being mistaken for a spy is played as pique rather than anxiety or fear. Nor are the antagonists all that menacing. They are very much in keeping with the tongue-in-cheek quality of the rest of the film.

Reindeer Games (2000), written by Ehren Krueger, the screenwriter of *Arlington Road* is a dark personal thriller. A prison parolee (Ben Affleck) takes on the identity of a fellow prisoner who is killed in prison. On the outside, his new identity makes him a "prisoner" again. He is expected to help a group of criminal types rob a casino. Danger, betrayal, death awaits all. He escapes with his life but the question is about how untrustworthy and dangerous a road life really is.

The Science Fiction Film

At its heart, the science fiction film is an optimistic take on the struggle of Humanity vs. Technology. The mad scientist of *Forbidden Planet* (1955) has been replaced by the products of technology who can be malevolent (*The Matrix*, 1999), benevolent (*The Rise of the Planet of the Apes*, 2010) or both (*Terminator 2*, 1991). Nevertheless, the core struggle in the science fiction film remains constant. Differences reside in tonal choices that imply the range from optimistic to pessimistic about the future and it's here that the greatest flexibility is exercised in the varied treatments of the theme that unites the genre. One complication to that thematic treatment is the presence of an inexplicable greater force, a reference to religion that is a presence in some but not all science fiction films. It is certainly central in *2001: A Space Odyssey* (1967) and in *The Matrix*.

Turning to the tonal treatments of character and plot in the genre, it's best to use a film such as *Gattaca* (1997) as a baseline, representing a more realistic or humanistic treatment of the central theme.

Vincent Freeman's (Ethan Hawke) blood test at birth suggests imperfection. He is likely to die of heart disease by age thirty. His brother Anton, genetically altered, is perfect and consequently privileged just as Vincent is destined to scrape by in life. But Vincent has willpower and he decides to "reach for the stars"; to become an astronaut. With the help of the perfect Jerome's (Jude Law) blood he will try to pass as perfect. Jerome, a paraplegic, has the blood but not the will for perfection. Vincent's success in *Gattaca* is about the triumph of will over science. The narrative treatment embraces Vincent's humanity as it triumphs over the human flaws in Jerome and Anton. *Gattaca* is realistic in its treatment of emotional complexity as the x factor that trumps the y factor in genetics.

Taking an emotionally lively but more optimistic take on "character" in humans and non-humans, *Star Trek* (2009) presents the young James Kirk, a cadet, immature and overshadowed by his father. Can he fulfill his potential and become the Captain Kirk and Admiral Kirk, of his later life? The answer is with the help of the non-human Spock struggling to deal with emotion, the overemotional Kirk, will succeed.

J. J. Abrams, the director uses an Action-Adventure plot that compliments the humanness of both Kirk and Spock. Relative to Andrew Niccols' *Gattaca*, where plot is not an equal partner in the narrative, *Star Trek* overflows with emotion as well as the excitement of plot. The lighter treatment makes *Star Trek* far more accessible to a wider audience than does the more realistic *Gattaca*.

A third tonal option, to go dark, is best illustrated by the Ridley Scott film *Blade Runner* (1982). Deckard (Harrison Ford) is a blade runner. He tracks down replicants (technologically created nonhuman workers). They run away because they begin to exhibit human traits. Deckard is cynical but effective. The replicants want to extend their fixed short-term lives (the human equivalent of hubris). If they can reach Dr. Tyrell, the head of the Tyrell Corporation that created them, they believe they can extend their lives. Deckard's job is to recognize the replicants (they look human) and destroy them. In doing so, however, he is losing his own humanity.

The complication for Deckard in *Blade Runner* is that he falls in love with Rachael (Sean Young) the most advanced version of the replicant. She too is destined for a short life (5 years). Will Deckard accept her fate and the fate of their relationship or not?

Blade Runner is a darker vision of the technology vs. humanity struggle. It's as if humanity is not enough to overcome the predictable mortality of the replicants, the most advanced products of technology.

The War Film

The war film is a genre that also exhibits a wide tonal range. Essentially, this story form focuses on the struggle of a character, civilian or military, caught in war. Will the character survive? Conversely, there are war films that pose the question, is there a war event or another person caught up in war, worth dying for? war films, particularly those made during a war, may take a patriotic position or an anti-war stance. This too becomes a motif in the war film. Another dimension, part of the advocacy of the war vs. the antagonism toward the war, drills down on the horror factor involved in combat. The physical as well as the psychological aspects of that horror also become elements in the narrative content of the war film.

One tonal category of the genre hones very close to the Adventure film. Here the main character and his comrades are heroes and in a cartoon-like sense, the enemy is disposable but not very challenging villains. Within this group there are comedic treatments of the narrative (*Kelly's Heroes*, 1970) and there are straightforward treatments for the narrative (*Where Eagles Dare*, 1968, and *The Guns of Navarone*, 1961). Although a writer such as Carl Foreman in *The Guns of Navarone*, injects speeches that are anti-war, what remains memorable in this film are the heroic characters and the exciting plot. As a group, these films are enjoyable enactments of the most positive qualities of men in war—bravery, camaraderie, decency. The dark exists elsewhere. The best modern representation of this kind of war film is David O. Russell's *Three Kings* (1999), set in the first Gulf war.

At the opposite extreme, there is the war film that focuses upon the overwhelming horror of war. Whether the focus is on the physical horror (*Letters from Iwo Jima*, 2006, *Come and See*, 1985, or *Full Metal Jacket*, 1987), the intensity of these film experiences is the opposite of the entertaining adventurous, enjoyable aspects of the former group of war films. Quite the contrary, this narrative style focuses on the waste, the destruction, the dehumanization of war. What should also be mentioned is that they take the critique of war to a level far beyond the literary anti-war message of *All Quiet on the Western Front* (1930) and *La Grande Illusion* (1937). These films have a more visceral quality, ill-making as an antidote to the condition.

These dark interpretations are marked by graphic representations of killing and dying as well as endless amounts of cruelty and violence. Every heroic idea the viewer ever had about war is attacked, liquidated. These films represent war showing its ugliest face.

In between the romantic and the grotesque tonal options, there is a realistic option. Early versions of this style include *Attack* (1956) and *Too Late the Hero* (1970), both from Robert Aldrich, *Hell is for Heroes* (1962) from Don Siegel and *Saving Private Ryan* (1998) from Steven Spielberg.

Here the focus is on neither glorifying nor criticizing war. These films portray human behavior under conditions of war. In each of these films camaraderie, cowardice, bravery is on full display. The best and the worst of human behavior pours out under the pressure of combat. None of these films flinch from the violence of war or from the horrible representations of maiming and dying in battle. These films chronicle rather than editorialize. In their ways they have great narrative power.

Key here is that in their tonal variations each group presents a very different experience for their audience. No genre better illustrates the flexibility and the results of that flexibility within a genre than the war film.

The Romantic Comedy

On its surface the romantic comedy would seem the most straightforward of genres, a genre where two opposites meet, repel each other, attract each other, concluding with their getting together. In the past, national differences, class differences were the sources of comedy. More recently the romantic comedy has been subject to considerable exploration to make these differences both more modern as well as more realistic.

As a result recent romantic comedies have explored the romance of two misfits, the romance between two men or two women as well as the romance between two characters whose psychological profiles make them more suitable for darker genre treatments. In short, the romantic comedy has become the epitome of flexibility.

The classic romantic comedy from the director whose career focus was the romantic comedy is *Ninotchka* (1939). Directed by Ernst Lubitsch, co-written by Billy Wilder, *Ninotchka* set in Paris, is the story of the romance between an austere Communist (Greta Garbo) and a hedonistic Capitalist (Melvyn Douglas). Not even their deeply held opposing beliefs can trump biology.

Judd Apatow's *Knocked Up* (2007) is a long way from Lubitsch. Lubitsch explored complex behavioral questions in his romantic comedies—is nonconformity an opportunity or a barrier to romance? (*Design for Living*, 1933). Is profession an opportunity or a barrier to romance? (*Trouble in Paradise*, 1932). What is more important to romance—public ambitions or secret desires? (*Shop around the Corner*, 1940). Apatow is more interested in making his romantic couple opposites and psychologically ill-suited. As a result in films such as *Knocked Up* (2007), the Apatow produced *Forgetting Sarah Marshall* (2008) and *I Love You, Man* (2009), he is exploring the less attractive features of men. In *Knocked Up*, an immature stoner, Ben (Seth Rogen) has a one-night stand with a drunken beauty, Allison (Katherine Heigl). Her consequent pregnancy poses the questions—what will she do? What will he do? And the larger question—Can such a refined beautiful young woman fall for a slob? He changes and so does she.

In *Forgetting Sarah Marshall*, it's the vulnerability of the male that is the barrier. At the beginning of the narrative the main character, Peter (Jason Segel) is abandoned by his famous girlfriend, Sarah Marshall (Kristen Bell). He falls apart, follows her to Hawaii, and there finds Rachel (Mila Kunis). She too is vulnerable. Nevertheless, these two wounded people eventually get together.

In *I Love You, Man* the romantic story is between two men. Peter (Paul Rudd) is engaged but friendless. He has a "female" side. He likes to hang out with his fiancée and be one of the girls. Who will be his best man at the wedding? He sets out to find a friend and he does. Sydney (Jason Segel) is a man's man. The rest of the narrative is their on–off relationship. The film ends with the two men embracing at Peter's wedding.

All three of these Apatow productions focus on male behavior—immature, insecure, gender blurring. By doing so, Apatow has enlarged the palate for the romantic comedy, making it more modern and more psychologically complex.

Other examples of flexibility include *500 Days of Summer* (2009), a film about the most romantic guy (Joseph Gordon-Levitt) falls for a young woman (Zooey Deschanel) who doesn't believe in love. Needless to say the relationship fails based on ideological incompatibility. At the opposite extreme is *Enchanted* (2007) where a New York divorce lawyer (Patrick Dempsey) who no longer believes in love falls for a fairy princess (Amy Adams) who is banished from her fantasyland to New York. She of course believes in love. The results are as you would expect in a Disney production.

The Biography Film

The biography film focuses upon a famous person. Whether the person is a scientist or a soldier, the task of the writer is to humanize a revered or reviled figure. This means the plot will focus on what made them famous while the character layer, the relational story, will humanize and emotionalize our relationship with the character. The 1930s were the classic period for the biography film, with the Warner Brothers Studio as the creative home for these films. Emile Zola, Louis Pasteur, Dr. Ehrlich, Juarez, all were subjects. More recently Gandhi, T. E. Lawrence, Jackson Pollack have been the basis for biography films. Generally, these films have been admiring of their subjects.

The genre has been stretched by the exploration of the weaknesses, flaws, and indeed the underside of characters that have captured the public imagination. It's here within the darker interpretations that different tonal treatments, less romanticized, have yielded a very different style of biography film. They also demonstrate that tonal variation yields useful options for the biography film.

When the classic biography adopts the melodrama option positioning the main character as a powerless character seeking power (or acknowledgement) from the power structure, the plot is the vehicle or means to make the main character heroic. Where the main character is less admirable, he or she needs to be surrounded by a character population that is even less admirable. Irony, humor, and exaggerations can push such a group of characters away from heroism toward satire. In short, distance us or provide enough distance from the main character to judge him rather than feel sorry for him.

The Hoax (2007) directed by Lasse Hallstrom and written by William Wheeler, is about Clifford Irving, the writer who in the 1970s claimed to be the official biographer of Howard Hughes. After release from prison he wrote *The Hoax*, a biography of his literary hoax.

Clifford Irving (Richard Gere), a modestly successful writer, loses a promised contract from McGraw-Hill, the publisher, as the story opens. Simultaneously his furniture is being repossessed and his marriage is as shaky as his finances. He needs a home run to solve his situation and to solve his ambition. He comes up with the idea of a biography of one of the world's richest men, Howard Hughes. The fact that Hughes is a recluse, in hiding from a damaging lawsuit, is an encouragement.

The narrative is a cliffhanger. Can this disreputable almost-been of a writer pull off this high wire hoax? He almost does. Wheeler, the writer creates a view of publishers and publishing that is far more greedy and manipulative than Clifford Irving. He also uses Clifford's co-writer, Richard (Alfred Molina) for humor. The surrounding character population, even those who help Irving—his mistress Nina (Julie Delpy), his wife Edith (Marcia Gay Harden), and Noah Dietrich (Eli Wallach), an associate of Hughes—are callow and shallow. As a consequence, the tone of *The Hoax* is smart and ironic. Wheeler and Hallstrom push the narrative toward a comment on the seventies. This is not quite as powerful as the portrait of Irving as a grandiose scoundrel. By making the character population even more grandiose and nasty, *The Hoax* becomes the anti-heroic biography film.

Another narrative strategy used to make the reprehensible main character of the biography film accessible is to use an on-screen narrator, a much more sympathetic character, as a guide. Both *The Last King of Scotland* (2006) and *The Devil's Double* (2011) use this strategy. In *The Last King of Scotland*, the subject is Idi Amin, the dictator of Uganda in the 1970s. His mass murder of his people scandalized the international community. The guide, Peter Morgan, the writer uses Amin's personal physician, Dr. Nicholas Garragan (James McAvoy). In *The Devil's Double* the subject is Uday Hussein, the murderous son of Saddam Hussein, the dictator of Iraq. The narrative guide is Latif, his double (Dominic Cooper). In both cases, there is considerable contrast between our guide and the biographical subject. Dr. Garragan is adventurous and engaged whereas Amin is primitive and given to impulsive action. Both characters have an appealing edge to them making each less than predictable. Uday Hussein and his double Latif are also opposites with Latif more conventionally good and Uday more conventionally evil. Uday is also impulsive, violent, and paranoid. He's dangerous in the same way Amin is dangerous. But Amin as played by Forest Whitaker has a sense of power that is not a presence in the Uday character.

There are also tonal differences between the two films. Kevin McDonald, the director of *The Last King of Scotland* opts for a sensuality that energizes both Amin and his doctor. When this sensuality links up with power, the violence in the film seems dangerous and unstable.

Lee Tamahori and his writer Michael Thomas opt to emphasize Uday's instability. He seems far more a comic character mired in unintelligence. The result is to trivialize Uday's acts of violence. As a result the narrative in general seems to shrink. These narrative choices have clear consequences for the impact of the overall narrative.

Other recent biography films that deploy the idea of an innocent narrator or guide include *The Last Station* (2009), focusing on Leo Tolstoy's last years; and *My Week with Marilyn*, a film about the making of *The Princess and the Showgirl* in England. In both films the narrator affords an easier entry into the complex subjects of these two biography films.

The Melodrama

Much attention will be given in a later chapter on melodrama. The focus here is on the classic treatment of melodrama. In this chapter, given our focus on the flexibility of genre, we will look to alternative treatments of the genre, treatments that change the mix of the narrative tools to yield a surprising experience that is no less true to the genre. To contextualize these "new" melodramas, an old melodrama will serve as a useful referent point.

A Place in the Sun (1951) directed by George Steven, written by Michael Wilson and Harry Brown, is based on the Theodore Dreiser 1920s novel, *An American Tragedy*. George Eastman (Montgomery Clift) travels east to take a job at his rich uncle's factory. He is uneducated but wants to move ahead. At the factory, he falls for a co-worker, Alice Tripp (Shelley Winters). He gets her pregnant. At a party at his uncle's house, a rich beauty, Angela Vickers (Elizabeth Taylor) falls in love with him.

He chooses to be with Angela. But to do so he chooses to get rid of Alice. He takes her out on a boat to drown her, but he can't do it. Afraid, she stands up and falls from the boat. She drowns. He is brought to trial for the drowning. He is found guilty and at the end of the narrative he is executed.

Given that he only thought to kill Alice but didn't actually kill her, he is executed for his intentions rather than his actions. Another interpretation is that by choosing Angel over Alice, he has expressed his desire to get ahead and he is punished in the end for that desire. *A Place in the Sun* is in every sense the classical melodrama—a struggle for power whose result in this case, is tragic.

Fatih Akin's *The Edge of Heaven* (2008) alters the structure of the narrative, but it too at its heart is a struggle for power ending with tragic results.

Akin divides the narrative into three chapters, titled *Yeter's Death*, *Lotte's Death*, and *The Edge of Heaven*. Two stories focus on a relationship that ends in death. The third story focuses on the forgiveness/acceptance of one generation for the behavior of the elder in one case, and of the younger in another.

The character population divides into three families, two Turkish and one German. In each case, there is a single parent of the same gender. The three younger characters are the main characters. Each shares the premise— am I traditional or am I modern? If I am traditional, I am intolerant; if I am modern, I am tolerant. Tolerance means acceptance across religious, cultural, and gender lines.

Yeter's Death focuses on the relationship of two Turks living in Germany. Yeter is a prostitute. Ali Aksu is retired. He has a son Najat, a professor of German. Nejat is one of the main characters. Ali asks Yeter to live with him, be his exclusively. Harrassed by two religious Muslims, Yeter sees Ali's offer as an escape from them. But Ali becomes possessive. When he has a heart attack he fears his son has slept with Yeter. He hits Yeter. She dies. Ali is deported back to Turkey.

Lotte's Death focuses on Yeter's daughter, Ayten. A radical in Turkey, Ayten is jailed. Before imprisonment she hides a pistol. Intimidated, Ayten names names and is released. She goes to Germany as an illegal. There she can't get on with the radical men who are her fellow radicals. She looks for her mother (who had said she worked selling shoes in Bremen). Not finding her, she meets Lotte at the university. They begin a relationship. Lotte, very liberal, invites Ayten to live with her. But Lotte's mother, Susanne, doesn't approve. They are picked up by the authorities who discover Ayten is an illegal. When Ayten is deported to Turkey, Lotte follows. At a prison visit in Turkey, Ayten alerts Lotte to the danger of the gun. She asks Lotte to retrieve the gun. She does, but her bag carrying the gun is stolen by street kids. One of them uses the gun, shooting Lotte. This ends with Lotte's body being returned to Germany.

The Edge of Heaven focuses on Nejat who has never forgiven his father. He goes to Istanbul to find Ayten. He wants to pay for her schooling. He doesn't find her. He buys a German bookshop and stays.

Suzanne, Lotte's mother, remorseful, comes to Istanbul to try to secure Ayten's freedom. She rents a room from Nejat. She visits Ayten. Her behavior moves Nejat. The film ends with his journey to reconcile with his father.

Each of the main characters is forced to deal with their anger with their parents. It's the parents who seem to be imprisoned by the values of tradition. It's the older generation—Yeter, Ali, and Susanne who suffer the tragedies that emanate from their rigid beliefs.

The question for Charlotte, Ayten, and Nejat is whether they wish to replicate their parents' rigidity. Each is angry and yet in the end each must find a way to forgive. Nejat must forgive his father, Ayten must forgive Susanne, and by doing so, forgive her own mother. Lotte and Yeter are the casualties of the violence that is at the center of traditional male values. They have consequences for women. They also have consequences for the men. Nejat chooses to be a modern man and to forgive his traditional father.

By using multiple main characters and a structure that is essentially three short films each with its own dramatic arc, Akin has deepened the narrative map of his melodrama. Rather than making it about a young person in a "parental" power structure, or a Turk in a German world, Akin has created a layered melodrama. Because there is no clear antagonist and because the main characters don't necessarily struggle deeply as their own antagonists, Akin has allowed the more general notion that it's the world they live in that is antagonistic to its young.

Asghar Farhadi in his film *A Separation* (2011) seems equally capable of creating a large palate for his intimate story of two families in contemporary Teheran. As in *The Edge of Heaven*, the traditional vs. modern, the young vs. the old, the secular vs. the religious, the female vs. the male; allow for an enormous amount of conflict in *A Separation*.

The middle class family in *A Separation* has one child, a girl. Simin, the wife, wants to leave Iran for the sake of their daughter and her future. The husband, Nader, does not. He must stay to care for his elderly father, already beset by Alzheimer's disease. She files for divorce but is disallowed from taking their daughter abroad without Nader's permission. Stalemate.

The working class family enters the story. Razieh, the wife, a religious woman, has a young daughter and an unemployed husband. She takes a job to mind Nader's father. Its a very uncomfortable job as Razieh must wash and touch the old man in a manner forbidden to a religious woman.

A complication is Razieh's pregnancy. Should she have a child or an abortion given her economic situation? One day she goes to the doctor, leaving Nader's father tied to the bed. Nader finds his father in this state, argues, and shoves Razieh on her return. She is rushed to the hospital. She loses the baby. Her unemployed husband sues Nader for manslaughter. A judge will decide Nader's fate.

A negotiation between the two families around blood money results in a settlement that would bankrupt Nader but keep him from jail. At the last moment, the religious Razieh confesses the child didn't die from Nader's actions. He is relieved. Now the danger is that Razieh's husband in his desperation will kill her or himself. The narrative ends with Nader and Simin awaiting a judge's decision about which of them will have custody of their daughter, a decision the judge leaves to the daughter.

A Separation begins at a critical moment in the life of one family and ends at a crisis point in the lives of two families. Although each of the six members of each family is trying to act in the interest of their family, they can't seem to help the members of their family. Although the two men seem rigid or harsh in their personal actions, Farhadi does not position them as antagonists. The members of each family suffer, not from the same causes, they suffer from being unable to find a way out of their suffering.

Each action, keeping a sick parent at home, trying to find financial solvency for the family, trying to secure a future for one's child, is simply a goal. The fact that there is no resolution emanating from trying to secure that goal, seems to go to the core of what this melodrama is about. Farhadi could have called his film *No Way Out*, and it would seem appropriate.

These characters attempt as do all main characters in the melodrama to secure power to improve their lives. In doing so they fail. So far these characters share the fate of their fellow main characters in classic melodramas.

What is different about *A Separation* is that the power these characters seek seems beyond the family. None of these characters seem to be able to help one another. The family unit, generally presented as the power grid in films such as *Once Were Warriors* or *The Heiress* is not the power grid in *A Separation*. Power seems to reside in a judge, a policeman, an official beyond the family. The result in *A Separation* is no resolution for these characters. They are caught in a system where family members are powerless. For all their efforts, the character population in *A Separation* are left suspended in conflict. This unbearable situation, the idea that there is no resolution for these characters, leaves the audience of *A Separation* to ponder whether life for these two families is sustainable and if it is, at what cost. Farhadi has fashioned a melodrama without resolution and in doing so he has taken his audience into the hell that is life for these two families. But he has done so without losing his empathy for the members of these two families, a remarkable achievement.

13

●　●　●　●　●　●　●　●

Genres of Voice

Voice, the editorial opinion of the writer about the story he is writing, can be deeply embedded, masked within the genre, or it can be foregrounded, superseding all the narrative elements of the script. In this chapter, we focus upon those genres that, in effect, aid the foregrounding process, thereby highlighting voice above all other narrative intentions. Before proceeding to those genres, it's important to establish that all genres exhibit voice but that most storytellers exercise voice within the boundaries of genre expectations. For example, if we look at film noir, the genre is all about betrayal. A main character makes a poor relational choice, and instead of being saved by the relationship, he is destroyed by it. The transgressional plot, whether robbery or murder, is for the main character not a transgression but rather a measure of the love he feels for the woman who is to save him.

Looking at how different writers have treated film noir, it's clear that Billy Wilder, in his work with Raymond Chandler in *Double Indemnity* and Charles Brackett in *Sunset Boulevard*, has emphasized the romantic dimension of film noir. Consequently, both Walter Neff and Joe Gilles are tragic heroes; victims of love. Clifford Odets and Ernest Lehman in their film *Sweet Smell of Success* are far more cynical about their main character. Sydney Falco is needy and greedy and consequently his fate and the voice of the writers are far darker than is Wilder's take on film noir. What we are suggesting is that there is a range for voice, from romantic to cynical, in this particular genre, and writers operate within that range.

Another example strengthens the case for voice functioning within genre expectations. The melodrama is the genre of a powerless person trying to gain power from the power structure. The struggle can be interpreted from a psychological or sociological or political perspective. Alvin Sargent focuses on the psychological barriers in his family melodrama, *Ordinary People*, whereas Michael Wilson embraces the social barriers for his main character in *A Place in the Sun*. Bud Schulberg, on the contrary, looks at the politics or power relationships in his screenplay of *A Face in the Crowd*, as does Robert Rossen in his screenplay for *All the King's Men*. The only observation we would make about these important melodramas is that the Sargeant approach in *Ordinary People* enhances our identification with the main character, whereas the Schulberg and Rossen approaches, as impressive as they are, leave us watching powerful characters that are difficult if not impossible to empathize with. The consequence is that the Rossen and Schulberg films have a more pronounced voice than do the Wilson and Sargeant screenplays, and yet each is a melodrama. This pattern of variability of voice operates in the majority of genres. Thrillers can be light or comic, as in *North by Northwest*, or they can be dark, as in *Arlington Road*. Action-adventure can be childlike and playful, as in *Gunga Din*, or it can be philosophical and tentative, as in *Only Angels Have Wings*. And yet these works remain thrillers or action-adventure films. Genres tend to exhibit this sort of range when it comes to voice. There is, however, another group of genres that are all about voice, and it is to those genres that we now turn.

There are five genres of voice:

- The satire
- The fable
- The docudrama
- The experimental narrative
- The non-linear film

The non-linear film is sufficiently unusual that we will focus upon its characteristics in the following chapter. The other genres will be our focus in this chapter. Before addressing the properties of these genres, it's important to understand why they have become so important. As suggested in *Global Scriptwriting*,[1] storytellers in the past 25 years have become bolder about putting forth their ideas, and consequently, genres that emphasize voice have become more attractive. Whether this is a result of the shifting demographics for films, or a reflection of growth in the perceived power of the medium, or both, the upshot has been that a new generation of storytellers—Quentin Tarantino, Lynn Ramsey, Wong Kar-Wai, and Tom Tykwer—has embraced voice-oriented genres. The fact that voice-oriented genres foreground in a bold fashion the ideas of these new storytellers has in no small measure contributed to their importance.

For voice to be foregrounded, it's critical to avoid or even to void central features of the classical narrative approach, specifically the nature of our relationship with the main character. In the classic thriller, an ordinary person is caught in an extraordinary circumstance. Just as we wouldn't want to be a victim in real life, we have to hope and care that the main character in the thriller does not become a victim. Whether he becomes a hero for surviving the pursuit or not, we have to identify with the main character in the thriller. And we have to hope that the main character in the horror film survives, and we have to see ourselves in the powerless main character of the melodrama. Identification and empathy characterize our relationship with the main character in these classic genres. In voice-oriented genres, identification and empathy must be replaced with emotional distance. We can watch Lola run in *Run Lola Run*, but caring whether she reaches her destination and its implications is another matter. The main character in these genres is the vehicle for the story but not the emotional core. Consider for a moment how you feel about the pregnant sheriff in *Fargo*, the leader of the convict escapees (George Clooney) in *O Brother Where Art Thou*, and the male and female lovers in *In the Mood for Love*. The best capture on all these characters is that you are watching them rather than emotionally attaching to them. Whether through narrative exaggeration or deployment of irony, there is a gate surrounding these characters, a gate that keeps the audience outside of the character. This is the central feature of the voice-oriented genres.

Other features of voice-oriented genres include structural as well as tonal differences. Again, the most useful measure for comparison is the classical genre. If the thriller is principally plot-oriented and the melodrama is principally character-driven, with film noir representing the mix of plot and character layers, the voice-oriented genre is different. The fable, for example, has a surplus of plot, probably enough plot for two or three thrillers. And the experimental narrative, whether plot-oriented or character-driven, tends toward open-ended narratives (Acts I–III or Acts I–II) as opposed to the classic linear three-act structure. Structural variance is significant in the voice-oriented genre. So too is the tone.

Classic genres exhibit a consistent tone. The melodrama tends to be realistic. The action-adventure films tend to be enabling, suitable for wish fulfillment, just as film noir tends to be excessive and passionate and the horror film tends to be excessive and violent, as suits a nightmare-oriented genre. Voice-oriented genres can be singular, romantic, as in Wong Kar-Wai's *2046* or Tykwer's *The Princess and the Warrior*, or they can be variable, embracing more than a single tone, as in Kubrick's *Dr. Strangelove*, which is, in parts, realistic, romantic, and nightmarish. Variability of tone is always a potential presence in the voice-oriented genre, just as a consistent tone is characteristic of classic genres.

As we move to the examination of the individual voice-oriented genres, it's useful to reiterate the characteristics of the classic genre:

1. The use of goal-oriented main characters who are inviting to identify with, either through their nature and their goal or through the situation they find themselves in.
2. The deployment of an antagonist whose goal is to oppose the main character.
3. The use of four to six characters who help or harm the main character. These secondary characters move the character to act or react.
4. A structural approach that leads us from critical moment to resolution, deploying plot and character layers to do so.
5. Plot is deployed against the goal of the main character to create a greater barrier to the achievement of that goal.
6. Character layer, when deployed, is used to explore the two options of the premise. The main character is deeply involved with two characters, each representing one of the options of the premise.

7. The Act II turning point represents the point in the structure where the main character makes their choice.
8. A consistent and genre-appropriate tone.

The Satire

When considering the satire, it is important to differentiate between the full-blown satire and the soft satire. Both are critical of a social or political target, and that target is the focal point for the voice of the writer. They differ, however, in the vigor of the application of voice. Examples of a full-blown satire would include the Chayefsky scripts, *The Hospital* and *Network*, the Southern–Kubrick script, *Dr. Strangelove*, and the Tolkin script, *The Player*. In each case, the anger of the writer invigorates his treatment of events and character. They are extreme. The soft satire, on the contrary, embraces a more gentle treatment of character and event. Examples include Juzo Itami's *A Taxing Woman* and *The Funeral*. Gentility, even affection for the characters, replaces the hard-edged "no-prisoners" treatment of the full-blown satire. Preston Sturges's *Hail the Conquering Hero* and *The Miracle of Morgan's Creek* also qualify as soft satires, as does Stanley Kubrick's *Lolita*.

Central to the core of the soft satire and the satire are the writer's opinion on an important—as opposed to trivial—social or political feature of life. Middle-class sexual mores are the target in *Lolita*. "Heroism" is the target in *Hail the Conquering Hero*. Nothing less than capitalism and its destructiveness is the core issue in the Anderson-Sherwin satire *O'Lucky Man*. And the power of television is the target in Chayefsky's *Network*; the character acts as our guide through the complex environment of the narrative. That environment is the real antagonist of the narrative. In *Short Cuts*, the ultra-urban Los Angeles dehumanizes its people and relationships and individuals degenerate accordingly. In *Dr. Strangelove*, the environment is the military–industrial complex of the United States, and once again individuals at every level misbehave in proportion to their responsibilities.

What is critical in these characterizations is the scale of the antagonists—its pervasiveness leaves no doubt as to what the central characters are up against. They have no choice but to be co-opted by the system, as in *The Player*, or to be destroyed by it, as they are in *Dr. Strangelove* and in *Short Cuts*. The vigor of our response to the film depends on the disproportionate relationship between antagonist and main character. The writer wants us to feel helpless and angered by that helplessness.

Structure

A number of structural elements mark the satire as different from other genres. The domination of plot is notable, but it is how plot is deployed that is different from its use in other genres. Plot begins realistically enough, but it veers like an out-of-control locomotive to absurdist results. The network's search for ratings starts with firing the old guard, moves on to psychotic news reporting, and concludes with on-air executions, all in search of ratings dominance in *Network*. This deployment of plot embraces narrative exaggeration as well as tonal shifts. Structure is organized along a rising action plot in the satire, requiring a heightened use of surprise and inventiveness, unusual in its creative challenge for the writer. Whether we look at *Short Cuts* or *Dr. Strangelove* or *The Player*, we note the level of inventiveness in their plots. The result is that the genre is dominated by plot, with the expected denigration of the character layer in the structure. Character layers imply choice for a main character. The main character, in effect, has no choice in the satire, and consequently relationships and character layers play a far lesser role in the satire than they do in more traditional genres.

Tone

Whereas tone is consistent throughout a conventional melodrama, it is not consistent in the satire. In fact, tonal shifts are typical in the satire. Blake Edwards' *SOB* is realistically comedic early on but rapidly enters an over-the-top tone that it keeps escalating until its resolution at the end of Act III. This pattern of shifting tone typifies the satire.

What makes tonal shifts (and structural variations) coherent and effective in the satire is the unifying effect of the voice of the writer. Anger—about the power of television, the negative impact of ultra-urbanization, or the dangers of nuclear Holocaust—has one purpose beyond a tale well-told and that is to move the audience to action. That is the deeper intention in using the satire as a story form.

The Fable

Fable has been referred to as a hyperdrama[2] and as a moral fable.[3] Although the intention is the same in each case, here we will refer to the form simply as "fable." If the satire is negative and intentionally agitating, the fable is the reverse; its intention is to make us feel good. What's important here is that although the voice has a different goal in the fable, the methodology is quite similar to that in the satire. Think of the two forms, fable and satire, as alter egos for each other—as negative and positive, to use the photography metaphor.

The fable has long been a favored form, but as in the case of the satire, the form is challenging to the writer. But when it works, the fable, as in the case of the satire, has provided us with some of the greatest examples of filmic storytelling. Chaplin's *Modern Times*, Baum's *The Wizard of Oz*, and Albert Hackett and Francis Goodrich's *It's a Wonderful Life* are early examples of the fable. Frederic Rafael's *Eyes Wide Shut*, Eric Roth's *Forrest Gump*, Roberto Benigni's *Life is Beautiful*, Tom Tykwer's *The Princess and the Warrior*, and Neil Jordan's *The End of an Affair* are examples of more current fables.

As in the case of the satire, the fable is fueled by the strengths of feeling of the writer about a particular issue, generally more personal than the sociopolitical frame for so many satires. Although Chaplin's frame in *Modern Times* is sociopolitical, the deeper psychology of Dorothy in *The Wizard of Oz*, or of George Bailey in *It's a Wonderful Life*, is more typical of the fable. It is as if the moral of the story is to convince the main character (Oscar in *The Tin Drum*) or his surrogate (the young son in *Life is Beautiful*) that adaptation—not growing in Oscar's case or a playful positive attitude passed from father to son in *Life is Beautiful*—will secure a more positive future. And it's the moral of the story that carries the writer's voice.

Character

The main character in the fable is the vehicle for the narrative, as in the satire. However, in the fable, the main character is more individuated, compared to the propensity for type in the satire. George Baily, in *It's a Wonderful Life*, has dreams, aspirations, and disappointments in his life. So too does Dorothy, in *The Wizard of Oz*. This complexity of characters deepens into the articulation of values in *Forrest Gump* and of beliefs in Arthur's character in *Excalibur*. Main characters in the fable are ultimately all too human, as is The Tramp in *Modern Times*. And they can be quite eccentric, as is Oscar in *The Tin Drum*. All these characters seem almost neurotic in their obsessions and ultimately recognizably human in their vulnerability. Main characters in the fable are more human than heroic, although their journeys in the fable make them heroic. Think of Neo in *The Matrix* and Guido in *Life is Beautiful*.

As in the satire, the environment—Fascist Italy in *Life is Beautiful* and the future over- and underworlds in *The Matrix*—provides the basis for the plot that will challenge the main character's goal. But unlike the satire, the antagonist more often has a face in the fable, such as the Nazi doctor in the concentration camp in *Life is Beautiful*. The technological replicant in *The Matrix* becomes the antagonist who acts against the main character. Unlike the satire, in which secondary characters rarely help the main character, there are helpers in the fable. Sara Miles in *The End of the Affair* and Morpheus and Trinity in *The Matrix* help the main character meet the challenge of the antagonist and the antagonistic forces in the fable. Because the outcome in the fable is positive, the interplay of characters and relationships becomes important, allowing Maurice to find faith in *The End of the Affair* and allowing Arthur to hold on to his idealism despite his jealousy and bad behavior in *Excalibur*.

Structure

As in the satire, the fable has an overabundance of plot. *Forrest Gump* is present at every important political event in America over a 40-year period. And in *The Tin Drum*, Oscar's lack of growth begins with the emergence of the Nazi party in the 1920s and ends (he begins to grow) when the Russians defeat the Nazis in 1945. *Excalibur* begins with Arthur's conception and ends with his death. But the scale of the plot has a particular purpose, and that is to enlarge the interior journey of the main character, to make that journey heroic. The larger the plot, consequently, the more significant the moral of the story. The moral of the story in *Forrest Gump* is that if a child is treated as special, he will be special. Forrest Gump, limited in intelligence, and a physical cripple until he is 12, is so gifted in his attitude that he saves all the normal people he comes into contact with, including his childhood girlfriend and his lieutenant in Vietnam. By placing *Forrest Gump* in the midst of social, political, and military turbulent times, we can see the value of his "special status" in relief.

It's not realistic, but the fable never pretends to be realistic. Indeed, it embraces the fabulous. An angel descends from heaven to save George Bailey in *It's a Wonderful Life*. And a prayer and a promise by Sara bring Maurice back from the dead in *The End of the Affair*. Magic and sorcerers play important roles in *The Wizard of Oz* and in *Excalibur*. In the fable, magic, the fabulous, and the imagined coexist with realism.

Plot is a critical part of structure in the fable, but, unlike the satire, so too are relationships. Character layers are central in the majority of the fables mentioned. Love relationships emotionalize *It's a Wonderful Life*, *The End of the Affair*, and *Life is Beautiful*. Without those relationships, the positive aspect of the fable would not be as vividly presented. In the fable, the main character cares, other characters care about the main character, and so we in the audience follow. Without a strong character layer, the moral of the story would not have as positive a ring. Plot and character layers are important in the fable.

Tone

As in the satire, tone tends to shift in the fable. Coline Serreau's *Chaos* provides a good example here. *Chaos* begins with a French couple witnessing the brutal beating of a young prostitute on a Paris street. The fact that she looks Semitic further complicates the situation. The wife wants to help, but the husband opts to clean the blood off his car's front window and drive off. The balance of the story will follow the wife's decision to help the young prostitute. What begins as a dark comic story evolves into a full-fledged war between man and woman across age, status, and community boundaries.

In terms of tone, the film begins realistically, flirts with situation comedy, and rapidly escalates into an enabling action-adventure where the women defeat all the men, the enemies of quality and choice, in each of their lives. Comedy, tragedy, and farce, all are fused by Serreau's passionate feeling that if all women don't help each other, they are doomed to fates determined by their fathers, husbands, and sons. The tonal shifts help portray in this case two women from two cultures as two heroes.

The fable is the positive take on the social, political, and personal issues that challenge each of us in our lives. And the fable has as its goal to help us—strengthen us—to carry on.

The Docudrama

The docudrama looks different than other classic genres in the sense that it adopts the veneer and structure of the documentary in order to heighten the credibility and the importance of the narrative presented. By importance is meant seriousness, gravitas, as opposed to the entertainment agenda generally implicit in so many narrative films. The documentary since the 1920s has explicitly had as its agenda education rather than entertainment. (Both Dziga Vertov, the father of cinema verité, and John Grierson, father of the social/political documentary, advocated an alternative goal for their filmmaking; see Dancyger, *The Technique of Film and Video Editing.*[4]) The development of light-weight video equipment together with the growth of television provided powerful incentives for the documentary. Not surprising then is the migration of documentary techniques into the mainstream narrative. So great has been that migration that the documentary style has promoted a movement (*Dogme*), and the veneer of the documentary has been used to mask familiar genres in order to make those narratives seem new and fresh (*The Blair Witch Project, Man Bites Dog*).

The docudrama proper has been associated with the work of Peter Watkins (*Culloden*), Ken Leach (*Poor Cow*), and John Cassavetes (*Shadows*). More recently, filmmakers such as Mary Harron (*I Shot Andy Warhol*), Frederick Fonteyne (*An Affair of Love*), and Kore-eda Hirokazu (*Afterlife*) have used the docudrama to powerfully present their narratives. Other writers, such as Chris Guest, have used the form for comedic purposes in their "mockumentaries" (*Best in Show, A Mighty Wind*).

Character

As for fable and satire, the main character is the vehicle for the narrative. The character can be empathic, as in *My Name is Joe, Sweet Sixteen*, and *Ratcatcher*, or simply can be the conveyer of the ideas of the writer, as in *Land and Freedom* and *Eduard Munch*. It is also a possibility that there can be no main character, as in *Culloden* and *The War Game*. In each of these cases, the main character, generally, is presented without a goal, and the consequence is that we watch the character deal with a life situation (*Ratcatcher*) or plot (*Land and Freedom*) in which he has little or no control.

The nature of the main character is dictated by the writer's intention in the narrative. The teenager in *Sweet Sixteen* is placed in an abusive home environment and the consequent violence points out how the teen and the stepfather are victims of that violence. In *Land and Freedom*, the Scottish laborer who wants to act on his leftist political beliefs goes off to fight for the Left in the Spanish Civil War. The reality of political organizations, whether Left or Right, unmasks his naivety and leads to his disillusionment and his departure from the war. In each case, the character serves the writer's purpose in organizing his narrative as a docudrama.

Because the main character is so often a victim of his situation (*Ratcatcher* and *Sweet Sixteen*) the question of the victimizer needs to be considered. In classic linear narratives, the victimizer tends to be a clear antagonist (the father in the family melodrama, *Once Were Warriors*) or a plot device (the sinking of the ship on its maiden voyage in *Titanic*). In the docudrama, there can be an antagonist (Prince William in *Culloden*) where there is a plot, or there can be a corrosive social or family dilemma (the garbage strike in 1970s Glasgow and a father's alcoholism in *Ratcatcher*). In both the cases, the focus is upon the victimization of the main character rather than upon the active role of an antagonist or life situation. As in the satire, it's the environment the main characters find themselves in that smothers hope and destroys ideals and/or lives.

Structure

As in the satire, the victimization of the main character forms the narrative structure of the docudrama. Unlike the satire, however, narrative exaggeration plays no role in the rising action of the structure. On the contrary, credibility of behavior and event drives every dimension of the docudrama. In general terms, it is best to think of the structure of the docudrama more as an echo of the structure of the documentary rather than as a traditional three-act structure. Think of the structure as akin in making a case for ideas on poverty, war, family relationships, art, class, age, and so on. The writer is making the case, and so the structure follows introduction; the points that make the case are organized in a rising action and are a restatement of the point of view of the writer. Threaded through this structure, there should be an information line and an emotion line. Together these two lines make the case credibly and emotionally.

The shape of the docudrama can follow an event, as in the last battle on British soil in *Culloden*, or a life, as in *Eduard Munch*, or the film can focus on a condition such as alcoholism, as in *My Name is Joe*. Whichever is chosen, the main character can be used to organize both the information and the emotional lines of the narrative. Consider the main character as the guide through the case that is being made in the docudrama. Where there is no main character, as in *Culloden*, a narrator becomes the guide. The narrator can be offscreen (the interviewer in *An Affair of Love*), or the narrator can be the main character (as in *Land and Freedom*). In both the cases, the narrator helps shape the narrative and focuses the voice of the writer.

Plot is very important in most docudramas. Examples include the battle in *Culloden*, the progress or lack of progress of career in *Eduard Munch*, and the strike in *Bread and Roses*. In fact, plot is more important than is the character layer, because plot works against the goal of the main character, and if victimization of the main character is purposeful to the case the writer makes, plot must be more effective than are the relationships in the narrative.

In terms of the character layer, it is also important that the character be more solitary, more unavailable to potential helpers. A good example here is Lynn Ramsey's *Ratcatcher*. James, an adolescent boy gets no help from his parents or his siblings in the trap of poverty in 1973 Glasgow. Although James dreams of a home in the suburbs, his only real friend is another outcast, Margaret Anne. She is older but she can't rescue James, and when his dream of a new home is shattered, he suicides. James' isolation and frustration and anger become understandably self-directed because of the thinness of the character layer. None of the characters can help themselves let alone another, and so their fate is sealed and the writers' voice about the issue of poverty is strengthened.

Tone

The tone of the docudrama is realistic. Incident and behavior are presented in as credible a style as possible. Although James's suburban dream is presented in heightened, almost hyper-realistic imagery, in *Ratcatcher* it doesn't detract from the presentation of James and his family's impoverished life. Presented as it is in the middle of the film, the suburban sequence gives life to the hope the character feels at that moment.

More generally, the docudrama uses realism and aural and visual strategies that underwrite a documentary feel, to reference the idea that this is real life and real people. For the writer of the docudrama, the framework of realism—the use of so specific a tone—adds weight to the argument made in the film about poverty, art, nationalism, or any other "ism."

The Experimental Narrative

The experimental narrative is quite different from the other voice-oriented genres. The story form has a distinctive style. Indeed, we could go so far as to say that the style overwhelms the content or, to phrase it another way, that it's a story form that maximizes style and minimizes content. The voice of the writer in this sense permeates the style.

Examples of experimental narrative would include Wong Kar-Wai's *In the Mood for Love* and *2046*, Peter Greenaway's *The Draughtsman's Contract* and *The Cook, The Thief and The Lover*, Tom Tykwer's *Run Lola Run*, Mike Figgis's *Time Code*, Atom Egoyan's *Calendar*, and Su Friedrich's *Sink or Swim*. The genre has links to the visual arts and seems often taken with issues of technology. Consequently, the non-verbal supersedes the verbal, and action supersedes characterization. One begins to see the origins of the experimental narrative in Dovshenko's *Earth*. Dovshenko's interest in a poetic style and his penchant for visual metaphor mark the pathway, through Maya Daren, to films such as Fellini's *8½* and Antonioni's *Blow-up* and eventually on to the recent work of Clara Law (*Autumn Moon*) and Guy Maddin (*Careful*).

Character

In Wong Kar-Wai's *In the Mood for Love*, the focus is on a love affair that begins in Hong Kong in the early 1960s and ends 10 years later. The male character is handsome, and the female is beautiful, but we never learn more than that each is abandoned by their spouse for the spouse of the other. The two characters remain stereotypes. So too do the lovers in *The Cook, The Thief and The Lover*, and so too does the married couple in *Calendar*. Stereotypes rather than full-blown characters are typical of the experimental narrative. Consequently, we rarely understand the behavior of the main characters or the characters who attract them, as in *In the Mood for Love*, or whose attraction they seek, as in *Sink or Swim*, or who frightens them, as in *The Cook, The Thief and The Lover*. The level of characterization keeps us watching them rather than relating more deeply to them.

Structure

Structure in the experimental narrative tends to the non-linear. Lola tries to save her boyfriend, Mani, three times, each with a different outcome, in *Run Lola Run*. Because time is advanced or retarded, the outcome varies each time. In *Calendar*, a photographer and his wife return to Armenia (from Canada) to take photographs of iconic churches for a calendar. The further into Armenia they go, the more the marriage suffers. He returns to Canada and she stays in Armenia. He tries to secure another relationship but continually fails. The Canada sequences are intercut (future) with the Armenian sequences (past), and what we're left with is the identity crisis of the photographer. Is he Canadian or is he Armenian?

Su Friedrich's *Sink or Swim* is a series of scenes from birth to adulthood of a young woman's relationship with her father. The relationship is vivid but unsatisfying for the girl, and the narrator (12-year-old girl) speculates about anthropology and life, mythology and biology, father and daughter. There is a chronology here, but the film structure remains exploratory and speculative.

Non-linearity—open-architecture structure—is the very opposite of classical linear structure. The very openness of the structure is so surprising and elusive that it leaves its audience open to the voice, the narrative intentions of its writer.

Tone

The tone of the experimental film is important and tends to add to our involvement in the film. *In the Mood for Love* is profoundly romantic, although we can't understand the characters. Greenaway eroticizes his tale of murder on an estate in *The Draughtsman's Contract*, making the film enjoyable despite not caring a pinch for the fate of its main character. And *Run Lola Run* has energy to burn. Playful about filmic conventions, Tykwer uses a plot device as an excuse for energizing the film. Tone is an important contributing factor to the articulation of the voice of the writer.

So what are these writers trying to say and how is the style they adopt helping them articulate their voice? In the case of Wong Kar-Wai, he is saying that relationships are impossible in overcrowded Hong Kong. Love is great but you'll never be able to hold on to it. In the case of Egoyan, he is concerned with identity in *Calendar* just as Greenaway is, commenting on the centrality of ownership and proprietorship in *The Draughtsman's Contract*. The artist may be talented, fierce, and sexy, but he'll always be the victim of monied people. Using style as a counterpoint to the content, the writer uses the experimental narrative to titillate and to preach to his audience about issues deep and frivolous.

Conclusion

Each of these genres of voice—the satire, the fable, the docu-drama, and the experimental narrative—in their own way use character, structure, and tone to reach out to their audience and to speak more directly with that audience. The audience accustomed to masked voice in the classical genres is thrilled to make more direct contact with the writer and his ideas: this is the strength of these voice-oriented genres.

References

1. K. Dancyger, "The Ascent of Voice," In *Global Scriptwriting* (Boston, MA: Focal Press, 2001), Chapter 11.
2. P. Cooper and K. Dancyger, *Writing the Short Film*, 3rd ed. (Boston, MA: Focal Press, 2004).
3. K. Dancyger, *Global Scriptwriting* (Boston, MA: Focal Press).
4. K. Dancyger, *The Technique of Film and Video Editing*, 3rd ed. (Boston, MA: Focal Press, 2003).

The Non-Linear Film

The non-linear film is a voice-oriented genre. As it tends to be quite open-ended in its characteristics, we devote this entire chapter to the form. In the years since *Pulp Fiction* debuted, the non-linear film has grown enormously in its influence, and its importance has been paralleled by the development of non-linear editing and of computer applications in special effects, animation, and video games. The latter technological developments have made more appealing the open-ended quality of the non-linear film. Beyond *Pulp Fiction*, important non-linear films include Paul Thomas Anderson's *Magnolia*, Terence Malick's *The Thin Red Line*, Atom Egoyan's *Exotica*, and Karen and Jill Sprecher's *13 Conversations About One Thing*. The open-ended quality of these films moves us away from their characters toward the voice of their writers.

The non-linear film is not a Quentin Tarantino creation. As early as 1929, Luis Buñuel and Salvador Dalí made *Un Chien Andalou*, the first non-linear film. That film, with its fragmented narrative, its leaps into fantasy, its shock juxtapositions, and its lack of narrative progression, provided an excellent vehicle for Buñuel and Dalí to voice their views on dreams, the Church, the Bourgeoisie, art, society, and anti-narrative narrative, leaving *Un Chien Andalou* open to various interpretations.

Also important in the evolution of the non-linear film is the work of Jean-Luc Godard. Since 1959, Godard has been using familiar genres—the gangster film, the war film, the melodrama, and the musical—as his narrative base. But in each case Godard subverts our genre expectations to voice his views on war, society, and capitalism and to polemicize for change.

What is important about both Buñuel and Godard is that they subverted plot and character in the same way contemporary non-linear storytellers do. Their work provides the models for non-linear storytelling. In order to understand the non-linear story fully, it's useful at this point to review linear storytelling, the analogue to the non-linear story.

Linear Storytelling

The linear narrative represents the commercial mid-point of storytelling. The experimental film and the documentary are at one edge of the mainstream and the docudrama, the fable, the experimental narrative, and the non-linear film are at the opposite edge. Underlying the experience of the linear narrative is the invitation for the viewer to identify with the main character. Whether the main character is a hero or a victim, the identification positions the viewer into a state that essentially renders the viewer passive. In that dream state, the viewer will not face choices but rather will move from the critical moment that opens the story to the resolution that in effect closes the story. Through a rising action, the viewer experiences the barriers, the challenges, and the eventual positive or negative resolution. The arc is predetermined and follows story form expectations. In this sense, the linear narrative is a safe experience, where the viewer makes no choice. Satisfaction, excitement, and the range of feeling depend on identification, and the predictability of the story form assures an exciting but safe arc of experience. Central to the experience of the linear narrative is that the viewer doesn't need to exercise choice (as opposed to the non-linear narrative).

The linear narrative also proceeds within established story form norms, within genres. Mainstream genres—the melodrama, the police story, the gangster film, film noir, situation comedy, romantic comedy, and the thriller—have established dramatic arcs known to the audience. For example, the romantic comedy will proceed along the arc of a relationship. Boy meets girl, or girl meets boy or boy meets boy kicks off the narrative. Because the film is a comedy, the narrative will have a positive outcome. The Farrelly brothers' *There's Something about Mary* and Richard Curtis' *Four Weddings and a Funeral* exemplify this genre. In the thriller, an ordinary person finds himself/herself in extraordinary circumstances. If he doesn't figure out who is pursuing him, he will die. The dramatic arc of the thriller is essentially a chase. Ernest Lehman's *North by Northwest* and Erin Krueger's *Arlington Road* exemplify the thriller. The dramatic arc of the police story is crime–investigation–solution. The dramatic arc of the gangster film follows the rise and fall of the gangster. The dramatic arc of the science fiction film follows the technology vs. humanity struggle. The audience, when it chooses a particular story form, knows how that experience will proceed. This is one of the strengths of the linear film. But as stated earlier, the key to the effectiveness of the linear film is the identification with the main character.

Whether the main character is an outsider or a professional (e.g., policeman), the writer will use particular strategies to enhance identification. First, the main character will have a goal, which he or she will pursue with vigor. Second, if the character is potentially victimized by an antagonist or by the structure of the plot, we will identify with that character. In real life, none of us likes to be victimized—so too in the film experience. And so we identify with the potential victim, the main character. The writer can also deploy other strategies, such as giving the main character a confessional private moment or, at the other extreme, a tragic flaw (such as overabundant ambition, as in *Macbeth*, or overabundant aggression, as seen in Jake La Motta in *Raging Bull*). Whatever the strategy or strategies employed, the identification with the main character will carry the audience through the dramatic arc to its resolution and by doing so the experience of the viewer will be whole and predetermined. This is both the strength and the weakness of the linear narrative for the viewer. In its predictability, there is no room for the viewer to exercise choice, to be more active or participatory, precisely the options the non-linear narrative affords the viewer.

The Non-Linear Narrative

To understand the properties of the non-linear story, it is best to consider them in light of the linear narrative. In terms of character, the non-linear story has multiple main characters rather than a single goal-directed main character. As the characters in the non-linear film may or may not have a goal, they do not necessarily proceed along a clear dramatic arc, as is the case in the linear narrative. An example will make the point: In Anderson's *Magnolia* (1998), there are eight characters who occupy the space of the main character. They group into three families and include at least one additional character, a policeman, who becomes emotionally involved with the daughter in one of those families. Some of the characters have a goal—a young boy ostensibly wants to win a television show competition (or does he?), two dying fathers want to reunite with their alienated son or daughter, a policeman wants to do his job effectively and in a humane fashion. The other characters do not have clear goals but rather find themselves in situations where they must make a decision. All eight characters seem to find themselves in a life crisis, disappointed in parents or not wishing to disappoint parents. This state of being is what the characters share, and if there is a dramatic shape to the story, it is to pose the question: What will each do and what will be the consequences of their actions?

In Atom Egoyan's *Exotica* (1995), a group of six characters is brought together in a place, a sex club. These characters are as despairing as Anderson's characters are. Their goals, however, are far more submerged or absent than is depicted in the Anderson film. More apparent are the goals of the characters in Malick's *The Thin Red Line* (1997). They are soldiers fighting on the American side in World War II. The battle is for the island of Guadalcanal, and their goals are principally to survive; although their Colonel has another goal, to use the outcome of the battle to achieve the promotion that has so long eluded him.

Key in the consideration of character in the non-linear film is that there will be multiple characters and that they may or may not have a goal. The consequence is that the viewer is observing character, rather than identifying with a character and moving with that character through a dramatic arc.

Turning to the issue of plot, there may or may not be a plot in the nonlinear narrative. There is a plot in *The Thin Red Line*: the progress of the war in the battle for Guadalcanal. In the linear film, plot works against the goal of the main character. As there are multiple main characters in

The Thin Red Line, we do not follow how a single character reacts against the pressure of plot. Consequently, the use of plot is muted. For the Colonel, the progress of the battle is an opportunity rather than a threat. But most of the soldiers seem indifferent to the progress of the battle. For one soldier who finds a tearful, terrified enemy in an overrun village, the progress of the battle reminds him of his own sorrow and pain, which he feels, rather than feeling empowered by victory. Because of the multiple and varied responses to the progress of the battle, plot is compromised as a dramatic device and consequently it is relegated to background rather than serving as the powerful narrative tool it can be in a linear film such as *Paths of Glory*. Similarly, the fact that there are multiple main characters in Julie Dash's *Daughters of the Dust* blunts the impact of the plot—the momentous day when a portion of the family will migrate from an island off of South Carolina to the mainland, principally the industrial Midwest of the United States.

Tarantino's *Pulp Fiction* (1994) offers a variation on the use of plot in three interconnected stories. There is plot in all three stories, each having to do with the professional activities of the main characters—killing off threats to the economic well-being of the gang. The middle story differs, as the main character is a boxer who fails to throw a fight; he both benefits and may suffer the consequences. Will he get away with it? Here plot operates as it does in a linear narrative, and it is quite effective. In the two stories that flank the middle story, however, plot proceeds as background, as it does in the other non-linear films described. In many non-linear films, including Egoyan's *Exotica* and Anderson's *Magnolia*, the plot element is so remote as to be de facto nonexistent. At best, it functions as background, but more often not even that. Most important is that the use of plot in the non-linear film rarely proceeds as it does in the linear film. It is simply not a vital narrative device.

The greatest consequence of this use of plot is to flatten the dramatic arc of the non-linear film. A war film such as *The Thin Red Line* changes from a progression from the beginning of a battle to its end, to a series of situations that may or may not be directly linked to the progress of the battle. The sense of time, so dramatically central to a linear war film such as *Apocalypse Now*, is totally different from the progression in *The Thin Red Line*. Chronological time is no longer critical. The same can be said for cause and effect. There is a randomness to the experience of the non-linear film. As a result, there is no dramatic arc. In its stead, we have a series of scenes or situations that are explored. The organization of those scenes will not necessarily be progressively linked. Consequently, our involvement will come from character rather than from plot, from the intensity of the individual scene rather than from the organization of progressive scenes. This puts much more emphasis on exploration than on exposition, on feeling and mood rather than on external events. The absence of the dramatic arc has far-reaching consequences for the writing of the non-linear film, an issue we will return to at the end of this chapter. For now, it poses this question: If there is no dramatic arc, what is the organizing principle of the structure of the non-linear film?

The first noticeable quality of the structure of the non-linear film is its elusiveness. It doesn't look like the clear structure of the linear film. But there is despite this a structure. That structure may be more shaping device than structure in the conventional sense of the word. The structure of *Pulp Fiction* might even be considered a counter-structure. The same characters appear in the three stories, but Tarantino has altered their chronology. Like a clock, we come back to the beginning of every 24 hours. In Tarantino's story, we come back to the beginning at the end (and go past that beginning hour!). Within the clock counter-structure, the three stories proceed out of sequence. There are, however, common characters in each story; primarily Marcellus is the inner circle of structure in *Pulp Fiction*.

The shaping device or loose structure in Malick's *The Thin Red Line* is the battle for Guadalcanal. There is lip service to chronology, but Malick chooses incidents and emphases that have little to do with that progression. Within this larger structure, the focus on a single platoon helps provide the inner shape Malick works with. The shaping device in Dash's *Daughters of the Dust* also references chronology, the day of migration for the Peazant family to leave Ebo Landing, an island off of South Carolina. Even Anderson pays lip service to chronology. Two fathers are dying, and they want to reconcile with their alienated children. Time is also a presence in the stories of the aging child star and the contemporary child "star" making his reputation in a TV quiz show. The inner core issues for all these characters, however, does not relate to time. It is their common condition—despair, ennui, a condition that does not relate to time but rather to inner life.

Place, rather than time, becomes the shaping event in Egoyan's *Exotica*. The sex club is the meeting place for the characters, but it is their inner state, each in crisis for a lost relationship or an impossible relationship, that gives the urgency and emotional depth to Egoyan's film. Place is also the outer skin for Karen and Jill Sprecher's *13 Conversations About One Thing*. Contemporary ultra-urban New York is the setting and as in the case of the Egoyan film, the inner emptiness or dissatisfaction of the characters is the common thread that gathers together its characters into a narrative.

Place is helpful but not enough in Schamus's *The Ice Storm* (1997). He uses time, the four days around Thanksgiving, 1973, and he uses family, specifically two families—husbands, wives, and two children, neighbors in an upper-middle-class Connecticut suburb. Tod Solondz follows the same structural choices in *Happiness* (1998), principally following a family for three generations, and adds a patient of the son-in-law psychiatrist in the family. New York/New Jersey/Florida is the geographical setting; the time setting is contemporary. The inner structure of these stories is principally the voices of Schamus and Solondz. For Schamus and director Ang Lee, they are interested and empathic about the unhappiness of their characters. Solondz, on the contrary, is more interested in skewering his characters with his unhappiness about their unhappiness.

The loosest structure of all is achieved by thematically affiliating different stories. In *Before the Rain*, Milcho Manchevski tells three stories about Macedonia (during the 1990s, of the Balkan wars, including Bosnia and Macedonia). The war generates parallel tensions between the two racial and religious minorities, the Albanian Muslims and the Christian Macedonians. The outer structure is similar to *Pulp Fiction*—the idea of a 24-hour clock. Within the clock, the three stories will proceed out of chronology, with the last story ending as the first story is about to begin. Consequently, in the course of the film, we feel we come full circle. Within that outer structure, three independent stories unfold, each story with its own internal integrity and progression. Two are love stories where two unlikely partners come together to help the other, and each story ends with the death of the unlikely partner. Each dies because she or he transgressed religious boundaries. They try to save a Muslim or a Christian, and one of their co-religionists kills them for crossing that boundary. The middle story, set in London, has a British couple going to a restaurant, where the wife tells her husband that she will leave him. An argument among the present staff and former staff (Macedonian, presumably Muslim) ensues, and the result is a shooting in which the innocent British husband is killed. The wife is now free due to the random local Balkan violence. In *Before the Rain*, it is the theme that provides the unity to the stories. Racial hatred destroys love. Theme rather than character or place provides the inner structure for *Before the Rain*.

An idea is also the shaping device for Don McKellar's and Francois Girard's *Thirty Two Short Films About Glenn Gould* (1994). The idea that genius is an eccentric, brilliant resistance to structural definition is captured by presenting Glenn Gould's life as a loose chronology of episodes, each of which differs from the other. A half-dozen episodes are documentary, at least three are animated, and the balance consists of dramatized episodes that differ considerably from each other. The film is reminiscent of an MTV approach to biography—32 self-contained episodes.

A more conventional but no less non-linear approach is taken by McKellar and Girard in their next film, *The Red Violin* (1998). An object, a violin, is followed from its nineteenth century creation to its current status. Episodes focus on the violin's owners through four centuries. Italy, Austria, England, China, and Canada locate the action. The episodes share neither tone nor idea. The only common thread is the violin itself. Because there is no deeper conceit, the film is less interesting, but it remains a non-linear narrative told along a loose chronology.

Natural Born Killers (1994) also uses a loose MTV idea for its structure. Here Oliver Stone uses the careers of two serial killers, Mickey and Mallory, as the outer structure. In the inner structure is a series of scenes unified by the notion that there is a link between media manipulation and violence. Are Mickey and Mallory a product of the media or is their career encouraged by the media? Stone links each MTV episode of the film to affiliate ideas about violence and media manipulation.

Whether the structure is loose or layered, it is critical to note the difference from the linear three-act structure. The non-linear film may be organized in two acts or without act breaks. More often it has numerous story lines that are integrated into two-act stories or into brief MTV-style short films loosely linked into the larger film. Again, key here is how very different the structure of the non-linear film is when compared to the linear film.

The last property that differentiates the non-linear film from the linear is tone. As mentioned in the previous chapter, tone tends to proceed along the story form expectations. The Western tends to be pastoral and poetic. The war film tends to be realistic. The thriller and the melodrama tend to be realistic. The horror film tends to be expressionistic, over the top. The tone adds to the credibility of the experience of the film.

Tone in the non-linear film tends to be less predictable. It can even vary within a story. What drives the tone is the writer's intentions and voice. Consequently, the tone of Anderson's *Magnolia* is in turn fabulous, then realistic, and, toward the end, when an intense storm yields a downpouring of frogs, it again becomes fabulous. Is Anderson using the melodrama or the fable as his story form base? Whichever it is, the non-linear narrative is the meta-genre that embraces the work. Similarly, Terence Malick uses a poetic meditative tone rather than realism in his war film *The Thin Red Line*. This variation in tone enables Malick to consider issues of life and death, permanence and impermanence, and the general issues of values in this war film. Critical here is that tone does not operate within story expectations as it does so often in the linear narrative. Consequently, the non-linear film is more malleable to the voice of the writer or writer and director.

Issues for the Non-Linear Screenplay

Character

The issue of writing a story in which the character may or may not have a goal immediately raises the issue of energy. In the linear film, the goal of the main character clashes with the goal of the antagonist. The plot additionally provides opposition to the goal of the main character. Conflict, and implicitly energy, abound, which in turn engages the viewer.

If the goal of the main character or multiple characters in the non-linear narrative is absent, where does the needed energy come from? Or to put it another way, audiences want to be involved with a story. Energy is attractive as well as involving. That energy has to be present in a narrative, in all stories, linear or non-linear. Goals simply make the creation of that involving energy easier. Take away the goals and the job of creating the needed energy becomes harder but nevertheless critical. So where and how does the non-linear storyteller create energy?

In order to address this issue, it's best to focus on the scene rather than on the narrative as a whole. First, the writer should be aware that energy can be created by positioning a character in a conflictual scene. The opening scene in *Happiness* has a young couple, clearly romantic in intention; perhaps a proposal is in the offing. Instead, one character breaks off the relationship with the other. We could look at this scene in another way by saying that the two characters in the scene have opposing intentions—one of them wants to cement the relationship, the other wants to end it. Similarly, if we look at a scene in *Magnolia*, the Tom Cruise character, a salesperson-guru for hypermasculinity, is being interviewed by a black female journalist. He begins the scene changing his clothing (provocative), being a sexual tease. Shortly after the interview begins, the journalist accuses Cruise's character of making up (and distorting) his past. She is calling him a liar. He is looking for yet another seduction, and she is looking for an expose, a good story.

A second strategy to create energy is to use dialogue in an unexpected way. Here *Pulp Fiction* provides a good example. Two hit men are going to kill someone for non-payment for drugs. What they talk about is eating, foot massages, and habits of the French. What they don't talk about is the job. Their gossip is a surprise and acts as a counterpoint to their intentions and consequently it creates tension and energy. Anderson uses dialogue precisely in the same way in *Magnolia*. The words, the pace of delivery—both will add to the emotionality and consequently to the energy level of the scene.

The Suitability of Plot

As mentioned earlier, plot may or may not be used in the non-linear story. When it is used, it is often background, as it is in the first and last stories in *Pulp Fiction*. In the fable and in the docudrama, however, plot is indispensable and vital. Plot can generate the energy that is not present in the characters. And plot is found in greater amounts in these two story forms. If a fable is the form being used, as in Tykwer's *The Princess and the Warrior* (2001), there may be different plots affiliated with particular characters. In Kusterica's *Underground* (1995), the entire post-war history of Yugoslavia provides the plot. Returning to the Tykwer film, a truck accident brings two characters together, one as victim and the other as rescuer. Later, a bank robbery plot reverses the roles—the character who was the victim in the first plot becomes a rescuer and the character who was the rescuer becomes the victim. Each plot serves a different purpose. In and of themselves, the plots seem almost arbitrary, but Tykwer brings them to bear on each of the characters.

What to realize about plot is that it is deployed very differently in the non-linear film than it is in the linear film.

The Importance of Voice

What has been implied so far is that the non-linear story has strengths (inviting more audience participation) and weaknesses (posting barriers to involvement); the key issue that can strengthen the experience of the non-linear story is the active presence of the voice of the writer. Voice not only supplants character as the key to the story experience, it also provides the writer with the kind of flexibility that can be liberating.

Again, the opposite illustrates the possibilities. In the linear narrative, the writer must conform first to the issue of identification with the main character and second to a structural approach that keeps us with the character. Having kept us with the character, the opportunity to share views of the writer becomes muted, indirect, and contained. What is so critical about the non-linear story is that its subversion of structure and character enables voice to be pronounced, clear, and important.

As mentioned earlier, the intention of Terence Malick in *The Thin Red Line* is to create a meditation on the value of life and the meaning of death, and consequently scenes are constructed not to focus on the progression of the battle but rather to emphasize the life and death views of Malick. In Jill and Karen Sprecher's *13 Conversations About One Thing*, the random stories of a half-dozen New Yorkers link modestly but thematically. Each story is a tale of dissatisfaction and urban angst. Voice unifies and makes urgent the four stories that are told. In the non-linear story, voice is central. Writers do use story forms that enable voice but are not restricted to those story forms. The Sprecher film is a melodrama, as is Wong Kar-Wai's *In the Mood for Love*. Kusterica's *Underground* is a fable, as is Tykwer's *The Princess and the Warrior*. The fable is far more malleable to voice than is the melodrama.

The Importance of the MTV Style

The MTV style focuses upon the scene and treats it as if it were a distinct, separate film. The emphasis is also on feeling rather than exposition. Again, the benefit is intensity. Given the looseness of the non-linear film and its shift away from character, the MTV style can generate the kind of intense involvement seen in the linear thriller, for example. The consequences of using the MTV approach are visible in vastly different films, including Stone's *Natural Born Killers*, Benigni's *Life is Beautiful*, and Solodnz's *Happiness*. In each case, this attitude toward the scene can help the writer overcome the less involving narrative strategies of the non-linear narrative (for a more detailed look at the MTV style, see Dancyger, *The Technique on Film and Video Editing*[1]).

Contentious Areas in the Non-Linear Story

Because the non-linear story so often has alternative narrative goals, there are issues that writers don't often need to address. If the writer is conscious of these problems, it is possible to work to counter them. The most obvious problem of the non-linear story is that it is less involving than the linear story is. Writers of non-linear video games provide choice for the player in order to encourage that involvement. Others go overboard on plot. Still others populate their stories with outrageous characters. All are taken up with the need to involve viewers in a story form that by its nature does not actively invite involvement. Whatever the strategy, it is critical for the writer to concern himself with the problem of involvement.

The attendant problem is boredom. Here writers look to plot, exaggeration, and over-the-top dialogue to avoid boredom. Certainly it worked in *Pulp Fiction*, but those who have tried to imitate *Pulp Fiction* have not been as fortunate. The novelty of being first benefited Tarantino's film; his imitators have not had such an advantage. The deeper solution to boredom is to involve us either with voice or to be different from the prevailing stories and approaches to a story. This is the reason Alan Ball was successful with *American Beauty*. It was different. Writers, especially writers of non-linear stories, need the edge of novelty.

Finally, writers have to acknowledge that the MTV impulse and the nonlinear story have yielded an emphasis on sensation (short term) over feeling (the story as a whole). Deeply felt narratives have come to be regarded as old-fashioned (read *linear*), whereas non-linear stories are rife with sensation through plot, dialogue, or tonal change. The issue for the non-linear writer is to try to overcome these problems endemic to the non-linear story—to find creative solutions that generate energy and creative difference to highlight the voice of the writer and to make unique the experience of the audience.

Reference

1. K. Dancyger, *The Technique on Film and Video Editing*, 3rd ed. (Boston, MA: Focal Press, 2002).

15

The Fable: A Case Study of Darkness: The Wizard of Oz and Pan's Labyrinth

The Wizard of Oz

Rare is the film where the children's world is the center and where children are more complex beings. The MGM film version of the Frank Baum classic *The Wizard of Oz* is such a film.

The Wizard of Oz is about a real world, Kansas, and an imagined world, Oz. Part musical and part fable, it audaciously pictorializes its main character, Dorothy's world. Structurally fables have an overabundance of plot relative to other genres, variable tone, and are unified by the moral of the story (see Chapter 13). It doesn't shirk from anxiety, and it relies on imaginatively doubling the characters in Dorothy's Kansas life with characters represented in her imagined life.

In the 1960s since *The Wizard of Oz* was created, it has taken on legendary stature.

Point of View

Childhood is a product of the past 200 years (see Edward Shorter's *The Making of the Modern Family*, 1977, on childhood). Before that there was birth, work, reproduction, and death. That period from birth to 12 years has developed in these 200 years as an incubation period where the child prepares for adult life. It's a protected period, a period of considerable practical and moral learning taking place. It is also a time of fear and anxiety as the ways of the world become increasingly clear. Whether this engenders security or insecurity in the child, is also a part of childhood.

The greatness of *The Wizard of Oz* lies in good part in its willingness to sidestep Hollywood stereotypes about children (as smaller adults) and vest itself in Dorothy's world, the child's world. This world is viewed as a bifurcated world—a world of good and bad, a world of protectors and of predators, a world where adults are mysterious and in terms of trustworthiness they are unpredictable, whereas animals are always predictable. As Dorothy is the only child in this world we cannot see a split between children and adults in terms of doing good and evil things. Bad behavior in her world seems to reside squarely in the adult world.

In terms of a more detailed presentation of the child's world, the film's narrative features flesh out that world. The first phase of the film takes place in Kansas. It's a dark brooding place with changes of weather threatening. Dorothy and her dog Toto live with her elderly aunt Emily and uncle Henry. Their threadbare farm has three workers, Hunk, Zeke, and Hickory.

This part of the story focuses on the local entrepreneur Miss Gulch's interdiction to have Dorothy's dog, Toto, destroyed. Dorothy's aunt and uncle comply and hand over the dog that promptly runs away from Miss Gulch back to Dorothy. Dorothy then runs away in order to save her dog. She visits Professor Marvel, a benevolent itinerant fortune-teller. He convinces her to return home. Upon her return, a tornado is blowing, and she imagines the entire farm and its surround are sucked up into the eye of the tornado, including Miss Gulch. She is then transported to the imagined world of Oz.

In this first sequence, Dorothy expresses anger at the injustice of the adult world. Miss Gulch has the power to punish, and no one stands against her. Dorothy is powerless, and she's anxious not only about Toto but also about the impotence of her aunt and uncle to protect her and Toto. Dorothy is also willful. She is willing to run away to save Toto. She's also young and impressionable. Professor Marvel easily convinces her to return home.

In this sequence, Dorothy is powerless but willful, angry but anxious; in short, she's a vulnerable child looking to protect what means most to her but fearful that the adult world will unjustly punish her. There is an underlying sense of disappointment here about adults in general.

In the next longer sequence of the film, the visit to Oz, Dorothy is on a journey of discovery. Oz the world divides more simply into a world of good and evil. There is a good witch, and there are two bad witches. The good witch is helpful to Dorothy as a benevolent "parent" would be, and the surviving Wicked Witch of the West, looking remarkably like Miss Gulch, is all about punishment and harming. And the world of Oz is presented in glorious Technicolor.

In order to find her way back to her world, Dorothy is advised to travel to the Emerald City to see the Wizard of Oz and seek his advice. To get to Emerald City, she must follow the yellow brick road. Along that road she meets three accomplices who like herself find themselves lacking. The Scarecrow (Ray Bolger) feels he has no brain. Perhaps the Wizard of Oz will tell him where he can find a brain. The Tin Man (Jack Haley) feels he has no heart. He will ask the wizard where he can find a heart. And the lion is a Cowardly Lion. He would like to know where he can find courage. Each is seeking an answer, as is Dorothy. The four travel to Emerald City, and after a confrontation with the Wicked Witch of the West, they find what they are seeking. The wizard tells them it's all inside themselves rather than out there in the world.

In the final sequence, it's the Good Witch of the North who tells Dorothy how to return to Kansas. All she has to do is repeat the phrase "there's no place like home." She does, and she's back home again with aunt Emily and uncle Henry, and their three workers. She repeats the phrase "there's no place like home," and the film ends.

In this part of the film, the life lesson of personal action enters Dorothy's repertoire. She learns that personal empowerment leads to a goal fulfilled. She also learns to appreciate home despite its shortcomings; it's still home. Acceptance of a life of limits is implicit in the conclusion.

What is notable about *The Wizard of Oz* is its focus on the anxious child and the role of anxiety in general in life. Let's turn to this central issue of the film.

Anxiety

If we were to ask the question whether Dorothy reflects a sense of belonging or mastery in her world, I would have to say she does not. In its stead, she seems to be anxious about her position in her world. The anxiety generates from different features of Dorothy's life and her behavior.

Above all, Dorothy is presented as a child without parents. Her aunt Emily and uncle Henry are custodians, but where are the parents? Both aunt and uncle seem older, another factor in the gap between Dorothy and her custodians.

A second feature of Dorothy's world is that there are no peers. No brothers or sisters, no school friends, no neighbors of a similar age. Dorothy is very much alone. Her best friend seems to be her dog, Toto. The prevalence of adults relative to children emphasizes Dorothy's aloneness.

A third feature of Dorothy's anxiety is the attitude of the adult world. The privileged Miss Gulch sees it as her desire to strip Dorothy of her only friend, Toto. Dorothy's custodians are powerless to intervene on her behalf.

Finally, the environment seems malevolent. Rather than being supportive or growth-oriented, in Dorothy's world, nature turns as violent as Miss Gulch, and uproots homes, and people. She cannot find respite from her anxiety anywhere.

In the second part of the film, in Oz the three friends, the Scarecrow, the Tin Man, and the Cowardly Lion become the repository of much of Dorothy's anxiety. Their anxieties are more focused, but nevertheless they are continually undone by that anxiety. They require reassurance particularly from Dorothy in order to cope with their anxiety.

Dorothy's own anxiety is focused on one goal, getting home. Here she has help from a parental figure, the Good Witch of the North who gives her special red shoes for protection. The negative forces whether they be human or natural are deposited in the Wicked Witch of the West. At least in this world, Dorothy has help to cope with the Wicked Witch. Dorothy also has a peer group, the Munchkins, the little people, that is, the children of Oz. They provide peers or allies for Dorothy in this imagined world.

Finally the whole of Oz, the imagined world, is a strategy for Dorothy to cope with her real world anxiety. The creation of Oz itself implies how very much anxiety inhabits Dorothy's world.

Two Worlds

A real world and an imagined world, this is the strategy created to help Dorothy contain her anxiety. In a sense, the analogy is to the toy animal the child uses as the positive polarity as she/he learns about the real world. The more vigorous that the attachment is to the toy animal, the greater the fear factor about the world at large. The toy animal pictorializes a defense against the fear. So, too, Dorothy's Oz.

Dorothy is not 2 years old. She's 12, on the cusp of entering the adult world. Whatever her age she is clearly a child using the imagined world to fill up the enormous void left by the features of her real world.

Her real world is a black and white (at best sepia) world. As such it's imagined as a world with a big storm brewing. The sky is not bright but rather ominous, threatening. A tornado in the making swirls in the deep background. This portrayal of powerful nature is the context. Her aunt and uncle's farm is Dorothy's corner of Kansas. Although there is an animal, there are also three workmen. Is this a make work project? The farm certainly does not look to be a prosperous working farm. The workers seem to be edgy, tense rather than benevolent. Bickering characterizes the employer–employee relationship. Are the aunt and uncle making ends meet? Because it's the Midwest, and it's the depression, the viability of the farm is dubious. And why do aunt Emily and uncle Henry look so grandparent-like in their appearance? Are they old before their time?

One can imagine aunt Emily and uncle Henry being worried about the viability of their farm. How else is one to understand their appearance, the bickering with the workers, their ready submission to the will of Miss Gulch, owner of so much of the town? Does Miss Gulch also hold the mortgage to their farm?

This is Dorothy's real world—a storm is brewing; her home, the farm, is vulnerable to economic storms; and her aunt, her de facto mother, feels and acts powerless. For Dorothy, the real world is a frightening place. And her future is as subject to whim as is the fate of her dog. Each can be taken away in an instant. The real world then is a very dark place.

Oz as a world is created as an antidote to the real world. The imagined world is a world in color, vivid, brilliant color. Roads are yellow, and cities are emerald green. And there are principally benevolent adult figures—the Witch of the North and the Wizard. The punitive figure of the Wicked Witch of the West at the very least has adult offset figures. As for the balance of the adult figures—the Scarecrow, the Tin Man, and the Cowardly Lion—each are incomplete, in sense adults in deficit figures. By allowing them to join her in her journey to the Emerald City to pose serious and personal questions to the Wizard, Dorothy has allies in her quest. She is also sharing anxiety with these adult figures. Her own anxiety by doing so is diminished compared to her presentation in the real world sequence. In a sense, her imagined world is occupied by bad, good, and anxious adults, again an improvement on her real world.

A bit of gender probing in these two worlds suggests gender differences in power. In Dorothy's real world, uncle Henry is ineffectual, whereas her aunt Emily seems to be the critical "parent." Another woman, Miss Gulch, is the repository of power in the community. The male workers seem as ineffectual as uncle Henry. Only Professor Marvel as a male holds out any possibility of power. Because he examines her handbag for information about Dorothy and then presents that information as "sighted" information or revealed through magic powers information, Professor Marvel is a male under suspicion. In this sense, he has no real power. All the males have no power, and hence, the only hope in Dorothy's real world lies with the females.

In the imagined world, it's the same. The men are anxious as her three co-travelers and the wizard like Professor Marvel (same actor) admits he's a benevolent fraud. He can't even take Dorothy home. He flies off before she's ready, which leaves the women, and here the women replicate the real world. The Good Witch is an empowered aunt Emily and the Wicked Witch of the West is Miss Gulch revisited (same actress).

In terms of gender, the women have it in them to be powerful in *The Wizard of Oz*. And the men need the women to empower them. For Dorothy, a female, empowerment is the answer. And that's just what happens in *The Wizard of Oz*.

The two worlds are used creatively. The imagined world helps the child contain her anxiety and provides her sufficient empowerment to accept her real world (and move on).

The Fable

The fable is not realistic. All that occurs in it from a story point of view serves the moral of the story. In *It's a Wonderful Life*, an angel comes down from heaven to talk a man out of committing suicide. *Forrest Gump* is all about a limited character whose mother treated him as special.

Consequently, he influences all the "normal" people in his life over a 60-year period. The moral of the story is that special is special regardless of physical or emotional deficits. *Life is Beautiful* is all about how you bring up your children. The right attitude will get you through all life's hardships; in this film, even a concentration camp.

Fables are all about the power of a single idea about meeting life. It can be physical, emotional, and spiritual. Whatever the moral is, it's the key to the fable. In *The Wizard of Oz*, the moral of the story is that the solution to life's problems is within us, not out there somewhere in the ether. It is inside. And this moral is what Dorothy will learn in the course of *The Wizard of Oz*.

The fable can have a dark tone such as Schlondorff's *The Tin Drum* or it can be light as is Benigni's *Life is Beautiful*. Generally the tone can also shift as it does in *The Wizard of Oz* from the characters of Dorothy's real world to the lightness of the imagined world of Oz.

Fables also tend to have a journey quality. The journey represents the metamorphosis of the main character from idealist to realist in Boorman's *Excalibur*, from innocent to political activist in Schlondorff's *The Lost Honor of Katerina Blum*. For Dorothy, the journey is from being paralyzed by anxiety to a stage where she can move on in life.

Fables also tend to have elaborate and complex plots and here too the bifurcated world and the journey to Oz is an intense elaborate trip for Dorothy.

What is critical to the fable is that all actions and characters serve the moral of the story. All the characters and events in Dorothy's imagined world are present to articulate and apply a strategy to overcome the problem posed in her real world. Fables have a constructed feel to them because we see the character constructing a coping strategy. "I will not grow" is Oscar's strategy in *The Tin Drum*. "Life is a game" is Guido's strategy in *Life is Beautiful*. The imagined world of Oz with its wisdom and good fairy help Dorothy realize that the answer lies within, not outside as she previously thought.

There is also a ritualistic quality to the fable, a constructed pathway to the moral of the story. The yellow brick road is one pathway just as the Emerald City is a destination. The disposition of the qualities needed to meet life, head, heart, and courage, each in three different characters, is an example of how the ritualization is constructed. The shaman role of Professor Marvel and the Wizard of Oz is also constructed. The division of good and evil in the witches, who occupy different geographical zones, is also a construction.

Ritual is critical in the fable, because it moves meaning away from realism. The fable is all about using metaphor to say something about life.

The Musical

The musical is a genre of wish fulfillment. It is about being a success in a relationship and in work. Generally, a performance on stage (*The Bandwagon*) or in a film (*Singing in the Rain*) is the enabling action to move from aspirant to actualized. The musical focuses on a performance skill—singing, dancing as the vehicle for success. The tone of the Musical is light and enabling. The music is often part of the performance focus of the film.

The Wizard of Oz is a different kind of musical. It is about a non-performing character. In this sense, it is more similar to *Oklahoma* and *Brigadoon* than it is to *Swing Time* or *Cabaret*. It is also much darker in terms of the material than the musical tends to be. There have been darker musicals—*Damn Yankees* (the Devil) and *Cabaret* (the Nazis), but they are in the minority.

It's best to look at the musical dimension of *The Wizard of Oz* as a promise that all will be well in the end. The tone of the musical, enabling, fulfilling the wish of the main character, is sustained in *The Wizard of Oz*. But the use of the music is interesting. "Over the Rainbow," for example, is a lament about the impossibility of things getting better in Dorothy's current life. A better life is always beyond reach, somewhere, over the rainbow.

Only when Dorothy reaches her imagined world Oz, does optimism enter. The song "Follow the Yellow Brick Road" brims with the optimism so lacking in the earlier song.

It is best to think of *The Wizard of Oz* as a musical about an internal issue rather than an external event. I'll explain. Generally the musical is about the external event of putting on a show in order to be an entertainment success in the world and to secure a love relationship, also out there in the world.

In *The Wizard of Oz*, the focus is on an interior journey rather than an external event. It is about Dorothy's state of mind rather about success or failure. This characteristic establishes *The Wizard of Oz* as a different kind of musical.

Another dimension to this difference is that most musicals use a play, a nightclub act, a cabaret act, or a movie as integral to their stature. Each of these forms have their own style of performance, the silent movie exaggerated acting style in *Singing in the Rain*, for example.

The Wizard of Oz is linked not to the theater as its performance base but rather to the circus. This may have to do with the fact that children don't go to a lot of plays or cabaret acts in their formative years. But they do go to the circus. To set a performance base in the circus for a children's sensibility in *The Wizard of Oz*, seems perfectly attuned. Chaplin in *The Circus* and Fellini in *La Strada* use the circus as their framework for character and behavior, but their work emanated from an adult sensibility for, in the most part, an adult audience. Mervyn LeRoy as the producer working with the writers, Noel Langley, Florence Ryerson, and Edgar Alan Woolf, was looking to capitalize on the Baum books and their pictorialization of the circus in the child's life.

Consequently, the basis for the Scarecrow, the Tin Man, and the Cowardly Lion becomes the clown. Each performs in a pantomime style of acting. Movements are exaggerated and physical. Expression and verbalization are equally exaggerated.

The Good Witch is the ringmaster. The Wicked Witch of the West is the exaggerated expression of evil, in her way, a different kind of clown.

If we consider the imagined world of Oz with all its color, exaggeration, and clowns as the population, we can see Oz—the circus—as the equivalent of the play in *The Bandwagon*. In *The Wizard of Oz*, the circus is the forum for Dorothy's internal life pageant. In *The Bandwagon*, the play is the vehicle for Tony's (Fred Astaire) life pageant.

The Musical Fable

The Wizard of Oz is a musical that is also a fable. Producers and writers mix story forms because of the ambition they have for their story. Among the most famous mixed genre films are *Blade Runner* (film noir and science fiction), *Crimes and Misdemeanors* (melodrama and situation comedy), and *Basic Instinct* (police story and film noir). *The Wizard of Oz*, as a Musical, uses the circus as the performance metaphor for Dorothy's journey. That journey is internal rather than external, understandable and meaningful from the fact that the main character, Dorothy, is a child. Oz is enabling for Dorothy, and its presentation is tonally in keeping with the musical; it's light, lively, and enabling.

But LeRoy and company are interested in more than an entertainment in *The Wizard of Oz*. The fable is all about the moral of the story. In *The Wizard of Oz*, we have a main character who is beset by anxiety. The moral of the story has as its goal to contain her anxiety. You cannot run away from your problems. You have to face them. And the best place to do so is at home. It does not say it in so many words, but if you do stay at home, you can begin to deal with those problems. The moral of the story is you can deal with the difficulties; the answers are all inside.

Pan's Labyrinth

As in the case of *The Wizard of Oz*, there are two worlds depicted in Guillermo del Toro's *Pan's Labyrinth* (2006). Seen through the eyes of Ofelia, an 11-year-old girl, one is real, and the other imagined.

Ofelia's real world is 1944 Spain. And it is populated by her pregnant mother, her new stepfather, Captain Vidal, and the captain's housekeeper, Mercedes. Its rural setting is not unlike Kansas in *The Wizard of Oz*. It's an unsettled frontier where the captain rules with an iron fist and where the population is compliant or in revolt against him.

The captain is cruel, controlling, and violent with no interest in Ofelia. His only interest in her mother is the son she will bear him. Ofelia's mother is beautiful and weak. Life has all but crushed her. Mercedes is strong and supportive of Ofelia's individuality. Ofelia is a rebellious dreamer. In her world, fairies and princesses make the world a better place.

In this real world, Ofelia experiences only loss. She tries to save her mother but cannot. And she tries to save her baby brother. That effort will cost her her life.

Although the guerilla war is ongoing, it is part of Mercedes' life rather than Ofelia's. Although the captain has become an important part of her mother's life, Ofelia never joins this reconstituted family. She is only interested in her mother and the baby. Ofelia's noncompliance with the new family order is her "guerilla attack."

In Ofelia's imagined world, she is a princess, mistakenly sent to live among humans. In the captain's rural setting, a fairy leads her into a labyrinth, where a faun challenges her to three difficult tasks before the next full moon. If she is successful, it will prove her essence is intact, she has not become mortal.

Unlike Dorothy's imagined world in *The Wizard of Oz*, Ofelia's imagined world is not beautiful, and there is no good witch. Her world is ugly and violent, and the faun seems every bit as menacing as the captain. This may be the immortal world, but for Ofelia, the journey is as dangerous as life is in her real world. In this sense, Ofelia's alternative world is a less optimistic alternative. The consequence is to force Ofelia to be more active in both worlds. The result is that more is at stake for Ofelia. In comparison, Dorothy's world seems more gentle and more child-like.

Dread vs. Anxiety

Dorothy in *The Wizard of Oz* uses her imagined world to help her manage the anxiety promoted in her real world where her family cannot act on her behalf. In her real world, she will be victimized by a powerful adult who will take her dog, the greatest comfort she has in her life.

Ofelia faces a very different real world prepared to deny her mother and her brother, all that is important to her. Nor can Mercedes protect her from the captain, a merciless destroyer of the beauty and the fantasy life Ofelia needs to sustain herself. Ofelia faces a dire and dangerous world. She knows bad things will happen. The only thing to be determined is when. In this sense, hers is a world filled with dread. Consequently, she throws herself into her imagined world to desperately escape. But unlike Dorothy's imagined world, Ofelia faces an unreliable dangerous imagined world. Dread has crept into this world as well.

The consequence is Ofelia's rebellious behavior in her imagined world. During her second task, although warned not to eat any of the food on display, she eats two grapes, making her environment even more threatening. Although she escapes, she is not chastened. During the third task, the faun asks her to turn over to him her baby brother. The faun, knife in hand, tells her no harm will come to the baby. He needs only a few drops of blood from an innocent. Ofelia refuses distrusting and disobeying the faun. She runs off to save the brother. At that point, the captain finds her and shoots her reclaiming her brother, his son.

If death is the ultimate outcome of dread, this is the moment when the two worlds, real and imagined, merge and when what is most feared occurs, the collapse of Ofelia's world.

The film's codicil, which by shedding her own innocent blood, Ofelia has qualified to reclaim her rightful place as a princess in a place where her mother is the queen, is open to interpretation. Is the reclaimed status the final imagined thought of the dying Ofelia? Is this moment her justification for her ultimate sacrifice made to save the life of her baby brother? Perhaps! Whichever interpretation the moment confirms how very dark is Ofelia's world, a world in which dread is partnered with hope, the more natural state of childhood.

Sexuality

Although Ofelia is prepubescent, sexuality is an important part of her life. This is not the case in Dorothy's world in *The Wizard of Oz*. Indeed sexuality is notably absent from Dorothy's world.

In Ofelia's real world, it's her mother who is the center of sexuality. Beyond how Ofelia sees her mother, as a beauty, her mother's pregnancy is the focal point of her sexuality. Del Toro pictorializes the state of her pregnancy, as well as the methods used to sustain the pregnancy, in sexual terms. Beyond the mother's weakened, vulnerable state, del Toro presents the pregnancy in terms of ingesting and expelling, a reenactment of the act that led to the pregnancy. Ofelia's mother bleeds, and in order not to expel the fetus prematurely, Ofelia uses the faun's recommendation to place a bowl of milk, herbs, and a replicate of the fetus (it moves as a real fetus might and is blood covered) under her mother's bed. This act of superstition (as opposed to science) helps the mother recover and sustain the pregnancy. The visualization of this act of saving is as sexual as del Toro dares to suggest.

In Ofelia's imagined world, ingesting and expelling are also the avenues del Toro uses to sexualize Ofelia's actions. The first task is to visit an obese frog that has a key that Ofelia will need. Her first contact with the frog is his tongue. He lashes out and touches Ofelia, leaving a sticky residue on her arm. She then finds him three stones that look like bugs, his food of choice. Upon ingesting the rocks, the frog all but explodes; expelling his innards on top of which Ofelia finds the key she needs. In effect, the key is birthed following the ingesting of rocks offered by Ofelia. The exchange even in logical terms is a visualization of the sexual act. This exchange between a male frog and an 11-year-old girl is every bit as grotesque as sexual union between the cruel captain and Ofelia's sensitive, feeling mother. Neither represents love; both, however, have biological beginnings and consequences, birth.

Violence

The center of violence in Ofelia's real world is her stepfather, Captain Vidal. The center of violence in Ofelia's imagined world is the faun. Both have an aggressively masculine physicality.

When we first see Ofelia with her stepfather, she offers her left hand to greet him. He grabs her right hand tightly conveying punishment for her lack of respect toward him. Hostility will be the basis of exchange between them throughout the story.

To establish the captain's true character, a violent character, del Toro uses the first scene where he interacts with two villagers, father and son. The father has been caught with a shotgun, recently fired in the woods. He is suspected of being a guerilla fighter. The son protests, claiming his father to be a poor farmer, who has only been hunting rabbits for food. Outraged the captain beats the son to death and then shoots the father. Searching his pouch, he does find two recently killed rabbits.

The captain's penchant for violence includes shooting the local doctor and later Ofelia. In an earlier scene, when accusing Mercedes of being a guerilla sympathizer, she stabs the captain. He stitches one of the wounds, a slice from his mouth to his cheek. Doing violence to others and repairing the damage of violence toward him highlight the centrality of violence in Ofelia's real world.

In Ofelia's imagined world, the appearance and behavior of the faun portend violence toward her and hers. Beyond his menacing appearance, the faun wields a knife toward Ofelia's infant brother. He doesn't carry through the threat, but his intentions clearly feel destructive toward Ofelia.

Tone and the Fable

As we state in an earlier chapter, the fable is positive about the impact of its character on others (*Forrest Gump*) or about the character's assessment of their life (*It's a Wonderful Life*). Tone that accumulation of narrative detail and events makes that interpretation of characters and their lives credible.

The moral of the story in *The Wizard of Oz* is about self-reliance, even in children. Self-reliance in a dark time or place will save you. When we turn to *Pan's Labyrinth*, the moral of the story is less clear.

A powerful antagonist, a weak mother, and a disloyal housekeeper make up the adult population. The negative power structure bodes poorly for Ofelia our main character-child. In fact, she is killed by the antagonist.

Nor is the imagined world an antidote for Ofelia's dire situation. The imagined world brims with violence, monstrous creatures, and an unreliable menacing guide, the faun.

What can be said about Ofelia in both her real world and her imagined world is that she is not a naïf. Yes, she does love books and the world of fairies and fauns and princesses. But this is presented as a way to see an alternative to a real world beset with darkness and disappointment. Her mother, who has given up hope, preaches a similar attitude for Ofelia, but Ofelia doesn't buy it. She actively rejects the captain and his values. She resists in the face of the poor condition of her mother, and allies herself with nonscientific remedies to help her mother. And she acts to protect her infant brother from the captain and from the faun.

Ofelia is in active resistance to the values she rejects in the real world. The captain is a product of the Falange victory in the Spanish Civil War. His militarism, his chauvinism, and his cruelty are all resisted and rejected by Ofelia. The moral of *Pan's Labyrinth* is to act as Ofelia does, to resist, embracing alternate virtuous values, even if it costs you your life. And use that better world, the world where you are, what you dream of (a princess) to cope with the hardships of the real world. Only by doing so will you be able to endure the pain, the losses, and the disappointments of the real world. This is the moral of del Toro's dark fable.

16

Reframing the Active/ Passive Character Distinction

On the most superficial level, film is a medium founded on the illusion of believability—what we see looks real (most of the time). Thus, the focus of the producer and, consequently, the writer is on making what we see as engaging as possible. Otherwise, they lose our attention. Whether one calls the connection between screen and audience engaging or electric, tame or gripping, it is the elusive characteristic that all producers look for as intensely as Francisco Pizarro looked for gold and Vasco da Gama looked for spices. In our business, it's what everyone wants.

What are the implications for the character? More particularly, does every main character have to be active, energetic, and attractive, as well as find herself in an abundance of conflicting situations? There is little question that this option offers us characters who are appealing and easy to identify with, but it also offers us characters we rarely meet and who we rarely find in our own lives.

In this chapter, we challenge the notion that the central character must be active and energetic to ensure sufficient conflict and drive to carry us through a 90+-minute narrative story. Instead, we suggest that there is a much broader set of options available to you.

We acknowledge that in particular genres it is more useful to have active, energetic main characters. It's hard to imagine how the plot of *Die Hard* would unfold if John McClane (Bruce Willis) were a reflective or passive character. But ambivalence and confession are very interesting in the Phillip Marlowe that Elliot Gould portrays in Robert Altman's *The Long Goodbye*. Indeed, this main character is a perfect reflection of Los Angeles in the 1970s; more than one form of pollution influences Marlowe's behavior. A wide range of options is available when you begin to move away from the active main character. To chart this path, we begin by studying the conventions that surround the main character.

Conventional Notions of Character

The troubled teenager, the ambitious lawyer, the poor prize-fighter, the belligerent police officer, all are characters we know. We see them in film after film, although they may enter their stories through various methods. Key to our discussion is that all these characters conform to our notion of the character. By profession and by nature, they are prone to act against barriers to their goals; each, in his own way, is keen to overcome his current situation in life. In a sense, these characters are not willing to wait, think, discuss, or feel paralyzed. They are characters who act.

The Active Character

Central to the conventions of characterization is the character who, in the superficial sense, will act. Not only does this type of character fit more easily into the event-filled story line, but in all likelihood his actions will help shape that story line. In this sense, the active character helps you do your job—to tell the story as effectively as possible.

The active character is, by nature, a character who gets involved in relationships and in events. Active characters are less predictable in their responses to people and events, and this involvement and potential for surprise are useful and helpful qualities for the screenwriter. It isn't surprising, then, that the active character has become a convention for screenwriters. Wyatt Earp in the John Ford version of the Earp saga, *My Darling Clementine*, is a good example of the active main character.

The Energetic Character

Second only to the active character is the energetic one. Clearly, a character who is energetic will respond quickly to a situation of conflict or to a barrier to her goals. This response may be anxious or aggressive. In either case, the response is useful dramatically, because it highlights the conflict. Generally, the more difficult the barrier, the more intense the character's response. The question in the audience's mind is whether the character can overcome the oppositional force.

Audiences relate quickly to energy. Energy is attractive. It needn't be negative or positive, but it does enhance the feeling that your character has power. This power is open-ended in a way that powerlessness is not. Consequently, the energetic character is a very inviting character for the audience. The Russian colonel, played by Nikita Mikhalkov in his *Burnt by the Sun*, is a good example of an energetic main character.

The Intentional Character

Although the active character and the energetic character are the most common conventions used to create a main character, they are incomplete unless the character has a goal. Intentional characters are those characters who have goals that motivate them. Most often, secondary characters have more clarified, singular functions in the screen story and, as a result, appear to be more intentional. Main characters are generally in conflict about their goals, and through the actions and events of people, they work through the conflicts and move toward their goals. The audience must understand the conflict as well as the character's goal. Only then, can the energetic efforts of the main character engage us in his struggle.

The active, energetic, goal-directed character is the conventional screen character. Charm, wit, and sexiness are all add-ons that deepen our engagement with the main character. Each invites us in different ways to get involved with the main character. Diello (James Mason) in *Five Fingers* is a good example of the intentional main character.

Real Life and Dramatic Life

In real life, we find the full gamut of characters—from active to passive, energetic to depressed, happy to angry, frustrated to fulfilled. These characters exist, whatever their state, in the ebb and flow of everyday life, with both its ordinariness and its excitement. Elemental tasks mix with significant events, and, as with many of us, these characters' lives are surrounded by the confusion that so often engulfs people and events. Dramatic life is considerably more shaped. Conflict, critical events, and intentional characters are codependent variables that make up the screen story.

One of our goals in this chapter is to suggest that how you interpret dramatic life in film can help you draw real-life characters into your stories. Before you can do this, however, you have to understand the limits and opportunities of real life and dramatic life.

Real-Life Characters

The primary problem for the screenwriter is that if the real-life character is not active, not particularly energetic, and does not have a goal, she is difficult to place in a screen story. Characters such as this, disinterested in their fate, are potentially unappealing. Consequently, they don't lend themselves to involve audiences with their story.

We have purposely overstated the traits of real-life characters. Often, we encounter active, energetic, and goal-directed people; they are people to whom we feel drawn. But what about all those other people who are in the middle, who are the opposite of the conventional main character? Must we discard all of them as potential main characters? The answer is no. Real-life characters appear as main characters in *Land and Freedom* and *Truly Madly Deeply* and in the works of Mike Leigh.

Movie Characters

The opposite of the real-life character is the movie character—the character to whom we have grown accustomed through our exposure to movies and television. Because we have had so much media exposure, writers are as likely to draw on a movie character for characterization as they are to draw on a character they know from their everyday lives.

Movie characters are an exaggeration of dramatic characters. They are shaped in ways characters in real life are not. Movie characters tend to be goal directed, energetic, and active, but they go even further. They are often charismatic, at least in the case of main characters, despite their proximity to a stereotype. Movie characters seek out resolutions to the conflicts they encounter, but they do so in an exaggerated way. They apply their energy with a vigor virtually unknown in real life. The complexities of everyday life are alien to these characters. Movie characters represent the opposite of the more complex characters we examine shortly, characters who represent a shift away from the active character, and characters who are more recognizable in real life. The main character in *The Last Action Hero* is a good example of a movie main character.

Dramatic Characters

Dramatic characters lie between movie characters and real-life characters; they are not as resolution oriented as movie characters are, but because of the conflicts in which they find themselves, they must find a resolution. Such characters may feel ambivalent; they may choose not to act or they may not exhibit the kind of energy we associate with conventional main characters. Dramatic characters may act as observers, they may be catalysts, and very often they are in the middle of the action of the story most reluctantly. They may not understand the forces at work in the situation, and they may not function well even if they do understand the situation.

We get involved with these characters, because they find themselves in the midst of crises that take over their lives. This dramatic situation allows us to engage with characters regardless of whether they are active or passive. The further the character is from the movie character, the more likely we will recognize him in our lives. Because of this identification, our response to this character is likely to be more complex than it would be toward a movie character. The dramatic character provides a wide range of options from which the writer can choose to engage the audience.

Real Life as Drama

One of the most powerful films of the early 1970s was a small domestic drama by Ken Loach entitled *Family Life*. The movie followed the life of a young woman who was falling into a schizophrenic state. Needless to say, she wasn't a very active character. Indeed, after 2 hours, she barely spoke. Yet, her story breaks the heart. Her conflict is multileveled. She is the younger of two daughters and is controlled rather than parented. Her stronger sister has broken out of the stranglehold of the family and has made a life for herself. The doctors who treat the young woman disagree on her psychological state.

A psychiatrist experimenting with treatments has luck with her, and she improves. However, when he loses his position to a more conventional doctor, the young woman moves from group therapy to shock treatment, and she is lost. The story has dramatic values at the level of interaction between family and institution (hospital). The character has a goal—to get better—but she is not strong enough to overcome the goal of her family (to keep her under control) and the goal of the institution (to keep people like her under control).

In real life, this young woman is quite recognizable, but she is a stranger and an exception to the screen story. The story works because of the nature of the dramatic situation, and because it has narrative drive.

Narrative Drive

Stories such as *Family Life* have a crisis that is sufficiently acute, and, if there is no quick resolution, the character will be lost forever. This sense of urgency is compelling and gives the story narrative drive.

A sense of urgency for the fate of a character can be replaced by a sense of urgency for the fate of a community (*Matewan*), of a society (*The China Syndrome*), or of the world (*WarGames*). In all cases, the sense of urgency creates the story parameters. Will the world be saved? Will the characters survive and thrive? However, a sense of urgency is not enough to grab the audience. There has to be an interesting story to tell. For example, the training of an assassin to kill on command and the execution of that command at the highest levels of government is the narrative drive of *The Manchurian Candidate*.

The more reflective or passive the character, the greater the writer's reliance on a sense of urgency and a strong story. *Psycho* is populated by characters of varying psychological states. The main character, portrayed by Janet Leigh, steals money and runs away. For 40 minutes of screen time, we are with her as she plots and ponders, decides, and finally changes her mind.

Guilt is her most prevalent characteristic. After 40 minutes, Hitchcock kills her off, and we are left without a main character. Yet the film remains etched in our memories. Why? Aside from Hitchcock's brilliant artistry, urgency and narrative drive are what capture our attention. Thus, the story doesn't end with the death of Marion Crane.

Narrative Energy

Often, a character's energy is the same as the story's energy. This is the case in *The Lady Eve*, in which Barbara Stanwyck's Eve is certain that she will wrap Henry Fonda's Adam around her pinky. The narrative energy is the way in which she goes about it. There is a lot of story to *The Lady Eve*. There are many other examples of this type of story, including *Papillon*, *The Great Escape*, *Champion*, and *Stella Dallas*.

Energy and drive, however important to the screen story, needn't reside in the main characters. The story and the secondary characters can compensate for the ambivalence or conflict of the central character. More often, we are presented with stories that have considerable narrative drive and characters who are ambivalent, conflicting, or reflective—the writer in *Sunset Boulevard*, the decent insurance clerk in *The Apartment*, or the reluctant book promoter in *Crossing Delancey*. In each of these stories, the drive or energy comes from the story. In each case, there is a secondary character who is driven and whose actions are critical to the evolution of the story. The most memorable of this trio of screen stories is *Sunset Boulevard*. Gloria Swanson's portrayal of the aging silent screen star is one of the greatest moments in cinematic history.

The Problem of Passivity

Avoid passive central characters: This is good advice for beginning screenwriters, who may face multiple problems of structure, language, and character, but it is too restrictive for writers who are comfortable with structure and storytelling. Clearly, the character who is totally passive leaves little room for opportunity to interact with the world. However, such characters have been the center of film stories—*Oblomov* and, more recently, a Polish film called *A Short Film About Love*. As mentioned earlier, other characters and the story have to compensate for passivity in the major character.

What is not possible—except in an Andy Warhol movie, perhaps—is a screen story in which all characters and the level of action and narrative remain quiescent. This does not leave much room to deal with stories in which characters are relatively passive, reflective, ambivalent, and unexpressive. In this type of story, the writer runs into real trouble. In the remainder of this chapter, we discuss examples of screen stories in which the active/passive balance clearly tilts toward passive characters.

■ ■ ■   ## A Case Study of a Passive Main Character I:
sex, lies, and videotape

The main character in Steven Soderbergh's *sex, lies, and videotape* is aware that she is unfulfilled but is totally unaware as to why. She is a passive main character. The young married woman is having sexual problems. She has a concerned therapist, a promiscuous sister, and a wandering husband. She is unaware and frightened by much of her behavior, particularly by her lack of sexual feelings.

An old friend arrives to stay with the woman's family and in his straightforward way alienates her husband, shares his sexual sublimation with her (he videotapes women talking about their sex lives), and stimulates her sister to new heights of arousal. His presence also destabilizes the young wife's slender hold on what passes for a married life. Her marriage collapses, she has a sexual experience with the voyeur, and becomes better friends with her sister.

This simple story parallels the *Sleeping Beauty* story, except here, Sleeping Beauty is awake—at least consciously—but she doesn't understand a thing about her life, about her failures, or about her potential. Total lack of awareness is not an active, reflective, or even reticent position for a major character. Indeed, it is a position that promises a character scorn or rejection. Only the despicable behavior of her husband and sister save her from such a fate. This is not the usual position for involvement and identification with the main character. The young wife is probably similar to young wives we know in real life—confused and a submerged personality—but she is not a character we often meet in movie life.

The old friend is hardly the typical Prince Charming. He is a voyeur with no clear means of support, and his position with the other characters is too ambiguous to make him appealing. He is, however, mysterious, which makes us curious about him and about his fate. But he doesn't replicate the powerful position that Georgia had in *Four Friends* or Ray had in *Who'll Stop the Rain?*

■ ■ ■   ## A Case Study of a Passive Main Character II:
My Own Private Idaho

The main character in Gus Van Sant's *My Own Private Idaho* is a narcoleptic. When there's a troubled situation, he goes to sleep. He is thus the antithesis of the type of goal-directed character whose goal and energy drive the story.

Mike (River Phoenix) is a street hustler in Portland, Oregon. He leads an unpredictable life, living moment to moment. He dreams of home—Idaho—and of a mother who will nurture him. When he meets Scott, a rich, rebellious street kid, Mike is attracted to him. Together, they search for Mike's mother. When they find Mike's brother, he tries unsuccessfully to disabuse Mike of his illusions of their mother. The search takes them to Italy, where Scott falls in love with a young woman. The two men part, Mike returning to his former way of life and Scott becoming what he always was—a person of privilege, a person who belongs. The film ends with Mike asleep on a road in Idaho. His search continues, but the road for Mike goes nowhere.

Mike is passive in a different sense than the wife is in *sex, lies, and videotape*. She is passive in her marriage and in her sexual modesty until she is transformed by a man who uses a camera as a wand to awaken her. There is no awakening for Mike in *My Own Private Idaho*. He not only remains on the margins of society but also seems to have little impact even on those with whom he has a relationship. Scott tolerates, even accepts his neediness, but Mike's brother does not. He is infuriated by Mike's unwillingness to face the truth of his life. Although there is one moment in the script when Mike attempts to be with another (Scott), he is for the most part withdrawn, acting out a psychodrama or actually sleeping in response to the pain of the moment. In the sense of realizable goals, Mike has none; he has only the desire to find his mother. Mike is a passive character in the most complex sense. It is far more difficult to relate to a passive character like Mike's than to a character who is eventually transformed. For the audience, therefore, he represents an emotional enigma who resists rescue because his mental state is his failed attempt to rescue himself.

■ ■ ■   A case study of main character as catalyst: "The Kids are Alright"

In Lisa Cholodenko's *"The Kids are Alright"* (2010), Julianne Moore portrays Jules, the "female" in a long term lesbian relationship. Jules and Nic (Annette Bening) have two adolescent children. The older of the tow, Joni wants to get to know their biological father, the sperm donor who provided the sperms for the two pregnancies. When she finds the donor, Paul (Mark Ruffalo), she invites him into her family's lives.

Although it is Joni's need to know that is he critical moment of "The Kids are Alright", it's Jules who explores the premise of the film. That premise, am I homosexual or heterosexual shakes up the stability of the family. The fact that Joni's mother explores he heterosexual option with Joni's biological father, Paul provides the exploration with its "rational" dimension as well as with its seismic emotional implications for Jules' longstanding relationship with Nic.

Jules' experiment in heterosexuality is grounded in a character that is tentative, insecure and more academic than pragmatic about career development. Jules is very much the emotionally labile female in her relationship with Nix. Nic on the other hand is the "stable, critical male". When Paul shows up and offers Jules he opportunity to redesign his backyard, Jules has the opportunity to prove she is not who Nic's criticism of her implies she is. Paul's bed and Paul are only a step away.

As a main character, Jules' impulsivity and physical need for affirmation make her more catalyst for what will follow, than a main character who genuinely changes through the exploration. Her actions nudge all the members of the family to take each other less for granted. The relationship with Paul ends. The relationship with Nic is re-established. All ends well in this dramedy that positions homosexuality and heterosexuality as opposites of the premise, only to find the two options not as emotionally different as one might have assumed.

▪ ▪ ▪ A case study of main character as catalyst II: *Goodbye Lenin*

The main character in Bernd Lichtenberg's "Goodbye Lenin" (2003) is Alexander Kerner. Alexander lives in East Berlin. The film begins in the 1970s when his father Robert escapes to the West and ends 20 years later after the two Germanys have been unified. Alexander's goal is to maintain his family or what's left of it no matter what happens. And a great deal happens.

His mother hospitalized by depression after that father leaves, threatens to leave Alexander emotionally. Her fragile state keeps Alex on family watch through his mother's enthusiasm to "improve" Communism, through his older sister's relationships, and through his mother's heart attack and coma in 1989, weeks before the Berlin Wall comes down.

Told when the mother awakens from her coma eight month later that any shock/change would kill her, Alex hatches a "no change" plan. In spite of the Wall coming down and the consequent flood of change in visual, material and economic facts, Alex decides to take his mother home, to redecorate the apartment in the pre-Wall style and in essence pretend everything is exactly the same.

This means recycling jars reclaimed from the trash and filling them with their newer Western versions. It means producing TV programs of old, and entering a subterfuge with neighbors, the mother's old students and with his sister, her new lover, and his own new girlfriend, a nurse who attended his mother in hospital.

The pretense works through to the end of the second Act and then unravels. The mother does suffer another heart attack and dies in Act 3 but not before Alex has found his father and attempted to reunite his nuclear family (in spite of father's new wife, children, life, in the West).

Alex remains steadfast in his original goal, rescue the family. Regardless of all the changes, political and personal, he clings to his original dream of family. Although Alex changes jobs and relational status, it's his original goal that stands out. In this sense he is the catalyst for a plot launched to save his mother. For Alex his personal goal trumps all else. It is in this sense that he is the catalyst for the clash of values (old vs. new, Capitalist vs. Communist) that dominate the plot, and it is his tenacity which highlights he priorities within the narrative.

▪ ▪ ▪ A Case Study of Main Character as Observer I: *Inside Moves*

Rory (John Savage) introduces himself to us by jumping out of a tenth-floor window and failing to kill himself. Disabled, he faces a limited life. This is a depressing beginning to one of the more uplifting films of the 1980s.

Rory is befriended by a group of disabled persons who hang out in an Oakland bar. One of them, Jerry, invites him to a basketball game where Rory is impressed by the expressiveness of his new friend. In fact, Jerry is a loudmouth who acts as if he can play the game better than the pros. He tells the star player how he blew the game and challenges the star, Alvin, to a one-on-one playoff. Alvin accepts and almost loses to Jerry. Rory watches and it begins to dawn on him that if Jerry (with a gimpy leg) can almost beat a pro, there are possibilities to his life.

Rory slowly begins to engage in his life; he takes an ownership stake in the bar. As Jerry's career ascends, Rory begins to grow. He becomes interested in a woman; the future is beginning to have options. But his ascent is tied to Jerry. Only after he has observed or responded to Jerry's achievements, does he try to broaden his life. Rory is always passive and observing. It is Jerry and the other disabled people who catalyze his final choice—to live fully, rather than in a limited way that is akin to suicide. The secondary characters are very active and energetic, despite being confined to wheelchairs, or blind, or even without arms. The narrative is elaborate and filled with events and people. There is a lot of story for Rory to observe and with which eventually to engage.

We never know Rory very well, but we can see his tentativeness, and we can relate to his emergence. He is never more than an observer. His condition doesn't permit him to play basketball like Jerry or to be a romantic activist with the waitress he loves. All of Rory's efforts are tentative. In the end, his efforts secure our respect for his decency and for his insight into himself and into Jerry, but it is late in the story for his character to win us over. Consequently, Rory is very far from the conventional main character in film, but he is never very far from characters we know in real life.

■ ■ ■   A Case Study of Main Character as Observer II: *Black Robe*

Brian Moore's *Black Robe*, set in early nineteenth-century Quebec, has as its main character Father Laforgue, a Catholic priest (Lothaire Bluteau). The priest is being taken inland to Huronia, and his guide is an Indian named Chomina (August Schellenberg). Accompanying him is a young fur trader, the family of Chomina, and several of his men.

The priest is an ascetic in a physical land, traveling with physical people. The Catholic priest believes in Jesus and organized Catholic religion; the Indians believe in the spirit of animals and the land. The journey to Huronia is a dangerous one, and the priest is totally dependent on his Indian guides. He also chooses not to experience the Indian values/interpretation of life. This is not so for his fur trader companion, who is quickly involved with Chomina's daughter. The priest watches, desires, and flagellates himself, so that he can transcend or avoid his earthly feelings.

The priest remains on the periphery of the action, always observing, but never entering it. Although he is present and is clearly the main character, his position remains as an observer. He does not change in the course of the story, which is unusual; he maintains his position as observer. He represents one corner of the spiritual struggle in the story; it seems the less fulsome interpretation of spirituality. Although the priest lives at the end, while Chomina dies, it is the spiritual life of the Indian that seems complex and appropriate to the primitiveness of the land. The priest's position in comparison seems outside the land—not transcendent, but residual. In this sense, his observer status as main character consolidates the narrative view that the coming of the white man and his religion to North America was not so much a progressive step as it was a new step, a different step, a misstep.

■ ■ ■   A Case Study of Main Character as Outsider: *Four Friends*

Steven Tesich wrote *Four Friends*, an autobiographical story that spans the 1950s to the 1970s. The story opens with young Danilo (Craig Wasson) and his mother joining their Yugoslavian father in East Chicago, Indiana, and takes us through the sexual revolution of the 1960s to when Danilo takes his parents to the boat on which they return to Yugoslavia; he remains to make his life in America.

Danilo's is an immigrant story. He stays quietly on the sidelines and allows his friends to speak for his rebelliousness and sexual expressiveness. He is alienated from his parents; against his father's wishes, he goes to college, where he befriends a rich American. He is engaged to his friend's sister, again against the wishes of his father. *Four Friends* ends with Danilo reconciled to his adolescent girlfriend, Georgia, and resigned to the idea that his father will never understand him.

Most of the story's action occurs around Danilo, and there is a lot of story to tell. The tale of the 1960s, from JFK to Vietnam, is interwoven with Danilo's story. Many of the characters are more vivid than Danilo. Georgia is the catalytic figure in the story. She is expressive, exploratory, and spontaneous—everything Danilo is not.

The story maintains Danilo as an outsider looking in on a society from an idealistic perspective. For him, America is the land of his dreams. What he sees rarely conforms to his dream, but that is because he remains on the outside. Danilo is passionate and energetic, but he simply cannot express those feelings; he is constrained by his posture as outsider. Consequently, he is a man on the margin, a position that poses various difficulties for a main character, not the least of which is identification.

One benefit of presenting the main character as outsider is the opportunity to reflect on the action of the story as well as to participate in it. Although this isn't taken up in Tesich's character, Danilo's inexpressiveness provides pauses where we can reflect on how he feels. Consequently, there is a constant tension (not knowing how the character will react) that is useful in maintaining our involvement. However, it is a tension that leads not to the concern for Danilo but to the curiosity about him and the story. This seems to be the fate of placing the main character in the position of outsider.

■ ■ ■   A Case Study of Main Character as Medium: *Field of Dreams*

Bill Kinsella (Kevin Costner), in *Field of Dreams*, is a main character who has a vision—he must build a baseball field in the middle of his Iowa cornfield. Kinsella is a three-dimensional character. He's a nice guy; he's a dreamer; he isn't materialistic. A series of voices and visions populate his thoughts, with Shoeless Joe Jackson and the other scandalized White Sox from the 1919 team accused of throwing the World Series. Kinsella calls upon a black writer (James Earl Jones) and an old doctor to assist him in his quest, and they eventually join the ghost players in the idealized diamond in the sky. Kinsella finally gets to see his dead father and reconcile himself to the former baseball player whose memory he had long scorned.

Perhaps we all long to say something to parents we have lost. Kinsella's wish isn't fulfilled until the end of the film, and until then, there isn't much to him. Unlike some of the other passive, reticent, or ambivalent main characters we have discussed, Kinsella's flatness is not compensated for by a rushing flow of narrative or by another major character who drives the story. The writer is interesting but too ambivalent to compensate for the shortcomings of the main character. Yet, the story has a powerful emotional resonance in Act III, despite the use of larger-than-life characters and a main character whose primary function is to act as a medium for this 1980s fantasy. Perhaps Kinsella, too, is recognizable as one of us.

■ ■ ■ A Case Study of Splitting the Main Character: *Mystic Pizza*

Another approach to the active/passive split in the main character is to challenge our involvement in a manner that fractures our identification with one character, whether that person is active or passive. In *Mystic Pizza*, there are three main characters—two sisters and a friend, all in their late teens and all preparing for their adult lives. Each character is different: One sister is loud and sexy; the other is quiet and cerebral; the friend is ambivalent. Character splitting offers us choices in terms of identification and involvement. On a continuum, the characters are active to passive around their sexuality, just as they are active to passive about a career, a husband, and their futures. The element that ties these three characters together is their need to work to secure a future. All of them come from working-class families, and all of them work in the restaurant named Mystic Pizza.

The story has none of the narrative drive or the overdeveloped secondary characters present in the films discussed previously in this chapter. What does propel us through the story is, in part, a choice of characters to identify with, the honesty of the characters, and the parallels of each character's story. In each case, the story unfolds through a relationship. The difference is the background of each character. Although there are significant differences among the three, their personal bond suggests that we concern ourselves with the fate of all three young women. These main characters are recognizable to us; they live among us and, in some cases, could be us.

■ ■ ■ A Case Study of Antagonist Compensating for Main Character: *The Little Foxes*

Alexandra (Teresa Wright), the young protagonist of Lillian Hellman's *The Little Foxes*, is an innocent. Her mother, Regina (Bette Davis), the antagonist, is anything but innocent. Regina is so worldwise, manipulative, and evil that we can't believe she has given birth to someone quite so angelic. This polarity is so extreme that it compensates for the slightness of the protagonist.

Set in the deep South in 1900, *The Little Foxes* tells the story of a wealthy Southern family. Their goal of growing richer is stymied by their reliance on the banker in the family, Alexandra's father (Herbert Marshall). The ailing man is urged to return from convalescence in Baltimore. Business dealings, particularly with his wife and her brothers, threaten his wealth and health, and cost him his life. Alexandra is witness to all these. The issue for her is whether she wants to remain an innocent or face up to the fact that her mother is willing to do anything and sacrifice anyone to fulfill her own ambition. This particular strategy has been frequently used to restructure the active/passive nature of a protagonist. The Luke Skywalker–Darth Vader relationship in *Star Wars* is one of the most famous examples of this very strategy.

Conclusion

In all the case studies discussed in this chapter, the main characters were not active or energized. Danilo (*Four Friends*) is a reactive character, and Rory (*Inside Moves*) and John (*Who'll Stop the Rain?*) are characters who act out of desperation. These actions bring each of them to the brink of disaster. They are reticent, passive, ambivalent main characters, and all are recognizable to us. They are tentative and all too human. They are flawed, and, in each case, they have been considered failures for much of their lives. Their commonality lies in their recognizability. They remind us of people we know rather than of movie characters.

In order to make these characters succeed dramatically, however, the writers had to modify their narrative approaches. These characters need dramatic situations and stories that are particularly energetic. The stories also needed memorable secondary characters, such as Ray Hicks in *Who'll Stop the Rain?* or Jerry in *Inside Moves*. Finally, these stories require a very special antagonist, an antagonist who in her nature can compensate for the shortcomings of the main character. Regina in *The Little Foxes* is but one of a long line of great antagonists.

The benefit, should you choose to use active/passive characters, is that you will move away from movie characters and move toward real-life characters. This shift, as we have seen, can take you toward other options for your character. In the next chapter, we discuss one of these options—identification with the main character.

17

Stretching the Limits of Character Identification

Audiences identify with characters who are in difficult situations and with characters they like or wish to be like. This identification is useful because it quickly simplifies the relationship between the audience and the story. The audience enters the story through the character with whom it can identify.

Identification also provides an umbrella of tolerance. Once involved with a character, viewers tend to overlook the more subtle issues of story credibility and are forgiving of the occasional use of coincidence. Writers don't want their viewers to become too aware of the various manipulations that are the mechanics of the screen story. This awareness is always a danger when identification with the main character is moderate or absent.

But what happens in a screen story when the main character is less than admirable? What is the balance between character exploration and audience empathy? Is there an underside to viewer identification? When does identification turn to voyeurism? We explore these character-related issues in this chapter.

Sympathy, Empathy, and Antipathy

Viewers relate to characters for different reasons. They relate to Sophie (Meryl Streep) in *Sophie's Choice* out of sympathy. She is a concentration camp survivor and her situation invites our sympathy. Sympathy means caring but not necessarily identification. Do we empathize with her? Do we identify with her? No. The same can be said about Sol Nazerman (Rod Steiger) in *The Pawnbroker* and Lena (Isabelle Huppert) in *Entre Nous*.

The factors that prevent us from becoming more deeply involved with these characters are different in each case. We don't empathize with Sophie because she is never very forthcoming. Whether one considers this withholding or lying is semantic. In the case of Sol Nazerman, he is too enraged, too angry at the whole world, to invite us to know him beyond his anger and his pain. In the case of Lena, she is a woman who makes a choice to marry in order to save her life. Later, she wants to escape from the man who provided her with her married life. We feel sorry for Lena, but we also feel sorry for her husband. There is little room for empathy.

In each case, the characters are trapped by past events, and their present life is hell. They escaped from one hell (e.g., the Holocaust) only to find another. The high level of tragedy in each of their lives precludes an empathetic identification and keeps our involvement with them at the level of sympathy.

Empathy is the step beyond sympathy. Empathy implies an identification with a character. Not only do we feel with them, often we feel like them. Wes Block (Clint Eastwood), a troubled detective in *Tightrope*, is a concerned single father as well as a professional with personal doubts. His flaws make him all too human, and, as a result, we empathize with him. The same can be said for Isabelle (Amy Irving) in *Crossing Delancey*. She is a professional person with no personal life. When an unorthodox opportunity arises to become involved with a man who cares about her, she doesn't know how to respond. Her vulnerability in this circumstance makes her appealing and empathetic. We care about her, just as we care about Wes Block.

In the majority of cases, the writer will use an empathetic, or at least sympathetic, main character. Occasionally, the writer will develop a character for whom our dislike outweighs our like. Antipathy for a main character is not as rare as we might think. We might feel ambivalent about Harry Mitchell (Roy Scheider) in *52 Pick-Up*, or hostile toward the manipulative Richard Boyle (James Woods) in *Salvador*, or loathing toward the cowardice of the conformist (Jean-Louis Trintignant) in *The Conformist*, but in each case, there is something about the character that involves us. The actors are portraying characters we like to hate—philanderers, manipulators, and cowards. Yet, we do get involved with them on some level. Harry Mitchell, in *52 Pick-Up*, is being blackmailed about an affair. The twist is that his girlfriend is part of the blackmail scheme. At risk is his marriage to a high-profile local politician. His wife's career is also at risk. His behavior is not admirable, but at least we can understand his desire to save his wife's reputation. Here lies the key to this type of character—there must be one redeeming quality that humanizes him. We can relate to that element.

When we look at Richard Boyle, in *Salvador*, we see the same quality. He will do anything for a story, but his love for a Salvadoran woman (he has a wife in the United States) is so intense, genuine, and different from the rest of his behavior that we can relate to this relationship and begin to see a more positive side to Boyle.

In the case of *The Conformist*, the title character's strong emotional relationship with a woman other than his wife is the quality to which we relate. The other woman is the wife of a political dissident in Paris, who the conformist must set up for assassination. His desire to save the politician's wife is so strong that we see a commitment for another not reflected elsewhere in the film. The fact that he allows her to be killed, despite her pleas to him, re-establishes his cowardice and is the most troubling moment in the film. Until then, however, this relationship is an attempt to reach us.

Identification vs. Voyeurism

Our relationship with main characters isn't always straightforward. Perhaps the person who understood that best was Alfred Hitchcock. He wanted us to be involved, to identify with his characters, but he also wanted us to see them, physically and emotionally, from a detached view—as if we were voyeurs. If we can sympathize with their plight, empathize with their positive attributes, yet objectively observe their obsessive tendencies, we become implicated in their downfall; we share their guilt.

Marion Crane (Janet Leigh) in *Psycho* and John Ferguson (James Stewart) in *Vertigo* are obsessed characters who steal or manipulate, and yet we are, in a complex and not always comforting way, involved with them. These two characters have a great deal in common with the most voyeuristic of Hitchcock's characters, L.B. Jeffries (James Stewart) in *Rear Window*. All three characters are straightforward, outwardly normal people who are trapped. In the case of Marion Crane, she is trapped in an extramarital affair that will only move ahead with enough money. So she steals the money and is then plagued by guilt. This guilt suddenly turns into expiation when she decides to return the money. Finally at peace with herself, she is killed by Norman Bates, and we are left in the position of voyeur and so are implicated in her death.

John Ferguson, in *Vertigo*, falls in love with a woman he has been hired to follow. As a policeman and now as a private detective, his fear of heights is exploited when his subject, Madeline (Kim Novak), falls from a window atop a tower, an apparent suicide. Riddled with guilt, he finds a woman who looks like Madeline, and in reality is Madeline, and makes her over to look like the woman he lost. When he discovers she has duped him, he returns to the scene of the first "death," but this time she does slip, fall, and die. His guilt is rekindled, and he is left standing atop the tower, looking down at the dead Madeline. He is a man suspended above the Earth, immersed in the realization that he has now caused the death of his loved one.

In both *Psycho* and *Vertigo*, each character has positive and negative characteristics. Through their negative actions, we are distanced from the characters and assume the position of voyeurs. As we distance ourselves, we begin to feel guilty, as if we were abandoning people to whom we had started to relate. Our guilt becomes particularly acute as the situations deteriorate (death for Crane, death of a loved one for Ferguson). Hitchcock has succeeded in implicating us in their guilt. Of course, this type of balance is not exclusive to Hitchcock, although it is most often found in this genre. *Bedroom Window*, *Blue Velvet*, and *Dead Ringers* are other examples of films that use this technique.

Self-Revelation

Another approach to overcome the negative qualities of a character is to provide him with an opportunity to reveal his real self. We generally see the social or public side of people. In everyday socializing, a person's true feelings, true self, is concealed. Hence, if a character is a rogue, writers usually give him some charm, and we come to think of him as something of a rascal, not as an evil or totally negative person. But if he is not charming, the moment of revelation is a very useful device to gain our understanding, complicity, or tolerance for the character. If this moment is particularly unexpected, the writer can even generate empathy for the character.

A good example of this type of character is Midge Kelly (Kirk Douglas) in *Champion*. This Carl Foreman screenplay chronicles the rise and fall of a world champion boxer. In the first half of the film, we sense that Kelly is a restless, ambitious man who wants to rise above his childhood poverty. He is opportunistic at every turn. Halfway through the film, Midge talks about what it was like to be a poor boy. The humiliation he suffered remains a vivid scar, and at that moment, we begin to forgive, or at least tolerate, his cruelty to those closest to him.

In *Blame it on Rio*, Matthew Hollis (Michael Caine) takes a vacation with a divorced friend and their teenage daughters. Matthew's marriage is foundering, and he takes solace in his friend's daughter. The affair that follows is kept from his friend but not from his own daughter. Matthew is not an admirable man in this Charlie Peters–Larry Gelbart script, but the writers give Matthew many moments of revelation. From the beginning of the film, Matthew begins to confess directly to us, and this continues periodically throughout the film. The result is that we tolerate his character.

Another approach to the moment of revelation is taken in *True Believer*. Edward Dodd (James Woods), a famous civil rights lawyer of the 1960s, is now a lawyer primarily for drug dealers. His moment of revelation comes when a new assistant, Roger Barron, chastises him for not taking on a controversial murder case. He is no longer the man whom Barron traveled to New York to work with. This is a humiliating moment for Dodd, who is hungry for the glory and publicity of those early days and now has to settle for less idealistic clients. We learn about Dodd's past and we sense who he was. Can he be that person again? Until this point in the story, Dodd is presented as a mesmerizing speaker in court but as a lawyer who has fallen from grace. He has talent but conviction without idealism seems ignoble. Can Dodd once again be noble? Although he is energetic, it is not possible to sympathize or empathize with him. Only when we learn who he was do we hope that he can recapture his idealism.

A moment of revelation is important for a less-than-sympathetic main character and is a device writers often use to involve us with character. These moments can also apply to more than just the main character. Virtually all the characters in John Patrick Stanley's *Moonstruck* have their moments of revelation, and the three key characters in David Mamet's *Things Change* have their moments as well. It is important to remember that the moment of revelation is very often associated with a story point in which the characters have undergone a humiliating experience. When they are vulnerable, they reveal their private sides. Then, whether saint or sinner, we are hooked by the character.

Heroism

A moment of revelation, particularly when a character is feeling vulnerable, requires courage. We don't mean Arnold Schwarzenegger's commando-type heroism but rather courage on a more human scale. Main characters, whether we identify with them to a greater or lesser degree, require a good measure of heroism in order to overcome the dramatic hurdles that stand in their way. Heroism can be defined, for our purposes here, as a main character's attitude plus action in surmounting challenges that prevent the character from achieving a goal. The use of heroism provides a means of viewing the character in a more sympathetic light and offsets our lack of empathy for the main character.

One route to heroism is the quality of the challenge. The challenge can take the form of a remarkable antagonist, like the Joker in *Batman*; it can be the setting, such as the land in *The Emigrants* and the desert in *Lawrence of Arabia*; or it can be class rigidity, as in *Pelle the Conqueror*. In each case, the level and quality of the challenge make the main character heroic.

However, not every character is as tenacious as T.E. Lawrence or as rich and talented as *Batman*. When we look at the rigid Colonel (Alec Guinness) in *The Bridge on the River Kwai* or the selfish captain (William Holden) in the same film, we find their behavior in the second half of the film no less heroic. The angry father (George C. Scott) in *Hardcore* is faced with the heroic search to find a teenage daughter who has run away from a religious home life to become an actress in hardcore pornographic films. The father has to overcome many qualities in his own background in order to proceed with his search.

One character we recognize as neither sympathetic nor empathic is Lyn McAdam (James Stewart) in *Winchester '73*. We don't know much about Lyn, other than that he is angry and is an excellent rifleman. Only as the story unfolds does the character have a number of moments of revelation. Each time, he tells us a little more. Then, in Act III, we finally learn the true source of his bitterness—his brother killed his father. In his attempt to confront and kill his brother, he has to overcome many challenges. During the course of his plight, he makes the transition from angry protagonist to vengeful hero. His challenges—outlaws, Indians, and more outlaws—seem increasingly daunting, yet his ability to overcome these challenges makes him increasingly empathetic.

Charisma

Whether a main character is empathetic or antagonistic, a quality that can be as useful as heroism is the elusive charisma that makes everyday people attractive. Although charisma is more often thought of in connection with politicians and movie stars, it can also be used in the development of characters. It is particularly important in the character, who, on first meeting, comes off in an unappealing light. Good examples of this quality range from the eccentric T.E. Lawrence in *Lawrence of Arabia* to Travis Bickle in *Taxi Driver*. Both are men with a mission seemingly beyond their own means. Screen stories naturally gravitate toward characters who have power (*Patton*) or who want power (*The Candidate*), and toward the famous (*All the President's Men*) and the infamous (*The Last Ten Days of Adolph Hitler*).

What is charisma, and how can it be developed in a character? Irvine Schiffer, in his book *Charisma*,[1] suggests certain characteristics that create charisma. They are as follows:

- An element of foreignness
- A subtle imperfection
- A calling or sense of mission
- Polarized aggression or intensity
- A sexual dimension
- An ability to convince others

The charismatic character, then, is somewhat different from other characters; he arouses our curiosity and attracts us with his intensity and sense of mission. Charismatic characters have a powerful sexual dimension, and they are not perfect. They might have a bad back, wear glasses, or be exceedingly short. The key element is that we quickly notice that they are different, but we are not put off by them; instead, we are curious about them. Charisma is helpful in balancing negative and positive characteristics, and it helps us get involved with a character.

The Tragic Flaw

Very often when a central character is portrayed in a negative light, our acceptance of him hinges on a tragic flaw in his character. Not dissimilar from Macbeth's sense of invincibility (some might call it susceptibility to delusion) or the lean and hungry look of Cassius in *Julius Caesar*, there is often an extreme quality that is the source of both strength and duplicity in these main characters. Lonesome Rhodes's (Andy Griffith) earnestness in Budd Schulberg's *A Face in the Crowd* is the basis for his wide appeal in small groups and then large groups (on television) but is also the source of his duplicity. Steven Gold's (Tom Hanks) immaturity in David Seltzer's *Punchline* is the source of his rage with people on stage and off, but it is also the source of his strength as a comic. The audience is attracted to the power, but repelled by the nature of the tragic flaw.

In order to better understand how the tragic flaw plays itself out in screen stories, it is useful for us to acknowledge that this quality is played out in a literary manner. A tragic flaw adds subtext and is the link between the character and the society that has produced this character. For example, Sidney Falco (Tony Curtis) is a New York press agent in Clifford Odets and Ernest Lehman's *Sweet Smell of Success*. Falco lives in a tough city in which he must depend on the kindness of gossip columnists to make a living. Unfortunately, there are no kind gossip columnists in New York. Sidney Falco's tragic flaw is his ambition. He will do anything and sacrifice anyone in order to succeed. On the other coast, Joe Gillis (William Holden), in Billy Wilder's *Sunset Boulevard*, wants the good life of Hollywood. He takes advantage of Norma Desmond's self-myopia and tries to rewrite her script for Mr. DeMille. Here, too, ambition leads Joe to desperation, opportunity, and finally to his own death.

The worldviews of Falco and Gillis, and the implicit worldview of the entertainment industry, are treated no more kindly than are the characters. In both cases, the viewer has a fascinating insight into character pathology and the cold ambition needed to succeed in the industry. And in both cases, the language and the dialogue are brittle, hard, and brilliant. The dialogue alone creates for us the excitement, the dynamism, of being inside the industry.

Falco and Gillis are men of their time and place. Other places and other times yield other memorable characters. King (George Segal), in Bryan Forbes's *King Rat*, lives in the world of the Japanese prisoner-of-war camp. Whereas others die, King, thanks to opportunism, thrives. Charles Tatum (Kirk Douglas), in Billy Wilder, Lesser Samuels, and Walter Newman's *Ace in the Hole* (later retitled *The Big Carnival*), is even more blinded by ambition than is Sidney Falco. Tatum is a New York newspaperman exiled because of his alcoholism to work in New Mexico. While there, he encounters a story that may take him back to New York. A man is trapped deep in a cave. The man could easily be rescued, but Tatum convinces the sheriff and others to delay in order to get some publicity for the town. Although the man slowly dies in the cave, a wave of pity carries the story to the national airwaves. People drive to the site; large equipment is set up to start the digging; admission is charged to gain entry to the site. Charlie finally makes it to the national airwaves and back to New York—until the man dies in the cave. Then, his story begins to unravel, and Charlie, the brilliant reporter, is turned into a murderer—all because of his immoral sense of ambition.

There are numerous other wonderful examples of the character with a tragic flaw—among them are the self-absorbed Blume (George Segal), in Paul Mazursky's *Blume in Love*, and the mad Rupert Popkin (Robert De Niro), in Paul Zimmerman's *King of Comedy*. The use of the tragic flaw attracts and repels the viewer, all the while making an unappealing main character tolerable.

▪ ▪ ▪ A Case Study of Charisma: *White Hunter, Black Heart*

White Hunter, Black Heart is the story of John Huston (as played by Clint Eastwood) in the making of *The African Queen*. Peter Viertel's novel is adapted by Viertel, James Bridges, and Burt Kennedy, and the focus of the screenplay is Huston's indifference to making a difficult location film in Africa and his total devotion at that time to shooting elephants. This ultimately leads to the death of a devoted black guide, and only then does Huston turn back to the purpose of his being in Africa—to make the film.

The screenplay does not dwell on the famous participants in the film—Bogart, Hepburn, Spiegel, and Harry Cohn. Rather, it stays with the character of Huston and his obsession. What is fascinating about the screenplay is Huston's vigorous narcissism. He loves to talk, challenge, bully, decide, contradict, all just to hear the tonal rhythms of his own speech. It's as if he's making up dialogue rather than behaving out of an ethos, a humanity. His speech on London and Nazi sympathizers during the Blitz, a tale told to an anti-Semitic British expatriate during an elegant dinner, is a classic example of liberal ideology and cynical manipulation. His is a character who loves to watch, and so do we. Whether it is his love of language or outrageous behavior, Huston is energetic, deterministic, and flawed—the perfect charismatic character.

The question here is whether these qualities are enough to draw us into the story. They certainly fascinate us, but the tragedy that befalls Huston (the loss of the guide) does not strike us as tragic for him, but rather tragic because of him. Consequently, we remain outside of his character, impressed by his energy but never identifying with him. The result is a bold experiment where we see what the character does but not how he feels.

▪ ▪ ▪ A Case Study of Charisma and Tragic Flaw: *Raging Bull*

Jake LaMotta (Robert De Niro), in Paul Schrader and Mardik Martin's *Raging Bull*, is a charismatic, but flawed, character. He is an intense Italian-American who, physically and emotionally, is always attacking. He has a primitive, animalistic aggression that is both the source of his power as a boxer and the poison to all his personal relationships.

As LaMotta moves toward the championship, he loses two wives and a brother—the people closest to him. Consequently, he loses everything. His impulsive aggressiveness results in the loss of his material goods as well as in his imprisonment. The film ends with LaMotta rehearsing his nightclub routine. He is the warm-up act for strippers—a far cry from being the champion boxer of the world. This character attracts and repels us at the same time. We are attracted to his restless energy, but we are repelled when it is used to beat up his wife. We are attracted by his ability to remain standing in the ring, no matter how badly he is beaten, but we are appalled by the savagery taking place. LaMotta is charismatic, but he is also terribly flawed. His flaw destroys him, leaving no more than a pathetic, second-rate comedian living off the remains of his sullied reputation.

■ ■ ■   ## A Case Study of Self-Revelation and Heroism: *The Manchurian Candidate*

Raymond Shaw (Lawrence Harvey), in George Axelrod's *The Manchurian Candidate*, is not a likable central character. He is arrogant, rude, and angry. He is also a man who has been brainwashed in Korea to be a Communist assassin. He is particularly dangerous because of his skill as a marksman, because of his unawareness of his chosen role, and because he is beyond suspicion. He is the stepson of a United States Senator, chosen to be the vice-presidential candidate of his party, and he is a Congressional Medal of Honor war hero.

Raymond's character, however, is of greatest interest to us. He is a negative character, and yet, by the end of the story, we empathize with a man who has killed at least five innocent people, including his own wife. This comes about in one key scene. The scene occurs when Raymond is drunk and opens up to his friend and commanding officer, Ben Marco (Frank Sinatra). In a state of utter despair, he repeatedly tells Ben that he knows he is not a lovable person. He then describes a time in his life when he was lovable. He describes meeting the woman, Josie Jordan, with whom he fell in love: As her father was the Senator that Raymond's mother once slandered as a Communist, the two families were at odds, but with Josie, Raymond laughed and became lovable; however, his mother finally broke up the relationship, and Raymond returned to his unlovable self. In this scene, Raymond also expresses his hatred for his mother and his inability to go against her.

Both his breakup with Josie and his relationship with his mother become critical in the second half of the film. Josie re-enters his life and Raymond enjoys a brief happiness when they marry. Then, his mother re-establishes her special hold over Raymond, and we learn that she is the Communist agent who controls Raymond, the assassin, in the United States.

The fact that Raymond reveals his inner self to us, the fact that his self is so totally different from the Raymond we have seen so far in the story, both shocks and moves us. He evolves from assassin to pawn, and we empathize with a character who was, up until that point, negative in every sense. As a pawn, we see Raymond in his Act III struggle with and against his mother, a heroic struggle of a weak son attempting to overcome an overpowering mother. At the end, in his struggle against his mother, Raymond becomes a real war hero who the Communists created.

■ ■ ■   ## A Case Study of Identification and the Negative Main Character: *Paper Mask*

The negative main character has a great deal in common with the classic main character. Each has energy, appeal, charm, and a goal, but the negative main character differs in the nature of that goal. Through an identification process, we understand and can share the positive goal of the classic main character. But through the same process, we can identify with the negative main character despite the nature of his goal.

Matthew Harris (Paul McGann), a hospital orderly in John Collee's *Paper Mask*, really admires the hospital's doctors: they own the hospital and have the respect of the women who work there. One night, Harris witnesses an automobile accident in which a young doctor is killed. He moves the body into the mortuary and steals the doctor's identification papers. The rest of the story is Harris's attempt to create a career as a doctor in two hospitals. At first he is awkward, but, helped by a veteran nurse, he almost succeeds, until an old acquaintance, a fellow orderly, moves to his new hospital. At this stage, so close to success, Matthew refuses to give up. He kills his friend, and the pretense goes on.

As one might imagine, Harris can be undone at any point—faulty medical practice being the primary problem. Equally possible is that he might slip up and reveal his false identity. There is also the recognition factor: How long can one hide from the past? Clearly, Harris's goal is to lie about himself and his profession. Even without proper training, he hopes to put himself in a position where people will trust him with their lives. Because of his lack of training, of course, they are at far higher risk than they realize. His goal makes him a negative main character.

Nevertheless, the vigor, the charm, and the relentlessness with which he pursues his goal create a certain amount of empathy for him, but not enough for us to identify with him. How then does writer John Collee create an identification with Harris? He uses the plot structure to create the necessary identification. Collee constantly puts Harris in danger of being caught—by a nurse, a hospital administrator, and a friend from the past; Harris is a man in constant danger. By using this plot device, we have no choice but to identify with him, because we identify with people who are in constant danger.

■ ■ ■   A Case of the Negative Main Character: *The Conformist*

The Conformist, Alberto Moravia's story of the making of a Fascist in Mussolini's prewar Italy of the 1930s, is the classic portrait of a negative main character. Marcello Clerici is an upper-class gentleman from an unorthodox family—his mother is a drug addict, and his mad father is confined to a mental institution. They once were people of standing, but Marcello does not identify with them; he wants order in his life. Hence, he becomes engaged to a flighty, nouveau riche young woman, and he wants to become a member of the Fascist party. Marrying the young woman requires only that he go to confession, a temporary return to the Catholic Church. Joining the Fascist party is more complex—he must go to Paris to trap his former professor, Quadri, a radical Fascist dissenter. Marcello agrees.

On his honeymoon in Paris, he goes to see the professor, befriends him and his wife, Anna, and then betrays them. Quadri and Anna are assassinated en route to their rural home. At the end of the war, Marcello decides that he no longer wants to be a Fascist; hence, so he betrays the blind friend who first introduced him to the party.

There is nothing admirable about Marcello. He is a coward and morally a cynic. He joins the Fascists to be empowered in the new society. He marries a woman for whom he has only contempt. And when he does fall in love, with Anna Quadri, he does nothing to prevent her death.

How, then, do the writers create empathy for Marcello? First, they show his scarred past—he is raped by the chauffeur, whom he believes he has killed in anger. In his present life, it is clear that neither his mother nor father were role models for him. Finally, the writers show us that Marcello knows what he is doing, but his self-contempt is so great that his negative actions fit in with his self-image. The writers show a level of consciousness, of choice, rather than desperation, in Marcello's actions. In this way, empathy is created for a character who has no admirable qualities, who is not charismatic, and whose goals are reprehensible.

■ ■ ■ A Case of an Ambivalent Main Character: "A Serious Man"

Although the classic main character and the negative main character share many qualities–except their goal–this is not the case with the ambivalent main character–often posing a distinct problem for the dramatic impact of the narrative.

In Joel and Ethan Coen's "A Serious Man" (2009), Larry Gopnik (Michael Stulburg) is a Midwestern physics professor. He has a wife, two children and is up for tenure. But life brims with dread for Larry Gopnik. Although he lives in Minnesota, he's never really left the shtetl. It's not that Larry Gopnik fears the worst. The worst is what happens to him. The question is how will he survive?

In short order, his wife announces she will leave him for a widower, the widower write anonymous letters to his tenure committee recommending Larry Gopnik be denied tenure, his son Danny is in trouble around non-payment for drugs, this in the year of his bar mitzvah, Larry's brother Arthur, with a record of transgressions, may have transgressed. Life seems to be piling on and it gets worse. An Asian student given a poor grade offers a bribe for better. He gives Larry an envelope, it's full of money. Not long after the boy's father arrives suggesting he take the money and change the grade or he'll have Larry charged with blackmail.

Although his competitor Sy dies in a car crash, Larry's wife insists he, Larry pay for the funeral. In despair Larry seeks out rabbinical counsel. Can religion, more belief save Larry from total destruction? The answer never comes clear and we are left with a Larry Gopnik neither saved nor condemned; ambivalence has infected the narrative as a whole. And it's in that state that we leave Larry Gopnik.

■ ■ ■ A Case Study of Identification and Voyeurism: *Blue Velvet*

Jeffrey Beaumont (Kyle MacLachlan), in David Lynch's *Blue Velvet*, seems to be a nice, middle-class young man in a small town. He is intelligent and curious. When he finds a severed ear in a field in Lumberton, he wants to find out to whom it belongs. His search leads him to a beautiful nightclub singer. Aided by the local police detective's daughter, he infiltrates the singer's home and begins to watch her. But he watches her not as a man with a mission but as a man in lust. He is aroused by her, and when she discovers he's broken into her apartment and has watched her undress, she turns the tables on him and rapes him.

This description of Act I begs a number of questions, not least of which is: Where is this story going? Of direct interest to us is that Jeffrey is a character with whom we can certainly identify; he has all the qualities we admire. But then he begins to behave like a voyeur. The events that Jeffrey watches are so violent, so unusual on the screen, that we are repelled and yet drawn to them.

As the story progresses and we return to the mystery (the missing ear), the behavior becomes more predictable. Jeffrey is again a protagonist we can admire, even if we don't fully understand why he is so driven (curiosity is not enough of an explanation). In this film, the role of the antagonist, Frank (Dennis Hopper), is important. He is a criminal, cruel, and misogynistic; he is unpredictable and vengeful. When Frank beats Jeffrey because of their mutual interest in the singer (as a jealous suitor would), we sympathize with Jeffrey's Boy Scout behavior. Jeffrey is earnest again, just the opposite of Frank. The antagonist takes over the voyeuristic dimensions (we become fascinated and repelled by him), and we identify with Jeffrey.

Lynch plays with identification and voyeurism throughout the film. As he is robbing us of our illusions of the sanctity of small-town life, there is little, if any, solace for the viewer. The best we can do is to identify with Jeffrey, even though he has raised our suspicions of his goals and motivations.

■ ■ ■   **A Case Study Beyond Voyeurism—The Discovery of Empathy: *The Boys of St. Vincent (Parts I & II)***

The Boys of St. Vincent, written by Des Walsh, John N. Smith, and Sam Grana, is an excellent example of the discovery of empathy in an absolutely vile character. The film is set in a Catholic orphanage in Newfoundland. In the first part of the two-part film, the focus is on the boys, and particularly on Kevin and his abuse at the hands of the orphanage director, Father Lavin. The first part concentrates on the investigation of suspicions of sexual abuse, how it is discovered and then covered up. The second part of the film, set 15 years later, focuses on the trial of Father Lavin. The main character in Part II is Father Lavin (Henry Czerney), who has now left the church and made a life in Montreal. He has two children, a wife, and a job—in sum, a new life. The charges and the trial pose questions of responsibility for both victim and victimizer. By focusing on Father Lavin, the film humanizes the perpetrator as it carries us beyond a voyeuristic position into a relationship with a character whose actions are despicable beyond description.

Although the writers do stay with Kevin and his struggle over whether to testify, they also create another main character in Father Lavin. His struggle is over whether to hide his past or to own up to it, particularly with his family (his wife). In terms of a negative main character, we have seen in Part I Lavin's goal, his sexual satisfaction, and his sadism played out in terms of his love object, Kevin. The Father Lavin we meet in Part II has a temper, but he seems to have overcome his desire for young boys. But what creates empathy for Father Lavin are his meetings with a psychiatrist, who has to assess him for the purposes of the trial. Those sessions create a good deal of empathy because Father Lavin provides us with a private moment, a confession, where we learn that he, too, was adopted and sexually abused as a young child. He did raise himself up in terms of class, education, and status, but the neglected child in Lavin is filled with the pain that fuels the adult Lavin's rage. That moment takes us past viewing him strictly as a repellent perpetrator and into a relationship with him. That empathetic relationship is shocking because of how negative our sense of the man, and his abuse of power and privilege (vis-à-vis young helpless boys), has been. Although he returns to his angry state when his wife at the end tells him she's leaving him, we remain acutely aware that this man is no longer a conventional negative character. He is complex, vulnerable, and sadistic. We have a relationship with him, empathy having replaced the distance of voyeurism.

Conclusion

The use of empathetic and energetic main characters is more widespread than it first seems. To establish the audience's identification with the main character, the writer can either create sympathy for the main character or present the vulnerable side of that character, to invite empathy. The writer can use a main character who challenges the audience's positive relationship with him and stretches the limits of identification. In order to do so, certain conditions must exist that allow the audience to become involved with such a character.

First, the main character should be charismatic. Jake LaMotta and George Patton are good examples. Second, the sense of mission the character exhibits implies an aura of heroism that is particularly appealing to audiences. These characters also generally have a tragic flaw that prevents them from being successful human beings. Generally, these characters exhibit an aloneness that implies a sense of tragedy. Finally, these characters tend to exhibit their flaw through self-revelation. This moment creates a vulnerable main character who may be unlikable, but who briefly becomes a fuller human being. Although these characters revert to their former selves soon thereafter, the audience's feelings toward them are never the same.

It is possible to use main characters who stretch the limits of identification. Certain conditions should prevail, however, to allow for the audience's engagement with the main character. If those conditions don't prevail, the writer will ensure that the viewers are voyeurs rather than participants.

Stories can function and remain interesting when the viewer is a voyeur. Particular filmmakers—Hitchcock, Lynch, and Godard—prefer that the viewer occupy both positions, voyeur and participant. The balance of the two positions depends on the narrative structure of the story as well as on the nature of the main character. If the writer wants the viewers to occupy the voyeuristic position, a more distant and unappealing main character will ensure that outcome. On the contrary, if the writer wants to place the viewers as participants, their identification with the main character must be challenged. The result is that the audience will relate to a wide range of main characters.

Reference

1.   I. Schiffer, *Charisma* (Toronto: University of Toronto Press, 1973).

18

Main and Secondary Characters

Traditionally, the main character is played against secondary ones in order to demonstrate that only the main character can surmount the obstacles posed in the story. This promotes the notion of a singular hero set against the world. By altering this relationship, a scriptwriter can suggest that no one character is privileged, and that the main character has to deal with the same limitations confronting all the other characters.

Classic Example: On the Waterfront

To explore this relationship, we first look at the classic example of the main character vs. secondary characters. In Budd Schulberg's *On the Waterfront*, the main character, Terry Malloy (Marlon Brando), faces a dilemma. He can be a criminal and a member of the union mob organization of which his brother is a part, or he can follow his more ethical instincts and try to lead a responsible (read *moral* or *anti-mob*) life. As with every good main character, Terry has it in him to go either way—criminal or good guy. He also has the energetic self-reflection to be troubled by his situation and is empathetic and charismatic. In short, he is the type of main character who focuses the story and helps tell the story.

The secondary characters line up on both sides of Terry's moral dilemma; they are either saints or sinners. The principal sinners are the head of the union, Johnny Friendly (Lee J. Cobb), and Charlie the Gent (Rod Steiger). Charlie, as Terry's brother, and Johnny, Terry's principal benefactor, are in positions to have particularly strong influence on Terry. Indeed, Terry's livelihood depends on the quality of his relationship with Charlie and Johnny. The screen story begins with Terry luring his friend Joey to a roof where the two raise pigeons. Johnny's henchmen proceed to throw Joey from the roof because he was ready to testify against union corruption and was therefore a threat to Johnny. Because Terry helped Johnny to get rid of Joey, he is immediately implicated. Although his conscience is troubled ("Joey wasn't a bad kid," he says),[1] Terry accepts a cozy job on the waterfront.

On the side of the saints are two important secondary characters: Joey's sister, Edie (Eva Marie Saint), and Father Barry (Karl Malden). Through his involvement with Edie, and the priest's call for moral warfare on the waterfront, Terry's conscience and consciousness are stirred. But it is only when Johnny forces Terry's brother Charlie to prevent Terry from speaking to the Crime Commission that the two brothers confront the nature of their relationship in the famous I-could-have-been-somebody speech. Now it is Charlie who suffers pangs of conscience. He releases Terry, an action that results in his own death. If there is one action that makes Terry's decision personal as well as moral, it is the death of his brother. Terry has made his choice to destroy Johnny. It almost costs him his life, but, in the end, Terry heroically acts on his choice.

All four of the secondary characters mentioned are strong characterizations, differentiated from Terry in their clear position as either saint or sinner. Only Charlie's character is uncertain. In this sense, Terry's choice is heroic because he has to overcome his own uncertainty. Each of the secondary characters acts as a catalyst to provoke Terry to act. They are foils that reveal different aspects of Terry's character, serve to illuminate Terry's conflict, and help him resolve his problem.

On the Waterfront represents the classic notion of main character and secondary characters. In no way does this notion suggest that secondary characters have to be uninteresting and maim the stature of the main character. Eve (Anne Baxter), in Joseph L. Mankiewicz's *All About Eve*, and Norma Desmond (Gloria Swanson), in Billy Wilder and Charles Brackett's *Sunset Boulevard*, are among the most memorable screen characters, yet both are secondary characters in classic dramas in which the main characters, Margo Channing (Bette Davis) and Joe Gillis (William Holden), respectively, are challenged to surmount the obstacles posed in the story.

Secondary characters can be interesting, and they can have their own goals (as Eve does in *All About Eve*). Often, their goals are so important and so oppositional to the main characters' goals that the secondary characters become the antagonists. Johnny Friendly, in *On the Waterfront*, and Eve, in *All About Eve*, both present themselves as antagonists. In doing so, such secondary characters often take on as complex a personality and passion as seen in the main characters. Indeed, the more powerful the antagonist, the more heroic the struggle of the main character and the more likely we are to confirm the main character's primacy in the world the film story creates.

At what point does dramatic democracy set in to promote a more complex view of the main character, who is one of the many characters struggling to work out a position during a particular film story? The answer depends on the writer. Many stories have explored this concept, and the result can be both interesting and confusing to the audience. It is in this type of drama that the level of skill and originality of the writer is tested, and we begin to move away from the classic balance between main characters and secondary characters.

▪ ▪ ▪   A Case Study of Dramatic Democracy: *Love with the Proper Stranger*

Arnold Schulman's *Love with the Proper Stranger* is a story in which two characters both attempt to resolve their dilemmas—to live life as their parents did (to marry) or to live a more independent life filled with sexual gratification (to be single). Angela (Natalie Wood) and Rocky (Steve McQueen) are Italian-Americans. Both come from immigrant parents who have instilled old-school values in the lives of their children. Both children are in full rebellion. But how serious is the rebellion? Will they ever be free? Do they want to be free?

The story has a very creative opening. In a busy musician's hiring hall, Rocky is looking for work. He wants to be paged to appear busy, and so he is. But it's not a scam; someone is really looking for him—Angela. He doesn't recognize her. Even after she tells him she's expecting his baby, he still doesn't recognize her. All she wants from him is the name of a doctor, so that she can get an abortion. This is not an auspicious beginning to a relationship that is the subject of the balance of the screen story. But, surprisingly, the film starts the relationship at a point where many other screen stories end.

We find out a great deal more about Angela's family life during the course of the film—her guilt-rendering mother, her overprotective, smothering brother—but we can't conclude that she is the main character. We also meet Rocky's parents and his latest girlfriend (Edie Adams). These characters present their unappealing version of domesticity. Both Angela and Rocky are on the run from domesticity, a view they associate with marriage.

Ironically, Angela and Rocky move through this story headed toward marriage, but when one proposes, the other opposes on the grounds of familiarity. Rocky offers to marry Angela because it is the right thing to do; Angela doesn't like the reason behind his offer. These two people, so intimate before the story began, learn to like each other and eventually fall in love. Whether they transcend the domesticity from which they ran is avoided in the romantic, open-ended conclusion, which leaves them kissing in front of a big crowd outside of Macy's.

What is most significant is that neither Rocky's nor Angela's struggle is made more heroic than the struggle of the other. These two characters find a solution, but we are not certain (as we would be if the ending were more heroic) that this is the end of their relationship problems. This is just the end of the film. We hope they will find happiness, but we have an uneasy feeling that their struggles will continue. This paradoxical conclusion is an inevitable result of following the plights of two equally balanced characters. This dramatic democracy is more credible, but it undermines the degree of resolution and catharsis one associates with the classic main character–secondary character balance.

▪ ▪ ▪   A Case Study of Plot Over Character: *Groundhog Day*

It is unusual when plot supersedes character in relation to our involvement in a story, but this is the case in Danny Rubin and Harold Ramis's *Groundhog Day*. As with the vigor of plotting in Dale Launer's work (*Blind Date*,

Ruthless People), *Groundhog Day* works with a powerful plot conceit to overcome the deficit of character in the screenplay.

Phil Conners (Bill Murray), a TV weatherman, has an inflated view of himself. When he is assigned once again to the annual live report from Punxsutawney, Pennsylvania, on Groundhog Day, it's too much. Accompanied by a producer (Andie McDowell) and a cameraman, Phil is obnoxious, uncooperative, and dying to get back to Pittsburgh. But a storm prevents his return, and when he wakes up the next morning, he finds himself living through a nightmare—it's Groundhog Day again. A few more repeats of the day and Phil realizes he's trapped in the worst day of his life. The rest of the screenplay relates to how he responds to being trapped.

Phil's character is clearly unappealing, and, although they differ, the producer and cameraman are not fascinating. She is ingenuous; the cameraman is sarcastic. Their characters do not compensate for Phil's flatness. What does compensate is the adventuresome quality of the plot. Phil is by turns cynical, opportunistic, and criminal. Once he discovers that he can't be punished for what he does, he becomes quite inventive about what he can get away with each day. This polar swing in behavior liberates the plot just as Phil himself is being trapped. Only when he experiences something he deeply wants—the love of his producer— does Phil regret being trapped in Groundhog Day. At that point, his behavior becomes saintly, too good to be stuck anywhere, and the day finally changes, just as Phil has.

The interesting element in the film is how plot development compensates for a main character who does not engage us empathetically. In *Groundhog Day*, only the plot and its inventiveness compensate for the lack of interesting characters; in this case, it is the plot, not the character, that saves the day.

▪ ▪ ▪ A Case Study of Multiple Main Characters: *Mystic Pizza*

Some films opt for three protagonists rather than one. An early example (1946) is Robert Sherwood's *The Best Years of Our Lives*. Postwar adjustments were thematically appropriate to that time. The more recent *Mystic Pizza* is appropriate to the 1980s. Feminism, upward mobility, acquisitiveness, and education all play parts in the film.

Kat (Annabeth Gish), Daisy (Julia Roberts), and Jo (Lili Taylor) are three young women who work at Mystic Pizza, in Mystic, Connecticut. Daisy and Kat are sisters. All three women wonder about the future and, through their male– female relationships, learn that there are no easy answers. All they have is an enduring affection for one another, which, they hope, will help them through their lives.

Having three main characters divides character identification as well as the capacity to make any one character's struggles heroic. Indeed, the fact that each meets her travails in a different fashion—Kat with a naive romanticism, Daisy with a street-smart aggressiveness, and Jo with an adolescent propensity for avoidance—suggests that all these women are dependent on one another. For example, if Kat had Daisy's street smarts, she wouldn't have fallen in love with a married man. These differences in character and approach to problem resolution threaten to destabilize the unity of the story, but they don't.

Because the time frame is short and because each character's story chronicles a relationship, there is a sense of unity. These stories are all slices of the same pizza, to use the metaphor from the movie. These are winning characters; their intentions and actions are understandable, not alienating. Their mutual friendship creates a net under the individual stories, and the result is an emotional unity that is as strong as a single-protagonist screen story.

The men in each relationship are the antagonists of this story. When the three women salute one another at the marriage that ends (and begins) the story, we admire them and resent those who come between them—their men. Writers Amy Jones, Perry Howze, Randy Howze, and Alfred Uhry have fashioned a sisterhood story that transcends the downside of using more than one main character and alleviates the consequences of the traditional main character–secondary character dynamic. This screen story is very much in balance.

▪ ▪ ▪ A case study of the main character as antagonist: *The Talented Mr. Ripley*

Does the negative main character need to be surrounded by one group of character even more negative and by another that is more positive? This is the central question posed from a narrative perspective by Anthony Minghella in his screenplay, "The Talented Mr. Ripley" (1999).

Base on Patricia Highsmith's novel of the same name, filmed in 1960 by Rene Clement as "Plein di Soleil", this story of Tom Riley down on his luck in New York. Mistaken for a classmate of a well-to-do playboy, Dickie Greenleaf, Tom is paid to go to Europe and convince Dickie to return home. This begins Tom Ripley's journey to pretend to be someone he's not.

In the course of that journey Tom will fall in love with Dickie and with his life. He kills Dickie when Dickie threatens to send him away, begins to impersonate Dickie in Italy, kills Freddy Miles, a friend of Dickie's when he threatens to unmask Tom, and finally kills a homosexual lover whose existence threatens to suggest he is ot the heterosexual Dickie.

In order to sustain the sense that part of the character population is more negative than Tom Ripley, both Dickie and Freddy are portrayed as shallow, callow and cruel. Whether this merits their fate is dubious. Both women in the story, Marge Sherwood and Meredith Logue are portrayed as possessions more than people. The character population, at least its younger characters are principally more negative than otherwise. Their positioning is similar to the publishers in "The Hoax" (2007) and the adults in Hanneke's "The White Ribbon" (2009). If you are powerful materially or in authority, skewing these groups toward the negative, creates some degree of sympathy for a negative main character, who is positioned as a victim of those in power.

▪ ▪ ▪   A case study of balance: *"Revanche"*

"Revanche" (2008) written by Gotz Spielmann, balances off the classic case of the main character dominating and driving the narrative. In "Revanche" the main character is Alex, an ex-con working in a bordello. To extricate himself from a dead end life, he chooses to liberate himself and his prostitute girlfriend, Tamara. To do so he will rob a bank in a small town close to the home of his grandfather, a farmer. Escaping from the robbery, Tamara is killed by a police bullet.

Balancing the narrative here is a secondary character, Susanne, with a goal, to have a child; her husband, Robert, the policeman who killed Tamara, is infertile. Both Alex and Susanne have good intentions but to execute those intentions each undertakes a transgressive strategy, a robbery and unfaithfulness (Suzanne sleeps with Alex and becomes pregnant).

Alex and Suzanne are very different as people. She is church-going, a good neighbor, and wife, seemingly bourgeois in lifestyle. Alex on the other hand, is sketchy. He works in the margins of society; he finds a love relationship in that margin, and he is willing to steal. His only conventional undertaking is to cut wood for his grandfather because his mother has asked him to help the grandfather. In this sense each is opposite to the other.

They are also opposite emotionally. Susanne is forthcoming, communicative, and social. Alex on the other hand, is sullen, angry and brimming to take revenge for Tamara's death. Revenge means killing Robert, and until the end we believe he will kill the policeman who killed his lover.

How then is it that he doesn't? In his sexual union with Susanne, Alex changes. He sees the baby room she and Robert furnished only to be proved impulsive when Susanne miscarried. He is impressed by her assertiveness in their relationship. And he is confused when she discovers that Alex's dead lover is the same woman that Robert killed. In spite of this knowledge she tells him that she will not betray him. She also tells him their affair is over. She has what she wants (a pregnancy). It's as if her pragmatism and tolerance opens up an option for Alex. Emotionality demands he kill Robert. Susanne's tolerance of Alex, suggests maybe he doesn't have to kill Robert. Perhaps he can live here with his grandfather. Perhaps he can have a new life, a different life. At this moment the film ends. By using balance between Alex the main character and Susanne as a subtle transformational secondary character, Spielmann has opened up new possibilities in "Revanche".

▪ ▪ ▪   A Case Study of Main Character as a Witness: *Full Metal Jacket*

Private Joker (Matthew Modine), in *Full Metal Jacket* (written by Stanley Kubrick, Michael Herr, and Gustav Hasford), is as much a witness as he is a main character. The story breaks down into two sections (another innovation of this screen story). The first part is the story of basic training; the second story is about combat in Vietnam, particularly concerning one patrol in Huê during the Tet Offensive.

In the first story, the sergeant and Private Lawrence are more important than Private Joker is. Joker is the witness to a psychodrama played out between the sergeant and Private Lawrence. The answer to how far the sergeant will go to turn his men into killing machines is very clear: he'll go to any lengths—including humiliation and destruction. The sergeant, the antagonist, succeeds in his goal by turning Lawrence into a killer. Lawrence kills the sergeant and then kills himself. Private Lawrence and the sergeant are protagonists and antagonists, depending on your point of view, even though Joker is the character through whom we experience the narrative. These two secondary characters take over the drama, and Private Joker survives as a witness and goes on to combat. Here the main character, Joker, is relegated to the position of observer.

This role is continued in the second act, the Battle of Huê. In combat, Joker is a photographer, a visual witness to a battle in which the antagonist is unclear. We never see the enemy, we only see the killing. The American patrol is whittled down one by one. The men of the patrol are frustrated, angry, and afraid. Finally, they capture the sniper. She is dying, and she is alone. Here, again, the members of the patrol, whether animalistic or rational, brave or cowardly, frightened or filled with bravado, are more complex and compelling than Joker is.

Joker does survive, as is appropriate for a witness, but the majority of secondary characters, who have faced life and death (mainly death), have struggled more expressively to surmount the obstacles placed before them. In *Full Metal Jacket*, it is clear that no one character is privileged. All characters are trying to survive, and all are limited by the same parameter—the war. Joker survives, but this outcome is neither heroic nor cathartic, a by-product of the narrative's two-act structure.

■ ■ ■ A Case Study of Interior Main Character and Exterior Secondary Characters: *Paris, Texas*

Travis (Harry Dean Stanton) is a 1980s poor version of Orson Welles's *Citizen Kane*. A relic from his past provides a key to his current behavior and character. Or does it? Sam Shepard and Wim Wender's *Paris, Texas* is the story of a man who has lost his memory and must reconstruct his life. His brother Walt (Dean Stockwell) and his son Hunter (Hunter Carson) help. It is not until Travis takes his son on a journey to find the boy's mother, Jane (Nastassja Kinski), that we get a true sense of Travis as a man who is incapable of coping with his own shortcomings. His possessiveness has cost him his wife; his self-absorption has robbed him of raising his son. Like Kane, Travis is fixated on the relationship of his parents and the circumstances surrounding his early life in *Paris, Texas*—where modern cosmopolitanism clashed with primitive ruralism. He cannot sustain the contradictions and has been among the walking wounded ever since.

In terms of character, Travis is lost, a position that is not conducive to mastery or primacy over other characters. The secondary characters seem more rooted (brother and sister-in-law) and more exposed (wife), and thereby more vital and engaged than Travis is. However, in the absence of primacy, Travis does occupy a dramatically more democratic position vis-à-vis the secondary characters. The secondary characters try to help Travis, but his conflict is internal; he has to help himself. For all their externalized actions, the secondary characters do not seem paralyzed by their deeper fears. Each is fearful, but each, including Travis's wife, is able to act in ways that elude Travis. As a result, Travis leaves his son with his mother at the story's end. Travis is alone and seems to realize the rightness of that stance. He has used his son to find his wife and realizes that although he may desire a traditional family life, his passivity prohibits him from having one.

■ ■ ■ A Case Study of Role Reversion: *Something Wild*

Charles Driggs (Jeff Daniels), the main character of Max Frye's *Something Wild*, is a closet rebel who happens to be a stockbroker. He is a conventional middle-class main character, and he allows himself to be accosted and then kidnapped by Lulu (Melanie Griffith). The ensuing adventure is filled with sadomasochistic dimensions. Lulu ties him up, has sex with him (he doesn't object), and eventually calls his boss, forcing Charles, naked and tied up, to make excuses for being away from the office for the afternoon. Later, Charles accompanies Lulu to her high school reunion and meets her ex-husband. He then almost loses his life in trying to take Lulu away from her ex-husband, a violent, unpredictable psychopath.

Charles is overwhelmed by Lulu, a dynamic, unpredictable woman whose sense of danger stimulates him. In a stereotypical sense, Lulu takes on male behavioral characteristics in Act I, whereas Charles assumes female behavioral characteristics. Because of this blurring, it's difficult to identify Charles with the classic main character (hero). Not until Lulu's ex-husband appears do we have a secondary character who is an antagonist—another requisite for prompting heroic action on the part of the main character.

The degree of role reversion intensifies when Lulu saves Charles from harm at the hands of her ex-husband. It is Lulu who decides whether she will have a relationship with Charles. To the degree that he has lied to Lulu about himself, Charles is as much a sociopath as she is. They are misanthropic and belong together in a relationship based on mutual deception and role reversion.

Charles, Lulu, and her ex-husband are all outsiders. In Charles case, he has been more repressed about it. Although these three are opposed to one another, their characters are quite similar. In this sense, they are different from classic secondary characters who represent different sides of the issue faced by the main character. These secondary characters, Lulu and her ex-husband, have a dark side, as does the main character, Charles. The lack of a clear-cut choice—to be an upright citizen and broker or to be a criminal or sinner—makes the resolution, the death of Lulu's ex-husband, less a climax than a relief from an untenable situation. His death, however, does not resolve the relationship issues between Charles and Lulu.

The central question with regard to the balance of main and secondary characters in *Something Wild* is this: Has the role reversion subverted the separateness of the main character, and is Charles defined enough to be further segregated (for heroic ends) by the active antagonist to qualify him as a classic protagonist? The answer is no. The role reversion has subverted Charles as a classic main character. His shared deception with Lulu has dramatically democratized Charles and Lulu. An argument could be made to consider Lulu the main character; although she isn't the main character, she is too much like Charles to be considered a conventional secondary character, either. Only the ex-husband's posture as antagonist works to save Charles status as a classic protagonist, but it isn't enough. The balance between main and secondary character has been successfully subverted.

Conclusion

In the classic screen structure, there is a particular balance between the main character and the secondary characters. The main character is in the midst of the drama, surrounded by secondary characters who articulate options for him. They may act as catalysts to promote a choice or they may provide examples of the options for the main character. In either case, the main character is implicitly big enough and complex enough to make a choice, and because he is implicitly larger than the secondary characters, his actions seem heroic.

What happens to this balance when the secondary characters are more important than the main character? Or when they are equivalent? The result of both cases is a form of dramatic democracy, where neither the main character nor the secondary characters appear to be more privileged. The trade-off, between the classic main character and the main character who shares the same quandaries and questions as the secondary character, is the loss of the hero. If one character is no more privileged than any other character, heroic action becomes, simply, action, and the dramatic struggle of the main character becomes, in one fashion or another, the struggle of each character.

When the main character is no greater an influence than any other character, various options ensue. Clearly, the writer has more freedom in the main character–secondary character balance simply because the conventional dynamic is constrained by formula. The secondary character who is the antagonist is pulled closer to the protagonist. The struggle between them flattens. Perhaps the similarities between protagonist and antagonist are more memorable than are the differences. There is a gap in the story that can move the writer to look to the interior struggles of all the characters, rather than to look to the externalized actions that confirm the primacy of the main character. The options are numerous and interesting.

Dramatic democracy allows for identification with the main character, but it robs the viewer of the satisfying catharsis of the classic screen story balance of main to secondary characters. In fact, the viewer may be left uneasy, as at the end of *Full Metal Jacket* or *Something Wild*, or emotionally exhausted, as at the end of *Paris, Texas* or *Who'll Stop the Rain?* This character dynamic is still obviously marketable, as evidenced by the works of such important artists as Woody Allen (*Crimes and Misdemeanors*) and Spike Lee (*Do the Right Thing*). The option (different stories, different outcomes, surprise) is a more encouraging one for those writers whose status is less secure.

Reference

1. B. Schulberg, screenwriter of the Columbia Pictures film, ON THE WATERFRONT, 1954.

19

Subtext, Action, and Character

The presentation of subtext, often associated with the interior dilemma of the character, is more often associated with theater than with film. However, subtext is an important dimension of good screen stories. Subtext always relates to character. In order to present a model of screenplay subtext, it is necessary to look at the structure of the screen story.

The structured screen story presents characters at a particular point in their lives, facing a particular problem. This problem is given dimension by the secondary characters, who articulate two options for the main character. The dilemma and character are supported by a story line that provides the opportunity for the main character not only to interact with the secondary characters but also to be confronted by events during the course of the action line that will help her to make a choice. If the story is properly structured, not only will there be a mounting sense of urgency about making that choice, but there will be major plot points that chart the way for the central character. So far, the story appears to be all action line. Where does the subtext develop, and does it interact with the action line?

Foreground and Background

To explain the subtext–action–character relationship, it is better to revert to other terminology. We will call the action line the foreground story. The foreground story is the plot that embraces people and action outside the character. The background story, which yields the subtext, relates to the main character's interior problem or issue. The central character works out this interior issue through her relationships with the secondary characters. A specific example of this foreground–background relationship is found in Jack Soward's *Star Trek: The Wrath of Khan*.

The foreground story is the struggle between Khan and Kirk. Khan, an aberrant genius long exiled to a desolate planet, is accidentally discovered by the starship Reliant. The Reliant has been on a scouting mission for the Genesis Project Scientific Station. Khan is only interested in getting revenge on his nemesis, Kirk. Khan takes over the Reliant and orders Carol Marcus, chief scientist of the Genesis Project, to hand over all scientific data. This is a highly irregular procedure, so Carol sends a distress signal to Admiral Kirk. Kirk, on a training mission with Captain Spock of the Enterprise, responds, and he and his inexperienced crew take off to the Genesis Station.

A struggle for control of the Genesis Project as well as a space duel between Kirk and Khan follow. To complicate matters, Kirk and Carol were lovers, and their child, David, now a grown man, works with his mother. David is not fond of Kirk, the father he never knew. Spock, however, is totally devoted to Kirk and to the fate of the Reliant. He sacrifices his life in order to save the crew members aboard the Enterprise. Spock's crypt is sent to the planet, created by the Genesis Effect, as his final resting place. This action line is the foreground story.

The background story is the interior issue of Admiral Kirk's aging. He no longer has a command, he has an administrative position, he needs glasses, and he seems to have a fondness for antiques—books by Dickens and Shakespeare. During the course of the story, Kirk echoes that he feels old. Taking command of the Enterprise, opposing an old adversary (Khan), and reconciling with his family are all challenges he must confront. At the end of the film, after the memorial ceremony honoring Spock, Carol asks him how he feels and Kirk answers, "Young. I feel young."

Clearly, the events in the action line can help or subvert this interior issue. In *Star Trek: The Wrath of Khan*, with so many young people playing important roles and with the Genesis Project providing the opportunity for the birth of a planet, the young–old dilemma is given dimension.

If we look at the balance of foreground and background, it is usually as follows: in Act I, both foreground and background stories are introduced; in Act II, the background story is fleshed out; in Act III, the foreground story is prominent, and the background story is resolved. The foreground story is action oriented. The background story, on the contrary, is emotion oriented; it is what the main character feels most deeply about.

In order to highlight the subtext, or background, story's relationship to character, it is useful to examine, in detail, Billy Wilder and I.A.L. Diamond's *The Apartment*. The foreground story is a tale of corporate advancement in a New York insurance company. C.C. Baxter (Jack Lemmon) is a low-level clerk. He is ambitious, and his colleagues give him the means for advancement. Baxter allows first one person, later four people, to use his apartment for trysts. Each promises recommendation to the head of personnel, J.J. Sheldrake (Fred MacMurray). When Sheldrake wants to use Baxter's apartment, Baxter's future is secured. At the beginning of Act II, Baxter is promoted. How far he advances in the company is now totally dependent on Sheldrake.

When Baxter takes care of a problem for Sheldrake (Sheldrake's girlfriend attempts suicide in Baxter's apartment), the reward is further advancement.

When a former girlfriend tells all to Sheldrake's wife, his feigned divorce becomes real, and he asks Baxter for his apartment. But Baxter refuses, because by now, he, too, is involved with Sheldrake's girlfriend. Baxter loses his job, and his advancement within the company is over.

The background story follows Baxter's interior dilemma—he wants a personal life, but his personal life is always negated by his will to advance. The focus for this personal dilemma is Fran (Shirley MacLaine), an elevator operator whom Baxter likes. When Baxter gets his first promotion, he asks her out. She agrees, telling him she has to see another man to say goodbye and will then join him in front of the theater. Fran never makes it to the theater. She gives into the charms of J.J. Sheldrake and goes with him to Baxter's apartment, leaving Baxter in front of the theater. She has stood him up and he's hurt but not discouraged. The opening of Act II follows Baxter's interest in Fran as well as Fran's relationship with Sheldrake.

In the first half of Act II, Fran and Sheldrake have a relationship, and Baxter is on the outside. Only during his second attempt to woo Fran (at the Christmas party) does Baxter realize she is Sheldrake's girlfriend. She uses a cracked makeup case he had returned to Sheldrake earlier in the story. Sheldrake jokes that women take these flings so seriously. Baxter, realizing the truth about Fran, leaves and gets drunk on Christmas Eve. Meanwhile, Sheldrake and Fran are arguing in Baxter's apartment. She presents him with a Christmas gift; he didn't remember to buy one for her; hence, he offers her a hundred dollars to buy herself a gift. Sheldrake then dashes off for an evening with the family, and Fran attempts suicide by taking Baxter's sleeping pills. When Baxter returns, a lovely woman on his arm, he finds Fran. With the help of the doctor next door, he revives her. The suicide attempt is the midpoint of Act II. The balance of the act focuses on Fran's recovery in Baxter's apartment and their developing relationship. Fran is not yet aware of the depth of their relationship, but Baxter is. He knows he wants a deeper connection with her, but his happiness is brief.

In Act III, Baxter rehearses his speech for Sheldrake. Because he loves her, Baxter will take Fran off Sheldrake's hands. However, when he sees Sheldrake, Sheldrake makes the speech. He tells Baxter that his wife threw him out and he's planning on getting a divorce and taking up more legitimately with Fran. It is at this point that Baxter faces his moment of truth. He chooses to give up his advancement and walks out on Sheldrake. He'll not be an accomplice to Sheldrake's plan, especially because he loves Fran. He is no longer willing to sacrifice his personal life for advancement.

Critical to the successful interplay of foreground and background is the nature of Baxter's character. We have to believe that he can be both an opportunist and a sensitive idealist. The story has to be structured in such a way as to provide scope for both sides of his character. Next, the quality of the secondary characters must allow for the two options—opportunist and idealist—to resonate. Sheldrake and the other insurance company executives are singularly opportunistic. Both Fran and Baxter's doctor neighbor, however, are idealistic; they are friendly and straightforward. They never manipulate, nor are they cruel. These two characters analyze the world: Fran categorizes people as "takers and those who get took," and the doctor sees those who are "mensch" (good human beings) and those who are not.

The subtext arises out of the interplay of the emotion-laden background story with the action-laden foreground story. The result is layered. How far is Baxter willing to go to succeed? Besides defining that limit, the subtext also suggests the degree of dehumanization the individual is willing to tolerate to improve his material well-being. But is it worth his spiritual well-being? In the end, Baxter opts to be a human being, and Fran decides to join him. They question their material well-being at this moment ("I don't have a job. I don't know where we'll go"), but the issue of spiritual sovereignty is, for these two characters, indisputable. They are whole, and they are happy; this is the implication of the background story and the source of satisfaction for the viewer.

In a sense, the deeper satisfaction for the viewer devolves from the subtext of the story rather than from the resolution of the plot. The subtext issue is the interior issue and is, therefore, more deeply associated with the main character. The plot, on the contrary, presents a line of action that is the surface of the story. The foreground story may be quite distant from the interior life of the main character. There are intersecting points of background and foreground, but the foreground story doesn't necessarily offer the viewer the level of involvement that is available from the subtext.

It is, however, not enough to believe that the character can go in one direction or the other. For subtext to be deeply meaningful, it must be interwoven with the character's foreground plight. An example will illustrate how this relationship between character and subtext works.

John Fusco's *Thunderheart* is the story of an FBI murder investigation on an Indian reservation in the Badlands of South Dakota. Roy Levoi (Val Kilmer) is the main character, an FBI agent assigned to look into the struggle between radical and conservative factions on the reservation, a struggle that has led to murder. The foreground story in *Thunderheart* is the investigation and solution of the murder. The background story is the struggle between primitive Indian values and commercial white values on the reservation. Fusco fuses the main character to this background story by making him half white, half Indian.

Those characters who relate to the white values in the story—the older FBI agent (Sam Shepard), who becomes the antagonist, and the conservative Indian faction he works with—definitely appeal to the side of Levoi that wants to be accepted as a white man. The other group of secondary characters, the Indian side, includes an Indian sheriff, a female Indian teacher, and the Indians' religious leader, all representing older values involved with magic, nature, and history. They represent the past for Levoi, and each in turn prods him to admit to his Indianness.

When the crime is solved and Levoi learns that his FBI partner is an accomplice to the murder, he is outraged. When the Indian teacher is killed, there is no turning back. He will go against his white partner, risk his life, and demand justice. By the end of the story, Levoi has accepted his Indian side and has implicitly devalued his white half. The subtext, or background, story to accept Indian values or white values, with their implications for the future, the environment, and the community, is at the center of *Thunderheart*. And because Roy Levoi is half white, half Indian, that struggle is all the more personal and meaningful. Thus, screen stories work best when subtext and character fuse as strongly as is the case in *Thunderheart*.

The Balance Between Foreground and Background

There are screen stories that are all foreground. These stories are plot intensive. In these stories, the character facilitates the plot, and her inner life isn't alluded to. *Ruthless People* and *Fatal Attraction* are two examples of films with a strong foreground script. In *Ruthless People*, the premise that money can't buy love attaches most easily to the wife (Bette Midler), but she experiences no deeper inner conflict, nor does the husband (Danny DeVito), who instigates the idea of murdering his wife for her money. What is interesting about *Ruthless People* is the difficulty in determining the identity of the main character, and, once that determination is made, how little the main character matters. Contrary to classic screen narrative, the main character's role in *Ruthless People* is incidental.

In *Fatal Attraction*, the premise that one-night stands can be fatal falls best on the shoulders of the husband (Michael Douglas). But again, there is no interior conflict. Both mistress (Glenn Close) and wife (Anne Archer) are important to the plot but are less critical to the interior life of the husband's character. His conflict is totally externalized. Noteworthy is the success of both *Ruthless People* and *Fatal Attraction*; both are well structured, compelling screenplays, but they do not have that additional layer, the background story, that involves the audience in a complex relationship with the main character. Other examples of screen stories that are all foreground include *Blind Date, Risky Business, Ferris Bueller's Day Off*, and *Back to the Future*.

Screen stories that allude to the main character's interior life, but for all intents and purposes are foreground treatments, include *Black Rain, The Accused, Presumed Innocent, Some Kind of Wonderful, Valmont*, and *Ghost*. In these screen stories, the effort at creating an interior conflict for the main character can confuse the viewer. In the cases of *Black Rain, Presumed Innocent*, and *Valmont*, the unfulfilled promise of greater complexity from the character eventually undermines the effectiveness of the foreground story. In *The Accused, Some Kind of Wonderful*, and *Ghost*, the main characters aren't complex; they are young innocents. The audience doesn't expect complex inner lives; consequently, these characterizations don't undermine the foreground stories.

A number of films do, however, try to introduce a modest background story that adds a layer to the story but does not derail the foreground story. These stories are primarily genre stories that are heavily plot dependent; thus, the effort put toward background story is surprising, yet in each case, the script is strengthened by the effort.

John Bishop's *The Package* is the story of a U.S.–Soviet military plot to assassinate Gorbachev and/or the U.S. president to promote a continuation of the Cold War. The cold warriors hire an assassin, a former covert military man (Tommy Lee Jones). The subversive plot, headed by an army colonel (John Heard), is organized with the help of top military officials on both sides. An army sergeant, Gallagher (Gene Hackman), is used as a dupe for the plot. But he doesn't want to be the victim of a traitorous plot, and he doesn't want to endanger all those close to him. In the end, he thwarts the assassination attempt and saves the day.

The Package has an elaborate, intelligent plot, but it is the background story that strengthens the film. Quietly, the sergeant's story is about the old-fashioned virtues of military life—the camaraderie, the loyalty, and the effectiveness. These virtues are undermined by the colonel's subversive political agenda. The sergeant doesn't want to get enmeshed in political scheming, he simply wants to be a good soldier, and, in the end, he is. But it requires disobedience and unlawful behavior and individual initiative—the very opposite of the values the military instilled in him. The background story follows his struggle with these contradictions.

The Package is a thriller, whereas *Striking Distance* is a police story. In the police story, there is a crime, and the plot chronicles the ensuing investigation until the crime is resolved and the criminal is apprehended. The background story in *Striking Distance* is about family values. Rowdy Hernington and Martin Kaplan have written a story about a Pittsburgh detective, Thomas Hardy (Bruce Willis), whose testimony indicts his partner and cousin for brutality. The result is that Hardy's colleagues on the police force shun him. The subsequent suicide of his partner and death of his father (also a policeman) in a high-speed chase, with Hardy at the wheel, lead Hardy to leave the force for the River Police, a demotion.

The foreground story concerns the hunt for a sadistic killer of women, all of whom were associated with Hardy. Through both phases of his career, in homicide and in the River Police, Hardy contends that the killer is a former policeman. The interesting background story about duty and family is played out effectively, because one of the accused is Hardy's cousin. His father and his uncle are career police officers, and, clearly, Hardy hopes to be a career police officer as well. The problem that divides the family and provides the background story is the role of his partner and cousin, Joey. Will Joey's father cover up the fact that his son is a criminal? And how should Hardy respond to the criminality of his partner and cousin? The choice between duty and family becomes the subtext and the background story.

Finally, we turn to a situation comedy, a genre that is also plot driven. Gary Ross's *Dave* is the story of Dave (Kevin Kline), a man who looks identical to the president of the United States. When the president, a self-serving political ne'er-do-well, has a stroke, Dave is recruited to act as his stand-in. Dave is decent and generous; even the president's wife notices how different the "president" has become. What will the fate of the nation be at the hands of Dave? Clearly, it's going to be better. But can Dave get away with this deception? This is the plot of the film.

The background story of *Dave* relates to the values the president should stand for. Should they be the idealistic, positive, Capra-esque values, or should they be modern, cynical, and self-serving? The background story provides a layer to the mistaken-identity plot of *Dave* and makes it far more meaningful to the audience. This is precisely the benefit in adding a background story. *The Package, Striking Distance,* and *Dave* are foreground-intensive stories, which are strengthened by the modest addition of an effective background story.

■ ■ ■ A Case Study of the Primacy of the Foreground Story: *Music Box*

Joe Eszterhas's *Music Box* is the story of a Hungarian-American accused of war crimes during World War II. If convicted, he will be stripped of his American citizenship. The majority of the story takes place in Chicago and pivots around the hearing during which Michael Lazlo (Armin Mueller-Stahl) is accused of lying on his American immigration application. He is specifically accused of being a Hungarian policeman who cruelly aided and abetted the deportations of Jews from Budapest in 1944. To the end of the film, he denies his complicity.

We enter the story through the eyes of his daughter, Ann Talbot, an attorney played by Jessica Lange. Lazlo asks her to defend him in the hearing. Reluctantly, Ann complies and, in her efforts to defend her father, learns more than she ever wanted to know. Whether she is prepared to deal with his past is her personal dilemma (the background story).

The presentation of the story is very straightforward. In the foreground, the father and daughter are introduced. We see that Ann Talbot is a successful, aggressive lawyer and a good daughter. Then her father is accused of war crimes. He invites his daughter to join him when he goes to see the immigration people. She agrees, already defensive about her father (the background story is introduced), and he asks her to defend him. Other characters are introduced—Ann's son, her ex-husband, her ex-father-in-law, the prosecuting lawyer, and her female assistant. The investigation begins, followed by the hearing, which includes a number of witnesses, survivors of the Holocaust, principally women. The hearing concludes in Budapest.

Throughout the story, Ann learns more facts that challenge her view of her father (the background story). Ann continues to function as a good lawyer, despite the credibility of the eyewitnesses. However, when her assistant turns up information about her father's finances, she begins to learn about his past associates. Finally, she pieces together the truth. Having gotten her father acquitted (the resolution of the foreground story), she is faced with a personal dilemma—to allow the acquittal to stand or to reveal what she has learned about her father. This is the moment of truth and the moment of resolution of the background story. Family solidarity or moral justice, which should she choose? As his daughter, her choice is that much more difficult to make, but in the end she turns against her father.

The foreground story in *Music Box* is elaborate and well plotted. The impact of the foreground story resolution is strengthened by the background story. The daughter's inner life—her view of herself as a daughter, and the solidarity and strength that comes from being a member of this immigrant family—is challenged by the choice she has to make. In *Music Box*, the foreground story is dominant, but the existence of the background story strengthens the screen story and results in a greater emotional resonance for both foreground and background.

■ ■ ■   **A Case Study of Subversion of the Foreground Story:**
Homicide

Homicide, written by David Mamet, is on one level a classic police story. Police stories tend to be plot intensive—crime, investigation, and apprehension. The story ends when the police officer or detective finds, takes into custody, or kills the bank robber or serial killer who has been the center of the investigation.

David Mamet is very taken up with the confused identity of his main character. Can one be both a police officer and a Jew? This is at the heart of the background story. Mamet builds up the background story as if it is another plot—the murder of an elderly Jewish storekeeper and the subsequent investigation. Nevertheless, its resolution is not at all clear in the way the foreground story is resolved. Indeed, the background story, with its overlay of Jewish terrorists, a neo-Nazi organization, and the effort to get Detective Gold (Joe Montegna), all but makes us forget about the foreground story. Gold suffers losses—his partner, his own well being—in expediting the foreground plot, which follows a murder investigation. Nevertheless, his confusion about his own Jewishness seems to supersede all other elements of the story. At the end, Gold is lost because he doesn't know who he is. The background story has posed a problem for him, and his failure to find an answer subverts resolution of the background story and makes us all but dismiss the plot, its resolution, and its importance in the narrative.

■ ■ ■   **A Case Study of Moving Toward a Greater**
Background Story: Q & A

There are particular genres where the plot is more critical than is the character layer or background story. The audience expects war, science fiction, and horror films to be plot driven. This is particularly true in gangster films; *Scarface* is a good example, whereas *The Godfather* is exceptional in its attempt to balance the foreground (plot) and background (character layer) stories. However, *Q & A*, written by Sidney Lumet, turns our expectations of the genre upside down. In *Q & A*, the background story (character layer) is more prominent and important than is the foreground story (plot).

The foreground story of *Q & A* is the investigation, by the district attorney's office, of a killing. A policeman, Mike Brennan (Nick Nolte), has shot and killed a Puerto Rican drug dealer in what he claims is self-defense. The investigation is commissioned by Quinn (Patrick O'Neal), the head of the department. Quinn assigns O'Reilly (Timothy Hutton), a recent law school graduate, to the case. O'Reilly, who has just joined the office, was a policeman and is the son of a policeman. This will be his first case.

The foreground story follows O'Reilly's investigation. He is assigned two police detectives to assist in what appears to be a straightforward investigation. But the investigation doesn't prove to be so straightforward. The dead man's boss, Bobby (Armand Assante), suggests that Brennan killed not in self-defense but in cold blood.

The story is further complicated by the fact that Bobby's wife is a woman that O'Reilly used to live with and who suddenly left him. Other complications are the loyalties that develop along lines of race, color, and culture. The case becomes even more complicated when the Mafia becomes involved. Finally, Brennan starts killing witnesses, and the plot—the killings and their investigation—accelerates. Can anyone stop this rogue cop? And will O'Reilly, the main character, come to appreciate the motive, which is racial hatred, rather than the pursuit of justice? In the end, Brennan and Quinn are implicated in the killings. The simple case of defensible homicide has become more complex; indeed, the extent of the killing defies rational explanation.

This foreground story provides the action line for a story that is more interior than it first appears. The background story that gradually unfolds is a story of prejudice and the hatred born of that prejudice. *Q & A* is populated by five ethnic groups—Puerto Ricans, Irish, blacks, Jews, and Italians. Each group is very loyal to its own members. Therefore, positioning O'Reilly, the main character, against Brennan, one of his own, immediately forces the main character to make a choice—be true to his own at all costs or go against his own. This is how Brennan and Quinn put his options to him. However, this particular conflict isn't as strong as that behind the reason O'Reilly's wife, Nancy, left him the night she first introduced him to her father. She had never told him, nor could he have guessed from her appearance, that her father was black. She saw his prejudice at that moment, and she left him. Seeing her again, O'Reilly is faced with his own prejudice.

The central conflict for O'Reilly is whether he can look beyond race and color to the person and situation, or whether he will remain prejudiced. The background story is rife with prejudice. Every group expresses hatred toward the other four groups, and their hatred is evidenced in language and in action. Simultaneously, the pressure within each group is to support the other members of the group, even if one member of that group is a criminal and another is a cop. Other cultures are present as well—the police culture, the criminal culture, and the transsexual culture. In each case, group solidarity and opposition to other groups are not just registered, they are demanded by members of the group.

Because of the dilemma faced by the main character, the story becomes not so much the story of a criminal investigation (foreground) as it is a study of a system choking on prejudice and hate (background). Can the individual maintain his nationality, humanity, and morality in such a system? There are no easy answers, and, as a result, the screen story ends posing more questions than it answers. But it does stir many emotions, principally because the background story is so powerful. In contrast, the outcome of the foreground story, the death of Brennan, is neither satisfying nor cathartic. The background story has displaced the foreground story in relative importance.

■ ■ ■ Case Studies of the Writer Elevating the Background Story: *The Fabulous Baker Boys* and *Flesh and Bone*

Steve Kloves has written two films, *The Fabulous Baker Boys* and *Flesh and Bone*, in which the interior life of the main character dominates the narrative. In the first film, a musician (Jeff Bridges) is passive relative to his business-minded brother and partner (Beau Bridges). Their music career is flagging, but when the business-minded brother decides to hire a female singer, their career improves. Two problems arise: as the passive brother is an inveterate womanizer, he falls for the woman (Michelle Pfeiffer); meanwhile, his career is a creative dead end. He does not have the self-confidence to pursue the jazz career he desires. When the story ends, he has broken off with his brother, the singer leaves him, and he may or may not pursue jazz.

In *Flesh and Bone*, a son (Arlis, Dennis Quaid) has a murky past. As a boy, the son helped his father, Roy (James Caan), burglarize farms in Texas. The story opens with a burglary gone wrong. The result is the killing of three of the farm occupants; only a baby girl lives. Twenty years later, the boy, now a man, is a small businessman in Texas. He keeps to himself. A woman enters his life (Meg Ryan), and later we discover she is the young baby who survived the killing. Arlis's father comes back, too, and on finding out about the girl's past, Roy wants to kill her. Despite his love for the girl, Arlis struggles with what he should do. In the end, he rescues her and kills his father. Whether he will take up with her and be happy is left unsaid.

Steve Kloves has chosen two main characters who are extremely interior and has placed them in stories with very little narrative. The background stories each have to do with individual vs. family obligation. How much should the individual give up on behalf of family? Should they give up creative aspiration, ethical consideration, and happiness? It's as if neither main character can be truly happy, and the background stories in each film provide one last chance at happiness. The attitude of these films is that of film noir, but the form is melodramatic with the parent/brother standing in as the power and the son/brother standing in as the transgressor.

In both *The Fabulous Baker Boys* and *Flesh and Bone*, Steve Kloves elevates the background story over the importance of foreground, and the result is a unique choice for character over plot at a time when plot over character dominates commercial screenwriting.

■ ■ ■   ## A Case Study of the Background Story: *Moonstruck*

John Patrick Shanley's *Moonstruck* is a good example of a background screen story. In the foreground, Loretta (Cher) is a mid-30s Italian-American who is about to marry for the second time. She agrees to marriage despite her lack of passion for her husband-to-be. Her husband-to-be (Danny Aiello) asks her to invite his estranged brother (Nicolas Cage) to the wedding, as he is flying to Sicily to tend to his dying mother. Loretta falls in love with the brother, and her passion is revived. Although everyone around her is looking for passion, Loretta finds it and keeps it.

The background story focuses on Loretta's pivotal search for passion. Her father, mother, aunt, and uncle, even an unknown NYU professor, all seek the same state—to be moonstruck. Loretta achieves this state by moving from a passionless relationship with one brother (Aiello) to a totally passionate relationship with the other (Cage). It is Cage, with his focus on opera (intense passion) and extreme emotions (love for Loretta and hate for his brother), who is the primary catalyst for Loretta.

Shanley is much more interested in exploring the state of being moonstruck (the background story) than he is in weaving an elaborate plot. Consequently, we have a very simple foreground story and a consistent meditation among each of the characters on the issue of the background story (being moonstruck). What is surprising about the story is the amount of feeling it generates, which is due to the appeal of the background story. It is very much like a fairy tale. Shanley wishes everyone could experience being moonstruck. It is interesting that director Norman Jewison has chosen "That's Amore," performed by Dean Martin, as the theme song. Could he be more direct about the background story?

Like *Moonstruck*, Sam Shepard's *Fool for Love* and David Mamet's *Things Change* also have dominant background stories, favoring the characters' interior lives over their actions. Noteworthy is the fact that all three films are written by playwrights. Indeed, Shanley, Shepard, and Mamet were probably three of the most interesting writers for both stage and film during the 1980s. We can look at the screen work of other playwrights—Paddy Chayefsky (*The Hospital*, *Network*), Peter Shaffer (*Amadeus*), and Herb Gardner (*A Thousand Clowns*)—and note that, in all cases, the background story is of great importance in their respective works.

"The Moment" and Subtext

As might be expected, stories with little foreground are accused of having no action, whereas stories that are all foreground are accused of having no character. The type of story that balances foreground and background offers the opportunity for both action and character. Harnessing the interplay of action and character, however, poses a very particular problem for the writer. To set up action and character, particularly characters with an interior dilemma, requires a strategy that we call "the moment." The moment is the point at which we join the screen story. Needless to say, there are thousands of points at which we can join a story or enter a character's life. The moment we refer to, however, is the point that launches us into the story in a gripping fashion.

For example, we join *The Apartment* at the moment when C.C. Baxter has so overcommitted his apartment that he is crowded out and has to sleep on a park bench instead of his bed. Clearly, the use of the apartment by corporate executives is out of hand. Does he want a personal life or not? In *Moonstruck*, we join the story at the point when Loretta receives a marriage proposal. The engagement sets into motion the events that follow and illustrates the lovelessness in Loretta's life, despite her being engaged. The moment in *Something Wild* is the point when Charles meets Lulu. She has accused him of stealing, and he is already on the defensive. The moment in *Mystic Pizza* is Jo's wedding. She faints, and the wedding is called off. The rest of the story has to do with three young women and their quest for either marriage or independence. The moment, then, can be called the critical moment, for in each case mentioned, the moment presents the character in a crisis. It highlights the nature of her dilemma and places the viewer right in the middle of the main character's quandary.

Important to note is that no background or insight into the main character is necessary to interpret the problem. We may not fully understand yet why the main character behaves as she does, but we soon will. The problem has been put forth, and we are curious as to how it will be resolved. Will Baxter opt for a personal life? Will Loretta be happy when she marries Jerry? Will Jo ever marry? In each case, the answer is yes or no. When the question posed during "the moment" is answered, the screen story is over. The moment, then, is critical in that it positions a main character in an untenable situation, given her interior life. The character's preferences become clear as the story unfolds, but the moment is used to intensify the character's tension and quickly involve us in the screen story.

▪ ▪ ▪   A Case Study of "The Moment": *My Beautiful Laundrette*

My Beautiful Laundrette is about Omar (Roshan Seth), who thinks of himself as a Briton, but the British think of him as a Pakistani. He is both and neither. The story begins—and this is the moment—when Omar tells his father he is dropping out of school and going to work for his father's brother, Nasser, whom his father thinks is a barbarian. Nasser puts Omar to work in a car wash, but Omar has other plans; he wants to be a businessman on his own. He talks Nasser into allowing him to take over one of his laundrettes. Located in a poor British neighborhood, this laundrette is destined for failure. But Omar has a strategy. He brings on a local boy named Johnny, a former classmate and lover, to help.

Johnny's fellow thugs feel that one of their own has betrayed them and gone over to the enemy. It is only a matter of time until the laundrette is subverted by the new colonialism—the Pakistanis as imperialists and the Brits as the new natives. Who is the colonized and who is the colonizer is very much at the heart of Hanif Kureishi's screen story.

The plot line, a young man's embrace of capitalism and its swift kick back, isn't very revealing or gripping, but the background story, Pakistani or Briton, is a critical internal issue, not only for Omar, but for all the other characters as well. All characters, including Nasser and Johnny, contemplate their identity. Nasser challenges his marriage by keeping a British mistress; Johnny challenges his friends by taking a Pakistani employer and lover. All three characters—Omar, Nasser, and Johnny—challenge the status quo and suffer for it in varying degrees. Nasser loses his mistress, Johnny loses his friends, and Omar loses his laundrette. However, in the end, Omar and Johnny are two outsiders taking solace in each other.

The moment unfolds two options—Omar will either succeed or fail. When one outcome occurs, the screen story is over. Although the screen story becomes somewhat more layered, the story ends with Omar's failure as a Brit. However, his British identity is replaced by another identity—his homosexuality—thereby leaving Omar as Pakistani but capable of a loving relationship with a Brit. The resolution is not a failure for the main character; rather, it is a success, as he has found a new, different, and more complex identity. The outcome was considerably more positive than was anticipated. The vitality of *My Beautiful Laundrette* derives from the inner lives of these characters (the background story). The use of the moment helps to involve us at a critical point, particularly in the life of Omar. The result is a screen story with considerable subtext.

The purpose served by the moment is to propel the story toward conflict and dramatic action. The character pits himself against prevailing expectations, thus situating himself in both the foreground and the background stories. The objective is to begin the character-intensive story in a compelling manner. Characters, as they are introduced, present the issue in a surprising fashion. The result is that the background story is fleshed out fully, whereas the foreground story is no more than a continuing device.

■ ■ ■ A Case Study of Subtext: "Lust Caution"

For James Schamus one of the writers of Ang Lee's "Lust Caution" (2007), the film was their second co-venture into Chinese language filmmaking, the first being "Crouching Tiger, Hidden Dragon". Both films have a vigorous plot that is used to mask a subtext particularly focused on the actions of their female main characters.

In "Lust, Caution", the main character is Wong Chai Chi. She is a freshman at Lingman University in 1938 when invited to join a patriotic drama club. In this second year of the Sino-Japanese war, there is clear pressure in the society, to choose sides. A Chinese Collaborationist government working for the Japanese already exists.

For Wong whose father and brother have left for England, the drama club offers companionship and a chance to be close to Kuang, its charismatic leader. Putting on plays is not enough. He suggests they would make a greater patriotic statement if they assassinated Mr. Yee, an official of the collaborationist government. He enlists Wong to be the bait. To assure Wong is the married woman she pretends to be Kuang enlists their only sexually experienced member to initiate the virginal Wong. He himself remains chaste as does their mutual interest in one another.

The attempt fails in Hong Kong. Kuang revives the plan in 1942 Shanghai this time with professional supervision from the Resistance. Wong's relationship with Mr. Yee progresses and a plan is developed to kill Mr. Yee at a jeweler's shop where he has had a ring created for Wong.

Wong cannot go through with the assassination. In the shop she urges Mr. Yee to "go now". He does. The would-be assassins including Wong are arrested and executed.

To this point the story has been about a young woman wishing to join in political action. Whether she does so to be close to Kuang, is implied rather than enacted. And it is clear, at least in the Hong Kong phase of the deception that Wong fully intends to see the plot through to a successful conclusion. In Shanghai however, to prove herself trustworthy to the rightly cautious Mr. Yee, she allows herself to get lost in the sexual relationship with him. And in getting lost, a feeling she fully confesses to her superiors, she wins Mr. Yee over. He is as lost as she is in the relationship.

In saving Mr. Yee, the subtext of the story becomes manifest, lust and sexual desire trumps all things rational—commitment to politics, to her drama club colleagues, to Kuang. She knows this means her own death and the death of her colleagues. Schamus and Lee add a codicil so as not to hang this outcome on women alone. As the narrative ends we see Mr. Yee also will pay a price for getting lost in a relationship. His deputy tells him he wavered in his commitment to his collaborationist cause. He will not be trusted in the future.

Conclusion

Screen stories can exist without subtext, but if the scriptwriter wants to tell a story that involves the inner life of the main character, the story must have subtext. To illuminate the subtext, the foreground story (the action line) must interweave with a background story. The degree of subtext is influenced by genre and by the writer's disposition toward action or character. It should be clear to the scriptwriter that subtext evolves in tandem with character. The writer should look for events that define character. If external events involve relationships, a subtext beyond plot is an option for the writer. The result can be a more emotionally satisfying experience for the viewer.

20

Exceptional, but Opaque Characters in Flattened Scripts

In the first fifteen minutes of *The Hurt Locker* (Katherine Bigelow, 2008), three members of a bomb squad serving in Iraq attempt to disarm a bomb. Their dialogue is tense and clipped; their fear covered by crude sexual humor. When they fail to destroy the bomb by robot, one of the soldiers, Thompson, must approach it in a bomb suit. The stage directions read, "Constrained by the eighty-pound suit, sweat in his eyes, Thompson LUMBERS down the road. . ."[1] We imagine the three characters feel much like we might in this situation—frightened, on the edge of losing control, counting the seconds before it is over. None of them stand out as distinct, unusual, or particularly driven. We wonder how these characters will sustain a narrative feature. The bomb is triggered before Thompson can clear the area and he is killed.

A replacement team member, James, is introduced. But when he approaches a bomb, it is described differently: "James heads downrange, a jaunty bounce to his step. . . In stark contrast to Thompson's cautious, lumbering gait, he seems eager, almost happy, to approach the bomb."[2] Unlike the others, and those of us who are not addicted to combat, he finds energy and purpose in the danger. He is the exemplification of the quote that opens the film, "The rush of battle is often a potent and lethal addiction, for war is a drug."[3] James provides the energy that sustains a narrative feature. Yet he is presented as opaque, distant, and unknowable by us.

We have talked in this book about flattened documentary style. This style tilts the balance between the individual and society, which in mainstream film tends to be weighted toward the individual, in the direction of the more impersonal forces of society. It allows the writer to use fiction to explore this abstract material, focusing on how the external forces of society tend to shape individuals rather than the other way around. To write this way requires a rethinking of character presentation. Rather than developing characters in the more traditional manner, with their individual internal decisions explored and driving the story, the writer in the flattened style has to find a way to keep them at a distance, inviting the viewer instead to pay attention to the external, impersonal forces shaping them.

The danger with this style is that these flattened characters may not have sufficient energy to carry the story. One way to overcome this is to create exceptional, driven characters, but to still present them at a distance, keeping them opaque, in order to allow the story to maintain its context. These characters frequently make up for the viewer's lack of access into their internal life by the force of their will. This chapter will look at four such characters, and ask how well this balance is maintained.

Winter's Bone

Written and directed by Debra Granik from a novel by Daniel Woodrell, *Winter's Bone* (2010) is set in an isolated Ozark community. All the external circumstances of her life—the male dominated community in which she lives with its excessive intermarrying, isolation, and code of silence—are stacked against the main character, seventeen-year old Ree. Further, because of her mother's depression, Ree must care for her two siblings, Ashlee and Sonny, while foregoing her own life. Yet, when she learns that her father, Jessup, has put their house up for bail and may not appear at his hearing, she does not hesitate. She sets out to find him. Ree eventually learns that not only is her father dead, but that he has been killed because he has violated the community's code of silence. Yet she ultimately succeeds in saving the house and finally assures her anxious siblings that she isn't going anywhere. "I'd be lost without the weight of you two on my back."[4]

If we examine Ree's growth in the course of the script, we find a deepening of her character, an increased sense of her own power, a greater understanding of the double-edged bind of kinship, but little that we would call significant character change. She willingly sacrifices for her siblings both at the beginning and at the end of the film, while her personal strength is also evident throughout. We see it as soon as she learns that Jessup is missing. When the sheriff warns she might lose the house and worries whether she will have another place to live, she refuses to consider that possibility, instead insisting, "I'll find him." "Girl, I've been looking," the sheriff says. "I said I'll find him," Ree corrects him.[5] She fearlessly confronts her meth-using uncle Teardrop who knows what has happened to Jessup and attempts to discourage her. This lack of significant character change adds to the flatness of the story, dampening events that could have been presented as an action film, and keeping the focus on the world in which Ree lives.

A second element that does this is that—despite her character strength and distinct from a mainstream film—Ree is unable to resolve the dramatic conflict on her own. Having learned that her father was a snitch, Ree retreats into a period of mourning. Resigned, she burns her father's belongings and ponders a love note that he sent to her mother. It is at this point that Merab, one of the central antagonists in the story, offers her help. Merab promises to take Ree to Jessup's body, allowing Ree to retrieve the needed evidence proving that her father's absence from his hearing was because he had died.

A third element that focuses on the larger social world is the film's treatment of gender. *Winter's Bone* is a story in which women play roles that have traditionally been assigned to men in more mainstream films. This has particular power given the patriarchal community in which it is set. For most of the script, Ree herself drives the story. As she begins her quest for her father, her friend Gail's husband refuses to let Ree borrow his truck. She confronts Gail about this, "Man, it is so sad to hear you say he won't let you do something, and then you don't do it."[6] But women also become obstacles, at least initially. After being discouraged by her uncle Teardrop, she visits other power brokers in the community; however, the gatekeepers to all these male characters are women. Protecting the community's most feared man, Merab first refuses Ree's access and then beats her up when she returns—yet Merab ultimately guides Ree to Jessup's body, bringing the story to resolution. Although the women may have originally disposed of Jessup's body, they project a richer sense of concern for the community than do the men. From their perspective, getting rid of a snitch may be necessary to preserve social order and that necessity is something that Ree may come to understand. The women step in when the community is at risk, but their concern is over cohesion rather than violence. Merab says, "We need to put a stop to all this nonsense talk about us we've been having to hear."[7]

There are many ways to interpret *Winter's Bone*. One reviewer reframes the argument about active female characters we make in the paragraph above, noting that the film is about the feminization of poverty, "illuminating how poverty's vice is harder to escape and more likely to ensnare when one is female."[8] From this perspective, what we are celebrating as the women's support of their community may be better understood as merely their maintenance of the town's male-dominated, status quo.

How we interpret this is up to the viewer. But no matter our interpretation, what is important for our purpose is how the treatment of character allows the larger ideas discussed above to so powerfully come to the surface.

The Hurt Locker

The other soldiers in his company count the days until they return home, but not James. When his tour is over, he has a short run of domesticity. He shops for cereal with his wife, washes mushrooms, puts his son to bed, and then cannot take it anymore. He returns to Iraq after three script pages as a civilian.

A vital, energetic solider, James is the embodiment of the quote that begins the film. He enjoys taking on missions that no one else wants to touch: defusing a daisy-chain ring of bombs, a car packed with explosives, or a bomb lab. He saves bomb parts that might have killed him and fights with his fellow soldier Sanborn to prove he is the toughest. The one discordant element in his characterization is his fascination with Beckham, the boy who sells him DVDs and whose body James is convinced has been made into a human bomb. The script describes James's attempt to find and avenge Beckham as a "jihad."[9]

The term "jihad" is important because the language that screenwriter Mark Boals uses in the script may raise some questions about the balance we are discussing. James's character description reads,

> In a world of outgoing young men, James seems markedly self-absorbed. Sanborn notices this trait instantly and is puzzled by it. The truth is that after so many years downrange, racking up kills and disarming bombs, James has lost some of the ability and most of the need to connect to other people.[10]

The first sentence is the kind of descriptive language appropriate for a screenplay. The second sentence, detailing Sanborn's reaction, also works to reinforce James's impact on the other soldiers. However, the last sentence reads more like a writer's note than a description in a screenplay—a projection of what the writers plan to accomplish in the course of the script. As a description, it raises a number of questions. How do we know that James has lost the ability to connect to other people? Why has he lost it? Did he once have it? Maybe more importantly for the purpose of his character—why has James lost it when Sanborn has not? Understanding this is important because it describes James's behavior not only with the other soldiers, but ultimately with his family. Yet, this characterization of James, which will chart his whole story, is presented as having already been decided, dramatized in the backstory.

The one present-tense hint that might help us understand James is his quest for Beckham. James's initial feelings for Beckham are demonstrated by the affectionate headlock he puts on the boy, the second time he sees him. This seems like a nice gesture, but hardly a sign of a deep friendship. Yet, when James believes Beckham's body has been turned into a human bomb, the script describes it with the italicized phrase, *The war has finally reached him.*[11] His subsequent attempts to find Beckham—his threatening of the older Iraqi now manning Beckham's table and frightening the professor that he assumes is Beckham's father—are aggressive and personal in contrast to his coolness when defusing bombs. Building on this, the script describes James's reaction when he comes upon a blown up tanker truck like this, "His faces hardens now in a way we haven't seen it before, and as the fire flicks on his features he seems lost in a private war of his own."[12] Finally, when he discovers Beckham alive, the description is, "His jihad was pointless. Insane."[13]

This suggests Beckham speaks to a deeper conflict in James. Given the technique of keeping the character at a distance, this would not need to be explained at this time, but we might assume that the boy reminds James of his own son. If true, this would make his subsequent return to Iraq more difficult. Yet, after all this investment in Beckham, James quickly returns to his old self. Nothing is made of the intensity of his reaction to the boy. And when James returns home, he appears only marginally interested in his son and does not seem to struggle over leaving him again.

James's opacity has the effect of shifting the focus of the story to the two other characters who attempt to understand him. "He's a rowdy boy," says Eldridge.[14] Sanborn calls him reckless. They are positioned as we are, outside, watching, trying to make sense of James's behavior. When Sanborn asks him why he takes the risks, James answers, "I don't know. I guess I don't think about it?" Then he asks Sanborn, "Do you know why—I am the way I am?" Sanborn does not. Instead the stage direction tells us, "They exchange a long look. Brothers at last."[15] Yet Sanborn is different than James. He has other things that matter.

This question of how to read James only deepens when we regard him as an embodiment of the opening quote, "The rush of battle is often a potent and lethal addiction, for war is a drug." If war is a drug, it must be strong enough to draw us away from other things that matter. Yet if nothing else matters to James, his addiction to war's power has limited significance to the rest of us. If James's reaction to Beckham is a glimpse into his character before the need for human contact had been burned out of him, we would like to see it further developed.

Goodbye Solo

Solo, the Senegalese cab driver featured in Ramin Bahrini's *Goodbye Solo* (2008) also has a powerful will. Yet unlike James, Solo learns to regain human contact by relinquishing some of it. When the film begins, we learn that Solo has already promised to drive his fare William out to Blowing Rock and to return without him. Blowing Rock is an overhang in the Blue Ridge mountains, so situated that air currents blow twigs up against gravity, and which in myth blew a suicide jumper back up to his lover. Realizing William's intention to jump, Solo spends most of the rest of the film attempting to talk him out of it. At the same time, Solo's own life falls apart. He separates from his Mexican wife, Quiera, and moves into William's motel. There he pries into William's past, seeking a motivation for his suicide. Furious at the intrusion, William replaces Solo with another driver, but Solo persists and succeeds in driving William. The film ends with Solo and his stepdaughter Alex leaving William at Blowing Rock and, subsequently, testing whether the wind currents are strong enough to blow back small sticks that Alex throws into the wind. They are not.

We do not fully understand why Solo's life is deteriorating at this time. On one hand, his wife is angry with him for seeking to become an airline steward, allowing William to spend the night on the couch, and leaving his disabled cab in the front yard. When she makes good on her threat to have her cousins fix the cab, Solo flees to William's motel room and fights with her on the phone. William, who has been kicked out by his wife thirty years before, is an unwitting witness to the conversation. We subsequently learn that William has now returned to his hometown to get a glimpse of his grandson who works in a local theater, his only connection to his family. On the other hand, Quiera wants Solo back, and it is he who has chosen to bring their relationship to a head. When Solo visits her at the hospital to see his new son, she comments on how happy he seems holding the baby and tells Solo that he cannot leave. He confronts her, explaining that he has always done things her way and now he wants to do things his way. This question of whose will is going to dominate, or more specifically Solo's initial inability to accept that relationships must always involve navigating differing wills, becomes the theme of the film.

We also never explicitly learn why Solo becomes obsessed with William in particular. Ramin Bahrini in his director's notes explains Solo's kindness is due to his cultural background and compares it to his own Iranian heritage.[16] The friendship causes Solo to begin to change, to accept another's will as no longer a challenge to his own—at the end of the film he stops trying to talk William out of his suicide. A key moment for Solo is when he finds and reads William's notebook, which contains observations of Solo. The observations are not revelatory in themselves—they merely report on Solo's activities— but the fact that Solo realizes that he exists in someone else's thoughts seems like a discovery to him. Like in *The Hurt Locker*, the observations of another, even those which fail to enlighten, give depth and presence to the opaque character—a depth that may ultimately be recognition as to how hard it is to penetrate another person's world.

Goodbye Solo consciously evokes Abbas Kiarostami's 1997 Iranian film *Taste of Cherry* about a man, who, having already dug his own grave, drives around Tehran seeking someone to cover him with dirt after his suicide. The man never discusses his reasons for wanting to kill himself and the film clearly is not interested in them. *Goodbye Solo* reverses the intended suicide—but both suggest that human connection requires the recognition, if not the acceptance, of the divergence of the other's will.

Our view is that *Goodbye Solo* works the balance between the individual and the social more deeply than does *The Hurt Locker*. James's lack of connection is established before the film begins and is reiterated, rather than developed, throughout. His reaction to Beckham suggests some opportunity for insight into his character, but this is ultimately not explored. As a result, its thematic resonance seems more static, determined by the opening quote. In learning to respect William's will, and maybe to escape framing the rest of his life as a battle of wills, Solo's movement through the story seems to demonstrate his growth. Yet the film never surrenders to the internal. The fact that Solo's change is presented at a distance allows the film to retain its resonance about an outsider attempting to find his place in a new country. We can infer that will for Solo is a tool, a way of engaging America. Paradoxically, it allows him to both explore the country while keeping it at a distance. His ability to finally relax it becomes a step in his coming closer to finding a new home, without the risk of losing where he came from.

Fish Tank

Unlike Solo, Mia, the fifteen-year old lead character in *Fish Tank* (Andrea Arnold, 2009) does not have the option of seeing herself reflected back through another's conscious. In the world of the film, written and directed by the English filmmaker Andrea Arnold, such sharing is not possible. Constantly jealous of her, Mia's mother throws at Mia the news that she planned to abort her daughter. Her mother's lover, Connor, flirts with Mia and eventually seduces her. After he runs off, Mia follows and discovers he lives a parallel life with a wife and child in a more comfortable suburban housing estate. Unable to express her rage in any other way, Mia pees on his carpet and then entices his young daughter, Keira, into the marshes of the Thames. In a subsequent fight, Mia first throws Keira into the river and then rescues her. The film is framed by Mia's attempt to free a horse from a traveler encampment and her subsequent relationship with Billy, the younger brother of the horse's owner. Learning that the horse has died near the end of the movie provides her the only moment to break down and cry. After a shared dance with her mother and her younger sister, the only connection that seems possible between them, she flees with Billy to go to Wales.

In some ways, Mia is the most disturbing of the four characters we have met because she is the most impulsive and the least self-aware. She is caught between adolescence and adulthood in a world that offers her no comfort or support. One of the most powerful scenes is paradoxically the most physically painful. Ignoring her mother's jealousy, she wades into a stream, catching a fish barehanded with Connor before slicing open her ankle. Connor bandages it and then carries her on his back across a grassy field. She lays her head on his. The scene is both childlike as we see the parental care that she is missing and sexual in the delicate intimacy of her head on his. But since ultimately Connor is not a character who Mia can trust, this moment is ephemeral—it merely serves as a contrast to the rest of her life.

In some way, Mia is the best example of the balance we discussed in the beginning of the chapter. Her drive—her attempts to free the horse, her competition with her mother, her decision to submit an audition tape to become a dancer, her almost uncontained rage toward Connor—all make us interested in her character and allow her to carry the story. The fact that the script proposes no explanations for the emotions driving these actions, however, keeps the story from becoming internal or psychological. We concentrate instead on the surface of her world—the cramped size and lack of privacy in their apartment, the blood on her head when she butts one of the girls dancing on the corner, the chained white horse in the middle of the city, the contrast between the urban world with the fishing stream meadow, the ferocity of the Thames, the way she dances with her mother and sister. We watch Mia drag Keira away from her home, stunned by the extent of her rage. In an unbearable world, it gives Mia life. When Mia leaves with Billy at the end of the movie, it does not seem like a change in her character as much as a momentary escape from an impossible reality. We do know not what change for her would be.

Summary

In this chapter, we discussed how characters presented with greater distance work well in flattened films because they allow the impersonal forces of society and culture to compete with characters' individual internal conflicts. But just because a character is presented to the viewer as distanced does not mean that she should be opaque or flat to the writer. In fact, working with such distance requires the writer to work harder in order to convince the viewer that the character has been fully imagined. Further we suggest that in order to sustain feature films, such opaque characters work best when they carry a great sense of drive and will.

References

1. Boal, Mark. "The Hurt Locker Shooting Draft June 7, 2008." Accessed June 10, 2012. http://content.thehurtlocker.com/20100103_01/hurtlocker_script.pdf, 8.
2. Ibid., 23.
3. Ibid., 1.
4. Granik, Debra and Anne Rosellini. "Winter's Bone." Accessed June 10, 2010. http://moviecultists.com/wp-content/uploads/screenplays/winters-bone.pdf, 73.
5. Ibid., 10.
6. Ibid., 14.
7. Ibid., 66.
8. Wilson, Natalie. August 3, 2010. "Chilling Truths in Winter's Bone," Ms. Blog. Accessed June 10, 2012. http://msmagazine.com/blog/blog/2010/08/03/chilling-truths-in-winter's-bone/.
9. Boal, op. cit., 102.
10. Ibid., 17.

11. Ibid., 84.
12. Ibid., 96.
13. Ibid., 102.
14. Ibid., 22.
15. Ibid., 113.
16. Bahrani, Ramin. "Director's Statement." Accessed June 10, 2008. http://www.raminbahrani.com/pdf/GoodbyeSolo.pdf, 4.

21

The Primacy of Character Over Action: The Non-American Screenplay

One of our goals with this book is to contextualize screenwriting as a form of storytelling related to and growing out of early forms of storytelling. Another of our goals is to challenge the myth that a single formula, form, or structure is sufficient to write a good screenplay. In this chapter, we challenge another myth—the myth that European and Asian films are a different type of screenplay and that what we have implicitly ascribed so far in this book is only applicable to American screenplays.

It is our goal to bring some clarity to the discussion of the non-American screenplay by illustrating how it is similar to as well as different from the American screenplay. In order to do so, however, it is critical to put forth the rationale for this chapter. The dramatized nature of the rationale is purposeful.

The Rationale

The contentious issues about non-American screenplays vs. American screenplays are best characterized by the following five statements:

1. European and Asian films differ so greatly from American films as to be considered a distinct form of storytelling. Often we see the observation made that European film is high culture and American film is pop culture. Many perceive European and Asian film as cultural and American film as purely entertainment.
2. Ideas about screenwriting, particularly those developed in the United States in the past 20 years, are not applicable to European and Asian film.
3. Both European/Asian and American films are forms of storytelling with more similarities than differences.

4. Those differences, where they do exist, are principally cultural and could be described as preferential storytelling strategies rather than as a different form of storytelling.
5. The dominance of American film in the past 20 years can be attributed to an international preference for action-oriented, foreground or plot-driven screen stories over background or character-driven screen stories.

By looking at European/Asian screen stories and by using case-study comparisons, we will explore these five propositions to arrive at our assessment of how wide a difference there is between the American screen story and the non-American screen story.

Classical European and Asian Film

When one looks over the breadth of classical European and Asian storytelling, one is struck by the literary quality of the work, whether considering the Tagore adaptations by Satyajit Ray or the Zola adaptations by Jean Renoir. Indeed, if we look at writers such as Dostoevsky, we can readily find French, Japanese, and American adaptations of their work. And if we look at a popular American writer such as Ed McBain, we can find Japanese as well as American adaptations of his work.

Our point here is that whether one is looking at an American version, a French version, a Russian version, or a Japanese version, the literary qualities, the storytelling virtues that made the original endure, transcend national boundaries. They are great stories and, in many cases, have become fine film stories. To explore this notion of a close, literary cross-national boundary to classical stories, we need to only look more closely at a number of great non-European writer-directors.

Beginning with the work of Ingmar Bergman, we can distill certain storytelling characteristics to his work. Bergman has a propensity for domestic melodrama and moralistic fables—in essence, life lessons. His style is very reminiscent of theater, in which he also works—his stories often have a dialogue-intensive quality. Referred to more than once as the spiritual descendant of August Strindberg, Bergman is distinct but easily identified in the mainstream of storytelling. Like all great storytellers, his insight into human behavior transcends national boundaries.

Frederico Fellini, at least in the first part of his career, had many of the same storytelling qualities as Bergman has. Working most often with cowriters Tullio Pinelli and Ennio Flaiano, Fellini was also influenced by theater, principally by Pirandello. Fellini's screen stories can be viewed as an exploration of particular character types—the fool, the clown, the brute, and the cynic and their attempted relationships—and the comedy and tragedy of everyday lives. His artistic point of view is unique, but as a storyteller, Fellini, too, is part of the larger tradition of storytelling.

We can draw similar comparisons between Luchino Visconti and Leo Tolstoy, and between François Truffaut and the great early French filmic storyteller Jean Vigo. And we can look at the relationship from another perspective—how literary figures, such as novelists and playwrights, have been the screenwriters of many of the most famous European films. Jacques Prévert wrote Marcel Carné's famous *Children of Paradise*; Charles Spaak, working with Renoir, was responsible for *La Grande Illusion*; and Raymond Chandler worked with Billy Wilder on *Double Indemnity*. What would the later career of Luis Buñuel be like without the storytelling skills of Jean-Claude Carrière? Would Volker Schlöndorff have been as successful without the script collaboration of his wife, Margaret Von Trotta? And what would Howard Hawks's classic film noir films have been like without the novelist Leigh Brackett? Whether American or European, the classic filmmakers have aligned themselves with the best writers possible. Their great work stands out internationally in the transnational tradition of storytelling.

Perhaps no filmmaker has been as international in his work as has Akira Kurosawa. As a writer-director, Kurosawa has adapted at least two Shakespearean plays; *Macbeth* became *Throne of Blood* and *King Lear* became *Ran*. Kurosawa also adapted Dostoevsky's *The Idiot* and Gorki's *The Lower Depths*. In addition, Kurosawa has adapted the work of Japanese writer Ryunosuke Akutagawa's *Rashômon* and has written original work as well.

To restate, classic European and Japanese screen stories tend to be part of the broader panorama of storytelling. In this sense, the international fame of Bergman, Fellini, and Kurosawa is far easier to understand.

Exceptions

Although we could apply the three-act structure, main character–secondary character, and foreground–background strategies to classical European and Asian films and determine that there are more similarities than differences, there are exceptions. As with the examples of much of Spike Lee's work in the feature film and of Su Friedrich's work in experimental narrative, there are filmmakers who disregard three-act structure for two-act structure and who seek vehicles beyond the main character to express their particular voices. Those filmmaker-writers, such as Alain Resnais, Michelangelo Antonioni, and Jean-Luc Godard, attempt to tell their stories in unique ways. Some, such as Godard and Buñuel, use the conventions of storytelling as their basis. In doing so, they subvert storytelling methodology as much as use it. Others, such as Antonioni, subvert our notions about character and plot. Still others, such as Éric Rohmer and Jacques Rivette, challenge a single narrative strategy and focus on how dialogue subverts the visual action (or vice versa), and yet others subvert the form of the genre, as Rainer Werner Fassbinder does in melodrama and Werner Herzog does in the adventure film, both in *Aguirre, Wrath of God* and in *Fitzcarraldo*.

At the heart of these exceptions is an exploratory narrative intention—with structure in the case of Resnais (*Muriel*) and Antonioni (*L'Eclisse*), with irony as applied to structure and character in the case of Buñuel (*The Discreet Charm of the Bourgeoisie*) and Godard (*Weekend*), and with character identification in the case of Oshima (*In the Realm of the Senses*) and Jodorowsky (*El Topo*). This impulse to experiment, to find interior stories, and to contradict convention is not exclusive to non-American film. There are many examples of experimental work in American film, yet it is more often associated in an evaluative sense with non-American film.

European and Asian Experiments in Foreground Stories

In spite of the superficial impression that European and Asian films are principally character driven, there have been many efforts in non-American film at foreground or plot-driven stories. Beyond the Indian musical and the Asian science fiction films, a number of important writers and directors have tried their hand at foreground stories.

François Truffaut made a thriller, *The Bride Wore Black*, while Akira Kurosawa made a gangster film, *High and Low*, as well as two films remade from classic Westerns, *The Seven Samurai*, remade as *The Magnificent Seven*, and *Yojimbo*, remade as *A Fistful of Dollars*. Phillipe de Broca made the adventure film *That Man From Rio*, and Luc Besson has even mixed genres in the thriller-police story *La Femme Nikita*. In addition, Bo Widerberg made a straightforward police story called *Man on the Roof*, and well-known writers such as Jean-Claude Carrière have written gangster films, including *Borsalino*. In fact, American genre films have been a mainstay in national European cinemas—the Western in Germany, the gangster film in Italy, and the situation comedy in France. All of these genres are principally foreground stories.

Our point here is that the foreground story hasn't been the exclusive domain of America, nor has background storytelling been the exclusive domain of non-Americans.

The Success of Old-Fashioned Storytelling: The Australian Case

Few countries have been as successful in exporting film talent and in capturing international attention as have Australia and New Zealand. Directors now working internationally include Phillip Noyce (*Clear and Present Danger*), Bruce Beresford (*Driving Miss Daisy*), Fred Schepisi (*Six Degrees of Separation*), Peter Weir (*Witness*), George Miller (*Lorenzo's Oil*), Roger Donaldson (*No Way Out*), Jane Campion (*The Piano*), and Paul Hogan

(*My Best Friend's Wedding*). From 1974 to 1994, the outpouring of fascinating narratives, from Miller's *The Road Warrior*, to Schepisi's *The Chant of Jimmy Blacksmith*, to Vincent Ward's *The Navigator: A Mediaeval Odyssey*, to Campion's *An Angel at My Table*, has been remarkable. It is our contention that the success of these non-American films as a whole is due to the storytelling skills exhibited. In a sense, these films and this movement represent storytelling at its old-fashioned best.

The virtues of storytelling can be grouped in three areas: character, structure, and voice. In all of these areas, the films of Australia and New Zealand have shared a vision that is striking. In terms of character, these narratives test the nature of both men and women against the prevailing power structure, whether it is the British mother country, the land itself, or, for female characters, the male power structure.

Character is explored in *Breaker Morant*, a story of three lieutenants who are accused of murder during the Boer War. The drama is not only enhanced by the severity of the charges, but is compounded by the fact that the lieutenants are Australians fighting as part of the British forces. In *Gallipoli*, this tension between British politics and Australian principle and sacrifice is also explored. The subject is played for adventure in *The Lighthorsemen*, but more often the British wars and the Australian role in them provide a layer of drama that strengthens the sense of the characters: they have not only the Germans or Boers to contend with, they also have the British. The resulting dramas make for a heroic sense of character. Individualistic, strong-willed but generous, the Australian main character is certainly appealing. The same sense of character infuses the female protagonists in *The Piano* and *My Brilliant Career*. Australian main characters in these films are goal directed, willful, and energetic; in short, they are appealing.

In terms of structure, character-driven stories such as *The Piano* also exhibit a boldness of dramatic clash as much as a vigor of plot, as in *The Chant of Jimmy Blacksmith*. Whether character driven or plot driven, these films use structure to intensify the narrative. *Breaker Morant* moves between the past (the events) and the present (the trial) of the three soldiers in a dynamic and urgent manner. Few foreground stories unfold as boldly as the adventure form does in *The Road Warrior*. Just as with character, there is a confident utilization of classical dramatic structure in these films. Attention is paid to joining the story at a useful critical moment.

Finally, these films have a tone that marks them as unique and committed. Beginning with a respect for genre, writer-directors such as George Miller bring an over-the-top zeal to making *The Road Warrior*, an adventure story to top all other adventure stories, while Jane Campion brings a poetic, complex feminism to the melodrama in all of her work, especially *The Piano*. Whether the racial rage in *The Chant of Jimmy Blacksmith* is due to Thomas Keneally's original novel or to Fred Schepisi's passion, there is a definite point of view that drives the narrative. Other countries deal with issues such as racism by using irony and metaphor; not so the Australians. They have a directness that makes the narrative incredible rather than simply credible. Tone, structure, and character have all been used in the old-fashioned or classic sense to tell tales we may recognize, but they are told in such a way that we don't forget them. This immediacy, passion, and storytelling strength—this approach explains the success of Australian and New Zealand films. It also explains why so many veterans of that movement are now prominent Hollywood filmmakers.

Success of Personal Storytelling: German French, and Hungarian Examples

The reputation of European and Asian film rests on the intimate storytelling identities of filmmakers such as Bergman, Fellini, Renoir, Mizoguchi, Ozu, and Ray. This tradition—call it personal vision—is so marked that, in the minds of many in the audience, European filmmaking is associated with personal filmmaking and with many others in the business of film art and its expression. This reputation is the context in which to consider a number of current European writer-directors, who are very much in the mold of the personal tradition.

Although many of the German filmmakers are essentially genre filmmakers (Fassbinder, melodrama; Wenders, the road subgenre of melodrama), there are writer-directors, such as Werner Herzog, who fall into the category of personal filmmaking. The result from a narrative perspective is that Herzog is likely to make adventure films with considerable background story (*Aguirre, Wrath of God*) and melodramas with considerable plot (*The Enigma of Kaspar Hauser*). In this sense, Herzog follows a different tradition—the artistic tradition of breaking the rules, challenging the conventions, and creating an artful alternative.

Like Herzog in Germany, Louis Malle and Éric Rohmer in France push the classic parameters of storytelling. Malle is as interested in the negative character in *Lacombe Lucien* as he was in *Le Feu Follet*. In *Atlantic City*, he challenges the story form and produces a gangster film with considerable background story and a motif twist: the gangster not only survives, he thrives. In *Murmur of the Heart*, he challenges the narrative tone of the classic war film. Malle makes his films his own by challenging narrative convention.

A similar pattern characterizes the moral tales of Éric Rohmer. Whether one considers *Claire's Knee* or *Summer*, and whether the issue is sexuality or the permanence of relationships, Rohmer uses ironic structure, character, and dialogue to probe the behavior of his characters in a series of melodramas he calls his moral tales. Although they are more difficult to identify with, his characters nevertheless have enough determination to keep us curious as to whether they will succeed or fail.

Finally, in Hungary, István Szabó has maintained a singularly personal view of life. As with Rohmer, there is an irony in Szabó's approach to character.

In *Father*, his concern is personal relations in a communist period; in *Mephisto*, his concern is personal relations in the Fascist period; in *Colonel Redl*, his concern is personal relations in an anti-Semitic period; and in his English-language film *Meeting Venus*, his concern is personal relations in an artistic period. Szabó, as you can assume, is always fascinated by the irony of human behavior, by the will to survive, and by the will to find love. Szabó's is an ironic approach to narrative, but as with his spiritual mentor, Luchino Visconti, he is capable of great feeling and empathy. In both cases, he follows his own personal direction in the tradition so well identified by Bergman and Fellini.

Case Studies

■ ■ ■ A Case Study of Classic Storytelling: Emir Kusterica's *Time of the Gypsies*

Emir Kusterica and Gordan Mihiś have written a classic melodrama in *Time of the Gypsies*. In exploring this film, we will determine how it is different from, and how it is similar to, American melodrama.

In scale, *Time of the Gypsies* is comparable to the work of the great novelists Dickens, Tolstoy, and Dreiser. A young boy, Pheran, is brought up by his grandmother. He wears thick glasses and looks sickly. His sister is physically disabled, and his mother died giving birth to her. Only a vagrant uncle provides a perspective on the gypsy adult male and family life. The story follows Pheran through his youthful romanticism to his adult paranoia. He joins a local gypsy criminal as he travels to Italy to make money. En route, they drop off Pheran's sister for medical treatment. Pheran leaves the girl whom he loves in the village, and her family totally rejects him.

Later, prosperous, Pheran returns and marries the girl. When he discovers she is pregnant, he does not believe it is his child, and his wife dies in childbirth. He also discovers that he has been deceived by his criminal patron. His sister was never medically treated but was instead used as a beggar on the streets of Rome. He sends his sister and his son back home and seeks out his former patron. As he kills him, he is also killed. At Pheran's funeral, his son, now 4 years old, steals the gold coins that cover Pheran's eyes.

This brief synopsis cannot do justice to the richness of the narrative of *Time of the Gypsies*. The detailing of the script creates a sense of the gypsy subculture and of the male character Pheran, who starts out optimistically but is doomed. He is doomed because he cannot accept his wife as faithful and as the mother of his child. This paranoia seems endemic among the men, who change wives as readily as Americans change jobs. But there is another unique quality to Pheran and to his culture—he has a primitive belief in a world that embraces superstition and magic. Consequently, in his world, personal will, divining, and magic all play an active part.

As with classic melodrama, there are characters who help Pheran, mainly the women, and there are characters who oppose him, mainly the men. The power structure that Pheran tries to challenge is the economic power structure of his village. The criminal is on top, with most of the villagers eking out a living. Only by establishing his base in Italy—that is, outside Yugoslavia—can the criminal enjoy prosperity. When Pheran attempts to join this power structure, the poison of deception infiltrates his ideology and he believes he has been deceived by his wife. In reality, he has been deceived by his patron, not his wife. Once he has crossed over to the model of his patron, Pheran is doomed.

As in classic melodrama, *Time of the Gypsies* has a strong background story. It differs from the classic melodrama in two areas: it has a far more elaborate plot than is usually found in melodrama, and it spends a great deal of Act One acclimatizing us to the gypsy culture before it introduces the main character. This latter decision may not be so much cultural subjectivity as much as essential exposition, given the lack of widespread knowledge about gypsy culture and its importance to the story. In tone, the film shares the ironic position so often used in central Europe. Consequently, humor plays a very important part in drawing us into what is essentially a tragic melodrama. Even after the death of Pheran, Kusterica uses humor in the last scenes—the stealing of the gold coins and the hasty departure of Pheran's uncle. Summing up, *Time of the Gypsies* is a classic melodrama with modifications in tone and in the pace of the story, particularly in Act One.

■ ■ ■ ### A Case Study of Ironic Structure: *The Double Life of Véronique*

As with so many other central European writers and directors, Krzysztof Kieślowski and Krzysztof Piesiewicz have deployed an ironic structure to explore the life of a contemporary young woman. Far more subtle in their irony than either Kusterica or Szabó, Kieślowski and Piesiewicz sidestep the political dynamics in favor of the psychological.

The Double Life of Véronique is about two young women, Véronique in France and Veronica in Poland. Both were born at the same time and grew up to look alike, but do not know each other, at least not consciously. Veronica is a musician, a gifted singer who dies in the midst of a performance. At that moment, Véronique is making love and suddenly feels a sense of loss. She gives up her voice lessons, without understanding or explaining why. The story that ensues is about Véronique falling in love with a man who is a puppeteer and writer. Véronique seems to know what he will do to reach out to her, even though she has only seen him once at a children's school performance. As the relationship develops, Véronique is aware of a level of knowing, of consciousness that anticipates emotion and events, as if she's had another life. Near the end, the puppeteer finds a picture he believes to be of Véronique from her visit to Krakow, but it is a picture of Veronica. Finally, there is a conscious acknowledgment of the other Veronica. The writers connect the two women beyond appearances. Each is very close to her father, each lost her mother at a young age, and each has a musical talent.

In terms of the structure, the notion of having a dramatic double invites the character and the viewer to reflect on the character. The double is the distancing device. The question in *The Double Life of Véronique* is: What purpose does irony serve? Véronique is lively, beautiful, appealing—an example of a positive life force.

And yet the double, Veronica, dies suddenly in Krakow. It's as if Kieślowski and Pie-siewicz are exploring, through a young, attractive woman, the loss, the fear of loss, and, inevitably, the fear of dying. By giving Véronique a double, the writers explore the dialectic between living and dying and, in the course of doing so, comment upon the quality of life. For Véronique to live means to love and to remember the other Veronica, who represents the cumulative losses in Véronique's life.

Another reading of the structure is to view the device as a way of depicting gain-ing control of events. When Véronique knows what will happen via the other Veronica, she can protect herself. This more cautious view of living is reflected in the puppeteer as well—he makes puppets of Véronique and Veronica, but tells Véronique that he uses the double only if injury or destruction occurs to the original during a performance. The artist, in this case the puppeteer and writer, is as cautious as Véronique is.

The *Double Life of Véronique* provides but one example of ironic structure. Kieślowski's work is often ironic in its structure—*White* and *A Short Film About Love* are powerful because they use ironic structure. But again, Kieślowski uses irony in a more delicate and subtle manner than do many other central European writers and directors.

■ ■ ■   **A Case Study in Foreground–Background Variation:**
Ghost and Truly, Madly, Deeply

Comparing American and non-American treatments of the same subject yields other insights into the deployment of the mix of narrative strategies. *Ghost*, written by American Bruce Joel Rubin, and *Truly, Madly, Deeply*, written by Briton Anthony Minghella, are both stories of male–female relationships in which the man dies unexpectedly. A major part of the story is how the woman copes with the loss. In both stories, the supernatural is invoked, and the dead male plays a significant role; in essence, the relationship continues in spite of death.

In *Ghost*, the main character (Patrick Swayze) is killed in a robbery. Unsatisfied with his departure from life, he hovers between worlds; he is in essence a ghost. He tries to communicate with his wife (Demi Moore), but only when he uses a medium (Whoopi Goldberg) does he communicate with her successfully. Before he goes to the other world, however, he must protect his wife from the advances of his best friend, and he discovers it was his friend who had him killed. Once he has settled the score, he can say good-bye and move on to the other world. In *Ghost*, the male is the main character and his goal is to move on with his loved one's affairs in order. By doing so, his love is confirmed in the life of his wife.

The main character in *Truly, Madly, Deeply* is a woman (Nina, Juliet Stevenson) who has lost her lover (Alan Rickman). Her goal is never to let go of her grief. All men, including her landlord and her boss, seem to love her, or at least want to protect her. But her grief is so deep that her lover returns as a ghost, and she is happy. At the same time, a teacher who works with limited young adults falls in love with Nina. He is the opposite of her lover—unsure, but startling in his hon-esty. Now Nina lives with a ghost and is pursued by an earnest mortal. Who she chooses is the substance of the second half of the script.

One clear difference between the two treatments of the story is the main character. *Ghost* is told from the point of view of the ghost; *Truly, Madly, Deeply* is told from the point of view of the survivor, the one who has to go on living in the light of the loss. This choice of main character puts the British film in the more realistic camp, while the use of a supernatural being as the main character makes *Ghost* principally a fantasy. This tonal difference is an issue we will return to.

Another difference between the stories is their emphasis. *Ghost* is plot intensive, while *Truly, Madly, Deeply* is character or background story intensive. In fact, *Ghost* has considerable foreground. The plot focuses on the killing of the main character, his own investigation of the killing, and the resolution of the foreground story—the killing of the best friend, who is the antagonist of the story. The background story of *Ghost* focuses on love and loss in the relationship between husband and wife. The believability and emotional complexity of the background story is seriously eroded by the dramatic device of a comic medium, which allows the dead husband and living wife to communicate with one another.

Truly, Madly, Deeply, on the other hand, has very little plot. The background story unfolds after the level of the main character's grief and longing are revealed. By Act Two, when her lover returns as a ghost and the teacher begins to pursue her, we proceed along the classic relationship triangle: Whom will she choose? Once she has made her choice for life, a choice to bear a child, her ghost lover recedes, and she begins her life again. The entire story has been, in essence, the main character's mourning over her loss. The resolution of the background story, her choice for life, ends this deeply emotional, painful story on an upbeat note. *Ghost*, on the other hand, ends with the admission of loss and the transcendence of the relationship beyond mortality into that realm best described as "foreverland." *Truly, Madly, Deeply*, having moved into the fantastic in Act Two, ends as it began, realistically, whereas *Ghost* ends reaching romantically for new heights in fantasy.

To sum up, the two films differ considerably. Not only is the point of view chosen by Minghella in *Truly, Madly, Deeply* more realistic, so, too, is the resolution of the story. By using background story over plot, Minghella creates more complex, believable characters, and he explores a difficult interior issue, loss. Rubin, on the other hand, has written a romantic fantasy about loss. *Ghost* is plot intensive, and its tone never veers from the fantastic. *Ghost* consequently requires an antagonist, whereas *Truly, Madly, Deeply* doesn't. The main character is both protagonist and antagonist. When she lets go of her grief, she overcomes her loss.

■ ■ ■   ## A Case Study of the Main Character's Position: *Dances With Wolves, Black Robe,* and *Close to Eden*

Generally, we expect a main character to sit in the middle of the screen story. The screen stories in this case study, however, differ. All three films, *Dances With Wolves, Black Robe,* and *Close to Eden* (*Urga*), position their characters differently. Each could be called an East-meets-West story.

Dances With Wolves, written by Michael Blake, is set in the post-Civil War West. The main character, Lieutenant John Dunbar (Kevin Costner), is a white man assigned to an abandoned fort. We sense he is fed up with war and the white man. He is first curious about and eventually utterly taken with his neighbors, the Sioux. The story is essentially about the clash of native culture with the dominant Eurocentric white culture. Dunbar clearly comes to admire and imitate the native culture. As a main character, he is an outsider who comes as close to being an insider as is possible. The foreground story follows Dunbar the soldier; the background story follows Dunbar the individual in search of his humanity. He finds this humanity in the Indian culture.

Black Robe is set 250 years earlier. The central character is a French priest, and, as in *Dances With Wolves*, the story deals with the clash of cultures and religions—the priest's religion is spiritual without the physical; the Indian religion is physical, spiritual, and animistic. In this story, the priest holds to his position. He does not enter the Indian culture; instead, he attempts to alter it. In terms of the story, since so much is taken up with articulating and validating the Indian culture, the priest remains an outsider. Consequently, we stand aside from the story, not quite in an ironic position, but far more distanced from the story than was the main character in *Dances With Wolves*. The result is that we don't see a victor in *Black Robe*. Whether this is more realistic or ascribable to cultural differences is worth considering.

Black Robe, written by Brian Moore, is an Australian–Canadian co-production made by Bruce Beresford, an exceptional filmmaker from Australia. Is the narrative distinctly non-American? The fact that almost all of the Indians (except Chomina and his family) are distinct threats to the priest's survival in *Black Robe* positions the main character on the periphery of the narrative. John Dunbar in *Dances With Wolves*, on the other hand, is a white man in a film about a culture dying because of the white man, and he enters centrally into the narrative.

Only when we turn to the third example, Nikita Mikhalkov and Rustam Ibragimbekov's *Close to Eden*, do we see a story of East meets West told entirely from the native's point of view. In *Close to Eden*, the main character is a Mongol herdsman in modern Mongolia. He lives with his family on the steppes. He rides a horse, and when he wants to have a child, he follows a ritual of chasing his wife on horseback, staking a suitable hill, and displaying his banner, the urga, the equivalent of a do-not-disturb sign. A Russian trucker gets lost, and the Mongol helps rescue him. The herdsman feeds him, and the ensuing contact between the European Russian and the Asiatic Mongol grows. The Mongol visits the Russian in the town. There, more trucks and the trappings of civilization make the Mongol look ridiculous. Nevertheless, he is not embarrassed, and he makes his way. In fact, he proves to be a man of means, and he purchases a television and other gifts for his family. On the steppes, he stares at the television, clearly considering its utility. He brings the gifts, but in the end, he is unsullied in his true interests in his family and in increasing its size. However, we are left with the sense that the next generation will not be able to resist modern life as well as he has.

As in *Black Robe*, the Mongol is spiritual, physical, open. He is not a fool, but he does seem a naïf next to the white man, and as in *Black Robe*, the gulf between the two cultures is enormous. The key difference between *Dances With Wolves*, *Black Robe*, and *Close to Eden* is that only *Close to Eden* tells the native story from the perspective of a native; the story is told from the inside rather than from the outside. Also notable is that both *Black Robe* and *Close to Eden* do not seek the kind of narrative closure used in *Dances With Wolves*. The shape of the story is more open-ended, a rarity in the Western, a genre often defined by the gunfight or battle that brings closure. Finally, the tone of *Black Robe* and *Close to Eden* is far less romantic than that of *Dances With Wolves*. Irony in both cases distances us enough to consider the actions and the fate of the main character.

■ ■ ■   ## Two Case Studies of Mixing Genres: *Schindler's List* and *Europa Europa*

Few movies have been as quickly acclaimed as was *Schindler's List*. The Steve Zaillian script, the Thomas Keneally book, and the Steven Spielberg direction each have been lauded. In this section, we will look at *Schindler's List* as an American war film. In addition, we will look at another recent war film from Eastern Europe, Agnieszka Holland's *Europa Europa*. Both are films about the Holocaust, and both mix genres, but for the purposes of our discussion, we will focus primarily on the war stories.

Zaillian's *Schindler's List* is a war film and a melodrama. The war film follows the chronology of events in Krakow from 1942 to 1945. It was throughout that period that the Jews were first placed in a ghetto; some killed there, and the survivors were shipped to concentration camps. In *Schindler's List*, the German industrialist Oskar Schindler uses Jewish labor in his factories. Those who work for him are in the end saved because he retains the permission of the authorities to use Jews for labor. The result is that those 1000 to 2000 Jews who worked for Schindler survived the war. In the typical war story, the protagonist does all he can to survive. In *Schindler's List*, the Jews as a group are the protagonist, and the antagonist is the Nazi commandant in charge of the Krakow labor camp. The Nazi commandant kills randomly, without pity. And for all the Jews he represents death.

In the melodrama, Schindler is the main character. He challenges the power structure of the Nazis by choosing to save Jews. Schindler's tragedy is that he can only save a handful out of the thousands who are killed. *Schindler's List* uses the war story as foreground, the plot to kill the Jews. The struggle of Oskar Schindler to save Jews from the Nazis becomes the melodramatic background story. The result is a realistic, powerful story that takes advantage of the strengths of both story forms—in essence, plot and character. The tone of the film is serious and realistic, as expected in both genres.

Europa Europa tells the story of a single Holocaust survivor, Solly Perel. He is a young adolescent, a German Jew, who does not look Jewish. His parents send him east when the war breaks out. He is separated from his older brother and taken into a Soviet boys' school. As the Nazis move into the area, he flees further east, but is captured by the Germans. He makes a decision to pose as a Russian of German descent. He is accepted and survives. As he travels with an army unit, a homosexual sergeant befriends him and discovers he is a Jew. The sergeant promises not to betray him, and Solly finally feels he has a friend, but the sergeant is soon killed. The captain of the unit, an anti-Semite, is taken with Solly and offers to send him to the Hitler Youth in Germany. He will also adopt him. Back in Germany, Solly strives once more to survive, knowing that his identity as a Jew will be apparent if his friends see him naked. He takes on elaborate measures to avoid detection. He seems to be a model young Nazi, as even his teacher, another anti-Semite, claims in front of his classmates.

The next threat to Solly, however, is love. He falls in love with a young German girl but arouses suspicion when he is unable to consummate the relationship. Overwhelmed with adolescent feelings of desire and anxiety, he confesses his identity to the girl's mother. Again, he is not given away. In fact, he eludes detection until the end of the war. About to be shot by the Russians and the Jews they have released, his brother, a survivor of a concentration camp, recognizes him and he is saved. Together they have survived the war.

Europa Europa follows a chronology, from Kristallnacht in Germany in 1938 to liberation in April 1945. A postscript shows the real Solomon Perel in Israel in 1990. As in the war film, there is a great deal of plot, or foreground story. Solly is clearly a protagonist trying to survive. The many settings and events suggest how dangerous the war is for him. His sister and later his parents and oldest brother are killed. Only his other brother survives. The war is presented in a surrealistic sense; however, since he is a non-combatant, there is a surreal quality to how relentless and eccentric death is to a boy so young.

The other genre used by Holland, however, is far less realistic and tends to exaggerate the surrealism of the story. The second layer of the film is a satire on race. Since Solly looks non-Jewish, he passes as an Aryan. His encounters with the captain and the teacher are deeply ironic, for each man professes an ability to clearly recognize anyone of Jewish descent, yet both mistake him for a non-Jewish German. Satire also allows Holland to be playful about Nazism. Solly is practicing the Nazi salute, which devolves into a jig. What is menacing to so many is amusing to him. We are reminded that he is still just a young boy, barely more than a child. Finally, the satire allows Holland to explore his fantasies, including his thoughts about Stalin and Hitler. The playfulness of the satire is of a different tone than that in the war film. Indeed, the jarring shifts in tone are such that we are left unsettled. Are we to believe this surreal tale, or is it a nightmare—imagined, not real? As we discovered with Szabó, Kusterica, and Kieślowski, irony is an important distancing device to reflect upon the fate of the character and the nature of events. The satire distances us from Solly, and we can consider the nature of the Holocaust as experienced by this one person.

Summing up, Zaillian's script mixes compatible genres for a realistic presentation of the Holocaust and of Schindler's role in saving Jews. Holland's script uses satire to undermine the sense of realism of the war story so that the audience considers Solly Perel's struggle for survival a nightmare on the level of Kosin'ski's *The Painted Bird*, a totally irrational experience modified by the will of one individual to do anything to survive. The experience of *Schindler's List* is dominated by realistic story forms; the experience of *Europa Europa* becomes more complicated as Holland distances us from the fate of the main character. *Schindler's List* reflects the American approach to genre, to work within genre expectations. Holland's script for Europa Europa deploys irony in its approach to the war film, an approach more typical of other middle European storytellers.

Conclusion

We cannot be definitive about storytelling strategies in non-American film. However, we can point out their linkages to storytelling in general, and we can discern preferences in the narrative strategy mix. Just as plot or action over character seems to be dominant in American film, we can see a clear preference for background story—character over plot—in many European films. This primacy is neither good nor bad; it simply appears to be the preference.

Also discernible is the use of irony in many central European films, and again, given the history of the region, that choice, too, seems understandable. We also note, as in the comparison of *Ghost* and *Truly, Madly, Deeply*, a preference in the United States for fantasy over realism and the preference for realism over fantasy in the British example.

American, European, and Asian films have much in common, but they also have distinct differences. Understanding these distinctive narrative qualities may help screenwriters learn more readily from one another.

22

The Subtleties and Implications of Screenplay Form

It is sometimes said that a screenplay has the same relationship to a finished film that a blueprint does to a completed building. Although this relationship may be true for the final shooting script, most screenplays lack a clear one-to-one correspondence to the finished film. Instead of being a precise list of specifications, screenplays have a language that suggests, but does not lay out, the actual shot structure of the film. A good screenplay must first succeed in evoking a strong emotional response from the reader.

Shots and Scenes

To understand the distinction between a screenplay and a shooting script, we need to review a basic distinction in fllmmaking—the difference between shots and scenes. A shot is a continuous strand of film. During the shooting process, a shot begins when the camera is turned on and ends when the camera is turned off. During the editing process, a shot is the space between cuts. Thus, assuming the camera is running at normal speed, a shot inscribes and relates real time and space. Revealing a different space within a shot always takes time, because the camera must be moved physically (e.g., tilted, panned, and dollied) to get to the new space.

A scene, on the contrary, is made up of one or more shots and is defined as implying, rather than inscribing, continuous time and a contiguous location. A scene takes place in one room, on one baseball field, in one car; however, within that space, the camera may cut to any angle or perspective without implying a lapse of time. The eyeline-match shots that make up many dialogue sequences are a good example. In this type of scene, the camera cuts back and forth from close-up to opposing close-up without any appreciable break in time to account for the change in angle. Of course, a scene may be made up of only one shot; in that case, it is inscribed with continuous time and space.

Shooting Scripts and Screenplays

As the advent of the addition of sound to films, the primary technical problem of screenwriting has been the integration of image and dialogue. Later in this chapter, we show that this is, in fact, a false distinction, because in a well-written, mainstream script, both image and dialogue function in the same way—as dramatic action or intention. But, for a moment, let's use the distinction between image and dialogue to help us understand the difference between a screenplay and a shooting script or, more specifically, between a scene-based and a shot-based script. Let's start with what comes last in the production process—the shooting script. Based on the completed screenplay, a shooting script is a shot-by-shot breakdown of what the finished, edited film will look like. In theory, it is possible to film a shooting script exactly as it is written, cut the shots together as planned, and have a complete coherent film. The following example is a shooting script from the 1958 film *I Want to Live*, written by Nelson Gidding and directed by Robert Wise.

```
1. INT. LIVING ROOM—CLOSE ON TH E BONGO PLAYER
now beating up a storm on his skins. He's a real cool
type—faded blue jeans, sandals.

2. ANGLE ON PEG
By the open window. She's brooding about her split up
with Barbara. She belts down half a tumblerful of
whiskey, then walks over to the bongo player and stares
at his flying hands.

                    PEG
          Give it some head, Joe.

The tattooed noncom grabs her and they join the wild
dance. The party is really getting into high gear.

3. OMIT

4. MED. SHOT
Barbara, ringed by an excited GROUP of men, dances almost
frenzied to the driving rhythm of the drums.

5. CLOSE SHOT
The drummer's hands flailing the skins faster and faster.

6. HEAD CLOSE-UP—BARBARA
reacting more and more excitedly to the increasing tempo.
In a sudden crash of abrupt silence, we.

                              STRAIGHT CUT TO[1]
```

The first and most important element of a shooting script is that the *slug lines*, the numbered lines of uppercase text that organize the flow of the script, describe shots rather than scenes. The example from Gidding's script is actually the continuation of a party scene that runs several pages. Within this one scene, the slug lines indicate many camera positions. As these numbers refer to the shooting schedule and script breakdowns, the script is not renumbered after a rewrite; rather, numbered slug lines are indicated as omitted. The dramatic tension between Barbara and Peg is clearly marked off by the slug lines. Both characters never appear in the same shot, and the alternation of shots focusing first on Peg and then on Barbara heightens this sense of separation.

A screenplay, on the contrary, is a more broadly visualized rendering of the film, which emphasizes the emotional and logical flow of the story over the breakdown of shots. Frequently called the *master scene-style*, slug lines in a screenplay indicate scenes rather than shots and are generally unnumbered. Even within a scene, the screenwriter rarely, if ever, indicates specific shots. Rather, a form of language has developed (we look at this in more detail later), which allows the writer to imply a pattern of shots, while still concentrating on the dramatic progression of the scene.

The following example is from Billy Wilder and I.A.L. Diamond's screenplay of *The Apartment*. We pick up the story at the scene in which Sheldrake asks to borrow Bud's apartment key, so that Sheldrake can take Miss Kubelik, with whom Bud is in love, to Bud's apartment. Bud owes his rise to the executive suite to his willingness to lend out his apartment. This is the obligatory scene.

```
[Picks up in middle of scene]

INT. SHELDRAKE'S OFFICE—DAY

                    SHELDRAKE
          I'm not bringing anybody—I'm
          bringing Miss Kubelik.

                    BUD
          Especially not Miss Kubelik.

                    SHELDRAKE
          How's that again?

                    BUD
                    (flatly)
          No key!

                    SHELDRAKE
          Baxter, I picked you for my
          team because I thought you
```

```
                         were a bright young man. You
                         realize what you're doing?
                         Not to me—but to yourself.
                         Normally it takes years
                         to work your way up to the
                         twenty-seventh floor—but it
                         takes only thirty seconds to
                         be out on the street again.
                         You dig?


                                   BUD
                         (nodding slowly) I dig.


                                SHELDRAKE
                         So what's it going to be?


             Without taking his eyes off Sheldrake, Bud reaches into
             his pocket, fishes out a key, drops it on the desk.


                                SHELDRAKE
                         Now you're being bright.²
```

In this example, the slug line marks the scene, not the shots. Yet, if we look carefully, we suspect that there must be more than one shot in this scene. Let's see if we can construct a shooting script from this screenplay. But before we do, let's think about the turning point of the scene—the moment when Bud gives Sheldrake the key. Clearly, this is not merely an unconsidered action on Bud's part. The fixedness of Bud's glance ("Without taking his eyes off Sheldrake...") suggests that something more is going on. Sure enough, in the next scene, we learn that Bud gave Sheldrake the key to the executive washroom instead of the key to his apartment. On the basis of this knowledge, we know that the pivotal moment in the scene is when Bud, backed into a corner and deciding what to do, regards Sheldrake before giving him the key.

One of the most useful guidelines for the writer is the principle of reaction that comes from the theater. It suggests that we tend to respond to something in a specific order—by looking, moving, and, lastly, speaking. Generally, by the time we speak, we have made our decisions. Thus, the reactions that precede speech—the looking and moving—are critical for the writer to capture, because this is where we see the character thinking.

In order to underscore this moment's importance, the shot must stop the action. This can be done by a close-up of Bud, intercut with his point-of-view shot of Sheldrake, followed by a return to the close-up in which Bud decides to move and a match cut to a wider shot of Bud taking his key out of his pocket. From here, we can fill in the rest of the scene. Sheldrake's long speech, his ace in the hole, will be most likely in a close-up, possibly cut with a reaction shot of Bud as he starts to weigh his decision. These shots will not break the flow of the action, nor will they be as tight as will be the decisive close-up on Bud. Somewhere at the beginning of the scene illustrated here, there will be a two-shot, not so much to set the spatial relationship between the two men (most likely that's already been set), but to relax the scene before its build to the final beat.

We have constructed a shooting script even though no actual shots were mentioned in the screenplay. Of course, our construction is really an interpretation. We have no confidence that these shots are exactly what the screenwriter had in mind.

Hence, does the screenwriter have the final say in how the film actually looks? Can a screenplay instruct the director in what to do? The answer is no. A screenplay exists to be interpreted. However, screenplays have evolved a connotative, expressive freedom that more than makes up for the proscriptive loss of the shooting script. Instead of being limited to describing the concrete details of individual frames, contemporary screenplays have developed a rich language that connects details to emotional impulse, pictures to feelings, and the rhythm of prose to the flow of the dramatic line of the film. The trick is to learn how to use the logic and structure of language to imply the logic and structure of the scene.

We said previously that shooting scripts are shot based, whereas screenplays are scene based. We can take this a step further and say that screenplays are not merely scene based, but are beat based. Beats are the smallest unit of coherent dramatic direction. They change when a character either succeeds with or gives up a line of pursuit, when another character takes over dominance of the scene, or when something new is introduced. In the scene from *The Apartment*, Sheldrake's attempt to convince Bud to loan out his apartment constitutes one large beat (this may be made up of a number of smaller beats in which they argue back and forth, or where Sheldrake changes strategy). The beat changes when Bud makes up his mind to give him the wrong key. Beat changes are marked in screenplays by stage directions and changes in rhythm.

Diamond and Wilder could have written the scene from *The Apartment* in the form of a shooting script, detailing each shot, so that the section we reviewed would run a number of pages. However, here is the key: Even though they would have more control over each shot, they would lose the impact that their screenplay conveys. In the shooting script, the shape of the scene, the rhythmic acceleration of the dialogue preceding the pause, and the change of beat when Bud makes up his mind would have been lost in the details. In the screenplay, the moment where Bud hesitates and then makes up his mind is inescapable—as it is in the film. Rather than conveying technical details, the screenplay dramatizes the line of the scene and the progression of the beats, so that its impact hits the reader. It is the director's job to find the exact visual equivalents for that impact.

The Basics of Screenplay Form

It is time, now, for details. We will start with a scene of pure whimsy. The easiest way to get screenplay layout correct is to use one of the screenwriting programs, such as Final Draft and Movie Magic. Shareware add-ins are available for word processing programs such as Microsoft Word.

- If you are using a word processor, set it to Courier 12 point.
- The line lengths for blocking should be 55 spaces, for dialogue 35, and for parentheticals 16.
- Set the left margin at 1.6″ and the right margin at 3/4″ in from the edge of the page.
- Set a tab for dialogue at 2.6″, for parentheticals at 3.3″, and for character name at 3.9″.[3]

When you print out the text, your page appears skewed to the right. In fact, a screenplay page is always printed with an additional binding margin to the left of the text, so that the script may be fastened with copper brads along the left edge and still be readable. In the following excerpt, the bracketed numbers refer to specific features of screenwriting; these will be explained following the excerpt. They should not appear in the script.

```
FADE IN[1]

[2]EXT.[3] OPIUM HEAVEN[4]—DAY[5]

[6]GEORGE[7], an ageless hippy, and WILLIE, 30[8] with
the largest pupils you ever did see[9] are [10] puffing
on a SEVENTEEN FOOT WATER PIPE[11]. The very clouds that
waft past their heads reflect the state they are in.

George passes the mouthpiece to SUSAN, late twenties, who
is not too happy.[12] She inhales, then coughs and gri-
maces. This is supposed to be heaven, but the weed just
doesn't smoke as sweet. Susan looks[13] at her friends.
Their bodies are already in seventh heaven. Who knows
where their heads are?[14]

Suddenly Susan rises and punches her fist through a
cloud.[15]

                        SUSAN[16]
                (Whining) [17]
                What fun is it to be high
                when everyone else is?

She lifts the filter from the water pipe and drops it off
the cloud.[18]
```

```
EXT. SHEA STADIUM—DAY

The PITCHER is in the middle of his windup when the MANNA
FROM HEAVEN lands at his feet.[19] He freezes.

                          UMP
                    Balk!
The pitcher ignores the UMP, picks up the filter, wets a
finger and then tastes it. He smiles. Looks up at heaven.
Some of the fielders move in to see what it is about.

Now the opposing dugout empties. The first fans climb
onto the field. The organist begins playing "Happy Days
Are Here Again."[20]

EXT. OPIUM HEAVEN—DAY
The commotion can be heard, however faintly, even up here
in heaven.[21]

                                        IRIS IN ON[22]
```

Excerpt Number Key

[1] Fade In—The traditional screenplay beginning; it no longer means a literal fade. Use it if you wish; it is useful if you don't like staring at a blank page.

[2] Each master scene starts with a slug line that indicates INTerior or EXTerior, location, and DAY or NIGHT. The slug line is in uppercase letters and is never underlined. Leave three line spaces between the end of the previous scene and the slug line. Leave two line spaces between the slug line and the start of a new scene. Generally, there is an em dash (—) between the location and DAY or NIGHT.

[3] EXT.—Outside.

[4] OPIUM HEAVEN—The location, wherever it might be.

[5] DAY or NIGHT—Even if there are no windows in an interior scene, it is important to know this to clarify the time flow of the script. You can indicate TWILIGHT or DAWN if we can see evidence in the sky. But you cannot put 3:42 P.M. because the slug line is what you want the viewer to be able to infer when she first looks at the scene. If you want the viewer to know that it is 3:42 P.M., you must explicitly indicate that in the body of the scene.

[6] Use a single-space setting. Use double spacing to separate paragraphs.

[7] GEORGE—Type the first introduction of each character in uppercase letters. From then on, capitalize only the first letter.

[8] Get in the habit of anticipating the kinds of questions you imagine your viewer will ask the first time the character appears on the screen. Generally, after determining gender, the first thing a viewer will seek to determine is age. You can answer this in a script with a newspaper-style age citation or a descriptive phrase (e.g., an ageless hippy).

[9] "The largest pupils you ever did see"—Try to limit your descriptive details to brief fragments that serve to place your characters in the reader's mind. Never indicate a precise, specific detail that doesn't pay off in the script.

[10] Everything must be written in the present tense. Describe only what the viewer will be able to see at a given moment. There is no direct equivalent to a linguistic past tense in film.

[11] Capitalize the first introduction of major props, especially those that are unusual.

[12] "Not too happy"—How do we know she is unhappy? Purists prefer to state a physical, external indication of her unhappiness, such as "Susan frowns" or "Susan kicks rocks" and let the viewer infer her state of mind. This is entirely a matter of taste.

[13] Looks—The word *looks* establishes point of view within a scene. It suggests some variant on a sequence that begins with a close shot of Susan's head turning, a longer shot of her friends that shows us what she sees, and a return shot of Susan for her reaction. It tends to make us regard the scene through the eyes and attitude of the character. We'll talk more about this later.

[14] Again, some screenwriters would find this paragraph too descriptive of internal state. But there is nothing described here that you cannot infer from the action. This is the test you want to apply to determine whether a particular descriptive phrase is filmable. We encourage you, particularly in early drafts, to overdo the emotional content of stage directions. More screenplays don't succeed because of a lack of emotional charge to their stage directions than because their scenes cannot be visualized. Put another way, it is almost impossible to visualize a scene that does not have an emotional charge. A scene with such a charge can almost always be brought to the screen. It is easier to cut a few lines in a later draft than to give life to meaningless movement.

[15] Beat change. Use movement to articulate beats. Stage directions are the screenwriter's best tool for dramatizing thought and change.

[16] SUSAN—The name of the person speaking is indicated in capital letters. There is no line space between the name and the parenthetical notes or dialogue that come after it.

[17] (Whining)—Instruction to the actor. It does not indicate a beat change. Keep these to a minimum. The character's attitude and intention should be inferable from the dramatic line of the script.

[18] It is what she does, not what she says, that makes the scene. In classic mainstream dramatic writing, the old cliché holds—action

is character. Movement is what brings this style of filmmaking to life. (This is also true in most, although not all, independent films). You want to top dialogue with movement. The inference in this excerpt is that Susan has complained for a long time, but this is the first time she has done anything about it.

[19] These three scenes inscribe continuous time. We indicate this by picking up the action in the previous scene (the dropping of the filter) and carrying it over to the next scene (the manna from heaven landing at the pitcher's feet).

[20] Capitalize the introduction of any major sound effect.

[21] When you return to the same scene, you want to come in with action. Remember, in most cases, film is a medium of images first and dialogue second. Always re-establish the physical layout; do not use, "Same as Scene 1."

[22] You may choose to connect scenes using optical effects. These may include LAP DISSOLVE TO:, FADE OUT:, FADE IN:, FADE TO BLACK:, WIPE TO:, and so on. You may also connect scenes by using the transition, CUT TO:. However, as the lack of any indicated transition implies CUT TO:, we suggest that you use it only between scene sequences (see next excerpt).

Scene Sequences and Transitions

When a group of scenes implies continuous action, as do the three scenes in the previous excerpt, we call them scene sequences. Within a scene sequence, the cuts between scenes are sometimes called non-nodal because our eye continues right through them, usually following a movement or sound cue. Scene sequences are frequently terminated by a nodal cut or transition. Such a transition serves as a marker, releasing us from one line of dramatic development and positioning us somewhere else. While non-nodal transitions suggest that the characters are carrying us from place to place, nodal transitions feel as though the filmmaker is picking us up and placing us down somewhere else. To continue using the previous excerpt, an example of nodal transition is as follows:

```
Now the opposing dugout empties. The first fans climb
onto the field. The organist begins playing "Happy Days
Are Here Again."

                                              CUT TO:

EXT. THE RUSSIAN STEPPE DAY
The vast expanse of Mother Russia. Nothing much grows in
these parts. We move down until we reach:
```

```
EXT. SOCCER FIELD—DAY
Or at least, what passes for one. The wind blows the
sandy soil. A lone BOY stands near a broken goal and
practices heading the ball. Nothing else is around.

Suddenly a huge image of a grinning STALIN appears in
the sky.
```

Notice the use of the word we in the stage directions. It implies the presence of the narrator or the filmmaker moving the camera. If we say, "Susan races along the cloud tops," we are implying that the camera is traveling invisibly with her. Our sense is that she is moving the camera—nothing calls our attention to the fact that the narrator outside the scene is actually responsible for this movement. However, if we say, "We move down until we reach," we are implying some form of crane shot that is overtly controlled by the director. Although the shot may be so smooth that it doesn't call attention to itself, this phrasing brings us into or out of a scene in a manner that a shot motivated by character does not.

Notice also how we indicate the nodal transition by stipulating "CUT TO." Although the transition between Scene 1 and Scene 2 is also made by a cut, we have used the direction "CUT TO" only to articulate the end of the scene sequence.

One more thing: we talked about using action as expressed through stage directions to articulate beat changes. Beat changes that take place within stage directions (i.e., the appearance of the vision of Stalin) are indicated by paragraph breaks.

Language

A screenwriter is an expressive writer, which means like all expressive writers, she uses language not only to describe but also to evoke. Evocation means allowing the reader (and the viewer) to draw as many inferences and connections as possible from the events you describe. Although the screenwriter is limited to describing scenes that can be visualized, such scenes can imply all kinds of unspoken details about the character's life and the screenwriter's attitude toward the issues of the screenplay.

The previous example, set in Opium Heaven, is a flip scene. Descriptive lines like "This is supposed to be heaven, but the weed just doesn't smoke as sweet" or "Their bodies are in seventh heaven" do not so much convey information as evoke the tone of the scene. "This is supposed to be heaven, but the weed just doesn't smoke as sweet" implies something of the author's playful attitude toward the scene. Clearly, this is not a serious polemic on drug abuse. As the line "Their bodies are in seventh heaven" comes after Susan's look, we assume that it represents her thoughts. Without having to say so explicitly, we imply a great deal about her attitude. By contrast, the following excerpt is a much more dead-on, serious scene.

INT. MATTHEW'S ROOM—NIGHT

WILLIAM, 39, darts a peek at his son MATTHEW, 14, who
lies silent, brooding next to him, but Matthew won't meet
his eyes. Instead, he stares up at the stars, hundreds
of them, projected from the small planetarium ball in the
center of the room.

                    WILLIAM
          Okay, so you won't tell me.

Giving up, William starts to his feet when Matthew
finally asks.

                    MATTHEW
          Dad, you can't catch AIDS
          holding a girl's hand?

Surprised by the question, William studies his son below
him.

                    WILLIAM
          No.

                    MATTHEW
          Just wanted to be sure.

The reflections of the stars in the dark room make
Matthew's eyes so unnaturally bright and clear that for a
precious moment, William believes he can see all the way
into them. Moved, he reaches to touch him.

Matthew relaxes. He takes a lighted pointer and points to
a cluster of stars.

                    MATTHEW (CONT'D)
          Look at that. The Keyhole
          Nebula.

Buddies again, William slides down next to his son.

                    WILLIAM
          What's her name?

                    MATTHEW
          Who?

                    WILLIAM
          The girl.

> MATTHEW
> You're grilling me, Dad.
>
> WILLIAM
> We're buddies, aren't we?
> There's Eta Argus up in the
> corner.
>
> MATTHEW
> Eta Cerinae. We're close.
>
> WILLIAM
> Damn close.

Matthew jumps up and flicks on the hall light behind him.

> MATTHEW (CONT'D)
> I've had it with stars.

William looks up at Matthew who stands with the light behind him, outlined, dark, and now totally inaccessible.

The prose of this scene is no longer flippant or unreliable, as evidenced in the following direction:

The reflections of the stars in the dark room make Matthew's eyes so unnaturally bright and clear that for a precious moment, William believes he can see all the way into them. Moved, he reaches to touch him.

Unlike Susan's, Matthew and William's reactions seem closer to our own. The expression "precious moment" implies sympathy with the character's desire. If the scene works, then we will see what he sees, and, more important, it will mean the same thing to us as it does to him. Without having to actually say so, we know how much this father wishes to communicate with his son and how difficult it has become. We also know that the screenwriter is asking us to take the father's desire for connection seriously.

Who is Seeing?

One of the critical differences between theater and film is the fact that the camera moves, positioning the viewer within a spectrum that runs from the objective position of the theatrical seat to the highly subjective point-of-view shot. Even when an actor in the theater reacts to a situation, we still see that situation through our own eyes. In film, however, we frequently see the situation unfolding in much the same way that the character does. These situations can be subjective to such an extent that the character appears to be describing or narrating the scene for us—the scene takes on the inflection or coloration that corresponds to the character's attitude. One of the major functions of screenwriting is to articulate this modulation from the objective to the more subjective point of view.

Once again, we can control this modulation through language. The use of the terms *we* or *the camera* in phrases like "The camera moves in on JOHNNY, the young man in the group" or "We see the gun before Marji does" suggests an omniscient point of view. Sometimes it implies dramatic irony, a situation in which the audience knows more than the character. At other times, the camera might be expressing the character's state of mind (e.g., "The camera pushes in on Max as he looks desperately from one to the other, searching for a clue") but still implying a narrative emphasis that comes from outside. However, if we describe a character's action directly (without identifying the camera or the viewer's position), as in "Delighted, Mary smiles as she skips across the room," we are implying that we are seeing the character with the minimum of narrative intervention. This means that if the camera moves, its movements will be timed to correspond to the character's. Such movements pass invisibly on the screen.

The use of the words *looks* or *watches*, as in "Johnny watches Jennifer take tiny bites of the steak," suggests some form of point-of-view sequence. There are many technical alternatives to point-of-view sequences, but they are all built around the same notion of replacing the omniscient narrator with a character narrator. The most common point-of-view structure is made up of three shots. For example, the character turns her head and looks; we cut to what she is looking at from an angle that matches (or nearly matches) her eyeline, and we return to a shot of the character (usually a reverse shot close to the eyeline) for her reaction. The effect of the reaction shot is to color what we see in the point-of-view shot with her attitude.

Technically, when a character in one location sees something in another location, we indicate it by using the acronym *POV* as illustrated in the following example.

```
INT. LORI'S BEDROOM—DAY

In disgust, Lori flings herself around only to freeze
when she catches sight of something out the window.

EXT. LORI'S FRONT YARD—LORI'S POV—DAY

Jacob looks uncertainly at the house. He is about to turn
away when he notices a baby robin squawking on the grass.
He bends down and tenderly holds the robin in his hand.
Then he starts toward the house.

INT. LORI'S BEDROOM—DAY
```

```
For a moment, Lori watches fascinated. Then quickly she
strides over to her vanity, picks up a tissue, and starts
wiping off her make-up.
```

The indication, "Lori's POV," specifies precisely how we see Jacob. It functions exactly like the direction, "Lori looks at Jacob," would function if they were both in the same location.

As POV functions by putting us in the character's position, it is important that there be some rhythmic or visual indication to take us from the more omniscient position we usually occupy. This is marked off by the change of rhythm in the stage direction, "In disgust, Lori flings herself around only to freeze when she catches sight of something out the window."

Dramatic Action

We said in the beginning of this chapter that one of the problems that usually confounds beginning screenwriters is relating dialogue and stage directions. We suggest that this problem is ultimately superficial, because dialogue and stage direction must function in the same way—as dramatic action. That is, every line of dialogue, like every movement, must come out of some need that can't be expressed any other way. Dialogue becomes movement, it becomes an expressive act. The content of the words is less important than is the need to speak.

The trick to good evocative writing is to make everything mean something. Everything you put down (or leave out), every change in rhythm (or its continuation), and every choice of word, sentence structure, descriptive detail, and character nuance conveys a point of view and is fair game for the audience reading your story. The more the audience feels they can ferret out, the more elements to which they respond, the more intrigued they will be, and the better chance the script has of being made into a film. If you are able to write a script in which characters do not move or speak and if the camera does not reveal anything unless there is a reason, then when your characters do move or speak or when we are shown something, we will pay particular attention. We will trust your screenplay and make the effort to respond to everything it contains.

We are not saying that before you write anything down, you understand exactly what it means. Many times an experienced writer will add things to the script, apparently without thinking, that end up being very important to the finished film. Instead, we are talking about a critically important writer's habit—a habit that a writer develops by constantly asking herself, "Do I see it?" If you see it, and if what you see is consistent with your story and your characters, then your staging automatically begins to have meaning.

Also, we are not saying that a character has to know the meaning of everything he does. Much of the movement of stories, in particular restorative three-act stories, centers on the character's gradual awareness of his motivations. Before this, the character acts more reactively, sometimes blindly. However, what the character knows has nothing to do with what you, as the writer, must know. We all do things in particular ways that define who we are, without being conscious of them. But a writer works to orchestrate this meaning.

Okay, now how does all this relate to the specifics of writing stage directions? Too often, writers lay out a scene entirely in dialogue. Only after the scene is spelled out, do they add stage directions as sort of obligatory filler to keep their scene visual. No matter how visual the details, no matter how full of action, the scene is not visual or active in the dramatic sense, unless the stage directions serve the story. Suppose we write the following dialogue fragment:

```
INT. STEAM BATH—DAY

                    SAUL
          And then it would take the
          burden off of you.

                    JAKE
          No.

                    SAUL
          Suppose, just suppose, I told
          you that I had made up with my
          father.

                    JAKE
          Is that a possibility?

                    SAUL
          We had dinner last night.

                    JAKE
          I see.
```

Now, let's throw in some stage directions and description.

```
INT. STEAM ROOM—DAY

A luxurious steam bath, at least 20 feet long, with gold
towel fixtures on one wall, a rack of newspapers on the
other. The whole room is full, mostly with older men, but
here and there we see a smug young face. JAKE and SAUL
enter. The steamer is bubbling, but hasn't yet emitted
much steam.

                    SAUL
          And then it would take the
          burden off of you.
```

Before we go further, let's look at what is implied by this description. First, it is omniscient; that is, it is shown to us independently of any characters in the scene. Second, it is indiscriminately descriptive; that is, the camera would need to pan the whole room, taking note of all the details mentioned in the description but giving weight to no detail in particular. Although one might want to set the location like this, there are several consequences to such omniscience. The first is that the description takes us out of the scene, by transferring the reaction to the steam room from the character to the audience. By the time the character comes in and reacts, we are already a beat ahead of him. The second consequence of this description is that it slows down the story. If we gave such a grand introduction to each location, all scenes will appear nodal, announced like chapter headings. What we need, here, is a point of view to organize the way in which the opening is written and, by extension, the way the camera sees.

```
INT. STEAM BATH—DAY

SAUL, a young man clearly out of his depth, follows the
older man, JAKE, into the steam bath. While Jake, at
home in his club, waves to his cronies, Saul pauses in
the doorway and stares in awe at the sheer grandeur of
the place. Gold towel fixtures and a newspaper rack in a
sauna! Then he pulls himself together and hurries over to
Jake, who turns away as he calmly spreads out a towel.
Saul finds himself speaking to the older man's back.

                    SAUL
              And then it would take the
              burden off of you.

Satisfied that the towel is even, Jake sits emphatically
on the bench, puts his head back, and places a rolled-up
towel over his eyes.

                    JAKE
              No.

                    SAUL
              Suppose, just suppose, I told
              you that I had made up with my
              father.

Jake raises the rolled-up towel slightly and casts a
withering glance at Saul.

                    JAKE
              Is that a possibility?

                    SAUL
              (Trying to hold up under
```

```
                           Jake's glance)
                           We had dinner last night.

        Dropping the rolled-up towel now altogether, Jake slides
        over on the spread-out towel and motions for Saul to sit
        next to him.

                                JAKE
                           I see.
```

Okay, now we are beginning to have a point of view. We start with Saul's awe as he looks around the steam bath, go to Jake as he emphatically shuts off Saul by putting the towel over his eyes, and then stay with Jake as he begins to respond to Saul's gambit. Description becomes a means of dramatizing Saul's state of mind rather than a catalog of details. This fragment of scene starts out as Saul's and ends up as Jake's. There is nothing wrong with such a change in perspective except that in this case, it seems to dilute the intensity of the scene. Let's limit our focus to Saul.

```
        INT. STEAM BATH—DAY

        SAUL, a young man clearly out of his depth, follows the
        older man, JAKE, into the steam bath. While Jake, at home
        in his club, waves to his cronies, Saul pauses in the
        doorway and stares in awe at the sheer grandeur of the
        place. Then he pulls himself together and hurries over to
        Jake, who turns away as he calmly spreads out a towel.
        Saul finds himself speaking to the older man's back.

                                SAUL
                           Then it would take the burden
                           off of you.

                                JAKE
                           No!
        Saul watches as, discussion over, Jake spreads himself
        out regally on the bench and takes a section of newspaper
        from the pile on the bench. Saul doesn't quite know what
        to do. Seeing that Jake's towel is wrinkled, Saul bends
        down to straighten it up. Without daring to look up, Saul
        mumbles.

                                SAUL
                           Suppose, just suppose, I told
                           You that I had made up with
                           my father.

                                JAKE
                           (After a pause—behind the
                           paper)
                           Is that a possibility?
```

```
Now that he's finally gotten Jake's attention, Saul takes
his time. Casually, he unbends and flicks some water on
the coals. A great cloud of steam hisses up, obscuring
the older man.
                    SAUL
          We had dinner last night.

                    JAKE
          (From somewhere in the steam)
          I see.
```

This version is focused entirely on Saul. We are with him as he is overcome by the steam bath, as he is brushed off by Jake, and, finally, when he enjoys himself after gaining Jake's attention. Notice several things. There is an unrelenting feeling to this version that we don't get with any of the others. This is achieved purely by the focus that staging brings to the scene. This focus is achieved by changing the rhythm and the emphasis of the previous version. Our movement from Saul to Jake in the earlier version is shown by the fact that Jake becomes the subject of the stage directions—for example, we go from "Saul pauses in the doorway" to "Jake sits emphatically." In the later version, Saul remains the subject of the directions—for example, "Saul pauses in the doorway," "Saul watches as . . . Jake spreads himself out," "Saul takes his time." Notice how a sentence like the one that starts "Saul watches" uses point of view to keep the beat focused on Saul (his watching), even though Jake is doing the action (spreading himself out).

Note also the importance of the moments of the transitions. Saul, unable to approach Jake head on, bends down to straighten the towel and only in the subservient position can bring himself to speak. When he's finally gotten Jake's attention, he straightens up and takes his time before speaking. Such transitions include us in the preparation for the character's action and bring us into the scene. It's as though we, along with Saul, look at Jake lying in front of us and don't know what to say. Looking around for any sort of connection with the older man, we see the towel needs straightening. Finally, feeling momentarily protected by looking down at the towel, we venture another request.

Staging for Beats

Dramatic actions are given shape by a progression of beats—for example, the movement of Saul, from when he has difficulty approaching Jake to when he takes his time before speaking once he has Jake's attention. This progression must be articulated in the staging.

Alternating dialogue sequences without stage directions are generally shot in some variant of eyeline matches—that is, in alternating reverse two-shots or close-ups. A sequence like this implies a single continuous beat. Character movement (indicated in the script by stage directions) or a new shot pattern breaks us out of these tight shots and causes a reframing. Such reframing indicates shifts in beats.

Alternatives to Screenplay Form

There are, of course, many ways to organize written material to be turned into a film. Some screenwriters eschew the master-scene technique and go directly to a shooting script, arguing that this gives them more control over the final film. Others use a half-literary, half-visual form of stream of consciousness to present a profusion of images that the viewer must reassemble. Other writers use a variation of the live-television, two-column script that has a column of visuals down the left side of the page opposite a parallel column of audio cues on the other side.

If you are producing and directing your own project, then you will be free to come up with whatever notational combination is useful to you. For instance, filmmakers making dance films have come up with a variation of the Laban dance notation to visualize their finished films. However, most of the independent, narrative films of which we have spoken in this book were written using conventional screenplay form. Unless you absolutely can't live without some hybrid form, we recommend that you stick to the conventional style. It's a matter of picking your battles. As the process of supporting and producing independent films is so difficult, it is usually not worth putting the additional obstacle of a "badly" formatted script in your way. Screenplay form frees you from the nuts and bolts of shots and editing sequences and allows you to evoke in your audience the most vivid mental image of the film you want made.

Conclusion

To write screenplays, you do not need to know a whole list of abbreviations for the technical details of filmmaking. In fact, the constant use of such details is the sure mark of an amateur writer. What you do have to understand is something that is ultimately much more difficult and more powerful: You need to know the way dramatic filmmaking articulates and controls the dramatic line of the story. To do this, you have to learn to see and write about what you see. Once you've learned this, everything else is just typing.

References

1. N. Gidding, *I Want To Live. From the Shooting Final Draft* United Artists (March 14, 1958), 15.
2. B. Wilder, and I. A. L. Diamond, *The Apartment* (MGM, United Artists, 1960), 135.
3. H. R. Cole, Jr., and J. H. Haag, *The Complete Guide to Standard Script Formats, Part I-Screenplays* (North Hollywood, CA: CMC Publishing, 1996), 4–5.

23

Agency and the Other

Agency and the Other

Near the end of Roman Polanski's *Chinatown* (1974), the detective, Jake Gittes, convinced of the guilt of his client/lover Evelyn Mulwray, charges into the house where she is staying. Mulwray's Chinese housekeeper tries to block Gittes from entering, but Gittes brushes him aside. As the housekeeper does not deter Gittes in any way, he does not "bend" the story. As a result, he does not have a beat[1]—he could just as well be a chair blocking the entrance, an inanimate object to be tossed away. This is the role that many minority, female, and marginalized characters have played throughout the history of film. It is the dramatic characterization of "the other."

"The other" is the term used by anthropologists, sociologists, and media theorists, among others, to represent classes of people that are alien to the self. The other is unknown and unknowable; as a result, the other functions as an unarticulated force in stories, as an object that is incapable of focusing consciousness. The motives and thoughts behind the actions of the other remain unexplored, and the actions themselves are usually futile. An obvious other, the Chinese housekeeper's inability to affect Gittes is, of course, ironic, given the detective's ultimate failure in *Chinatown*. However, even though Gittes fails in *Chinatown*, his failure concerns a white love interest and a white villain. The idea of the Chinese and the section of the city where they live remains opaque to both of the white characters in the film and to the viewer. Although in some ways the antagonist throughout the film, Chinatown as a place and a culture is voiceless.

To give the housekeeper (and the neighborhood) power would mean giving him (and it) a beat. A beat would allow the housekeeper to stop Gittes in some way, to cause him to rethink his plan. It would gift the housekeeper with some subjectivity, some personhood. The term for this is *agency*, the ability of a character to act on his own, to exhibit will, to change the direction of the story. The housekeeper's failure to have an effect on Gittes is a failure of the particular kind of agency we will call *action agency*.

In addition to action agency, there is a *reflective agency*, a form of subjectivity in which a character does not directly affect the action line, but rather one in which his reaction shapes the viewer's understanding of the scene. If after failing to stop Gittes, the housekeeper had instead watched him disappear into the house and the camera remained on the housekeeper, watching, there would be a point where the viewer's perspective would shift to that of the housekeeper. The housekeeper would have a beat, not of action, but of reflection. He would have been given agency, not to control the line of the story, but to shift our perception of the story.

In most films in which we are brought into character, we are given both forms of agency. The *reflective agency* prepares us for action, whereas the *action agency* drives the scene. It is the reflective agency that makes the viewer feel she is participating in the thought process that leads to the action. Even when we see reflective agency but do not understand the logic underlying a main character's action, it is usually subsequently explained. For instance, in an earlier *Chinatown* scene, we participate with Gittes's decision to break the taillight of Evelyn Mulwray's car, even if we don't fully understand why (because the white light, shining through the broken red taillight, will make it easier to trail Mulwray) until later.

But let's return to the portrayal of the Chinese housekeeper. Contrast his treatment to the treatment of the Iraqi other in David O. Russell's *Three Kings* (1999).[2] In the torture scene, the Iraqi captor, Captain Said (played by Saïd Taghmaoui), discusses his dead child with the American prisoner, Sfc. Troy Barlow (played by Mark Wahlberg). Said is no longer a father, because his child was killed in an American bomb blast; Barlow has a new child back home. As Said has Barlow tied and wired for electric shock, there is no question that Said has action agency. But Said also controls reflective agency and, through this, is able to achieve a more profound action agency than physical force—the control of Barlow's imagination. Said describes the death of his son, which motivates a cut to the boy's crib being destroyed by a bomb blast. We read this as Said's imagined image of what happened to his son. Next he provokes Barlow into thinking about his own wife and daughter walking along a calm, American suburban street. Here is where the reflective agency becomes action agency. Said pushes the American to imagine his daughter being blown up. We cut to a quick image of an explosion racking the calm suburban street. We read this as Barlow's flash of an unimaginable horror, and it suggests that Said is not only able to exert action agency through controlling the torture, but even to impose deeper action agency by manipulating Barlow's subjectivity, causing him to imagine what he does not desire.

To an American audience and to the American characters in the film, Said is an other. Yet, the film first breaks down our understanding of how we identify with, and who is seen as, the other, by putting us into Said's head, allowing us access to his subjective experience, and then giving him the power to modify the subjective imagination of the character whose frame of reference usually informs our focus.

The comparison between *Chinatown* and *Three Kings* is not to suggest that *Three Kings* is the better film but rather serves to demonstrate an evolution in the presentation of the subjectivity and agency of the other. Beyond being a faceless captor, an unknown force of evil, Said is developed as a character who can not only feel his own pain but also cause another character to imagine it.

In the rest of this chapter, we look at means of developing action and reflective agency through script examples.

Character Agency—An In-Depth Exploration

Let's start with a simple sequence in which our fictional characters Robert and David, both 19, are road tripping across the desert.

```
INT. CAR—DAY

Robert steers with his knee and fools with the radio.
There ain't much good out here.

                    DAVID (O. S.)
          Girl!

Robert's head springs up.

EXT. DESERT HIGHWAY—ROBERT'S POV—DAY

Through the windshield, he can just make out a woman with
a suitcase at her feet. She is turned away, only her
back is visible.

                    ROBERT (O. S.)
          Nice.

INT. CAR—DAY

Robert swings the wheel toward the side of the road.

EXT. CAR—DAY

Before the car comes to a complete halt, David is out the
door. In his anxiety, he stumbles and falls to his knees.
```

The boys in the car have agency; the woman does not. The boys' actions drive the scene; the woman's actions have no effect on it. Furthermore, the woman is not characterized, except as to her gender, which is used against her by the fact that we are seeing through the boys' eyes—they identify her as a girl. Presented this way, she might as well be an inanimate object of desire named by the beholder. Although David's agency is active (we do not see him reflect on his actions), Robert's agency is both reflective and active. We experience with him the seeing, processing, and then taking the subsequent action.

Now we can add a little characterization to the woman.

```
EXT. DESERT HIGHWAY—ROBERT'S POV—DAY

Through the windshield, he can just make out a woman with
a suitcase at her feet. She is turned away, only her back
is visible.

Now they are close enough to see her. Even from behind,
the woman's posture hints at a youthful grace that draws
Robert's attention.

                    ROBERT (O. S.)
          Nice.
```

But the characteristic of youthful grace does not give the woman agency. In fact, this rewrite serves only to further emphasize Robert's reflective agency, because it is his movement (or that of the car which he controls) that allows us to see more and reinforces the fact that we are seeing through his eyes. The characteristic of youthful grace is not so much a property held by the woman as it is a characterization imposed on her by Robert.

Now suppose we give the woman the simplest action.

```
EXT. DESERT HIGHWAY—ROBERT'S POV—DAY

Through the windshield, he can just make out a woman with
a suitcase at her feet. She is turned away, only her
back is visible.

Now they are close enough to see her. As the car
approaches, she turns. She is a beautiful young woman,
maybe 25 years old.

                    ROBERT (O. S.)
          Nice.
```

She acts: Is this agency? Only if it has an effect on something else in the scene. So let's rewrite it, so that it is clear that the guys would not have stopped unless she turned.

```
EXT. DESERT HIGHWAY—ROBERT'S POV—DAY

Through the windshield, he can just make out a woman with
a suitcase at her feet. She is turned away, only her back
is visible.

                    ROBERT (O. S.)
          So . . .
```

```
He guns it.

Now they are close enough to see her. As the car
approaches, she turns. She is a beautiful young woman,
maybe 25 years old.

Robert hits the brakes.
```

Finally, the woman has agency, even if she merely turned reflexively at the sound of the car. Her action "bends" the story, causing the boys to stop. We mark agency by its effects on the story.

Now suppose we give texture to her reaction.

```
EXT. DESERT HIGHWAY—ROBERT'S POV—DAY

Through the windshield, he can just make out a woman with
a suitcase at her feet. She is turned away, only her back
is visible.

Now they are close enough to see her. As the car
approaches, she turns. She is a beautiful young woman,
maybe 25 years old.

                    ROBERT (O. S.)
          Nice.

Although almost joyful when she turns, as she focuses in
on their car, her face clouds with rage.
```

This is the beginning of reflexive agency. We don't know why her face changes, but we begin to suspect that her view of this event is ambivalent enough to make us wonder how to look at it. Her reaction creates backstory, a sense that the character is part of a specific world that predates this event. In fact, when I wrote it, I imagined a backstory to motivate her reaction. In the backstory, she had a fight with a friend, and he had taken off in anger, leaving her by the side of the road. The expectation that once he cooled he would come back to pick her up causes her joyful reaction. Discovering someone other than her friend explains her rage. It is not important that readers/viewers understand these specific details; rather, they must get the feel of the backstory, so that they can fill in the pieces later.

But does a character have to take physical action to convey active agency? Not necessarily. Let's take a step back and look at the fact that the woman does not turn around in early versions of this script. Initially, we may read the not turning around as her not hearing the car, but there is some point at which her refusal to recognize the boys becomes willful. This makes it a form of agency conveyed by her very refusal to move.

EXT. DESERT HIGHWAY—ROBERT'S POV—DAY

Through the windshield, he can just make out a woman with
a suitcase at her feet. She is turned away, only her back
is visible.

Now they are close enough to see her. Even from behind,
the woman's posture hints at a youthful grace that draws
Robert's attention.

                         ROBERT (O. S.)
               Nice.

INT. CAR—DAY

Robert swings the wheel toward the side of the road.

EXT. CAR—DAY

Before the car comes to a complete halt, David is out the
door. In his anxiety, he stumbles and falls to his knees,
not ten feet from where she stands. When he looks up, he
sees her back. She still has not turned.

In these scenes, we can make an argument that the story is being driven
not by the boys' activity but by the woman's refusal to move. Her lack of
action becomes a form of active agency—our attention and interest focus on
what is motivating her rigidity. This form of agency through inaction is frequently described in "real" life as passive–aggressive behavior.

Before we get deeper into reflexive agency, we want to look at how the
implied point of view in the screenplay is used to focus agency. For instance,
let's make one change in what the young woman is doing.

EXT. DESERT HIGHWAY—ROBERT'S POV—DAY

Through the windshield, he can just make out a car with
its hood up. A young woman is working on the engine.

                         ROBERT (O. S.)
               Nice.

INT. CAR—DAY

Robert swings the wheel toward the side of the road.

EXT. DESERT HIGHWAY—DAY

Before the car comes to a complete halt, David is out the
door. In his anxiety, he stumbles and falls to his knees.

```
Looking over, he sees that the woman is continuing her
work on the engine. She does not look up.
```

In all the versions thus far, the axis of tension projects out from the boys to the young woman. She is the object of their gaze, and the questions raised by the scene are defined by what they see. Is she interesting to them? Will she respond to them? In this version, we have given her a concrete task. Yet, the fact that she may be able to overcome the obstacle of her car breaking down, an act of agency in many other situations, has no impact here. From this perspective, she does not assert any agency, because nothing that she does affects the boys' actions, which are foregrounded by the scene.

So let's flip it:

```
EXT. DESERT HIGHWAY—DAY

Karen reaches under the hood of her old Chevy Impala. She
checks each spark plug wire, then moves to the distribu-
tor cap. That's it. The coil wire is disconnected.

She leans back out of the engine and wipes the sweat off
her forehead.

Behind her, we see a new Toyota 4Runner pull to the side
of the road.

Paying no attention, Karen leans back under the hood.
Where is that damn wire? She reaches deeper into the
engine.

Vaguely she hears the sound of someone behind her
as she feeds the wire back up to the distributor. It is
caught on something. She has to reach back under the
engine.
```

As she ceases to be the object of the boys' gazes and moves from being the object of a second-order observation (we see the boys and they see her) to being the subject of a first-order one (we see her and she sees the engine), the young woman earns a name. This serves to immediately collapse the narrative distance we felt when we only saw her through the boys' gaze as a "woman." Karen's active agency is foregrounded by the concentration on the detail of her working on the car. In fact, we have emphasized this by using reactive phrases ("That's it." "Where is that damn wire?") designed to pull the reader into the immediacy of the scene as Karen perceives it. Karen controls what we are able to see. The approaching car is only visible in the background by virtue of her leaning out of the engine.

All these result from our shifting the axis of tension. The dramatic question becomes whether Karen will be able to fix the car (and maybe whether she will be able to do so before the boys arrive). As a result, not only does Karen have active agency, but she also has reflective agency. Her thoughts drive her action and condition how we take the scene.

We should note, however, that, unlike the versions that focused on the boys' point of view, this one is not a purely character-driven scene, because the reader/viewer sees more than Karen does. The scene also points out the difference between the use of image and sound in a screenplay. In the early versions, Karen's decision not to turn when she *hears* someone behind her falling represents a willful ignoring of something we assume she has perceived, because sound, within hearing distance, is ubiquitous. By contrast, her lack of response to the car behind her in this version probably comes from her not noticing. As she doesn't notice, her lack of response does not seem the same as the willful ignoring we saw previously.

Now let's give explicit Karen agency of both kinds, and let it drive a fully character-driven scene.

```
EXT. DESERT HIGHWAY—DAY

Karen reaches under the hood of her old Chevy Impala.
She checks each spark plug wire, then moves to the
distributor cap. It is cracked.

She leans back out of the engine and looks down the road.
It is empty as far as she can see.

She looks the other direction. A Toyota 4Runner is
approaching. She looks back into the engine. There is
nothing she can do.

She slams the trunk, turns to the road, and sticks her
thumb out.
```

Not only is Karen now driving the scene, but we have also dramatized her transition, the moment of decision or reflective agency that leads her to act. Unlike the narrated position of the previous version of the scene, where we see the car but she doesn't, now she is the one responsible for directing our gaze. We can develop this use of point of view further.

```
EXT. DESERT HIGHWAY—DAY

Karen pops the hood of her old Chevy Impala. She ducks
her head underneath.

After a moment, she pulls her head out, disgusted. She
looks down the road. It is empty as far as she can see.
```

```
She looks in the other direction. A Toyota 4Runner is
approaching. She turns to the road and sticks her thumb
out.

Seeing the car begin to slow, she raises her arm higher.
This seems to work because the car now begins to pull
over.

Finally, it is close enough to see inside. Two
guys have their faces pressed to the windshield. She can
almost hear them panting.

Her arm drops. She ducks her head behind the raised hood
for a moment.

When she pulls her head out, her smile is dazzling. She
slams the hood and thrusts her thumb up defiantly as the
car pulls to a stop in front of her.
```

It is now not simply the identification of a possible ride that drives this scene, but Karen's mixed feelings about these two guys. Yet in this version, we are left out of her key thought process when she hides beyond the hood. Suppose we now take advantage of the camera's mobility and give her a private moment where we can see what the guys cannot.

```
EXT. DESERT HIGHWAY—DAY

Karen pops the hood of her old Chevy Impala.

She reaches under the hood, checks each spark plug wire,
then moves to the distributor cap. It is cracked

She leans back out of the engine and looks down the road.
It is empty as far as she can see.

She turns in the other direction. A Toyota 4Runner
approaches in the distance. She smiles and sticks her
thumb out.

Seeing the car begin to slow, she raises her arm higher
This seems to work because the car now begins to pull
over.

Finally, it is close enough so she can see inside. Two
guys have their faces pressed to the windshield. She can
almost hear them panting.

Her arm drops. She ducks her head behind the raised hood
for a moment. Her smile fades. She looks out across the
barren landscape. She is absolutely alone. She looks
```

```
back at the engine. She taps the distributor cap, but the
crack won't go away. She'll never fix it.

Making up her mind, she steps back out and slams the
hood. She thrusts her thumb up defiantly as the car pulls
to a stop in front of her. Her smile is dazzling.
```

Of course, the private moment can reveal more than just a change of mood. Depending on the story, Karen might be cocking the gun she has hidden in the engine compartment. The important thing is we are with her at a period of emotional uncertainty and experience her decision to act.

Now we have built both reflective and active agency in a character that had been previously passive, but we are still treating the boys in the car as a single unit. Let's go back and consider what we can do to characterize each of them.

```
INT. CAR—DAY

Robert steers with his knee and fools with the radio.
There ain't much good out here. When he raises his head,
he sees that David is staring out the window.


                         ROBERT
              What?


                         DAVID)
              There's someone. Hitching.

Robert looks.


                         ROBERT
              Why didn't you say something?

David shrugs, turns away. Robert continues to stare out
the window.

EXT. DESERT HIGHWAY—ROBERT'S POV—DAY

He can just make out that the hitcher is a young woman
standing by the raised hood of an old Impala.


                         ROBERT (O. S.)
              Nice.

Now they are close enough to see her. The hitcher is a
beautiful young woman, maybe 25 years old. She smiles
seductively at them.
```

```
INT. CAR—DAY

Robert begins to spin the wheel. David turns back to him.


                    DAVID
          Wait.

He puts his hand on Robert's arm to stop him. But Robert
is already pulling off the road.
```

Now we've split the boys, giving them each a different attitude to the woman they see on the road. This immediately characterizes them, making them distinct in their desires, even if we do not yet understand what is driving them. It also makes them seem less monolithic and more characterized; more human, less a threat.

But what about the woman's hesitation we have developed in the previous version? Can it further articulate the tension between Robert and David?

```
EXT. DESERT HIGHWAY—ROBERT'S POV—DAY

He can just make out that the hitcher is a young woman
standing by the raised hood of an old Impala.

                    ROBERT (O. S.)
          Nice.

Now they are close enough to see her. She is attractive,
maybe 25 years old, but before Robert can register
anything else, she drops her thumb and disappears behind
the raised hood of the car.

INT. CAR—DAY

Robert turns back to David. David puts his hand on
Robert's arm.

                    DAVID
          Forget it. It's getting dark.
          We're lost.

                    ROBERT
          Yeah.

As Robert starts to speed up, he glances off to the side
of the road again.

                    ROBERT (CONT'D)
          Wait.
```

EXT. DESERT HIGHWAY—ROBERT'S POV—DAY

The woman has her thumb held high. Her smile is dazzling.

INT. CAR—DAY

Robert begins to spin the wheel. David puts his hand on
Robert's arm.

> DAVID
> Not now.

But Robert is already pulling off the road.

Until now, we have been making an arbitrary distinction between point
of view. Although there are certain times when you will want to remain in
a single point of view, most of the time you will free the camera to assume
multiple points of view. We'll end this sequence by rewriting the scene to
shift points of view.

EXT. DESERT HIGHWAY—ROBERT'S POV—DAY

He can just make out that the hitcher is a young woman
standing by the raised hood of an old Impala.

> ROBERT (O. S.)
> Nice.

Now they are close enough to see her. She is attractive,
maybe 25 years old, but before Robert can register
anything else, she drops her thumb . . .

EXT. DESERT HIGHWAY—DAY

. . . and ducks her head under the raised hood of the
car. Her smile fades. The young woman, KAREN, looks out
across the barren landscape. She is absolutely alone. She
looks back at the engine. She taps the distributor cap,
but the crack won't go away. She'll never fix it.

Making up her mind, she steps back out and slams the
hood.

INT. CAR—DAY

David flicks off the radio.

> DAVID
> Forget it. It's getting dark.
> We're lost.

```
                    ROBERT
          Yeah.
```

As Robert starts to speed up, he glances off to the side
of the road again.

```
                    ROBERT (CONT'D)
          Wait.
```

EXT. DESERT HIGHWAY—ROBERT'S POV—DAY

The woman has her thumb held high. Her smile is dazzling.

INT. CAR—DAY

Robert begins to spin the wheel. David turns back to him.

```
                    DAVID
          Not now.
```

He puts his hand on Robert's arm to stop him.

EXT. DESERT HIGHWAY—DAY

Karen drops her thumb and grins as she watches the car
pull off the road.

In these shifts of point of view, it is useful to think like an editor. In the first transition from the boys to Karen, we cut from Robert's point of view to the omniscient perspective on Karen using the action of the arm drop. A match cut. This covers the first shift, usually the hardest one to make, and helps it flow better. The cut back to the boys comes off the action of slamming the hood matched with cutting off the radio. This is intentionally abrupt, making the connection much more obvious. Karen has made her move. Now what are the boys going to do? The cut back to Karen at the end is one of dramatic inevitability. Karen and the reader know she has won. We want to see her savor it. Early in the scene, before the dramatic connection between characters has become as strong as it will be, we cover the transition through a smooth match cut. Later, as the dramatic tension rises and the habit of cross-cutting has been established, the cuts can be more abrupt, signaling the flow of dramatic meaning.

We have run through a number of permutations, demonstrating different ways the writer can shift agency and refocus the scene. We want to end this section by noting that if you attempt to articulate every beat of every character, your scene will lose dramatic focus. You must decide on the line of the scene, the sequences of beats marking character agency that best tells your story. Once decided, you will dramatize the appropriate beats of agency accordingly.

Withheld Agency

Much of drama comes from discovery. It might be interesting to present Karen initially as an apparently compliant character with few dramatic edges, only to have her reveal herself later. However, this does not mean you will want to withhold information. Usually, it is more interesting to hint at the growing need to act by emphasizing reflective rather than active agency. We can do this omnisciently:

```
INT. CAR—NIGHT

David and Robert are engaged in radio wars, each fighting
for a desired station. The car swerves as Robert reaches
for the knob.

David pushes Robert's hand away, but not before the car
fills with rancid country music, played loud.

Karen, sitting in the back, flinches at the sound. Then
she stills herself and calmly watches the two boys.

David, having gained control, switches to loud, grating
sports talk.
```

The flinch might be because of the music. Or it might suggest an edgy character, nervous and ready to be triggered. We can also do this with another character clued in:

```
INT. CAR—NIGHT

David and Robert are engaged in radio wars, each fighting
for a desired station. The car swerves as Robert reaches
for the knob.

David pushes Robert's hand away, but not before the car
fills with rancid country music, played loud.

Karen, sitting in the back, flinches at the sound. In so
doing, she drops her purse which she has been holding on
her lap.

David looks behind him. Karen covers with a sweet smile,
but not before David sees her restlessness underneath.

David drops his hand and lets the country continue to
play.
```

Narrative Distance

So far, we have been concentrating on character-driven scenes in which the agency is transferred from the narrative perspective to that of the characters. But suppose you want to emphasize the narrative voice? Suppose you want viewers to read the scene as an archetype of the American West, rather than as a story of particular characters? In that case, you would give the camera increased agency.

```
EXT. THE WEST—DAY

We fly up over the commercial strip of a Western town.
Shiny, gas-guzzling, SUVs pull into shiny, retro
drive-ins.

We reach high enough to see the town is surrounded by
desert. A lone horseman walks slowly around the town.

Now we are moving through the desert. The town recedes.
There is nothing around.

In the distance, we see a person standing alone by a car.
As we come closer, we see the hood is up and the wind is
whipping through the person's hair.

Closer still, we see that she is a woman, alone in the
desert. But don't worry—help is on the way.

A 4Runner slams on its brakes. As the woman runs to
the truck, we move back up to the mesa towering over
the scene, where we see a roadrunner being chased by
a coyote.
```

Patterns of Agency

It is very unlikely that we can conclude anything about how a script portrays "the other" by citing any one encounter. Most scripts contain a range of characters, none of which can be said to represent the script's point of view as a whole. However, in sections with a dominant narrative voice, we can sometimes see patterns of agency that, inadvertently or not, begin to suggest a point of view.

For instance, the following version of a narrative-voiced sequence of a number of encounters might suggest that sexual initiative is solely the providence of males.

INT. NY BAR—NIGHT

Across the bar, a guy slides over to a girl drinking a
red Metropolitan. He taps her glass.

                                        SWISH PAN TO:

EXT. HOTEL POOL—DAY

A young man watches a young woman in a bikini slather
suntan lotion on her legs. She turns.

The man hikes his suit and saunters over.

                                        SWISH PAN TO:

EXT. DESERT—DAY

Two guys get out of a 4Runner and stroll over to the
woman hitch-hiker. One picks up the woman's suitcase. The
other takes her arm. They help her into the truck.

                                        SWISH PAN TO:

INT. CASINO—NIGHT

A young man watches a twenty-one player who can't decide
what to do. He smiles at her.

A simple adjustment changes what you are saying:

INT. NY BAR—NIGHT

Across the bar, a guy slides over to a girl drinking a
red Metropolitan. He taps her glass.

                                        SWISH PAN TO:

EXT. HOTEL POOL—DAY

A young woman watches a young man in bikini briefs
slather suntan lotion on his legs. He turns.

The young woman adjusts her bikini and saunters over.

                                        SWISH PAN TO:

EXT. DESERT—DAY

```
Two guys get out of a 4Runner and stroll over to the
woman hitch-hiker. One picks up the woman's suitcase. The
other takes her arm. they help her into the truck.

                                          SWISH PAN TO:


INT. CASINO—NIGHT


A young woman watches a twenty-one player who can't
decide what to do. She smiles at him.
```

In dramatic scenes, the writer's treatment of the other may be disguised because it comes through a character. Our reading of the author's attitude toward the character is essential to our interpreting the script. For instance, if the preceding all-male libido version was told to us by a male character that we felt the writer was posing as an ideal of behavior, we would wonder about the point of view of the script. We would have less of a problem if we understood that the character was being presented as insecure and uncertain about his own virility.

A good writer will use subtle devices to separate him/herself from the character. Here is an example from Jon Favreau's script for *Swingers* (1996):

```
52 INT. MIKE'S APARTMENT—LATER THAT NIGHT              52


Mike opens the door and flicks on the lights in his
sparsely furnished single.

He drops his keys on the table and makes a bee line to
the answering machine.

He pushes the button.

                    ANSWERING MACHINE
                    (synthesized voice)
              She didn't call.

Mike collapses into his futon and lights a smoke.

Beat.

He pulls out the COCKTAIL NAPKIN. He stares at the num-
ber.

He looks at the clock. 2:20 AM.

He looks at the napkin.

He thinks better of it, and puts the napkin away.
```

Beat.

He takes out the napkin and picks up the phone.

> ANSWERING MACHINE
> (synthesized voice)
> Don't do it, Mike.

> MIKE
> Shut up.

He dials.

It rings twice, then. . .

> NIKKI
> (recorded)
> Hi. This is Nikki. Leave a
> message.

> (beep)

> MIKE
> Hi, Nikki. This is Mike. I met
> you tonight at the Dresden. I,
> uh, just called to say I, uh,
> I'm really glad we met and you
> should give me a call. So call
> me tomorrow, or, like, in two
> days, whatever. My number is
> 213-555-4679. . .
> (beep)

Mike hangs up.

Beat.

He dials again.

> NIKKI
> (recorded)
> Hi. This is Nikki. Leave a
> message.
> (beep)

> MIKE
> Hi, Nikki. This is Mike,
> again. I just called because
> it sounded like your machine
> might've cut me off before I
> gave you my number, and also

```
          to say sorry for calling so
          late, but you were still there
          when I left the Dresden, so I
          knew I'd get your machine.
          Anyway, my number is. . .
                    (beep)

Mike calls back right away.

                    NIKKI
                    (recorded)
          Hi. This is Nikki. Leave
          a message.
                    (beep)

                    MIKE
          213-555-4679. That's all. I
          just wanted to leave my num-
          ber. I don't want you to think
          I'm weird, or desperate or
          something. . .
                    (he regrets saying
                    it immediately)
          . . . I mean, you know, we
          should just hang out. That's it.
          No expectations. Just, you know,
          hang out. Bye.
```

This continues until Nikki finally answers the phone and blows him off. The writer is able to dramatize Mike's desperation while also commenting on it and do all this with humor. Anthropomorphizing the phone machine—so that not only can it talk to Mike, but it can also give him the advice we would give him—allows the writer to enjoy Mike's passion while positioning the audience outside of it. The progressive phone calls to Nikki, each one built on unfinished business from the call before, not only are funny, but simultaneously let us watch Mike's building desperation, and laugh at it. We care and suffer with Mike, but we also understand the script's point of view toward his behavior.

Otherness is More Complex Than We Can Fairly Treat Here

The notion of *us versus them* is premised on a clear demarcation between those who have power and those who do not. Power in this case means the ability to make a representation, to create characters in our image—power comes from the ability to see through the eyes of our characters; *the other* is that which is seen. The historic impact of the Hollywood production/distribution apparatus and the developed world's access to the technologies of representation has led many to believe that they will always dominate media representation. They will always define the other as not them.

However, this thinking has been challenged in recent years. The availability of the Internet and more recently of blogging has given voice to those traditionally regarded as other. Also, the re-representation of the First World by many Third World societies has raised the question as to whether representational power only flows in one direction. Michael Taussig[3] cites the Panamanian Cuna tribe as an example, who, in their pictorial cloth molas that are often made into decorative blouses or dresses, have redrawn some of the icons of Western advertising power and reflected back to us images of how the other sees us. The Cuna's redrawing of the RCA Victor "Talking Dog" icon transforms the staid image of the dog listening to the gramophone against a black background into a frenzy of color and geometric patterns. Taussig speaks of the intense pleasure this modification brings to Westerners today, the delighted laugh when we see the original ad and the mola side by side. He notes, "the possibility that this sudden laugh from nowhere registers a tremor in cultural identity, and not only in identity but in the security of Being itself"; for Taussig "Being" is the certainty of the superiority of the developed world.

One can also turn this perspective entirely around. In the Western desire to represent otherness from the inside, have we presumed to dramatize motivations that we do not deeply understand? Stephen Gaghan's *Syriana* (2005) relates the story of three young Muslim men who become terrorists. They are portrayed as the opposite of the oil people, as pure as the oil industry is corrupt. The treatment of American business as universally corrupt is a trope, something that we are used to seeing in film. Pretending to show us the three terrorists up close, but reducing them to a similar trope, the opposite side of the corruption, reduces them to the same post-modern cliche as is represented by the oil men. It allows us to feel that we understand and have assimilated something that we do not. It is not so much an exploration of the other, as a reduction of the other to the comfortable categorization of the opposite side of greed.

Conclusion

There are no simple answers when it comes to dramatizing the other. All we can ultimately ask is that the writer imagine all participants in a scene, even if the writer is only focused on a few of them. The writer is responsible for meanings, both intended and not.

You cannot give every character agency all the time or your story will have no focus. But if you find you are repeating patterns in which you deny agency to a class of characters—that is, all women cannot speak up in a relationship—you and your script may be saying something about your view of the world that you are not aware of and which you did not mean to say. You must first learn to sensitize yourself to unintended messages or find a trusted reader who can point them out to you. If you discover that you are inadvertently suggesting a more limited view of voice than you intend, then you want to add agency to those characters who are denied, using some of the techniques discussed in this chapter.

Ultimately, the question of otherness is very complex, and simple answers do not work. All we can ask is that you as a writer listen for the range of perspectives and explore how you can give agency to the widest range of voices in your script.

References

1. This was brought to my attention by my former student, the media maker Charlene Gilbert who is currently an Associate Professor of Film and Media Arts at American University.
2. The example of *Three Kings* was brought to my attention by Dr. Christine Holmland, Lindsay Young Professor and Chair of Cinema Studies at University of Tennessee.
3. M. T. Taussig, *Mimesis and Alterity: A Particular History of the Senses* (New York, NY: Routlege, 1993), 226.

24

Character, History, and Politics

In Richard Leacock's 1964 documentary *Campaign Manager*, a heated, meal-time strategy session slides into an equally intense argument over who ordered the medium-rare steak. A similar scene is dramatized in Michael Ritchie's 1972 feature film *The Candidate*.[1] Because these two films have virtually identical content, they enable us to study how mainstream scripts have traditionally transformed historical and political material into fiction. In this chapter, we pay particular attention to three transforming techniques—the filling in of missing spaces, the use of rhythm to heighten articulation, and the personalization of decision making. We then look at how these techniques serve to diminish the historic overview that makes documentary reality so powerful. Finally, we examine some alternative transformations that, while dramatizing the tension within individual personality, still affirm documentary reality.

We now accept it as a critical commonplace that the traditional distinction between documentary and narrative—articulated as truth vs. fiction—is problematic. However true the events of a documentary may be when they are filmed, the act of filming transforms them into recorded, mediated, formally constructed representations. Such representations necessarily convey an interpretative meaning independent of the truth of their subject. All the filmmaking choices—selection, framing, focal length, photographic quality, editing sequence, shot length, and sound mix—inscribe such a point of view.

Rather than looking at the question of truth, we, instead, approach the distinction in terms of the representation of individual motive. The restorative three-act structure locates the source and the meaning of action within the psychology of character. All else is subordinated to this causality. Documentary, on the contrary, deals with the material world's resistance to such a clear-cut sense of individual causality. This may or may not be acknowledged, but although both fiction and documentary construct their representation to reveal, a documentary is always constrained by the fact that it must recognize that its subject has an existence independent of the film. Of course, it is such limitation, such a sense that meaning is not fully accounted for and contained within the film, that brings documentary closer to history.

We must recognize this limitation if we are to make fictional films that speak to the interactions between the individual and the larger world.

■ ■ ■ A Case Study of Form: Campaign Manager and The Candidate

Mainstream films have certainly represented the larger world, but by and large, they have addressed it on the level of content rather than of form. In other words, the subject is made overtly political or social, but the means and manner of storytelling remain located within character. This suggests that history, politics, and society are primarily individual problems. We can clearly see this when we look closer at the *Campaign Manager* and *The Candidate* scenes.

Shot in black-and-white, direct-cinema style, the mealtime strategy scene from *Campaign Manager* (mentioned in the opening paragraph of this chapter) feels fragmentary, incidentally observed—voices come from off-screen, images linger behind the overt content of the scene, and the camera concentrates on details, such as the way a man listens, and the way his fingers play across his cheek, whereas another man shifts restlessly in his seat. The scene captures the behavior of a body of men rather than any particular personality. We do not see the food cart being rolled in; instead, it is revealed in a wider shot. Voices overlap, so that the debate on campaign strategy, someone offering the black waiter a tip, and the discussion about how the steaks are cooked all run together. The rhythm is continuous, moving without a break from the Virginia primary to who ordered what. The scene ends in a disquieting manner, by focusing on a man who grins and shakes his head as he looks self-consciously at the camera.

By contrast, *The Candidate* personalizes this scene by setting up a spatial and dramatic tension between the campaign manager and the other members of the campaign staff. Presenting strategy, the manager stands alone in front of the others, who are seated below him. The food cart defines the space between them as it is rolled into the room. Although the waiters try to get the food orders straight, the manager keeps up the campaign discussion until he is finally interrupted by someone who asks whether they can get this thing straightened out. There is a dramatic pause, a threatening silence, a series of expectant shots, and then, in close-up, the character asks, "Who has the medium rare?" Merely a joke.

Campaign Manager reads like a parody of the political personality in general, rather than a comment on a specific group of individuals. This focus is reinforced by the casual overlapping of dialogue, the camera's interest in character quirks at the expense of the line of action, the sense of seeing events that have been discovered rather than set up, the suspicion that important moments might have been missed, the lack of rhythmic articulation of beats, the equality in the way the participants are presented, and the one participant's awareness of the camera at the end of the scene. *The Candidate* reads more like a personal dispute, the embodiment of a power struggle between a dry campaign manager and one of the campaign workers—the group's clown. Although *Campaign Manager* seems casual and haphazard in its design, *The Candidate* is rigorously and obviously structured. The character of the campaign manager is set against the other characters through staging and dialogue, the speed with which everyone else turns to their food, the fact that the food cart is rolled between them (prefiguring the dispute), and the rhythmic articulation (the expectant pause) that leads to the final humor of the last beat.

This raises a series of questions critical to any film that attempts to deal with social and political issues: Is history made by individual conflict or by larger and more impersonal forces that in some way act on individuals? Are stories about what we can control or what is bigger than we are? Can power be fully explained by personal quirks? Experience suggests a very complex and ever-changing interaction between these two perspectives. The problem with fully personalized, mainstream filmmaking is that its very technique, its means of involving us in and explaining the story, simply does not speak to this tension.

Filling in, Rhythmic Articulation, and Personalization

To demonstrate why mainstream screenwriting does not speak to this tension, we will show what happens when you use three techniques— filling in missing spaces, heightening articulation through rhythm, and personalizing decisions—to transform historical material into fiction. The following transcript is from a section of documentary footage taken from the fifth episode of the PBS documentary on the Civil Rights movement, *Eyes on the Prize – Mississippi: Is This America? (1962–1964).*[2] The scene is from the training camp for the Mississippi Freedom Summer, run by veteran civil rights workers at Miami University in Oxford, Ohio, during June 1964.

```
M.S. of Afro-American man speaking left to right across
the frame. He is identified by supered title as JIM
FORMAN of SNCC. Other civil rights organizers stand behind
him. Hand-held, black-and-white, news footage.

FORMAN: We're going down there, trying to face a real
situation that will occur; mainly there'll be a mob at
the courthouse. And we want you to get used to this, used
to people jeering at us, and we also want the white stu-
dents who will be playing the mob to get used to saying
things, calling out epithets, calling people niggers and
nigger lovers.

CUT TO LATER. A paper sign reading "Courthouse" taped to
a tree. Jeering over. Camera zooms out between two lines
of white students standing on either side of the tree,
yelling and gesturing towards camera.

CUT TO LATER. White students now gathered around and push-
ing civil rights leaders to the ground. Jeering continues.
```

```
Camera seems to be on edge of crowd, looking up and over.
Hand-held.

CUT TO LATER. Some confusion. The African-American leaders
seem to be standing up. Camera is walked around an
arc so we move from behind James Forman until he is once
again in profile. Laughing. Embarrassment. Ends similarly
to first shot.

FORMAN: Okay, that was very good. (Laughter) Because that
happens ... (drowned out)

(Pause)

FORMAN: That was very good because you all got carried
away, see. I mean you were just supposed to yell and you
started hitting us and you got out your frustration. But
that's what happens, you know.

WHITE STUDENT: Isn't that the way it really happens down
there?

FORMAN: Hey it happens, you know, people begin shouting,
then somebody lurches forward, and then everybody begins
to lurch forward so that was even better than we had
anticipated.
```

Does this scene illustrate a residual racism lingering in America, so that even America's apparently most liberal white children are susceptible to it? Or is it a moment where one individual, for whatever personal reason, gets angry (we don't see this, but we can imagine it) and starts pushing and provoking everyone else? Or is it just an accident of confusion, without any meaning beyond the event itself? There is, of course, no single answer, but the openendedness that characterizes this direct-cinema documentary technique allows, even forces, a number of interpretations. Even if we finally reject those interpretations that suggest a disturbing and ironic indictment of racism in American society, we must at least consider them as possibilities.

We are now going to rewrite the previous transcript into a mainstream fictional scene, by centering our attention almost exclusively on character, in order to show how such rewriting restricts our range of interpretation. Normally when rewriting, we would first ask ourselves: What effect we want to achieve? Once we answer this, we would know what to change. However, for purposes of illustration, we are going to work backwards here—making changes and then analyzing their effects.

When we look at the previous transcription, we see that two important stretches of time are not represented. The transition between Forman asking the students to role-play and their presumably subsequent gathering by the mock courthouse has been cut out (or more likely, not filmed), and, although we see the crowd beginning to collapse around the civil rights leaders, we do not actually observe the leaders being knocked to the ground. The fact that they stand up and brush themselves off in the next sequence allows us to assume that this happened.

Let's now reconstruct this scene in screenplay form, filling in these missing moments with imagined transitions. This filling in of transitions is one of the ways we traditionally transform fragmented historical material into fiction. Six beats have been marked for subsequent discussion.

```
Version #1

EXT. COLLEGE CAMPUS—OXFORD, OHIO, JUNE, 1964—DAY

A bucolic college campus on a lovely summer's day. A
group of white college-age students cluster reverently
around an African-American civil rights LEADER. Several
other African-American leaders stand with him.

                    LEADER
          We're trying to give you expe-
          rience with a real situation
          that will occur when you get
          down to Mississippi. We'll do
          a little role playing, see.
               [Beat #1]

LEADER #2 slaps a scribbled sign that says "Courthouse" on
the trunk of a large oak tree that dominates the campus.

                    A WHITE STUDENT
          Hah. Hah. "Courthouse."

                    LEADER #2
          You're the mob, you got it.
               [Beat #2]

The students play at being the bad guys while Leader
#2 retreats to join the other African-American leaders.

                    A WHITE STUDENT
          You catch any Neeeeegroes in
          your cotton fields? Hah. Hah.

                    2ND WHITE STUDENT
          I get my hands on one of them
          agitators, I'll rope 'em to
          my plow.

                    A THIRD
          Hah. Hah. Draw and quarter 'em.
```

>   LEADER
>   Now yell.
>   [Beat #3]

The students cut loose, yelling insults at the
African-American Leaders watching them.

>   WHITE STUDENTS
>   Hey idiots. Fools. Your mother
>   sucks tomatoes.

>   LEADER
>   Louder. You've got to get
>   used to saying things.

>   WHITE STUDENTS
>   Assholes. Mother fuckers.

>   LEADER
>   Niggers! Nigger lovers!
>   Things you wouldn't say in
>   your worst dreams.
>   [Beat #4]

The white students go silent. They giggle, but they can't
begin to say it.

>   [Beat #5]

Finally, one of them whispers.

>   STUDENT
>   Nigger.
>   [Beat #6]

The earth does not open under their feet. Still hesitating, the others pick it up.

>   WHITE STUDENTS
>   Nigger. Nigger lover.

>   LEADER
>   All right. Now here we come,
>   just like it'll be for you
>   when you're trying to register
>   a few voters.

The Leader and the other African-Americans begin to move
toward the "Courthouse." The white students yell louder,
their voices growing.

```
                    WHITE STUDENTS
          Nigger lover. Nigger. Coon.
```

The African-American leaders push through the students who
refuse to give them room.

```
                    WHITE STUDENTS
          Darkie. Nigger. Boy.
```

The students begin to push back. For a moment, there is a
standoff as the two groups shove against one another.

Suddenly, the white students burst forward, collapsing in
on the African-American leaders. With unexpected viciousness, they knock them to the ground. The Leader's voice
calls out, sharp, commanding.

```
                    LEADER
          Hey. Hey.
```

Stung, the white students freeze, then step back. The
African-American leaders break free. For a long and
uncomfortable moment, the two groups eye each other suspiciously. Then the Leader laughs.

```
                    LEADER (CONT'D)
          You all got carried away,
          see? I mean you were just
          supposed to yell and you
          started hitting us. But
          that's what happens, you know.
```

Relieved, everyone begins to joke. The camera is quick,
hand-held. It moves over faces, vital, alert, but nervous
in their grinning, everything just a little too fast.

```
                    WHITE STUDENT
          That's the way it's supposed
          to happen, right?
```

Without personalizing the group of white students anymore than is
strictly necessary (we will do that in the next section), we have fleshed out—
"milked," if you will—the transitions merely implied by the documentary
footage, shaping them by rhythmic articulation. Let's look closely at how the
first transition works.

In Beat 1, Leader 2 slaps the "Courthouse" sign on the tree without telling the students what they are supposed to do. Figuring it out, the students
play (Beat 2) at being southern rednecks. A general trick is used here. A tight
script avoids doubling; that is, it avoids an explanation followed by an action
played out precisely to the specifications of that explanation. Rather than

have Leader 2 tell the white students what to do and then show the students doing it, we achieve a tighter scene by having Leader 2 hint and then having the students show us, as they (and we) figure it out. If you do place the explanation first, you will want to show us something that does not go according to plan.

In the third beat, the Leader challenges the white students to cut loose, then in the fourth beat, he ups the ante by asking them to yell the word nigger. They go silent. Note the use of contrast here. The silence after the leader asks them to say the word nigger becomes much more powerful, because the intensity of the white students yelling has been jacked up by the previous beat. Only in the fifth beat can one person finally step forward and say it; and only in the sixth beat, do the rest of the students dare to join in.

The beats were written to create a logical momentum that leads the white students to break their taboo and say the one word that is most difficult for them to say. The logic builds like this: Beat 1—The civil rights leaders are asking the students to lean forward by hinting at what they want the students to do but not telling them outright. Beat 2—The students figure it out and play at being bad guys. Making the leap on their own to playing rednecks establishes the eagerness of the students to do what is expected of them. It suggests an energy and a willingness to throw themselves into childlike game-playing that will be intensified by Beat 3 and will ultimately lead to Beat 6. After the boisterous acceleration of Beats 2 and 3, Beat 4 closes in silence. The silence inscribes a space, a clear moment of expectation that not only fills in the transition but also directs us to its most important moment. When the white student finally says *nigger*, the importance of this action has already been carefully framed.

In the transcription of the actual film, we saw how the sense of historical inevitability developed, in large part, due to the omissions of the transition scenes. Lacking their particularity, we are led to generalize and fill in on our own. Rather than focus on character for motivation, we look to the historical situation.

By dramatizing the omitted transitions, we begin to reduce the sense of historical inevitability in favor of narrative causality. Something specific happens, events evolve from that, and this specificity makes us less confident about the kind of historical generalizations we can make.

We have added detail to the script, but we have not yet tied it to a specific personality. Although we have filled in the transition, the movement toward the fight remains completely impersonal. The white students act, but we do not know why. The motivation comes rhythmically from the previous beats; the buildup of excitement and anticipation in Beats 2 and 3 generates a momentum that is irresistible, if uncharacterized. We have no idea why one specific student volunteers and the rest do not.

Now we'll go deeper into the screenplay and lay in a specific character motivation. As you no doubt can guess, this takes us even farther from historical representation.

Version #2

EXT. COLLEGE CAMPUS—OXFORD, OHIO, JUNE, 1964—DAY

A bucolic college campus on a lovely summer's day. DAVID, 21, a white student, intense and eager, his hair buzzed down to a crew cut, scurries to keep up with JOHN, 24, who coolly saunters through the campus, almost oblivious to the younger man at his heels.

> DAVID
> That bad?

> JOHN
> Worse.

> DAVID
> I can't believe you want to go back.

> JOHN
> (Flat)
> A man has to do what needs to be done.

David nods in respect at the older man's cool, then follows him into a group of white college-age students clustered near a dorm. They greet John enthusiastically while paying no attention to David.

> STUDENT
> Hey, John.

> ANOTHER STUDENT
> How's it going?

Before John can answer, an African-American civil rights LEADER, along with several other African-American leaders, struts out from the dorm.

> LEADER
> Okay, listen up.

Not wishing to miss a word, the students go dead silent. David pushes to the front of the group where he gazes at the Leader in awe.

> LEADER (CONT'D)
> We want to give you experi-
> ence with a real situation
> that will occur when you get
> down to Mississippi. We'll do

                    a little role playing, see.
                    [Beat #1]

One of the other African-Americans slaps a scribbled sign
that says "Courthouse" on the trunk of a large oak tree.
Confused, David looks at John, who laughs.

                         JOHN
                    Always the bad guys?

                        LEADER #2
                    I ain't gonna play no redneck.

                         JOHN
                    (With an exaggerated drawl)
                    You catch any Neeeeegroes in
                    your cotton fields? Hah. Hah.
                    [Beat #2]
David turns to the others who don't seem to know what to
do.

                      JOHN (O. S.)*
                    I get my hands on one of them
                    agitators, I'll rope 'em to
                    my plow.

Then David looks back to John who continues to play at
his notion of southern redneck behavior. Now David turns
the words in his mouth.

                        DAVID
                    Hah. Hah. Draw and quarter
                    'em.
                        [Beat #3]

The Leader steps forward.

                        LEADER
                    That's right. Now yell.

Encouraged, the others pick it up.

_____

*The parenthetical phrase O. S. stands for Off-Screen. It is used to show that
a character within the scene is speaking, but is not currently on camera.
This is distinct from the parenthetical indication V. O., which stands for
Voice-Over. V. O. means that the character speaking is either not physically
present in the scene, or that the dialogue is a rendering of the character's
internal voice. O. S. is a useful designation if you want to keep the beat
focused on the character reacting (the one described by the stage directions)
rather than on the character speaking (the one whose dialogue is off-screen).

                        WHITE STUDENT #1
          Hey idiots. Fools.

                        DAVID
          Your mother sucks tomatoes.

                        LEADER
          Louder. You've got to get used
          to saying things.

                        WHITE STUDENTS
          Shit heads. Mother fuckers.

                        DAVID
          Assholes.

                        LEADER
          Niggers! Nigger lovers! Things
          you wouldn't say in your worst
          dreams.
                    [Beat #4]

The white students go silent. Nervously David looks at
the others. All they can do is giggle; they can't begin
to say the word.

                    [Beat #5]

Finally, John steps forward.

                        JOHN
              Nigger.
                    [Beat #6]

But no one picks it up. The word itself overwhelms them.
David looks between his tongue-tied peers and John, who
casually stands alone between the two groups, apparently
not bothered.

                        DAVID
              It's only a game, isn't it?

                        JOHN
          Only a game.

                        DAVID
          (Experimentally) Nigger.

                        JOHN
              That's it.
                    [Beat #7]

David beams. The others look at him with new respect as he struts out to join John.

DAVID

Nigger.

JOHN

Nigger lover.

DAVID

Polack.

JOHN

Kike.

They clasp hands in newfound solidarity.

[Beat #8]

Seeing that, the others finally pick it up.

WHITE STUDENTS
Nigger. Nigger lover.

The Leader and the other African-Americans begin to move toward the "Courthouse." The white students yell louder, their voices growing firm.

WHITE STUDENTS
Nigger lover. Nigger. Coon.

The African-American leaders push through the students who step back gingerly under their pressure. Only John refuses to give them room. For a moment, there is a standoff as John shoves against the African-American leaders.

JOHN
Darkie. Nigger. Boy.

When David sees this, he lunges forward again to join the fray. But just at this moment, John and the African-American leaders ease off, giving up the role-playing. The force of David's lunge knocks the unprepared Leader back against another African-American who falls to the ground.

In what seems to be a reflex action, the Leader's hands come up and knock David back against the group of white students, toppling one of them. The other students burst forward. For a moment, all we see are flailing bodies. Then the Leader's voice calls out, sharp, commanding.

> LEADER
>
> Hey.Hey.

Stung, the white students freeze, then step back. With
David stuck between them, the two groups eye each other
suspiciously. Finally David breaks the standoff.

> DAVID
>
> That's the way it's supposed
> to happen, right?

The Leader looks at him for just a moment too long, then
grins.

> LEADER
>
> You all got carried away,
> see. I mean you were just
> supposed to yell and you
> started hitting us. But
> that's what happens, you know.

Relieved, everyone begins to joke. The camera is quick,
hand-held. It moves over faces, vital, alert, but nervous
in their grinning, everything just a little too fast,
until we reach David. He is still somber, stunned by
what happened. We pass over his face, then reverse direction and come back on him as he finally lets the giddiness
swash over him and breaks into a grin.

By opening the scene on David's attempt to get a reaction from an
indifferent John, this new version immediately frames the issue in terms of
character. Although our interpretative position in the first dramatized version remains ambiguous (we see the transitions, but we do not understand
individual motivation), this version leaves us with little doubt about how we
are meant to enter the scene. In the first version, we wonder what will happen between these groups of whites and blacks given the history of American
race relations and the lack of anything turning us in other directions. In the
second version, we wonder why David is so eager for affirmation and how
this eagerness will condition his subsequent actions in the context of this
moment in the history of American race relations.

This difference in focus actually serves to change the location of the
meaning. In the first version, our initial interest is in the content of the Leader's words. The opening shot holds our attention even though it runs much
longer than we would expect in a narrative film. But in the second version,
the words are less important than is the physical relationship, with David
trailing after John, all the while seeking his recognition. In the documentary,
we would be lost without dialogue, while the opening beats of the fictional
screenplay would be quite intelligible without sound.

The first beat dramatizes John's cool familiarity with the role-playing. He is the only white student to know what Leader 2 is suggesting. When David picks it up in Beat 2, he plays off of John, not off of the leader. This is a critically important transformation—the leader has been reduced to the "other," the unknown character who remains in the background. The force that David responds to is no longer the African-American man, but John, a potential white friend. The unspoken implication is that, although intellectually David might be here for the racial equality of the civil rights movement, emotionally he is still more eager for approval from the older white man he understands, rather than from the African-American leaders he apparently has come to work with. This relationship is reinforced in Beat 6, during which David seeks permission to say the word *nigger* ("It's only a game?")—not from the African-American leader who has asked him to say it, but from John.

The cumulative effect of this is to give a public act a private meaning. We have personalized David's decision to say the word *nigger*—we have given it subtext. The paradox is that, normally, subtext is a sign of the writer's success; it implies there is more to the character's private life than meets the eye. But if we want to maintain focus on more abstracted social issues, on an historical perspective, we cannot explain everything in terms of the character's personal life. We must suggest that larger, more impersonal circumstances have something to do with the outcome.

We have taken a documentary scene that we are inclined to read as an expression of a moment of racial intolerance and have turned it into a personal story about an insecure character named David, who is seeking approval through his involvement in the Civil Rights movement. Of course, we have no way of knowing what really happened in Oxford, Ohio, that day in June 1964. The issue here, though, is not what actually happened, but what is suggested by different forms of representation, because it is these forms of representation that we can control. By using the mainstream model and placing the character story in the foreground, we bring to this event a greater individual specificity that may involve us more in the story, but the cost is considerable. History becomes secondary to personal will. The possibility that this scene might represent anything greater than David's psychological needs is diminished. Far from being indifferent or cruel, the world becomes highly responsive to our individuality. It becomes expressive of an internal state. If we want to maintain historical causality, the sense that at times we are moved by forces larger than ourselves, we have to find some way to flatten the story, to diminish character motivation, and create some space for a broader range of motivation.

Before we go on, we need to add one more thing. A fictional film that maintained the distance of this documentary segment for its whole length would bore the most discriminating viewer. Storytelling assumes modulation of distance to achieve its effects. An indiscriminate use of such distance would be read as a lack of filmmaking control. However, used selectively, the flattening, the sense of inevitability suggested by the documentary, is a tool that the fictional filmmaker can use for considerable effect.

Using Narrative Distance to Suggest the Impersonality of History

To control narrative distance, we have to find a means to establish a tension between the personal and the more formal, distant voice characterized by the documentary. One way to bring about tension is to account for the narration by presenting the scene as though it were actually a documentary seen by a character within the story. This is very useful, because it can suggest two, apparently simultaneous, orders of reality—the documentary itself and the dramatic space in which the documentary is viewed. Framing the event as a documentary within a dramatic film also frees the camera to assume a more open, documentary form without having to otherwise account for the radical change in style.

Holes do not have to be filled in, rhythms do not have to be articulated, the documentary scene does not have to be personalized. While at the same time, the framing dramatic scene can serve all three techniques without disturbing the fragmentary quality of the documentary. The following example is a scene in which a middle-aged man, having used the memories aroused by looking at a tape of himself as a young man to revive his own sense of social commitment, begins to realize that the moment in Mississippi was not as clear-cut as he remembered. The content mixes in another documentary scene from the same episode of *Eyes on the Prize*.

```
Version #3 (Picks up a section of script in progress.)

INT. DAVID'S OFFICE—DAY

DAVID, 42, enters the office. The videotape hasn't been
touched since the day he first received it. The tape
itself lies on his desk. He puts it in the VCR and turns
it on.

The screen breaks up for a moment, then settles down to
grainy black-and-white documentary footage. Under the
supered title Mississippi Delta—1964, the camera pans
over flat-bottom land and a wide swollen river until it
finally settles on a boy-man, intense and eager, his hair
buzzed down to a crew cut, his surprisingly innocent face
leaning determinedly toward the camera. David Fish at 21.

                    YOUNG DAVID
            I'm down here because I
            believe that my freedom is
            very much entangled with the
            freedom of every other man.

The older David watches intently.
```

                    YOUNG DAVID (CONT'D)
               And that if another man's not
               free, then I'm not free. So
               I'm fighting for my own free-
               dom down here.

                         REPORTER
                    Are you scared?

The young David hesitates.

                         YOUNG DAVID
                    Yeah, I'm very much afraid.
                    Everyone here is.

In perfect solidarity with his younger self, David raises
his fist.

                         DAVID
               Yeah.

David turns away from the monitor and picks up the phone.
Behind him, the video goes to snow. Then something else
comes up.

A college campus, Oxford, Ohio, 1964. A group of white
college-age students cluster around a large oak tree and
yell at several African-American civil rights leaders.

                    WHITE STUDENTS
               (Faint) Hey idiots. Fools.
               Your mother sucks tomatoes.

David begins to dial, paying no attention to the TV.

                         LEADER
               Louder. You've got to get used
               to saying things.

                    WHITE STUDENTS
               Assholes. Mother fuckers.

                         LEADER
               Things you wouldn't say in
               your worst dreams. Niggers!
               Nigger lovers!

Phone in hand, David turns on the word and stares at the TV.

The white students go silent. They giggle, but they
can't begin to say it. The young David is among them.
He whispers.

                    YOUNG DAVID
          Nigger.

Still hesitating, the others pick it up.

                    WHITE STUDENTS
          Nigger. Nigger lover.

                    LEADER
          All right. Now here we come,
          just like it'll be for you
          when you're trying to register
          a few voters.

The Leader and the other African-Americans begin to move
toward the "Courthouse." The white students yell louder,
their voices growing firm.

                    WHITE STUDENTS
          Nigger lover. Nigger. Coon.

The African-American leaders push through the students who
refuse to give them room.

The older David watches, the phone still in his hand. We
can hear it ring.

                    WHITE STUDENTS
          Darkie. Nigger. Boy.

The students begin to push back. For a moment, there is a
standoff as the two groups shove against one another.

                    VOICE ON PHONE
          Hello? Hello?

But David ignores it.

On screen, the students suddenly burst forward, collapsing in on the African-American leaders. With unexpected
viciousness, they knock them to the ground. The Leader's
voice calls out, sharp, commanding.

                    LEADER
          Hey. Hey.

Stung, the white students freeze, then step back. The
African-American leaders break free. The two groups look
at one another, stunned. Still staring at the tape, David
replaces the receiver without answering.

There is another technique that can be used to distance the viewer from a scene without actually throwing the scene into the past. We can play it almost exactly as before, but, by exaggerating the pattern of the scene, we call attention to its formal qualities, to the fact that it is not quite natural. This conscious lack of naturalism suggests that there is more going on here than a specific character's story.

```
Version #4

COLLEGE CAMPUS—OXFORD, OHIO, JUNE, 1964—DAY
A bucolic college campus on a lovely summer's day. A
group of white college-age students cluster reverently
around an African-American civil rights LEADER. Several
other African-American leaders stand with him.

                    LEADER
          We're trying to give you
          experience with a real situ-
          ation that will occur when
          you get down to Mississippi.
          We'll do a little role play-
          ing, see.
                    [Beat #1]

LEADER #2 slaps a scribbled sign that says "Courthouse"
on the trunk of a large oak tree which dominates the
campus.

                    A WHITE STUDENT
          Hah. Hah. "Courthouse."

                    LEADER
          #2 You're the mob; you got it.
                    [Beat #2]

The students look at each other now uncertain what to
do, while Leader #2 retreats to join the other African-
American leaders.

                    LEADER
          Hey, come on now.

Finally one of them volunteers ...

                    A WHITE STUDENT
          You catch any Neeeeegroes in
          your cotton fields? Hah. Hah.
                    [Beat #3]

The others pick it up.
```

                    2ND WHITE STUDENT
          I get my hands on one of them
          agitators, I'll rope 'em to
          my plow.

                    A THIRD
          Hah. Hah. Draw and quarter
          'em.
                    [Beat #4]

                    LEADER
          Now yell.

The students cut loose, yelling insults across at the
black leaders watching them.

                    WHITE STUDENTS
                    (Faint)
          Hey idiots. Fools. Your
          mother sucks tomatoes.

                    LEADER
          Louder. You've got to get
          used to saying things.

                    WHITE STUDENTS
          Assholes. Mother fuckers.
                    [Beat #5]

                    LEADER
          Niggers! Nigger lovers!
          Things you wouldn't say in
          your worst dreams.

The white students go silent. They giggle, but they can't
begin to say it.

                    LEADER (CONT'D)
          Hey, come on.
                    [Beat #6]

Finally, the same person who volunteered before whispers.

                    STUDENT
          Nigger.

Still hesitating, the others pick it up.

                    WHITE STUDENTS
          Nigger. Nigger lover.

In Beat 1, Leader 2 slaps the "Courthouse" sign to the tree, leaving the white students uncertain about what they are to do. Only after the Leader's encouragement does one student tentatively take a stab at it (Beat 2). The Leader affirms the student's action. Because it is okay, the other students join in (Beat 3), pretending to be southern rednecks. In Beat 4, the leader challenges the white students to cut loose; in Beat 5, he ups the ante by asking them to yell the word *nigger*. They go absolutely silent. Only after almost identical encouragement in Beat 6 can the same white student finally step forward and say it.

Notice the intentional repeating of motif in Beats 1–3 and Beats 5–7. These two sets of beats stop the action and focus on the same individual who hesitates, receives identical encouragement, and finally acts. The success of that individual's action then frees the others to follow. The repetition of the motif can be placed in the foreground (especially if the motif is repeated a third time), so that the viewer's attention is unconsciously taken from the question of individual motivation to the broader sense of a patterned or formal motivation. The scene will begin to seem artificial, intentionally stagy. Such artificiality displaces the motivation. The scene will seem to come, not from the story world (i.e., not from a character's specific motivations), but from some imposed outside world. Because the scene is so distant, this outside world may supply the necessary perspective without consciously breaking the immediateness of the story. We will end with a few examples of films that use these techniques.

The film *Swoon* gets its historical perspective, not by updating the case of Leopold and Loeb or presenting it as though we were there, but by foregrounding the distance between then and now by introducing a number of historical anachronisms into the story, which emphasizes the difficulty in a historic recreation. It starts and ends with a scene of recreation in which actors circle around one another in front of a backdrop while we see modern film equipment at the edges of the frame—the whole thing is a performance.

Sometimes, the performance comes from the script, as in the choice of framing the story with these two scenes. Sometimes, it comes from the directing. As Leopold waits in the car, Loeb draws the boy they will kill into the car. The camera remains with Leopold in the car. But outside of anyone's point of view, the camera twice slides over to a lake and goes out of focus. The feeling it conveys is not only a lyric expression of what the character is feeling but also an acknowledgment of the act of narration which distances the scene, reminding us that it is a historic recreation. Instead of seamlessly appearing to enter history, we are constantly aware of the tension between our perspective today and the not fully explainable quality of this moment in our past.

Daughters of the Dust achieves its historic perspective in a number of ways. By opening with a title that sets the historical situation and its outcome, the film functions much like the titles in Brecht's *Mutter Courage und ihre Kinder* (*Mother Courage*), which tell us exactly what will happen in each scene. In one critical scene in *Daughters of the Dust*, Nana Peazant, the island's matriarch, confronts her great grandson, Eli. After Eli moves away, Nana begs him to return. At first, he does not, and a series of cross-cuts builds the tension between the two characters. However, as this scene reaches what seems like a climax, we cut away from it altogether to a group of women in white dancing on the beach. This imagery becomes processed and slowed down; hence, we read it not as emphasizing individual characters but rather the dance—the act and joy of ritual itself. We cut back to Nana Peazant as she holds her hands out to Eli. After a beat, he takes them.

A character changes in this sequence, but we do not see the moment of change. Instead, it happens while we watch the imagery of the dancing woman. Instead of the motivation coming at the individual level, the effect of this design is to displace the meaning to the interaction between the individual and his history. Eli's decision is motivated by some combination of his own circumstances and the history of his people.

Conclusion

As we move beyond the simple truth/fiction distinction, we can see that documentary approaches open up subjects and forms that may be borrowed by fictional filmmakers. At the same time, documentary filmmakers' increasing awareness of the constructed nature of their work has led them to appropriate devices that had been traditionally limited to narrative films. But it is important for filmmakers to realize that while the old truth/fiction distinction is no longer automatically applicable, there is a sense in which documentary suggests a very different worldview than do mainstream fictional films. To truly use documentary as a source for fiction, we not only have to appropriate its content, but we have to think about using its form to expand the possibilities and range of fictional filmmaking.

References

1. We would like to thank Professor Warren Bass of Temple University for calling this to our attention at the 1990 Symposium on Screenwriting and the Academy, in New Orleans.
2. *Eyes on the Prize – Mississippi: Is This America? (1962–1964).* Transcription of the fifth episode.

25

∎ ∎ ∎ ∎ ∎ ∎ ∎ ∎

Tone: The
Inescapability of Irony

In Chapter 17, we established the relationship between screenplay form and dramatic intention. In this chapter, we look at dramatic intention and examine how it is presented through character, dialogue, atmosphere, and narrative structure.

The screenwriter uses tone to imply directionality. Generally, in the treatment phase, the writer is faced with pinning down many dimensions of the story. This process continues into the first draft, and perhaps the second. (Events subsequent to this phase are the subjects of Chapter 25.) In further drafts, the writer, or the writer, producer, and director, introduce the directionality (voice) that leads the reader, and, later, the viewer, to interpretation. Of course, interpretation is not singular; there are many ways to construe material, and each yields a different interpretation. Two of the screen versions of the 1782 novel *Les Liaisons dangereuses* (director Stephen Frears's *Dangerous Liaisons* and Miloš Forman's *Valmont*) are good examples of differing interpretations.

The principle of interpretation is carried forward by the director and actors in the production phase of the script, and later by the editor in the post-production phase. It is critical to the viability of the film that the various phases be organic, and that further development and maturation of the ideas and intentions of the screenplay take place. When the process works well, it results in a film like *The Godfather*; when it doesn't, there are many participants to whom to apportion the blame.

In this chapter, we concern ourselves with the early phase of the screenplay—between treatment and the first few drafts. This is the phase in which tone is a critical factor in rooting the screen story. When writing a screenplay, the writer is faced with many hurdles. The first is credibility. Do I, the reader, believe this story (no matter the genre used)? Second, do I care what happens in the story? Third, am I stimulated by the story? All these issues—credibility, involvement, and stimulation—are strongly influenced by the tone of the screen story. In this chapter, we examine how character, dialogue, atmosphere, and narrative structure are used to establish the tone of the story, and how looking for alternative options inevitably takes the writer to an ironic mode or approach toward the material.

Character

The primary question of character, as it influences the tone of your screen story, is the relationship of your main character to the screen story. The choice of a character is not simply a question of a suitable main character; you must ensure that the screen story amplifies and breathes life into his central conflict. It's not enough that the main character as observer becomes involved in a series of events that constitute the plot line. It is critical that a more symbiotic relationship between character and plot exists. If this relationship does exist, your task as a writer is to flesh out both character and plot in ways that amplify that symbiotic relationship. Dominant physical and behavioral characteristics help create a more three-dimensional character. If these qualities are relevant to the plot line, you are making choices that help foster credibility and involvement with your character and your story.

For example, Steven Martin's *Roxanne* is a modern version of Edmund Rostand's classic *Cyrano de Bergerac*. Although Martin's screenplay is a situation comedy, rather than a melodrama (as was the original), the basic story line has remained the same. Fireman Charlie Bales, complete with lengthy proboscis, loves Roxanne (Daryl Hannah). Charlie is poetic and romantic, but he has no confidence. He helps a better-looking, but verbally inept, co-worker win over Roxanne. The only modification to the original version is that Charlie survives and wins the hand of Roxanne.

The key to the relationship of Martin's character and the screen story is to project Charlie's physical shortcoming (the length of his nose) together with his behavioral passion—he is both a romantic and a poet. When Martin's character helps the other fireman, the story takes on a poignancy that forges an even stronger link between us and the Martin character. When the most beautiful woman in town, Roxanne, returns his love, the goals of the character and the screen story are synonymous. For the audience, the sense of satisfaction is pervasive.

Dialogue

The language that you use may reflect character function, but it is important for you, the writer, to realize that dialogue can create credibility for your character, a credibility every bit as great as that achieved by the techniques of dominant characteristics and function-oriented actions. Regionality, culture, class, profession, as well as personality and disposition, all color what a character says. Part of your task at this stage is to use dialogue to make your character credible. Your choice of words can reflect the idiom of a region. The complexity of the idiom can tell us the class of the speaker. Finally, the balance of emotion and socialized (sanitized) language tells us about the nature of the speaker. Power implications also are reflected in the choice of words and how they are put together. All of these elements—regionality, culture, class, status—build a grid that, together, supports or undermines a particular character's image. The dialogue you choose helps set the tone of the script and certainly supports characterization.

The film we discuss as an example is neither overly literary nor memorable in terms of the language, but it is an effective classical use of dialogue. Howard Franklin's *Someone to Watch Over Me* tells the story of Detective Mike Keegan (Tom Berenger). Keegan, a Brooklyn-bred police officer, has just been promoted to detective and is assigned to the Upper East Side in Manhattan. His first job is to protect Claire Gregory (Mimi Rogers), a material witness to a murder. Since she has been sighted by the murderer, Joey Venza, Keegan and his colleagues have to provide Claire with 24-hour protection. In the course of his duties, the married detective falls in love with Claire, and he has to decide whether he will remain in his own culture (Queens), with his wife and son, or whether he will leave it for another woman and another world, the Upper East Side. In the foreground, the story of murder–protection–capture unfolds.

The element critical to the tone of the story is the use of the dialogue to help create the two worlds in which Keegan lives. In the world of Queens, intensity and violence are key. Swearing, explosive dialogue, as well as a kind of lower class simplicity to the language contrast sharply with the quiet, controlled, cerebral language of the Upper East Side. Since Keegan lives in both worlds, he can swear like a trooper or be as sensitive as a psychoanalyst. Franklin's dialogue is consciously class driven. He makes very clear the origins of each character. As is so often the case, the dialogue helps develop a core of believability that supports the central issue for Keegan: Who (or where) do you want to be, Queens or the Upper East Side?

Atmosphere

If dialogue provides the verbal cues to support character, atmosphere provides the non-verbal equivalent. In *Someone to Watch Over Me*, the atmosphere is the two worlds—Queens and the Upper East Side. It is critical for the credibility of the main character that these two worlds be visually articulated. We have to sense the world from which Keegan comes, his home and his neighborhood. In this film, the key atmospheric elements are the lack of class together with the potential for violence. Color, furnishings, noise—all are referred to in the script to highlight the characteristics of Queens, as they are useful to the screen story. Later, the art director, director, and cinematographer articulate the non-verbal vision for viewers. It is equally important that the affluent, opulent, high-technology life of Claire Gregory be clearly articulated for Keegan. The Upper East Side has to be strongly presented so that the alternative is credible and understood. Interestingly, the first few times we see Keegan in this milieu, he is either lost or burning toast. This is how far Franklin wants to go to illustrate how Keegan is out of place in Claire's apartment, her world.

Similarly, in *Roxanne*, it is critical that the setting (in this case, Nelson, British Columbia) is conducive to a romantic fairy tale. In fact, Martin goes to great lengths to ensure that the only challenge to Roxanne's beauty is the beauty of the town. We believe that this story would occur in such a setting. Critical, then, to the credibility of the story is the non-verbal building of visual evidence. Just as dialogue makes a character credible, atmosphere helps make narrative credible.

Narrative Structure

When a writer chooses to write a screen story in a particular genre, she is making a choice that elicits particular viewer response. When Howard Franklin chooses to write a police story, the viewer expects an urban crime-and-punishment tale. In *Someone to Watch Over Me*, Franklin adds a love story, but we know that a solution to the crime will be found. The class dimensions of the story are very much in keeping with the classic gangster story (the basis for the development of the police story). When Steve Martin chooses situation comedy, we understand that the story will work out to the protagonist's advantage (thus challenging our expectations that *Roxanne* will be a repeat of the Rostand original).

Narrative structure affects the tone of the screen story to the extent that the viewer has particular expectations about the antagonist, the nature of the protagonist–antagonist relationship, and how their struggle relates to the resolution of the story. In both genres (gangster and situation comedy), these relationships are attenuated by the expectation that realism, as opposed to fantasy, is the modus operandi. People and events seem real. If they are not, the genre expectation is broken.

At this point, we are concerned with the classic case, where the genre expectation is not broken. This is critical to help the writer understand how narrative structure helps set the tone for the screen story. Up until this point, the emphasis has been on the classic relationship of character, dialogue, atmosphere, and narrative structure, and how they influence the tone of the screenplay, particularly in the early writing phase. But what if the writer is looking to create a different kind of story, a story that opts to challenge the conventional approach? When the writer does attempt to alter tonal expectations, inevitably she begins to write more ironically. Irony is a writing style that, in its farcical description, is tongue-in-cheek, but in its more serious manifestation is profound.

According to Northrop Frye, "Irony never says precisely what it means."[1] It often presents a content that is undermined or contradicted by its style. The same principle can be applied to a character that functions against our expectations of the character in a role, or a character that speaks in a manner that undermines his authority or credibility or that of the person to whom he is speaking. Irony, when applied to realistic genres, implies what is underneath the realistic veneer. Inevitably, one person is designated to seek out what is underneath. In its extreme, comic irony becomes satire. Ironic writing, according to Frye, also has implications for how we use the main character. Often, the main character is the innocent victim and the events that happen to him are far greater than anything he has provoked. We suggest that as you move against conventional writing, you begin to write ironically. Our task for the balance of this chapter is to illustrate how this manifests itself.

The Ironic Touch

Particular screenwriters have become known, during the course of their careers, for using a pronounced sense of irony in their writing. Samuel Raphaelson's work (*Trouble in Paradise*) is a good example, along with that of Ben Hecht (*Design for Living*) and Billy Wilder (*Ninotchka*). Interestingly, all three screenwriters wrote for Ernst Lubitsch. Lubitsch is the master of having his characters speak and project a meaning that is quite different from the literal meaning of the dialogue. He is also known for staging visual action that has a meaning that is somewhat different from its most superficial meaning. This tendency of distancing meaning from content, the ironic mode, was taken up by writer-director Billy Wilder in his work with I.A.L. Diamond (*The Apartment, Some Like It Hot*), by writer-director Joseph Mankiewicz in his late 1940s and early 1950s films (*A Letter to Three Wives, All About Eve, Five Fingers*), and by writer Herman J. Mankiewicz (*Citizen Kane*). This tradition has also been explored more recently by David Lynch (*Blue Velvet*), David Hare (*Strapless*), Harold Pinter (*The French Lieutenant's Woman*), and Hanif Kureishi (*Sammy and Rosie Get Laid*), among others.

To exemplify how irony works in setting the tone through character, dialogue, atmosphere, and narrative structure, we use the work of two writer-directors and one director. Up until this point in this book, we have emphasized scriptwriters, by quoting films referenced to writers rather than to directors. At this point, we are going to emphasize works by directors and writer-directors, such as Preston Sturges, Stanley Kubrick, and Jonathan Demme. Sturges is the sole writer of the films he directs. Kubrick is often the co-writer, and in some films the sole writer, of the films he directs. Only Jonathan Demme does not receive writer credit on his films. He is the sole exception to the pattern we have tried to establish.

The Ironic Character

There are a number of ways to use an ironic character. The most obvious is the sidekick role performed by so many comedians and character actors. From Stan Laurel to Jerry Lewis, the idiot savant commenting on the serious endeavors of his partner has provided the viewer an instant alternate insight into the unfolding dramatic situation. In numerous films, this tradition manifests itself in the characters played by actors such as Tony Randall or Donald O'Connor, who is the quintessential ironic character in *Singin' in the Rain*. Other manifestations include Mary Stuart Masterson in *Some Kind of Wonderful* and Nick Nolte in *Down and Out in Beverly Hills*.

The ironic main character is more of a challenge and less of a tradition in screen stories. Referring back to Frye, the ironic character is something of an innocent who unleashes a course of events that "punish him or her" far beyond what we might expect given their actions.[2] What makes the ironic main character interesting is that her positioning in the story is so important that her ingenuousness as a character leads us to ask naturalistic questions: Is she for real? Is she mad? Can anyone truly be as innocent or as ingenuous as she is? Think for a moment about the Keith Carradine character in Alan Rudolph's *Choose Me*, or the Burt Lancaster character in John Guare's *Atlantic City*, or Paul Le Mat as Melvin in Bo Goldman's *Melvin and Howard*. They seem too honest or naive to be believable; they must actually be deceptive or manipulative. This first impression is wrong. They are precisely what they present. What is notable about ironic main characters is that their very nature can shift our perceptions from viewing *Atlantic City* simply as a gangster film, or *Choose Me* as a melodrama, to fantasy. As Frye claims, the story is then pushed toward myth.[3]

The ironic main character is somewhat different from the conventional main character. Whereas the traditional main character is someone we are visually encouraged to identify with, the ironic main character is somewhat distanced from us. She may seem likable, but her actions convince us that she is also foolish. The ironic main character acts opposite to the traditional heroic action of the main character (even main characters who are not necessarily likable or empathic). The ironic main character unleashes action that, in its results, undermines her intentions, with results that are often closer to tragic than to heroic.

In the work of Preston Sturges, Charles Pike (Henry Fonda) plays the ironic main character in *The Lady Eve*. Woodrow (Eddie Bracken) is the central character of *Hail the Conquering Hero* and John L. Sullivan (Joel McCrea) portrays the ironic central character in *Sullivan's Travels*. Although we can also highlight the Barry Lyndon (Ryan O'Neal) character in *Barry Lyndon*, or Alex (Malcolm McDowell) in *A Clockwork Orange*, or Joker (Matthew Modine) in *Full Metal Jacket*, we will concentrate on the Sturges characters for the moment.

Charles Pike in *The Lady Eve* is a naive, rich young man who would rather affiliate with snakes than women. On a sea cruise, Jean (Barbara Stanwyck), a professional gambler, prepares this lamb for slaughter, but she inadvertently falls in love with him. He, meanwhile, has discovered what he considers her true intentions—to marry him for his money—and he breaks off the relationship. To avenge herself, she visits his family, pretending to be British nobility. Pike falls for the transparent ruse and once again proposes.

This time, she confesses a history of marriages (on the wedding night) that, in its extensiveness, insults his masculinity. Again, the relationship is off. But Charles, a true innocent, takes another cruise and falls in love with the same woman, claiming to be the original gambler. The film ends with Pike taking a third stab at this relationship. We can only hope for the best. In true quintessential fashion, Sturges has created an Adam and Eve story that maintains the illusion of the Garden of Eden but admits some contemporary qualifications—that money skews vision and perception. Pike moves from an innocent to wronged young man, to a spiteful and then naive young man, with abandon. As the main character, he seems remarkably unaware and impulsive, and he does not have a very clear goal. Nor is he a pillar of strength; he is a flawed innocent.

The same type of description can be claimed for John L. Sullivan (Joel McCrea), the main character in *Sullivan's Travels*. Sullivan is an accomplished film director whose success is based on his comedies. However, Sullivan doesn't feel directing comedies is appropriate during the Depression. He wants to do a serious film based on an important book. As he knows nothing about the down-and-out people in society, the subject of the book, he goes out into society to do research. The studio, to protect its investment, sends a team of public relations and medical people to look after him. In order to lose them, Sullivan hops a train headed south. Aroused from sleep by a train guard who takes him for a hobo, he is arrested and imprisoned. A real hobo is killed by the train, and the body is presumed to be Sullivan's. Sullivan, now in a southern prison, is mourned by his friends and employers.

The film turns very serious as Sullivan suffers as a prisoner. He only regains his perspective on himself when, one night, together with the prisoners, he watches cartoons in the local church. He laughs and he realizes the importance of laughter. When he is released from prison, he acknowledges his inability to make serious films and celebrates the importance of laughter.

Sullivan functions as a stand-in for Hollywood success stories that don't relate to the world outside of Hollywood. They take themselves seriously, often too seriously, and elevate superficially important things and downgrade ordinary life. Just as Sullivan doesn't have a good grasp of the reality in society, neither does Hollywood. In many ways, Sturges is poking fun at himself through Sullivan's character. Again, the ironic character is far from heroic.

In *Hail the Conquering Hero*, Woodrow (Eddie Bracken) can't get into the army (he has allergies), but his father was a World War I hero. Now that World War II is upon him, it's his turn. He can't face telling his mother or his sweetheart the truth, so he begins a deception. He works in a military plant a few hours from his hometown, but he has soldiers who are shipping out mail letters home from Guadalcanal for him. His family thinks he is a soldier. One night, he meets a group of Marines with very little spending money and he buys them drinks. The Sergeant (William Demerest) knew Woodrow's father in World War I, and vows to make the situation better. He telegraphs Woodrow's family to notify them that Woodrow has been discharged due to a war wound and will be coming home. The Marines will go home with him.

An elaborate deception ensues, which Woodrow resists. He becomes war hero to both his loved ones and the town. Some people in the town want him to become the new mayor; others resist. Woodrow's original deception has grown so elaborate that the family's reputation, not just his own, is at stake. When he finally confesses the truth, he faces his humiliation squarely. But the town needs a hero and they claim him as one in spite of his lack of a military war record. Whether the ending of the film comments on war, small towns, heroism, the issue of deception in public life, or on all of these things, Woodrow is as far from John Wayne in *The Sands of Iwo Jima* as he can get. As an ironic character, Woodrow is an innocent who is deceptive to prevent hurting his loved ones, but, in the end, he humiliates them and himself.

No matter the outcome of the narrative ending, the ironic character plants doubt in our minds, and we are left with a sense of unease. We are also as far from identifying with the character as we would be if the main character were unsympathetic. The ironic main character is quite far from the conventional main character.

What we have described so far are essentially unusual characters who are positioned in the story in such a way that they are ironic. Another approach to ironic character is to allow for less identification with the character because of the nature of the character. For example, Janet Frame, a writer, is portrayed as unattractive and disturbed and at all times eccentric in Jane Campion's film of the Laura Jones screenplay *An Angel at My Table*. This intense portrayal of the early life (leading up to her commercial success) of the writer is troubling in that she is rejected by everyone in her life. As a consequence of these rejections and of her behavior, Janet is positioned as an ironic character.

Rejection also plays a role in how we view Forrest Gump (Tom Hanks) in Eric Roth's screenplay *Forrest Gump*. He seems to be influencing major historical events while not possessing a true understanding of what is transpiring around him. The consequences of his interactions and the death of characters who tolerate him are such that he seems detached from those events and people. It is the ultimate irony of the story that he has such an impact on people and events because of that detachment. Forrest Gump is certainly an ironic character.

Finally, we turn to an unusual example of an ironic character. Bruno Ramirez and Paul Tana have used the striking device of shifting main characters at the end of Act One in order to reflect on the fate of both main characters. Their film *La Sarrasine* is a Canadian film set at the turn of the century. In Montreal, an Italian immigrant, a successful tailor who is very paternal about his employees, who are fellow immigrants, is intimidated by a local Quebec man. An argument between one of the employees and this man escalates into violence. It is the conciliatory tailor who acts. He kills the man. The resulting trial confirms the guilt of the tailor. At this stage, the story shifts to the tailor's wife. She, too, wishes to survive, but as her husband struggles for dignity, she is the person who insists on fighting. She will not return to Italy; she will fight for her husband's life. In the end, she fails. The tailor commits suicide in jail, and she decides to stay and make a life for herself.

The shift from one character to the other at the end of Act One works because both characters share the same goal—to survive. However, because we shift from one character to the other, we are distanced from the tailor, and we can reflect on the implication of the cultural, social, and legal struggles of both the tailor and his wife, if not all Italian immigrants in Quebec. The shift allows husband and wife to become icons of the immigrant experience. This results in a power unexpected in the story. The use of ironic character, once again, has made our response to the screen story more complex.

Irony and Dialogue

Dialogue often relates to the function of the character speaking in the screenplay. It can be used for purposes of characterization or plot advancement, or it can be used simply as humor to alleviate the tension in a scene. When dialogue is used ironically, it yields results similar to those attained by the ironic character. Ironic dialogue draws attention to itself. It distances us from the unfolding story, and, by taking us out of the scene, we think about the content of the scene or about the dissonance between character and language, character and character, or what the characters knows in relation to what we know.

Perhaps the simplest way to study ironic dialogue is to look at it in its simplest form. In *The Lady Eve*, everyone on the ocean liner is aware that Charles Pike is very rich. Consequently, every woman on the ocean liner (and in the film) is consumed with trying to marry Charles Pike. In the rush for bar orders for dinner, the following brief conversation takes place between the bartender and a steward:

```
             A STEWARD
             (coming up to the
             bar)
       Six more Pike's Pale, and
       snappy, my lad.


             BARTENDER
       What are you trying to do,
       embarrass me? We're all out of
       Pike's. Work something else
       off on them.
```

```
                THE STEWARD
     They don't want nothing else.
     They want the ale that won for
     Yale ... rah, rah, rah!


                BARTENDER
     Well, tell them to go to
     Harvard.⁴
```

It is clear that the bartender is not suggesting his recommendation literally. In fact, his response suggests his loss of patience with the patronizing efforts of all of the shipmates trying to ingratiate themselves to an indifferent Charles Pike. The request is ruining the bartender's ability to serve, and his professional pride induces the ironic comment about Harvard.

Moving to a more complex use of dialogue, the relationship of function to character, we turn to *Sullivan's Travels*. The following exchange takes place between Sullivan and his butler:

```
                SULLIVAN
     I'm going out on the road to
     find out what it's like to be
     poor and needy . . . and then
     I'm going to make a picture
     about it.


                THE BUTLER
     If you'll permit me to say,
     Sir: the subject is not an
     interesting one. The poor
     know all about poverty and
     only the morbid rich would
     find the topic glamorous.⁵
```

The function of the butler is to serve his employer, Sullivan; but in this scene, he challenges Sullivan's goal to make a serious film. The butler suggests Sullivan is one of those morbid rich people who find poverty glamorous, and he goes on to lecture his employer about poverty. The exchange points out Sullivan's naiveté and sets up a pattern in which all of Sullivan's expectations are undermined (as they are in the narrative).

Another purpose of dialogue is to characterize. In the excerpt that follows, a young woman, a fledgling actress, buys breakfast for a hobo in Hollywood. The hobo is John L. Sullivan, a Hollywood director, but she doesn't know it yet:

```
                THE GIRL
     Say, who's being sorry for
     who? Are you buying me the
     eggs or am I buying them for
     you?
```

                    SULLIVAN
          I'd like to repay you for
          them.

                    THE GIRL
          All right, give me a letter
          of introduction to Lubitsch.

                    SULLIVAN
          I might be able to do that
          too . . . Who is Lubitsch?

                    THE GIRL
          Eat your eggs.

                    SULLIVAN
                    (with his mouth
                    full)
          Can you act?

                    THE GIRL
          What did you say?

                    SULLIVAN
                    (swallowing)
          I said, can you act?

                    THE GIRL
          Sure I can act. Would you
          like me to give you a
          recitation?

                    SULLIVAN
          Go ahead.

                    THE GIRL
                    (not expecting to be
                    taken seriously)
          Skip it. My next act will be
          an impersonation of a young
          lady going home . . . on the
          thumb.

                    SULLIVAN
          In that outfit?

                    THE GIRL
          How about your own outfit?

                    SULLIVAN
                    (after a moment)
          Haven't you got a car?

                    THE GIRL
        No. Have you?

                    SULLIVAN
        Well . . . no . . . but . . .

                    THE GIRL
        Then don't get ritzie. And
        I'll tell you some other
        things I haven't got. I
        haven't got a yacht, or a
        pearl necklace, or a fur
        coat, or a country seat or
        even a winter seat. And I
        could use a girdle, too.

                    SULLIVAN
        I wish I could give you a few
        of the things you need.

                    THE GIRL
        You're not trying to lead me
        astray, are you? You big, bad
        wolf!
        (Sullivan laughs sheepishly)

                    THE GIRL
        You know, the nice thing
        about buying food for a man
        is you don't have to laugh at
        his jokes. Just think, if
        you were some big shot like
        a casting director or some-
        thing, I'd be staring into
        your bridgework . . .[6]

In this sequence, we get a sense of the girl's generosity, as well as her spirit. Another level of meaning is added because the girl doesn't know Sullivan's true identity. Ironically, she can be herself and so can Sullivan. Consequently, the dialogue shifts from emphasizing the relationship between director and actress to that between man and woman, and keeps shifting. The relationship advances much more rapidly than it would otherwise. It's as if both characters dropped their public personalities for their personal ones. The result is an intimate feeling between these two characters.

Finally, dialogue is used for plot advancement. The following excerpt from *The Lady Eve* characterizes the first meeting of Jean and Charles Pike, and also reflects the primacy of Jean. Jean is looking into her mirror as women all over the room are attempting to command Pike's attention. He is oblivious or indifferent.

JEAN'S HAND, A MIRROR. SHOT OF CHARLES IN MIRROR.

                    JEAN
          That's right . . . pick it up
          . . . it was worth trying
          anyway, wasn't it? . . . Look
          at the girl over to his left
          . . . look over to your left,
          bookworm . . . there's a girl
          pining for you . . . a little
          further . . . just a little
          further, there! Now, wasn't
          that worth looking for? See
          those nice store teeth, all
          beaming at you? Why, she rec
          ognizes you! She's up . . .
          she's down . . . she can't
          make up her mind. She's up
          again! She recognizes you!
          She's coming over to speak to
          you. The suspense is killing
          me. "Why, for heaven's sake!
          Aren't you Fuzzy Oathammer I
          went to manual training school
          with in Louisville? Oh, you're
          not? Well, you certainly look
          exactly like him . . . it's
          certainly a remarkable resem
          blance, but if you're not
          going to ask me to sit down;
          I suppose you're not going to
          ask me to sit down . . . I'm
          very sorry. I certainly hope
          I haven't caused you any em
          barrassment, you so-and-so
          . . . ." So he goes back to the
          table. Imagine thinking she
          could get away with anything
          like that with me. I wonder
          if my tie's on straight . . .
          I certainly upset them, don't
          I? Now, who else is after me?
          Ah, the lady champion
          wrestler, wouldn't she make an
          armful . . . Oh, you don't
          like her either. Well, what
          are you going to do about it?
          Oh, you just can't stand it
          anymore . . . you're leaving
          . . . these women just don't
          give you a moment's peace, do
          they? Well, go ahead! Go sulk
          in your cabin! Go soak your
          head and see if I care.

```
CLOSE SHOT—CHARLES
He rises, places a finger in his book and starts for the
door of the main dining room. The CAMERA PANS with him. As
he gets a little distance away from Jean and her father—

POINT-OF-VIEWSHOT
Jean and her father watch us rigidly. Suddenly, Jean gets
lower in her seat as she stretches out under the table.
Charles goes hurtling PAST THE CAMERA and we hear a
frightful crash.

                        JEAN
                    (half-rising)
              Why don't you look where
              you're going?
              Charles being helped to his
              feet.

                        CHARLES
              Why don't I look . . .?

He walks toward Jean.

                        JEAN
              Look what you did to my shoe.
              You knocked the heel off.

                        CHARLES
              I did? Well, I'm . . . cer-
              tainly very sorry.

                        JEAN
              You did and you can just take
              me right to my cabin for an-
              other pair of slippers.

                        CHARLES
                    (slightly rattled)
              Oh . . . well . . . certainly
              . . . I guess it's the least
              I can do . . . by the way my
              name is Pike.

                        JEAN
              Everybody knows about that
              . . . nobody's talking about
              anything else. This is my fa-
              ther, Colonel Harrington. My
              name is Jean. It's really
              Eugenia.
                    (she takes his arm)
              Come on.⁷
```

In this scene, the dialogue suggests a passive viewer, at best, editorializing about the efforts of the women in the room to meet Charles Pike. Toward the end of the excerpt, when Jean trips Pike and blames him for the fall, not only does she move from passive commentator to participant, but she actually moves into command of the situation. He will, of course, take her to her cabin for a change of slippers. She not only meets him, she isolates him, a man who has been in the jungle for a year, and gets him alone with her in her cabin.

We, in the audience, are privileged. We know things that Charles does not. The irony is that Jean is totally controlling the situation. Her dialogue does not convey her true intentions. We understand her intentions, but not Charles. He remains the innocent and is about to be victimized by Jean. In this scene, the plot is advanced to the next phase of the relationship.

Irony and Atmosphere

If non-verbal detail creates a sense of atmosphere that supports the credibility of the narrative, the use of detail in an ironic manner subverts the most obvious direction of the narrative. The result is to alter meaning through a tonal shift. The use of irony widens the gap between the foreground and background stories. We have no choice but to adjust our interpretation of the screen story.

Few writers or directors use irony as deftly as does Stanley Kubrick. In *2001: A Space Odyssey*, Kubrick presents a future world in which a computer, Hal, exhibits more humanity than do the two astronauts who are his masters. Indeed, when he senses that their distrust will lead to his destruction, Hal sets out to destroy his destroyers.

This role reversal, the humanizing of the machine and the dehumanization of man in this futuristic setting, is rife with irony. What is critical for the credibility of both perceptions is the presentation of the spaceship. Its interior, as well as the behavior of the astronauts, has been stripped of feeling. The cool white planes of the spaceship contrast sharply with Hal's red eye, his operational light, and the voice that acknowledges that Hal is in operation. Kubrick contrasts the antiseptic world of the humans with the passion of the computer. Both the sound and visual dimensions of Hal are limited, but they allow our imagination to conjure up the degree of Hal's humanity.

In *Lolita*, Kubrick uses irony to portray the two worlds of Humbert Humbert and America. Humbert is a guest to America and is a lecturer in poetry at an American college. When he stops at a guesthouse to vacation prior to the school year, he falls in love with Lolita, the 15-year-old daughter of the guesthouse owner. Humbert is a man consumed by his obsession and his passion. All the while, the place and the people (including Lolita) are somewhat sterile. The clash between Humbert's feelings and the milieu of the characters is so great that we are left wondering about the reality and meaning of his passion for a nymphet. Without this clash, the irony of Nabakov's screenplay wouldn't resonate with the powerful commentary about sexuality in post-war America.

Irony and Genre

As suggested in Chapters 7, 8, and 9, genres lend themselves to consistent narrative structures. What happens when a writer sets out to alter a motif or challenge a convention? Whether this occurs through mixing genres or altering a single motif, the resulting genre violation is similar to the result of using an ironic character or dialogue. Meaning is altered. At times, this enhances the richness of the genre experience. At other times, it can depreciate the experience. In all cases, the viewer is moved away from the expectations that genre films imply.

Genre violation is probably the most typical ironic challenge to narrative structure. Jonathan Demme seems very attracted to this approach. In his film of Max Frye's script for *Something Wild*, Demme mixes film noir with screwball comedy. The result is both more than and less than the sum of the two parts. The main character, as victim (a characteristic of film noir), does reconcile with the ironic main character; but after the midpoint of the film, the main character begins to entertain heroic action. The result is inconsistent. We don't know whether to admire or pity the main character. In the end, we have a mixed feeling toward the main character and, as a result, his heroic efforts in the second part of the film don't yield the results for which Demme may have hoped. However, the film does have the patina of freshness for having attempted to mix genres.

Demme has more success with Bo Goldman's *Melvin and Howard*. This story, of the consequences of the encounter Melvin, a simple Westerner, has with Howard Hughes, is rife with irony. Melvin, in possession of what he views to be the Last Will and Testament of Howard Hughes, attempts to become what society suggests is the pinnacle of success—to be rich and, therefore, happy. But Melvin's efforts are those of an innocent. Where money is concerned, happiness proves elusive. There are many people who want Howard Hughes's legacy, and Melvin has neither the guile nor the resources to be rich like Howard Hughes.

In *Melvin and Howard*, Demme and Goldman portray Melvin as the ironic character, and they achieve in this film a feeling for the mythology that made America the richest nation on the face of the Earth. We feel for the myth and the man. In the end, however, Melvin is the tragic main character of the melodrama. Because of the use of ironic main character, the film moves in the direction of satire. The dissonance between the two genres, melodrama and satire, elevates the film beyond melodrama, but not quite so far as to attain the aggressive aftertaste of satire.

It is useful to explore this notion of irony and genre further by focusing on genre violation at the level of the nature, goal, and fate of the protagonist. When the expectation that Bill Munny will be a classic Western protagonist is upset in *Unforgiven*, we are distanced from him and we reflect upon his goal—financial gain—in the light of the Western hero's classical goals, moral equilibrium and an individualistic sense of freedom. Munny's goal debases his character in our eyes and dims the sense of pastoral myth with it; consequently, our experience of the story form, the Western, is altered.

This is the pattern of irony when applied to genre. In melodrama, the classic character challenges the authority of the power structure and is punished accordingly. Good examples of this kind of character are the Donald Sutherland character in Euzhan Palcy and Colin Welland's *A Dry White Season* and the Richard Gere character in Nicholas Meyer and Sarah Kernochan's *Sommersby*. In *A Dry White Season*, the Sutherland character challenges apartheid in the South Africa of the 1970s and is killed, while the Richard Gere character in *Sommersby* challenges the power of property and marriage when he pretends he is another man. Both characters suffer the classic fate of the main character in the melodrama.

However, in Steven Soderbergh's *King of the Hill*, the young man who is the film's main character will do anything to survive the travails of the Depression in St. Louis in the 1930s—and he does survive. By layering the fate of this main character, Soderbergh subtly shifts our attention to the unfairness and the cruelty of this period. He makes something of a hero out of the boy by celebrating his survivalism. Many who were kind or helpful to him are not so lucky in this grim portrait of the time and place. A similar result occurs in Alison Anders's *Gas Food Lodging*. This story of survival focuses on a single mother's attempt to raise two daughters in the modern West. The mother's ability to survive against a power structure that is skewed against women makes the story more poignant and more believable, compared to Callie Khouri's *Thelma & Louise*. Anders's melodrama is far more suited for such a message than the mix of Khouri's road film (adventure) and melodrama allows for. And again, the survival of the protagonist in Anders's melodrama poses a wish for a better life for the three women in the story.

A more distanced and complex alteration of a main character's fate occurs in John Guare's *Six Degrees of Separation*. A young black man pays a visit to a wealthy older married couple. He claims to be the son of Sidney Poitier and a friend of their son. He is soon all but adopted into the family. When they find out he is an impostor, they all turn against him—except for the wife. She feels a loyalty to him that is totally absent from her relationship with her own children. The main character in this Upper East Side New York melodrama is the wife. Her goal in the earlier part of the story stems from a status most clearly associated with great wealth. Having passed through the phase of wanting to associate with Sidney Poitier, she transcends her disappointment and sense of betrayal and works toward a relationship with the young impostor. Whether this is another deception or a liberal feint at race and age reconciliation is unclear. What is clear is that the main character does not suffer the classic fate of the main character in melodrama. The consequent distancing poses reflective questions about economic, social, and political standing in the community. Irony is not deployed critically here, but as a more conciliatory device—and the results are surprising.

The fate of the protagonist is also surprising in Don McKellar's *Highway 61*. A gentle mix of melodrama and road movie (adventure), *Highway 61* tells the story of a young Canadian rural barber (Don McKellar) who is convinced, without much pressure, to drive a young woman (Valerie Buhagiar) and "her dead brother" to New Orleans, for burial of the body. What the barber doesn't know is that the woman is using the body to transport drugs across the border. They meet an assorted and sordid group of characters. The emphasis of the journey is on eccentricity (the tone is definitely ironic). The young barber, a man with musical aspirations, succeeds in transcending his own meekness. Since his fate is more indicative of an adventure story than of a melodrama, McKellar successfully incorporates elements of both genres, thus illustrating that melodrama doesn't always need to end in tragedy. The result is an ironic meditation on the fate of the main character in melodrama. Funny and surprising, *Highway 61* is in every way fresh. Irony succeeds in the breech of genre expectation.

Three-Act Structure

In *Full Metal Jacket*, Stanley Kubrick challenges the traditional structure by presenting the story in two acts. Act One is basic training; Act Two is the battle of Hué in Vietnam. By moving away from the introduction–confrontation–resolution to introduction–confrontation, Kubrick opts for an open-ended conclusion to the film—there is no catharsis. This troubling result is compatible with the use of ironic secondary characters: the drill sergeant in Act One becomes the enemy, rather than the father figure, and the sniper in Act Two proves to be a slight woman who is near death. She is not presented as the enemy usually is presented. Given the death she has inflicted, we expect that the enemy is an invincible, larger-than-life force. But, ironically, the enemy is this young girl. In both cases, the characters subvert our expectations and support a structure that offers no resolution.

Woody Allen, as mentioned in previous chapters, chooses to subvert structure and genre in *Crimes and Misdemeanors*. Two stories, both written in three acts, intertwine freely, the point of view of one undermining that of the other. Although melodrama and situation comedy are flip sides of each other, the happy ending to the melodrama (when our genre expectation is a tragic ending) and the tragic ending to the situation comedy (when our genre expectation is a happy ending) subvert each other and make the final scene, the meeting of Cliff and Judah, ironic. Woody Allen uses, as did Stanley Kubrick in *Full Metal Jacket*, structural and genre violations in order to produce the ironic tone that unsettles the viewer to reflect upon issues beyond genre—war, morality, and quality of life. Both *Crimes and Misdemeanors* and *Full Metal Jacket* are serious films that use tone and irony to invite meaning beyond what is apparent in the narrative.

A number of writers have experimented successfully with structure. The most commercially successful experiment is Richard Curtis's *Four Weddings and a Funeral* (1994). An argument can be made that this film actually follows conventional three-act form—boy meets girl, boy doesn't want girl, boy finally decides he really does want girl. But we would like to suggest that, on another narrative level, Curtis does organize the entire story around a series of special events—weddings, proposed weddings, and a funeral. By doing so, he has contextualized the personal issue (commitment to a relationship) into a social context—that is, the weddings and the funeral.

As a genre, *Four Weddings and a Funeral* is clearly a situation comedy with the main character challenging the values of marriage. The story has a clear protagonist, the male, Charles (Hugh Grant). The challenge to storytelling conventions of structure comes from the theatrical device of organizing the entire story around five social events. Superficially, the implication is five acts, but actually, the film neatly divides into three acts, with turning points just after the two characters have slept together for the first time: the female lead, Carrie (Andie MacDowell), poses the issue of commitment, and Charles rejects it. The next turning point occurs after Carrie's marriage: Charles confesses his love for her, but now she is married and the possibility of a relationship has never seemed more distant.

The dissonance between the formal structure of the film (five acts) and the dramatic structure (three acts) makes the film seem novel and inventive. The dissonance between the two structures also allows the audience to consider more powerfully the clash of personal and social goals as represented principally by Hugh Grant's character.

Another recent experiment with structure is Don McKeller's *Thirty Two Short Films About Glenn Gould*. This unusual mix of recreated dramatic episodes, together with documentary segments, is 32 episodes about the life of the great Canadian interpreter of Bach, Glenn Gould. The film for the most part follows the chronology of Gould's life and career. Particular episodes—his decision to stop performing live and his last concert—are much longer than are other episodes. By mixing documentary and drama, by altering lengths, and by shifting tone in 32 self-contained films within a single story, *Thirty Two Short Films About Glenn Gould* becomes an example in which rules are broken in the name of creating a complex, creative, bold pastiche of a man who defied categorization. Because of the structural violation, McKellar and director François Girard force us to consider the undefinable nature of genius and the playful core of creativity. The film undermines structural expectation and creates its own structure in order to move us beyond convention.

Jean-Claude Lauzon, in his meditation on the limits of family and the opportunity of art, *Léolo*, travels more deeply down a path not dissimilar from that of McKellar and Girard. *Léolo* tells the story of a young boy growing up in Quebec within a family that is limited both mentally and spiritually. Consequently, the young boy conjures up a new identity for himself: he is really an Italian born out of an unusual alliance. In Sicily, a young Italian masturbates on a fresh shipment of tomatoes. In Montreal, the boy's mother falls on those same tomatoes, and Léolo, as he calls himself, is born of this union. He denies he is his father's son. Faced with a primitivism, emotional violence, and illness, and a sterility of life he cannot accept, Léolo imagines another life, a better life, an Italian life—an artistic effort to escape his physical reality.

Lauzon has structured his film along a foreground story that highlights the physical reality of Léolo's life, and a background story that reflects his artistic efforts at a rich spiritual life. The dissonance between the two story lines, between fact and fiction, between reality and fantasy, is so great, so vivid, that we enter a relationship with Léolo's hopes and dreams. Lauzon manages to use the ironic shifts in tone between the two to create a rich interior life for the boy, a world where dreams can overcome despair. Our involvement becomes so visceral that it is quite a shock when *Léolo* ends with the boy being hospitalized for the same schizophrenia that afflicts his siblings. It is a remarkable creative achievement that Lauzon's structural violation and contradictions are as effective as are the 32 short films used by McKellar and Girard in creating a complex, rich, creative inner life in the main character.

A similar range of tonal shift for purposes of satire can be found in Robert Altman's *Short Cuts*. This meditation on the urban nightmare, set in Los Angeles, attempts to underscore the cost to one's humanity. No one is immune. A mother diapers her child while dispensing phone sex. A police officer harasses a young woman driver with the threat of fines; he will dispense with the fine in return for sexual favors. Mothers are indifferent to their daughters, and fathers are self-serving and narcissistic. The sons will clearly pay a price in the future. Alternating between humor and emotional violence, Altman creates an equivalent to Hieronymous Bosch's hell in today's Los Angeles.

It is useful to contrast Altman's effectiveness in *Short Cuts* with a less extreme presentation of humanity in the urban context—John Sayles's *City of Hope*. Because Sayles does not employ an extreme tonal shift in order to present a more realistic portrait of personal and political corruption in an unnamed eastern city, the effectiveness of *City of Hope* is blunted when one compares it with *Short Cuts*. As with the work of Anderson and Kubrick, satire, when applied to a critical social issue, can be a remarkably powerful story form.

Satire

Perhaps no genre offers more freedom to the writer than does satire. Satire is the extreme case of deploying irony in the screen story. The writer is free to use an ironic main character, but, beyond the characters, the writer can move as far from realism as she desires. Whether one references film satire as Terry Gilliam's *Brazil* or Stanley Kubrick's *Dr. Strangelove or: How I Learned to Stop Worrying and Love the Bomb*, the healthy irreverence of these writers is generated from their passion about the issues—the future and the bomb in the aforementioned films—and from their ferocious use of humor. Satire affords the writer with the ultimate opportunity for irony in a screen story. The tonal violation is so great that satire shakes the viewer's sense of security.

David Sherwin's *O'Lucky Man!* is the story of Mick, a young coffee sales-man who is interested in getting ahead. He is earnest, but the barriers that prevent him from getting ahead include friends, lovers, employers, and total strangers. He is almost killed on a highway and lands in a hospital. He is arrested for the malfeasance of his employer, and when he tries to reform himself after prison, he is attacked by the very homeless he helps feed. The world is more than cruel—it's lethal. Naturally, Mick decides to become an actor, and there the story ends.

This brief description doesn't do justice to this modern Candide with musical interludes. The story is savage in its portrayal of the alienating forces active in our modern lives. Although not Luddite in its goals, it's certainly a modern equivalent. Sherwin uses Mick as an ironic main character, the inno-cent victim of an economic system certainly determined to exhaust him, but more likely to destroy him.

The narrative structure of *O'Lucky Man!* is constantly challenged. Almost spontaneously, we break away in sequence to a musical interlude. Eventually, the musician who performs the interludes, Alan Price, is intro-duced as a character in the narrative. Transgressions follow transgressions and the narrative progresses readily away from realism. Satire is the extreme case of tonal violation and its primary quality is its use of irony.

Conclusion

Tone is a crucial factor for the screenwriter to consider. Tone should concern you early in your writing. In the treatment to first-draft phase, your attitude toward the characters, their language, and the narrative structure prompts you to make choices about the tone of your script. These choices are critical signposts for a film's viewer; they point in the direction of the interpretation of the story. They don't provide enough information to fully interpret the story, but they do point toward the interpretation.

As a writer, you can create a conventional tone by using the classic empathic main character, functional dialogue, the expected three-act struc-ture, and genre. Or, you can challenge those notions, in which case the use of irony comes into play. In extreme cases, you can use satire, the ultimate genre application of irony. Or you can challenge our expectations by using an ironic main character. The use of this type of character will result in a more distanced relationship between viewer and character. Whether the result is to reflect upon the actions of the character or to seek out alternate meanings for his role in the narrative, the use of the ironic main character yields very different, often more complex, results than does the use of the conventional main character.

Additional meaning can also result from the use of ironic dialogue. Ironic dialogue is certainly the result of genre violations and mixed genres, rather than of conventional narrative patterns. In all cases, tonal shifts alter meaning as well as the audience's experience of the screen story. Whether the shifts are verbal (dialogue) or non-verbal (atmosphere), both point out the critical role tone plays in setting up the audience to relate to the screen story.

References

1. Herman Northrop Frye, *Anatomy of Criticism* (Princeton, NJ: Princeton University Press, 1957), 47.
2. Ibid.
3. Ibid.
4. Preston Sturges, "The Lady Eve," in *Five Screenplays by Preston Sturges*, ed. Brian Henderson (Los Angeles: University of California Press, 1985), 362.
5. Preston Sturges, "Sullivan's Travels," in *Five Screenplays by Preston Sturges*, ed. Brian Henderson (Los Angeles: University of California Press, 1985), 552–553.
6. Ibid., 589–590.
7. Preston Sturges, "The Lady Eve," in *Five Screenplays by Preston Sturges*, ed. Brian Henderson (Los Angeles: University of California Press, 1985), 364–366.

26

Dramatic Voice/ Narrative Voice

David Burdwell notes that maintstream film subordinates everything to narrative causality and character motivation. "In Hollywood cinema, a specific sort of narrative causality operates as the dominant, making temporal and spatial systems vehicles for it."[1] These subordinated temporal and spatial systems—the actual elements of film language—are rendered transparent by the functioning of a conventional structure that creates the illusion that the story would happen exactly the same way regardless of whether the camera were there. Most of our dramatic concerns—the plausibility of motivation, the consistency of character, the avoidance of overt coincidence, the construction of a believable backstory—come out of the conceit that we are spying on a pre-existing event. As we discussed in Chapter 2, this conceit is deeply embedded in nineteenth-century notions of realism and naturalism, and, like the restorative three-act structure, can be traced back to the well-made play.[2]

For our purposes, we identify a scene that seems to tell itself—one that plays without making us conscious that it is being narrated—as a scene that is dominated by the dramatic voice. But as we said earlier, even a scene using the dramatic voice must be given shape by some form of narrating agency that organizes the presentation of events. No matter how realistic the representation, we are not watching reality—the act of representing the world implies narration. The narrating may be overt or virtually invisible, but it is always present.

The use of the terms *narrator* and *narrative voice* in film is problematic. First, a narrator in film is most often understood as a voiceover narrator. Relatively few films use such voiceovers, and if our comments pertained only to them, we would be addressing a very narrow concern. Second, the narrative voice is problematic in film because it is deeply embedded in literature and refers to the manner in which the writer speaks directly to us. Such simple and direct authorial address is not possible in most films because there are too many intermediating agencies in the mass media production process to speak of a unified, singular filmmaker's voice. Also, in most films, the articulation of the narrative voice is much less direct than it is in literature.[3]

However, even given these reservations, we find that *voice* and *narration* are the only terms that speak to the independent filmmaker's desire to be heard, to express a personal vision while still using the storytelling ability of narrative (as opposed to experimental) filmmaking. Thus, we use these terms to refer to the agency that communicates the story to us, whether overtly or not. In fact, the literary antecedents are useful to us because we can understand the development of narrative voice in mainstream film by looking at the movement from the classic nineteenth-century omniscient narration to the limited, three-person narrator of Henry James and Gustave Flaubert. The classic omniscient narrator of the nineteenth century was not only all knowing, but also all judgmental—not only able to spy on all aspects of this pre-existing world, but also capable of commenting and evaluating. For instance, George Eliot opens *Middlemarch* with this sentence:

> Who that cares much to know the history of man, and how the mysterious mixture behaves under the varying experiments of Time, has not dwelt, at least briefly, on the life of Saint Theresa, has not smiled with some gentleness at the thought of the little girl walking forth one morning hand-in-hand with her still smaller brother, to go and seek martyrdom in the country of the Moors?[4]

Not only does this sentence serve to introduce Theresa, it also introduces a style of narration in which the narrator is willing to admit to a clear sense of what is important. This is evident in its flat declaration that the character, Theresa, like the saint, is going out to seek martyrdom.

Today, we probably find such pre-judgment by the narrative voice old-fashioned, preferring instead to make our own judgment as the story plays out. In effect, we would rather infer the quality of the character by the dramatic voice, rather than be told by the narrator. Even if we wanted to, it would be very hard to communicate this omniscient judgment directly in film. How would we show Theresa as a saint? With the superimposition of a statue, church music, and animated halo? All of these expressionistic devices have been tried and, for the most part, were found to be heavy handed and literal. In the 1927 Soviet film *Oktober*, director Eisenstein's mocking of the pompous revolutionary leader Kerensky, by superimposing his walk with the strut of a cock, has historical interest but does not suggest much of a practical alternative to us today. Does this mean, then, that a filmmaker cannot suggest a point of view without being so mannered? No. The late nineteenth-century development of the narrator within the story provides an analogy for the classic film style.

Reacting against the overt authorial presence of writers such as Charles Dickens and George Eliot, many novelists (foremost among them Gustave Flaubert and Henry James) looked for another way to narrate stories. They shifted their interest from the question of what we know to how we know it, and, as a result, they saw the omniscient, judging narrator as problematic, asking: Where does this voice of God come from? What explains the certainty with which an omniscient narrator creats and claims to know the fictive world? Though it was possible for a reader to judge the characters' trustworthiness (based on their actions, about which an opinion could be formed), how could it be possible to engage the narrator who injected a point of view, but stood outside the story? Thus, instead of commenting directly on the action, Henry James came up with the notion of the *reflector character*, or the narrator within the story—a character who was presented quite neutrally by the writer, but who was allowed to recount and make judgments about the events in which she was involved. This character provides narrative in place of the writer, but since she exists in the fictive world of the story, it would be possible for the reader to engage with her even as she is presenting information.

We can see how this works when we contrast this sentence of Henry James's *The Ambassadors* to the *Middlemarch* sentence quoted previously: "Strether's first question, when he reached the hotel, was about his friend; yet on his learning that Waymarsh was apparently not to arrive till evening he was not wholly disconcerted."[5] Notice, immediately, how little direct authorial judgment this sentence makes (of course, there are implications of narrative voice in the syntax, word usage, length of the sentence, etc.). The emotion directly described is Strether's, an emotion that we take to be one of which the character is fully conscious and thus is in a position to describe. By contrast, in *Middlemarch*, the judgments are authorial; nothing there allows us to assume that the young Theresa regards herself as a saint.

Strether's not being "wholly disconcerted" is taken up over the next few pages of *The Ambassadors*, developed, as it were, through Strether's consciousness, so that we learn, as he figures out the reason for being "not wholly disconcerted":

> ...the fruit of a sharp sense that, delightful as it would be to find himself looking, after so much separation, into his comrade's [Waymarsh's] face, his business would be a trifle bungled should he simply arrange for this countenance to present itself to the nearing steamer as the first 'note' of Europe.[6]

Strether is, in effect, setting (narrating) his own situation—we enter the dominant voice of the book with his plotting his own expectations of how he wants to first meet Europe.[7]

The classic film style draws on this idea of allowing the character to, in effect, narrate his or her own story, without forcing the filmmaker to overtly comment. For instance, there is a scene in *The Verdict* in which Galvin enters the victim's hospital room with the intention of taking Polaroids that he can use to get more money from the out-of-court settlement. As he takes the pictures, however, he moves slower and slower until he finally stops altogether, staring at one picture of the victim as it develops in front of his eyes. We know that this is the important moment of the scene, the moment where he begins to realize he must take the case to trial. But how do we know? Without in any way calling attention to them, the narrator employs a number of devices (rhythm, lighting, cutting pattern) that emphasize the importance of this decision, but because they all seem to be at the service of Galvin's realization, we get the sense that Galvin is not only making a decision, but he, not the narrator, is also directing our attention to its importance.

Hiding the narrator agent behind the character also explains one of the paradoxes of the classic style—that, although the story appears to be driven by character, the camera expresses very little of the character's emotion on its own. The lens is almost never distorted by subjectivity, and rarely do we see extreme angle interpretative shots. Rather, the narrative agency sets the stage for the character perspective by its use of point-of-view and eyeline-match sequences, structuring a series of neutral shots and reverse shots that are carefully tied to the line of the character's emotion. Our movement through the film is made up of our progressive awareness of the character's (as opposed to the filmmaker's) attitude toward the action. It's as though the filmmaker, much like Flaubert and James, is unwilling to say anything directly, preferring instead to let the characters tell their own story.

This method of storytelling, during which the narrator apparently cedes emotional control of the story to his character (remember, the outside narrator never disappears; he only appears to), raises a major obstacle for the independent narrative filmmaker. Independent films are made out of the desire of the filmmaker to speak in his own voice (whether this is possible is another topic). However, by emphasizing the dramatic voice over the narrative, by concealing the filmmaker's voice behind the characters', the effaced narrator of the classic film style restricts direct lyrical expression. The independent filmmaker who is seeking her own voice must find a way to assert the narrative voice over the dramatic pull of events. This may be harder in film (and video) than in all other arts because of the inherent naturalism and apparent transparency of the camera's image.[8]

Voice and Structure

Clearly, much of what we are calling voice in film is under the control of the director. The relative realism of color scheme, the lighting contrast ratios, the set design, the casting, the balance of ambient sounds to dialogue, and the final editing pattern are beyond the realm of the writer. Still, it is possible to construct a script that emphasizes the narrative voice at the level of the story. As before, we have to start with structure.

We said that in classic film style, overt narration tends to be hidden behind a structure that functions to organize the meaning of events without calling attention to itself. If we want to place the narrative voice in the foreground, we must reduce the primacy of this unacknowledged structural drive.

However, if we reduce the dependence on the restorative three-act structure, we must find other ways to supply a narrative voice.

To simplify, we might say that structure is a pattern designed to focus the questions we want the viewer to ask as the story unfolds. Although structure is tied up with character-driven plot in classic Hollywood film, it does not necessarily have to be used that way. Structure is pattern. It may be made of anything that organizes our attention—a repeated line of dialogue, a recurrent situation, a musical theme, an external historical moment, a radio in the background, a return to the same location. The less structure relates to plot, the more formal it seems to be. The more external to the action, the more structure reads as the filmmaker's voice.

The realistic use of patterns, which we identify as mainstream structure, functions in two distinct and apparently self-contradicting ways. Structure tells us what is necessary for the movie to come to an end, while at the same time it must not call attention to itself. We know, for instance, that in *Wall Street*, Bud must come to terms with his father before the movie can end, but when he does, we must feel that this is an inevitable outgrowth of character, not an overt manipulation by the filmmaker giving order to what would otherwise be an ambiguous circumstance.

To play against the structural dominance of mainstream film, then, we have to uncouple plot structure from simple story closure (or at least twist it) and find a way to call attention to its patterning. This sounds like it requires a radical approach to filmmaking, but this is not necessarily so, as evidenced in an apparently mainstream example, Alfred Hitchcock's *Vertigo*. Scottie, a former police lawyer, falls in love with Madeleine, the woman he has been employed to protect. Obsessed by bizarre suicide fantasies, she apparently kills herself by jumping from a church bell tower. Overcome by guilt, Scottie breaks down and is unable to pull himself together until he sees a woman who reminds him of Madeleine, and Scottie seeks to remake her as Madeleine. We are told that this new woman, Judy, actually had originally disguised herself as the very Madeleine whom Scottie thought had fallen to her death, to cover a murder plot. Scottie doesn't know this and proceeds to make Judy over to recreate an image of Madeleine. When Scottie finally realizes what has happened, he takes Judy back to the bell tower where, after having it out, she convinces him that she loves him. As they begin to kiss, a nun, having overheard them, suddenly appears and causes the startled Judy to fall to her death, mimicking the bell tower "suicide" earlier in the film.

The film is divided in half, which suggests a kind of oppositional binary structure (the action in the first half, the reconstruction of the action in the second) different from traditional three-act structure. Scottie's recreation of Madeleine seems to succeed. The traditional pattern of transgression, recognition, and redemption has been overturned—Judy looks like she will get away with murder, and Scottie, with his obsessive remaking. Then the nun appears and Judy tumbles to her death. The nun's appearance seems both realistic and self-consciously tacked on to the film. Although the death from the bell tower has certainly been set up, the dominant dramatic force throughout the second half of the film is the question of Scottie's relationship to Judy. Their final embrace seems to resolve the dilemma, but this would be a disorienting resolution. If they make it together, how are we to take the murder and the illicit perversity of Scottie? Does crime actually pay? Yes and no; Judy's death implies "no." But suppose we don't read the nun's appearance with the same sense of realism as we did in the rest of the film? Suppose we have a sense that some agency outside of the fictive world told her to come in, as if Hitchcock quite boldly is saying, "It is time to end the film now and to restore order." Then would the message of the film be that crime does not pay? Or would we be getting a much richer, more self-conscious and fascinatingly ambiguous message that seems to be primly acceptable, while at the same time winks at the simple morality of more traditional endings? Such a possibility takes us out of the realm of plausible storytelling and leaves us with a lingering, overt, and much more bitter perception of the decorative veneer of story closure and its attendant romance.

Psycho, too, provides an interesting example of what happens when the apparent structural pattern is turned around. Much has been written about how Janet Leigh's murder gains particular power because it breaks the genre expectation that the main character will survive. But the murder does something else. By breaking the apparent dramatic drive of the story, it leaves us confused, uncertain what to look for or whom to follow. Left on our own, the dark tonalities of the film rise to the foreground and we feel a loss of direction that makes us even more anxious than the murders themselves would warrant.

Although he twists our expectations, Hitchcock still works within (and at times against) classic narrative cinema. A much more extreme example can be seen in Antonioni's *L'Eclisse* (*Eclipse*). This film, which charts a skittish love affair between Vittoria, a nervous woman played by Monica Vitti, and an unimaginative stockbroker, is more about urban space and how it distorts intimacy than it is about character and relationships. The lovers meet twice at the same intersection. Both times, nothing appears to happen between them; instead, the camera seems more interested in the surroundings—a race horse trotting by, the emptiness of the streets, the permanence of the physical location in contrast to the tentativeness of the characters. The camera, far from being neutral, regards the lovers with the same sense of formal distance with which it regards everything else; hence, the dominant emotional force comes from the camera, not from the characters. By the second visit, Vittoria senses that there is a relationship between this desolation and her own life. It's almost as if she is becoming aware of the camera's distance.

Toward the end of the film, the lovers agree to meet at the intersection for a third time. They never show up, but Antonioni does. In a famous 8-minute sequence, he films the intersection as it appears without the lovers.

It slowly darkens and the streetlights come on (representing an actual eclipse or merely dusk, we never know). Over the sparse electronic music, the shots become increasingly abstracted and fragmentary until the sequence ends with an extreme close-up of a light bulb going on, which then dissolves into the grain of the film. The characters have disappeared; they are not important anymore. What had been a narrative film becomes an experimental one—the dramatic voice is completely taken over by the narrative. The only logic informing the shots is the filmmaker's. There appears to be no fictive world, only a lyrical documentary of the street.

This ending is surprisingly powerful. Although the characters do not appear, somehow the filmmaking has taken on the characters' feelings. Or, more accurately, the characters have taken on the feelings expressed all along by the filmmaking. The devolution of image in the last sequence seems to be a direct personal expression of the filmmaker's sense of the ineffability of emotional experience against the mass meaninglessness of the landscape. The character and the narrator have merged.

Conclusion

We have used the distinction between dramatic and narrative voice to talk about the relative foregrounding of the organizing agency in the story. We note that all films use a combination of these two voices. Mainstream filmmaking tends to follow Henry James's edict for literature—"Dramatize, dramatize, dramatize"—and particularly emphasizes the effaced narrator and the character's narration of his own story by using the point-of-view sequence and the eye match.

We suggest that the independent filmmaker who wants her voice to be heard tip the scales back toward emphasizing the narrative voice. This requires finding ways to uncouple traditional structure's one-to-one linkage with plot. We have demonstrated that such uncoupling requires only the slightest shift in balance, as in Hitchcock's *Vertigo*, or a great commitment to almost lyric experimentation, as in Antonioni's *L'Eclisse*.

References

1. David Bordwell, Janet Staiger, and Kristin Thompson, *The Classical Hollywood Cinema, Film Style and Mode of Production to 1960* (New York: Columbia University Press, 1985), 12.
2. Of course, it can be traced back to Aristotle, but as Erich Auerbach points out in *Mimesis: The Representation of Reality in Western Literature* (translated from the German by Willard Trask, Garden City, NY: Doubleday, 1957), the combining of "low mimetic forms" and tragic forms, which define what we call realism, comes after the French Revolution.

3. In *Narration in the Fiction Film* by David Bordwell (Madison, WI: University of Wisconsin Press, 1987). David Bordwell has an interesting set of chapters that contrast the dramatic model of narration with the more narrative model. He concludes that neither model is theoretically satisfactory; a conclusion with which we agree, although we suspect there will never be a fully satisfactory way to talk about this from the writer's perspective.

4. George Eliot, *Middlemarch* (New York: Penguin Books, 1979), 25.

5. Henry James, *The Ambassadors* (London: Penguin Books, 1974), 5.

6. Ibid., 5.

7. We are simplifying very complex material in order to present it here. We don't want to imply that the narrator outside the story has been replaced by Strether, only that another level of narration has been cloned (Strether's), which allows the narrator outside the story (there must always be one) to be less evident. These assumptions of the objective, non-commenting narrator also came under attack in literature. A pivotal book, Wayne Booth's *The Rhetoric of Fiction* (Chicago: University of Chicago Press, 1961) demonstrates just how involved the so-called invisible narrators actually are.

8. Rudolf Arnheim made a more general instance of this argument in his book *Film As Art* (Berkeley: University of California Press, 1957), but he was dealing with experimental film and the whole question of modifying the image per se. We are dealing with a narrative situation rather than experimental film and will suggest that this may be done by story construction.

27

■ ■ ■ ■ ■ ■ ■ ■

Digital Features

About one year after the dot-com crash, the first crest of excitement over digital features had passed. Whether this was a reflection on the films at that time or on a culture oversaturated by the digital medium, few believed that the long-term outlook for digital features would dim. The question became what kind of films the wide-scale availability of digital features would bring. At the time, we proposed least three different categories:

1. High-end features that push the technologies and budget to create smoothly rendered fantasies. These features will allow the making of ever more constructed worlds at the content level, although the visual styles that communicate these worlds will remain conservative.
2. Mainstream features that depend on standardized high-end, digital production technology, and ultimately widespread digital projection. These video films will replace features as we know them, but there is little that can be done creatively in this style that cannot be done on film, and for such productions, the savings that digital video might bring are a minimal element in the budget.
3. Independent features made in digital video. These independent features can be divided into those that might have been shot on film, but for financial reasons are not, and those that are conceived from the ground up as digital features, and whose writing and design are constructed around the particular aesthetic of digital video.

At the time of writing the present edition of this book, the digital revolution has developed...witness *Star Wars: Episode III – Revenge of the Sith*. In this chapter, we look at the early independent features constructed to take advantage of the aesthetic of digital video. However, we should start with a large caveat. In other chapters, in discussing specific techniques, we have pointed to alternative films that use those techniques to create mature, well-conceived artistic films. With early digital features, we cannot be so definitive. Some films reach this level, but most of the films that we consider in this chapter are those that hint at, but may not have fully realized, the possibilities of the digital format. We examine these as precursors of what has evolved and then consider how the writer might design for digital video format today.

Of course, our focus is the story. But how story differs in digital features will take a little untangling. The excitement over digital features has concentrated on issues such as economics, projection, shooting style, lighting, digital manipulation, and transfer back to film; the script has not received as much attention. But, if we are to consider features that seek to develop a style or point of view based on digital imagery, we need to ask how best to construct stories for them.

So, what does a writer need to know about digital imagery to write digital features? How does this compare with what a writer needs to know about film? As we have noted, although the mainstream screenplay writer has to learn to think in terms of the flow of visualized moments that make up the film, she describes these images through linguistic syntax, not through the technical description of camera angles. In the very personal media-making that we talk about in Chapter 28, the distinction between writer and director frequently breaks down completely as the writer constructs a framework to build a film within. By contrast, in the video examples we will look at first, the most important thing is for the writer to understand the different cultural uses of film and video and to structure a script that takes advantage of them. This goes beyond technology and deals with a sensitivity to how the media function in our society. Rather than worrying about, say, the difference between a wide or a telephoto lens, the writer of digital features should be aware of distinctions of usage and convention that differentiate genres such as video as home record, video as diary, video as cheap ad, video as local news feature, and video as investigative television. And the writer should be aware of these or other video conventions in contrast to those of different film styles, such as the look of the wide-screen 35-millimeter feature film or that of the academy frame of the 16-millimeter student film.

Writing for video features can be far more like constructing similes between story meaning and self-conscious camera styles than is traditional film writing. Rather than worry about the technical details, the writer cites the point or usage of the medium. A description of an exaggerated voiceover might include the text and then add, "As in a cheap car dealership ad shown on late night cable TV." A character's use of an amateur video camera in a film might be described as, "We look through the viewfinder of camera as Eddy wildly pans around the room, not lingering long enough on any one character for us to become oriented. He zooms further in, searching for something. Now all we see are details. Frustrated, he sweeps the camera once more across the room, then he snaps it off." The emphasis is not only on what's revealed by the action but also on how the character's use of the camera reveals the character to us and on what it shows us about her comfort in, and mastery of, the video culture in which she lives.

Intertextuality vs. Formalism

Before we go forward, let us consider more broadly the implications of the preceding discussion. When we talked about writing for film in Chapter 17, we made a distinction between the shooting script and the screenplay. The shooting script requires a very specific sense of film language, because the writer indicates shot by shot how a film would be put together, whereas while the screenplay, which is a much less technical form, requires that the writer learn to see the movie run in her head and then find the language to convey this information to the reader. Not only both of these forms but also our discussion of them focused on the formal elements of film—that is, how the writer uses specific blocking or shots to convey meaning within the context of this particular film.

Much has changed in the years since the first edition of *Alternative Scriptwriting* was published. Not only have we seen films that incorporate video, but a much more intertextual, post-modern critical approach[1] has come to dominate the way we talk about film and the broader culture. Even films that do not use video are much more dependent on their relationship with other films, genres, and cultural elements to generate meaning. Because we don't all interpret this relationship in the same way, meanings have become much more open.

Video—particularly those films that use both film and video—has taken this dependence much further. While Although there are many formal differences between film and video images—film allows wider shots with greater detail, more subtlety in color, and a greater contrast range than does video—they have led to small adjustments in framing rather than to a radical rethinking of classic storytelling. Instead, the differences appear in the way that film and video scenes reference other uses of their respective media, or in the difference between production circumstances—we understand that a slick, well-made, 35-millimeter studio film implies a different level of planning, production team, and economic base than does a handheld, small-format video. Hence, the contrast between film and video is less in the film language per se and more in the cultural connotations that each medium carries.

This relates to authority. Whether true or not, studio productions tend to connote corporate authority, great production control, and the primacy of market over vision; hence, it is not surprising that the actual making of images in most films is presented as beyond the character's control. Put another way, film characters are almost always objects of, rather than the "creators" of, the shot. The classical point-of-view sequence provides an illustration of this. There are many variations, but the basic model includes a combination of a shot that shows a character looking, a shot that reveals what a character is seeing, and a shot that indicates the character's reaction. These sequences are generally shot with the camera near, but not fully on, the axis between the character and what she is seeing. The effect of this is to split responsibility for the point of view—the character is establishing the optical position of the camera and supplying the reaction, but the filmmaker remains responsible for the shot.

In small-format video, this separation may be broken down. The camera may not only represent the character's point of view—it may literally be perched on her shoulder. Not only is the camera light enough to be manipulated by one person, but also the economic system of creating and reproducing video images makes the format accessible to individuals. The power of image-making is available to the consumer—media literacy movements, community video outlets, and public-access stations around the country have altered our culture. Translated to narrative films, this means that we can imagine characters who are able, by making contrasting[2] images on their own, to contest with the filmmaker for control of the story.

Mixed Media

We will start by looking at two films that use both film and video or regular video in contrast to video designed to look like film. In these examples, the juxtaposition of media is designed into the film at the story level and shapes its narrative structure. *The Last Broadcast* was shot in Digital Video (DV), edited on Adobe Premiere, and released through satellite in October 1998. It preceded *The Blair Witch Project* both in release date and in its structuring a story that "justifies" its video look.

The Last Broadcast purports to be an investigative report of the unexplained deaths of two public-access reporters covering the Jersey Devil, a mythical figure said to inhabit the Southern New Jersey Pine Barrens. All but the last 5 minutes of the film are shot in the style of the video footage that is supposed to make up the investigative report we are watching—this includes the original, first-person footage gathered by the public-access crew, documentary interviews, reconstruction of damaged video footage taken from the scene, and stand-ups developed by the filmmaker constructing the investigative report. The first-person footage is quite self-conscious, because it explicitly references the reporter/videomaker's personal desire to get to the bottom of the story; still, we sense that something is going on that is not accounted for by the conceit of the reporter getting the story. The last 5 minutes reveal what this is: suddenly the film changes perspective, the implied authority controlling the camera switches to an outside voice (we know this, because we see the reporter in long-shot as a character rather than as the narrator who controls the camera), the aspect ratio changes to widescreen, and the colors become muted and more film-like. This happens right at the moment when we learn that the killer is in fact the reporter—thereby doubling the story's meaning. The shift to the outside perspective of "film" does not merely reveal the killer but exposes the limits of the video broadcast perspective.

In a film like *The Last Broadcast*, digital production allows us to rethink the use of point of view. Not only does point of view show us the spatial approximation of what the point-of-view character can see within the fictive world, but it also represents what the character as narrator is choosing to show us (and of course what the writer thinks the character would be likely to show us). Thus, the writer has an additional expressive tool to work with— almost as if she were writing a novel from entirely within a character's head; what is shown (or, in most cases, hidden) by the character is as important as what happens.

Once introduced, this contrast in voices between what the filmmaker and what the character show us becomes a major dynamic driving the story. Whatever else the writer does, she must play out the audience's expectation that something is being shaped by this. As the character controlling the camera has an agenda, a subtext, the story maintains interest precisely, because we in the audience are invited to engage it, to make inferences about why things are being presented to us in exactly this way, much in the same way we watch a character's behavior to discover whether there might be more going on than the dialogue reveals. Ultimately, this tension is not sufficiently developed in a film like *The Last Broadcast*. The withholding of the second, or outside, perspective makes it a bit of a one-joke story. Instead of our engaging the double perspective throughout, we are surprised when it appears at the end.

Connected to this is the way the film so neatly ties up its resolution. As long as we suspect that the video voice within the film of *The Last Broadcast* is in tension with some other way of knowing, the use of the video invites our speculation, our sense that there must be something more. This directs us to a number of broader issues, such as the nature of investigative reporting, how individual perspective tends to blur truth, and questions of whether we can ever know these answers. These issues die with the switch to "film." Besides revealing the killer, the resolution of *The Last Broadcast* restores a rather conservative notion of representation—that the low-cost, portable video camera through which the filmmaker/killer has been conducting his investigation is less reliable and less "true" than is the implied "objective" narrative filmmaker who not only uses wide screen, muted color, and smoother shots, but also stands outside the action and reveals all. The idea that this position is only achievable through the shift to "film" has the effect of sanctifying the high-end, impersonal perspective that alternative film is best positioned to critique.

It is precisely because it does not resolve this tension between media that *The Blair Witch Project* takes the potential of using video and film much further. Unlike *The Last Broadcast*, *Blair Witch*, which follows a team of student filmmakers as they attempt to document the elusive Blair Witch, was shot in two medias, black-and-white 16-millimeter film and Hi8 video, and it moves back and forth between them. Initially, the two media have two distinct narrative functions: the video is a personal diary, documenting the student project, for a presumed audience of friends and family, an audience that knows the characters, whereas the film is the product, a more formal media work constructed for a class that has no "outside" knowledge of the filmmakers. The tension between, and ultimate collapse of, these distinctions is one of the conflicts that drive the film.

In *Blair Witch*, Heather's video camera functions as a diary, providing a reflection on the students' desperation as they lose their way in the woods. By the end, this changes. The video camera becomes not so much a diary, reflecting back to the maker, but a means of communication, a message in a bottle to the outside world. We see this shift when Heather apologizes directly to her mother through the video camera. "I just want to apologize to ... my mom and I'm sorry to everyone. I was very naive. ... I am so scared. What was that? I'm scared to close my eyes and I'm scared to open them. I'm going to die out here."[3] This is a moment of extraordinary double address: Heather addresses both the imagined characters within the film's fictive world (her mother and all the people who know her) and us. What makes this so powerful is the directness of this address to the audience. Here we are no longer positioned close, but off to the side, as we would be in a point-of-view sequence. Instead, Heather is speaking to her mother directly through us. She is both in her own story at the same time that she is recording that story. Additionally, we experience the intimacy of the diary combined with the directness of a confession. The closest equivalent to this experience is that of reading an epistolary novel, where a character exists both as a player in the story-world and as the composer of the letters that serve to create the story-world.

The dual media add another level of meaning to *Blair Witch*. In some sense, *Blair Witch* transcends its literal story and becomes a meditation on the contrast between film and video. Although *The Last Broadcast* doesn't introduce the voice of "film" until the last 5 minutes of the story, *Blair Witch* constantly cuts back and forth between the two media, suggesting that the resolution between their perspectives will figure in the closure of the film. The closure in *The Last Broadcast* comes from the "deus ex machina" change in perspective—the sudden introduction of the film voice late in the story. As we mentioned previously, it is an ending that shuts out any additional ambiguity. Once the film voice asserts itself, we have no opportunity to see any other reality than that presented by the film—the outside perspective reveals all. Not only does the story have a complete sense of closure, but the tension between the media is also fully resolved. Video is revealed as transitory, hopelessly inflected by the personal, unable to reveal the true. Film, on the contrary, is presented as the ultimately reliable narrator. The resolution of the story is a resolution of a battle of forms.

When it opens, too, *Blair Witch* suggests that video will be second to film in its reliability as a medium. Film is the voice that is suitable for pronouncement. Reaching the entrance to the forest, Heather stands on Coffin Rock, picks up "The Blair Witch Cult" book, and begins to read with great authority, "They went into the woods prepared to find death, what they found was a desecration to humanity."[4] This is to be the introduction to the film that the students are making. By contrast, video is for behind-the-scenes moments, such as Heather panning around her room, saying, "This is my home. Which I am leaving the comforts of, for the week to explore the Blair Witch."[5] Yet ultimately, the power of *Blair Witch* may come from the way it reveals that film has no more of a monopoly on truth than does video. The film camera teases us with its potential as savior, as evidence of the importance of the project, of the truth that will allow the characters to escape the woods. But when it can reveal no more at the end than that revealed by the home video camera, our sense of media hierarchy is overturned.

Before we move on, we need to note one thing: *Blair Witch* was created out of a series of improvised moments with the video camera. The function of the writer, of course, changes in improvised productions, to the designing of situations and dramatic problems for actors. We have seen this before in other improvised films, but we need to note one difference of great power to the video maker. In a film-based, improvised feature, the improvisation, whether live in front of the camera or developed over time and then "written" to be shot, is an improvisation of performance for the camera. In a film such as *Blair Witch*, we start to see not merely an improvisation of performance for the camera, but improvisation of the camera itself. What is most suggestive in this film is not so much the way the actors participated in developing its content, but rather their active role in developing its narrative voice by their control of the camera.

Mixed Media: Expression of Character or Media Critique?

One thing a writer might want to consider is whether she wishes to use mixed media as an expression of character or as a larger examination of the media. We can see the difference in these approaches by looking at the script and the film[6] of *American Beauty*. *American Beauty* is structured around the last year in the life of Lester Burnham, a suburban trade magazine copywriter who—as a result of the general deterioration of his life and inspired by his sexual fantasies about his daughter's friend Angela—quits his high-pressure job, remakes his life, and seems to find some kind of self-realization before he is abruptly killed. In the script, the story is framed by Lester's daughter Jane and her boyfriend Ricky's trial for Lester's murder. During this trial, Ricky's father, Colonel Fitts, not satisfied that Jane and Ricky will be convicted, turns over to the police a copy of the video tape in which Jane, speaking out of context, seems to commission Ricky to kill her father. When we later learn the circumstances of the killing, we are inclined to even more deeply suspect Colonel Fitts's motives. The film does not include the framing story.

A scene that received much attention when the film came out is the one in which Ricky shows Jane his vision of beauty—a videotape of a plastic bag, caught by the wind and circling in front of a brick wall. By looking at this scene closely, we can see how the video in the script functions much more as a media critique than it does in the movie, where it used as a revelation of character. In the script, after Ricky says "Want to see the most beautiful thing I've ever filmed?" we cut to a description of the video of the plastic bag. The description of its action is fairly neutral, "We follow it as the wind carries it in a circle around us, sometimes whipping it around violently, or, without warning, sending it soaring skyward, then letting it float gracefully gown to the ground...." Then we go to Jane sitting on the bed, watching "Ricky's WIDE-SCREEN TV, her brow furrowed, *trying to figure out why this is beautiful*" [italics mine].[7] Not certain she can find an answer in the image, Jane turns to Ricky, watching the cold intensity of his fascination. It is only then, as a result of her watching him, they connect. Thus, the video itself is separated out from the plotting; it is removed from serving as merely the means by which two characters get together. In fact, the possibility is raised that the video might be totally opaque, a form of impenetrable adolescent poetry that communicates nothing to Jane. Not only does the video not serve to connect them, but the script is also raising questions about aesthetics and truth. This critique of video runs through the rest of the script—the Court TV presentation of Jane and Ricky's trial, the highlighting of the incriminating lines in the video, the Colonel's use of the video as a weapon—the whole fact of video is presented as something as dangerous as it is beautiful, as much a manipulator as a recorder of reality.

In the film, video functions quite differently. After Ricky asks Jane if she wants to see something beautiful, we cut to a shot from behind of the two characters watching the TV image. The image plays, the camera gradually pushes in, and much of the dialogue runs over this. By the time we cut around in front of the characters and Jane turns to Ricky, the image has done its work and she looks at him with awe. Unlike the script, which suggests that she is responding to Ricky's explanation of what the video means to him rather than the video itself, her response in the movie is one of being moved by the images themselves and then connecting them to Ricky. The feeling is that the film's voice is endorsing the beauty of the video by showing us how deeply it affects the story's most sympathetic character. Taken along with the lack of the courtroom frame, the lack of the video serving as evidence, and the diminished role for Colonel Fitts, video is presented in the film as something that unambiguously expresses our deepest sense of beauty.

In the film, Ricky's artistic vision is contained; it functions like a character's painting or photograph might in a traditional film—as a way of learning something about that person rather than as some consideration of the medium itself. In the script, however, the writer has given the video some range to declare itself as a medium in its own right. It may be evidence of beauty or manipulation—the script is not quite clear—but video as a medium is shown to have power to challenge our easy assumptions about it.

Although it probably does not take this critique far enough—much of the video has the same farcical quality as does the surrounding film—the script does demonstrate how a writer can address the particular qualities of the video medium itself.

To explore this further, let's contrast *American Beauty* with Atom Egoyan's film *Calendar*. With very few exceptions, *Calendar* uses just three perspectives to tell the story of a photographer and his wife, both of Armenian origin who go back to Armenia to photograph picturesque churches for a photo calendar. Once there, they are joined by an Armenian guide. In translating the guide's loving accounts of the churches, the wife becomes aware of her husband's lack of interest in their common history. The film takes place over the following year when the husband, having returned without his wife, seems to be auditioning young women who must make an imaginary phone call. As they speak, we see the calendar of the Armenian churches, marking the progression of the year, in the background. The story is told through the following three perspectives:

1. The locked-down, picture-postcard shots of Armenian churches, all classically composed and lit.
2. Videotape, taken almost entirely by the husband, of his wife and the guide in Armenia.
3. Formal shots of the photographer as he auditions women, one a month, for something (we do not know what) that involves a fictional phone conversation.

The locked-down camera in the first perspective circumscribes static frames of picture-postcard beauty through which the wife and the guide pass. The camera never moves to follow them. This contrasts with the video camera in the second perspective, which is handheld, free, and clearly reflects the interest of the photographer, its operator. Egoyan has said he wanted to deal with three levels of national consciousness: nationalist, diasporan, and assimilationist,[8] which he represents through the three major characters. He also seems to position the characters in terms of their relationship to verbal and visual language. The guide, the nationalist, is verbal, relaxed. The wife, the diasporan, mediates between language and image. The husband, while visually in control, seems verbally so uptight that he might almost be mute.

Early in the film, we watch a long video shot taken through a car window as the car drives by what seems to be an endless herd of sheep. The movement of the car, the endless flow of sheep, and the softer focus of the video all create a hypnotic effect on the viewer. This image returns several times and suggests the husband's control of the film. Yet at the movie's conclusion, we learn through the wife's letters that it was during this moment with the sheep that the guide put his hand on hers. The woman contrasts the intensity with which the guide gripped her hand to that with which the photographer gripped the camera.

Watching the wife and guide move through the formal compositions of the churches, we are able to infer that something is going on between them. But the husband is unable to see or respond to this, because his vision is fixed by his need to see everything through a camera. The film explores the husband's loss, but even more it examines the limits of understanding the world through the various prisms of image making, by demonstrating that the husband's control of the camera has missed the true subject of his trip.

In *American Beauty*, the film is not interested in media itself but concentrates on using video to communicate Ricky's character. It searches not for the essence of the form but for what it allows us to see—for example, the sequence where Ricky controls the video images so that he can see Jane in her bedroom, rather than the posing Angela, who seeks to "steal" his view. *Calendar*, on the contrary, foregrounds the difference between experience and a mediated, composed view of reality. The locked-down, "professional" images of the churches and the casual video image of the sheep are both shown to miss the point. The film flips the priorities of *American Beauty*. Rather than use form to articulate character, the husband's dependence on media becomes a critique on the limitations of mediated form itself.

Four Frames at a Time

Time Code (also marketed as *Timecode*) presents us with a screen divided into quadrants, with each quadrant following a converging line of action in real time. The multiple-image effect has been used in other films, most notably *Klute* and *Bullitt*, in which the screen is fragmented into an increasing number of divisions, and, of course, a two-screen split was once the conventional staple for representing telephone conversations. The multiple-image effect has also been used in experimental films whose purpose is not to develop a narrative line but to explore visual textures in relationship to one another. What makes it different in *Time Code* are the extended long takes, the sustained narrative line, and the use of a television shooting style that concentrates on close and mid-shots. Also, unlike most other examples, *Time Code* sustains four separate sound tracks; in fact, the sound tracks are so important that the mix between them is used to modulate and direct our attention to a specific set of images.

The choice of four images not only splits the screen, but it also mirrors four-part harmony, the most fundamental pattern of Western music. Developing this as a design motif, writer-director Mike Figgis has explained that he used "music paper, a string quartet format where each bar line represented one minute of real time."[9] In the published examples of his script, we can see the way red lines run through the score to signify the major plot action or melody. For instance, we can see red lines joining all the staffs at the point where the earthquakes strike and two red marks over each other in the place where a character from one story calls the other. When the plot is vamping in one or more particular staffs, something less specific—*DV Magazine* calls it "improvised background dialog, or rhythm, if you like"[10]—fills the score.

So how do these voices or lines play against one another? What do we get from their simultaneous presence on the screen that we would not get if they were arranged sequentially? Since the film refers us to music, let's look that way. Think of opera (it may take some getting used to, but opera, along with dance—both forms that abstract out from story—have much to teach filmmakers). Get a tape of Mozart's *Marriage of Figaro* and listen to the finale of the second act, a scene that has up to eight voices, all singing at once. Even if you do not know the story, after a few hearings, you will be able to track the dramatic line of the scene. With the score open in front of you, you can see, almost as if they were marked with the red lines of Figgis's script, quite clearly the dramatic demarcations—here the character of Figaro is isolated and protesting his innocence, while at this point Susanna and the Countess urge the Count to get on with Figaro and Susanna's wedding, and then later on, the place where the gardener takes the Count aside, and so on. What makes this form work, however, is not merely that we can track the line but that the simultaneity of the voices, even as they are fighting one another, creates a musical whole that melds the constant shifting story tensions into a unity of sound that is greater than any one moment or one line of character. This harmonic whole is what lifts at times rather banal opera stories (*Figaro* is clearly an exception—very few opera libretti are much more complex than basic melodrama or comedies of mistaken identity) above the literal to something whose form speaks beyond the limitations of story.

The potential power, then, of *Time Code* lies in a similar dynamic relationship between the horizontal or plotted line of the action unfolding in time and the vertical or harmonic whole of the four images across the screen. If this were achieved, it would not only create a totality that goes beyond the individual stories but would suggest that *Time Code* permits a more open reading than that of mainstream film. Like in music, we would find we are striking a different balance between the melody and the harmony every time we watch *Time Code*; sometimes our attention would focus on the melody, the plot as expressed in one of the quadrants at a time; other times we would concentrate on the harmony, the relationship of each quadrant to the whole. In fact, Mike Figgis seems to want to encourage this, saying, "I don't believe in one interpretation—that's not rich enough for us today."[11] And one of the advertising taglines for the film was, "Who do you want to watch?"

The threshold for where a work opens itself up to many interpretations is, of course, a subjective experience that will vary for each of us. For us, however, *Time Code* does not achieve the multiple interpretations that Mike Figgis seems to be striving for, precisely because it substitutes narrative coherence for the power of the commenting or contrasting voices. At any given time, we are clearly directed to follow one of the four stories, none of which ever seems to rise above the limited self-obsession of the characters. The fact that the film is a Hollywood insider story only makes this limited perspective seem more hermetic.

Let's examine one transition by way of an example: There is a critical scene when, after making love, the aspiring actress Rose asks her lover, the producer Alex, to get her an audition (call this quadrant A). In the other screen quadrants, we see Lauren, the lover whom Rose is betraying, restlessly waiting in her limo listening to Rose through a bug (quadrant B), while the security guard wanders off in a daze (quadrant C), and the aspiring actress Emma passes through a bookstore into the bathroom (quadrant D). After the scene between Rose and Alex resolves, Emma in quadrant D looks into a bathroom mirror and begins to cry.

There is plenty of story here. Yet it is a sequential, not a simultaneous, story. Rose's failure to get an audition in quadrant A is the key story beat. Everything else, her lover, Lauren's listening in, Emma passing the bookstore, and, of course, the security guard, is secondary. These moments would have functioned just as well had they been cutaways. Seeing them at the same time as we see Rose adds little to the scene, because the tension they generate is horizontal, time- or story-based, rather than vertical, providing a timeless spatial commentary on the action. After the scene between Rose and Alex resolves, we could just as well cut to the sequence where Emma looks in the bathroom mirror and begins to cry. Nothing in this is really simultaneous, and nothing would not work if it were structured as interwoven stories, presented consecutively as they would be in a script such as *Short Cuts* (see Chapter 26).

When we compare *Time Code* to Mozart, we are, of course, unfairly putting up an enduring work with one of the first attempts at developing a new film form, but this may be a result of our excitement in considering what a multi-framed, long-take production might open up for the filmmaker. Success in this will depend on developing the harmonic relationship between the screens as well as the plotted forward line. If we imagine Mozart's second-act finale stretched out sequentially, without all the voices weaving back and forth between one another, we would be left with a thin schematic of the opera. If we imagine *Time Code* stretched out that way, with one quadrant after the other filling the entire frame, we would not lose much. We encourage the video writers and directors of the future to construct sufficient complexity and tension between the screens, so that a multi-framed story of the future might truly fill us with wonder.

Voice in Digital Features

In Chapter 22, we talked about narrative and dramatic voices, identifying the former as the perspective of the agent (the narrator) that organizes the story, and the latter as that of the characters whose experience we enter. All stories represent some combination of these voices; their balance has a large role in determining how the story affects us. Video provides an expressive tool that allows us to reset this balance. We can see this in a film such as *Festen* (*The Celebration*), written and directed by Thomas Vinterberg. *The Celebration* is a self-proclaimed Dogma 95 (a filmmaking ideology instituted in 1995) film. However seriously we take Vinterberg's adherence to it, the Dogma manifesto, a self-conscious declaration of filmmaking principles written by Danish media maker Lars von Trier along with Vinterberg, suggests something about the appeal of video features. The manifesto, the so-called vow of chastity, has a number of strictures, including that films should[12]:

1. Be shot on location.
2. Use direct sound.
3. Use handheld cameras.
4. Use only color film. (Special lighting is not acceptable.)
5. Forbid optical work and filters.
6. Use no superficial action.
7. Tell stories set in the here and now.
8. Avoid genre stories.
9. Be shot using academy ratio [the 1.33:1 ratio used in standard broadcast TV, as opposed to the wide-screen ratio (usually 1.85:1 or higher) seen in most theaters].
10. Not credit directors.

Taken together, these principles suggest a desire to re-embrace cinematic materialism—the concept that the physical act of shooting, the indexical nature of the photographic or videographic image, be preserved in the making of the film. This cleansing of filmmaking from the artificiality of the studio (forbidding the use of sets and the sweetening of sound, and avoiding smooth camera moves, heightened lighting, and special effects) is not new to film history—we see it, for example, in Italian neo-realism and in the French New Wave's reaction to the highly produced, tony French studio film. The impulse seems to be to reclaim the signifying act, the camera's explicit narrative presence.

Video provides a surprisingly powerful way to do this. The video image, particularly when it contains a light source in the frame, can have a certain thickness, almost a translucency, that film does not have. Whether this will remain a distinct video signature or become so conventionalized is hardly noticed, which we do not yet know, but at least it has expressive qualities that the screenwriter may well use. *The Celebration* plays simultaneously with two distinct moods. The dominant mood of satire, an over-the-top celebration of a patriarch's sixtieth birthday, is contrasted with a more character-based mood played out through Christian, who struggles with the recent death of his twin sister. He finally announces to the assembled guests that her suicide was to avoid continued, unwanted sexual advances by the very patriarch for whom the party is being held. No one seems overly concerned. The tragedy as experienced by Christian is constantly contrasted with the party, for whom this announcement is nothing more than a bit of inconvenience.

The section we will look at occurs right after Christian's revelation, when the guests begin to dance. This transition from drama to farce is covered by a close shot of a match lighting a candle. The resultant lens flares create a net, rays or fibers of light between us and the candle. As the music starts, the camera pans across a large, empty room to the dancers at the other end. The focus pull is extreme and obvious as the automatic mechanism of the video camera snaps in. Even at this distance, the lens flares serve to sculpt the intervening space, creating a sense of substance between the camera and the subject. Vinterberg cuts. The camera angles up at the dancers toward a candle-lit chandelier. The light scatters. The air feels thick and congested.

The thickness of imagery seems to capture the paradoxical quality of the video. At one level, the images are more real than are those in film, in that they seem causal, unlit, almost accidental—the kind of pictures that anyone would take. But maybe not. After all, our interpretation of reality is a conventional process. What we take for reality in feature films tends to be well-lit, smoothly shot images backed by carefully laid-in ambient sound, so, by contrast, these apparently crude video images actually seem more stylized, further away from experience, more painterly. We note this same contrast, for instance, in an early shot of Christian walking in the sun. The shot seems both thrown-off, immediate in its casualness and almost garish in the neon contrast of his red florid flesh tones to the sky's cobalt blue. This doubling of effect—apparently real, yet artificially heightened—seems key to the way video can work on us. Later, we are shown a dream sequence between Christian and his dead sister, lit by the flame of a cigarette lighter that Christian holds in his hand. Brother and sister float in a pool of blackness; the inconsistency of the flame alternately heightens and diminishes their presence, their images moving into and out of focus. The lighter itself has a nimbus around it—the light feels substantial, almost as if we can grasp it. At times, all we see is the flame suspended in darkness.

Both of these scenes suggest something of the particle effect we see in many mainstream films; the difference being that the particle effect is motivated from fog or dust that might be in the fictional environment, whereas the quality of light in *The Celebration* is motivated by the filmmaking process. It is narrative or more explicitly expressionistic in origin. Thus, the particle effect makes us feel more deeply the emotional values coming from the scene, whereas the digital thickness directs our attention to the filmmaker's voice or perspective.

There is something about the way this digital thickness captures both the natural and the constructed, the immediate and the theatrical that makes it distinct. This is where the screenwriter of digital features might best position herself—the paradox of photographic styles virtually demands a juxtaposition of genres. A script that is either all "real" or "parodic" would not speak the same language as does this visual voice. Exaggerating the pull between the dramatic and the narrative is central to this style of filmmaking. This balance of contrasting voices must be carefully maintained. We need to feel that, at some level, there is both a story world that we can enter, along with a narrative force pulling us away. In some cases, the narrative voice is so strong that we lose this balance, and the film becomes overcontrolled. Once this happens, the narrative agent can do whatever it wants with the story, and, as the film has not generated any life of its own, we won't care.

We see this in Hal Hartley's *The Book of Life*, which carries the video look to the extreme. Shots are smudged by movement captured at low shutter speed, the edges of the details blend together, and the images lose their specificity. At other times, scenes are shot in natural light against windows that create contrast ratios too great for video, so that details go black or are washed out. Indeed, we are more aware of light itself than of individual characters. The images are both beautiful and abstracted by the lack of detail. Characters seem to be moving through a sea of light, displacing it and then letting it fall back into place. It isn't the look but the lack of tonal contrast that limits the resonance of the film. *The Book of Life* is resolutely allegorical. It tells the story of Christ's decision to spare the world on the last day of the twentieth century. The allegory is established immediately when the first character we meet, the airport preacher as John the Baptist, turns and recognizes the returning Christ, and it is reinforced by Christ's voiceover, which is suitably abstract, "I could never get used to that part of the job. The power and the glory. The divine vengeance." The supporting cast includes characters named Magdalena, Satan, the true believer, and the martyr.

Because the images are so abstract and the quality of light so much a physical presence, *The Book of Life* does not quite exist on a "real" plane. We watch and cannot quite penetrate the images. Neither can we get very deep into the story, which, because it is largely a theological discussion, gives us very little in terms of character involvement. The abstraction of the images and the allegorical nature of the story work to reinforce one another rather than to create the contrast that would drive the story. The film never appears to be fully grounded. Nor does it ever surprise us. We go passively to where the narrator takes us, but, as in other overdetermined stories, we are not quite convinced by the journey.

Conclusion

Video used in feature films is a means of production, not necessarily an aesthetic. At the high end, using customized cameras, it has been used to construct fantasy images for films such as *Star Wars: Episode III— Revenge of the Sith*, whereas at the low end, using broadcast and even consumer technology, it is being substituted as a low-budget alternative for stories better made as films.

In this chapter, we have concentrated on video as a form in itself, one that uses its distinct visual qualities to define its own aesthetic. The aesthetic is not so much one that rejects or transforms feature film's narrative language, but rather one that builds on its distinct cultural resonance or uses its juxtaposition of the causal and the manipulated to contrast genre and style.

In films such as *The Blair Witch Project*, *American Beauty*, and *Calendar*, we have seen how the video look is contrasted to that of film, whereas in *The Celebration* and *The Book of Life*, we have studied how the look itself encourages tension between genre and voice. In either case, like most other alternative forms, these shifts evoke a distinct narrative voice that becomes a major part of the story. They direct our attention into the fictional world, not from the perspective of the omniscient film production entity wielding the apparatus of production, but through the eyes of characters in the field wielding consumer video gear or the eyes of makers who ask us to re-see space, the apparent emptiness around us, itself.

References

1. This approach had been critically dominant even before the first edition of *Alternative Scriptwriting* appeared, but it had not had much direct effect on screenwriting. Now, it is part of almost all story evaluations.
2. Of course, this is a conventional practice. No contrasting image in a film is literally put there by a character, but still we recognize that it might contrast with the film's narrative agent.
3. D. Myrick and E. Sánchez, *The Blair Witch Project*, 1999, accessed December 20, 2012, http://sfy.ru/sfy.html?script=blair_ witch
4. Ibid.
5. Ibid.
6. I would like to thank my student, Marsha Walker, for bringing this film to my attention.
7. A. Ball, *American Beauty* (1998) 76, accessed December 20, 2012, http://www.script-o-rama.com/snazzy/dircut.html.
8. Quoted in J. Rosenbaum, *Tribal Trouble*, 1995, accessed December 20, 2012, http://members.cruzio.com/~akreyche/ttrbl.html#topttrbl.
9. K. Reed, "Time Code," *DV Magazine*, 2000. Originally online at http://www.dv.com/magazine/2000/0800/reed0800.html (now available through the Internet Archive Wayback Machine at http://www.archive.org/web/web.php).
10. Ibid.
11. "*Time Code*: Digital Storytelling in 4/4 Time," 2000. Originally online at http://www.apple.com/hotnews/articles/2000/04/timecode (now available through the Internet Archive Wayback Machine at http://www.archive.org/web/web.php).
12. L. v. Trier and T. Vinterberg, *The Vow of Chastity* (1995), accessed December 20, 2012, http://pov.imv.au.dk/Issue_10/section_1/artc1A.html.

28

Writing the
Narrative Voice

In this chapter, we look at some of the practical consequences of placing the narrative voice in the foreground. However, we need to make one warning before we go on. As we said earlier in the book, most of the traditional screenwriting rules are designed to feature the dramatic voice. Because we will be looking instead at the narrative voice, some of the ideas in this chapter will not only seem different but will also be a violation of those traditional rules. This is intentional. Remember, the purpose of this book is not to ask you to adopt all these thoughts on alternative screenwriting but to make you aware of what is possible, so that you might look further. Then, if you decide to write a mainstream script, you make a conscious decision to do so.

Openings

Exposition in Mainstream Scripts

The beginning of any story must establish the tone, the relationships between the characters, and any necessary prior history (called *backstory*). Exposition is traditionally handled as invisibly as possible—the action is never stopped to explain backstory. This treatment of exposition is based on two concerns:

1. You want to keep up story interest by moving forward, even when conveying past information.
2. You want to preserve the realism of the dramatic voice.

If the convention is that characters are being inadvertently observed in their day-to-day activities (if you assume they know one another and have a common past), then the characters would have no need to explain their pasts to each other; rather, they would simply act on them. By creating this implied commonality, you allow your audience to project the characters back in time. This gives your film a feeling of extension that goes beyond the 2 hours on the screen.

In practice, the writing of traditional exposition is very difficult, precisely because it must convey information without calling attention to itself. The amount of attention you can get away with varies with which voice you are emphasizing. If you emphasize the dramatic voice (the poet speaking in the voice of the characters), the exposition has to be nearly invisible. When you use the narrative voice (the poet speaking to the audience), you can be quite explicit about the handling of exposition. In *Psycho*, for instance, we have no problem with the subtitle identifying the time and place of the story, because it is superimposed over the opening panoramic shots of Phoenix that move us into Janet Leigh's hotel room. Such a series of shots is overtly narrative. They seem to be saying to us, "At 2:43 P.M. on a typically beautiful day, Friday, December 11th in Phoenix, Arizona, two people have just finished making love in a hotel room." However, if the same title superimposition occurred over the dramatic dialogue scene between Janet Leigh and Anthony Perkins in the lobby of the Bates Motel, we would be annoyed at the authorial intrusion pulling us out of the ongoing drama.

Exposition using the dramatic voice generally comes from character ex-change. When the characters are new to one another, exposition can be quite easy and natural. The customs official in *Niagara* can ask Marilyn Monroe and Joseph Cotton why they are heading to the Canadian side of the border, because we assume this is something that customs officials do. In *Melvin and Howard*, Howard Hughes can ask Melvin Dummar where he's going or what he does for a living, because it is the first time they have met. However, Galvin's drinking buddies in *The Verdict* cannot credibly ask how long he has been a drunk, because we assume they have been drinking together for a long time and have no need to ask.

Exposition may be revealed between characters that know one another by heightening the conflict between them to such an extent that the conveyed information seems less important than does the subtext motivating the conflict. For instance, the angry Mickey, Galvin's ex-partner in *The Verdict*, can reveal that he has been helping Galvin when he yells at the hungover lawyer, "I got you a good case, it's a moneymaker. You do it right and it will take care of you. But I'm through. I'm sorry, Joe, this is the end."[1] This does not feel like naked exposition, because our attention goes to the subtext, the disappointment and disgust that motivates Mickey's outburst. Trying to read Mickey's rage and Galvin's reaction involves us, makes us active viewers. The dialogue has motivation; it does not merely sit there. Only incidentally do we pick up the information.

Another form of exposition is called unreliable direct exposition. We expect a detective story to open with a client presenting a problem to the detective. This may be as up-front as possible; the only thing given is that the information has to be wrong or incomplete. As we, along with the detective, are known to be skeptical, we are actively involved in looking for holes in the story.

We can generalize and say that, except for small amounts of exposition that occur between people who don't know one another (these scenes tend to have little dramatic interest and cannot be sustained), the trick to handling exposition is to misdirect our attention. If the writer develops sufficient conflict between characters, the reader will respond to the subtext, the unspoken tension between them, and absorb expository information without noticing it. If the writer doesn't develop conflict, the dramatic voice is broken, and the reader can almost see the writer speaking directly and letting the reader in on what he needs to know and what the writer failed to dramatize.

Exposition in Alternative Scripts

Predictably, as many alternative films want to heighten the narrative voice, they don't hesitate to use blatant exposition that intention-ally lets us know that we are watching a film. In *She's Gotta Have It*, we push in on Nola Darling's bed as she sits up. Initially, we may read this move as a narrative device (the filmmaker is bringing us in) leading into a dramatic scene (we expect Nola to react to someone in her room). But instead of responding to another character, Nola speaks into the lens, announcing her position in the movie. "I want you to know the only reason I'm consenting to this is be-cause I wish to clear my name, not that I care what people think, but enough is enough.'" Not only is information placed in the foreground even in this apparently dramatic mode, but also the whole convention of realistic cinema is exposed by Nola's looking into the camera and speaking directly to us.

In *Blue Velvet*, the only thing we know about the hero's father, Mr. Beaumont, comes from what we infer from the montage of idealized small-town life that opens the film. Presumably, Mr. Beaumont is the personification of this innocence. The narrative voice is placed so much in the foreground, is so intent on making us see the connections it wants us to see (rather than those we infer from the action), that, as Mr. Beaumont has his stroke, the camera glides away from him and sneaks up on the insects busily fighting on the grass below. As the insects function as symbols rather than as antagonists (they didn't cause the stroke), the camera movement serves not so much to introduce conflict in the story, but more to make a self-conscious metaphor by comparing the generalized small-town innocence to the brutal nature that lurks below. Because the shot is so self-conscious, we view it as a wink at us, a connection made between filmmaker and audience, at the expense of the characters in the film.

The Location of Conflict

Let's carry this idea of winking a little further. When Ben runs out of the party in *The Graduate*, the camera holds for a moment on Mrs. Robinson watching greedily from behind. She looks at Ben, not at us; if we had to draw a line to detail the tension of the scene, we would draw it from her look to Ben's departing back. The tension remains with the protagonists and antagonists who inhabit the story world. But the tension does not have to remain imbedded in the fictive world. We can shift the conflict so that it runs between the characters in the story and the narrator, who frequently seems to stand in for us. *Blue Velvet* and *She's Gotta Have It* both implicate us to a greater degree than do more classic scripts. We (as opposed to a character) look down, fascinated at the terrifying insects. We feel we must have maligned Nola and caused her to direct her opening outburst at us. As we will see, this has a profound effect on how we respond to the story.

A theoretical aside: In his famous essay on deep focus,[3] André Bazin praised the "ambiguity" of deep focus, which allows the viewer to choose what he or she would look at. Using narrative voice to lead us would seem to violate Bazin's concerns, but we would argue that this is not the case. Deep focus or not, all films organize space to lead us through the frame. The question is to what extent the viewer is conscious of being led. The assertion of the narrative voice that we are talking about implies a certain self-consciousness. These films work by, in effect, posing a dramatic voice and a narrative voice in conflict with one another. The viewer must progressively decide to which voice she is giving most credence. A film whose narrative voice totally and consistently dominates the dramatic voice would have no interest to us.

Development

Focus and Build

One of the great paradoxes of dramatic writing is that even if you want to write a script that touches on issues that go beyond the events of the story, you first need to make the story strong and clearly focused. Instead of freeing the viewer, a script that wanders all over the place is generally so hard to follow that it loses its ability to stretch and take on larger issues. Therefore, no matter what your approach, we certainly encourage you to write with focus. However, we suggest a broader definition of what is being focused on. The trick to being able to write the middle of a story is to deepen the conflict set up in the opening of the film. In mainstream films, this deepening is driven largely by the forward motion of the plot. However, a script might also be organized around character insight, theme, irony, recurring motif, and even childish wonder—but it is not easy.

A number of scripts start with this looser sense of organization, but then the writer, fearing the lack of a story, seems to panic and reach for melodrama. The first 40 minutes of Steven Spielberg's *E.T. the Extra-Terrestrial* are as loosely structured as is any independent film, delightfully avoiding any single strong dramatic conflict, while instead concentrating on the wonder the children feel in dealing with the alien and, to a lesser extent, the problem of hiding it from their mother. A few shots of people searching the landing site with flashlights are thrown in to prepare us for the melodrama that comes later. But the central dramatic issue is how Elliott, so awkward around his older brother's friends, finds an identity with E.T. Once the villainous adult scientists arrive, however, this issue gets lost under the mechanics of the quarantine, the operation, and the final chase. The first bicycle-flying scene, in which Elliott feels the transcendence of all human limitations, resonates with much greater richness than does the second flying scene, when the joy is framed in terms of kids escaping from evil adults.

Many writers consider the middle to be the hardest part to write, because it calls most directly on the resources of imagination. However you start, the trick is to carry through with the implications of the questions you've opened up. Sigmund Freud once said that his goal was to study something over and over again until it spoke for itself. This kind of unflinching, honest attention is necessary for a story to develop. Gross plot manipulation will always be a temptation for the writer seeking to keep the middle of her story alive. This must be rejected. The mechanics of drug dealing, the violence between the Pakistanis and the English, and the lurid details of the homosexual relationship between Omar and Johnny might all have taken over *My Beautiful Laundrette*, but they are not allowed to. By progressively unraveling the complex determination, ambition, and love that make up Omar's character, while at the same time keeping the movie focused on the paradox of the well-to-do former colonial subjects and the poor English lower-class, the film sustains and develops its extraordinary resonance and insight.

John Waters's *Polyester* plays out in the opposite direction but is still true to the absurdity of its opening. Francine Fishpaw loses her husband to another woman, sees her son arrested for foot-stomping, and sends her pregnant daughter to a nunnery. Then, everything reverses—her children reform and she marries the dreamboat, Todd Tomorrow. When this falls apart, when her mother and Todd Tomorrow lie murdered at Francine's feet, she can still stare up into the craning camera and yell, "We are still family." Although we feel a surprising amount of tenderness for Francine, she has not reformed and the movie is not allowed to surrender to sentimentality. By the time Waters made *Hairspray* in 1988, his edge had softened and, unlike in *Polyester*, we are invited to regard the happy ending without irony.

Meaning and Action

In the traditional script, meaning must flow from action. Characters are defined by what they do, not by what they say. In an alternative script, there is greater freedom to bend the rules. In fact, such scripts frequently gain their power from proposing several competing locations for meaning. Where exactly does the meaning lie in Louis Malle's *My Dinner with Andre*? Is it purely in the talk? Or in the reaction shots? Is it in the new way that Wallace Shawn sees the city after spending the evening with Andre Gregory? Or is it in the lack of action that makes us wonder whether Wallace Shawn's insight, no matter how overwhelming, will lead to anything?

The Aristotelian notion that "action is character" becomes much more complex. What do we mean by action? Is character defined only by the capability to act (the classical notion)? Or might it be defined by the gaining of insight? Must character be at the center of film at all? Might not the organizing principle be one of theme, of the twisting of the family melodrama clichés, as in *Polyester*, of the narrative voice, or of some rich amalgam of character, theme, history, and society, as in *My Beautiful Laundrette*?

Closure

How We Know It's Over

The music swells, the plot resolves, the hero and heroine kiss, the lights come up, and the movie's over. After years of experience, we can pop in on an ongoing movie and know instantly whether it is about to end. A number of formal elements contribute to our sense of ending. One trick in writing effective third-act scenes is to cut down the scene's opening. This pruning accelerates the rhythm and heightens the immediacy of the conflict. Of course, by this time in the movie, we should be sufficiently oriented so as not to need to be set up.

The restorative three-act model suggests that by the beginning of the third act, most of the character conflict has been resolved. Thus, third-act scenes tend to be external, the playing out of the stakes that were raised in the second act rather than the working through of character. Tactics are placed in the foreground. Hesitation tends to be directed toward overcoming obstacles, not scruples. We wonder how the character is going to achieve his goal, not what that goal is, or whether it is right or wrong. Of course, we are familiar with the tying up of plot: stop the film in the middle and try to identify all the questions raised. In most mainstream films, these questions will be quite clear-cut. If you make a list, you will find that invariably they are answered (or at least finessed) by the end of the film.

Most independent films do not end with such a complete sense of closure. These open-ended works make a different demand on the viewer. Mainstream films tend to generate a great amount of moment-to-moment tension, which explains their hold on us. But once they end, the hold tends to vanish. This how-does-it-come-out style of moviemaking is an essential consequence of restorative three-act structure. If you stop a more offbeat film in the middle, it is generally not as easy to pinpoint the tension that must be resolved, because the tension tends to be less urgent while at the same time more broadly resonant. The ending in such a script does not have to resolve one monolithic flow, as much as it has to finish one element of a multi-stranded flow while letting the others continue to play out in the viewer's mind. Thus, the whole notion of story structure has to be rethought in open-ended scripts. Part of this requires displacing the location of the conflict.

The Relocation of Conflict

As we have said, in restorative three-act scripts, the conflict remains almost entirely with the character and the character's particular situation. Rarely is there a cultural, social, historical, class, or gender-based element to the conflict. If the conflict exists totally within the story (i.e., totally within the control of the writer who is inventing fictional characters and giving them problems to solve), there is nothing to keep the conflict from being fully resolved. But if the conflict is designed to touch on the larger world right from the beginning, if we are asked to see the individual's problems against an ongoing historical process, then we don't expect the same kind of complete resolution. In fact, if we get it, we tend to think that the writer is naive for ignoring the long-term persistence of such problems in the world beyond the story.

In his excellent piece on open endings and ideology, the Israeli Eran Preis talks about writing a script on the Lebanon invasion.[4] Preis's lead character chooses to hide his hospitalization for paranoia, because to reveal it would mean that he has to leave the army, which is socially unacceptable in Israel. Yet word gets out. As he becomes increasingly ostracized in the army, he comes to see the problems of the militarized Israeli society. The film ends with him stripping off his army uniform and standing in the road as the tanks drive off. All we know is that he is no longer in the army. How he will live in the society that he no longer trusts and that no longer trusts him remains unresolved.

Maintaining enough resolution to satisfy, while still keeping the story open, is very tricky. Generally, the immediate dramatic problem has to be solved, so that it must be posed in such a way that the larger issues still resonate. In a mainstream script, these issues, because they exist completely in the world of the story, are clearly resolved. We feel comfortable in guessing that, in *Wall Street*, Bud will get out of jail and that his father will remain proud of him. The Gekkos of the world will be written off as bad guys. There won't be an analysis of American society or any suggestion that Gekko represents something that we all might share. By contrast, although the character in Preis's film has solved the problem of whether he will remain in the army, we have no idea how he will deal with his society in the future. The question of how to live with Israel's current militant response to a long and impotent history cannot be so easily answered.

In Godard's *Vivre sa Vie: Film en Douze Tableaux* (in North America, *My Life to Live*), the character Nana insists that she is responsible for her own actions and her eventual fate. A prostitute by choice, she falls in love and wishes to leave the business. But before she can, her pimp inexplicably seeks to trade her for money. The exchange is made, but the money is not what was promised, and Nana is killed, by accident, in the ensuing gunfight. The film ends. The arbitrary randomness of Nana's death makes for a powerful and appropriate ending for this film. However, the very arbitrariness would be a disaster in a more mainstream script, because it does not answer such questions as: What motivated the killing? Who were the other guys? Why weren't they set up earlier in the story? These would be fair questions, because mainstream scripts are based on clear-cut principles of causality and clear expectations set up in the first act.

If we want to deal with the randomness and lack of simple causality, we must establish these elements at the beginning of our film, and we must not raise expectations of answers to questions raised in the first act (unless we are planning to subvert these expectations). It is not enough to declare that the world doesn't make sense anymore; we must incorporate this breakdown of order into the questions raised by the structure itself. For instance, the script of *Platoon* fails to chart the arbitrary lunacy of Vietnam (although there are some brilliant moments in which the filmmaking depicts this), because its structure—a clear villain in this most morally ambiguous war and an avenger who is able to take his revenge—is so old-fashioned and comforting. This dislocation must take place in the way the story is told, the way the narration is asserted.

In *Vivre sa Vie*, Nana's claim, "I am responsible," raises the whole question of our freedom of will in a mass society; the filmmaker's intervention and explicit foregrounding of the narrative voice raise the question of the freedom of the characters from the narrating agency. This has a profound effect on how we understand stories. The form—the way the story is told—becomes as important (or more important) than the story. In effect, an equation is being made—the society that gives shape to our lives acts, in some way, as a narrator acts toward a character. Society educates us, presents us with choices, and determines what we fight against.

Narration defines, whether overtly or not, a similar range of choices for the characters contained within its story. If, as in a mainstream script, the narration is not acknowledged, then the characters are given the illusion of being free while we, as onlookers, know exactly what they have to face up to. This displacement leaves us protected, entertained but never implicated by the film. If, however, the narration is foregrounded, as it is in *Vivre sa Vie* (and, as discussed in earlier chapters, in *Vertigo*), then we have to pay attention to it. We must ask from where it is coming. It is coming from a direct extension of our wish to have a story. It is in part an expression of our own desires. Thus, the conflict extends from the story world out to us. Rather than being left unscathed by the story, we are forced to question our desire to look on and enjoy.

Conclusion

The mainstream script tends to use structure as the invisible narrator of the story. This structure provides organization and meaning as though it evolved logically from the characters and the situations of the story. The alternative script tends to foreground structure as the voice of the self-conscious narrator organizing the material. With this change, the location of meaning tends to shift from being fully contained within the fictive world to running between the fictive world and the narrator.

This shift allows us to rethink how we can actually use structure. If the narrative voice is in the foreground, then exposition, typically rendered invisible in a mainstream script, can become an expression of the narrator's presence. Development can be broader, apparent not only in how the characters act, but in their insights and perceptions. Closure can become much more open ended. In this chapter, we have only touched the surface of available options. But by identifying the location of the conflict and by figuring out exactly what you want to say, you can use structure as an expressive form, not as a predetermined given.

References

1. D. Mamet, *The Verdict* (Twentieth Century Fox, 1982), 6, http://www.imsdb.com/scripts/Verdict,-The.html..
2. S. Lee, *She's Gotta Have It* (New York, NY: Simon and Schuster, 1987), 279.
3. A. Bazin, "The evolution of the language of cinema," In *What Is Cinema?* Vol. 1 (Berkeley, CA: University of California Press, 1968), 23.
4. E. Preis, "Not Such a Happy Ending," *Journal of Film and Video* 42, no. 3 (Fall 1990): 18, 23.

29

Rewriting

Once we subject the mainstream rules to scrutiny, we are left without a map upon which we can depend. By what standards do we critique our own work? How do we get ourselves out of trouble? What guides our rewrites? We don't want to minimize how difficult it is to work without guidance. Models do provide an important framework. For instance, in her book *Making a Good Script Great*, Linda Seger offers a very good checklist of what each act should accomplish: "What kinds of action points are within my script? Barriers? Complications? Reversals? Where do they occur, and how often?"[1] are a few of the questions she asks about Act II. These questions are very helpful to a writer. However, we feel that checking your script against a list of questions does not address the fundamental issue. It presumes that the rules are more important than is the life or urgency that we hope will be created by your script. Anyone who has read amateur scripts will bear witness to this misappropriation of values. Most amateur scripts contain every one of the prescribed act breaks, and many would pass the checklist for act accomplishments, yet most of them are absolutely dead.

Screenplays fail not because they break the rules but because the writer has failed to imagine and see clearly. Screenplays fail because they lack urgency and life. The reason we talk about rules at all is because no one can directly teach you (much less talk about) how to imagine and how to generate urgency and life, especially in a book. We don't pretend to be able to do so here. All we ask is that you don't substitute preconceived models for the apparently formless chaos that, at some point, is a component of all truly creative projects. Time consuming or not, any screenplay that has life has to be invented from the ground up and has to discover its own rules.

So how do you rewrite? Beyond everything else, you seek to recapture the impulse that brought you to your particular script in the first place. Where do you get this impulse? Anywhere and everywhere. It depends on you, but it must be there. This is so critical that many books on fiction writing dedicate whole chapters to it. For instance, R.V. Cassill, in his excellent book *Writing Fiction*, worries about students getting sidetracked by sensational melodramatic subjects that have nothing to do with their own experience[2]:

> I never quite understood why students should waste their time and mine on efforts so far off the right track. Sometimes I guessed that they might be afraid to discover how little of their own experience they had actually possessed, how little of their own lives they had grasped.... But the choice of becoming a writer is the choice to face some fears, including the fear of being a hollow or a dull person with nothing to say.

Harsh words, but true. If you don't command the emotional resources to respond, to worry, to be obsessive over your experience, you will find it very difficult to write. We are not making the old argument that you should write only about what you know. Although this may (or may not) be useful in fiction writing, it would unduly limit the scope of your scriptwriting, because film requires a larger audience than does fiction. Rather, we are saying write only about things you feel passionate about, things you haven't fully worked out, things you don't mind going back to, again and again. Get down on paper words that express these feelings. Anything—an image, a scene, a moment of characterization, blocking, sound, conflict that embodies the story you want to tell.

Only when you put down such a concrete moment have you truly started to write. But once you have, you already have something greater than any abstract knowledge of structure will ever give you. You can continue to go back to that moment to recapture the impulse that brought you to your story in the first place. Eventually, as your story line grows clearer, you may want to replace this initial moment with another that seems to come closer to what you are after. But that doesn't matter. You have started. Now you can build from there.

How do you do that? By trial and error. There is no other way. By going forward until you get lost. By going back to where it works, rekindling your ideas, recapturing your thread, and going forward again. This process of keeping the whole story in front of you is no easy task. Many writers use a bulletin board covered with scene cards to remind them of how the story is moving. Others write paragraphs summarizing the development of plot, theme, and character. Use whatever works, but learn the technique of stepping back from your story and seeing it in its totality.

Most writers will tell you that developing the middle of a story is the hardest part. Here again, we urge you not to worry about abstractions such as complications, barriers, and reversals but rather to go back to your initial impulse. The reason the middle is so difficult is because you've taken your original story idea as far as you can imagine and now you have to go even further. You might be working out of character. In that case, try to identify what you have only hinted at but not fully explored. What are the rough edges? The dark sides? The unspoken or misunderstood motivations? How can the character be pushed so that these are uncovered and how can the fullness of characterization be revealed? You might work thematically. In that case, try to identify what you are really trying to get at. What ambiguity or confusion in the situation has not yet been examined? What contradictions are there to be explored? What is always assumed but never examined? Suck everything you possibly can out of your material.

As you gain more experience, there will be much less trial and error. You will come up with possible solutions and quickly play them out in your head to see whether they will work for you. However, even as you do, you want to be careful. Writing is not like learning to tune a car—once learned, then many times repeated. To write well, you must go through the feeling of learning to write each time you start a new script. You must discover for yourself why the strategies you decide to use work for your particular story.

Taking Suggestions

You should feel as confident about rejecting suggestions as you feel about accepting them. A writer must have the ego, the toughness, to stand up and say, "This is my idea." Otherwise, your script becomes an amalgam of all the responses to it. However, it is very important to learn to listen to suggestions. This requires getting over the natural defensiveness we all feel when we are criticized, in addition to understanding how to decipher someone else's ideas.

Any criticism you can get is worth having. Note exactly what your reader is having difficulty with and pay particular attention to how the objections and suggestions are phrased. It is useful to write down the exact wording. If several readers object to the same thing, make sure you look at it closely. Don't bother responding (otherwise, readers will start critiquing your comments rather than your script). Rather, study the suggestions when you are alone. A caveat: unless your critic is another writer whom you respect, never take suggestions at face value. The reason that we respond the way we do is frequently deeply embedded in the structure and development of the script. In most cases, it is very difficult for an untrained reader (and even a trained reader won't know the script the way you do) to take into account the implications of making a change. Instead of taking your critics' suggestions at face value, try to use them to figure out exactly what isn't working. Frequently, you will find that you have inadvertently set up a line of expectation 20 pages before the scene your reader/critic is talking about, and that is what needs to be changed. Or an earlier moment that may be perfectly clear to you is read as something entirely different, which affects all that comes after it.

Once you make your corrections, it is tempting to go back to readers and ask them whether your fix of the earlier scene helps the problem, but in most cases you will be disappointed. Rather than showing them the earlier scene, you might want to ask your critics to read the whole script again. If you have made the right prior adjustments, they may come to the identical scene they complained about before and remark on how much better it is.

Sample Exercises

We have purposely kept this chapter general, because we don't want to inadvertently propose a series of rules to replace those we are asking you to reconsider. We will, however, end with some sample exercises. These exercises are designed not so much to help you solve specific problems as much as they are to help you regard your work from varying perspectives. Once again, we believe that you get stuck when your vision fails. If you can see anew, you can discover solutions on your own.

Closing Distance: Write Out Subtext

The mechanics of screenwriting can seem quite clumsy. You may find yourself so concerned with visualizing and blocking that you forget what is going on with your characters. If you are writing a character-driven script, you want to avoid such loss of internal life. One solution is to use a stream-of-consciousness style to write the flow of your character's thoughts under each piece of action or line of dialogue. Compare this to what is actually going on. You may discover several things:

1. Your character has no thoughts or has thoughts of no particular urgency. In this case, ask yourself: What is the point of the scene? If it doesn't have a dramatic function, if it doesn't cost the character something, cut it.
2. The thoughts are a mere rehash of the dialogue. You've got no subtext and the scene will probably be dead. Remember, characters need not know exactly why they are speaking, or their reasons may contradict the viewer's sense of their motivation. However, there must be some skew between dialogue and thought. Consider pushing the conflict harder to give your character reasons not to speak everything on her mind.
3. The thoughts don't correspond to the actions that are supposed to express them. This is not as much of a problem as it may seem, because it means you know what the scene is about, but you just haven't visualized it successfully. Try to imagine your character free of anything governing her actions except her thoughts. Let them move her. Use the camera to underscore this movement; reveal a sense of motivation to the viewer without exposing it to other characters in the scene.

Sometimes it is useful to start writing the character's stream of consciousness from scratch. Write only the progression of the point-of-view character's thoughts against the dialogue of the other characters. Only after you have the line of the thoughts written down do you want to write the dialogue that goes with them.

Gaining Distance: Shift the Point-of-View Character

Sometimes writers have the opposite problem—they are too close to a character. In a character-driven story, most often you will be writing from the perspective of a point-of-view character. Try arbitrarily reversing this. Write the scene from a totally different perspective. Use this new perspective to see your original point-of-view character from the outside. This technique is useful because writers frequently get so close to their point-of-view characters that the characters cease to exist in the concrete world. But remember, we will be seeing them on the screen. What will they be doing? How do they react and how are they reacted to? How will their thoughts be communicated or suppressed?

Gaining Even More Distance: Write a Totally Unreliable Scene

Do you want us to be with the character at a particular moment? Do you want us to understand that you approve of what the character is doing? This closeness can be harder than it looks, because all writers have a tendency to fall in love with their characters. When this happens, viewers tend to check out. Who cares about a paragon of virtue? Someone who only appears to be a paragon—now that's interesting.

One way to avoid falling in love with your characters is to artificially distance yourself. Add some irony to the scene; have other characters contest your character; let your character do something you don't feel all that happy about. Establishing distance can be enormously freeing. By implicitly telling your viewers that you don't stand behind everything your character does, you don't fall into the trap of trying to present yourself.

Easing Exposition: Rewrite an Early Scene as a Late Scene

Expository scenes are very difficult to bring to life. After several rewrites, it becomes difficult to sort out what is the bare minimum of information that must be communicated to make the script work. As the line of the script may have changed through your rewrites, you may be carrying much more expository weight than is needed.

One solution is to strip the scene of any expository function. Cut down the beginning of the scene and write the whole scene with the economy of a later scene. Assume we know enough to follow the scene. Now go back and identify exactly what information you need to communicate. Frequently, you will find that by stripping down the scene, you have so increased its dramatic urgency that it becomes easier to add the now-limited expository information.

Reshaping: Shift the Story Frame

Imagine your script starting on page 10 or page 20. Consider what this does for your story. Even if you don't make these cuts, you may find that a great deal of information in the beginning of your script can be trimmed down. Now look at the end of your script. Have you gone far enough? Have you truly squeezed everything out of the story? Sometimes, after you've finished a draft, the whole window of the story can be adjusted to take in more of the story and less of the setup.

Visualizing: Write with Dialogue Crossed Out

You may want a scene to be stagy or talky. For example, *Stranger Than Paradise* is structured in single-shot scenes, with the camera looking in (as opposed to being in) on the action. By its very refusal to yield more insight into the characters through camera placement and cutting, this style becomes an expression of the material, insensate, physical world that denies us the romantic release of penetration into character. However, when you want to bring the camera inside your story, your staging should reveal the fundamental tension of each scene. The best way to make sure you are doing this is to cross out the dialogue, so that you can't read its content (although you are still aware of its placement). Reading just the stage directions, you should still be able to identify the scene's basic dramatic movement, the dominant character, and the beat where the scene turns.

Giving the Scene Some Breathing Room: Rewrite with an Opposite Outcome

One of the great (and true) clichés of realistic narrative writing is that you want to create scenes that have the possibility of coming out in at least two different ways, and you want to sustain such a possibility for as long as you can. This balancing of choices allows the viewer to participate in the drama by constantly weighing and rethinking the possible outcome.

Try rewriting a scene and intentionally reverse the outcome. If you have written a scene in which the outcome is determined too early, you will have to do a great deal of rewriting to reverse it. Once you do, go back and, with the minimum of changes, restore the original direction of your ending. You will find that the tension now sustains itself to the end of the scene. Such a technique is also useful for characters written as all dark (evil). Try reversing them and see what dimension emerges.

Taking the Curse Off: Write with Overt Reasons, Not to Explain

Sometimes writers—more often than not, sensitive writers—cannot resist the opportunity of having the characters explain exactly what they feel. The explanations may even be extended to include little essays on the theme. We see no problem with this if there are conflicting viewpoints presented with equal authorial authority. As long as the viewer has to work to synthesize meaning, multiple voices can only contribute to the richness of the script.[3] Think how resonant the contrasting perspectives of Omar and Johnny are in *My Beautiful Laundrette*. However, you want to avoid head-on, reliable exegeses in which you tell us exactly what you think about the situation. Such commentary is impossible to play, causing actors to use the term *taking the curse off* when they find a way to diminish the obviousness of these lines.

The solution is simple. Find an overt reason in the scene that keeps the character from explaining. A man who tells a woman that he desires her but is afraid of losing her is a lot less interesting (to us and to her) than is the man who avoids such a confession, because he knows that is precisely what would doom him.

Breaking Out of the Narrow Mind-Set: Ask a Whole Group to Rewrite Your Scene

It takes considerable courage to have a class or workshop rewrite your scene, but it can prove to be very worthwhile. You are not looking for answers; rather, you want to break out of the narrow mind-set with which you have approached the scene, by seeing in just how many directions it might actually go. You won't believe what people will discover in a scene that you felt you had already thought through.

Conclusion

Writing beyond the rules requires that you approach any given rule with skepticism and that you don't use a rule until you are satisfied that it works for you. The difficulty with such an approach is that you have no authority, no place to go for guidance. We suggest that you learn to look at the strength of your own impulses for guidance and that you build from this through trial and error. Although this is more frightening than working with a preconceived model, it encourages you to do the real exploration necessary to write material that is truly original and alive.

References

1. L. Seger, *Making a Good Script Great* (New York, NY: Dodd, Mead & Company, 1987), 58.
2. R. V. Cassill, *Writing Fiction* (New York, NY: Prentice Hall, 1975), 11–12.
3. See M. M. Bakhtin, "Discourse in the Novel," In *The Dialogic Imagination: Four Essays* ed. M. Holquist, trans. and ed. V. Liapunov, trans. K. Brostrom (Austin, TX: University of Texas Press, 1985), 259–422.

30

Adaptations from Contemporary Literature

It is a commonplace that literary fiction that depends on internal voice or that is highly stylized does not translate well into a mainstream film. This is because these literary techniques need a channel, a means to communicate, in addition to that provided by the story. In fiction, this channel is frequently provided by the narrative voice, but, as we have discussed, mainstream films tend to subordinate narrative voice to the more dominant dramatic voice. Beyond voice, the other element that limits the translation of literary fiction is that mainstream films impose a much more circumscribed notion of how far characters can stray before they will threaten audience identification. Thus, the moral ambiguity of complex characters that feature in literary fiction is frequently reduced in mainstream films, simplifying the potential richness of the adapted stories.

The availability of an expressive channel that comes from heightened narrative voice in alternative films, along with a greater willingness to risk audience identification, means that alternative films frequently allow more complex adaptations than do mainstream films.

The expressive channel more directly represents the effect of language, rhythm, and internal dialogue that we see in literary fiction. Further, whether because of its audience's assumptions, its lack of established stars, or its conventional flexibility, alternative filmmaking tends to be more comfortable with ambiguous treatment of character and situation than does mainstream film, allowing this style of filmmaking to track stories of greater moral complexity and more ambiguous narrative centers.

In this chapter, we examine these differences by looking closely at two film adaptations, *L.A. Confidential* and *Trainspotting*. Both of the novels from which these adaptations were made pose challenges of voice and ambiguity, yet their translations to film are quite different. We will consider how each was translated; one was adapted to a traditional film and the other to a more alternative film.

Successful Adaptations

Before we start, we need to consider two different approaches to evaluating adaptations. One is to ask that the film accurately reflect the content or the story of the book. This is used in judging adaptations of popular novels that have developed a strong following on their own. Many viewers of such adaptations are looking for a retelling of a story they remember, and are angered or disappointed by significant deviation. A second way to evaluate adaptations is to step back and take a broader look at how the novel works. More voiced or literary novels tend to reveal their essence not only through story, but also through style. In such adaptations, a literal recapturing of the story alone would miss the point. In fact, in such novels, the storyline itself, reduced to its essence of action and reaction, can be quite thin or not easily reconstructed. The narrative elements of language and perspective and their way of constructing the imaginary world give these novels their depth.

We have picked two novels whose pleasure we believe comes in part from these narrative elements. While both of these novels could be reduced to their story alone, neither storyline would command our attention in the same way had it not been filtered through its highly inflected narrative voice. James Ellroy's 1990 novel *L.A. Confidential* is a self-conscious noir set in the Los Angeles of the 1950s. Written in a clipped, reactive style, it follows three members of the Los Angeles Police Department through three major investigations spanning most of the decade during which the contemporary city of freeways and theme parks began to emerge. The novel is self-conscious in its writing style, transforming the elaborate similes of Los Angeles noir writer Raymond Chandler into clipped, broken phrases influenced by bebop jazz. *L.A. Confidential*, the Warner Bros. Studios movie, was adapted by Brian Helgeland and Curtis Hanson, directed by Curtis Hanson, and released in 1997.

Trainspotting, a 1992 novel by Scottish writer Irvine Welsh, follows the disintegration of a gang of working-class junkies from Edinburgh, told from a number of different perspectives. The writing is in a Scottish street slang, dense enough to warrant a glossary. Holding the story together is the character Mark Renton, whose gradual disillusion with and separation from his friends' world is tied to a degree of self-awareness that the other characters do not possess. *Trainspotting*, the Miramax Films movie, was adapted by John Hodge, directed by Danny Boyle, and released in 1996.

Narrative Voice

There are a number of ways to approach the concept of narrative voice. One is to separate two different acts involved in storytelling: representation and interpretation. *Representation* is the creation of the fictional world for the viewer; it concentrates on showing us where characters are and what is happening. *Interpretation* provides an attitude or way to understand that world. Ultimately, these two acts are inseparable—all representation implies an interpretation—but it can be useful to think of them as posing different analytical perspectives.

In mainstream films, we are generally directed to pay attention to interpretation rather than representation. That is, interpretation, when it is apparent, is made obvious; it is manifest through overt acts of narrative intervention such as music, crane shots, montages, titles, and so on. The rest of the time it is there but is held in the background and expressed more covertly through character moves and positioning, and the conventions of shot-reverse shots and storytelling. But in all cases, representation itself is portrayed as neutral or uninflected—the fictional world seems to exist, but we are asked not to think much about how it got there. Continuity is never disrupted, tone is consistent, and even shots that call attention to themselves make sense within the implied space of the fictional world. We are looking in at a place and a scene that would supposedly be there regardless of whether a movie was being made. Put another way, we rarely ask questions of where we are, who is seeing, or what is happening that are not ultimately answered by the forward movement of the story.

By contrast, many alternative films and voiced novels intentionally merge interpretation and representation—they challenge representational practice itself and make it the source of interpretation. In such films, we are frequently aware of being confused over location and point of view; we feel gaps, and aspects of the story remain unexplained. Not only is continuity sometimes disrupted, shots also do not always follow logically and tonal consistency is often ignored. Yet these gaps are part of the meaning of the story; they suggest something of the disorientation, contrasts, or hesitations contained in the dramatic situation. Ultimately, if the film succeeds for us, we come to understand that this confusion contributes to its overall feel and meaning.

To make this clear, let's look at a scene from the screenplay of *L.A. Confidential.*[1] In this scene, Bud White, one of the three police officers whom we are following, joins the Christmas Massacre prison riot, the first of the three police events that structure the story:

```
INT. SQUAD ROOM—NIGHT
Bud types his report with one finger. Jack looks in.

                    JACK
          White, you better get a leash
          on Stens before he kills
          someone.


INT. CELL BLOCK—NIGHT
Followed by Jack, Bud forces his way through the crowd.
The men who see it's him quickly clear a path.
```

This is very clean screenwriting. The sentences direct our attention to what the camera will photograph, and the action is very easy to follow. We open with a shot of Bud typing. Jack takes the camera when he looks in, and the cut to him prepares us for his dialogue. The scene in the squad room cuts away before Bud reacts to Jack's request, but it is very easy to reconstruct it from the next scene, where Bud is driving the action. The first sentence in the second scene uses complex sentence structure to focus our attention. The dominant action, Bud's forcing his way through the crowd, makes up the sentence's independent clause while the modifying action, "followed by Jack," is rendered secondary through its dependent grammatical position. The shot we can see in our head features Bud pushing between the men in the foreground as the camera dollies back to emphasize the force of his action. Jack is in background, nipping at Bud's heals. The subsequent clearing of a path by the men in the last sentence is clearly in reaction to Bud.

If we look at the interpretative elements of the scene, we can see that they are designed to foreground character. The most inflected verb is "forces," which emphasizes the determination of Bud's walk. It also tells the director to structure the shot to highlight the aggression of Bud's action—this means initially using the men as obstacles to be plowed through, and then reinterpreting their subsequent clearing as a sign of their respect for him. Finally, the representational elements of the scene are economical and precise. We need to see Bud quietly typing at first to contrast this action with his assertiveness when he moves through the crowd. The crowd itself is not detailed because it does not need to be; rather, it is presented as a whole, first to serve as a foil to Bud's movement and then to underscore the respect in which he is held by the men. Representation serves the interpretative line of the scene without calling attention to itself. We know exactly where everyone is and what they are doing. We do not see anything in either location that does not advance either character or story. Character action takes us from location to location. Cause and effect drives the creation of the fictional world. Our sense of "reality" is never disturbed. Furthermore, we know exactly where we, as viewers, stand. We are put in the best place to observe the action, but remain onlookers, placed a little outside, so we can put it all together. There is no confusion about either the character's motivation or the narrator's motivation for positioning us where we are. We feel we see what we need to see.

Let's contrast this to the novel. We are picking up with Bud standing outside the cellblock[2]:

> The music inside went off key-wrong, not really music. Bud caught screeches—screams from the jail.
>
> The noise doubled, tripled. Bud saw a stampede: muster room to cellblock. A flash: Stens going crazy, booze, a jamboree—bash the cop bashers. He ran over, hit the door at a sprint.

The catwalk packed tight, cell doors open, lines forming. Exley shouting for order, pressing into the swarm, getting nowhere.

Later, we read[3]:

Cops shoved cell to cell. Elmer Lentz, blood splattered, grinning. Jack Vincennes by the watch commander's office—Lieutenant Frieling snoring at his desk.

Here the action and syntax are much less clear. Many of the sentences describe sense fragments rather than causality. Description might not be the right word; rather, the prose itself conveys the rhythm of the senses, the jarring disconnection of the scene. We experience discrete fragments of images and sound, out of context. No longer are we standing outside from a safe distance and looking in; rather, our perceptions, too, are suspect. The technique has the effect of pulling us into the scene by encouraging us to experience the same sense of confusion and immediacy that Bud does.

Further, there is no attempt to separate the representative from the interpretative elements of the narration. The language here mixes both functions of narrative. In representing the world, telling us how fragmented it looks and sounds, the language conveys the slant of its interpretation—the chaos that Bud feels. We have a sense of reactive action rather than character motivation driving the scene. We are not necessarily put in the right place to observe—in fact, it may take several readings to have any idea what is happening. Rather than constructing a world in which we are watching from close in but still outside the character perceptions, which is the classic mode of mainstream film, the novel brings us much closer to the direct experience of the characters.

Whatever be our take on the adaptation of *L.A. Confidential* and how well it succeeds in conveying the novel's story (more on that later), we would argue that it does not succeed in conveying the novel's voice, and thus is not successful by our second criterion of adaptation. The chaos of experience, the fragmented representation, the sense of a world that lacks a clear point of view that we experience so strongly in the novel (and it is a world that gets increasingly more fragmented in Ellroy's subsequent novels)—these are smoothed out in the film. The clear connections of the images to motivation and the smooth texture of the film language convey a feel that does not match the texture of the novel.

In the novel *Trainspotting*, we get a similar emphasis on voice. Mark Renton, about to come down from heroin and needing a carry-over fix, stuffs himself with opium suppositories. Walking home, he suddenly realizes he needs to go to the bathroom. In both the book and the film, he dashes into a filthy public lavatory where, in his desire for abdominal relief, he forgets about the suppositories. In both cases, he must reach into the toilet to retrieve the suppositories.

In the novel, Renton relieves himself, saying, "Ah empty ma guts, feeling as if everything; bowel, stomach, intestines, spleen, liver, kidneys, heart, lungs and fucking brains are aw falling through ma arsehole intae the bowl."[4] Then he catches a fly, crushes it between his fingers, and smears on the wall the word, "Hibs," the name of his favorite football team. Having done this, he admires his work and notes, "The vile bluebottle, which caused me a great deal of distress, has been transformed intae a work of art which give me much pleasure tae look at. Ah am speculatively thinking about this as a positive metaphor for other things in my life, when the realization ay what ah've done sends a paralyzing jolt ay raw fear though ma body."[5] He rolls up his sleeve, plunges his hand into the toilet, and retrieves the suppositories, noting "Ma brown-stained airm reminds us ay the classic t-shirt tan. The line goes right up past ma elbow as ah hud tae go right around the bend."[6] This is not the chaotic language of *L.A. Confidential*, but it is highly voiced nonetheless, describing action in such a way as to emphasize the character's wry self-awareness. It is gross, casual, immediate on one hand, and surprisingly funny and reflective on the other. It moves very freely between representation and interpretation, telling us what Renton does and how he feels about it. The language itself becomes a form of action, an expression of character—meet Renton, smearer of bug's bodies and self-conscious commenter on his own vile existence.

In the script, we're told that Renton, "drops his trousers, sits on the bowl and closes his eyes." This is followed by[7]:

```
MONTAGE
A lorry on a building site dumps a load of bricks, B52's
shed their load on Vietnam, the Blue Peter elephant, etc.

INT. CUBICLE—DAY
Renton has his eyes closed. They snap open.

He looks down between his legs.

He drops to his knees in front of the bowl and rolls his
sleeves up.

With no more hesitation, he plunges his arm into the bowl
and trawls for suppositories.

It seems to take ages. He cannot find them. He sticks his
arm further and further into the toilet, moving his whole
body close. He strains to find it.

His head is over the bowl now. Gradually he reaches still
further until his head is lowered into the bowl, followed
by his neck, torso, other arm, and finally his legs, all
disappearing.
```

```
The cubicle is empty.

INT. UNDERWATER—DAY
Renton, dressed as before, swims through murky depths
until he reaches the bottom, where he picks up the sup-
positories, which glow like luminous pearls, before head-
ing up towards the surface again.

INT. HORRIBLE TOILET CUBICLE—DAY
The toilet is empty.

Suddenly Renton appears through the bowl, then his arms
as he lifts himself out. Still clasping his two supposi-
tories, he walks out of the toilet.
```

The opening montage is a fairly literal translation of the novel, but the trip underwater is an invention of the screenwriter that serves to render the quality of Renton's voice into visual language. Through this invention, the scriptwriter has found a narrative device to express the dual nature of Renton's character—the addicted and the whimsical.

Representation, the way the world is presented to us, becomes expressive, interpretative rather than literal. Our sense of "reality" is shifted. We don't actually know how to take the trip down the toilet; it is not explained as a traditional fantasy and it certainly doesn't vibe as "real" within the conventions of this film's world. Yet it changes this desperate act into something more. Somehow, in both novel and film, the act of fishing dope out of a toilet full of shit becomes transformed into a moment of peace and reflection. This is the essence of literary adaptation—not literally to be faithful to the book, but to find ways to translate its voice into the language of film.

Reduction of Moral Ambiguity

We frequently hear that audiences need to identify with main characters. The mechanism of identification is a subject of much critical literature and won't be dealt with here. Our concern will be with how the need to sustain identification affects the construction of film stories made from novels that treat characters more ambiguously. We are not arguing that main characters do not need to be interesting—in most cases, this is a given of storytelling. Rather, they don't necessarily need to be likable or morally unambiguous. Yet, characters' rough edges are frequently rubbed off in mainstream adaptations.

We can see how this works by looking at *L.A. Confidential*. In the novel, the only characters that emerge with any moral claims are Bud, who, injured to the point of not being able to speak, goes off with the woman he has shared with Exley, and Jack, the cop who has found redemption but is shot in service to the law. The main character, Exley, is thoroughly compromised. By

necessity, the film simplifies and compresses the story, combining characters and events to reduce the sprawl and strengthen its line. Some of this,
such as the combining of relatively minor characters like Dick Stensland and
Duke Cathcart, works without affecting the fundamental thrust of the story.
However, smoothing out the moral complexity of Exley, the character whose
arc sustains both book and film, radically reduces the ambiguity suggested by
the book. Let's look at three examples of this:

1. The false resolution of the Nite Owl case, one of the three police
   incidents that structure the story, turns on the shooting of three
   African-American subjects who are tapped as fall guys by the police.
   Exley's career is made by gunning them down after they escape. In the
   book, Exley arrives alone and shoots the unarmed men in cold blood,
   driven by the taunting he has received from one of several women who
   do not love him back. In the screenplay, the killing of the three men
   is handled very differently. Exley is accompanied by another officer, a
   corrupt cop. The first shot, fired by this officer, is triggered by the accidental crash of a beer bottle. Subsequent to his shot, the other suspects
   pull guns. It is only after the corrupt cop is hit that Exley shoots back.
   What had been a gratuitous shooting triggered by Exley's need to prove
   himself to a woman who does not love him becomes a measured and
   careful act of self-defense.

2. Both novel and film turn on the subsequent reopening of the Nite Owl
   investigation. In the film, Exley begins pushing for the reopening a
   short half script page after the shooting, trying to find out what really
   happened when everyone else thinks the case is closed. Three pages
   later he is saying, "Something's wrong. I feel it inside,"[8] and just a
   short time afterwards, he is questioning suspects. In contrast to the
   film, where the reopening is driven by Exley's guilt, in the book, he
   does everything he can to stop it. The case is not reopened until 5 years
   after the crime, brought on by circumstances Exley cannot control.

3. In the movie, the villain Dudley Smith is killed when Exley shoots
   him in the back after Smith tries to take him and Bud down in a raid.
   The question of whether Exley is capable of shooting someone in the
   back has been raised earlier by Dudley, and the fact that Exley does it
   at least raises a hint of Exley's possible corruption. However, Dudley's
   evil is so egregiously dramatized that Exley's killing him is sufficiently
   justified. It is experienced more as a relief than as a descent into corruption. With Dudley out of the way and Exley made Chief of Detectives,
   the conflict seems resolved. Exley has succeeded in cleaning up the
   police force. Contrast this to the novel, which ends in a standoff. Dudley not only lives, he looks on as Exley is made Chief of Detectives.
   Dudley beams at his protégé, who Dudley is still certain he will be able
   to control. Exley's rise and his potential for reform are tainted by being
   held under the eyes of, and in forced collusion with, his archenemy.

These three changes transform Exley from a morally compromised, complex cop working in a corrupted system to a movie hero who roots out corruption without it rubbing off on him. Further, the cost to Exley in the novel is played out in his personal life. Whereas in the novel he fails romantically with two women, both of whom he shares with Bud, in the film, his failure is just with one woman. The film plays this as a love triangle—Bud wins, Exley loses. However, the double failure in the novel suggests something more— Exley succeeds as a cop precisely because he is incapable of loving anyone.

Thus, *L.A. Confidential* the film and *L.A. Confidential* the novel tell very different stories. The film suggests that, while Exley has suffered and his simple ideals are somewhat tarnished, he has still brought justice to L.A. The novel charts the story of a terminally unhappy man, incapable of love, and morally complex enough to bring a deeply compromised city under some kind of control.

By contrast, Renton's actions in *Trainspotting*—his successive kicking, resuming, and then rekicking the heroin habit; his affair with an underage schoolgirl; his arrest; and his running off with the money at the end—match those of the book. The movie is not as complex as the novel is (for instance, the movie eliminates all of the other voices in favor of Renton's), but it does not smooth out or sugarcoat Renton's character. Unlike with Exley, who in *L.A. Confidential* the movie is a straight read, we do not always know how to take Renton. His weakness, moral ambiguity, and need are part of his character—even his fleeing at the end reads simultaneously as an escape from and a betrayal of his past. Exley grows harder and more able to assume control, but the temptations he faces, the darkness in him, are considerably reduced from the novel, and so is his complexity as a character. In *Trainspotting*, Renton is able to move beyond his habit and the limitations of his world in the novel in a way that he cannot at the beginning of the movie. His growth in both the novel and film seems much more richly earned because we feel just how far he is capable of falling.

We have chosen two aspects of adaptation, the articulation of narrative voice and the reduction of moral ambiguity, to demonstrate some of the differences between mainstream and alternative translations of literary novels. There are, of course, other issues that deserve the same kind of treatment. We will end by summarizing a few examples that illustrate some of these.

The Sweet Hereafter Russell Banks's novel *The Sweet Hereafter* tells the story of a school bus accident and its effect on the town of Sam Dent, New York. It is structured around five first-person narrators, the first and last being the voice of Dolores Driscoll, the school bus driver, and one of the others being that of Mitchell Stephens, the New York City lawyer who briefly represents some of the townspeople. The accident itself is hardly touched upon; the dramatized scenes all take place before or after the accident occurs, although there is one deeply moving scene after the children have been recovered and their bodies are laid out on the ice. The writing is almost entirely scenic, but its presentation is exclusively filtered through the voice of the narrators and hence is highly inflected.

Because the narration of Dolores Driscoll frames the story, her perspective may be what we take with us most. However flawed it will be, we have a sense that she has begun her reintegration into Sam Dent when the men of her community volunteer to help carry her husband's wheelchair down from the county fair grandstand, as the novel ends. Atom Egoyan's script shifts the focus to the lawyer Stephens. In the novel, we learn that Stephens is estranged from his daughter through his internal reflections triggered by her disturbed phone calls. Egoyan fills in this information by adding an airplane scene, a conversation between Stephens and a friend of his daughter, in which he recounts an old story where he had to confront the possibility of cutting into his infant daughter's throat to save her. This scene, intercut throughout the script, recapitulates the narrated quality of the novel, framing the immediacy of Stephens's experience in Sam Dent with his memories. We are not immediately sure when this airplane scene takes place and only learn near the end that it is 2 years after the events in Sam Dent.

In the novel, we think that Dolores might reintegrate back into her town; in the movie, there is no such hope. Instead, the movie draws a different sort of complicity between Dolores and Stephens when, after getting off the plane, he discovers her driving a hotel minibus at an anonymous airport. At the end, they both are isolated, he from his daughter, she from the town she loves. Since the film lacks the narrative frame that drives the novel, we would not fully understand the depth of their isolation without the addition of Stephens's account of his infant daughter and the subsequent scene where he discovers Dolores in the airport. These additions restore the depth of loss so important to the book.

Smoke Signals *Smoke Signals* is adapted from a short story in the collection *The Lone Ranger and Tonto Fistfight in Heaven*, by Sherman Alexie. The story, "This Is What It Means to Say Phoenix, Arizona," is the structural template designed to contain a number of other stories from the collection. *Smoke Signals* is most successful when it evokes a larger context of history and time, and Alexie finds a way to do this by embedding a storyteller into the narrative. He uses one of his main characters, Thomas, whose flaw—and reason for the tension between him and the other main character, Victor—is the fact that he is incessantly telling stories. This is annoying to Victor because not only are Thomas's stories mannered, but because Thomas, through his stories, claims a connection to Victor's father that Victor himself does not have. However, Thomas also possesses a sense of the reservation's history that no one else can claim, and the writer Alexie is able to use this to convey a context and a relation to the larger culture that he would not be able to convey in any other way. Thus, for instance, Thomas's story of how his father was "the perfect hippie, since all hippies were trying to be Indians"[9] both functions to delineate his relationship to the other characters in the story and also speaks to a time in American culture in which the image, at least, of the Native American had a cachet that it does not have today.

By developing storytelling as a dramatic trait in the character, Alexie is able to bring the stories into the film, without using an intrusive narrative voice. This makes a critical political point. Had the voice of self-conscious-ness been represented by a narrator standing outside the story, the film would have communicated a sense of a community that had little awareness of its own mythology. Instead, by putting the stories into Thomas's mouth, Alexie is able to suggest a self-awareness that transcends the poverty we are shown in the film images of the reservation.

Short Cuts It is arguable that *Short Cuts*, Robert Altman and Frank Barhydt's adaptation of a collection of Raymond Carver's short stories, fundamentally violates the quality of the stories by setting them in Los Ange-les. Carver's stories, which are about anonymous people set in unnamed, anonymous towns, largely in borderline financial situations, seem radically altered when set within the glamour that we associate with Los Angeles. Even if one accepts that city as the setting, there is another aspect to *Short Cuts* that seems to challenge the spirit of Carver's stories. We can speculate that Carver chose to write stories, as opposed to novels, in order to explore individual lives or families set in limbo. This form kept him from having to deal with surrounding community. In choosing to construct a feature film using the "grand hotel" technique that ties the stories together, Altman and Barhydt have inevitably created connections that were not originally there. This sense of larger world undercuts the isolation that runs so strongly through the individual stories.

Yet, there is another, in some ways more subtle, level in which this adaptation succeeds. Let's take an example from Carver's story, "They're Not Your Husband," which provides the basis for the *Short Cuts* characters played by Lily Tomlin and Lyle Lovett. In this story, Earl (Tom Waits), visit-ing his waitress wife, Doreen (Lily Tomlin), overhears two men at the coffee shop where Doreen works, commenting on her body. He departs suddenly. "When she began shaking the can of whipped cream, Earl got up, leaving his food, and headed for the door."[10] The action is abrupt, its motivation opaque, and its connection to Doreen shaking the can unclear. Yet this concentration on external details and the refusal to go into the psychological specifics of motivation are characteristic of many Carver stories.

In the film, the sequence is handled as follows. In the first three-shot, one of the men turns from Doreen and looks over to Earl. In a single reverse shot, Earl returns the look. He never looks back to Doreen. This is followed by a wider shot in which Doreen turns away and calls out her order. And then in a wider shot still, Earl suddenly gets up and leaves, his place taken by another man. In a more mainstream construction of this sequence, we might have been with Earl as he looks back at his wife, considers, and leaves. The lack of this reaction, or even a glance at Doreen, gives the scene something of the abruptness that we feel in the story, and in this way, Altman is able to capture some of Carver's distinct voice. Altman uses this technique throughout the film, which despite its setting, is able to evoke the fragile, "surfacy" characters who live in the anonymous town that Carver celebrates.

Conclusion

The common understanding about literary novels making poor mainstream film holds true in our experience. While somewhat successful as pure stories, films such as *L.A. Confidential, The English Patient,* and *The Talented Mr. Ripley* have very little of the textual richness or complexity that the novels from which they were adapted do. We believe that this is largely a result of a style that privileges the dramatic, or story, voice over that of the narrative voice. This more transparent approach reduces the personal perspectives that convey the richness of the literary voice.

Alternative films, by more explicitly foregrounding the voice of the maker, provide richer opportunities—more communication channels, if you like—to convey not only story, but also some element of the teller's perspective on the story. They also allow a greater range of character and moral ambiguity, giving these scripts, and their subsequent films, a greater sense of thickness. Whether it is the surreal toilet swim in *Trainspotting*, the constructed narration and meeting between Stephens and Dolores in *The Sweet Hereafter*, the storyteller within the text in *Smoke Signals*, or the abrupt style of *Short Cuts*, the screenwriters have found ways to use the language of alternative film to extend their adaptations, thereby finding filmic equivalents to the richness of literary fiction.

References

1. Brian Helgeland, *L.A. Confidential,* (1995), 19. Script originally online at http://bamzone.bizland.com/scripts/ellay-confidential_early.html, (now available through the Internet Archive Wayback Machine at http://www.archive.org/web/web.php; archived on July 2, 2001).
2. James Ellroy, *L.A. Confidential* (New York: Warner Books, 1990), 28.
3. Ibid.
4. Irvine Welsh, *Trainspotting* (New York: W.W. Norton & Company, 1993), 25.
5. Ibid.

6. Ibid., 26.
7. John Hodge, *Trainspotting* (1997). Original screenplay available online at http://www.godamongdirectors.com/scripts/trainspotting.shtml.
8. Helgeland, op. cit., p. 69.
9. Sherman Alexie, *The Lone Ranger and Tonto Fistfight in Heaven* (New York: HarperPerennial, 1993), 24.
10. Raymond Carver, "They're not your husband," in *Will You Please Be Quiet, Please?* (New York: McGraw-Hill, 1976), 21.

31
. . . .

Personal Scriptwriting: The Edge

William Goldman, in his amusing book about screenwriting, *Adventures in the Screen Trade*, advises that new screenwriters realize that an excellent screenplay is a well-structured screenplay, but no one knows what constitutes a successful screenplay.[1] An entire world of difference exists between these two desirable adjectives—excellent and successful. Many elements beyond your control determine whether your screenplay is excellent and successful. Agents, producers, directors, and, above all, actors, influence the outcome of your screenplay.

If Goldman's proscription is dire, it certainly isn't overly dramatic. Screenwriting is not akin to a lottery, but time is pushing it in that direction. As successful screenwriters are paid more and more for their screenplays, the risk factor in production suggests an increasingly conservative attitude toward screenplays and screenwriters. Film is already (given its economic structure) the most conservative of the arts! Does this mean that the screenwriter must study and write for the market? Only partially. The search by studios for the successful screenplay is more urgent than ever. Therefore, screenwriters, more than ever before, will have to strive to differentiate themselves from the rest of the marketplace.

All producers expect well-structured screenplays. As a writer, you can't avoid structure. But because producers read with an eye on emulating the latest great success at the box office, you have to capture their interest by writing something different. In the end, the only source of inspiration is those screenplays that are different. This is the reason for the meteoric rise of Spike Lee and John Patrick Shanley. As a writer, you have a choice—to imitate, as do so many others in the marketplace, or to innovate. We suggest that you innovate. If you do, you'll have a better opportunity to obtain excellence and success. This means that you have to move your screenplay beyond structure. It also means that you take on a more personal form of storytelling.

In this chapter, we reiterate screen story conventions and how to write against those conventions. We look at form, character, language, and tone, and highlight narrative strategies that yield fresh options. We also highlight how the other arts provide sources of options to strengthen your screen story. We want to stress that there is no strictly technical solution to writing a successful screenplay. Screenplays are a mix of technical form, good story, characters by whom you are fascinated, and a deep interest on your part in inviting the audience to stay with your characters for 2 hours. During these 2 hours, you want the audience to feel pain and pleasure, and at the end of the experience, you want them to leave stimulated or exhausted. You want the audience to think and to feel, and, in doing so, to feel a level of satisfaction for having spent 2 hours with your story.

If this stimulation is missing, you have failed. If it is present, you have worked a small miracle, given the distractions of modern life. You will have convinced, hopefully, a large paying group to suspend their sense of the present and enter the world you've created. After 2 hours of escape into your world, they've been entertained, stimulated, and may leave not quite the same as when they entered. This change may last 20 seconds or 20 years. This is the extent of your influence.

Your Story

Whatever the source for your screen story, whatever your motivation for writing the story, it has to reach an audience, or it remains incomplete. Unlike a novel, which can be published modestly, or a play, which can be produced locally, a film requires an infrastructure for production, distribution, and exhibition. Consequently, the economics of production preclude the vast majority of screenplays from being produced. With producers, distributors, and exhibitors all eyeing audiences to determine what will sell, screenwriters are constantly pressed to do this as well. The results are screenplays that are strongly influenced by current issues, be they social, political, or economic. Almost any personality or event that has significantly captured the public's interest, even for an instant, merits screen consideration.

Your story, however, doesn't have to be a direct rendering of such an event. The perspective you choose, along with everything else, is up to you. This is where your individuality can yield an interesting angle. This is where you begin to apply the range of narrative strategies that best suit your story. This is where your life experience helps you coax an unusual perspective from your story.

This individualism explains the powerful moral fervor of the scripts of Paul Schrader. Whether the subject is Jesus Christ (*The Last Temptation of Christ*), a high-priced male prostitute (*American Gigolo*), or pornography (*Hardcore*), Schrader's perspective makes his screenplays intense, probing, and unpredictable. He's made the subject his own. However we feel about his treatment of the subject, the films differ dramatically from other screenplays about similar subject matter.

Turning to another writer, Blake Edwards, who grew up in Hollywood, we notice that whatever the subject matter or genre, Edwards's screenplays are, first and foremost, entertaining. His desire to entertain rather than to risk offending blunts the intensity of his subject matter—for example, his films about sexual identity (*Victor/Victoria*) and middle-age crises (*10*)—but the subject matter is as serious as is that of Schrader's scripts. Edwards, above all, wants to entertain, so he uses the situation comedy, rather than the melodrama, to provide entertainment values that are much stronger than are those in a Schrader screenplay.

The key point here is that these two screenwriters are serious, but their priorities and approaches differ from one another. Both are successful, individualistic screenwriters. The best approach to your story is the approach that respects your individuality and seeks to differentiate your story from those about the same subject.

Approaches to Structure

The respect paid to structure in contemporary produced screenplays grows every day. Respectfully, structure has become Hollywood's eleventh commandment. Challenge to the structural model has been tempting only to those who are established in the industry. No studio is going to tell Woody Allen or Spike Lee that it will not finance his next film. Allen's and Lee's patterns of experimentation mark the route of Fellini and Bergman. Having reached their audience, all of these writer-directors want to experiment. The result is that they often challenge our notions of structure and allude to what structure can be.

We are not suggesting that you should rail and rebel against Syd Field or Bob McKee. But, we are saying that audiences today are very media-wise and they tire of repetition. You can help your career and foster your creativity by varying your structural approach. Structural options begin to develop once you have a main character, a premise, and the nature of the story (i.e., the genre). Immediately, you face two issues: at what point will your audience enter the story and, if you sense a possible ending, what is the end point or climax?

Whether you opt for a three-act structure depends on how open ended you want your story to be. If you see a story with a resolution, a three-act structure is called for. However, if you don't find a resolution necessary or interesting, you may opt for a two-act structure. If you do, realize that this choice has implications for every other element in your screenplay. To make a two-act screenplay work, you need gripping characters whom we won't mind spending time with. Since there is less action, particularly rising action, in the two-act approach, your audience will demand more from your dialogue as well as from your characters. The conflict that doesn't happen visually must be manifested in the language.

The decrease in action also has implications for the number of plot points and the number of plot-oriented devices you employ (i.e., reversals and surprise). Because the amount of plot is lessened in the two-act approach, there will be less need for reversals and surprises. The audience's involvement will come from their involvement with your characters, not from their involvement with your plot.

If you *do* choose the three-act structure, there remain many structural options available to you. Rather than writing within the context of genre, you can challenge or alter a primary genre motif. One example is *Raising Arizona*, by the Coen brothers. The main character (Nicolas Cage) isn't driven by material success like the classic gangster is. He is a man who is driven by his love for his wife. She wants a baby, so he steals a baby for her. His sweetness is an element that is foreign to the main character in the gangster genre, whose transgressions are carried out to get ahead materially in society. Yet *Raising Arizona* remains, at least partially, a gangster film.

Another option available to the writer is to mix genres. This approach is rapidly becoming an industry standard. The mix of the science fiction and gangster genres is the most popular. But the most unusual of combinations have proved successful. Certainly, audiences have found mixed-genre films to be an appealing novelty. The issue for you, whether you alter a motif or mix genres, is whether it improves your story. This is a critical question. If you alter a motif or mix genres for novelty's sake, the benefit to your story remains superficial. If, on the other hand, the mix helps reach another level of meaning that makes your story more credible and revealing, then the structural shift has served you well.

The protagonist–antagonist mix is a power struggle of considerable force in the melodrama. *Kramer vs. Kramer* is an example in which both protagonist and antagonist are members of the same family—husband and wife. This same approach is taken in *Music Box*, but this film has a twist. In *Music Box*, daughter–father are protagonist–antagonist, but the daughter doesn't know it. In fact, for the majority of the screen story, she is her father's lawyer. Only at the end of Act Three does she face the truth about her father and his Nazi past. This twist of bringing protagonist and antagonist close together within the melodrama lends a force to the story that would not be present if this choice hadn't been employed by a screenwriter such as Joe Eszterhas. It also helps create the background story of the film. The key is that the motif shift brings us into the story in a deeper way than if the same story were presented with the daughter, father, and the father's lawyer. In *Music Box*, the motif shift adds an additional layer of meaning to the melodrama.

If we look at Errol Morris's mixed-genre film *The Thin Blue Line*, the use of the dramatic form of the police story together with the investigative documentary makes the film both realistic and stylized. The artifice of the drama makes the viewer ask the question: Am I being manipulated or did this really happen? The viewer is invited to consider who is manipulating whom. Consequently, *The Thin Blue Line*, in using a mixed-genre approach to structure, makes the central theme of the documentary come alive for the viewer. Who are we to believe? Randall, his accuser, the police, or the filmmakers?

Remember: the strength of challenging a motif or a mixed-genre approach lies in what the narrative strategy adds to your story. Does it make the story deeper? Does the approach give us new insights about your main character? Does the approach help sidestep audience expectations? If it does, you are on your way to writing a unique screen story.

Approaches to Character

Perhaps the most important decision you make about your screenplay is the identity of your main character. You must then ask yourself why you have chosen this person to tell your story. The appropriateness and flexibility of your main character can't be overestimated. Not only does the audience enter the story through that character, they also relate to the story to the degree in which they become involved (positively or negatively) with that character.

Your decision about character has many implications about the nature of the other characters, as well as the degree of plot in your story. The specificity of your character—the socio-economical, regional, cultural, political, and psychological qualities of that character—affects the nature of the dialogue.

Real Drama and Unreal Life

At the baseline, your character has to convince us of her credibility. This doesn't necessarily mean you need to take a slice-of-life approach to the nature of the character. Indeed, too literal a view of realism yields an unrealistic character in dramatic terms. To put it simply, drama and real life are distant cousins; they are not synonymous. Drama is, in a sense, compressed real life complete with coincidence. Real life might be dramatic, but more likely the dramatic incidents are stretched out over a long length of time.

Screenwriters have to use compression, coincidence, and conflict in order to create dramatic situations. Dramatic situations are the meat and potatoes of audience expectations. We experience the long stretches of filler in our lives. We won't pay to see more of the same thing; we want drama. So your characters have to be credible. In order to be credible to the audience, they have to get involved in events and with other characters far beyond what might be called credible. This contradiction is willingly overcome if you fascinate us and convince us to suspend our sense of realism in order to enter into, with your character, the screen story.

The Role of Dilemma

When George (Bob Hoskins), the main character in Neil Jordan and David Leland's *Mona Lisa*, returns from 7 years in prison, he finds that his wife has thrown him out and his mobster boss, for whom he suffered imprisonment, is no longer interested in employing him. George's dilemma is that he is free, but he feels betrayed by his two principal sources of support—his wife and his boss. How George deals with this dilemma is the subject of the balance of the film. The fact that George is both violent and tender adds dimension to this gangster film centered in London.

The dilemma serves to very quickly bring us into the story and to see George as disadvantaged. In spite of his being a gangster, his callous rejection by his wife and the corporate style of gangster life seem to justify George's outbursts. He yearns for life as it was. The dilemma helps us identify with George. Once this identification has taken place, we are ready to follow George through the story, hoping that he will be able to resolve his problem. Whether the dilemma is coincidental, as it is in Dalton Trumbo's *Lonely are the Brave*, or logical, as in *Mona Lisa*, the role of the dilemma is to bring us into the story quickly and to get us to identify with the main character.

The Role of Charisma

As we have mentioned earlier in the book, whether one describes the main character as appealing or charming, main characters need charisma. The sense of energy that the character displays may develop out of a sense of commitment or out of an intensity that may be sexual, aggressive, or both. It is valuable to the writer when the main character isn't likable, but the character does have to attract the viewer; he has to be charismatic.

While dilemma gets us involved with your character, charisma keeps us involved. In William Inge's *Splendor in the Grass*, the main character's intensity is sexual. In John Steinbeck's *Viva Zapata!*, the character's intensity is political. In Elia Kazan's *America, America*, the character's intensity is born out of a will to survive. In each case, the main character has an honesty as well as an intensity that shows the character's vulnerability. The result is that we remain involved with each of these characters throughout the screen story.

The Tradition of Non-conformity

In America, non-conformity as a philosophy of life has always had appeal. This is not lost on screenwriters. Often, they will position the main character in such a way that he appears to be a non-conformist. Whether we view the country singer, portrayed by Robert Duvall in Horton Foote's *Tender Mercies*, as a stranger to the community or as a man with an unconventional vocation, he doesn't quite fit into the community. He is an outsider. So, too, are Pelle, in Billie August's *Pelle the Conqueror*, and Pike Bishop, in Walon Green's *The Wild Bunch*.

It is useful to the writer to create an additional layer of conflict when the main character's position is that of a non-conformist. Nola, in Spike Lee's *She's Gotta Have It*, and Bree Daniels, in Andy and David Lewis's *Klute*, both pursue non-conformist behavior. The non-conformist main character has a natural appeal in a country where non-conformity, or individualism, has a historical backdrop. The fact that American culture has always embraced the non-conformist does much to explain the popularity of the anti-hero—the cowboy and the gangster. The usefulness of non-conformity in behavior and appearance is dramatic and appealing. Indeed, the writing tradition suggests that the use of a non-conformist as your main character enhances his appeal.

Character Versus Plot

An issue you will continually face has to do with the primacy of character over plot or plot over character—the foreground–background dilemma. As we mentioned, stories are enhanced by having both foreground and background. However, particular stories and genres need more of one than the other. Adventure films, farce, satire, and musicals do not need complex characters, but they do need elaborate plots. Other genres, such as the melodrama and film noir, depend on the complexity of the characters. Consequently, the screen time spent with characterization rather than with plot in melodrama and film noir is much greater.

When the background story takes precedence over the foreground story, such as in Sam Shepard's *Fool for Love*, character becomes everything, and the plot—the foreground story—withers in importance. In the extreme case of background story primacy, such as in John Patrick Shanley's *Moonstruck*, the plot can be described in two lines. In these cases, where the background story is prevalent, the nature of the character, the role of charisma, and the role of dilemma become even more important. The consequence is a reliance on character.

Implied in the reliance on character is the increased reliance on dialogue. Your dialogue in background stories has to be exceptionally charged and appealing to compensate for the simpler plot. The audience's need for stimulation is no less in the strong background screen story than it is in the foreground screen story. You should keep in mind the tradeoff between plot and character. What does your story need? Does it need more of one than the other?

Character Types

There are particular character types that may be useful as you consider the nature of your main character.

The Marginal Character

As mentioned earlier, audiences find the outsider appealing as a main character. The sense of mystery and surprise this character brings to your story is useful. But marginality only works when it interacts with the larger society or with mainstream ideas. If Nola in *She's Gotta Have It* didn't flirt with the idea of a life with one of her three men, there would be no personal conflict and, consequently, no story. Likewise, Mozart may be a musical genius in Peter Shaffer's *Amadeus*, but his manners and behavior are far below the expectations of the Viennese court in which he seeks fame and fortune. He is an outsider looking to breach the social order, and his failure leads to his death.

Whether your main characters are prostitutes, pimps, or princes, the marginalized position in which they find themselves comes alive when you create dramatic situations in which margin and center clash in terms of characters.

The Mad Character

An extreme example of a marginal character is a mad character. Whether madness is the subject matter of the story, as in Ken Loach's *Family Life*, or the posture taken by the character to meet the world, as in Julius Epstein's *Reuben, Reuben*, the mad character places the viewer in a challenging position. The mad character is not charismatic; in fact, he is the opposite. This character pushes us away to reflect on his plight and the reasons for it.

Often, the writer will use the mad character to comment on significant relationships or on society. Robert Klane uses mad behavior and mad characters to comment on society. His screenplays for *Where's Poppa?* and *Weekend at Bernie's* use humor to make the mad behavior more palatable. Essentially, the behavior of the mad character remains irrational. However, the fact that he experiences humiliation causes us to feel sympathy for him. The benefit of using a mad character is the distance between the character and the audience. This distance allows the viewer to reflect upon events. In this sense, the mad character is useful in the same way the ironic character is useful.

One last point: Because of the extreme behavior of the mad character, the writer has a volatile unpredictability that can be useful to rouse the feelings of the viewers beyond the usual experience. Bo Goldman uses this powerful quality in *One Flew Over the Cuckoo's Nest* and *Shoot the Moon*.

The Victim

In many ways, the mad character is the ultimate victim. But many other screen stories present the main character as a victim without the overlay of madness. The screwball comedy, film noir, the horror film, the satire, the melodrama, the war film, and the situation comedy can all present the main character as a victim. Who can forget Felix in Neil Simon's *The Odd Couple*? The benefit of using this position for the main character is the inherent conflict of the position. If the character is being exploited by a situation or a person, we can readily hope he will not only survive, but will also overcome his dilemma. It's the old story of rooting for the underdog.

There are stories where the character is being victimized by himself. The main character in Roger Simon and Paul Mazursky's *Enemies: A Love Story* needn't go on acting like the victim, but a mixture of living in the past and fearing the present maintains his position as a victim. As long as you can avoid a position in which the character accepts being a victim, the main character as victim is useful to you. Just as the marginal character needs the center to rail against, the victim needs to struggle against the oppressor. As long as the character struggles, we hope for the best and fear for the worst, a useful position for the writer to have us in.

The Hero

The natural position for the main character is the hero. This is probably the easiest character with which to work. The hero is attractive, has charisma, and, by virtue of the dilemma in which you place him, his struggle can be easily presented as heroic. We are not suggesting that this is the position most useful for your screenplay. Rather, we are suggesting that the presentation of the main character as a hero needn't be like James Bond or Josie Wales. It does mean that the behavior of Rory, in *Inside Moves*, in his decision to make something of his life rather than remain a victim, is heroic. Rory is a hero in spite of his passivity. Regina's decision to go against her mother in Lillian Hellman's *The Little Foxes* also makes Regina a hero.

In order to make the main character, even a passive character, a hero, you need a plot that suggests the many barriers to heroic action. You also need an antagonist who is so formidable that the behavior of a Rory or a Regina will seem heroic. Heroic action does not need superhuman effort. From a writer's perspective, this option only needs proper positioning of the character and plotting of the story. The main character as a hero probably offers you the strongest formula for identification, but to be credible, it challenges you to create a story that, on a personal level, seems like the climb up Mt. Everest; it's tough, but worth a try.

Your Attitude Toward Character

Your attitude toward the character is the most important decision you'll make in your screenplay. You don't have to love your character, but you should be fascinated by him—so fascinated that exploring the facets of that person is very real for you. If the character grips you, your audience should follow readily.

A variety of positions can help you set up your character so that conflict flows more readily. The marginal character and the mad character are positioned to fight the values of the center, the society. This struggle brings us into their stories. The victim and the hero are more readily viewed as characters with whom we can easily identify. Again, the situation in which they find themselves is a conflict; therefore, we can enter their story quickly. This is where tone becomes very important when articulating your relationship (and ours) with the main character. Will it be a tone in accord with genre expectations or will you deploy an ironic tone?

Seduction and Scriptwriting

It is not enough to make us care about your character. It is not enough that you grip us with your character. If your screenplay is to succeed, we have to experience all the ups and downs with your main character. To be more specific, we suggest that most successful screenplays tend to acknowledge a special relationship between you, the writer, and the viewer. We intentionally call this relationship between writer and audience *seduction and scriptwriting*. The hyperbolic term *seduction* is used to focus your attention on the devices you use to involve us in your screen story. To capture our attention, we suggest that you involve us in an intense relationship with your main character, and that in the course of the screen story, we in the audience have to live through an emotional relationship with that screen story. The relationship needs many of the satisfactions of intense personal relationships. We need to love and hate and to resolve the state of the relationship. Our contention is that without this level of intensity, structure, plotting, character, and elegant language will not be enough to link us to the screen story.

To illustrate what we mean, we will look at five screen stories dealing with the same story. Essentially we want to illustrate why *Wyatt Earp*, the Lawrence Kasdan and Dan Gordon version of the Wyatt Earp story, failed. We contend that it failed because it did not establish a deep relationship with the main character, Wyatt Earp. By looking at four other versions, we will show how important it is for the writer to create and maintain an intense relationship between us and the main character.

The four other versions of the Wyatt Earp story are *Tombstone*, written by Kevin Jarre; *Hour of the Gun*, written by Edward Anhalt; *The Gunfight at the OK Corral*, written by Leon Uris; and *My Darling Clementine*, written by Samuel G. Engel. These and *Wyatt Earp* share the following elements:

1. Wyatt Earp is the central character.
2. He is the sheriff of Tombstone, Arizona.

3. He was formerly the sheriff of Dodge City, Kansas, where he earned a reputation as a lawman.
4. He worked closely with his brothers, Virgil and Morgan, as both sheriff and deputy.
5. He struck up a friendship with Doc Holliday, a gunfighter who was a gambler and former dentist in the East.
6. Tombstone is a tough frontier town. The cowboys, including the Clantons, the McLowerys, Curly Bill, and Johnny Ringo, were the dominant outlaw force in the territory.
7. The famous gunfight at the OK Corral is fought in Tombstone. The Earps and Doc Holliday fought against the Clantons and the McLowerys.
8. As a consequence of the gunfight, Morgan Earp is assassinated.
9. Wyatt Earp wreaks revenge on the cowboys by destroying those who stood against him, and Doc Holliday continues to help.
10. Wyatt Earp, although he believes in his family, is a man with rough edges. He functions well as a lawman because he is as ruthless as the cowboys.
11. All of the Earp stories focus on the 1880 period when he is sheriff of Tombstone.

These are the story elements of all five screen versions. Each of them works with the historical record, some more literally than others. The two versions that attempt the greatest verisimilitude—Anhalt's *Hour of the Gun* and Kasdan and Gordon's *Wyatt Earp*—are the weakest screenplays.

The Anhalt version opens with the actual gunfight at the OK Corral and focuses on its aftermath. It's not quite docudrama, but the historical events are the focus of this version. The Gordon–Kasdan version covers 40 years in Earp's life, beginning with him as an adolescent and ending with him in middle age. The events of the OK Corral gunfight occur shortly after the midpoint, although the preparations for the fight open the film. The goal here seems to be to look at Earp the man while dismantling Earp the legend. The three other versions each take a particular dramatic approach to the story.

In typical John Ford fashion, Samuel G. Engel's script, *My Darling Clementine*, approaches the story as a struggle of two families, the Earps and the Clantons. The Earps represent family values—loyalty, responsibility, and morality—while the Clantons, although loyal to one another, are cattle thieves and murderers who kill James Earp at the beginning of the story. The gunfight at the OK Corral becomes the ritual that purges Tombstone of its immoral element and establishes the primacy of the Earp family values as American, as a source of strength of the individual, Wyatt Earp.

Leon Uris's *Gunfight at the OK Corral*, as with *My Darling Clementine*, takes place principally in Tombstone. This version focuses on the evolution of the friendship of Wyatt Earp and Doc Holliday. Although Holliday is important in all of the versions, no single version focuses on him as much. Indeed, the friendship supersedes the antagonists whether they are the Clantons, Curly Bill, or Johnny Ringo. Friendship and personal sacrifice are all that count in this version.

Kevin Jarre's *Tombstone* focuses on Wyatt Earp as a man with material ambitions for himself and his family. Those ambitions take him to Tombstone and away from the law. However, in Tombstone, the power of the cowboys is such that they stand in the way of his material climb. He takes up the law to protect what he views as his material well being. The cowboys are so relentless and vengeful that all who stand in their way become their targets; they force the confrontation with the Earps. (In this version, Wyatt is deputized by Virgil in order to fight as a lawman at the OK Corral.) Doc Holliday, Wyatt's friend, fights as well. Only the assassination of Morgan forces Wyatt to eliminate the cowboys. He uses all means, and his ruthlessness is necessary for his survival. In the end, he has lost the very thing he came to Tombstone for: prosperity.

In the most successful versions—*My Darling Clementine* and *Tombstone*—there is a natural progression in our relationship with the main character. Each film begins with a clear articulation of the goal of the main character—prosperity for the family. In *My Darling Clementine*, prosperity involves a cattle drive. In *Tombstone*, it involves buying into a gambling emporium/saloon. In each version, a bully taunts the ordinary citizenry of Tombstone. And in each case, the objectionable person is easily overcome by Earp. The consequence is that Earp is a highly desirable person for the position of sheriff. In *My Darling Clementine*, he accepts; in Tombstone, he does not. In each film, we see Earp struggle to maintain his position in Tombstone as either lawman or businessman. And in each case, a clear antagonist emerges to position himself against Earp. In both films, that character is Ike Clanton (although Curly Bill and Johnny Ringo are more prominent co-antagonists in *Tombstone*). Our point here is that the clarity, persistence, and cruelty of the antagonist(s) in *My Darling Clementine* and *Tombstone* draw us closer to the main character, Wyatt Earp.

Another dimension of our relationship with Wyatt Earp is to see his vulnerability in a love relationship. In *My Darling Clementine*, it is Earp's unrequited love for Clementine that makes him seem vulnerable. In *Tombstone*, it is his attraction to Josie, the actress, that makes him vulnerable. Since Earp has an ongoing relationship with the prostitute Mattie, he doesn't take up a simultaneous relationship with Josie. He is loyal—and, consequently, lonely. Therefore, in both of these versions, Earp seems a man incapable of finding love. The loss enables his sense of responsibility to his family and to Mattie.

Finally, there are the concepts of family and friendship. Earp works closely with his brothers, and in both versions he is strongly supported by an alter ego, the educated, articulate killer Doc Holliday. In *My Darling Clementine*, Doc dies in the gunfight. In *Tombstone*, Doc fights on with Earp against the cowboys after the famous gunfight. In the latter version, Earp is present at the sanitarium when Holliday is near death. Although much is made of family, it is the friendship and its dignity that emotionalizes both *My Darling Clementine* and *Tombstone* (as it did in *The Gunfight at the OK Corral*); the two men are opposites, but friendship remains important to both. Their mutual commitment in the midst of a hostile environment, Tombstone, makes them both appealing. Their relationship humanizes and serves to ennoble the notion of friendship and, in this case, its object, Wyatt Earp.

Returning for the moment to the concept of family, this issue is much more powerful in *My Darling Clementine*, where it is two families, the Earps and the Clantons, who sum up the struggle of good against evil in Tombstone. Consequently, family is very important in *My Darling Clementine* and it serves to root and ennoble the Wyatt Earp character.

We turn now to the flaws in the Gordon–Kasdan version, which essentially come down to our lack of involvement with the main character. This version fails for the reasons that the Jarre and Engel versions succeed.

The Latest Version: Lawrence Kasdan's Wyatt Earp

First let's look at the issue of the main character's goal. In the Engel and Jarre versions, we learn the goal of the main character right away. This is not the case in the Gordon–Kasdan version, where we first see the young Earp trying to run off to war. For the first hour of the film, we understand him as a character struggling between what he wants to do and what his father wants him to do. He experiences disappointments and tragedy (the loss of his first wife), but we never do know what his goal is. We have to assume that he is a character without a clear goal, an ambivalent character rather than a character who wants material success for his family, as the Earp character does at the outset of *My Darling Clementine* and *Tombstone*.

A second problem in the Gordon–Kasdan script is that there is no clear antagonist. The Clantons, the McLowerys, Curly Bill, and Johnny Ringo are present in Tombstone, but we never understand the antipathy of the Earps toward them, nor do we understand what they are fighting about. It is as if Gordon and Kasdan are so concerned with debunking the myth of Earp that they make him his own antagonist. The consequence is that we do not understand Earp in his struggle. We watch as observers on the sidelines rather than as participants in Earp's struggle.

And what of Wyatt Earp the lover-in-waiting of *My Darling Clementine* and *Tombstone*? This is not the Earp we meet in the Gordon–Kasdan version. Instead, we find a man who never recovers from the loss of his first wife—he takes up with a prostitute, Mattie, and simultaneously begins to sleep with the actress, Josie. Instead of Earp the vulnerable male, here we have Earp the selfish male. Instead of caring, he seems cruel. Instead of vulnerable, he is cold and calculating. This is not a character we want to be involved with.

Turning to the issues of family and friendship, we find a similar Earp. In the Gordon–Kasdan version, as in the others, Wyatt does work with his brothers. However, the brothers' wives constantly complain that Wyatt runs their lives and eventually ruins them. In this version, Wyatt Earp is in a constant power struggle for control of his family. This is hardly the ideal Earp family portrayed in Engel's *My Darling Clementine*. As with Wyatt the unrequited lover, here Wyatt the family man is unattractive.

This leaves only the issue of Earp's friendship with Doc Holliday as a source of audience empathy for Earp. There is friendship here, but it's a case of too little too late. Earp seems so impervious to feeling that the empathetic Holliday appears marginal and pathetic. Given Holliday's fragility, the friendship says more about the Holliday character. Consequently, it does not help our relationship with the Earp character as it does in the more successful versions.

At all levels, the Gordon–Kasdan version of the Wyatt Earp character deflects us from an active involvement and empathy with the character. Without that intense relationship with Earp, the screen story fails. Indeed, in any screen story, if the writer does not seek and cultivate a special relationship between the main character and the audience, the story will fail. To succeed, the audience needs that special relationship; writers can cultivate that relationship by understanding the dramatic means to achieve it.

How to Make Your Script Your Own

If the narrative strategy you've employed takes advantage of your character choice and your structural choice surprises and delights the viewer, all that remains to making the script your own is to infuse the script with details that mean something to you and with language that allows your emotions to speak. This may sound optimistic, but it isn't.

What we are saying is that having a good feeling for the structural choice and character type that best suits your story isn't quite enough to make it unique. You have to be willing to invest more feeling in the story. This effort is akin to the mechanical adjustment you can make to alter a character who is a stereotype. Move away from the idealistic professor who is curious about everything to the idealistic professor who follows up his curiosity with action and you've got Indiana Jones. But it isn't until Jeffrey Boam begins to probe the conflicting relationship between Jones and his father that we begin to understand Jones's quick frustration and misunderstanding in his relationships. This move humanizes Jones and makes the third film in the series, *Indiana Jones and the Last Crusade*, seem fresher. Jones is now far from stereotype. This is the sort of creative metamorphosis that makes the story seem new and appealing. This is the path Alvin Sargent follows in *Julia*, and Sam Shepard and Wim Wenders follow in *Paris, Texas*. It's the path Julius Epstein has followed from *Casablanca* to *Reuben, Reuben*.

Screenwriting and the Other Arts

Screenwriters are storytellers who write stories for film. Some make a great deal of money but get very little respect from their peers. Most make very little money and get very little respect from their peers. It has always been perplexing, but that's the way it is. Nevertheless, writing talents such as Clifford Odets, Sam Raphaelson, Preston Sturges, and Harold Pinter have been attracted to the form. The works of Billy Wilder, Joseph Mankiewicz, and Ben Hecht remain vital and artful, especially from today's vantage point.

Just as other industries compartmentalize function, so, too, do the arts. A screenwriter is no longer a writer from a community of storytellers. She is a screenwriter. However, it is important that the screenwriter reconsider her links with other communicative and popular arts. We have much to learn from playwrights, novelists, and journalists, just as they have something to learn from us. Whether their interests are social action or a good laugh, they share our interest in capturing our audience. They, and screenwriters, live in a world of ideas.

Screenwriters can strengthen their foreground stories by telling them clearly and quickly, as do journalists, who have to maintain reader interest to the end of the story: at any point, a reader can set aside a newspaper. Likewise, screenwriters can learn much from the strength the playwright brings to the background story. Character and language are all that the playwright employs to keep his audience. Consequently, these elements have to be amusing, stimulating, and must compensate for the relative loss in action the stage suffers relative to film. Screenwriters can also benefit from the use of stronger background stories. Screenwriters can be emboldened by the structural experiments of writers such as Ann Beattie (*Picturing Will*) and Don DeLillo (*Libra*). These structural experiments add layers of meaning to the content of the work, just as the structural experiments of screenwriters such as Stanley Kubrick and Spike Lee add meaning to their work.

Screenwriters and the Market

In *Broadcast News*, James Brooks begins the film with three small vignettes about the three characters of the story as adolescents. After this prologue, the film shifts to the time period of the film, some 15 years later. Brooks's point is that characters come from somewhere and go somewhere. They have regional, cultural, sexual, and behavioral differences. The same can be said for writers. Unfortunately, if you were to watch all of the films released in any 3-month period, you'd hardly know it. You'd think all screenwriters grew up a 10-minute drive from Universal Studios, were all the same sex, and were born minutes apart.

Our point, here, is that you are the only *you* there is, and your script will be better if it reflects your individuality rather than what you think is selling today. This isn't a particularly radical thought. If you look at cinematographers and directors, notice how many come from Australia, England, The Netherlands, and Germany. Hollywood has always sought out talent wherever it was available. The only thing American writers have going for them is their ease at writing colloquial English. This will change as English becomes more and more widespread and will end the American writers' monopoly on screenwriting—unless, of course, we start writing better scripts.

Ann Beattie, Richard Ford, Bharati Mukherjee, and Margaret Atwood are all exceptional world-class novelists. Playwrights such as Sam Shepard and Neil Simon have also made their mark around the world. Will the art of screenwriting follow suit? It will when screenwriters tell stronger, more personal stories. To compete in the fickle entertainment market, screenwriters have to be as innovative as are novelists and playwrights.

We hope you will be.

We know you can be.

Note

1. William Goldman, *Adventures in the Screen Trade* (New York: Warner Books, 1983).

32

Personal Scriptwriting: Beyond the Edge

Up until this point, we have primarily been discussing the scripts for feature-length theatrical films written in standard screenplay form so that others might direct them. However, with the growth of alternative sources of funding and the low-tech production opportunities afforded by Hi8 video, super16, or even Fisher Price Pixelvision, we are seeing an explosion of productions of varying lengths, intended for a wide range of audiences, many of them written to be directed by the writer. Although some of these are so personal as to be elaborate home movies, others have demonstrated new ways to speak from experience and, in so doing, they have redefined our notion of the possibilities of the personal script.

In addition to their raising questions of screenwriting technique, these alternative, self-made forms have served as vehicles for underrepresented peoples to express a voice that otherwise may have been denied them. Many times, such expression unites directing and writing, suggesting that the way we see and the stories we use to organize our seeing have to be developed together. Thus, many of these alternative films open up story structures to provide opportunities to explore moments of visualization and rhythm that can be prepared for through writing, but cannot be directly expressed through writing alone. Working through distribution channels such as Deep Dish TV and Women Make Movies, women, historically minimally employed as mainstream film and television writers and directors, have transformed low-tech video into an expressive form in its own right, while Third World Newsreel has provided distribution to emerging writers and directors of color.

We would like to conclude *Alternative Scriptwriting* with a brief consideration of a few short films, paying particular attention to their development of new narrative languages that serve as expression of voices not traditionally heard. But we cannot do this without first considering once more the power and the problems associated with working close to personal experience. As we have said before, one of the central premises of this book has been to encourage writing out of the self, because that is where the deepest possibilities for self-expression and originality lie. But, as writing teachers, we see everyday examples of what can get created under the notion of the personal—highly self-involved stories whose authors write with the same blindness that cripples their characters. The approach to the personal we are talking about must find a way to counter this by requiring both immediacy and reflection. Without the immediacy, our work will have neither heart nor drive. However, without the reflection, our work risks being only an immature self-justification of the particular limitations that bedevil our life. To break out of this, we must find some way to look with clarity at the very personal experience from which we are writing.

Seeing Oneself

Undigested, our lives, our personal perceptions, and our experiences communicate nothing. Without any prior extra-textual interest in the author, we cannot expect our audience to care. That which is purely personal is, by definition, inherently uninteresting to others. Although this is not true of textbooks in fiction writing, most texts on screenwriting warn against this personal writing for exactly this reason—in a medium that needs to reach millions of viewers, it is assumed we cannot find something in the details of our lives that is sufficiently broad.

Screenplay texts stress conceptual issues such as structure, act breaks, and even external conceptions of character as a means of separating writers from the personal, of concentrating on communication practices rather than on the extraction of meaning from what we know best. Screenplay texts do this for a number of reasons, of which two are important to us here. The first is that mainstream film, almost by definition, substitutes the broad and the general for the individual. The second is that while it is possible to guide writers by making general statements about structure in a textbook, it is not possible to discuss how to make meaningful and universal the individual experiences that make up our lives and that we seek to transform into story. While we will provide some examples, we have no illusions we can do that here.

Being aware of the danger must not keep us from working out of our own sense of the world, because without doing so, we have little true investment in our work. We must learn, however, that while we fully embrace our experience, we also must stand outside it and understand what the viewer might make of it. The central issue here is not one of technique but rather one of courage and honesty in looking at ourselves. We all have areas of darkness where our motivations are not clear or our self-perceptions serve to hide our disappointments. This can be rich and powerful stuff, but it can also be terrifying to examine. But we cannot write about these areas without honest self-awareness.

Characters may in fact never escape this trap of self-delusion, but we, as writers, cannot let ourselves fall in. We must push our characters to the point where they either must see or be lost.

The Intensely Personal: A Few Short Films *Peel* and *Molly's Pilgrim*

We will start as we did in Chapters 2 and 3, by comparing a traditional short film with an alternative short film.

In *Molly's Pilgrim*,[1] a recent Russian Jewish immigrant girl is teased by her schoolmates because of her accent and her misunderstanding of American culture. Assigned to make a Pilgrim doll for Thanksgiving, she brings in instead a doll dressed in a Russian folk costume. Her class and her teacher laugh at her misunderstanding of how a Pilgrim should look, until Molly explains that she has come to America to seek freedom and that makes her a Pilgrim also. The teacher, realizing that it has been a mistake to laugh at Molly, then connects the Thanksgiving feast to the Jewish Festival of the Tabernacle, and Molly's classmates come to accept her as one of their own.

Jane Campion's *Peel*[2] is much more difficult to summarize. A man, his sister, and his son, driving back from viewing a piece of land, fight, pull off the road, and, although the alliances change, continue to fight. The film ends with the son jumping on the car's roof as the sister sulks inside and the brother sits dejectedly on the rear bumper. On one level, looking at *Peel* and *Molly's Pilgrim* together is unfair, because *Molly's Pilgrim* is designed for a young adult audience while *Peel* is not. Yet *Molly's Pilgrim* is valuable to us because it illustrates in a short form some of the elements we have talked about as characteristic of mainstream film:

- Problems are shown to belong to individuals, not to society at large.
- When individuals overcome the problems, the problems vanish.
- Stories have a clear beginning, middle, and end that shape experience in a satisfying way.
- The individual voice of the filmmaker is concealed behind the working out of the story.
- The implied perspective of the filmmaker regards the class's ultimate acceptance of Molly as right and proper, as does the viewer.
- This eventual acceptance is set up as the correct answer in the beginning, and the story serves to bring us to its realization.

We can see the clarity of this design by considering the way *Molly's Pilgrim* begins. Molly stares at a music box that we read as representing her Russian past. Her mother enters and begins to speak Russian; Molly interrupts, asking her mother to speak English. The two-part split represented by the music box and by speaking English resolves at the end of the story, when Molly has both her Russian Pilgrim and her English friends.

Peel works on totally different levels. The character tension develops first between the man and his son, because the son refuses to stop throwing an orange peel out the window, and then, after the son has been sent off to gather the discarded peel, the tension shifts to the man and his sister. The text of the ensuing argument is trivial—the sister is angry that she has gone on this expedition with the brother because she will miss a favorite television program. The argument appears continuous, without end, and seems to conceal more than it reveals. Finally, an added element of tension that drives the story is the threat from the cars that are whizzing past on the highway.

Let's look at the conflict a little closer. In a mainstream film, the main characters are thought to be in a transitory state—the playing out of the story is designed to bring them to resolution. If the conflict does not resolve, the characters will remain undefined and the film will not appear to be over. (Think, for instance, of how vague the character of Rick in *Casablanca* would be if the film ended before he made his final decision about Ilsa). Thus, conflict functions as an obstacle for resolution; it must be transcended for the story to end.

As the character moves to resolution, several things tend to happen. First, the subtext emerges and in most cases is confronted head-on. This is part of what gives many mainstream films a "self-help" feel—confronting feelings leads to overcoming them. (It is what makes a film such as *sex, lies, and videotape*, which initially feels original, so predictable and pat at the end). Thus, the class's recognition of how unfairly they have misjudged Molly in rejecting her Pilgrim is a necessary precursor to accepting her in the end.

Second, a lurking potential for resolution that has been set up earlier in the story becomes activated. Molly is initially rejected by a number of classmates, who represent a spectrum of attitudes; some classmates project outright hostility, others just go along with the group. When the story resolves, the classmate who has been most tentative in rejecting Molly—not the classmate who has been most hostile—is now the one who first hugs her. By introducing a spectrum of characters, the potential for change has been set up right from the beginning.

In *Peel*, however, the text of the argument is about nothing that is intrinsically important, and the subtext seems to imply a whole history of specific irritations rather than one conflict that can be overcome. Nothing deeper than the surface conflict is even engaged; there is no suggestion that something might be overcome. Arguments cannot be transcended here as they are in mainstream films, because arguments and a kind of low-grade tension are precisely what define the characters and the experience of their life. Thus, the argument in *Peel* provides a kind of centrifugal force, a sense of what makes families spin apart.

But stop. Anyone who has seen student films or read student stories knows about this centrifugal force. At a certain age and with a certain mindset, young writers and filmmakers always construct a world in which everything falls apart. Anxiety is glorified, despair celebrated. Stories end with suicides or lonely walks in the sand; they do not recognize the needs that work to hold us together. If this is what we mean by personal filmmaking, then why should anyone be interested? It is not what we mean. It is precisely the perspective that the writer gains by being able to look back on her experience that provides an answer to this.

Recognizing the limitations of presenting disintegration as an easy way out, Campion proves a contrasting centripetal force by dramatizing the cost of the tension driving the family apart in *Peel*. In doing so, she brings a perspective to the disintegration. The boy—confronted with his aunt sitting motionless behind the wheel, and his father, head in hand, on the rear bumper—stares into both of their mute faces, looking for similarities, apparently seeking to connect their faces with his own. The shots that Campion gives us go beyond the boy's individual point of view to represent a more general meditation on commonality and difference. As the boy touches the faces, the camera frames them with great tenderness, caressing them in such a way as to suggest it is seeking a connection between father and aunt and the reverse shot of the boy. At this moment, although the conflict does not end, we see, directly expressed by the narrator, the forces that keep us from spinning entirely apart. Conflict is not transcended, definition is not static. Rather, life is seen as a movement between forces of disintegration and the need for cohesion.

Finally, *Peel* is not a work in which we can separate script from final film. The dialogue is minimal and hardly consequential; there is not a clear and readable progression of beats that serve to bring us into character, nor is the action focused to provide revelation. The quality of shots in which we examine the faces at the end could not really be anticipated in writing. All this is not to negate the importance of the writing or the design of the piece, but rather to reposition it. Although it is achieved without a traditional script or relationship between writer and director, we are still witnessing a masterful act of storytelling that has been constructed to allow shots to resonate far beyond their literal meaning.

Sink or Swim

Su Friedrich's *Sink or Swim*[3] is structured in 26 sections, each of which is introduced with a short title. The titles begin with the letter z and work through the alphabet in reverse order, "Zygote," "Y Chromosome," "X Chromosome," "Witness," etc. Over these sections, a young girl's voice narrates the story of a woman whom we come to regard as the central character. Gradually, the narrated story focuses on the relationship between this woman and her father. We learn of the precariousness of their relationship, the cruel tenderness that marked their dealings with one another (after learning to swim by being thrown into a pool, she and her father celebrate their enjoyment of swimming together before her father frightens her by impossible tales of water moccasins lurking in the lake), and the hurt the woman feels when her father leaves her mother and, later, when her father sends the woman home early after an abortive vacation in Mexico. Struggling with subsequent unsatisfactory contacts with her father, the woman finally is able to declare herself and begin to live her own life.

Told this way, the story sounds as specific and private as do the stories of many of our friends. It is so personal that our reaction might be to think: What a difficult situation living with a father like that, but we all have our problems and we can only listen to so much that does not directly concern us. Friedrich counters this by finding moments of broader resonance that make the actual narrative less important than what she sets against it. This narrative space is created by various formal strategies that serve to modulate the distance with which we regard the story.

The voiceover itself is stylized in a number of ways. Using another character to narrate the woman's story suggests a distance that could not be achieved if the woman narrated the story herself. The effect is almost that of the close-in, third-person narrator used by Henry James; for much of the film, we are so close that we feel as though the story is being narrated by the woman herself, then suddenly something shifts and we become aware of the narrator that stands between us and the woman. Sometimes the film uses its greater narrative distance for irony, as in the passage where the girl tells us that the woman looked up her father's work to see what he had written at the time of the divorce. "She discovered that two of the articles written that year involve the study of kinship systems."[4] No comment. No reaction. The girl does not probe the woman's mind and we are left to fill in the irony for her. At other times, we move in very close and the sudden collapse of distance is very powerful, as in the section where we watch the woman type a letter to her father without any comment from the girl narrator. The effect of this movement is to constantly make us consider our position relative to the woman character. Sometimes we see it as purely her story; at other times we are pulled back and invited to consider more broadly the marks a parent leaves on a child.

Making the narrator a young girl contrasts with the controlled, at times formal, diction of the voiceovers. It adds a sense of longing to the film, a sense of a simplicity that seeks to speak directly, but that cannot. We tie this blockage to the woman's difficulty in speaking about her father. Using the reverse alphabet serves to organize the story around language, providing another way to extend the story beyond the events it describes. Language itself is seen as a way for the woman to come to terms with her father. Finally, individual sections use a wide variety of narrative techniques, including a recounting of myths, spoken and sung nursery rhymes, Schubert lieder, and a letter.

The images are as diverse as is the narrative style. Some are almost literal, such as the roller-coaster ride that plays against her father's taking the woman to a terrifying movie. But most images function to open a space between voiceover and image. For instance, after the title "Kinship," we hear a scratchy recording of Schubert's song "Gretchen am Spinnrad," music that we later learn evokes her mother's love for her father. We see images from a plane window, then we move to a deserted landscape, then to the same landscape seen from a car, then to women in a shower, then to strangely floating birds, then circle back to the women embracing in the shower, back to the desert, then to women drying themselves and laughing in the shower, and finally to baked, cracked desert soil. There is no way to summarize all that this communicates except to note that this moment, which we will retrospectively come to regard as the moment when the woman's father left her mother, is associated with a more generalized feeling of space, of the ramifications of sexual identity and a kind of parched dryness that transforms a specific personal event into a celebration of much greater beauty and meaning.

Daughter Rite

Michelle Citron's 1979 *Daughter Rite*,[5] a personal hybrid documentary/fiction, intercuts Citron's processed home movies of her childhood under voiceover meditations on her mother, with a series of acted improvisations based on the background of Citron and her sister. We identify the voiceover with the filmmaker. "I started this film when I was 28," is the first thing she tells us. She goes on to explain that 28 was her mother's age when the filmmaker was born, and connects her own need to make the film with this coinciding of their ages.

The voiceover meditations are written and delivered with no irony or narrative distance and, considered alone, they are a bit too complete in their understanding of the mother. Within these sections, little challenges the voiceover. Although the filmmaker describes her mother's actions, we have no basis for seeing them except as the narrator instructs us to. We do not pick up on any inadvertent slips or contradictions that betray the authority of the narrative perspective. We can relate this to our discussion about the tension between the narrative and dramatic voice in Chapter 22. If the narrative voice so dominates a film that it makes other readings difficult, we would say the film is "overdetermined" or without "air." Another way to talk about this is to say that such a film provides the viewer no opportunity to work within the context of the film. We can take it or leave it, but we cannot engage it.

The particular power of the fictional forms we have been discussing is that, by balancing narrative voice with dramatic voice, they allow us to hear what the narrative voice is declaring; at the same time, by considering our engagement with the dramatic voice, we can challenge and read behind the narrative voice. If *Daughter Rite* remains overdetermined, this tension would be denied it. This is where the use of the improvised footage comes in. In the scenes, we are privy to a great deal more than the voiceover gives us. While sharing great intimacy with the filmmaker, the sister's take on the mother is much more forgiving than is Citron's. At times, the sister seems naive relative to the filmmaker, but at other times, she acts to expose sides of the filmmaker that we do not get in the voiceover. We have to weigh the contrasting perspectives.

Here again, we see a tension playing out between the immediately personal voice, with its prejudices and shortsightedness, as expressed in the voiceover, to the slightly less personal voice, which uses constructed dramatized sequence to imply a multiplicity of perspectives that the single voice could not convey. Our sense of the meaning of the film lies in the space between these two presentational styles.

Family Gathering

While *Daughter Rite* is dynamic in its effect on the audience, the structure of the film remains the same throughout. Lise Yasui's *Family Gathering*[6] changes right before our eyes. This leads us to another generalization about personal filmmaking—that one of the ways to start from the personal and move to the more universal is through the introduction of elements that are outside the writer's control.

Family Gathering is a study of the filmmaker's grandfather, a survivor of the American internment camps for citizens of Japanese descent during World War II. About halfway through the film, and about halfway through the filmmaker's progress of making the film, the filmmaker learns that her grandfather's death was actually a suicide, which came as a direct result of his experience in the internment camp, a family secret that she has not known. At this point, the filmmaker's unraveling of the grandfather's story stops. The issue abruptly becomes one that affects the making of the film itself. Confronted with this new knowledge, can the filmmaker go on and complete the film? Does she want to document her discovery of this family secret? Or is it too great a violation of her family's history and therefore should not be exposed?

The viewer feels strangely ambivalent, sympathizing with the filmmaker's dilemma while at the same time wanting the story to move to completion. Eventually it does. But now we watch the film differently. Before, although we had been told that the filmmaker was attempting to reconstruct a past that she did not know, her authority still carried us along. Now, the whole dramatic structure of the piece functions to reveal just how little control the filmmaker actually has and how affected she is by the rawness of what she has discovered. The acute personal nature of her story is given an extra resonance because we witness the immediacy of history's impact on an individual's life and understand that as much as we try to define ourselves on our own terms, there are also forces greater than we can control that cause us to discover ourselves as we react to them.

Nice Coloured Girls

Sometimes the tension between history and the individual is played out more explicitly. Tracey Moffatt's film *Nice Coloured Girls*[7] follows four story lines—in contemporary Sidney, aboriginal women pick up a guy in a dance club and ply him with drinks; a voice reads an account of an early British landing on Australian shores; a black-and-white picture of that landing is shown hanging on a wall while performances of the actions depicted in the readings are played out against it; and an aboriginal woman standing on a beach stares into the camera.

The Sidney scene is edited without synch sound. Instead, we are given what looks to be subtitled documentary comments by the aboriginal women about their experiences picking up men they mockingly refer to as "captains." The irony of the piece is generated by the resonance of this reversal—the present-day captains are powerless against the aboriginal natives. However, the juxtaposition of the reading of the landing account against the contemporary scene adds an additional twist to this shifting of power. The Western settlers believe they have brought control and civility to this wild land. But the film cuts back a number of times to the woman on the beach staring into the camera with a force that denies anyone's domination. This, combined with the Sydney scenes, makes us listen more closely to the reading of the landing account and, as we do, we realize that in each encounter described, the English sailors are really acting on the dictates of the aboriginal women. While this does not deny the history of Western colonization, it suggests a much more complex dynamic of power than that which is traditionally presented.

Summary

We have ended *Alternative Scriptwriting* by looking at a different notion of writing than that discussed in the earlier chapters. We present this for two reasons. The first is that these works demand serious attention in their own right. These pieces, along with many others not described here, have contributed to a new visual and narrative expression by peoples not traditionally in control of media. The second is that these pieces all suggest means of exploring the tension between the narrative and dramatic voice that writers, no matter what their genre, may learn from and use.

Although these works are not written in standard screenplay form, are usually designed to be directed only by the writer, and are not feature length, they are logical extensions of the concerns of this book in their intensely personal nature. They provide examples of solving the problem that confronts all independent writers, which is how to embrace our own experience while at the same time gaining sufficient perspective on it to make it significant beyond the facts of our life. This—taking what is ours and learning to make it over so that it resonates for others—is the ultimate and most important thing we hope you take from this book.

Notes

1. Distributed by Phoenix Learning Resources (Phoenix Learning Group, Inc.), 2349 Chaffee Drive, St. Louis, MO 63146; (800) 221-1274.
2. Distributed by Women Make Movies, 462 Broadway, Suite 500W, New York, NY 10013 (212) 925–0606.
3. Ibid.
4. Su Friedrich, *Sink or Swim* (1990), quoted in Scott MacDonald, *Screen Writings: Scripts and Texts by Independent Filmmakers* (Berkeley: University of California Press, 1995), 253.
5. Distributed by Women Make Movies.
6. Distributed by National Asian-American Telecommunications Association, 346 9th Street, 2nd Floor, San Francisco, CA 94103; (415) 863-0814.
7. Distributed by Women Make Movies.

Index